AF734644

COLLEGE IN CALIFORNIA: *The Inside Track*™

The Comprehensive and Practical GUIDE for Students, Parents, and Educators

3rd Edition

Dedication ...

College in California: The Inside Track is dedicated to my partner in life, my husband, Gene, who spent more than a year reading, editing, and formatting this Guide. Without his commitment, expertise, and invaluable assistance College in California would never have been completed.

I dedicate this book, also, to my mother for her love and support and for teaching me the patience to research; to my father who gave me the courage to take risks; to my dear friend now gone, Betty Shively, who shared her knowledge of college guidance with me at the beginning of my career and for her sustaining faith in me; and to my many friends and colleagues, for their encouragement and understanding.

3rd Edition

COLLEGE IN CALIFORNIA™

THE INSIDE TRACK

The Comprehensive and Practical GUIDE for Students, Parents, and Educators

1995

Rochelle S. Rosen, M.A.

Routledge
Taylor & Francis Group
NEW YORK AND LONDON

First published 1992 by Baywood House Inc.

Published 2021 by Routledge
605 Third Avenue, New York, NY 10017
2 Park Square, Milton Park, Abingdon, Oxon OX14 4RN

Routledge is an imprint of the Taylor & Francis Group, an informa business

Library of Congress LCCN 94-094379

ISBN 13: 978-1-880403-13-6 (pbk)

What others say about this book ...

"This comprehensive guide provides students with a great resource to help select from among the many post-secondary education opportunities in California."

Sally Mentor, Deputy Superintendent
Curriculum and Instructional Leadership
California Department of Education

"Very practical, well-researched and readable. We can find everything regarding California colleges and admission in one book and we know we can trust that the facts are all accurate. What a wealth of information!"

Daniel Meyer, Ph.D., Counselor
Susie Anderson, Counselor
Educational Counseling Associates

"This book is great! I just wish I had started reading College in California when my daughters were freshmen and our planning for college began. It is the only book I would have needed"

Ginny Marley, Parent

"Included in College in California are the answers to questions most frequently asked by students. All the information is presented in an appealing and clean format."

Jeannie Yang, High School Senior

"The most comprehensive book I have seen and should prove to be a worthwhile tool to anyone exploring educational opportunities in California."

James Maraviglia
Director of Admissions and Evaluations
Cal Poly San Luis Obispo

"How often I have heard that the California college system is a mystery. Rochelle Rosen's book, College in California, puts a huge dent in this mystery."

Frederick E. Rugg, Author
Rugg's Recommendations on the Colleges

"This book walks a student through the college admission process beginning with the eighth grade through the senior year. Information about colleges in California, independent or public, is all inclusive and current. College in California is must reading."

Margy Arthur, Director
College Campus Tours

Education is a social process ....

Education is growth ....

Education is not preparation for life; education is life itself.

John Dewey

Contents

Chapter 10: CALIFORNIA STATE UNIVERSITY (continued ...)

WORKSHEETS ...

About the author ...

Rochelle S. Rosen, M.A., a counselor for more than twenty years, specializes in college and career guidance. She provides her professional services in northern California as a counselor at both the high school and community college levels.

The recipient of awards and recognition for her effective college guidance programs, Rochelle uses her expertise to assist students to formulate and realize their college plans. Over the years, she has guided her students through the process of preparing for and being admitted to the finest educational institutions in California and throughout the United States. Her students have received extensive financial aid.

Throughout her career, Rochelle has expanded and updated her knowledge of college and financial aid requirements and procedures. She constantly hones her skills through specialized training, relevant conferences, and continuing discussion with her peers and the admissions and financial aid officers of many of California's public and private educational institutions. She is a member of the Western Association of College Admission Counselors and the National Association of College Admission Counselors.

Rochelle Rosen received her Bachelor of Science degree in Psychological Tests and Measurements from Simmons College in Boston. After moving to California with her family, she continued her education at Stanford University, where she received her Master of Arts degree in Guidance and Counseling.

Her comprehensive understanding of the public California college and university systems, thorough familiarity with California independent colleges, and her extensive knowledge of college application and financial aid strategies make Rochelle S. Rosen highly qualified to write this book.

Acknowledgments ...

The material used in this book is drawn from many sources including the author's extensive personal knowledge, experience, and research. For completeness and accuracy, selected extracts from several publications that are in the public domain and others that are protected by United States copyright law are incorporated in the author's own work to create a uniquely useful reference source for students, parents, and educators.

The author wishes to thank the following organizations for providing the most current information and for granting permission to use certain extracts from their own copyrighted publications and materials.

ACT — The American College Testing Program
Iowa City, Iowa

ACT — The American College Testing Program
Financial Aid Services
Iowa City, Iowa

College Entrance
Examination Board
New York, New York

College Entrance
Examination Board
Western Regional Office
San Jose, California

College Entrance
Examination Board
College Scholarship Service (CSS)
Princeton, New Jersey

Educational Testing Service
Princeton, New Jersey

NAIA — National Association
of Intercollegiate Athletics
Kansas City, Missouri

NCAA — National Collegiate
Athletic Association
Overland Park, Kansas

NCAA Initial-
Eligibility Clearinghouse
Iowa City, Iowa

The Directors of Admissions of the following colleges have been most helpful by granting permission to reproduce essay questions from their admission applications.

Dominican College
Harvey Mudd College
Pomona College
Scripps College
University of the Pacific

The author wishes to thank the following organizations and the many professionals within them for their cooperation in providing the most current information.

California Community Colleges
Office of the Chancellor
Sacramento, California

California State University
Office of the Chancellor
Long Beach, California

University of California
Office of the President
Oakland, California

Admissions, Financial Aid,
Relations with Schools, and
Student Research Offices of each campus of
California State University and
the University of California

Admissions, Financial Aid, and
Public Affairs Offices of the
Independent Colleges of California

AICCU — Association of
Independent California Colleges
and Universities
Sacramento, California

Western Association of Schools and Colleges (WASC)
Accrediting Commission
Aptos, California

California Student Aid Commission
Sacramento, California

ROTC Programs of the Army, Navy-Marines, and
Air Force

California Department of Education
Sacramento, California

U. S. Department of Education
Office of Region 9
San Francisco, California

U.S. Department of Education
Washington, D.C.

Illustrations by
Richard Bernstein
Hayward, California

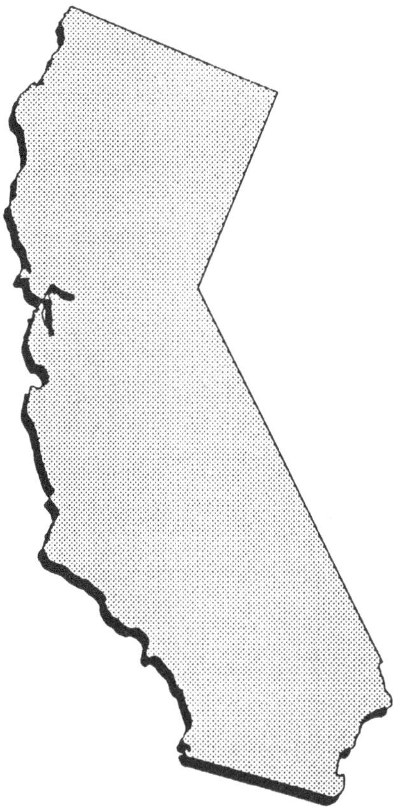

Introduction

WHAT THIS BOOK CAN DO FOR YOU

What classes should I take in high school?

What are the differences between the University of California, the California State Universities, and the independent colleges?

How important are my grades? My test scores?

What about recommendations? Extracurricular activities? Do they really matter?

What tests should I take and when?

How do I select a major? When do I need to?

Which colleges have strong programs in my major?

How do I know to which colleges to apply?

What are my chances for admission to this college? How can I improve my chances?

What are the colleges looking for in students they admit?

To get accepted to college, what must I do in my senior year? In my junior year? Earlier?

How do the transfer programs at the community college work?

How do I complete my application? Write my essay? Get recommendations?

Can I afford to go to college? How can I get financial aid?

Are these questions on your mind? You probably have many others also. I wrote **COLLEGE IN CALIFORNIA:** ***The Inside Track*** to give you detailed, factual, and timely answers to your critical questions. You need answers that you can act on. You need a plan that will help you succeed in whatever you set for your college goals. In this comprehensive Guide are the information and tips I have learned over many years as a specialist in college guidance in both high school and community college counseling positions.

As you read and use this book you will see that planning ahead for college is essential. You must make numerous decisions throughout your high school years.

If you know in advance what you need, what to expect, and how to proceed, you can reduce the tension of choosing and getting into a California college. Most importantly, you will not make critical and costly mistakes. A well-prepared and well-informed applicant is a successful applicant!

In a straightforward, easy-to-read style, **COLLEGE IN CALIFORNIA:** ***The Inside Track*** provides authoritative, up-to-date specifics on what it takes to plan for and go to college in California and how to pay for it. The emphasis is on what to do, why, how, and when. Every topic necessary to completing the process of becoming a California college student is covered in depth. You learn step-by-step strategies. This Guide will help you through the process. You can make the process work for you!

To get the most out of my GUIDE ...

Take a few minutes to scan the entire book to develop a sense of its organization and contents. To help you find the facts you need, I have provided a table of contents at the front of each chapter. I have also included numerous charts, worksheets, checklists, forms, and diagrams.

Use this book as a reference. Read a chapter only as you perceive the need to do so. Each chapter is largely self-contained and you do not need to read the book from beginning to end to make sense of it. However, read each chapter completely. You need the foundation of materials presented early in a chapter to understand topics presented later in it.

COLLEGE IN CALIFORNIA: ***The Inside Track*** **at a glance ...**

Chapter 1: ***Your Action Plans*** helps you understand the sequence of actions you must take and the optimum time to take them as you proceed through high school. It tells what to do and when. Other chapters of the book explain in detail how and why.

Chapter 2: ***Choosing Your College*** describes college choices and helps you select and evaluate factors to consider to determine which colleges suit your needs.

Chapter 3: ***Choosing Your Major*** explains majors and the self-knowledge you should develop to select your major and determine your career goals.

Chapter 4: ***Paying for College*** emphasizes how to get financial aid. Sources and procedures are described in detail.

Chapter 5: ***Athletics*** describes how to get the attention of recruiters and what to look for in athletic programs. NCAA and NAIA eligibility requirements are explained. The NCAA Initial Eligibility Clearinghouse application procedures are reviewed

Chapter 6: ***College Entrance Tests*** covers (1) Admissions tests: the PSAT, the SAT I: Reasoning Test, ACT, SAT II: Subject Tests, and (2) Placement tests such as the Advanced Placement examinations. Test content, which ones to take, when to take them, and the meaning of your scores are described in detail.

Chapter 7: ***Steps in the Application Process*** emphasizes the how of applying to college. Step-by-step procedures for applying, writing your essay, getting recommendations, interviewing, and handling the wait-list are covered.

Chapter 8: Educational Opportunities for the minority and/or educationally-disadvantaged student, the disabled student, and the international student are presented.

Chapter 9: California Community Colleges describes what the community college has to offer and emphasizes what you need to do to prepare for transfer to a four-year institution.

Chapter 10: California State University explains admission requirements, selection criteria for impacted campuses and programs, application procedures, costs, financial aid, housing, support services, international programs, and placement tests. Detailed profiles of all twenty CSU campuses and a listing of majors conclude the chapter.

Chapter 11: University of California explains admission requirements, selection criteria of each campus, application procedures, costs, housing, support services, study abroad, and placement tests. Detailed profiles of all nine campuses conclude the chapter.

Chapter 12: California Independent Colleges reviews the advantages of the independent college and criteria for admission. Detailed profiles of one-hundred-seven independent colleges and their majors conclude the chapter.

Share this book with your parents. It is important that they know what you need to do to help you through the process.

Seek individual assistance from your counselor, guidance administrator, career center technician, or whoever provides college guidance in your school.

Although I have attempted to thoroughly cover the many details about the colleges and the admission process and to answer many of the questions that can occur, you may have specific unique needs that require special attention. Included in this *GUIDE* are phone numbers and addresses of many sources of information. Do not hesitate to contact these sources for help with your special circumstances.

COLLEGE IN CALIFORNIA: ***The Inside Track*** includes the most up-to-date information available to me as of publication time. The college admissions picture is always changing. Even during the course of the school year, procedures, requirements, and deadlines change. Ultimately, you must verify your plans and your decisions by contacting the appropriate information source. An updated version of this book is published every September.

There is no guarantee, either explicit or implied, that using the information and following guidelines contained in this book will guarantee you admission to the college of your choice or financial aid. But, the more informed you can make yourself, the more you improve your opportunity for success.

I am very interested in your suggestions for making this book even more helpful. Please write to me in care of Baywood House Inc.

The author.

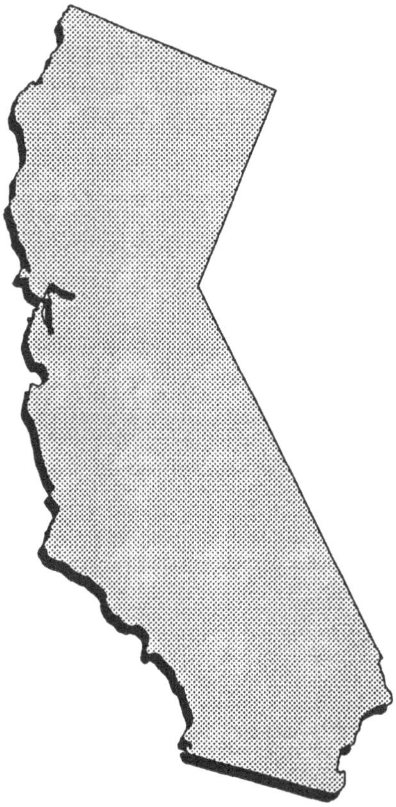

Chapter 1

YOUR ACTION PLANS

You are in charge of getting yourself into college. You have decisions to make, actions to take, and deadlines to meet. To accomplish your educational goals you must be organized, use your time effectively, and keep careful records of each step. Specific action plans are your guidelines to follow as you progress through the steps.

OVERVIEW

The process of getting into the college of your choice begins as early as the eighth grade and continues through high school graduation. It is important that you follow each step of the process carefully so that you are organized and do not miss any important procedures or deadlines. You must plan your courses, achieve the highest grades of which you are capable, and take advantage of enrichment opportunities to strengthen your qualifications. Action plans help you to know what to do and when. Specific actions for you to take beginning in grade eight are listed chronologically in this chapter. *For a full explanation of the meaning of each step and how to complete it, refer to the appropriate chapters of this guide.* The various worksheets that you must use to follow your plan may also be found in these chapters. Check the Table of Contents on page *xiii* for a complete listing of worksheets and their page numbers.

The process of getting into the college of your choice begins as early as the eighth grade and continues through high school graduation.

HIGH SCHOOL COLLEGE PREPARATORY PROGRAM

Taking appropriate high school courses and the grades you achieve make a difference in the college choices available to you. Your high school has a list of college-preparatory courses to use as a guideline for planning your course schedule. Not every course offered by your high school counts toward college admission requirements. It is important that you use your high school list in your planning.

The pattern of high school courses in the college-preparatory program shown here is the minimum recommended to prepare you for college admission and for success in your college studies. Your high school may use different titles for some of these courses. Advanced algebra might be called algebra 2, English classes probably have titles such as American literature, and world history might be called global history. Use the courses from your high school college-preparatory list to meet these requirements. Your high school counselor or administrator can help you define which courses fit into which category.

Completing this pattern presents a strong record for admission to college. Colleges may differ in the classes they require. For example, some schools do not require a foreign language. A college or major emphasizing a technical program might require more mathematics or science courses for admission.

COLLEGE PREPARATORY PROGRAM	
English	4 years of college-preparatory English
Science	2 years of lab science (college-preparatory introduction to lab science, biology, chemistry, physics, anatomy and physiology)
Mathematics	3 years (algebra, geometry, advanced algebra, analytical geometry, trigonometry, pre-calculus, calculus)
History	2 years (world history, United States history, government)
Foreign Language	2 years of the same language
Fine Arts	1 year (art, music, drama)
Additional courses in any of these areas	1 year

This pattern of courses adds up to a total of 15 one-year, college-preparatory courses. Some colleges expect more than 15 courses, others accept less. This list is a basic set of courses which meet the admission requirements of most colleges.

MY FOUR-YEAR PLAN

9th Grade Courses	
Semester 1	Semester 2
English	English
Summer School	

10th Grade Courses	
Semester 1	Semester 2
English	English
Summer School	

11th Grade Courses	
Semester 1	Semester 2
English	English
Summer School	

12th Grade Courses	
Semester 1	Semester 2
English	English
Summer School	

Develop a four-year plan which identifies the courses you need for high school graduation and the classes to meet college entrance requirements. Usually, college entrance requirements also meet graduation requirements. Your plan can easily satisfy both sets of requirements simultaneously.

Although it is important to take college-preparatory courses, do not take any classes that may be too advanced for you and for which you may not be adequately prepared. Listen to the advice of your parents, teachers, counselors, and administrators about the level of class you should take in English, foreign language, mathematics, or science. Only grades of C or better count toward meeting college requirements. If you take a class that is too advanced and get a D or F grade, your academic record will suffer, and the course will not count toward college admission requirements. You will need to repeat it and raise your grade to C or better for it to qualify. It may be better to wait a year and develop your background for the more difficult classes.

Develop a four-year plan which identifies the courses you need for high school graduation and the classes to meet college entrance requirements.

Review your four-year plan each year. You may change it as you proceed through high school depending upon your success in classes and the goals, interests, and strengths you develop. Review the classes you have listed. Are they too difficult? Too easy? Is the plan realistic for you?

Use the worksheet, MY FOUR-YEAR PLAN, on the opposite page to formulate your plan.

STRATEGIES FOR GETTING THE BEST GRADES

You want to achieve the highest grades possible in your classes. A competitive academic record will help you get into the colleges of interest to you. The following suggestions will assist you.

SPECIFIC GRADE GOALS

Set specific grade goals for each of your classes. Decide what grade you are aiming for in each of your classes and make a contest of attaining it. Talk to your parents about a reward if you achieve your goals. Tailor the reward to your interests and recreational pleasures. It might be special privileges, money, gifts, excursions, TV watching, or no monitoring of your study time by your parents. You decide what works for you. Some students set up contests among themselves and reward each other with a treat to lunch or some other fun activity. You may find that achieving the grade you want is rewarding in itself and you do not require additional motivation.

Set specific grade goals for each of your classes.

STUDY SKILLS

Study smart! You can learn strategies to get the most out of your study time. Talk to your counselor, administrators, and teachers about materials and programs available in your school to teach you how to improve study skills.

TIME MANAGEMENT

You are involved in many responsibilities and activities. They all take time. You may sometimes feel you have so much to do you do not know what to do first. You may be disorganized or tend to procrastinate. These feelings and habits prevent you from making your best grades. Recreational activities compete with your academics for your time.

Make the most effective use of your time by planning and writing a schedule. Use the worksheet, MY PERSONAL TIME SCHEDULE, on the next page. When planning your schedule be sure to include:

Make the most effective use of your time by planning and writing a schedule.

- Time for eating, sleeping, school, exercise, recreation, socializing, work, study, and home responsibilities.
- Uninterrupted study time each day at a time when you are most productive. Do you study best after school? Just before dinner? After dinner? Late in the evening?
- Flexibility. Prepare your schedule in pencil. Review it frequently. Do not hesitate to change it as you learn more about what works best for you.
- Time for unexpected activities. Allow for uncommitted time to use for an unplanned special recreational opportunity, extra study time for a test or big project, or simply to reschedule your studying.

Select a handy place for your schedule where you can easily see it and often refer to it.

ENRICHMENT OPPORTUNITIES

COLLEGE COURSES

If you have the opportunity, take courses at your local community college while you are still in high school. You can experience how college classes are taught and learn what is expected of students. You will have a broadening experience by attending classes with college students of all backgrounds and ages. College classes strengthen your record by showing that you seek enrichment and challenge.

SUMMER COURSES

Take college classes for enrichment and challenge.

Many colleges offer special summer programs for high school students. Take advantage of these programs if possible. If the program is at a college away from home, you can experience dormitory life to see what it is like to live away at school. You will meet students from other places and make new friends. Community colleges near your home offer summer courses as well.

If you spend the summer at a college to which you are interested in applying, you will gain insight into what that institution is really like. The experience will also help you define what you are looking for in a college.

MY PERSONAL TIME SCHEDULE

	Monday	Tuesday	Wednesday	Thursday	Friday	Saturday	Sunday
7:00 AM							
7:30 AM							
8:00 AM							
8:30 AM							
9:00 AM							
9:30 AM							
10:00 AM							
10:30 AM							
11:00 AM							
11:30 AM							
12:00 Noon							
12:30 PM							
1:00 PM							
1:30 PM							
2:00 PM							
2:30 PM							
3:00 PM							
3:30 PM							
4:00 PM							
4:30 PM							
5:00 PM							
5:30 PM							
6:00 PM							
6:30 PM							
7:00 PM							
7:30 PM							
8:00 PM							
8:30 PM							
9:00 PM							
9:30 PM							
10:00 PM							

COLLEGE IN CALIFORNIA: *The Inside Track*

ACTIVITIES

It is important to involve yourself in activities both at and outside of school. Activities make your high school years more fun and meaningful. Further, the colleges prefer to see well-rounded students who can add enriched experiences to their student body.

The colleges are not interested in just a list of your activities. They look for depth of involvement.

The colleges are not interested in just a list of your numerous clubs, sports, or outside activities. They are interested in depth of involvement. You might be in only one activity in which you have thoroughly participated, taken a leadership role, and gained a great deal of personal growth. Great! Be ready to describe your activity, what you learned from it, how you developed, and what you accomplished. Were you a leader? A team player? Did you make a significant contribution? Why was it important to you? Did you have a paid job in which you learned to handle money or to take special responsibility?

Got the idea? Quality of involvement — not quantity — is what colleges look for.

YOUR ACTION PLANS

GRADE EIGHT

In the spring of your eighth grade, seek advice and information for setting the goals you would like to achieve in high school.

grade 8

- ❒ ***Talk about your college plans.*** Talk to your parents, your teachers, your counselor. Get everybody alerted to your goals!
- ❒ ***Attend college information workshops with your parents.*** Workshops may be given by your school or the high school you will attend. They are generally offered in the spring.
- ❒ ***Develop your worksheet,*** MY FOUR-YEAR PLAN, for all four years of high school. Include all required courses for college admission and high school graduation. You may change your plan each year to meet developing needs.
- ❒ ***Talk to older brothers, sisters, cousins, and friends*** about your desire to go to college, your course selections, and your concerns about high school. Learn from their experiences!
- ❒ ***Discuss the costs of college with your parents*** and their plans for helping you to pay them. Encourage them to seek expert advise from an accountant or financial planner.

GRADE NINE

Grade nine is the year of adjusting to the high school environment, courses, and expectations. Learn about the opportunities and programs your high school offers to help you meet your college admission goals.

❒ ***Develop your worksheet,*** MY PERSONAL TIME SCHEDULE, your plan for the most effective use of your time.

❒ ***Set goals for the grades you want in each of your courses.***

❒ ***Learn about the extracurricular activities*** available at your school and in the community. Join clubs, activities, and sports programs of interest to you.

❒ ***Begin keeping your worksheet,*** MY ACTIVITIES, the record of your school and outside activities.

❒ ***Review your worksheet,*** MY FOUR-YEAR PLAN, after you receive your first-semester grades. Think about classes for next year. If you have not yet developed your worksheet, MY FOUR-YEAR PLAN, do it now.

❒ ***Visit your career center*** to become familiar with college and career publications, videotapes, and computerized information.

❒ ***Attend college representative programs*** on your high school campus or in the community. You must learn about college opportunities and admission requirements.

❒ ***Seek college guidance*** from high school staff members who can help you with planning for college — your counselor, the career center technician, administrators.

❒ ***Monitor your progress*** to meet college admission requirements. Start filling in course names and your grades on your worksheet, MY COURSE PLAN: CSU SUBJECT REQUIREMENT for CSU or MY COURSE PLAN: "a-f" SUBJECT REQUIREMENT for UC. Review the independent college requirements in chapter 12: CALIFORNIA INDEPENDENT COLLEGES.

❒ ***Consider taking the SAT II: Subject Tests*** at the end of the school year in the appropriate courses in which you are enrolled if you are planning to attend a four-year college that requires or recommends them.

❒ ***Discuss the costs of college with your parents*** and their plans for helping you to pay them. Encourage them to seek expert advise from an accountant or financial planner.

GRADE TEN

Grade ten is the year for researching. Review your academic qualifications and determine your interests, values, and abilities. Take advantage of every opportunity to become knowledgeable about your college options.

grade 10

- ❐ ***Develop your worksheet,*** MY PERSONAL TIME SCHEDULE, your plan for the most effective use of your time.
- ❐ ***Set goals for the grades you want in each course.***
- ❐ ***Consider taking the PSAT in October for practice.***
- ❐ ***Take the PSAT practice test,*** which you receive when you register for the PSAT, to become familiar with the types of questions and materials covered.
- ❐ ***Attend PSAT score explanation workshops*** presented by your counselor or assistant principal. These usually take place during the first two weeks of December.
- ❐ ***Review your PSAT test booklet and your answers.*** Where are your weaknesses? Talk to your teachers for help in finding study materials to strengthen your skills.
- ❐ ***Review your PSAT scores with your counselor*** to determine what your results indicate about your qualifications for the colleges which interest you.
- ❐ ***Join more activities or get more involved*** in the ones in which you already participate. You may decide to take a leadership role.
- ❐ ***Update your worksheet,*** MY ACTIVITIES. Do not forget to include your activities this past summer — jobs, enrichment courses, summer camp counseling ....
- ❐ ***Visit your career center*** to utilize college and career publications, videotapes, and computerized information.
- ❐ ***Review your worksheet,*** MY FOUR-YEAR PLAN, after you receive your first-semester grades. Think about your classes for next year and revise your plan if necessary. If you have not yet developed your worksheet, MY FOUR-YEAR PLAN, do it now.
- ❐ ***Attend college representative programs*** on your high school campus or in the community. You must learn about college opportunities and admission requirements.
- ❐ ***Seek out career self-assessment activities*** available in your school. Learn about your interests, values, personality, abilities, and the college majors and careers that fit you.

❒ ***Request college guidance*** from your counselor, the career center technician, and/or administrators. They can answer many of your questions.

❒ ***Review your school record*** to help you define the competitiveness of the colleges for which you might qualify.

❒ ***Monitor your progress*** to meet college admission requirements. Start filling in course names and grades on your worksheet, MY COURSE PLAN: CSU SUBJECT REQUIREMENT for CSU or MY COURSE PLAN: "a-f" SUBJECT REQUIREMENT for UC. Review the independent college requirements in chapter 12: CALIFORNIA INDEPENDENT COLLEGES.

grade **10**

❒ ***Consider taking the SAT II: Subject Tests*** at the end of the school year in the appropriate courses in which you are enrolled if you are planning to attend a four-year college which requires or recommends them.

❒ ***Visit colleges this summer.***

❒ ***Find a summer job*** to earn money to pay for your college education.

❒ ***Discuss the costs of college with your parents*** and their plans for helping you to pay them. Encourage them to seek expert advise from an accountant or financial planner.

GRADE ELEVEN

Grade eleven is the year to begin your serious planning and decision-making. There are specific actions to be taken each month to prepare for your goals.

SEPTEMBER

❒ ***Get your social security number.*** It will serve as a major means of identification on your college applications and testing registration.

❒ ***Develop your worksheet,*** MY PERSONAL TIME SCHEDULE, your plan for the most effective use of your time.

grade **11**

❒ ***Set goals for the grades you want in each course.***

❒ ***Join more activities, or get more involved*** in the ones in which you already participate. You may decide to take a leadership role.

❒ ***Update your worksheet,*** MY ACTIVITIES. Do not forget to include your activities this past summer — jobs, enrichment courses, summer camp counseling ....

- ❐ ***Think about your qualifications for college:*** Your courses, grades, GPA, rank in class, test scores, extracurricular activities, and goals.
- ❐ ***Narrow down your educational goals:*** Four-year college, two-year college? Public, private? In-state, out-of-state? Transfer program? Career training program?
- ❐ ***Meet with your counselor or administrator*** to review your schedule and your past academic record. What are your chances of admission to the schools which interest you? How can you improve your chances?
- ❐ ***Set goals for the grades you want in each of your courses.***
- ❐ ***Visit your career center*** to utilize college and career publications, videotapes, and computerized information.
- ❐ ***Sign up for college and career speakers*** who will be coming to your campus. Do this every month.

OCTOBER

grade 11

- ❐ ***Sign up for the PSAT*** at your high school. The PSAT experience will help you prepare for the SAT I tests you will take this spring, and your scores may make you eligible for special scholarship opportunities.
- ❐ ***Take the PSAT practice test,*** which you receive when you register for the PSAT, to become familiar with the types of questions and the material covered.
- ❐ ***Consider signing up for Student Search Service*** when you take the PSAT. Colleges will review your background and interests and send you information about their schools in the spring.
- ❐ ***Attend fall college fairs with your parents.*** College representatives give out materials, answer questions, and make presentations.
- ❐ ***Attend college representative programs*** on your high school campus or in the community. You must learn about college opportunities and admission requirements.
- ❐ ***Seek out career self-assessment activities*** available in your school. Learn about your interests, values, personality, abilities, and the college majors and careers that fit you.

NOVEMBER

- ❐ ***Visit your career center*** and look over college catalogues and brochures. Begin to clarify what you want in a college.

- ❐ ***Attend college representative programs*** on your high school campus or in the community. You must learn about college opportunities and admission requirements.

- ❐ ***Review your worksheet,*** CHOOSING MY COLLEGE, and begin to fill it in.

DECEMBER

- ❐ ***Attend PSAT score explanation workshops*** presented by your counselor or assistant principal.

- ❐ ***Review your PSAT test booklet and your answers.*** What are your weaknesses? Talk to your teachers for help in finding study materials to strengthen your skills.

- ❐ ***Review your PSAT scores with your counselor*** to determine what your results indicate about your qualifications for the colleges which interest you.

- ❐ ***Attend college representative programs*** on your high school campus or in the community. Keep your college criteria in mind and do not hesitate to ask questions.

- ❐ ***Talk to students home from college:*** Your brothers, sisters, cousins, friends. Find out what they like and do not like about their school. Learn from their experiences!

- ❐ ***Visit colleges during your Christmas vacation.***

grade 11

JANUARY

- ❐ ***Focus on your grades. Focus on your finals.***

FEBRUARY

- ❐ ***Monitor your progress*** to meet college admission requirements. Fill in course names and grades on your worksheet, MY COURSE PLAN: CSU SUBJECT REQUIREMENT for CSU or MY COURSE PLAN: "a-f" SUBJECT REQUIREMENT for UC.

- ❐ ***Fill in your worksheet,*** CHOOSING MY COLLEGE. It is time to decide what are the most important characteristics to you of a college.

- ❐ ***Register to take your college admissions tests*** this spring. Pick up registration forms from your guidance office or career center. Mail them in time to meet the regular application filing period.

- ❐ ***Register for the TOEFL*** if you are an international student or if your native language is not English. Pick up your registration form from your guidance office or career center. Mail it in time to meet the regular application filing period.

- ❐ ***Attend college representative programs*** on your high school campus or in the community. Keep your college criteria in mind and do not hesitate to ask questions.

MARCH

- ❐ ***Decide which Advanced Placement Examinations to take.*** Inform your teachers so that examinations will be ordered for you.
- ❐ ***Register for April and May admissions tests.***
- ❐ ***Evaluate the information colleges mail to you*** about themselves. Share your information and opinions with your parents. Ask for their impressions and suggestions.
- ❐ ***Look into summer enrichment activities.*** Several colleges and universities offer courses and programs for students who will be entering their senior year of high school in the fall. Your career center will have this information.
- ❐ ***Attend college representative programs*** on your high school campus or in the community. Keep your college criteria in mind and do not hesitate to ask questions.

grade 11

APRIL

- ❐ ***Take admissions tests for which you have registered.***
- ❐ ***Register for the June admissions tests.***
- ❐ ***Develop a preliminary list of the colleges*** that interest you, and write to them for information and brochures.
- ❐ ***Develop a plan to visit colleges this coming summer.***
- ❐ ***Attend spring college information nights and fairs*** with your parents. Your high school may have special college information nights for juniors.
- ❐ ***Attend admissions testing preparation programs*** offered by your school. Check with your guidance or career center for information and dates. Not all schools offer this opportunity.

MAY

- ❐ ***Take the admissions tests for which you have registered.***
- ❐ ***Register for the June admissions tests.***
- ❐ ***Continue to fill in your worksheet,*** CHOOSING MY COLLEGE, as you become more informed about college opportunities and profiles.

- ❐ ***Take your Advanced Placement Examinations.*** Ask your AP teachers for exact dates for specific examinations.

- ❐ ***Plan for recommendations from teachers.*** Mention to some of your current teachers that you will be asking them to write recommendations for you next fall. They may want to jot down ideas about you in preparation.

JUNE

- ❐ ***Take the admissions tests for which you have registered.***

- ❐ ***Make serious plans to visit colleges during the summer.***

- ❐ ***Find a summer job*** to earn money to pay for your college education.

- ❐ ***Focus on your grades. Focus on your finals.***

- ❐ ***Discuss the costs of college with your parents*** and their plans for helping you to pay them. Encourage them to seek expert advice from an accountant or financial planner.

grade 11

SUMMER

- ❐ ***Take college summer classes.***

- ❐ ***Visit colleges.***

- ❐ ***Write to the independent colleges*** to which you plan to apply for information and application materials.

- ❐ ***Begin work on your college application essays.***

- ❐ ***Work at a summer job*** to earn money to pay for your college education.

GRADE TWELVE

Use your senior year to make your college admissions happen! The twelfth grade is a busy and stressful time. You are in challenging courses with homework and projects, involved in extracurricular activities, and may be holding down a part-time job. You need to make decisions about colleges to which to apply. You have numerous applications and forms to complete and deadlines to keep. You are taking college admissions tests. There are extra expenses involved: Fees for admissions testing and college applications, and deposits for college and housing.

grade 12

In the spring you will need to make your final decision about which college to attend. Then one day, probably sometime in late May, it will hit you — you will be leaving the familiarity and security of high school, your old friends, and possibly your parents and home. Next year you truly will be on your own making your own decisions about schedules, what to eat, friends, classes ....

To get through this year and make a successful effort to get into college you must follow a plan of action so that you do not miss any procedures or deadlines. If you are well-organized and use your time efficiently, you will succeed in reaching your college goals. Keep track of college, test, and scholarship application materials, deadlines, test dates, dates materials are submitted, dates recommendation forms are distributed, transcript requests, college visit and interview dates. Use your worksheet, MY APPLICATION CHECKLIST, in chapter 7: STEPS IN THE APPLICATION PROCESS, page 7--28 to monitor your progress.

grade 12

YOUR SENIOR YEAR AT A GLANCE	
September through December	Apply for and take your college admissions tests.
September through December	Submit application materials for early scholarship opportunities.
November	Apply to CSU and UC.
November through December	Apply to independent colleges and universities.
November through December	Have transcripts sent to colleges to which you are applying, if required.
December	Have recommendations and Secondary School Reports sent to the colleges to which you are applying, if required.
January through February	Have seventh semester transcripts and Seventh Semester School Reports sent to the colleges to which you are applying, if required.
January through May	Submit application materials for the majority of your scholarship and financial aid opportunities.
March 2nd	Submit your FAFSA, FAF, and GPA Verification Form to apply for financial aid.
January through mid-April	You will be notified of admission, rejection, wait-listing, or other options.
January through June	You will be notified of results of scholarship, grant, and financial aid opportunities.
May 1st	Generally-accepted deadline for you to inform colleges of whether or not you intend to enroll.

SEPTEMBER

❐ ***Begin your worksheet,*** MY APPLICATION CHECKLIST. Record application deadlines and your filing dates.

❐ ***Determine the admissions test requirements of the colleges*** to which you are likely to apply.

❐ ***Register for the October and November admissions tests.*** Pick up your registration forms from your guidance office or career center. Mail them in time to meet the regular application filing period.

❐ ***Register for the TOEFL*** if you are an international student or if your native language is not English.

❐ ***Review college information*** that you have accumulated. Visit the career center.

❐ ***Think about your qualifications for college:*** Review your courses, grades, GPA, rank in class, test scores, extracurricular activities, and your goals.

❐ ***Narrow your college choices to five to six schools*** and complete your worksheet, CHOOSING MY COLLEGE.

❐ ***Obtain CSU and UC applications*** at your career center or guidance office in late September or early October. You will not need to send for them.

grade 12

❐ ***Write to the independent colleges for application materials*** and information.

❐ ***Begin your application essays.*** Think about what you want to write about yourself and how you want to say it. Ask your English teacher for help.

❐ ***Watch for scholarship announcements.*** Find out where the latest information on scholarships is routinely presented and get in the habit of checking this source on a regular basis, perhaps weekly.

❐ ***Talk to your parents about scholarship opportunities*** offered by their employers, organizations, and clubs.

OCTOBER

❐ ***Record deadlines and filing dates on your worksheet,*** MY APPLICATION CHECKLIST.

❐ ***Take the admissions tests for which you have registered.***

❐ ***Register for November and December admissions tests.***

- ❒ ***Obtain CSU and UC applications*** from your career center or guidance office and begin to complete them.
- ❒ ***Start working on your applications for the independent colleges.*** Write to the independent colleges for your applications if you have not already done so.
- ❒ ***Prepare a resume about yourself*** from information on your worksheets, MY ACTIVITIES and MY PERSONAL INFORMATION, to give to those people writing recommendations for you.
- ❒ ***Request recommendations*** from your teachers, counselor, administrators, and/or employers. Ask for them at least a month before they are due.
- ❒ ***Submit the Secondary School Report form*** from the independent colleges to your counselor or administrator for completion and mailing. It is generally due at the colleges between December 15th and January 15th.
- ❒ ***Give serious attention to your essay.*** Complete it this month so that it is ready for inclusion in the college admission applications that you will submit in November.
- ❒ ***Attend fall college fairs with your parents.*** You may obtain information to help with the process of applying to and deciding among colleges.

grade 12

- ❒ ***Attend college representative programs*** on your high school campus or in the community. Ask questions to help you make decisions and properly follow application procedures.
- ❒ ***Watch for scholarship announcements.***
- ❒ ***Submit scholarship application materials by their deadlines.***

NOVEMBER

- ❒ ***Record deadlines and filing dates on your worksheet,*** MY APPLICATION CHECKLIST.
- ❒ ***Take the admissions tests for which you have registered.***
- ❒ ***Register for the December admissions tests.***
- ❒ ***Attend admission application workshops.*** These are generally presented at your school.
- ❒ ***Submit your college applications this month!***

All University of California campuses, impacted California State University campuses and majors, and some independent colleges have November 30th deadlines.

- ❒ ***Submit Early Action or Early Decision applications*** to independent colleges. These are usually due by a specific date during the first two weeks of November or earlier.
- ❒ ***Make photocopies of applications for your files.***
- ❒ ***Get a Certificate of Mailing*** when you mail your CSU, UC, and independent college applications. It is a receipt provided by the post office to prove you mailed your application by the deadline in case any question arises.
- ❒ ***Request that your 6th semester transcript be sent*** by your high school registrar to those colleges which require it. Review your college application materials to determine if this transcript is required.
- ❒ ***Make sure your admissions test scores are sent to the colleges*** to which you have decided to apply. Your official Score Report forms lists the colleges that have received your scores.
- ❒ ***Review housing application requirements.*** Is there a place to request housing on your admission application form? Do you need to file a separate application? If so, request it immediately. Note deadlines.
- ❒ ***Contact the financial aid offices*** of the colleges to which you are applying. Do you need to file a special institutional financial aid application? If so, request it immediately. Note deadlines.
- ❒ ***Request recommendations*** from your teachers, counselor, administrators, and/or employers. Ask for them at least a month before they are due.
- ❒ ***Submit the Secondary School Report form*** from the independent colleges to your counselor or administrator for completion and mailing. It is generally due at the colleges between December 15th and January 15th.
- ❒ ***Attend college representative meetings*** on your high school campus and in the community.
- ❒ ***Watch for scholarship announcements.***
- ❒ ***Submit scholarship application materials by their deadlines.***

DECEMBER

grade 12

- ❒ ***Record deadlines and filing dates on your worksheet,*** MY APPLICATION CHECKLIST.
- ❒ ***Take the admissions tests for which you have registered.***
- ❒ ***Register for January admissions tests.***
- ❒ ***Submit all college applications*** that were not required to be filed by November 30th. Watch your deadlines!
- ❒ ***Request that your 6th semester transcript*** be sent by your high school registrar to those colleges that require it. Review your college application materials to determine if this transcript is required.
- ❒ ***Pick up your FAFSA — Free Application for Federal Student Aid, FAF — Financial Aid Form, and GPA Verification Form (required for Cal Grant consideration)*** from the guidance office or career center to begin the financial aid process.
- ❒ ***Attend financial aid nights with your parents.*** They may take place at your high school or in your community. Suggestions for filling out the FAFSA and FAF are usually covered.
- ❒ ***Discuss your financial circumstances*** with your counselor or other person in charge of scholarship information in your school. Alert them to your needs.
- ❒ ***Check with your recommendation writers:*** The administrators, counselor, and/or teachers who are writing recommendations for you. Politely remind them of deadlines.
- ❒ ***Make sure your transcripts have been sent*** by the registrar as you requested.
- ❒ ***Attend college representative meetings*** on your high school campus and in your community. You may gain information to help you decide which college to attend.
- ❒ ***Talk to students home from college:*** Brothers, sisters, cousins, friends. Find out what they like and do not like about their school. What tips can they give you? Learn from their experiences!
- ❒ ***Visit colleges during your Christmas vacation.***
- ❒ ***Watch for scholarship announcements.***
- ❒ ***Submit scholarship application materials by their deadlines.***

JANUARY

- ❒ ***Record deadlines and filing dates on your worksheet,*** MY APPLICATION CHECKLIST.
- ❒ ***Take the admissions tests for which you have registered.***
- ❒ ***Register for February admissions tests.***
- ❒ ***Pick up your FAFSA — Free Application for Federal Student Aid, FAF — Financial Aid Form, and GPA Verification Form*** (required for Cal Grant consideration) from the guidance office or career center.
- ❒ ***Attend financial aid nights with your parents.*** They may take place at your high school or in your community. Suggestions for filling out the FAFSA and FAF are usually covered.
- ❒ ***Your parents should begin filling in the FAFSA and FAF*** at this time. The deadline for filing these forms and the GPA Verification Form is March 2nd.
- ❒ ***Complete college financial aid forms*** required by the colleges to which you are applying. Note the deadlines stated on the forms.
- ❒ ***Send your 7th semester transcript and/or the 7th Semester School Report*** to the colleges that require them.
- ❒ ***Watch for space reservation notices from the CSU campuses*** to which you applied. Call the campuses if you have not received reservations by late January.
- ❒ ***Watch for an acknowledgment from UC*** to confirm the receipt of your application. Call (800) 523-2048 if you have not received this acknowledgment by January 1st.
- ❒ ***Watch for scholarship announcements.***
- ❒ ***Submit scholarship application materials by their deadlines.***

grade 12

FEBRUARY

- ❒ ***Record deadlines and filing dates on your worksheet,*** MY APPLICATION CHECKLIST.
- ❒ ***Take the admissions tests for which you have registered.***
- ❒ ***Register for April and May admissions tests.***
- ❒ ***Confirm that your 7th semester transcript, and/or the 7th Semester School Report*** has been sent by your registrar.

- ❒ ***Complete the FAFSA, the FAF, and the GPA Verification Form.*** The deadline is March 2nd and February is a short month.
- ❒ ***Complete college financial aid forms*** required by the colleges to which you are applying. Note the deadlines stated on the forms.
- ❒ ***Complete housing applications*** by the required deadlines for priority consideration. Note the deadlines stated on the forms.
- ❒ ***Watch for notices of admission from CSU, UC, and independent colleges.***
- ❒ ***Continue researching colleges*** to help you decide which one to attend.
- ❒ ***Get California Community College information and applications*** from the guidance office, career center, or the community college itself.
- ❒ ***Watch for scholarship announcements.***
- ❒ ***Submit scholarship application materials by their deadlines.***

MARCH

grade 12

- ❒ ***Record deadlines and filing dates on your worksheet,*** MY APPLICATION CHECKLIST.
- ❒ ***Register for April and May admissions tests.***
- ❒ ***File your FAFSA, FAF and GPA Verification Form by March 2nd.***
- ❒ ***Watch for the Student Aid Report*** from the Need Analysis Processor to which you sent your FAFSA. Review the information on this report for accuracy and send necessary corrections.
- ❒ ***Decide which Advanced Placement Examinations to take*** and inform your teachers so that examinations will be ordered for you.
- ❒ ***Watch for notices of admission from CSU, UC, and independent colleges.*** You should hear by mid-March if you have been accepted to the CSU or UC campuses to which you applied.
- ❒ ***Continue researching your colleges*** to help you decide which one to attend.
- ❒ ***Submit admission applications to California Community Colleges.*** Get your application from the guidance center, career center, or the community college itself.
- ❒ ***Sign up for community college placement tests and orientation.***
- ❒ ***Watch for scholarship announcements.***
- ❒ ***Submit scholarship application materials by their deadlines.***

APRIL

- ❒ ***Record deadlines and filing dates on your worksheet,*** MY APPLICATION CHECKLIST.
- ❒ ***Take the admissions tests for which you have registered.***
- ❒ ***Expect to hear from the independent colleges by mid-April*** regarding your admission status and your financial aid packages.
- ❒ ***Review your admission and financial aid offers carefully*** as you decide which college to attend.
- ❒ ***Discuss your financial aid package with the college*** if you are not satisfied with it. You may be able to negotiate some aspects of it.
- ❒ ***Contact the colleges at which you are wait-listed*** to determine your chances, how you can strengthen your application, and when you will know if you are admitted.
- ❒ ***Make the big decision about which college to attend.*** Review college videotapes and brochures, talk to students who attend, and visit the campuses, if possible.
- ❒ ***Notify the colleges of your decisions by May 1st.*** Inform the colleges you will not be attending of your decision as well as the one you have decided upon.
- ❒ ***Review housing application requirements*** of the college you will attend. Submit your housing application by the deadline.
- ❒ ***Send your commitment deposit by the deadline required*** by the college you plan to attend.
- ❒ ***Watch for notices from the Cal Grant A and Cal Grant B programs.*** They state whether you are a recipient of an award.
- ❒ ***Notify the Cal Grant program of the college you plan to attend.***
- ❒ ***Submit your admission applications to California Community Colleges.*** Get your applications from the guidance office, the career center, or the community colleges themselves.
- ❒ ***Sign up for community college placement tests and orientation.***
- ❒ ***Attend any community college open houses or tours*** to become familiar with programs and opportunities.
- ❒ ***Watch for scholarship announcements.***
- ❒ ***Submit scholarship application materials by their deadlines.***

grade **12**

YOUR ACTION PLANS

MAY

- ❒ ***Record deadlines and filing dates on your worksheet,*** MY APPLICATION CHECKLIST.
- ❒ ***Take the admissions tests for which you have registered.***
- ❒ ***Submit your community college applications.***
- ❒ ***Sign up for community college placement testing and orientation.***
- ❒ ***Inform the colleges you will not be attending of your decision.***
- ❒ ***Take placement examinations if required*** — English Placement Test (EPT) and the Entry Level Math (ELM) for CSU, Subject A for UC.
- ❒ ***Check on placement examinations for independent colleges.***
- ❒ ***Take your Advanced Placement Examinations.*** Ask your AP teachers for exact dates for specific examinations.
- ❒ ***Inform all of the high school staff members who helped you*** with the college admission process of your decisions and the scholarships you received. They will be delighted they helped you succeed in your goals!
- ❒ ***Request that your final transcript marked "graduated" be sent*** to the college you will be attending as soon as your final grades are available and you have graduated.
- ❒ ***Watch for scholarship announcements.***
- ❒ ***Submit scholarship application materials by their deadlines.***
- ❒ ***Sign up for the college orientation*** at the college you will attend. This program will help you to learn more about the college and to select your courses.

grade 12

JUNE

- ❒ ***Thank all those who helped you through this challenging year:*** Your family, friends, teachers, counselors, administrators, career center specialist, registrar, clerical staff, employers ....

Well you made it!

Off to college you go!

Congratulations!

Chapter 2

CHOOSING YOUR COLLEGE

There are more than two-hundred undergraduate colleges and universities in California. Do not be overwhelmed! Not just one college will fit your educational needs perfectly; several will come very close. Your challenge is to narrow down your possible choices to those most likely to satisfy your personal priorities. Clearly defined and evaluated criteria will help you through the maze of college options.

OVERVIEW

When thinking about the colleges that might be right for you, consider your abilities, motivations, interests, needs, and goals. Eleven criteria are outlined in this chapter to help you define what you want and need in a college. Some of these criteria may be very important to you, while others may have no importance at all. Narrowing down the field of college choices can be a fun research project. If you do it well, your decisions will be based upon factors critical to you. You will increase the likelihood of choosing colleges that "fit" you and provide the learning and social environment that maximizes your potential for success.

Review college catalogues and brochures, go to college fairs to obtain materials and talk with college representatives, attend college presentations at your high school, and talk with other students about their college experiences. Do you know former graduates attending a school you are considering? Write or call them. Have any of your classmates visited a school of interest to you? What were their impressions? Talk to your high school counselor, career center specialist, or administrator. They may have information about the experiences of prior graduates as well as a full library of reference materials and college catalogues.

Visiting the college campuses is one of the most effective ways to decide upon your schools.

Visiting college campuses is a most effective way to decide upon schools. Many families take a vacation, and together, visit colleges ... a "family campus tour." Your family will enjoy touring schools and discussing your options with you. Call the admissions offices of the colleges you wish to visit. They will set up a guided tour and arrange appointments with admissions and financial aid personnel. When visiting a college campus, sit in on some classes and observe how they are conducted. How does the instructor interact with students? Make arrangements with the admissions office to stay overnight in a dormitory to get a feeling for its atmosphere. For guidelines to get the most from your college visit, review the section, Your College Visit, on page 2--15.

NARROWING YOUR CHOICES

To How Many Colleges Should You Apply?

Narrow your choices to five to six schools to which to apply.

After exploring the colleges in which you are initially interested, narrow your choices to five to six schools to which to apply. You may decide to apply to more. Sort these colleges into three groups:

Group A: The colleges which are on your *"dream list,"* but are a reach for you, either because they are extremely competitive to get into, or because your qualifications are just on the edge of their requirements.

Group B: The colleges that interest you and which offer you a *"good, but not certain chance of admission."*

Group C: At least one college acceptable to you for which you are *"fairly certain of admission."* This third group will give you the safety schools, the ones in your *"hip pocket,"* in case none of your group A or group B choices accept you.

How many schools you place in each group depends upon your qualifications. Be sure to apply to at least one school in the *"hip pocket"* group.

College Comparisons

The following information will help you understand some of the differences among the many college opportunities in California.

UC — THE UNIVERSITY OF CALIFORNIA

Number of campuses	9, statewide.
Programs offered	Certificate, Bachelor's, Master's, Credential, First Professional, and Doctoral degree programs.
System supported by	Public tax money.
Costs	California resident: $3,799 enrollment fee, not including room and board, for a 1994-95 full-time student. Non-California resident: $7,699 tuition plus other fees.

The University of California is committed to admitting the top 12.5% of California high school graduates. Every qualified student who is a resident of California is entitled to admission at one of the University's campuses, although not necessarily at the campus of choice.

The University of California emphasizes research and academic theory.

The University focuses upon research and academic theory. Academics are theoretical, not practical. The emphasis is upon teaching you how to think, and how to abstract theories and apply them. The campuses are the state's primary, state-supported academic agency for research. Most faculty members both teach and conduct research. The University of California is the only California public system offering graduate instruction in dentistry, law, medicine, and veterinary medicine. Among the state's public institutions, it is the only one granting the Doctoral degree, except in a few fields where it awards joint Doctoral degrees with the California State University system.

CSU — CALIFORNIA STATE UNIVERSITY

Number of campuses	22, statewide.
Programs offered	Certificate, Bachelor's, Master's, Credential, and Doctoral degree programs.
System supported by	Public tax money.
Costs	California resident: $1,584 enrollment fee, not including room and board, for a 1994-95 full-time student. Non-California resident: $246 per semester unit/$164 per quarter unit plus other fees.

California State University is committed to admitting the top 33% of California high school graduates. Every qualified student who is a resident of California is entitled to admission at one of the University's campuses, although not necessarily at the campus of choice.

A degree from CSU has dual purposes: (1) Provide a broad liberal education. (2) Prepare students for specific professional and occupational goals. The focus is on blending classroom learning with practical application of the knowledge gained. Faculty members are committed to instruction as a main focus.

The California State University focuses upon practical application of knowledge.

The primary function of California State University is instruction of undergraduate and graduate degree students in the liberal arts and sciences, applied fields, and professions, including teaching. A limited number of programs leading to the Doctoral degree are also offered jointly with the University of California and private institutions.

CCC — CALIFORNIA COMMUNITY COLLEGES

Number of campuses.......	107, statewide.
Programs offered	Certificate and Associates degree occupational programs. Transfer programs to four-year institutions. Classes may be taken for personal or professional growth.
System supported by	Public tax money.
Costs	California resident: $13 per semester/$9 per quarter unit enrollment fee, not including room and board, for 1994-95. Non-California resident: $112 per semester unit/$75 per quarter unit.

California Community Colleges are open to anyone who has a high school diploma, a General Education Diploma (GED), a high school Proficiency Certificate, or, is eighteen years of age or older and shows evidence of being able to profit from instruction.

Community colleges emphasize transfer, occupational, and personal enrichment programs.

Community colleges emphasize transfer, occupational, and personal enrichment programs. They also serve as comprehensive community centers offering broad educational opportunities to meet local educational needs. Instruction covers, but does not go beyond, college-level freshman and sophomore courses. The community colleges grant vocational and technical certificates and the Associates degree. Community service and adult education programs offer noncredit classes.

CALIFORNIA INDEPENDENT COLLEGES

Number of campuses	Over 130 accredited, diverse undergraduate colleges, statewide.
Programs offered	Certificate, Associates, Bachelor's, Master's, Credential, First Professional, and Doctoral degree programs.
System supported by	Private funds, not public tax money.
Costs	Tuition for a full-time student, not including room and board, for 1994-95 varies from $4,600 to $18,669. There is no difference in tuition costs for California residents and nonresidents.

Admissions standards and requirements differ widely among the independent colleges. Some are highly selective, accepting only the most talented students; others admit the majority who apply.

California independent colleges are very different from one another in academic emphasis, programs, environment, and focus. They include nonsectarian and religiously affiliated, nonprofit and for-profit, technically-oriented, and liberal arts and sciences institutions. A full array of Bachelor's, Master's, and Doctoral degrees are offered, depending upon the specific school.

Independent colleges are very different from one another in academic emphasis, programs, environment, and focus.

Criteria For Choosing Your College

Here are eleven criteria to consider when choosing your college.

College type
Location and environment
College size
Competitiveness
Majors
Instruction
Support services
Student satisfaction and success
Extra curricular opportunities
Physical facilities
Costs

Each of these criteria is presented on the following pages with questions to help you understand what it means, how important it is to you, and what you need to know to evaluate it with respect to the colleges.

Additional questions will occur to you. Add them to the appropriate criteria — you cannot ask too many questions. A complete examination is essential to making an informed college decision.

As you review these criteria, rank them to help you define your priorities.

As you read through the criteria, rank them. Jot down notes in the margins. Which criteria are most important? Which are of no importance at all? This ranking can help you define your priorities. You will learn what questions and factors to emphasize as you evaluate colleges and their appeal to you. You will begin to focus your thinking.

At the end of this chapter is a worksheet, CHOOSING MY COLLEGE. This worksheet will help you organize your college search and make comparisons among schools during your screening process. It provides a system for you to objectively evaluate and rank the institutions you are considering.

COLLEGE TYPE

❒ Do you want to attend a four-year college immediately after high school?

❒ Do you want to begin your education at a community college and transfer later? If this is your plan, make sure the four-year college in which you are interested accepts transfer students. What courses will you be required to take at the community college to prepare for transfer?

❒ Do you wish to attend a public, private nonsectarian, or private religiously-affiliated school?

❒ Do you want a college that focuses on the liberal arts with a wide variety of subject areas, or one that is more limited in scope and concentrates, for example, on an art, business, science, technical, or engineering education?

❒ Do you want to attend an all-women or all-men institution?

LOCATION AND ENVIRONMENT

❒ Do you want to attend a college close to home or farther away?

❒ In what part of California would you like to attend college? Northern? Central? Southern?

❒ What type of campus setting appeals to you?

- A major city campus (urban)?
- Located close to but not in a major city?
- Located in a small- to medium-sized city?
- Located in a small town?
- Located in a rural area?
- Near water? The mountains? Farm country?

❒ Is the physical size and appearance of the campus important? Spread over many acres? Compact? Modern? Traditional?

❒ Are there museums, theaters, or other cultural activities nearby?

❒ Is there a program of speakers and/or cultural events on-campus or nearby? Remember that there may be fewer social and cultural activities in rural areas.

❒ What recreational activities are available? Snow? Mountains? Ocean? Bicycle trails? Shopping?

❒ Are climate, living pace, and/or environmental issues important considerations?

COLLEGE SIZE

❒ What size college do you wish to attend?

Size	Number of Students
Very Small	Less than 1,000
Small	1,000 to 5,000
Medium	5,000 to 10,000
Large	10,000 to 20,000
Very Large	More than 20,000

Smaller schools generally offer a closer student-teacher relationship, smaller classes, sometimes with a student/teacher ratio as low as 8/1, more individual attention, and the opportunity to become really active and well-known.

Larger campuses generally offer more majors and more varied course offerings, more cultural events such as speakers on campus, larger classes (lectures with perhaps two hundred to eight hundred students in them), more anonymity, and a more dynamic environment.

COMPETITIVENESS

❒ How competitive a college do you wish to attend? How much academic challenge do you want? Review the overall entrance difficulty of the college and the academic data of entering freshmen.

- What is the pattern of course work required for admission?
- How many college-preparatory classes are required?
- How many students apply? How many and what percentage of those who apply are accepted?
- Did most students come from the top 10% of their high school class? Top 25%? Top 50%?
- Which college admissions tests are required? ACT? SAT I: Reasoning Test? SAT II: Subject Tests? TOEFL?
- What percentage of entering freshmen scored over 600 on the SAT I: Verbal? Over 600 on the SAT I: Mathematics? Over 500?
- Did the middle fifty percent of entering freshmen score over 600, between 500 and 600, or between 400 and 500 on the verbal and mathematics SAT I tests?

❒ Is the prestige of the college important to you? When a college develops a strong reputation, it attracts more student applicants. The more applicants it has, the more selective it becomes. Generally, the more selective the college, the more highly regarded it is.

❒ Can you rank the reputation of the colleges and universities you are considering?

MAJORS

- ❐ Does the school offer the majors you are considering?
- ❐ Does it offer a wide range of courses and specialties in these majors?
- ❐ How many instructors are there in the departments of these majors?
- ❐ If you are not really decided upon your major, does the school offer a variety of options in your general areas of interest?
- ❐ What majors are most popular at the college?
- ❐ What majors are considered strong at the college? Weak?
- ❐ Can you create your own major with the aid of an advisor?
- ❐ Is an interdisciplinary major offered?
- ❐ Are internships available in your major?

INSTRUCTION

- ❐ What is the student/teacher ratio?
- ❐ What is the average class size? How many students are in lectures? Labs? Classes? Discussion groups?
- ❐ Are there opportunities to work with faculty on research?
- ❐ Are freshman and sophomore classes and labs taught by graduate assistants (graduate students) rather than regular faculty? Particularly at larger universities, lectures may be given by professors to large numbers of students (from one hundred to several hundred). Small group discussions are led by graduate assistants.
- ❐ Can you develop a close relationship with faculty? Are they friendly, concerned, and well-qualified? Are there informal, out-of-class opportunities to interact with the faculty?
- ❐ What percentage of the faculty have Ph.D.'s?
- ❐ Is the college on a semester, quarter, or trimester system, or another type of schedule?

  Colleges operate on an academic calendar. You may wish to consider the college calendar in choosing your college.

  Semester system: The school year is divided into two semesters, each generally seventeen to eighteen weeks long. Summer session is usually available.

4-1-4 system: The school year is divided into two semesters, each sixteen weeks long, and one interterm in January of one month's duration. Summer session is usually available.

Quarter system: The school year is divided into four quarters, each eleven to twelve weeks long. Students usually attend for three quarters per year. You may complete units faster if you attend the summer quarter as well.

Trimester system: The school year is divided into three trimesters, each about fifteen weeks long. Students usually attend two trimesters per year. You may complete units faster if you attend the summer trimester as well.

- ❐ Are there any special programs unique to the school? Grading procedures? Schedules? Majors? Seminars? Others?

SUPPORT SERVICES

- ❐ Is there a well-planned orientation program for new students, and possibly, parents as well?
- ❐ Are you assigned an advisor to help with course and major information? Is the advisor a faculty member or a counselor? Does advising occur frequently and informally? Can you choose your advisor?
- ❐ Are you assigned a peer counselor, an upper class "sister" or "brother," to help you with your adjustment to college, your concerns, and questions?
- ❐ Are there support programs for educationally-disadvantaged students and underrepresented students? Counseling? Peer assistance?
- ❐ Are there services for learning-disabled students? For physically-disabled students?
- ❐ Is tutoring available?
- ❐ Does the college have a well-organized and professionally staffed career center for career research?
- ❐ What is the track record of the placement center? Are part-time jobs available? How successful is the center in placing graduates in jobs?
- ❐ Is personal counseling available for adjustment problems?

STUDENT SATISFACTION AND SUCCESS

- ❐ Are students successful in enrolling in classes they need and want?
- ❐ What percentage of entering freshmen complete their degree at the college within four years? Within five years?
- ❐ Does the school offer a program of guaranteeing graduation within four years?
- ❐ What percentage of the senior class continues on to graduate school?

- ❐ What percentage of graduates who apply are accepted into medical school? Law school? Business school? Graduate school?

EXTRA CURRICULAR POSSIBILITIES

- ❐ What percentage of the student body is involved in extracurricular activities?
- ❐ In what intramural/intercollegiate sports does the school participate?
- ❐ To what athletic associations does the school belong?
- ❐ What kinds of clubs, organizations, and social activities are on campus? How many?
- ❐ Are there sororities/fraternities on campus? How important are they to school social life?
- ❐ Do you need a car or a bicycle to get around between classes? Into town?
- ❐ Does the school offer study programs in other countries or on other college campuses in the United States? Which ones? Are the programs for the summer, for one term, or for a full year?
- ❐ What degree of political and/or ethical activism occurs on the campus?

PHYSICAL FACILITIES

- ❐ What is the on-campus housing situation? Is housing difficult to get? Is there a lottery for determining priority in selecting housing?
- ❐ What types of on-campus housing facilities are available? Singles? Doubles? Suites? Apartments? High-rise? Low-rise?
- ❐ Are the dorms co-ed?
- ❐ Are you allowed to live off campus?
- ❐ Are there off-campus living facilities nearby?
- ❐ Is the library well-stocked and convenient?
- ❐ Are the science labs up-to-date and well-equipped?
- ❐ Are computer facilities available?
- ❐ What religious facilities are available on campus? Nearby?

COSTS

- ❒ What are the costs for tuition and fees for a year of school?
- ❒ What does it cost to live in the dormitory?
- ❒ Are there different board (food) plans and different numbers of meals-per-week if you are living in a dorm? Fourteen meals/week or twenty-one meals/week rates?
- ❒ What are off-campus housing costs? Is the college in an area of low, medium, or high-cost housing?
- ❒ Will you have expensive transportation costs to visit your family during vacations?
- ❒ What is the college's estimate of total expenses for one academic year?
- ❒ What kinds of financial aid are available?
- ❒ What percentage of the student body receives financial aid? How much is the average financial aid package?
- ❒ Does the school have any special procedures to apply for financial aid?

At college fairs, representatives from various colleges assemble in one location to disseminate information and materials about their schools.

COLLEGE FAIRS/ COLLEGE REPRESENTATIVES ON CAMPUS

College fairs and college representatives, who visit your high school, provide wonderful opportunities to learn about colleges.

At college fairs, representatives from various colleges throughout California and the country assemble in one location at a local high school or community college to disseminate information and materials about their schools. Each college is usually set up at a table with materials about its institution. One or more representatives from the school are available at the table to answer your questions. Additionally, there is often a program of large group presentations about the community colleges, the California State University system, the University of California system, the independent colleges, entrance testing, and financial aid.

Decide ahead of time which colleges you want to learn about, and prepare questions in advance.

In a separate program, college representatives visit high schools throughout the state to give college information presentations to groups of students. These presentations usually take place in the high school career center, library, or auditorium and last about a period. In some cases, the college representative may visit particular classes or have a table set up on your high school campus. Your high school will inform you of which representatives will be coming and how to sign up to meet them. The representatives welcome questions and sincere interest in their schools.

To get the most from the college fair:

- Fairs can have as many as one-hundred or more representatives and can attract from one to several thousand students and parents. They can be crowded and confusing. If you plan in advance, you can look for the schools of most interest and talk to those representatives first.

- Decide ahead of time from which colleges you want to gather information. Use your school career center to research the schools. Write down any questions unanswered by the college materials on hand and plan to ask them of the college representatives.

- If your parents are interested in attending, bring them along. Encourage them to participate. By attending workshops and meeting the campus representatives, they can get a firsthand understanding of the admissions process and college educational and financial aid opportunities. Later, they can help you in your decision-making.

- Go to the fair early, preferably just after it opens. This is your best chance of getting your specific questions answered from the representatives of your first choice schools. The fairs usually take place in late afternoon and evening; they often are very crowded after 6:30 P.M.

- You may find that the representative with whom you wish to speak is surrounded by a crowd of students and parents. You can learn a lot by listening to the questions others ask and the responses to them.

If your parents are interested in attending, bring them along. The college representatives are delighted to talk to them.

REQUEST FOR INFORMATION

Name ______________________ Soc. Sec. # (optional) ______________

Street Address ______________________________________

City ______________________ State ________ Zip ______________

Telephone ______________________ Male ☐ Female ☐

High School now attending ______________ City ______________ State ________

Estimated overall GPA ☐ PSAT verbal ☐ PSAT math ☐

ACT composite ☐ SAT I verbal ☐ SAT I math ☐

Possible majors ______________________________________

Extracurricular activities ______________________________________

I plan to enter as a ☐ First-time freshman. ☐ Transfer student. Fall ☐ Winter ☐ Spring ☐ of 199 ___

Ethnic origin (optional): ☐ American Indian/Native Alaskan ☐ Asian or Pacific Islander ☐ Black/African-American ☐ Hispanic/Latino ☐ Other

COLLEGE IN CALIFORNIA: *The Inside Track*

Scan the materials while you are at the fair to prompt yourself to ask additional on-the-spot questions.

- Collect written materials, brochures, and flyers to read later when you get home. Scan the materials while you are at the fair to prompt yourself to ask additional on-the-spot questions.

- Shown on the previous page is a sample of an information card that you should prepare in advance to give to college representatives. Giving them the completed card saves time and immediately places you on their mailing lists for information and application materials.

- Many of these same strategies are useful when attending a college representative's presentation on your campus.

NACAC/WACAC 1995 College Fairs

The National Association of College Administrators (NACAC) and the Western Association of College Admissions Counselors (WACAC) together sponsor NACAC/WACAC College Fairs throughout the western United States. College representatives are present to disseminate information and make presentations about colleges, admissions procedures, testing, and financial aid. These fairs are aimed especially at juniors, although students from all grade levels are welcome. Invite your parents to come with you. It is important that they are involved with your college research. Fairs occur in April and May according to the schedule shown here.

Before attending a college fair or college representative presentations, research schools and prepare questions.

NACAC/WACAC COLLEGE FAIR SCHEDULE SPRING 1995		
Date	County	Location
Wednesday, April 26th	Santa Clara	Santa Clara University
Thursday, April 27th	Alameda, Contra Costa	Saint Mary' s College
Friday, April 28th	Sonoma	Sonoma State University
Sunday, April 30th Monday, May 1st	Sacramento	UC Davis
Monday, May 1st	San Francisco	To be announced
Wednesday, May 3	San Diego	San Diego Convention Center
Thursday, May 4th,	Riverside, San Bernardino	Riverside Convention Center
Sunday, May 7th	Orange	Anaheim Convention Center
Tuesday, May 9th Wednesday, May 10th	Los Angeles	Pasadena Convention Center

YOUR COLLEGE VISIT

The college visit may be the best way to determine if a particular college will satisfy the selection criteria you have decided are most important to you. What could be better? You can see firsthand what a college looks and feels like and talk directly with students and faculty to get your questions answered.

There are two parts to the college visit. The first is a tour of the campus. Talk with students and teachers, visit classes, stay in the dormitory, and check out the physical facilities. The second part is a meeting with an admissions representative to answer your questions and concerns.

Take the campus tour first. It will suggest additional questions and clarifications you will need addressed during your subsequent interview with an admissions representative. It will also familiarize you with the school so that you can respond to the interviewer's questions in an informed manner. See chapter 7: STEPS IN THE APPLICATION PROCESS, Your Interview, page 7--19.

To get a sense of campus touring, first visit colleges close to home and only of moderate interest. Save the schools in which you have the greatest interest until last. By then, you will be more sophisticated about what is important to you, and you will know what to look for at the schools.

First visit colleges close to home and of only moderate interest. Save the schools in which you have the greatest interest until last when you are more experienced in the selection process.

YOUR CAMPUS TOUR

Call several weeks in advance to arrange for your visit. Campuses often have the largest number of visitors in the fall months.

Determine in advance what you want to know about the school, and what you hope to gain from your visit. Bring your worksheet, CHOOSING MY COLLEGE, with you to use as your prioritized list of important criteria. It will keep you focused on the questions you most want answered about the school. Jot down questions and comments during the tour so you do not forget anything of critical importance. Fill in the worksheet as you go or at the end of the tour when the information is fresh in your mind. This is especially important if you have scheduled yourself to visit several campuses in succession. After two or three college visits, facts and impressions will blur. Writing notes can help keep your information and reactions clear.

Determine in advance what you want to know about the school. Bring your worksheet, CHOOSING MY COLLEGE, ***to help you focus your questions.***

Visit the college during the week. Plan to attend classes in session to observe what the school is like with students present and activities occurring. The atmosphere and culture of the campus will be evident. Faculty and coaches will be available to meet with you.

Stay overnight in a dormitory. Make arrangements to eat in the dining hall. These experiences can give you a realistic view of college life and the opportunity to talk informally with the students.

The campus tour will usually take one to one-and-one-half hours. Leave time to explore on your own. Get a map of the campus and visit areas of special interest.

Observe more than one class in subject areas of interest to you. Get to the classes a little early and stay awhile afterwards. Do students talk informally with the instructor before and after class? Are students encouraged to ask questions during the lecture? How big are the classes? Are you welcomed?

Your campus tour guide will undoubtedly be a student at the college. Freely ask him or her whatever questions occur to you. These students are knowledgeable about their school and familiar with procedures, activities, and the practical aspects you will want to know about from the perspective of a student. Presented below are some questions to ask of your guide. These will get you started. You will think of others. Note the responses on your worksheet, CHOOSING MY COLLEGE.

- ❒ How accessible is the faculty? Do you need an appointment far in advance, or are you able to meet with staff members informally and frequently? Do they mingle with students in the cafeteria? Do they include juniors and seniors in research projects?
- ❒ How tough are the classes? How much studying is expected? How does your campus guide compare this college experience to high school?
- ❒ Do freshmen have difficulty enrolling in courses because classes are overcrowded and priority registration is given to upperclassmen? If so, which subjects are particularly crowded?
- ❒ Who teaches freshman and sophomore classes? Experienced professors? Graduate students?
- ❒ What are weekends like? Are activities planned? Do most students generally go home?
- ❒ What is the overall atmosphere? Party school? Studious? Balanced between the two? How is the social life? Are students friendly?
- ❒ What does your campus tour guide like best about the school? Least?
- ❒ To what other schools did your campus tour guide apply? Why did he or she come to this one? Has it met his or her expectations?
- ❒ Can you get any tips for your interview?
- ❒ How is the dormitory food? Any good restaurants nearby?
- ❒ What if you have personal or academic problems? What kind of help is available?
- ❒ Is the campus safe?
- ❒ Are there any rules or regulations you should know about?

Staying overnight in a dormitory and eating in the dining hall will give you a realistic view of college life. You will have the opportunity to talk informally with students.

Be sure your tour includes the library, computer center, student center, bookstore, and any other areas of particular interest such as the athletic facilities, laboratories, and your major's department.

Your parents are undoubtedly interested and involved in your college decision-making and may accompany you on your campus tours. This is very acceptable to the colleges. If you meet with an admissions representative to talk about the school, your parents can join you to have their questions answered. However, if you go in for your formal admissions interview, your parents should leave you alone with the interviewer. See chapter 7: STEPS IN THE APPLICATION PROCESS, Your Interview, page 7--19.

Immediately after your tour, write down your general impressions.

Immediately after your tour, write down your general impressions, concerns, enthusiasms. What appeals to you? What does not? Are you comfortable with what you have learned? Can you visualize yourself as a student there? How does the school compare in the criteria important to you with others you have visited?

Talk over your impressions of the school with your parents. Share your worksheet and your general impressions with them. Seek their reactions and opinions.

CHOOSING MY COLLEGE WORKSHEET

Use the worksheet, CHOOSING MY COLLEGE, on the next pages to help you determine the colleges to which to apply, and after acceptance, to help you select the actual college to attend. Review the criteria and mark those most important to you. Across the top of the worksheet list the colleges you wish to compare according to these criteria. Jot down notes on the worksheet as you research the colleges through written materials, meetings with college representatives, campus visits, and conversations with current students. Record your impressions from your campus visits and interviews.

CHOOSING MY COLLEGE

COLLEGE NAME:	US Fransis	SONOMA STATE UNIVERSITY	UNIVERSITY OF SAN DIEGO	HUMBOLTD STATE UNIVERSITY		
CHANCE OF ADMISSION:						
COLLEGE TYPE:						
Public, Private, Religious						
Liberal Arts, Technical						
Two-Year Or Four-Year	FOUR YEAR	FOUR YEAR	FOUR YEAR	FOUR YEAR		
LOCATION & ENVIRONMENT:						
Where In California	SAN FRAN	NAPA VALLEY	SAN DIEGO	NEAR EUREKA		
Campus Setting						
Cultural Opportunities						
Recreational Opportunities						
COLLEGE SIZE:						
Number Of Students				6,000		
COMPETITIVENESS:						
Required College-Preparatory Courses						
Required Admissions Tests						
Freshmen Class Standing . . .						
% From Top 10% Of Class						
% From Top 50% Of Class						
Freshmen Verbal/Math SAT I Scores . . .						
% Over 600	/	/	/	/	/	/
Range Of Middle 50%-V	–	–	–	–	–	–
Range Of Middle 50%-M	–	–	–	–	–	–
# Of Applicants						
# Of Applicants Accepted						
School Prestige . . . High, Average, Low						
Other						
MAJORS:						
Has The Major You Want						
# Of Courses In Your Major						
# Of Instructors In Your Major						
# Of Specializations In Your Major						
Broad Curriculum For Undeclared Majors						
Other						

COLLEGE IN CALIFORNIA: *The Inside Track*

COLLEGE NAME:						
INSTRUCTION:						
Student/Teacher Ratio	/	/	/	/	/	/
Average Class Size						
# Of Students In Lectures, Labs						
Teaching Assistants						
Student/Faculty Relationships						
Semester/Quarter System						
SUPPORT SERVICES:						
Orientation For New Students						
Faculty Or Peer Advisors						
Career Center						
Counseling Services						
Job Placement						
Other						
STUDENT SATISFACTION & SUCCESS:						
Success in Enrolling in Needed Classes						
% of Freshmen Completing A Degree Within 5 Years						
% Of Graduates Going On To Graduate School						
Other						
EXTRA-CURRICULAR PROGRAMS:						
Sports						
# & Type Of Clubs						
Sororities/Fraternities						
Study Abroad						
Other						
PHYSICAL FACILITIES:						
Availability Of Dormitory Space						
Availability Of Off-Campus Housing						
Religious Facilities						
Other						
COSTS:						
Tuition/Fees						
Housing						
College-Estimated Total Annual Expenses						
% Students on Financial Aid						
Average Financial Aid Package						

CHOOSING YOUR COLLEGE

CHOOSING YOUR COLLEGE

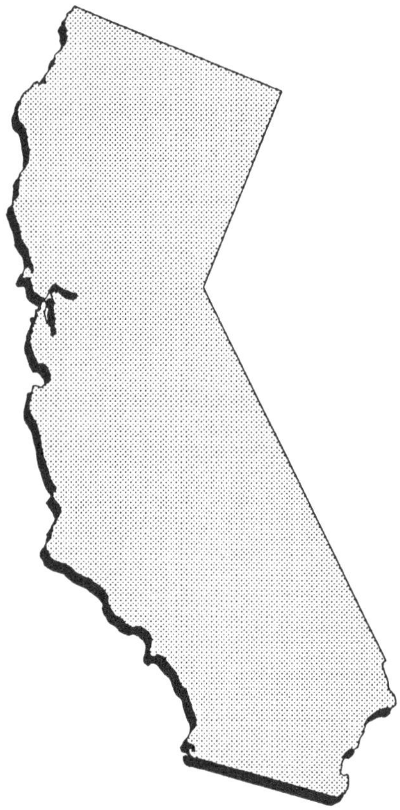

Chapter 3

CHOOSING YOUR MAJOR

CHOOSING YOUR MAJOR

"What do you want to major in?" is a question you probably think about often and hear from others. Your parents most likely are concerned about your choice. If your major fits your interests, activities, and long-term goals, it will keep you motivated and challenged in college.

OVERVIEW

As you consider continuing your education, you are probably trying to decide upon a major. You may select a major that prepares you for a particular career, or you may choose one because the subject and curriculum for the degree interest you.

Your decision about a major is not necessarily a lifelong commitment to a specific career goal. A major can lead to any number of careers. Many college graduates choose careers unrelated to their college major, especially in liberal arts. The broad background presented in liberal arts majors develops in you a number of skills that fit a wide variety of career choices.

Your decision about a major is not necessarily a lifelong commitment to a specific career goal.

Majors in such fields as engineering, computer science, science, and health usually do prepare you for specific job areas. However, even in these areas there is a great deal of choice regarding the particular career you select. For example, a biology major might become a teacher, medical researcher, pharmaceutical products salesperson, physician, physical therapist, or dietician.

Choose a major that fits your interests, abilities, long-term goals, and very importantly, one which will keep you motivated and challenged in college.

COLLEGE DEGREES

In selecting a major, consider how many years of college you are willing to complete. You can pursue some majors through a certificate program and enter a job upon its completion. Others may require a Doctoral degree to obtain a position in one of its related careers.

College programs differ in:

- The type of courses required.
- The number of units required in these courses.
- The total number of units required for program completion.
- The length of time necessary to complete the units.
- The degree you receive upon completion.

Progress through college is measured by the number of units you complete, just as progress through high school is measured by the number of credits you complete.

Progress through college is measured by the number of units you complete, just as progress through high school is measured by the number of credits you complete. Typically, the number of units earned in a college class correlates with the number of hours per week the class meets. For example, a three-unit class meets three class hours per week, a four-unit class meets four class hours per week. Generally, college classes vary from one-half unit to five units. Half-units are often given for physical education classes, five units are often given for laboratory science classes.

College courses taken to complete the units for a program fall into three categories: general education, your major, and electives. Programs differ in how many units toward the total must be completed in each of these three areas. These categories are explained fully in chapter 9: CALIFORNIA COMMUNITY COLLEGES, Components Of A Transfer Program, page 9--12.

Certificate of Completion: The Certificate of Completion in a specific career program varies in the number of units required for completion. The unit requirement can range from 15 to 40 semester units/24 to 60 quarter units or more. Courses are taken in your major for career preparation.

In selecting a major, consider how many years of college you are willing to complete.

Associates Degree: The Associates degree generally is a two-year degree program, although it may take longer to complete if you attend part-time. Completion usually requires 60 semester/90 quarter units. Required courses are taken in general education and your major. Electives are optional.

Bachelor's Degree: The Bachelor's degree generally is a four-year program, although it may take longer to complete if you attend part-time. Completion requires a minimum of 124 to 136 semester units/180 to 200 quarter units. Courses are taken in general education and your major. Electives are optional.

Credential Program: The Teacher Credential Program in California is made up of a sequence of requirements, which may take as long as six years to complete. This time includes the four years needed to earn a Bachelor's degree. See this chapter, page 3--11 for a full description of Credential requirements.

Master's Degree: The Master's degree generally is a one- to two-year program requiring 36 to 60 semester units/48 to 90 quarter units beyond a Bachelor's degree. The program may take longer to complete if you attend part-time. Courses are taken in your major.

First Professional Degree: The First Professional degree generally is a program totalling at least six years. For admission to it, you must have completed the first two years of college. Courses are taken in your major. Completion indicates completion of academic requirements for the practice of Chiropractic, Dentistry, Law, Medicine, Pharmacy, Podiatry, Theology, or Veterinary Medicine.

Doctoral Degree: The Doctoral degree is the highest degree awarded. It is generally a three to six year program requiring 90 or more semester/135 or more quarter units beyond a Bachelor's degree, or 60 or more semester/90 or more quarter units beyond the Master's degree. It requires advanced courses in your major and a research project, known as a dissertation or thesis.

A college major is a field of study or a discipline that represents your principal academic interest.

COLLEGE MAJORS

A college major is a field of study or a discipline that represents your principal academic interest. The curriculum required in your major focuses your course of study so that you develop a thorough knowledge of your chosen major.

College majors fall into the following general disciplines:

Agriculture	Engineering
Architecture, Natural Resources, and Environmental Design	Food, Nutrition, and Consumer Sciences
Arts: Applied, Fine, and Performing	Health Sciences
Area and Ethnic Studies	Humanities
Biological and Life Sciences	Foreign Language and Literature
Business and Management	Mathematics
Communications	Physical Education
Computer and Information Sciences	Physical Sciences
Education	Social Sciences

Within these disciplines are specializations.

Within these disciplines are specializations. For example, among the specializations in Area and Ethnic Studies are African Studies, Latin American Studies, and American Indian Studies. Among the specializations in Business and Management are Accounting, Hotel and Restaurant Management, and Economics.

Frequently confusing are specializations known by different names. Administration of Justice, Criminal Justice, and Law Enforcement in college catalogues generally refer to the same major. Unless you are familiar with its alternate names, you may have difficulty determining if a particular major is offered at the college you are considering. If you believe a major is offered and you cannot find it listed, think of other names for it. If your research does not answer your questions, call the school and inquire.

DECIDING UPON A MAJOR

Deciding upon a major is a three step process ...

Step 1. Assess yourself. Review your high school years and think about what you have learned about your interests, personality, abilities, and values.

Assess yourself — your interests, personality, abilities, and values.

- ❐ Which courses do you like best? Least?
- ❐ Which classes are your strongest? Which ones are your weakest?
- ❐ Are there any areas that you study on your own initiative?
- ❐ What extracurricular activities do you enjoy? Why?
- ❐ Do your hobbies relate to a major?
- ❐ Do you want to work mostly with people? With data? With things?
- ❐ How hard do you like to study?
- ❐ What are the things you do best? Express yourself well in writing or speaking? Relate easily to other people? Help others? Use computational skills? Do research? Create new ideas or things? Plan and manage projects? Supervise others?

- ❐ What do you want from your career? Money? Travel? Time for family? Adventure? Security?
- ❐ Do you want to work for someone else or own your own business?

Step 2. Evaluate the curriculum required by each of the majors of interest to you. Review college catalogs and talk to college representatives.

Review college catalogs and talk to college representatives about majors.

- ❐ What courses are you required to take in the major?
- ❐ Do these courses appeal to you? Do they stimulate your interest?
- ❐ Does the major require many courses you would dislike? Is this a serious problem?
- ❐ Does the major require many courses that would be overly difficult for you? Is this a serious problem?
- ❐ Would you feel challenged by the courses in the major?
- ❐ Does the major allow much opportunity to take electives? Is this important to you?
- ❐ What degrees are required for careers based upon this major? Do these educational requirements fit your plans?

Step 3. Research careers related to majors. Visit your high school career center. Based upon your self-assessment, review possible career options for each of the majors of interest to you. How well do these careers fit you?

COMMONLY ASKED QUESTIONS ABOUT MAJORS

MUST I CHOOSE A MAJOR WHEN I ENTER A FOUR-YEAR COLLEGE?

Unless you are preparing for a major that requires numerous preparatory courses, you usually do not need to declare a major until the end of your sophomore year.

Unless you are preparing for a major that requires numerous preparatory courses — for example, majors in engineering or science — you usually do not have to declare a major until the end of your sophomore year of college. During your first two years of school, you are exposed to a wide range of areas of study for the first time. You are required to complete lower-division (freshman and sophomore) General Education/Breadth courses, which are graduation requirements expected of all students regardless of major. General Education/Breadth requirements are explained in chapter 9: CALIFORNIA COMMUNITY COLLEGES, Components Of A Transfer Program, page 9--12. Use your freshman and sophomore college years to explore the variety of options open to you. You may become interested in a concentration previously unknown to you.

HAVE MOST STUDENTS WHO ENTER FOUR-YEAR COLLEGES DECIDED UPON A MAJOR?

No. Many, many students who enter four-year colleges have not definitely decided upon a major. Many who do have one in mind, change it when they get to college. If you are one of the many who do not have a definite major selected, be sure to enroll in a school offering a broad curriculum. You will be able to try out various courses and expose yourself to new fields. When you decide upon your major, you will not have to change institutions to pursue it.

If you do not have a college major selected before enrolling, choose a college offering a broad curriculum.

WILL I BE ABLE TO CHANGE MY MAJOR ONCE I AM IN COLLEGE?

Usually, changing your major is easily accomplished unless you wish to change to one which requires a heavy concentration in science, technical, or specific preparatory courses during the first two years. If you do choose a major requiring extensive freshman and sophomore prerequisite courses, you may have some coursework to make up when you change majors. The number of years needed to complete your program could be extended. Also, it may be difficult to change to a major that is already full on your campus.

HOW CAN I FIND OUT WHICH COLLEGES OFFER THE BEST PROGRAMS IN THE MAJOR I HAVE IN MIND?

Here are some strategies to help you answer this question.

- Look up the major you are considering in the catalogues of the colleges of interest to you. Arrange all the catalogues in front of you. Compare the programs with each other using the following criteria:

Specializations: How many areas of specialization are in the department? Can you specialize in your area of interest? A program with several specializations generally has a larger selection of courses to choose from. For example, a psychology major might offer the following concentrations: Clinical, social, developmental, school. There may be more.

Look up the major you are considering in the catalogues of the colleges of interest to you and compare programs.

Courses: How many courses are listed? How extensive are the range and variety of courses? What is the emphasis? For example, if you are interested in majoring in business with an emphasis on small business, determine how many and what type of classes are available with small business as a focus.

Professors: How many professors are in the department? How many have Ph.D.'s? What proportion of the total teaching staff of the school teaches in your department of interest? These numbers can give you an idea of the size and strength of the department.

Student data: What percentage of the student body majors in your field? How many apply for and get into graduate school? These figures can give you a sense of how important and how successful the major is in the school.

- The size of the colleges you are comparing is important. If one school is much larger than the others, it could present a more comprehensive program just because of its size. On the other hand, a small, specialized college may offer a strong program because of its emphasis upon a particular discipline.

- You may want to contact the admissions office at each school to discuss your areas of interest and your particular concerns. How responsive are the personnel and faculty to your call and your questions? When you visit the college, visit the department. Be sure to talk to students in the program.

Many career opportunities require thinking and people skills rather than specialized technical skills.

WILL I BE ABLE TO GET A JOB IF I MAJOR IN A LIBERAL ARTS SUBJECT?

As a liberal arts major, you will develop skills in research, writing, interpersonal relationships, and critical thinking that are widely applicable to a number of professions. These skills are highly regarded by employers. Many career opportunities require thinking and people skills rather than specialized technical skills. You may wish to take courses in computing or business to enhance your qualifications. Your college extracurricular activities, internships, jobs and volunteer work, and independent study projects all improve your chances in the job market.

MUST I MAJOR IN PRE-MEDICINE, PRE-DENTAL, PRE-VETERINARY, OR PRE-LAW TO GET INTO GRADUATE PROGRAMS IN THESE FIELDS?

No. These graduate school majors may require that you complete certain preparatory courses as an undergraduate, but in most cases they do not require a specific major. More information on these majors is presented on the following pages.

SHOULD I CHOOSE A MAJOR THAT LEADS TO A CAREER WITH STRONG DEMAND IN THE MARKETPLACE?

A career that is in demand now may not be in demand four or ten years from now.

This factor may be an important criteria for you. However, job trends change. A career that is in demand now may not be in demand four or ten years from now. Also, new careers will emerge in the future. You must know yourself to choose a career that suits you. Knowing yourself means reviewing your interests, your values, your personality and your abilities. These factors should be just as important to you in making your major and career choices, as future job opportunities.

WHERE CAN I GET HELP IN CHOOSING A MAJOR?

Your high school counselor and/or career center has materials to help you learn about yourself and the majors and careers to consider. Up-to-date information about various career opportunities and job trends should be found there as well.

Colleges have career centers with personnel to provide career guidance. College advisors, counselors, and job-placement officers are all resources to tap. Many colleges offer courses in career decision-making and workshops on choosing a major. These programs are designed to help you learn more about yourself so that you can define the direction that best fits you. When investigating colleges ask about their career guidance services.

PRE-PROFESSIONAL PROGRAMS

PRE-MEDICAL, PRE-DENTAL, PRE-VETERINARY

No specific major is required to get into medical, law, or business schools.

Medical school is a four-year program after you have completed at least three years of undergraduate college — four years and a Bachelor's degree are preferred for admission. The term "pre" indicates that you must take certain courses as an undergraduate to prepare you for admission to medical school, but there is no preferred undergraduate college major. These required courses can be included in your major or in your electives.

Most medical schools expect, as a minimum, that you have completed these college courses: One year each of English, biology, inorganic chemistry, organic chemistry, physics, and math (calculus and statistics). Other courses that may be required are vertebrate embryology, genetics, cell or molecular biology, biochemistry, comparative anatomy, developmental physiology, and computer science. Additional English and a foreign language (especially Spanish in California) may be required or recommended.

When you read that a college offers premedical, pre-dental, or pre-veterinary science, the college is indicating that it offers the courses just listed as part of their curriculum. You can major in any subject you wish. Students often do major in a biological science because the coursework for this major mirrors to a great extent those courses required for medical school admission.

The term "pre" indicates that you must take certain courses as an undergraduate to prepare you for admission to medical school, but there is no preferred undergraduate college major.

Many students believe that if they wish to go to a particular medical school, they should choose that same school for their undergraduate preparatory work to gain preferential consideration. Medical schools say there is no preferential admission for students from their own undergraduate school. They review an entire set of factors reflecting your undergraduate college record and the degree of your commitment to becoming a physician: College coursework and GPA, Medical College Admissions Test (MCAT) scores, application essay, interview, letters of recommendation, experience in health fields, extracurricular activities, and research.

Acceptance to medical school is extremely competitive. Some undergraduate colleges have more success in getting their graduates into medical schools than others. Ask the colleges you are considering about their success rate. What percentage of their graduates who apply to medical school are admitted? Also find out what type of premedical advising is available as you prepare for medical school and complete your application process.

If medical school is your ultimate goal, be sure to include in your high school curriculum as many courses as possible in biology, chemistry, physics, and mathematics to prepare you for the college-level courses in these subjects. Also, get some experience, either as a paid employee or as a volunteer, in a health service setting such as a clinic or hospital, or a veterinary, dental, or medical office. Doing so can help you decide if a health career is appropriate for you, and it will allow you to state evidence of early interest and commitment on your medical school application.

CHOOSING YOUR MAJOR

Pre-Law

Major in a subject of interest to you in which you can excel.

Law school is a three-year program after you receive your Bachelor's degree. No specific or pre-law undergraduate major is necessary for admission to law school. Major in a subject of interest to you in which you can excel. Many students planning on law school major in the humanities, social sciences, business, or natural sciences. Courses that help develop your reading and writing skills, and your ability to analyze and reason logically, can help you do well in law school entrance examinations and in your law school courses.

Admission to law school is very competitive. A four-year Bachelor's degree is required. Law schools do not give preference to graduates from their own undergraduate schools. When reviewing applicants, law schools consider your grades, Law School Admission Test (LSAT) score, personal statement on your law school application, letters of recommendation, extracurricular activities, and work experience.

Some undergraduate colleges have more success in getting their graduates into law schools than others. Ask the colleges you are considering about their success rate. What percentage of their graduates who apply to law school are admitted? Also find out what type of pre-law advising is available as you proceed through your undergraduate program and complete the application process.

In high school, enroll in classes and activities that can develop your writing, speaking, and reasoning skills. English composition and oral communication classes as well as participation in debate and student government, are some suggestions. A job in a law office can give you firsthand knowledge and experience in the field you can cite on your law school application.

Business Administration/ Business Management

Full-time work experience is becoming increasingly important for admission to business schools.

A Master's degree program in business administration or management requires two years of additional study after you receive your Bachelor's degree. You may major in business in undergraduate school, although no specific undergraduate major is required for admission and no preference is given to any field of study. Skills in writing, oral communication, and mathematics are important for admission, and courses in micro- and macro-economics, accounting, statistics, and calculus may be prerequisites for acceptance.

Just like medical and law school, admission to business school is very competitive. A four-year Bachelor's degree is required. Business schools do not give preference to graduates from their own undergraduate schools. When reviewing applicants, the schools consider your grades, test scores on the Graduate Management Admissions Test (GMAT), letters of recommendation, and evidence of leadership potential and organizational skills. Full-time work experience is increasingly important for admission. Some of the most prestigious business programs have initiated a process of deferred admission to ensure that students have the necessary work experience before they undertake graduate study.

In high school, enroll in classes that can develop your writing, speaking, and mathematics background. Extracurricular activities such as participation in student government, clubs, and work experience demonstrate leadership and practical organizational skills.

California Teaching Credentials

Colleges offer credential programs to prepare you to teach at the elementary level or the secondary level. There are two basic teaching credentials:

There are two basic teaching credentials in California: The Multiple Subject Credential to teach elementary and middle school, and the Single Subject Credential to teach departmentalized junior or senior high school.

Multiple Subject Credential: The Multiple Subject Credential authorizes you to teach in a classroom where many different subjects are taught by a single individual. You typically teach in an elementary or middle school.

Single Subject Credential: The Single Subject Credential authorizes you to teach in a classroom where only one subject is taught. You typically teach in a departmentalized junior high or high school.

You may study for either or both credentials.

Both credentials have two levels: the Preliminary and the Professional Clear. You can earn the Preliminary Credential in a four-year Bachelor's degree program. The Preliminary Credential authorizes you to begin teaching. Within five years of the issuance of your Preliminary Credential you must attend college for a fifth year to earn a Professional Clear Credential.

Preliminary Credential: To meet the minimum requirements for the Preliminary Credential, you must do the following:

a. Earn a Bachelor's degree in a field other than professional education. According to California law, any major other than education can be selected. To teach at the elementary level most students interested in a Multiple Subject Credential select Liberal Studies or Child Development as a major. Majors in the social sciences, humanities, or natural sciences also can be excellent backgrounds for careers in elementary education. To teach at the secondary level most students interested in a Single Subject Credential complete the degree major closest to the subject field in which they wish to teach.

b. Complete an approved program of teacher preparation, including supervised student teaching for two semesters or quarters with a minimum grade of B on a five point scale.

c. Pass the California Basic Education Skills Test (CBEST), a test of reading, writing, critical thinking, and mathematics skills.

d. Demonstrate subject matter competency appropriate to the specific credential which is awarded. Competency required for the Multiple Subject Credential is a broad general knowledge of the arts, humanities, social sciences, mathematics, language arts, and natural sciences. Competency required for the Single Subject Credential is a knowledge of the subject you plan to teach.

You may demonstrate this competency by either passing a state-approved subject matter examination or by completing a state-approved academic program, a "waiver program." Your degree program may or may not satisfy this requirement. Seek academic advising for assistance in meeting degree and waiver program requirements.

e. Satisfactorily complete a course on the United States Constitution (2 semester/ 3 quarter units) or pass a test on this subject.

f. Complete a course in the methods of teaching reading, or pass the National Teacher Examination entitled "Introduction to the Teaching of Reading."

Professional Clear Credential: To meet the minimum requirements for the Professional Clear Credential, you must do the following:

To complete the Professional Clear Credential you must complete a fifth year of study after the Bachelor's degree.

a. Complete a fifth year of study after the Bachelor's degree. This must be done within five years of receipt of your Preliminary Credential.

b. Complete a unit requirement in health education.

c. Complete a requirement in the needs and methods of providing educational opportunities to individuals with exceptional needs (mainstreaming).

d. Satisfactorily complete computer education coursework, which includes general and specialized skills in the use of computers in educational settings.

You must earn a GPA of C on a five-point scale or the GPA required by your college, whichever is higher, in all coursework offered toward fulfillment of credential requirements.

Chapter 4

PAYING FOR COLLEGE

PAYING FOR COLLEGE

Although college costs increase each year, it is possible for you to afford to attend. More than half the students now in college receive some type of financial aid. The money is available to assist you, but you must go after it. Organize your search, investigate the various options, and complete your applications in a timely manner. Think about your college education as an investment in your future and make it happen!

OVERVIEW

When you talk about preparing for and choosing colleges, your parents probably get excited about your plans and want to support your educational goals. Undoubtedly, they also become concerned about how to pay for your college expenses. Do not let the high costs of a college education discourage you or them — affording college is possible. There are several ways to pay for college. One is financial aid, money from outside sources to pay for part or all of your education. Outside sources may be the federal and state governments, colleges, private organizations, companies, and/or lending institutions. Another way to help pay for college is based upon your personal financial strategies to reduce your costs. Still a third emphasizes allocating your money to maximize its use in meeting your needs. Your financial plan may include one of these methods or a combination of several.

Do not let the high costs of a college education discourage you — affording college is possible.

You and your parents should review the various possibilities presented in this chapter and determine which ones best suit your needs, your qualifications, and your family's financial circumstances.

WAYS TO PAY

FINANCIAL AID

Financial aid refers to several different types of programs offered by outside sources of money to assist you to pay for college. These include outright awards of money that do not need to be paid back, loans that must be repaid with interest, and self-help, work-study opportunities.

- **Grants:** Awards of money based upon your financial need. Academic achievement or other factors *may* be considered in addition to need. Grants need not be paid back.

- **Scholarships:** Awards of money based upon your grades or other achievements. Financial need *may* or *may not* be a criteria. Scholarships need not be paid back.

- **Educational Loans:** Moneys that you, your parents and/or guardians borrow to pay for your educational expenses. Loans *must* be paid back with interest.

- **Work-Study:** Part-time job programs to earn money for college expenses.

Financial aid includes awards of money that do not need to be repaid, loans that must be paid back with interest, and self-help, work-study opportunities.

COLLEGE COST REDUCTION

You can reduce your costs of attending college to some extent by a number of techniques including (a) attending a less expensive college, (b) attending college for fewer years, and (c) diligently budgeting your sources of money and your expenses.

CREATIVE FINANCIAL PLANNING

Creative financial planning can reduce the adverse impact of your college expenses on your family's cash flow and assets. However, the effectiveness of this option depends upon various strategies best explained to you and your parents by an accountant or financial planner.

PAYING FOR COLLEGE

SOURCES OF FINANCIAL AID

Sources of financial aid to pay for college are numerous and varied. The United States government, the State of California, the colleges and universities themselves, financial institutions, and private sources such as the business community, churches, clubs, and ethnic groups have programs to assist students with their college expenses.

Sources of financial aid to pay for college are numerous and varied.

THE UNITED STATES GOVERNMENT

Some federal programs provide assistance directly from the United States government to you — you apply directly to the government for this aid. Others are administered by the schools and colleges or the state of California, which determine how to use available federal programs to meet students' financial needs.

Eligibility Requirements

To receive financial aid from the United States government you must meet certain eligibility requirements.

In order to receive federal financial aid or borrow a California guaranteed loan under the federal loan program you must...

- have a high school diploma, a GED, or demonstrate the ability to benefit from the program or training offered;
- be enrolled in college at least halftime; i.e., six semester or quarter hours per term;
- be enrolled as a regular student in an eligible school (one that takes part in federal financial aid programs) in a course of study that leads to a degree or certificate;
- make satisfactory academic progress;
- sign a statement that if you are required to register with the selective service, you have done so;
- sign a statement certifying that you will not make, distribute, dispense, possess, or use drugs during the period covered by your grant;
- not be in default or owe a refund on a federal grant or educational loan; and
- be one of the following:

  a. United States citizen
  b. United States national including natives of American Samoa or Swain's Island
  c. United States permanent resident who has an Alien Registration Receipt Card (I-151, I-551, or I-551C).

  If you are not in one of these categories, you must have an Arrival-Departure Record (I-94) from the United States Immigration and Naturalization Service (INS) showing one of the following designations:

  a. "Refugee"
  b. "Asylum Granted"
  c. "Indefinite Parole" and/or "Humanitarian Parole"
  d. "Cuban-Haitian Entrant, Status Pending,"
  e. "Conditional Entrant" (valid only if issued before April 1, 1980)
  f. Other eligible noncitizen with a temporary residency card (I-688)

  Or, you can be eligible based on the Family Unity Status category, with approved I-797s (Voluntary Departure and Immigrant Petition).

Also, you remain eligible for federal student aid if you have a suspension of deportation case pending before Congress.

If you have only a Notice of Approval to Apply for Permanent Residence (I-171 or I-464 A), you are not eligible for federal student aid.

If you are in the United States on an F1 or F2 student visa only, or on a J1 or J2 exchange visitor visa only, you cannot get federal student aid. Also, if you have a G series visa (pertaining to international organizations), you are not eligible for federal student aid.

Permanent residents of the Trust Territory of the Pacific (Palau) may be eligible for all federal student aid programs.

If you are a citizen of the Marshall Islands, the Federated States of Micronesia, or Palau, you are eligible for Federal Pell Grants, Federal Supplemental Opportunity Grants, or Federal Work-Study only.

For answers to questions about federal student aid, call this toll free number: (800) 4-FED-AID (800-433-3243) between 9:00 A.M. and 5:30 P.M., eastern time, Monday through Friday. Obtain the booklet, *The Student Guide: Financial Aid From The United States Department of Education* for a full description of federal financial aid programs.

STATE OF CALIFORNIA

The State of California, through the California Student Aid Commission, sponsors financial aid programs for students seeking a postsecondary education. With the exception of the Federal Stafford Loans and the Federal Parents Loan For Students (PLUS) described later in this chapter, all California Student Aid Commission awards are available only to California residents who attend California colleges, universities, or postsecondary vocational schools. Stafford and PLUS loans may be used by California residents for out-of-state colleges. See appendix A: CALIFORNIA RESIDENCY REQUIREMENTS.

The California Student Aid Commission sponsors financial aid programs for California students.

For answers to questions about California student aid call the California Student Aid Commission in Sacramento, CA at (916) 445-0880.

SCHOOLS AND COLLEGES

The public and independent California colleges and universities have financial aid programs that offer all types of financial aid including college grants, scholarships, loans, and work-study.

FINANCIAL INSTITUTIONS

Lenders such as banks may offer educational loans and other financing options including home equity loans and lines of credit.

PRIVATE ORGANIZATIONS

Community organizations, labor unions, business groups, ethnic groups, churches, professional and trade associations, and employers are important sources of scholarship and grant awards. Public libraries have books listing scholarships.

DETERMINING FINANCIAL NEED

Your college expenses are more than just tuition/fees and room and board. Books, supplies, transportation and personal expenses are also included.

YOUR COLLEGE EXPENSES

Your college expenses are more than just tuition/fees, and room and board. Moreover, they vary according to your needs and circumstances.

- Whether you live at home, in a college dormitory, or off campus in an apartment with other students makes a difference in your costs. Furthermore, some areas of California are more expensive to live in than others.

- You must pay for books and supplies wherever you go. You can buy used books and/or sell books you no longer need to save money.

- Personal expenses such as clothing, laundry, recreation, entertainment, and medical costs vary based upon your personal life style and special needs.

- If you commute to college, your actual transportation costs to and from school will depend upon your use of a car or public transportation. You might car pool to save money. Will you be attending a college far from home in another part of the state that requires extra expenses for transportation? Will you own a car on campus?

The colleges *estimate* how much it costs the typical student to attend their school for one academic year of two semesters/three quarters or twelve months for year-round students. Their estimate includes tuition/fees, room and board, and amounts for books, supplies, transportation, and personal expenses such as clothing, laundry, and entertainment.

The colleges estimate how much it costs the typical student to attend their school for one academic year of nine to ten months.

AVERAGE COLLEGE COSTS IN CALIFORNIA FOR 1994-95

	Living at Home and Commuting	Living Off Campus	Living On Campus
Community Colleges	$5,226	$8,682	$6,700
California State University	$6,840	$10,291	$9,642
University of California	$9,194	$12,919	$12,604
Independent Colleges	$9,870 to $22,598	$13,230 to $26,510	$10,355 to $26,475
Private Vocational Schools	$7,700 to $20,810	$11,148 to $25,702	not available (1)

Notes: 1. Low figure is for a six-month, vocational course; high figure is for one academic year.
2. Figures are approximate. Contact each school for their specific costs.

For information about estimated costs of various institutions, review college costs in chapters 9, 10, 11, and 12: CALIFORNIA COMMUNITY COLLEGES, CALIFORNIA STATE UNIVERSITY, UNIVERSITY OF CALIFORNIA, and CALIFORNIA INDEPENDENT COLLEGES in this *GUIDE*. You can also obtain the most up-to-date information about total college expenses of the colleges in which you are interested by checking their most recent college catalogs or calling the colleges directly.

Use the worksheet, MY COLLEGE EXPENSES, on the facing page to record and compare the expenses for one academic year of the colleges which interest you.

MY COLLEGE EXPENSES						
COLLEGE NAME						
Tuition & Fees						
Food & Housing						
Books & Supplies						
Transportation						
Miscellaneous (Personal, Recreational, Clothes, etc.)						
MY TOTAL COLLEGE EXPENSES						

COLLEGE IN CALIFORNIA: *The Inside Track*

EFC — YOUR EXPECTED FAMILY CONTRIBUTION

There is the expectation that you and your parents pay some amount toward your education regardless of your financial circumstances. This amount, your "expected family contribution" — EFC — is what you and your family can reasonably be expected to contribute toward your expenses for one academic year of two semesters/three quarters. It can vary from one-hundred to several thousand dollars per year depending upon family income, assets, and other financial criteria. Paying some amount of your own and your parents' money for your education is an investment in you and a commitment that you and your parents make toward your educational goals.

The amount of your expected family contribution (EFC) for one academic year is the same regardless of the cost of attending the college you choose.

Your EFC for one academic year is a constant. It is the same regardless of which college you choose and how much it costs to go there. If you and your parents together can afford $4,000 toward your year at college, then this amount is all you can spend, whether you decide to go to an expensive, independent school or a relatively inexpensive California Community College.

YOUR FINANCIAL NEED

The amount of money you need from outside sources to help defray your college expenses is called "your financial need." Your financial need is the difference between what it costs to attend a particular college and your expected family contribution. To determine the amount of your financial need, you must subtract your EFC for one academic year from your total college expenses for one academic year.

PAYING FOR COLLEGE

	YOUR TOTAL COLLEGE EXPENSES	(For one academic year.)
−	YOUR EXPECTED FAMILY CONTRIBUTION (EFC)	(What you and your family can pay for one academic year.)
=	YOUR FINANCIAL NEED	(The total amount of money you need from sources other than yourself and your family to help pay for your academic year at college.

Your total college expenses at the college you choose to attend affects your financial need. You can see this in these examples for two different colleges. Dollar amounts are for one academic year.

		College "A"	College "B"
	YOUR TOTAL COLLEGE EXPENSES	$10,000	$18,000
−	YOUR EXPECTED FAMILY CONTRIBUTION (EFC)	$4,000	$4,000
=	YOUR FINANCIAL NEED	$6,000	$14,000

Financial Aid

Ninety percent or more of financial aid is awarded to students who demonstrate financial need. Less than ten percent is merit-based.

If you determine that you have financial need and require assistance from outside sources to help pay for your college education, seek financial aid. Financial aid is available in the form of scholarships, grants, loans, and part-time jobs. Most financial aid programs are based upon financial need. In fact, less than ten percent of financial aid is awarded for high academic achievement or for merit in an area such as athletics or music. Ninety percent or more is awarded to students who demonstrate that they need financial assistance to attend college.

This may surprise you. Many students believe they must be academic scholars to qualify for aid. Because their grades are average, they do not apply even though their need is great. This erroneous thinking can be costly. If you qualify for admission to a college and demonstrate that you need money to attend, you are very likely to be eligible for financial assistance even if you did not get the highest grades in high school.

You do not have to be poor or from a family with low income to qualify as having financial need. You do need to demonstrate that you require financial support to further your education. You must submit financial aid applications to demonstrate your need.

APPLYING FOR FINANCIAL AID

A form called the Free Application for Federal Student Aid, FAFSA, is now the primary application for applying for federal, state, and college-based financial aid. The Higher Education Amendment of 1992 requires that the United States government consider no other application for federal aid. The state and college-aid programs also must use this form. Information you and your parents provide on the FAFSA determines your expected family contribution, EFC, for one academic year. You list on this form up to six college, federal, and state programs to which you are applying for financial aid and request that your FAFSA information and its analysis be sent to them.

The FAFSA is the primary application for applying for federal, state, and college-based financial aid.

PAYING FOR COLLEGE

FAFSA — FREE APPLICATION FOR FEDERAL STUDENT AID

Questions on the FAFSA cover information that the federal government needs to determine your expected family contribution, EFC, according to federal guidelines. FAFSA questions to determine your EFC for the 1995-96 academic year cover the following topics:

- Your father's and mother's income for the 1994 tax year, including salary and wages, pensions, dividends, interest, Aid to Families with Dependent Children payments, unemployment insurance payments, and Social Security benefits.
- Your income for the 1994 tax year, including salary and wages, pensions, dividends, interest, Aid to Families with Dependent Children payments, unemployment insurance payments, and Social Security benefits.
- 1994 taxes for both you and your parents.
- Family assets and your assets, include checking account balances, savings, stocks, bonds, real estate investments, business ownership, corporate farms, and trusts. Home and family farm equity are not considered as assets for federal, state, California Community College, California State University, and University of California aid. Many independent colleges do consider home and family farm equity as assets in determining your EFC and will ask for this information on supplemental applications. These policies as well as other policies regarding the inclusion of assets in the calculation of expected family contribution are explained more fully later in this chapter in the section: Commonly Asked Questions about Financial Aid, page 4--18.
- Your parents' age and their need for retirement income.
- The number of children and other dependents in the family household.
- The number of family members in college.
- Your status as a dependent (on parents) or independent student.

Questions on the FAFSA cover information that the federal government needs to determine your expected family contribution, EFC.

PAYING FOR COLLEGE

NEED ANALYSIS PROCESSORS

A "Need Analysis Processor" processes the data you and your parents provide on the FAFSA. These are the "Need Analysis Processors" in California:

The College Scholarship Service (CSS)	American College Testing
Federal Student Aid Programs	Federal Student Aid Programs
P.O. Box 6376	P.O. Box 4005
Princeton, New Jersey 08541	Iowa City, Iowa 52243-4005
(609) 951-1025	(916) 361-0656

California Community Colleges, CSU, UC, the California Student Aid Commission, the federal government, and the independent institutions accept the need analysis results from either of these sources.

Both processors distribute identical versions, in both content and format, of the FAFSA. California Community Colleges, CSU, UC, the California Student Aid Commission, the federal government, and the independent institutions accept the need analysis results from either of these sources.

The FAFSA is available from your high school counselor, guidance or career center, college financial aid offices, and the processors. Mail the completed FAFSA to the Need Analysis Processor — CSS or ACT — depending upon whose version you use. The Need Analysis Processor assembles your data and sends it to the Central Processing System, which calculates an initial estimate of your expected family contribution. This contribution is the amount you and your family can reasonably be expected to contribute toward your educational costs for one academic year.

FEDERAL METHODOLOGY

The Central Processing System uses a standard formula, described by law and known as the "Federal Methodology," to perform the need analysis and estimate your expected family contribution. The Central Processor also checks your selective service status, and immigration status for both federal and state financial aid. The Central Processor sends the results of this analysis back to the Need Analysis Processor to which you submitted your FAFSA. Your Need Analysis Processor prepares reports for you and for the college and scholarship programs to which you have applied.

The Need Analysis Processor assembles your data and sends it to the Central Processing System, which calculates an initial estimate of your expected family contribution.

The expected family contribution figure developed using the Federal Methodology is the basis for determining federal and state awards and financial aid from the community colleges, CSU, and UC. Many independent colleges consider additional data in determining institutional financial aid awards. See Institutional Methodology explained on the next page.

REPORTS MAILED TO FINANCIAL AID SOURCES BY THE NEED ANALYSIS PROCESSOR

The Need Analysis Processor sends a Need Analysis Report, calculated based upon the Federal Methodology, to the colleges and scholarship programs you listed on your FAFSA to receive this analysis. The FAFSA allows you to list up to six recipients of this analysis. This report states your estimated family contribution, a calculation based upon the information you provide on your FAFSA.

REPORTS MAILED TO YOU BY THE NEED ANALYSIS PROCESSOR

Within four to five weeks of submitting your FAFSA, the Need Analysis Processor sends you a Student Aid Report (SAR), which is an acknowledgment of receipt of your materials.

The Student Aid Report (SAR) states the amount of your expected family contribution.

SAR — STUDENT AID REPORT

The Student Aid Report (SAR) states the amount of your expected family contribution and tells you if you qualify for a Federal Pell Grant. It also presents a detailed review of the information you and your parents submit on your FAFSA. This report provides you with the opportunity to recheck your data and make revisions if necessary. You may need to make changes because of errors or because your financial circumstances have changed since you submitted your FAFSA. You may also add the names of additional colleges and programs to receive your SAR.

If revisions are necessary, mail the revised data to the Need Analysis Processor. The Processor then reevaluates your data and revises the estimate of your need. A revised SAR is returned to you. The reprocessing of your application will take two to three weeks.

If you apply for Cal Grants and have already received a notification letter of an award, contact the financial aid office of the college directly with any corrections. See this chapter: The Cal Grant Program — A, B, and C, page 4--29.

Make copies of the final, correct version of your SAR and submit them to all the colleges to which you have applied for financial aid. Save the original to submit to the college you finally decide to attend. The colleges use the SAR information together with data from the "Need Analysis Report", and the information from any required supplemental financial aid applications to determine the types and amounts of financial aid to award to you. Call (301) 722-9200 to order duplicate SAR's at no cost.

Your Student Aid Report gives you the opportunity to add additional colleges and programs to receive your SAR.

SUPPLEMENTARY FINANCIAL AID APPLICATIONS

INSTITUTIONAL METHODOLOGY

Many independent colleges and private scholarship programs require supplementary data to derive more information than is requested on the FAFSA and to analyze your financial circumstances in more detail. They add this additional data to the information provided by the Federal Methodology and *recalculate* your expected family contribution using the "Institutional Methodology." This adjusted figure is the basis for awarding institutional financial aid awards.

To gather information about these additional factors, the independent institutions *may* require you to complete either or both of the following:

1. Their own institutional financial aid applications. Contact the financial aid office of each institution to which you are applying to determine if additional forms are required.

2. The Financial Aid Form (FAF) disseminated by the College Scholarship Service.

PAYING FOR COLLEGE

FAF — THE FINANCIAL AID FORM

Many independent colleges and private scholarship programs require supplementary data to derive more information than is requested on the FAFSA

The College Scholarship Service (CSS) of the College Board designed the FAF to supplement the information you submit on your FAFSA.

FAF questions cover the following topics:

- Estimated income for the next calendar year for both you and your parents.
- Home and family farm equity (current market value minus all amounts owed on all mortgages).
- Assets such as cash on hand, checking account balances, savings, stocks, bonds, real estate investments, business ownership, corporate farms, and trusts. This information is requested regardless of your family income. On the FAFSA you must include this information only if you or your parents' income is $50,000 or more.
- Private elementary, junior high, and high school tuition paid for other students in your family.

There is a space to explain any unusual expenses such as high medical or dental expenses, educational and other debts, or special circumstances.

Obtain the FAF from your high school counselor, guidance or career center, college financial aid office, or CSS directly. It comes with an instruction booklet and a mailing envelope. Mail it separately from the FAFSA.

You may list up to eight colleges and programs to which CSS will send information from the FAF. There is a fee for each institution or private scholarship to which you send a report. A listing of colleges that require or accept the FAF, in addition to the FAFSA, comes with the FAF packet. Contact the independent colleges to which you are applying to determine if they *require* you to complete the FAF as part of your financial aid application process. This information may come with your college admission application packet.

A listing of colleges that require or accept the FAF, in addition to the FAFSA, comes with the FAF packet.

The California Community Colleges, California State University, University of California, and the California Student Aid Commission, which administers the Cal Grant Program, *do not require* a FAF. They require only the FAFSA. See this chapter: The Cal Grant Program, page 4--29.

FAF FEE

The FAF fee varies according to the number of colleges and programs to which you submit your FAF information. In 1993-94 the filing fee was $13.75 for the first college or program and $9.75 for each additional one. The fees will increase in 1994-95.

1993-94 FAF FEES	
Number of Colleges	FAF Fee
1	$13.75
2	$23.50
3	$33.25
4	$43.00
5	$52.75
6	$62.50
7	$72.25
8	$82.00

If you feel you might qualify for a fee waiver to pay FAF fees, inquire at the colleges to which you will be submitting your FAF. Each college establishes its own fee waiver criteria and can distribute the waiver directly to you.

About four weeks after you submit your FAF, CSS sends you a CSS Acknowledgment which lists the colleges and programs to which your FAF information was sent. If you later wish to have your FAF information sent to additional institutions or programs, use the Additional College Request Form on your CSS Acknowledgment. After you receive your CSS Acknowledgment, you may contact CSS with any questions. Call CSS in New Jersey at (609) 951-1025. If you are hearing impaired you may call the TDD number: (609) 734-9013.

You may list up to eight colleges and programs to which CSS will send information from the FAF.

YOUR FINANCIAL AID PACKAGE

The state and federal governments inform the colleges you list on your FAFSA of any scholarships, grants, or loans they award to you. Many private scholarships also inform the college financial aid offices of awards made to you. Some awards come directly to you, and you are expected to inform the colleges of them.

The colleges and scholarship programs use information from your Need Analysis Report, together with data gathered from their own additional institutional applications (if required), and the FAF (if required) to determine your financial need. The college financial aid office then assembles the information about the cost of attending its college, your financial need, your expected family contribution, the scholarships you receive from private sources, and the financial aid you receive from the state and the federal governments.

There is a fee for each institution or private scholarship to which you send a report.

The colleges add their own institutional scholarships, grants, loans, and work-study grants to the amount you receive from outside sources and offer you a financial aid package that lists your awards and the sources of them. Each institution develops a total financial aid package to meet your financial need so you can afford to attend their school. However, the content of your financial aid package may vary from college to college. Furthermore, some schools may not be able to meet your full financial need with the resources available.

The table at the top of the next page depicts three representative examples of student financial aid packages at an independent college. Although the financial circumstances of these students vary widely, so do their financial aid packages. In each case, the total financial aid package adds up to meet the student's financial need.

EXAMPLES OF FINANCIAL AID PACKAGES FOR THREE STUDENTS	Maria	David	Kim
Total College Expenses	$18,500	$18,500	$18,500
Expected Family Contribution	$5,800	$3,100	$1,400
FINANCIAL NEED	$12,700	$15,400	$17,100
Financial Aid Package			
Cal Grant A	$5,250	$5,250	$5,250
Federal Pell Grant	$2,400	$0	$2,400
College Grants/Scholarships	$2,050	$6,800	$5,500
Loans	$3,000	$2,150	$2,550
College Work-Study	$0	$1,200	$1,400
TOTAL FINANCIAL AID PACKAGE	$12,700	$15,400	$17,100

The colleges add their own institutional scholarships, grants, loans, and work-study grants to the amount you receive from outside sources and offer you a financial aid package

DEADLINES

The financial aid application process for the 1995-96 academic year begins January 1, 1995. The FAFSA must be submitted between January 1st and March 2nd of each year for aid for the following school year beginning in September. To apply for financial aid for fall 1995, submit your FAFSA between January 1, 1995 and March 2, 1995.

Because you and your parents must provide income tax information through December 31, 1994, you cannot submit the FAFSA earlier than January 1, 1995. CSS and ACT do not accept it earlier. March 2, 1995 is the deadline for the Cal Grant Program. See this chapter: The Cal Grant Program — A, B, And C, page 4--29. March 2nd also is the generally accepted deadline to apply for most college financial aid programs in California.

To apply for financial aid for fall 1995, submit your FAFSA between January 1, 1995 and March 2, 1995.

Some colleges may want your completed FAFSA at an earlier time. Also, the colleges may have special deadlines for the FAF and institutional applications. Check with them. The federal government will accept the FAFSA for federal aid programs as late as May 1, 1996 during the first year you are in college. See chapter 10: CALIFORNIA STATE UNIVERSITY, Financial Aid, page 10--48; chapter 11: UNIVERSITY OF CALIFORNIA, Financial Aid, page 11--62; and chapter 12; CALIFORNIA INDEPENDENT COLLEGES, College Profiles, page 12--12 to 12--75.

THE PROCESS OF APPLYING FOR FINANCIAL AID IN CALIFORNIA

START HERE

FAFSA

A form you and your parents complete. Send it not later than March 2nd to the Need Analysis Processor at either CSS or ACT (depending upon the FAFSA version you use).

NEED ANALYSIS PROCESSOR

(either at CSS or ACT)

Receives your completed FAFSA and prepares two reports based upon calculations done by the Central Processing System, which analyzes your data using the Federal Methodology.

NEED ANALYSIS REPORT

Sent by the Need Analysis Processor to your listed colleges and scholarships and also to the Federal Pell Grant Program and the Cal Grant Program. Contains an analysis of your FAFSA information and states your expected family contribution.

SAR - STUDENT AID REPORT

Sent to you by the Need Analysis Processor. Contains a detailed review of your FAFSA information. Provides the opportunity to correct or update your information. Also indicates your expected family contribution.

FEDERAL PELL GRANT

CAL GRANTS

A State of California Grant Program.

FAFSA-LISTED SCHOLARSHIPS, GRANTS, LOANS

Programs that you listed on your FAFSA.

YOUR PRIVATE SCHOLARSHIPS, GRANTS, LOANS

Programs that you applied to directly and did not list on your FAFSA. Notify your colleges of any financial aid you are awarded from these sources.

YOUR COLLEGES

Those you list on your FAFSA receive a copy of your "Need Analysis Report" from the Need Analysis Processor, and award information from the Federal Pell Grant and Cal Grant Programs. The FAF and/or institutional applications may also be required. You notify the colleges of additional private scholarships/grants/loans you receive. Coordinate and determine your total financial aid package including their own scholarships, grants, loans, and work-study programs.

YOUR FINANCIAL AID PACKAGE

Prepared by your colleges and awarded to you. It may consist of federal, state, private, and college scholarships, grants, and/or loans as well as work-study.

PAYING FOR COLLEGE

Completing The FAFSA And Supplementary Applications

Several useful strategies can aid you in completing and submitting the FAFSA and required supplementary applications — FAF and institutional applications. By attending workshops and contacting the resources listed later in this chapter in the section: Commonly Asked Questions About Financial Aid, page 4--18, you can complete the forms correctly and to your best advantage. Here are some suggestions:

Submit only one FAFSA. Send it to whichever Need Analysis Processor you have selected — CSS or ACT.

- Submit only *one* FAFSA. Send it to whichever Need Analysis Processor you have selected — CSS or ACT. It must be mailed and postmarked by the March 2nd deadline for Cal Grant Program consideration. See this chapter: The Cal Grant Program — A, B, And C, page 4--29. This deadline is critical. Furthermore, this date gives you priority consideration for financial aid at California State University and University of California campuses. With priority consideration, your financial aid application materials are reviewed early and you receive the first award moneys to be allocated. This is very important. The colleges have a predetermined amount of money for financial aid; once it is completely awarded, late applicants receive either limited or no financial assistance.

The public and independent colleges may have additional and/or different priority filing dates; these dates may be earlier than March 2nd. Contact them for specific information.

To file for financial aid for fall 1995, you must report your family's financial information for the 1994 tax year.

- Your parents should assemble their income tax information as soon after January 1st as possible so they can accurately answer the questions on the FAFSA and supplemental applications. The FAFSA requires your family's income and tax data for the tax year ending December 31st. For example, to file the FAFSA for aid for the 1995-96 school year you must report your family's financial information for the 1994 tax year ending December 31, 1994. If your parents' tax forms are not available by March 2nd, your parents may use their best estimates to complete the FAFSA. Their 1993 income tax return can be helpful if their financial situation has not changed significantly in the past year. They have an opportunity to amend the FAFSA with more accurate information when you receive your Student Aid Report.

- Complete the FAFSA and supplementary applications as accurately as possible. If your parents make errors that later need correction, processing is slowed. The sooner the colleges get the information from your financial aid applications, the sooner they can assemble your financial aid package. The colleges have more money to distribute early in the cycle of preparing and awarding financial aid packages. As funds are awarded, they may become less generous.

- Both CSS and ACT include specific written information about each of the questions on the FAFSA. Your parents should read this material carefully to fully understand what is being asked. The FAF also comes with an information booklet.

- Fill in every blank unless instructed to do otherwise. If your parents omit answers to questions, the Need Analysis Processor and the colleges may conclude that data has been mistakenly left out. Enter a zero ,"0", to indicate that a question has been considered and no answer is appropriate.

- The FAFSA is sent automatically to the United States Department of Education, which verifies your citizenship and eligible noncitizen status with the Immigration and Naturalization Service (INS). Answer the questions regarding citizenship carefully. See appendix A: CALIFORNIA RESIDENCY REQUIREMENTS.

The FAFSA is sent automatically to the United States Department of Education, which verifies your citizenship and eligible noncitizen status.

- Do not include any attachments with your FAFSA; they will be thrown away. If you have special circumstances that your parents wish to explain or that should be emphasized, send a letter to each college financial aid office. Be sure to include your (student) name and social security number on any correspondence. If a FAF is required, there is space on this form to explain your special circumstances. The college notifies the Cal Grant Program of this information. Do *not* write to the Cal Grant Program directly.

- Your FAFSA is automatically submitted to the federal government for Federal Pell Grant consideration. If you list a California college to receive the FAFSA analysis and otherwise qualify, you will automatically apply for the Cal Grant Program. See this chapter, The Cal Grant Program — A, B, and C, page 4--29.

- Be sure to list all colleges and programs that you wish to receive information from your FAFSA. You may add additional ones later when you receive your SAR, but it is more efficient to include them on your initial application.

- Be sure to list on your FAF all colleges that require it. You may add additional ones later, but it is more efficient to include them on your initial application.

- If you do not yet have a job for the summer or the school year, enter zero where you are asked for summer/school-year income on the FAF.

- You *and* at least one parent or guardian must sign all forms; otherwise, the applications are invalid and will not be processed. If you are unable to get a parent or guardian's signature, speak to your counselor or assistant principal about alternatives. Call the Need Analysis Processor about your circumstances to obtain advice about how to meet the signature requirement on the FAFSA. If your parent is out of town, sign the FAFSA and submit it by March 2nd. You will receive a follow-up form later for your parent's signature.

You and *at least one parent or guardian must sign the FAFSA; otherwise, the applications are invalid and will not be processed.*

- The FAFSA is free. There is no processing fee. However, there is a fee for the FAF and there may be fees for institutional applications.

- You may wish to reapply for aid for each year you are in college. To do this, you will not need to complete an entire FAFSA. However, you will need to update information supplied on previous forms. The Need Analysis Processor to which you send your FAFSA will automatically send you the Renewal FAFSA each year. About seventy-five percent of the information will be preprinted on the form and will be the same as the information you gave on your 1994-95 application. You will only have to write in information that has changed from 1994-95. If you do not receive your Renewal FAFSA by early January, contact your college financial aid office for a new FAFSA form. You and your parents will want to refer back to forms completed in past years to assist them in updating. Keep a copy of your FAFSA, FAF, and institutional applications for future reference. Save your acknowledgments and any other correspondence for future reference.

- Get a Certificate of Mailing from the post office when you mail the FAFSA. It is a receipt, which proves you have met the March 2nd deadline.

- Review very carefully the Student Aid Report, which you receive from the Need Analysis Processor, to make sure the information your parents submitted on your FAFSA is reported accurately. If there are errors, send in corrections immediately.

- Keep your acknowledgments and any other correspondence for future reference.

COMMONLY ASKED QUESTIONS ABOUT FINANCIAL AID

WHERE CAN I GET HELP WITH QUESTIONS ABOUT FINANCIAL AID PROGRAMS, APPLICATIONS, AND PROCEDURES?

Your high school counselor or guidance administrator can answer many of your questions. The following telephone numbers can be helpful to you as well.

IMPORTANT TELEPHONE NUMBERS

To ask about ...

Your FAFSA:

To get a FAFSA or for information about a form submitted:

CSS (in New Jersey — Eastern time) .... (609) 951-1025

ACT (in Iowa — Central time) .... (319) 337-1200

The status of the processing of your application by either CSS or ACT:

(in Maryland — Eastern time) .... (301) 722-9200

The Cal Grant Program, student loans, and other state financial aid programs:

California Student Aid Commission

(in Sacramento, California — Pacific time) .... (916) 445-0880

General information regarding federal aid:

(Washington, D.C. — Eastern time)................................ (800) 433-3243

Hearing Impaired .... (800) 730-8913

To request ...

a duplicate SAR (no fee):

Federal Information Center .... (301) 722-9200

If your school holds a financial aid night for parents, encourage your parents to attend.

THE FAFSA AND FAF LOOK COMPLICATED. WHERE CAN I GET HELP TO COMPLETE THEM?

Most likely, an assistant principal or guidance counselor at your high school is knowledgeable about the FAFSA and FAF and the financial aid process. The California Student Aid Commission, CSS, and ACT hold workshops for high school and college professionals to review the forms and the latest information regarding financial aid. If your school holds a financial aid night for parents, encourage your parents to attend to get an understanding of the forms and to get their questions answered. College financial aid offices also are excellent sources of information about the FAFSA and FAF.

SINCE OUR FAMILY INCOME IS $------, SHOULD MY PARENTS SUBMIT A FAFSA AND, IF REQUIRED, A FAF?

Yes. You have nothing to lose, and unless your family is very affluent, a great deal to gain. For a moderate expenditure of time, you gain the opportunity of being considered for aid. Whether or not you qualify for assistance depends upon many factors including your family circumstances and the costs of the particular colleges to which you apply. Do not try to outguess the criteria. Let the experts in need analysis at the Central Processing System and at the colleges evaluate your situation. The worst that can happen is you will not get any need-based aid. On the other hand, you will have begun the process of pursuing non-need-based loans — and other strategies, described later in this chapter — to reduce the burden of your college expenses.

You have nothing to lose, and unless your family is very affluent, a great deal to gain by submitting the FAFSA and, if required, a FAF. Do not try to outguess the criteria.

HOW CAN I QUICKLY OBTAIN AN ESTIMATE OF MY EFC USING THE FEDERAL METHODOLOGY?

ACT offers a service for dependent students called Financial Aid Need Estimator. The service can help you quickly determine if you are likely to be eligible for financial aid. Send in a simple one-page form and you will receive an estimate based on the Federal Methodology of your expected family contribution and your eligibility for a Federal Pell Grant. You also will receive the estimated costs of up to three colleges which you list on the form, your estimated financial need at these colleges, and admissions information and financial aid deadlines at the schools you are considering. A mail response will arrive within five to seven business days. If you FAX your report and want your results by FAX, it will take an hour or less after receipt of your form. The fee for 1994-95 is $5.00 for a mail response; $8.00 for a FAX response. Obtain a Financial Aid Need Estimator brochure and form from your counselor, career center, or guidance administrator or contact:

ACT Financial Aid Need Estimator
2255 North Dubuque Road
P.O. Box 4029
Iowa City, Iowa 52244-9935
(319) 337-1615
FAX (800) 525-6927

or,

ACT Financial Aid Need Estimator
10419 Old Placerville Road, Suite 262
Sacramento, California 95827-0656
(916) 361-0656

HOW ARE ASSETS CONSIDERED IN DETERMINING MY EFC USING THE FEDERAL METHODOLOGY?

Using the Federal Methodology assets such as cash-on-hand, savings and checking accounts, stocks, bonds, real estate investments business ownership, trusts, and corporate farms may be calculated as part of your expected family contribution.

- Equity in the family home — the value of the home minus all mortgage amounts — and in the family farm are *excluded* as assets when determining expected family contribution regardless of family income. This is a major change from past practices and greatly helps Californians who have a large amount of home or family farm equity.

Equity in the family home and family farm are excluded as assets when determining expected family contribution using the Federal Methodology.

If your parents' adjusted gross income is $50,000 or more, the value of their assets is considered.

PAYING FOR COLLEGE

- If your parents' adjusted gross income is $49,999 or less, and neither you nor they will file an income tax form 1040, you do not have to answer questions on the FAFSA regarding assets. Your (student) income is not included in this calculation. If your family meets these conditions, no assets are considered for determining the expected family contribution.

- If your parents' adjusted gross income is $50,000 or more, the value of their assets is considered. However, a portion of these assets is protected. The government expects families to use their assets for a variety of reasons, including educational expenses, retirement, and emergencies. Therefore, there is an Educational Savings and Asset Protection Allowance. This allowance is subtracted from total assets to protect a portion of your family assets for these purposes. The amount of the allowance varies according to the age of your oldest parent. The older your parent, the larger the allowance. Twelve percent of your parents' assets, after the subtraction of the allowance, is used in the calculation of your expected family contribution.

- Thirty-five percent of student assets are calculated as part of your expected family contribution. If you own a home or family farm, the equity in these properties is not counted in your assets.

HOW IS STUDENT INCOME CONSIDERED IN DETERMINING MY EFC USING THE FEDERAL METHODOLOGY?

The Federal Methodology uses a student Income Protection Allowance of $1,750, which is subtracted from student income. After the allowance is subtracted, fifty percent of the remainder is included in the calculation of your expected *family* contribution. There is no automatic minimum student contribution.

ARE THERE ANY ALLOWANCES FOR MEDICAL OR DENTAL EXPENSES IN DETERMINING MY EFC USING THE FEDERAL METHODOLOGY?

No. The Federal Methodology does not allow for medical or dental expenses.

ARE THERE ANY ALLOWANCES FOR ELEMENTARY, JUNIOR HIGH, AND HIGH SCHOOL TUITION EXPENSES IN DETERMINING MY EFC USING THE FEDERAL METHODOLOGY?

Most independent colleges recalculating your EFC using the Institutional Methodology will include home equity in their formula.

No. The Federal Methodology does not allow for elementary and secondary school tuition expenses for students other than the applicant.

WHAT ARE THE DIFFERENCES IN THE CALCULATION OF EFC USING THE FEDERAL METHODOLOGY VERSUS THE INSTITUTIONAL METHODOLOGY?

When the independent colleges use the Institutional Methodology to calculate your EFC, they incorporate the information from your FAFSA and the EFC calculated from it. They also may choose to include home and family farm equity, a portion of your parents' and your assets regardless of adjusted gross income, medical and dental expenses, a higher percentage of your (student) earnings, and allowances for elementary, junior high, and high school tuition for other students in the family. Most independent colleges include home equity in their formula when recalculating your EFC using the Institutional Methodology. This will likely result in a higher EFC figure than that calculated using the Federal Methodology. The EFC derived from using all or some of these additional factors is the basis for awarding *institutional* financial aid dollars.

FEDERAL METHODOLOGY	uses FAFSA data to calculate EFC which is basis for determining federal, state, UC, CSU, CCC, and Cal Grant awards.
INSTITUTIONAL METHODOLOGY	uses FAFSA and supplementary applications (institutional applications and/or FAF) data to recalculate EFC which is the basis for determining campus-based aid.

Most colleges have a need-blind admission procedure.

SHOULD I WAIT UNTIL I AM ACCEPTED TO A COLLEGE BEFORE I APPLY FOR FINANCIAL AID?

Definitely not. Apply for aid to all the colleges to which you have applied for admission as soon after January 1st as possible and before March 2nd. Check with the colleges to see if, in addition to the FAFSA, they require the FAF or their own institutional financial aid applications. Also check to see if they have their own earlier deadlines.

DOES THE FACT THAT I NEED FINANCIAL AID TO ATTEND COLLEGE AFFECT MY CHANCES FOR ADMISSION?

The college admission process is generally separate from the financial aid process. Most colleges have a need-blind admission procedure; they review your academic and personal qualifications for admission without any consideration of whether you need financial aid. The admissions office informs the financial aid office of your admission. The financial aid office then assembles your financial aid package. However, some independent colleges *do* consider financial circumstances when making admission decisions.

The FAFSA is a national form. Contact out-of-state institutions to determine if they require the FAF and to obtain any institutional financial aid applications they may require.

I AM APPLYING TO OUT-OF-STATE COLLEGES AS WELL AS CALIFORNIA SCHOOLS. DO I NEED TO SUBMIT OTHER FINANCIAL AID APPLICATIONS IN ADDITION TO THE FAFSA?

The FAFSA is a national form. Contact out-of-state institutions to determine if they require the FAF and to obtain any institutional financial aid applications they may require.

PAYING FOR COLLEGE

MY PARENTS ARE DIVORCED. WHOSE FINANCIAL INFORMATION SHOULD BE USED TO ANSWER QUESTIONS ON THE FAFSA AND SUPPLEMENTARY APPLICATIONS?

Report financial information about the parent with whom you are living.

Report financial information about the parent with whom you are living. If you live alternately with each parent, report information about the parent who provides most of your support. If the parent with whom you are living has remarried, the income of this parent *and* his or her spouse must be used. If your parents are separated or divorced, there is a special form that you may need to complete. This form is sent to you By the colleges, if they require it, after they receive your FAFSA information from the Need Analysis Processor. If you can make a strong case for not using step-parent money in your EFC calculation using the Institutional Methodology, the college financial aid officer has the option of not considering this income.

HOW ARE MY FAFSA AND SUPPLEMENTARY APPLICATIONS AFFECTED IF I AM AN INDEPENDENT STUDENT? WHAT IS THE DEFINITION OF AN INDEPENDENT STUDENT?

If you qualify as an independent student, you may complete the FAFSA and supplementary applications with information regarding *your* income and asset information. You do not include your parents' information on the form. Because your income and assets are probably considerably less than those of your parents, there is a definite advantage to you in declaring yourself independent. However, the definition of independent student is very specific and has been set forth by the United States Congress.

To be considered an independent student for state, federal, and college aid you must meet *any one* of the following criteria:

The definition of an independent student is very specific. It has been set forth by the United States Congress.

1. You must be twenty-four years or older by December 31st of the award year; for example, December 31, 1994 for the college enrollment period beginning between July 1, 1995 and June 30, 1996.

2. You must be an orphan or ward of the court.

3. You must be a veteran of the United States Armed Forces.

4. You must have legal dependents other than a spouse.

5. You must be married and will not be claimed as an income tax exemption by your parents for the 1994 tax year.

6. You must be a graduate or professional student.

7. You have circumstances that the financial aid administrator has documented as unusual and qualify you as independent of your parents. An official at your high school, such as an administrator or guidance counselor who knows your circumstances, can send a letter to the college financial aid office explaining your situation and supporting your request to be considered independent. A community person such as a social worker or church official can also verify your independent status. The financial aid administrator at the college may use professional judgement to determine if you are an independent student. The decision is final and cannot be appealed to the U.S. Department of Education.

I AM NOT A UNITED STATES CITIZEN.
SHOULD I SUBMIT A FAFSA?

Yes. The colleges and the state and federal governments require it. Your status as a noncitizen may have no effect upon your eligibility for college-based aid, even though it might disqualify you for government assistance programs.

Your status as a noncitizen may have no effect upon your eligibility for college-based aid.

The FAFSA contains questions about your alien status to determine your eligibility for federal and state aid. Are you a permanent resident or an eligible noncitizen? These categories are defined on page 4--4. The United States government automatically verifies your citizenship and eligible noncitizenship status when you submit the FAFSA. Are you an undocumented alien? As of January 1991, undocumented aliens are not considered state residents and are not eligible for new Cal Grants. This rule is under appeal in the courts. Renewal recipients are not affected by this recent ruling. See chapter 10: CALIFORNIA STATE UNIVERSITY, Financial aid, page 10--48 and chapter 11: UNIVERSITY OF CALIFORNIA, Financial Aid, page 11--62 for special instructions.

I DO NOT THINK I CAN QUALIFY FOR THE FEDERAL PELL GRANT
OR THE CAL GRANT PROGRAM,
BUT I AM HOPING FOR CAMPUS-BASED AID. MUST I APPLY FOR
THE FEDERAL PELL GRANT AND THE CAL GRANT PROGRAM?

Yes, definitely. Many California colleges require you to apply for both the Federal Pell Grant and the Cal Grants using the FAFSA before they will consider you for any campus-based aid programs. This assures the college that you have attempted to get government support for your education before they tap their funds to assist you.

Many California colleges require you to apply for the Federal Pell Grant and the Cal Grants before they consider you for campus-based aid.

MY PARENTS' FINANCIAL CIRCUMSTANCES WILL BE
VERY DIFFERENT IN 1995. THEIR INCOME WILL BE MUCH LOWER.
IS THIS CONSIDERED IN CALCULATING OUR EXPECTED FAMILY
CONTRIBUTION USING THE FEDERAL METHODOLOGY?

The FAFSA and the Federal Methodology do not consider future income in calculating family contribution. The FAF requests this information. Financial aid professionals at the colleges may use professional judgement on a case-by-case basis in making awards. Inform the colleges of your circumstances so they may be considered in determining your financial aid qualifications.

In some cases, the financial aid administrator may adjust your cost of education or data elements of your Expected Family Contribution to take into account circumstances that might affect the amount you and your family would be expected to contribute toward your education. These circumstances might include unusual medical or dental expenses, tuition expenses for children attending a private elementary or secondary school, or loss of a job by either of your parents. There have to be very good reasons for the aid administrator to make any adjustments, and you will have to provide adequate proof to support those adjustments. The aid administrator's decision is final and cannot be appealed to the U.S. Department of Education.

DO MY PARENTS NEED TO SUBMIT COPIES OF THEIR INCOME TAX FORMS TO VERIFY THE INFORMATION ON THE FAFSA?

The colleges usually require copies of your income tax returns to verify your FAFSA and supplementary application information. They will contact you directly for this documentation.

When your parents sign the FAFSA, they state that the information provided on it is true and complete, and if required, they will submit proof of the information. Generally, this proof is in the form of copies of federal, state, and/or local income tax returns. If your parents refuse to provide this proof when requested, you could be denied aid. *Do not send copies of income tax returns with the FAFSA.* The schools usually do require this proof and notify you to send it directly to them. Wait to be asked. Presently, the Cal Grant Program requests tax returns only infrequently.

HOW DO THE SCHOLARSHIPS I RECEIVE FROM PRIVATE SOURCES COUNT IN MY FINANCIAL AID PACKAGE FROM THE COLLEGES?

Most colleges count these moneys toward the self-help part of your financial aid package, thereby reducing the amount of your loans or your work-study awards. However, some campuses reduce the amount of grant money they offer, or they reduce both the self-help portion and the grant award. For example, a college might use half of your outside scholarship money to reduce your loan and/or work-study award. The remaining half might be allocated to lower the amount of college grant money awarded to you. Your financial need is the figure they work toward meeting, and they reassemble your package as necessary to meet it.

Contact the colleges in which you are interested to find out what approach they use for private scholarships. As you receive these scholarships and let the colleges know about them, discuss your preferences about how these scholarships might be used in your financial aid package. Each college makes the final decision on the structure of its package, although your input is considered within any policies it must follow. The colleges inform the Cal Grant Program of scholarships you receive from private sources. This could affect your Cal Grant award.

WILL I KNOW ABOUT MY FINANCIAL AID PACKAGES IN AMPLE TIME TO MAKE MY DECISION ABOUT WHICH COLLEGE TO ATTEND?

Many college financial aid offices send a statement of your financial aid package with your admission letter from the admissions office.

Yes, you will. Many college financial aid offices send a statement of your financial aid package with your admission letter from the admissions office. Some send it separately, but very soon after they have been notified by the admissions office that you are accepted. If you applied for financial aid on time, you should have all the information you need to make an informed decision by the required deadlines.

WHAT IS A TENTATIVE AWARD LETTER?

Sometimes, the college sends a tentative award letter to you early in the admissions/award cycle to give you some idea of the type of package the college is considering for you. This letter is usually an accurate representation of your offer, although it is not official. Receiving this information early can help you in planning and in comparing offers.

I HAVE RECEIVED FINANCIAL AID PACKAGES FROM SEVERAL COLLEGES. HOW DO I COMPARE THEM AND DECIDE WHICH ONE TO ACCEPT?

There is often a considerable amount of similarity between financial aid packages offered by the colleges. When this occurs, make your college choice based upon your interest in the school itself. When the packages differ significantly, compare the amount of grant and scholarship moneys offered, the types and amounts of loans planned, and consider how much you must earn yourself.

Use the worksheet, MY FINANCIAL PLAN, *on page 4--26 to compare financial aid packages.*

What is the ratio between grants and loans? Will the school make a commitment to offer you a similar package in future years if your need remains the same? Are the grants and scholarships renewable? What is the cost to you and your parents at each school? Are you willing to pay more to attend one school than another? Try to negotiate a better package at the college you really wish to attend if the package it has offered is not adequate to meet your needs. You can negotiate by informing one college of what another has offered. This tactic may improve your package, particularly at independent colleges.

Use the worksheet, MY FINANCIAL PLAN, on page 4--26 to compare financial aid packages. Organizing your information in this way permits you to compare how well your expenses will be met at the various colleges. Further, it provides you with a clear basis for negotiating a better package at the institution you wish to attend. When filling in your expected family contribution, put down your EFC calculated using Federal Methodology next to FM, and your EFC calculated using Institutional Methodology next to IM.

THE AMOUNT OF EXPECTED FAMILY CONTRIBUTION CALCULATED FOR MY FAMILY SEEMS MUCH TOO HIGH. THE FINANCIAL AID PACKAGE DEVELOPED BY THE COLLEGE I WISH TO ATTEND DOES NOT MEET MY NEEDS. WHAT CAN I DO?

If you feel the financial aid package put together by the college is not adequate to allow you to attend that college, contact their financial aid office and discuss your concerns. If the college has accepted you, they really want you to attend. In these years of decreasing enrollment, they are competing with other colleges to enroll you. This is particularly true of independent colleges. The colleges can use professional judgment on a case-by-case basis to interpret the information on your financial aid application.

If you feel the financial aid package put together by the college is not adequate to allow you to attend, contact the financial aid office and discuss your concerns. There is a strong possibility for negotiating.

Your parents may be able to negotiate with the college for a revision of your financial aid package. Your parents may call and say, "This is not an accurate judgement of what we can pay." They can then state their case explaining why they cannot meet the amount stated as your expected family contribution. Or, perhaps they feel the loan expectation is too high. Or, maybe they do not want you to work during your first year of college.

Your parents should state what they think is a realistic figure for your expected family contribution — what they really can afford. How large a loan are they willing to take? Do they want you to work during the academic year? Is there a limit to the number of hours they want you to work? The financial aid office will consider this appeal and may make changes in your financial aid package based upon their professional judgement.

There is a strong possibility for negotiating. It is certainly worth a try.

MY FINANCIAL PLAN

COLLEGE NAME							
My Total College Expenses							
My Expected Family Contribution (EFC)	FM						
	IM						
MY FINANCIAL NEED							
GRANTS							
SCHOLARSHIPS							
LOANS							
WORK STUDY							
MY FINANCIAL AID PACKAGE							

FINANCIAL AID PROGRAMS

PROGRAM	ELIGIBILITY REQUIREMENTS	AWARDS 1994-95
GRANTS		
Federal Pell Grant	Financial need	Maximum $2,300
Federal SEOG	Exceptional financial need	$100-$4,000
Cal Grant A - CA	Low and middle income, GPA	$1,584-$5,250 Tuition/fees, renewable
Cal Grant B - CA	Disadvantaged and low income	$1,410 Subsistence first year,in subsequent years also pays tuition/fees
Cal Grant C - CA	Vocational student, low and middle income	$2,360 Tuition/fees, $530 Training
BOGG (CCC) - Campus	Exceptional financial need	Enrollment fees
EOPS (CCC) - Campus	Disadvantaged and low income	Maximum $900
EOP (CSU) - Campus	Disadvantaged and low income	$400-$1,000
Law Enforcement Personnel Dependents Grant - CA	Dependents of law enforcement officers and firefighters killed or disabled on duty	$100-$1,500
Bureau of Indian Affairs Grant - Federal	Member of federally-recognized CA tribe	Varies
College Grants - Campus	Determined by college	Varies
SCHOLARSHIPS		
Paul Douglas Teacher	Top 10% of class, minimum 3.00 GPA, committed to career in teaching	$5,000 a year, up to 4 years
Robert Byrd Honors	Merit-based - GPA, SAT I	$1,500 a year, up to 4 years
College	Determined by college	Varies
Private Organizations	Determined by organization	Varies
ROTC-Armed Services	Commitment to serve as officer, GPA, SAT I	Tuition, fees, subsistence
LOANS		
Federal Perkins	Financial need	$3,000 a year, up to 5 years
Federal Stafford	Need-based and non-need based	$2,625-$5,500
Federal PLUS	Loan for parents, creditworthy	Cost of education minus other aid
Federal Consolidation	$7,500 or more in loans	Varies
APLE-CA	Enrolled in teacher education program	Pays off educational loans to $8,000
Child Development-CA	Enrolled in child center education program	Pays off educational loans $1,000-$2,000
Private Organizations	Creditworthy	Varies
WORK-STUDY		
Federal	Financial need	Current federal minimum wage
State	Financial need	Varies
College Co-op	Integrated program of study and work	Varies

CA - California based aid
Federal - U. S. Government based aid
Campus - Campus based aid

COLLEGE IN CALIFORNIA: *The Inside Track*

PAYING FOR COLLEGE

GRANTS

Grants are awards of money based upon financial need. Academic achievement or other factors *may* be considered in addition to need. Grants do not need to be repaid.

FEDERAL PELL GRANT

SOURCE

A federal government program with funds administered by the federal government.

ELIGIBILITY REQUIREMENTS

Eligibility is based upon financial need.

ADDITIONAL REQUIREMENTS AND INFORMATION

The Federal Pell Grant is the largest of the federal student grant programs.

You must meet federal requirements described on page 4--4.

An award is usually limited to five to six full years of study. You must reapply each year to demonstrate financial need and satisfactory academic progress.

ANNUAL AWARD AMOUNTS

The United States Department of Education uses the Federal Methodology to evaluate the information you report when applying for a Federal Pell Grant. The Federal Methodology produces an Expected Family Contribution (EFC) number. If your EFC figure is 2100 or less you may receive a Federal Pell Grant.

How much you actually receive depends upon your expected family income, the cost of education at your college, whether you are a full-time or part-time student, and how many terms you are enrolled during the academic year. The college determines the exact amount of your award.

The federal government guarantees that it will provide enough funds to pay the Pell Grants of students at each participating school. Awards depend upon federal funding levels.

These are the maximum Federal Pell Grant Awards authorized by the law:

$3,900 for the academic year 1994-95.

$4,100 for the academic year 1995-96.

$4,300 for the academic year 1996-97.

$4,500 for the academic year 1997-98.

However, the amount of funds appropriated for the Pell Grant by Congress each year determines the actual award levels. For the 1994-95 academic year, the maximum Pell Grant award is $2,300.

If you participate in a study-abroad program that costs more than the cost of education at your home school, you may be able to get more Federal Pell Grant aid to cover those costs, as long as the extra Pell amount does not exceed the maximum Pell award. Your study-abroad course must be approved for credit by your home school.

PAYMENT OF AWARDS

Your college credits your award to your college account, pays you directly, or uses a combination of these methods. Schools must pay at least once per term — semester, trimester, or quarter. Schools that do not use formally-defined traditional terms must pay at least twice per academic year.

APPLICATION PROCEDURES AND DEADLINES

Application: Submit the FAFSA.

Deadline: The deadline is March 2, 1995 for the 1995-96 school year, if you wish to apply for state and college aid in addition to a Federal Pell Grant. Applying for state and college aid is recommended. You might as well apply for all aid available through this single form.

If you miss the March 2nd deadline, you have until May 2, 1996 to file the FAFSA for a Pell Grant for the 1995-96 academic year.

Notification: You receive your Expected Family Contribution figure with your Student Aid Report from the Need Analysis Processor about four to six weeks after submitting your FAFSA.

FSEOG — Federal Supplemental Educational Opportunity Grants

SOURCE

A federal government program with funds administered by the colleges. It is a campus-based program; the colleges select recipients and determine award amounts.

ELIGIBILITY REQUIREMENTS

Eligibility is based upon exceptional financial need with priority given to Federal Pell Grant recipients. This grant is a supplement for other sources of financial aid.

ADDITIONAL REQUIREMENTS AND INFORMATION

You must meet the federal requirements described on page 4--4.

You may receive an award even if you are enrolled less than halftime.

ANNUAL AWARD AMOUNTS

The amount of your award is based upon your need and the availability of funds. Each college receives a set amount of money for FSEOG's and determines which students receive awards.

Awards range from $100-$4,000 per award year.

If you are participating in a study abroad program approved for credit by your home school, you may receive up to $4,400 if your study abroad costs exceed the cost of education at your home school.

PAYMENT OF AWARDS

Your college credits your FSEOG award to your college account, pays you directly, or uses a combination of these methods. Schools must pay you at least once per term — semester, trimester, or quarter. Schools that do not use traditional terms must pay at least twice during the academic year. There is one exception: If the total FSEOG aid you receive is $500 or less, your school may choose to pay you just once during the year.

APPLICATION PROCEDURES AND DEADLINES

Application: Submit the FAFSA.

Deadline: Each college establishes its own financial aid application deadline. Because each school has a predetermined amount of FSEOG funds, it is important to file on time. A college is unable to make further FSEOG awards for the year once it uses its allotment of money for this program.

Notification: The financial aid package you receive from the college specifies your FSEOG award.

The Cal Grant Program — A, B, and C

The California Grant Program provides financial assistance to California students seeking a postsecondary education. There are three Cal Grant Programs — A, B, and C — each serving a specifically-defined segment of the student population.

SOURCE

A State of California program with funds administered by the California Student Aid Commission.

ELIGIBILITY REQUIREMENTS

To apply for Cal Grants A, B, or C, you must be a California resident attending an eligible California high school, college, university, or postsecondary vocational school. A Cal Grant cannot be used at an out-of-state college. It has been specifically developed for California students attending California colleges and universities.

- You may apply for a new Cal Grant during your last year of high school or after you begin college.
- You must attend college on at least a halftime basis as defined by your school.
- You must not owe a refund on any state or federal educational grant or have defaulted on a student loan.
- If you are an eligible noncitizen (defined by federal law on page 4--4) and, you have a visa type that prevents you from seeking permanent United States residence, you are not eligible to participate in the Cal Grant Program. The disqualifying visa types are as follows:

B - Visitor
C - Alien Traveler
D - Alien Crewman
F - Student
H - Temporary Worker
J - Exchange Visitor
M - Vocational Student

Undocumented aliens cannot be considered for new Cal Grants because the California Court of Appeal has recently ruled that undocumented aliens do not meet California residency requirements. This decision is under appeal in the courts.

ADDITIONAL REQUIREMENTS AND INFORMATION

In 1994, the California Student Aid Commission received over 356,000 applications for the 31,000 new Cal Grant awards authorized by law. The large volume of applications received each year makes the Cal Grant program highly competitive.

You must enroll for at least halftime as determined by your school for the fall semester or quarter or, your Cal Grant will be withdrawn. If your enrollment is officially deferred by the college because of illness or campus overcrowding, you may defer activating your Cal Grant until the following term. Contact your school or the California Student Aid Commission for the appropriate form.

Your award amount may be adjusted downward if you attend less than full time.

You may qualify for more than one Cal Grant, but you can accept only one. For example, you might qualify for Grants A and B, or B and C.

The Commission notifies you of your award on the California Aid Report (CAR). The report states which Grants you are eligible for and the amount of those awards at up to three of the Cal Grant eligible colleges you listed on your FAFSA. The Cal Grant that lists a dollar amount indicates that it is the Grant that would be the best choice for you at that particular school. If you qualify for another Cal Grant, it will be marked "1". Unless you otherwise notify the Commission with the Recipient Change Form accompanying your award letter, you automatically accept the Cal Grant designated for you with the dollar amount.

The New Cal Grant Recipient Change Form allows you to correct your name, address, and social security number. It also permits you to change your college choice and to change your Cal Grant program from the one designated for you to the one marked "1". If you make changes on your Recipient Change Form, sign, date, and return it to the Commission within 21 days of the date of your CAR.

Before you change your Cal Grant choice, contact the financial aid office of the college in which you will be enrolling to discuss your change. Your campus financial aid officer's signature is required. The deadline for submitting your request to change your Grant Program is July 31, 1995.

OVERSEAS PROGRAMS

You may apply your Cal Grant A to international programs provided you are officially registered at a California college. You may apply a Cal Grant B to international programs that are regularly accredited and recognized by your home campus.

Your student budget is not automatically increased by the California Student Aid Commission to match the additional expenses of overseas study. However, your school, at its discretion, may choose to adjust your budget.

APPLICATION PROCEDURES AND DEADLINES

Application: Apply for all three Cal Grants — A, B, and C — using the same two forms: The FAFSA and the GPA Verification Form. The FAFSA must be mailed to the Need Analysis Processor. See this chapter, page 4--10. The GPA Verification Form must be mailed to the California Student Aid Commission.

Deadlines: The deadline for the FAFSA and the GPA Verification Form is March 2, 1995 for awards for the 1995-96 academic year.

Notification: Cal Grant A and B notifications begin in May and June. Cal Grant C notifications occur in July. If you are not chosen for an award, the reason will be stated on the CAR.

FAFSA

You are automatically considered for all three Cal Grants if you

a) file a FAFSA,

b) indicate on it that you will be a legal California resident for at least one year as of September 20, 1995,

c) list at least one California college in the FAFSA section, which allows you to list at least six colleges, and

d) give permission on your FAFSA for your information to be forwarded to the California Student Aid Commission.

The first-listed, eligible California school choice on your FAFSA is used to determine grant eligibility. Write the name of the most expensive school you are considering. The amount of your Cal Grant award is based on the cost of this school. If you later decide to attend a less expensive college, the California Student Aid Commission may adjust your Cal Grant downward.

However, if you decide to attend a more expensive school, it may not be possible to adjust your grant upward. If you list a community college as your response and later decide to attend a four-year college, the Commission does not allow you to change your choice from a community college to a four-year school for Cal Grant consideration after March 2nd

GPA VERIFICATION FORM

You must submit a GPA Verification Form signed by you and your school official. It must state your GPA according to very specific criteria. Mail it separately from the FAFSA. Your school may expect you to mail the signed form or they may collect them and mail several at the same time. It is important that you give this form to your school counselor, guidance administrator, registrar, or other designated school official early enough so they have ample time to complete it. If you do not submit a GPA, a GPA of 2.00 will be assigned to you by the Student Aid Commission. Mail the GPA Verification Form to:

The California Student Aid Commission
Initial Processing Branch
P.O. Box 510621
Sacramento, California 94245-0621

CRITERIA FOR COMPUTING YOUR GPA

To compute your GPA for use on the GPA Verification Form, the following rules must be followed:

- Calculate your GPA to two decimal places on a 4.00 grading scale. *Do not give honors-level and Advanced Placement course grades extra points when calculating your GPA.*

- In no case may grades from the academic year prior to the award year be used. If applying for the 1995-96 award year, grades from the 1994-95 academic year may not be used.

- If you are enrolled in a nongraded program with no available GPA, have been out of high school ten years or more, or have completed courses while attending a foreign school, you may submit the SAT I: Reasoning Test, ACT, or General Education Development (GED) test scores.

PAYING FOR COLLEGE

Mail a copy of the testing organization's score report to the California Student Aid Commission along with the GPA Verification Form by the March 2nd deadline. Arrange to have official copies sent by the College Board or ACT by the March 2nd deadline.

High School Students

- If you apply as a high school senior, you must include *all* grades from your sophomore and junior years — *except physical education and ROTC* — in your GPA.
- If you are an accelerating junior, graduating in the spring of your junior year, list only your sophomore grades.
- You cannot use grades you earn during your last year of high school just prior to entering college.
- Include summer courses only if they are considered part of your sophomore or junior year. The summer prior to a particular school year is usually considered the same grade as that year. Do not include summer grades posted after your eleventh grade — your junior year.

High School Graduates and College Freshmen

If you apply after graduating from high school, include high school sophomore, junior, and senior grades — *except those for physical education and ROTC.* If you have completed twenty-four college semester units — thirty-six quarter units — or more prior to fall 1994, your GPA must be based upon only your college grades.

Other Cal Grant Undergraduates

If you have completed at least twenty-four college semester units — thirty-six quarter units — include

a) all college grades, *or*

b) all college grades excluding nontransferable courses and those courses not counted in the computation for admissions of a transfer student.

New Cal Grants are not awarded for the senior year of college.

CAL GRANT A

ELIGIBILITY REQUIREMENTS

The Cal Grant A is designed to help low- and middle-income students meet tuition/fee costs at California State University, the University of California, and California independent schools and colleges. Financial need *and* grade point average are criteria.

FAMILY INCOME AND ASSET CEILINGS

Certification of financial need is the first step in the selection process. If you are evaluated as having financial need, you are then ranked according to your GPA. Award recipients are selected from those applicants with the highest grades. The minimum GPA for entering college freshmen in 1994 was 3.24; for entering sophomore and junior winners, 3.21. Information about computing your GPA appears on the previous page.

Dependent Students and Independent Students with Dependents (other than a spouse)

To receive a Cal Grant A for the 1994-95 academic year, total family income, including taxable and nontaxable income and benefits, could not exceed these income ceilings:

Family Size	Income Ceiling
3 or fewer	$52,000
4	$55,000
5	$58,000
6	$61,000

Total family assets including cash, checking and savings accounts, equity in real estate other than your home or family farm, and investments could not exceed $42,000. Equity in your home or farm is not considered in computing total assets.

Independent Students without Children or other Dependents (other than a spouse)

To receive a Cal Grant A for the 1994-95 academic year, total family income, including taxable and nontaxable income and benefits, could not exceed these income ceilings: $21,000 for single students, $24,000 for married students.

Total family assets including cash, checking and savings accounts, equity in real estate other than your home or family farm, and investments could not exceed $20,000. Equity in your home or family farm is not considered in computing total assets.

ADDITIONAL REQUIREMENTS AND INFORMATION

The California Student Aid Commission awards 17,400 new Cal Grant A's each academic year. To be a first-time recipient you must enroll in the fall term of the year for which the award is made and be in a program that takes at least two academic years to complete.

You can receive a Cal Grant A for up to four full years of undergraduate study. It will pay for the fifth year of a teacher credentialing program or mandatory five-year programs. You must reapply for renewal each year to demonstrate continued need and satisfactory academic progress as evaluated by your college. There is no minimum GPA for renewal. You submit a financial aid application to your college to reassess your financial eligibility.

SPECIAL AWARD CATEGORY: COMMUNITY COLLEGE RESERVE

If you attend a community college at least halftime, you may place your Cal Grant A in "reserve" for a minimum of one year, but not more than two years. You may activate it when you enter a school that charges tuition/fees. This activation is not automatic; you must demonstrate your financial eligibility by submitting a financial aid application — one your college uses to verify your financial need. This option may be a good alternative because competition for Cal Grants historically has been tougher for those who defer applying until after enrolling in college.

ANNUAL AWARD AMOUNTS

A Cal Grant A pays tuition/fee costs only. Each year the California State Legislature appropriates funds to pay the Grants. Cal Grant A awards for the 1994-95 academic year are

a) $1,584 at California State University,

b) $3,799 at the University of California, and

c) up to $5,250 at California independent colleges.

Your Cal Grant A award may be adjusted from year to year if your need for financial assistance changes or if state budget allocations for student financial assistance are reduced or increased.

PAYMENT OF AWARDS

Tuition/fee payments are paid directly to your school on your behalf by term — semester or quarter — and are never more than the tuition/fees charged by your school.

Your payments and Cal Grant A award may be adjusted based upon your attendance status: Fulltime or halftime.

CAL GRANT B

ELIGIBILITY REQUIREMENTS

Cal Grant B is designed to help students from disadvantaged/low-income families who are not able to attend a postsecondary school or college without aid. Financial need, ratio of family income to family size, parental education level, two-parent or single-parent family, and GPA are criteria for selection. See this chapter: Computing Your Cal Grant GPA, page 4--31.

Certification of financial need is the first step in the selection process. Applicants with financial need are selected based upon a composite scoring system that includes consideration of low income, disadvantaged background, and grades. The average family income of financially dependent Cal Grant B recipients in 1993-94 was $12,580. Eighty-five percent were minorities. These figures are typical of recent years.

Many recipients are the first in their families to attend college. Recent program trends show that only the most disadvantaged and highest achieving applicants receive a Cal Grant B award.

FAMILY INCOME AND ASSET CEILINGS

Dependent Students and Independent Students with Dependents (other than a spouse)

To receive a Cal Grant B for the 1994-95 academic year, total family income, including taxable and nontaxable income and benefits, could not exceed these income ceilings.

Family Size	Income Ceiling
1	$21,849
2	$23,324
3	$26,299
4	$29,274
5 or more	$32,249

Total family net assets including cash, checking and savings accounts, equity in real estate — other than your home or family farm — and investments could not exceed $42,000. Equity in your home or family farm is not considered in computing total assets.

Independent Students without Children or other Dependents (other than a spouse)

To receive a Cal Grant B for the 1994-95 academic year, total family income, including taxable and nontaxable income and benefits, could not exceed these income ceilings: $21,000 for single students and $24,000 for married students.

Total family assets including cash, checking and savings accounts, equity in real estate — other than your home or family farm — and investments could not exceed $20,000. Equity in your home or family farm is not considered in computing total assets.

ADDITIONAL REQUIREMENTS AND INFORMATION

Each year the California Student Aid Commission awards 12,250 new Cal Grant B's.

At least fifty-one percent of Cal Grant B awards are given to recipients who begin their college education at a California Community College. Not more than forty-nine percent are awarded to students attending other eligible schools.

You must enroll at least halftime in the fall term of the year for which the award is made. You may continue to receive annual Cal Grant B awards until completion of your BA/BS degree or completion of the equivalent of four years of full-time study. You must reapply for renewal each year to demonstrate continued need and satisfactory academic progress as evaluated by your college. You submit a financial aid application to your college, which reassesses your financial eligibility.

You may receive a fifth-year, Cal Grant B award for a teacher credentialing program or a mandatory five year program.

ANNUAL AWARD AMOUNTS

Freshman awards are usually limited to nontuition costs of attending college — living expenses, books, supplies, and transportation. There is tuition/fee assistance for unusually needy or disadvantaged students.

The Cal Grant B may also cover all or part of tuition/fee costs for sophomore, junior, and senior recipients. If, after completing one or two years at a California Community College, you transfer your grant to a tuition-/fee-charging school, your grant may be increased to cover all or part of the increase in tuition/fees. There is no increase in funds to cover living expenses.

Each year the California State Legislature appropriates funds to pay the Grants. Cal Grant B subsistence awards for the 1994-95 academic year are $1,410. If you qualify for tuition/fee awards, they are the same as for Cal Grant A. The total award amount printed on your notification letter may be a combination of a subsistence award and a tuition/fee award. The maximum total award is $6,660.

PAYMENT OF AWARDS

A subsistence award is paid to you through your college. You must pick up your payment in person at disbursement time at your institution. Contact the financial aid office on your campus for information about when, where, and how payments are made.

Your payments and Cal Grant B award may be adjusted based upon your attendance status: Full-time or halftime.

CAL GRANT C

ELIGIBILITY REQUIREMENTS

The Cal Grant C is designed for vocationally-oriented students from low- and middle-income families. Selection is based upon financial need, work and/or academic references, prior work experience, educational history, and GPA. See this chapter: Computing Your Cal Grant GPA, page 4--31. Family income and asset ceilings are the same as those for Cal Grant A. See this chapter: Cal Grant A, page 4--32.

If you are financially eligible based upon your FAFSA, you receive an additional application form in May or June. On it you provide a description of your educational plans and your work and educational history. In addition, you must submit one occupational/educational recommendation from a teacher, counselor, school official, employer, or other responsible person who knows you well and can comment knowledgeably about your interest or achievement in occupational/technical areas. You must return the form within twenty-one days of the date on the accompanying letter to remain in consideration for an award.

CAL GRANTS

	CAL GRANT A	CAL GRANT B	CAL GRANT C
Eligibility	Students from low and middle income families with financial need and academic ability.	High-potential students from disadvantaged and low income families.	Vocationally oriented students from low and middle income families.
Selection Criteria	Based upon financial need and GPA.	Based upon financial need, GPA, ratio of family income to family size, parents' education level, and whether or not student is from a single- parent family.	Based upon financial need, work and/or academic references, prior work experience, educational history, and GPA.
Maximum Awards	Pays tuition/fees for programs of at least two years. May be held in reserve while you attend a California Community College. 17,400 new Cal Grant A' s awarded each year, not including community college reserve awards. ANNUAL AWARD AMOUNTS FOR 1994-1995 <u>Tuition/Fees</u> UC: Awards - $3,799 CSU: Awards - $1,584 Independent Colleges - $5,250	Pays only subsistence awards in the first year; tuition/fees and subsistence awards thereafter for programs of at least one year. Tuition/fees assistance is available for the first year to unusually needy or disadvant- aged cases. 12,250 new Cal Grant B' s awarded for each year. ANNUAL AWARD AMOUNTS FOR 1994-1995 <u>Tuition/Fees</u> Same as Cal Grant A. <u>Subsistence Awards:</u> Awards up to $1410	Pays tuition/fees and training costs (books and supplies) for vocational programs of four to twenty-four months. Not available to students pursuing a four-year college program, course prerequisites, or general education. 1,570 new Cal Grant C' s awarded for each year. ANNUAL AWARD AMOUNTS FOR 1994-1995 <u>Tuition/Fees</u> $2,360. <u>Training-Related Costs:</u> Allowances range up to $530.

ADDITIONAL REQUIREMENTS AND INFORMATION

The California Student Aid Commission awards 1,570 new Cal Grant C's each academic year.

You must be enrolled at least halftime in a vocational program of four months to twenty-four months at a community college, independent college, or vocational school in California.

You must enroll at least halftime in the fall term of the year for which the award is made.

Your award cannot be used to pursue a four-year degree, course prerequisites or General Education/Breadth requirements. It must be used to acquire marketable job skills through short-term, highly specialized vocational training in the shortest feasible time.

The Cal Grant C is awarded for the length of the course to a maximum of two years if you maintain satisfactory progress. You do not need to formally renew your award.

ANNUAL AWARD AMOUNTS

Cal Grant C pays a tools, books, and equipment allowance of up to $530 (maximum) and tuition/fee awards of $2,360.

The total award amount printed on the notification letter may be a combination of a books and supplies award and a tuition/fee award.

These award amounts are the maximum authorized by law. Each year the California State Legislature appropriates funds to pay the Grants. The amount of funds appropriated may not be enough to pay the maximum awards authorized.

Grants are limited to $530 at community colleges.

PAYMENT OF AWARDS

Tuition/fee awards are paid directly to your school on your behalf. Books and supplies payments are paid to you by your school. You must pick up your payments in person at disbursement time at your institution. Contact the financial aid office on your campus for information about when, where, and how payments are made.

Your payments and Cal Grant C award may be adjusted based upon your attendance status: Full-time or halftime.

You may be eligible for a 1995-96 summer payment. If you plan to be enrolled at least half time in the summer term, you and your school must contact the California Student Aid Commission by phone or in writing to request summer payment.

BOGG — BOARD OF GOVERNORS GRANT

SOURCE

A State of California program with funds administered by the California Community Colleges.

ELIGIBILITY REQUIREMENTS

The BOGG is a program for California Community College students only.

You must be a California resident and meet one of the following criteria:

1. Demonstrate financial need and already have qualified for financial assistance from other federal and/or state need-based financial aid programs, such as the Federal Pell Grant, SEOG, Cal Grant, or EOPS; or,

2. Receive benefits from AFDC, SSI, or General Assistance/General Relief Program, or be eligible for a Deceased/Disabled Veteran's Dependent Fee Waiver; or,

3. Meet specific income levels shown in the table at the top of the next page.

Number In Your Household Including Yourself	Total Family Income Last Year (Note 1.)
1	$7,500 or less
2	$15,000 or less
3	$16,000 or less
4	$17,000 or less
5	$18,000 or less
6	$19,000 or less
7	$20,000 or less
8	$21,000 or less
9	$22,000 or less
10 (Note 2.)	$23,000 or less

Notes: 1. Adjusted gross income and/or nontaxed income.
2. Add $1,000 for each additional dependent.

Dependents of deceased or disabled veterans who are eligible for benefits — under the California Veterans Dependents Educational Assistance Program — and dependents of deceased or disabled California National Guard members certified by the Adjutant General's Office can also have California Community College enrollment fees waived with a BOGG.

ANNUAL AWARD AMOUNTS

The BOGG awards are equal to the total of California Community College enrollment fees.

Once qualified for a BOGG, your California Community College enrollment fees are paid for the rest of the school year, including summer, whether you are taking one class or a full-time program.

PAYMENT OF AWARD

The community college credits your college account each term when you enroll.

APPLICATION PROCEDURES AND DEADLINES

Application: Apply through your community college financial aid office.

Deadline: The deadline is established by your community college.

Notification: Your community college notifies you of your award.

EOP — Educational Opportunity Program And Grant

EOPS — Extended Opportunity Programs And Services And Grant

SOURCE

EOP - CSU

A California State University program with funds administered by the EOP.

EOPS - CCC

A California Community Colleges program with funds administered by the EOPS.

ELIGIBILITY REQUIREMENTS

EOP and EOPS serve low-income and underrepresented ethnic students who are disadvantaged because of economic and educational background.

For EOP eligibility, you must be enrolled at a California State University campus. If enrolled less than half time, approval of the EOP director is needed.

For EOPS eligibility, you must be enrolled full-time at a California Community College.

ADDITIONAL REQUIREMENTS AND INFORMATION

In addition to EOP and EOPS Grants, admissions assistance, counseling, and tutorial services are available through the EOP/EOPS offices on the college campuses.

EOP income guidelines for participation in the California State University EOP program are reviewed in chapter 10: CALIFORNIA STATE UNIVERSITY, EOP, page 10--33.

Income guidelines for the California Community College EOPS are the same as those used for the BOGG described on the previous page.

Campus EOP/EOPS offices may have additional specific eligibility requirements.

Counseling and/or tutorial services are provided though the campus EOP at the University of California. The UC financial aid office rather than the EOP office provides financial assistance.

ANNUAL AWARD AMOUNTS

EOP Grants at California State University range from $400 to $1,000 per year depending upon need and the availability of funds.

EOPS Grants at California Community Colleges can be as high as $900 per year depending upon the school.

PAYMENT OF AWARDS

Your college has its own plan for disbursement of funds. Funds are credited to your college account and/or disbursed to you. Contact the EOP or EOPS office and/or the financial aid office for specific information.

APPLICATION PROCEDURES AND DEADLINES

EOP - CSU

Application: Submit the FAFSA.

Deadline: Apply as soon as possible after January 1, 1995 and before the financial aid priority date of March 2, 1995. EOP Grants are awarded only while funds are available. You have a much better chance of receiving an EOP Grant if you apply early in the application cycle and before March 2, 1995. Call the EOP office of your CSU campus to verify these dates; some campuses may have earlier filing periods.

Notification: You receive notice of your award in May or June.

EOPS - CCC

Application: Submit the FAFSA.

Deadline: Apply by March 2, 1995 if you also are applying for a Cal Grant. If you miss the March 2nd deadline, submit the FAFSA to apply for community college aid and a Federal Pell Grant.

Notification: Notification varies with the school.

LAW ENFORCEMENT PERSONNEL DEPENDENTS GRANT

SOURCE

A State of California program with funds administered by the California Student Aid Commission.

ELIGIBILITY REQUIREMENTS

This program provides educational grants to needy dependents and spouses of California city, county, and state law enforcement officers, and permanent and full-time firefighters who have been killed or totally disabled in the line of duty. Eligible law enforcement officers include peace officers, and officers and employees of the California Department of Corrections and the California Youth Authority. Death or disablement must have been the result of an accident or injury caused by external violence or physical force incurred in the performance of duty. You must demonstrate financial need.

ADDITIONAL REQUIREMENTS AND INFORMATION

Awards may be used to attend any postsecondary college-level institution in California accredited by the Western Association of Schools and Colleges.

Awards may be used for tuition, subsistence, books, and supplies.

ANNUAL AWARD AMOUNTS

Awards to attend a four-year college or university range from $100 to $1,500 per academic year based upon financial need and may not exceed a cumulative maximum of $6,000 in a six-year period.

Awards to attend a California Community College range from $100 to $500 per year based upon your financial need and may not exceed a cumulative maximum of $2,000 over four years.

PAYMENT OF AWARDS

A check is issued to the college in your name. When you enroll in school, sign for the check at the college financial aid office.

APPLICATION PROCEDURES AND DEADLINES

Application: Submit a FAFSA together with a special application obtained from the state. For the special application write directly to:

California Student Aid Commission
P.O. Box 510624
Sacramento, Ca. 94245-0624

Deadline: The deadline for the FAFSA is March 2, 1995 if you are applying for other financial aid. Otherwise, you may apply for this grant at any time before the end of the academic year.

Notification: You are notified of your award about a month after all application materials are received by the California Student Aid Commission.

BUREAU OF INDIAN AFFAIRS GRANTS

SOURCE

A federal government program with funds administered by the federal Bureau of Indian Affairs (BIA).

ELIGIBILITY REQUIREMENTS

To receive benefits in California you must prove that you are a member of a federally recognized California tribe.

ADDITIONAL REQUIREMENTS AND INFORMATION

The Bureau of Indian Affairs requires you to apply first for a Federal Pell Grant. You are also encouraged to apply for Cal Grants.

APPLICATION PROCEDURES AND DEADLINES

For applications and information regarding award amounts, payment procedures, application procedures and deadlines write to

Office of Indian Education
2800 Cottage Way
Sacramento, CA 95825
(916) 978-4680

BENEFITS FOR DEPENDENTS OF DECEASED OR DISABLED VETERANS

Both the federal and state governments provide benefits for dependents of veterans who died in the service, have service-connected disabilities, or who died of a service-connected disability. If qualified, you may receive benefits from both the federal and state programs.

PAYING FOR COLLEGE

FEDERAL EDUCATION BENEFITS

Educational benefits are available to veterans' dependents if the veteran (a spouse or parent) died in the service, was totally disabled, or is still listed as missing in action. This benefit pays eligible veterans' dependents up to $404 per month for full-time study, $304 per month for three-quarter time study, and $202 per month for halftime study. Contact the local office of the U.S. Veterans Administration or call (800) 827-1000.

CALIFORNIA EDUCATION BENEFITS

SOURCE

A State of California program with funds administered by the California Department of Veterans Affairs.

ELIGIBILITY REQUIREMENTS

You must be the child of a veteran of the United States military

a) with a current service-connected disability, or

b) who died of a service related death.

ANNUAL AWARD AMOUNTS

The benefit available is a waiver of tuition and registration fees to any California Community College, California State University, or the University of California.

APPLICATION PROCEDURES AND DEADLINES

Application: An application and additional information may be obtained by contacting a county veterans service officer, listed in the telephone directory under county government. Information is also available from:

California Division of Veterans Affairs
Division of Veterans Services
P.O. Box 942895
Sacramento, CA 94295-0001
(916) 445-2573

COLLEGE GRANTS

SOURCE

Programs originate at and funds are administered by the public and independent colleges and universities.

ELIGIBILITY REQUIREMENTS

Eligibility requirements for college grants vary from college to college and are determined by the college financial aid offices.

ADDITIONAL REQUIREMENTS AND INFORMATION

Colleges may award grants to supplement federal, state, and private scholarship aid and also to encourage students to attend their schools.

ANNUAL AWARD AMOUNTS

Award amounts vary from college to college and are established by their financial aid offices. The amount of your college grant is stated in your financial aid package, which you receive from the college.

PAYMENT OF AWARDS

Procedures vary from college to college and are established by the college financial aid offices.

APPLICATION PROCEDURES AND DEADLINES

Application: Submit the FAFSA and the FAF, if required.

Deadline: The deadline for the FAFSA is March 2, 1995 for the 1995-96 school year.

Additional Application: Institutional application materials may be required. You receive these materials directly from the colleges. Contact the financial aid offices of the institutions to which you are applying for information and appropriate application materials.

Deadline: Deadlines vary according to individual college guidelines.

SCHOLARSHIPS

Scholarships are awards of money based upon your grades or achievements. Financial need may or may not be a criterion. Scholarships generally are not repaid.

PAUL DOUGLAS TEACHER SCHOLARSHIP PROGRAM

SOURCE

A federally funded program with funds administered by the California Student Aid Commission.

ELIGIBILITY REQUIREMENTS

You must be an outstanding high school graduate who demonstrates a commitment to pursue a teaching career at the preschool, elementary, or secondary school level.

You must have achieved a minimum high school GPA of 3.00 based upon a 4.00 scale.

You must be in the top ten percent of your high school class or receive a GED average standard score of 62 or higher.

You must be enrolled in and attend on a full-time basis an accredited United States postsecondary school with a teacher credentialing program.

You must be formally accepted or continue in a full-time teacher credential program beginning with the fall term of the award year if all your Bachelor's degree requirements are completed.

You are required to sign an agreement to teach two years full time for each year you receive the scholarship. This requirement may be reduced by fifty percent if your teaching is done in a teacher shortage area identified by the United States Department of Education.

If you do not fulfill the teaching requirement, you must repay all or part of the scholarship plus interest and collection fees.

You must be a United States citizen or eligible noncitizen as described on page 4--4.

You must be a legal resident of California.

You must not be in default on a federal loan or owe a refund on a federal or state grant.

ADDITIONAL REQUIREMENTS AND INFORMATION

The following students are encouraged to apply:

Ethnic and racial minority students,

Individuals with disabilities,

Other individuals from groups historically underrepresented in teaching

Those willing to teach in rural, urban or other schools having less than average academic results or which serves large numbers of economically disadvantaged students,

Women and minorities interested in mathematics and sciences teaching careers.

ANNUAL AWARD AMOUNTS

Scholarships of up to $5,000 a year may be awarded for up to four academic years beginning in your freshman year of college and cannot exceed your cost of attendance.

Acceptance of this award may affect other financial aid, including Cal Grants. You have the option of requesting that the amount of your award be reduced.

PAYMENT OF AWARDS

Payments begin in your freshman year of college. Contact the financial aid office of your college for their payment policies and procedures.

APPLICATION PROCEDURES AND DEADLINES

Application: Applications are available at your high school after January 1, 1995. Submit your application to your high school counselor or appropriate administrator. Your high school screens applications and nominates one student to compete in a statewide competition.

College students may apply for this scholarship through the financial aid office of their college.

Deadline: Your high school sets its own deadline for submission of your application. Your high school coordinator must submit your school's nomination to the California Student Aid Commission postmarked by July 15, 1995.

Notification: You are notified in September 1995 if you are awarded this scholarship.

ROBERT C. BYRD HONORS SCHOLARSHIP PROGRAM

SOURCE

A federally funded program with funds administered by the California Student Aid Commission.

ELIGIBILITY REQUIREMENTS

The Robert C. Byrd Honors Scholarship is awarded to high school graduates who have demonstrated outstanding academic achievement in high school and who show promise of continued academic achievement in college. This is a merit-based scholarship. Your unweighted GPA (no extra weight given for grades in honors classes) and your SAT I scores are the criteria for selection of recipients.

ADDITIONAL REQUIREMENTS AND INFORMATION

You must be a United States citizen or eligible noncitizen as described on page 4--4.

You must be a legal resident of California.

You must graduate from high school between July 1, 1994 and June 30, 1995 or receive an equivalent GED/high school proficiency examination certificate between September 1, 1994 and March 31, 1995.

You must enroll at and attend any United States public or private, nonprofit postsecondary institution full time during your first year of college. You are not limited to colleges in California. Nonprofit institutions that only provide training programs of less than one year and proprietary (for profit) institutions are not eligible.

You must be considered a freshman beginning in the fall term of the 1995-96 academic year.

You must fulfill United States Selective Service registration requirements.

ANNUAL AWARD AMOUNTS

$1,500 renewable scholarships are awarded for four years of undergraduate study at any public or private nonprofit institution in the United States. The amount of the Byrd Scholarship plus any other aid your receive cannot exceed the total cost of your education.

Scholarships are awarded, in part, according to the county in which you reside.

PAYMENT OF AWARDS

A check is issued to your college in your name. When you enroll in school, sign for the check at the college financial aid office.

APPLICATION PROCEDURES AND DEADLINES

Application: Robert C. Byrd Honors Scholarship Program applications are available at your high school after January 1, 1995. Submit your application to your high school counselor or appropriate administrator. Your school screens applications and nominates two students to participate in a statewide competition.

Deadline: Your school sets its own deadline for submission of your application to them. Your high school coordinator must submit your school's two nominations to the California Student Aid Commission, postmarked by April 30, 1995.

Notification: You are notified by May 1995 if selected as a Robert C. Byrd Honors Scholarship recipient.

College Scholarships

SOURCE

Programs originate at and funds are administered by the public and independent colleges and universities.

ELIGIBILITY REQUIREMENTS

Colleges may award scholarships to (a) students with exceptional academic ability, (b) skilled athletes, (c) students with specific backgrounds, (d) those with a specific major or career objective, (e) those with specific talents, (f) those from certain geographic locations, or (g) those meeting any other criteria that the colleges develop.

ADDITIONAL PROCEDURES AND INFORMATION

Many of these scholarships are merit-based. Each school establishes its own criteria such as GPA, entrance test scores, high school curriculum, and special talent. Frequently, merit-based scholarships do not consider financial need as a criterion.

The University of California provides complete information in their application packet about all scholarships offered by the university. Criteria and required supporting documentation — letters of recommendation, transcripts, an essay — are outlined for each scholarship and for each campus. See chapter 11: UNIVERSITY OF CALIFORNIA, Financial Aid, page 11--62.

For scholarship information at California State University and all other colleges and universities, contact their financial aid offices for complete information. Many of the independent colleges send financial aid information with their admissions application materials.

ANNUAL AWARD AMOUNTS

Amounts vary from college to college. Some merit-based scholarships are very generous. The colleges want to attract the most able students and make strong offers to enroll them. Amounts of college scholarships are listed in your financial aid package.

PAYMENT OF AWARDS

Colleges credit awards to your college account and/or disburse funds directly to you according to their published schedule for the academic year. Contact the financial aid office of the college you will attend for specific information.

APPLICATION PROCEDURES AND DEADLINES

UNIVERSITY OF CALIFORNIA

Application: Complete the section designated on the admissions application form to apply for all scholarships offered by the university. Supporting documentation required for each scholarship at each campus is specified in the admissions application booklet.

Deadline: The admissions application deadline is November 30th for the following fall. The deadline for scholarship supporting documentation is January 11th.

Notification: You are notified of awards in your financial aid packages from the campuses.

ALL OTHER COLLEGES AND UNIVERSITIES

Application: Contact the college financial aid offices to receive scholarship information and institutional application materials.

Deadline: Deadlines vary from college to college.

Notification: You are notified of awards in your financial aid packages from the colleges.

Private Scholarships

SOURCE

Moneys are offered by a wide variety of private sources including community organizations such as Rotary, Elks Club, Chamber of Commerce, and PTA; employers; professional, career, and trade associations such as unions; churches; and national foundations. Also, your high school or school district may participate in a community scholarship program.

ELIGIBILITY REQUIREMENTS

Awards may be based upon grades, entrance test scores, rank in class, leadership ability, country or state of birth, ethnic background, church affiliation, artistic talent, athletic abilities, special skills, special examination scores, career goals, college major, an essay on a selected topic, a research project, parent organization membership, or a combination of these criteria.

Some scholarships require financial need, many do not.

ADDITIONAL REQUIREMENTS AND INFORMATION

Scholarships from private sources are often small. Researching them requires time and effort. Budget your time carefully; applications may require you to write an essay or autobiography, and/or obtain recommendations. Your first priority is to apply for the major sources of aid: Federal Pell Grants, Cal Grants, and campus-based financial aid programs.

Your high school counselor, administrator, or career center technician has descriptions of scholarship opportunities. College financial aid offices are also a good source of information.

Go to your school library, career center, or the public library and research scholarships, grants, and loans to develop a list of opportunities for which you may qualify.

Urge your parents to inquire if their employers offer any special scholarships for children of employees. Many businesses do. Your parents should also contact their church and any organizations to which they belong.

Contact organizations having chapters in your local area that may offer scholarships to students living in their city or neighborhood.

ANNUAL AWARD AMOUNTS

Awards vary considerably from one hundred to several hundred dollars, but generally are not sufficient to cover all of your college costs. However, the amounts you receive from several scholarships do add up. Furthermore, they provide needed moneys that would otherwise be borrowed and repaid at a later time. These awards can also reduce the number of hours you must work.

PAYMENT OF AWARDS

Some awards from private sources are paid directly to you; others are paid to the college financial aid office after you have sent the scholarship source proof of your enrollment in the college.

Colleges ask that you inform them of any awards made directly to you. These scholarships are calculated into your financial aid package. For information about how colleges handle outside scholarships see this chapter: Commonly Asked Questions About Financial Aid, page 4--18.

APPLICATION PROCEDURES AND DEADLINES

Every week or so check your high school scholarship bulletin board (or other announcement system used in your high school) for flyers and announcements about scholarship opportunities.

Application: Scholarships are generally announced four to eight weeks before their application deadlines. Your high school counselor, guidance administrator, or career center has application materials. You may have to call or write directly to some of the sources for applications and further information.

Deadline: Deadlines vary. Stay alert for opportunities and quickly pursue them.

ROTC — Reserve Officers Training Corps Scholarships And Officer Training Programs

SOURCE

Federally funded programs with funds administered by the United States Armed Services: Army, Navy-Marine Corps, Air Force.

If the armed services are of interest to you, several scholarship and officer training programs are available to help you defray your college expenses:

- Four-year ROTC scholarship programs.
- One-, two-, and three-year ROTC scholarship programs.
- Two- and four-year officer training programs.

FOUR-YEAR ROTC SCHOLARSHIP PROGRAM

ELIGIBILITY REQUIREMENTS

CITIZENSHIP

You must be a United States citizen.

AGE REQUIREMENTS

Army: You must be seventeen years of age before the scholarship becomes effective. Also, you must be able to complete all course and training requirements for an Army officer's commission and a college degree, and be under twenty-five years of age on June 30th of the year you graduate and receive an officer's commission. An extension of up to four years is possible for enlisted military service.

Navy-Marine Corps: You must be seventeen years of age by September 1st and less than twenty-one on June 30th of the year you start college. Also, you must not have reached your twenty-fifth birthday by June 30th of the year you expect to graduate from college and receive an officer's commission.

Air Force: You must be seventeen years of age to receive a scholarship and under twenty-five years of age on June 30th of the year you plan to graduate and receive your commission.

EDUCATION REQUIREMENTS

You must be a high school graduate or possess an equivalency certificate by the fall term of the same year you enter into the program. The specific deadlines by service are:

Army .... Fall term
Navy-Marines Corps .... August 1st
Air Force .... Fall term

You must have four academic years remaining to earn your Bachelor's degree.

You must apply for and gain admission to a college offering the program.

PERSONAL REQUIREMENTS

You must be in excellent physical and mental condition and pass physical standards established by the particular service branch.

You must have no moral obligations or personal convictions that prevent your conscientious bearing of arms, and supporting and defending the Constitution of the United States against all enemies, foreign or domestic.

SELECTION CRITERIA

Selection is extremely competitive. Consideration is given to high school GPA, class standing, pattern of high school courses, SAT I or ACT scores, extracurricular activities, and leadership qualities. Interviews and recommendations are required.

PAYING FOR COLLEGE

Army: Take the SAT I: Reasoning Test or ACT no later than November of the year you apply. You must achieve a minimum SAT I total score of 850 (verbal plus mathematics) or an ACT composite score of 19 to qualify for competition. Army four-year ROTC scholarship recipients for the 1994-95 academic year had an average SAT total score of 1323 (verbal plus mathematics), and an average ACT composite of 29.

Navy-Marine Corps: Initial screening is based upon SAT I or ACT scores. The program must receive your test scores no later than December 31st of the year you apply.

To apply for a Navy ROTC four-year scholarship, you need a minimum SAT I verbal score of 450 and a minimum mathematics score of 500; or an ACT English score of 22 and a mathematics score of 22. Recipients for the 1994-95 academic year had an average SAT total score of 1250 (verbal plus mathematics), an average verbal score of 570, and an average mathematics score of 680. To be competitive, winners needed an average high school GPA between 3.60 and 3.80. 78% were in the top 10% or their class; 88% were in the top 20% of their class.

To apply for a Marines ROTC four-year scholarship, you need a minimum SAT I verbal and mathematics score combined of 1000 or an ACT English and mathematics score combined of 45. Marines ROTC four-year scholarship recipients for the 1994-95 academic year had average SAT total scores (verbal plus mathematics) for men of 1214, for women of 1197. The average ACT score of English plus mathematics for men was 56, for women 58. 85.4% of men were in the top twenty percent of their class; 71.4% of the women were in the top twenty percent of their class.

Air Force: Complete your SAT I: Reasoning Test or ACT tests by November of the year you apply. Plan to test in your junior year or early in your senior year. You must achieve the following minimum SAT I scores or ACT scores.

SAT I Scores		ACT Scores	
Mathematics	500	Mathematics	21
Verbal	450	Verbal	21
Total score	1000	Composite	24

You must have a minimum GPA of 2.50 out of 4.00 and be in the top twenty-five percent of your class.

Air Force four-year scholarship recipients for the 1994-95 academic year had an average SAT total score (verbal plus mathematics) of 1170. The average ACT composite score was 28; the average high school GPA was 3.65.

ADDITIONAL REQUIREMENTS AND INFORMATION

During the four years of your college education, you must take a program of military training courses in addition to your regular college curriculum. Paid summer training periods are also required.

Army: Special consideration for an Army ROTC scholarship is given to students pursuing degrees in nursing, engineering and the physical sciences. If you receive a scholarship on the basis of your major, you are expected to earn an undergraduate degree in the same field.

Navy-Marines Corps: You may apply for either Navy- or Marine Corps-option scholarships, but not both. Apply through a Navy recruiting office for the Navy option or through a Marine Corps recruiting office for the Marine Corps option. The Navy offers special four-year scholarships to students planning to study nursing.

Air Force: One year scholarships are available for students majoring in career fields in which the Air Force has a shortage, such as law and nursing. Two-to four-year scholarships are available for students pursuing degrees in certain fields of engineering, science, math and nursing. Limited scholarships are available to those who enroll in certain nontechnical degree programs such as business administration, accounting, economics, and management.

MILITARY SERVICE OBLIGATION

Upon graduation from college, you receive a commission as an officer in the branch of the service in which you were trained. You then have a military service obligation as outlined here.

The service commitment of number of years of active verses reserve duty is subject to change depending upon world affairs and the needs of the United States and its armed services.

Army: You must serve in the Army for a period of eight years. This service may be fulfilled by

a) serving on active duty two to four years and then serving in the reserves of the Army National Guard or the Army for the remaining years, *or*

b) by serving eight years in the Army National Guard or the Army Reserves, preceded by active duty for an officer's basic course.

Navy-Marine Corps: You must serve in the Navy-Marine Corps for a period of eight years, at least four of which are in active duty.

Air Force: You must serve in the Air Force for at least four years on active duty and a total of four years in reserves.

ANNUAL AWARD AMOUNTS

The four-year ROTC scholarship provides tuition assistance for up to four years of undergraduate study, costs of textbooks, fees of an instructional nature, and a nontaxable subsistence allowance of $100 per month for a maximum of forty academic months — ten school months each year. You are also paid for your summer months of training. Maximum tuition payments may be less than your actual costs. If you win a four-year ROTC scholarship, check carefully with the service branch to determine exactly how much money you will receive.

Because the subsistence allowance is usually not sufficient to pay all your college expenses, plan for additional money to cover your total costs.

APPLICATION PROCEDURES AND DEADLINES

Application: Get application materials by

a) contacting the recruiting office of the services in which you are interested, or

b) sending a special request card that you find in your high school career center or other area in your high school that houses college and scholarship information, or

c) contacting the ROTC program at a college or university for application materials and further information.

Deadline:

Army: Request your application between March 1st and November 1st.

Early Decision: Your completed application must be postmarked by July 15th of the summer before your senior year of high school. Winners are announced about November 1st.

Regular Decision: Your application is considered in a regular admissions cycle if received by December 1st of your senior year of high school. Winners are notified in March.

Navy-Marine Corps: Apply between March 1st of your junior year and December 1st of your senior year of high school. You are notified by April 15th if you are a winner.

Air Force: Your application package must be completed by December 1st of your senior year of high school. The selection boards meet periodically between November and February.

The earlier you apply, the sooner the Service Scholarship Board, which reviews and screens applicants, notifies you if you are a recipient.

ONE-, TWO-, AND THREE-YEAR ROTC SCHOLARSHIPS

In addition to ROTC four-year scholarships, the armed services offer other scholarship programs to help you with college expenses.

Army: The Army offers two- and three-year scholarship to students who are already in college. Scholarship benefits and obligations are similar to those for their four-year scholarships.

Navy-Marine Corps: The Navy-Marine Corps offers three-year scholarship programs to students who are already in college. Scholarship benefits and obligations are similar to those for their four-year scholarships.

Air Force: The Air Force offers one-, two-, and three-year scholarships to students who are already in college. Scholarship benefits and obligations are similar to those for their four-year scholarships.

TWO- AND FOUR-YEAR OFFICER TRAINING PROGRAMS

All three branches of the service offer officer training programs. These are two- and four-year ROTC programs, which train you to be an officer, although they are not considered scholarship programs. The programs pay for your uniforms and all books required for your military science courses. During your junior and senior years of college, you receive a nontaxable $100 monthly allowance for a maximum of twenty academic months. Upon graduation, you are commissioned as an officer and have a service obligation.

CALIFORNIA COLLEGES OFFERING ROTC TRAINING

Many of the colleges listed here are host schools, which offer students from nearby colleges and universities an opportunity to attend the host school's ROTC program. These arrangements are called "crosstown or cross-enrolled agreements." Call the host school nearest to the college in which you are interested to find out if it has an agreement with your institution.

Army

California Polytechnic State University, San Luis Obispo
California State University, Fresno
California State University, Long Beach
San Diego State University, San Diego
San Jose State University, San Jose
Santa Clara University, Santa Clara
The Claremont Colleges — Claremont
University of California, Berkeley
University of California, Davis
University of California, Los Angeles
University of California, Santa Barbara
University of San Francisco, San Francisco
University of Southern California, Los Angeles

Navy-Marine Corps

University of California, Berkeley
University of California, Los Angeles
University of San Diego/San Diego State University Consortium, San Diego
University of Southern California, Los Angeles

Air Force

California State University, Fresno
California State University, Long Beach
California State University, Sacramento
Loyola Marymount University, Los Angeles
San Diego State University, San Diego
San Jose State University, San Jose
University of California, Berkeley
University of California, Los Angeles
University of Southern California, Los Angeles

THE ARMED SERVICES SCHOLARSHIPS

There are several generous scholarships and student aid programs in addition to ROTC if you are willing to serve in the United States armed services. In some cases, you can receive an education first and serve an equivalent amount of military time after graduation. Some programs allow for accumulation of money for an education while completing an enlistment period.

All services pay up to seventy-five percent of tuition costs (depending on rank and length of service) for qualified servicemen/women who take approved college courses while in the service. Academic, vocational, technical, and independent study courses are eligible. Armed forces reservists are eligible for educational assistance after completing one-hundred-eighty days of a six-year enlistment.

Under the new G.I. Bill program, service personnel on active duty can save up to $14,400 toward future college or technical training costs, with the government contributing $12.00 for every $1.00 saved by the individual.

Under the Army College Fund, up to $15,600 is added to the new G.I. Bill for qualified enlistees in specific job categories. The Navy College Fund will add $10,800. The U.S. Coast Guard has a scholarship designed to increase ethnic minority representation in its commissioning program. Recipients are enlisted in the Coast Guard and have college costs covered for up to two academic years in addition to full pay and allowances.

Under the Army Loan Repayment Program, qualified applicants may reduce their student loan debt — Federal Perkins or Stafford — by one third or $1,500, whichever is greater, for each year of active service. Every year of Army reserve service reduces indebtedness by fifteen percent or $500, whichever is greater.

Veterans disabled in the service are eligible for educational or training-for-employment benefits. The monthly subsistence allowance is $333 for full-time study, $250 for three-quarter time study, and $166 for halftime study. Payment varies depending upon the number of dependents.

For further information contact an armed forces recruiting office or the local office of the United States Veterans Administration.

EDUCATIONAL LOANS

Educational loans are moneys that you or your parents or guardian borrow for educational expenses. Loans must be paid back with interest.

SHOULD YOU BORROW?

An educational loan is a serious commitment. You must make payments until the loan and interest are fully paid.

Consider loans only after you have exhausted other possible strategies such as grants, scholarships, and/or a job. You are making a decision to pay for your present education with money you will earn in the future. Have you thoroughly researched all sources of grants and scholarships? Can you work more hours while in college?

Only borrow what you absolutely need to meet your college expenses. If you overborrow, you will have excessive debt to pay back later when you may have a family and other needs for your income.

Even if you do not graduate or are displeased with your education, you still are required to repay your student loans.

WHERE TO OBTAIN LOANS

There are many banks, savings and loan associations, and credit unions making loans to students in California. Contact the financial aid office of the school you will attend for their list of lenders that participate in educational loan programs.

Subsidized and Unsubsidized Stafford Loans are guaranteed by the State of California; others, made by lending institutions, may be insured by the United States government. For these, the government stands behind your loan and assures the lending institution it will recover its money in the event you do not repay your loan.

Many loan plans are between just you and a bank; you enter into a private contract with a bank that does not involve either your college or the government.

If you can, stay with one lender to simplify repayment of your loans. You must keep your lender informed of changes in your name, address, enrollment, school, and graduation date — much easier to do when dealing with only one lender.

QUESTIONS TO ASK ABOUT LOAN PROGRAMS

- ❐ What is the maximum total amount the loan program will lend for your full education? What is the maximum loan amount per year?
- ❐ What is the interest rate? Is it fixed for the duration of the loan, or does it vary according to some formula tied to prevailing economic conditions?

- ❒ When must you begin making payments toward interest? Toward principal? Loans have different "grace periods," the amount of time after you receive loan money during which you do not have to begin repaying your loan. Some loans require you to begin repayment with interest within a short time after receiving your funds; others will wait until you are no longer in school.

  Some loans allow you to pay just interest while attending school, deferring repayment of principal until after you have left school or become enrolled less than half time. If you are allowed to defer interest payments while in school, will you owe interest on this interest you have not paid? If so, the total amount you must pay back is increased.

- ❒ How many years do you have to repay the loan? The longer you have, the smaller the amount of the monthly payment. However, the total amount, which is ultimately repaid, is increased.

- ❒ Is there a penalty for repaying the loan early?

- ❒ Can you defer paying your loan? A deferment allows you to postpone the repayment of your loan for a period of time because of economic hardship. Interest on the loan does not accumulate during the deferment period. What deferment plan is available?

  Some possible reasons for deferment include service in the United States armed services, Peace Corps, or Vista; temporary total disability; or unemployment. Check with your financial aid office and/or your lender for other qualifying reasons for deferment.

  If you are not qualified for a deferment and you are unable to make payments, you may apply to your lender for a hardship extension or "forbearance," a postponement of payments. Interest on the loan continues to accumulate during the period of forbearance.

- ❒ Who can borrow? Must it be you, the student, or can it be anyone willing to finance your education — your parents, grandparents, brother? Some loans are designed for students, others for parents or guardians.

- ❒ Are there any restrictions on who can borrow? United States citizen? Enrolled at least halftime? Minimum income level? Maximum income level? Your credit worthiness? Your parents' credit worthiness?

- ❒ Do you have to demonstrate financial need to obtain the loan, or is it available to any student or parent who is credit worthy?

- ❒ Is your college involved in the loan program or is it just between you and the lender?

- ❒ Do the loan funds come directly to you or are they sent to your college? When is the money disbursed — once a year, monthly, by term?

- ❒ Is there any restriction on which education-related expenses the funds must be used? Books? Fees? Room and board? Transportation? Or, are you free to use the funds to pay for your education in any way you prefer?

- ❒ Are there fees for obtaining the loan? Origination fees? Insurance premiums? Application fees? Closing costs? Administrative charges? Legal fees? Creditworthiness evaluation fees? Points? These fees increase the total amount of money that you borrow — money that you do not receive, but must pay back.

- ❒ Must your college complete special forms that certify that you are accepted, enrolled, and/or are making satisfactory academic progress?

- ❒ Is life insurance available to repay the loan in case the borrower dies?

Contact several lenders to learn about the particulars of their loan plans.

TIMELINES

It generally takes one or two weeks to process a loan after your completed application reaches the lender. Your school may take several weeks to determine your financial need and confirm your enrollment and/or satisfactory academic progress.

If your loan is guaranteed by the state or federal government, a lender can make a loan only after receiving a government guarantee. Also, the lender must disburse your loan in several checks at intervals during the covered educational period. The lender mails checks to the college financial aid office, which cannot release the loan funds until ten days prior to the start of instruction. Thus, it could take a month or more before you receive funds. Do not plan on loan moneys to pay preregistration fees or make early deposits to the school.

POSSIBLE CONSEQUENCES OF NOT MAKING LOAN PAYMENTS

Should you default on your loan (by not making payments as they become due), your school, private lender, state, and/or federal government can take action to recover the money. If the loan is government-guaranteed, the lender can notify national credit bureaus of your default. The lender can turn your loan over to the state or federal government for collection. The entire amount, including principal and interest accrued, becomes due and payable. The State of California clearly stipulates that it will take all steps necessary to collect the money owed, including taking you to court if necessary.

Consequences of a defaulted loan include no further financial aid, and/or no income tax refunds from either the state or the federal government. Income tax refunds are applied against your defaulted loans. Also, you could be given a bad credit rating, which might affect your future borrowing power for such financial commitments as an automobile loan, housing loan, or credit card.

LOAN ENTRANCE COUNSELING

Your college is required by federal regulation to provide you with entrance counseling, either in person or by videotape, prior to releasing the first disbursement of your loan. This counseling emphasizes the seriousness and importance of your repayment obligations, describes the consequences of default, and your responsibility to repay your loans, even if you do not finish or are dissatisfied with your educational program, or you do not obtain employment upon completion of your education.

LOAN REPAYMENT TABLE

To give you an idea of your future financial commitment, the table on the next page shows the size of monthly repayments for interest rates from five to twelve percent for repayment periods of five to ten years. The table is based on a loan of $1,000. However, you can use the table to project payments for any loan amount by multiplying. For example, if you are considering a total loan amount of $10,000 multiply the monthly payment by ten.

FEDERAL PERKINS LOANS

The Federal Perkins Loans are low interest loans for undergraduate and graduate students.

SOURCE

A federally funded program with funds administered through your college financial aid office.

ELIGIBILITY REQUIREMENTS

You must have financial need and be enrolled at a participating college or vocational school.

You must meet the federal eligibility requirements described on page 4-4.

REMEMBER, WHEN YOU ACCEPT A LOAN, YOU ARE ACCEPTING RESPONSIBILITY FOR REPAYING IT PLUS INTEREST. MAKE THIS DECISION WITH CARE.

MONTHLY LOAN PAYMENTS ($1,000 LOAN)

ANNUAL INTEREST RATE	LOAN TERM					
	5 Years	6 Years	7 Years	8 Years	9 Years	10 Years
5%	$18.87	$16.10	$14.13	$12.66	$11.52	$10.61
6%	$19.33	$16.57	$14.61	$13.14	$12.01	$11.10
7%	$19.80	$17.05	$15.09	$13.63	$12.51	$11.61
8%	$20.28	$17.53	$15.59	$14.14	$13.02	$12.13
9%	$20.76	$18.03	$16.09	$14.65	$13.54	$12.67
10%	$21.25	$18.53	$16.60	$15.17	$14.08	$13.22
11%	$21.74	$19.03	$17.12	$15.71	$14.63	$13.78
12%	$22.24	$19.55	$17.65	$16.25	$15.18	$14.35

NOTES: 1. Payments shown are for a fully amortized loan over the indicated loan term.
2. Monthly payment amount is fixed for the term of the loan.
3. Interest is compounded monthly on the unpaid loan balance.

ADDITIONAL REQUIREMENTS AND INFORMATION

The Federal Perkins Loan is a low interest loan. Currently, the annual rate is five percent.

Repayment begins nine months after you graduate, leave school, or drop below half-time enrollment. Interest is paid by the federal government until you begin making loan payments.

You are allowed up to ten years to repay. Your school has the option of making you pay at least $40 per month. The actual payment amount depends upon the size of the debt and the length of the repayment period. Your monthly payment is made to your school.

The school is your lender. Each year, participating schools receive a predetermined amount of federal funds to be used in awarding Federal Perkins Loans. The schools determine the number of loans and amount of loan money given to their students based upon the total money available.

LOAN AMOUNTS AND REPAYMENT PLANS

Depending upon the amount of your financial need, the availability of funds at your college, and the amount of other aid you receive, you may borrow up to

- $3,000 annually as an undergraduate student with an aggregate loan limit of $15,000, and
- $5,000 annually for graduate or professional study with an aggregate loan limit of $30,000. (This amount includes any Perkins Loans received for undergraduate study.)

You may be able to borrow more than these amounts if you are attending a school that has a default rate no higher the 7.5%. Check with your school.

If you participate in a study-abroad program approved for credit by your home school, the annual and total debt limits may be exceeded by 20%.

The amount of each payment depends upon the size of your debt and the length of your repayment period. Usually, you must pay at least $40 per month. In special cases — for example, if you are unemployed or ill for a long period of time — your school may allow you to make payments of less than $40 per month, or may extend your repayment period. Determine what the monthly payments are before you take out the loan so you will know what to expect.

Under certain conditions you may be able to defer (postpone) repayment of your Federal Perkins Loan. Check with your lender.

There are several conditions under which up to 100% of your loan may be cancelled:

- You become a full-time teacher in a designated elementary or secondary school serving students from low-income families.
- You become a full-time special education teacher.
- You become a full-time professional provider of early intervention services for the disabled.
- You become a full-time teacher of mathematics, science, foreign languages, bilingual education, or in other fields designated as teacher shortage areas.
- You become a full-time employee of a public or nonprofit child or family service agency, providing services to high-risk children and their families from low-income communities.
- You become a full-time nurse or medical technician.
- You become a full-time law enforcement or corrections officer.
- You die or become totally and permanently disabled.

Although not a cancellation, if you serve as an enlisted person in certain specialties of the United States Army, the Army Reserves, the Army National Guard, or the Air National Guard, the Department of Defense will repay a portion of your Perkins Loan.

PAYMENT OF LOAN MONEYS

After you sign a promissory note agreeing to repay your loan, your school will either pay you directly or credit your college account. You receive the loan amount in at least two payments during the academic year. There is one exception: If the total Perkins Loan you receive is $500 or less, the school may choose to pay you just once during the year.

APPLICATION PROCEDURES AND DEADLINES

Application: Submit the FAFSA. Contact your college financial aid office for additional loan application materials and further information.

Deadline: Apply as soon as possible after January 1, 1995 but not later than March 2, 1995 if you apply for Cal Grant and institution aid as well. Submit the FAFSA not later than May 1, 1996 if you apply only for a Federal Perkins Loan. Contact your college financial aid office for further deadline information.

Notification: The college notifies you of your loan in the financial aid package it sends to you.

FEDERAL STAFFORD LOANS

The Federal Stafford Loan Program offers government subsidized and unsubsidized, low-interest loans to undergraduate, graduate, vocational, or professional students. You qualify for a *subsidized* loan if you can demonstrate financial need. The *unsubsidized* loan is designed so that all students, regardless of income, can obtain a student loan.

SOURCE

Loans are made by a lender such as a bank, credit union, or savings and loan association.

These loans are insured by the California Student Aid Commission, the "Guarantee Agency" in California, and reinsured by the federal government. This means that both the State of California and the United States government protect the lender from losses if you do not pay back your loan.

ELIGIBILITY REQUIREMENTS

You must meet the federal eligibility requirements described on page 4--4.

You must (a) be a California resident enrolled in a college in California, outside the state, or in another country that is approved by the United States Department of Education and the California Student Aid Commission, or (b) be a resident of another state attending a California school.

SUBSIDIZED

Your college financial aid office must determine that you have a financial need in accordance with federal regulations.

You must first apply for a Federal Pell Grant and receive a determination of whether you qualify for it.

Although the subsidized Stafford Loan generally is made by a bank, credit union, or savings and loan association, the determination of eligibility is made by the financial aid office of your college.

UNSUBSIDIZED

Financial need is not a factor in qualifying for the unsubsidized loan. You may borrow the difference between expected cost of attendance and reasonable available financial assistance up to the maximum available loan limits. This program helps middle- and higher- income students borrow for education costs.

ADDITIONAL REQUIREMENTS AND INFORMATION

You may obtain both a subsidized Federal Stafford Loan and an unsubsidized Federal Stafford Loan. The aggregate amounts of both cannot exceed the loan limits shown below.

LOAN AMOUNTS AND REPAYMENT PLANS

Depending upon the amount of your financial need, the amount of other aid you receive, and program length, you may borrow up to the following Federal Stafford Loan limits.

Dependent Undergraduate Students

- first-year borrowers
  $2,625 (full academic year),
  $1,750 (2/3 of academic year),
  $875 (1/3 of academic year).

- second-year borrowers
  $3,500 (full academic year),
  $2,325 (2/3 of academic year),
  $1,175 (1/3 of academic year).

- remainder of undergraduate studies
  $5,500 (full academic year),
  $3,675 (2/3 of academic year),
  $1,825 (1/3 of academic year).

Additional Unsubsidized Stafford Loans Available to Independent Undergraduate Students:

- first-year borrowers
  $4,000 (full academic year)

- second year borrowers
  $4,000 (full academic year)

- remainder of undergraduate studies
  $5,000 (full academic year)

Graduate or Professional Study Students:

- $18,500 ($8,500 subsidized, $10,000 unsubsidized) per year.

You cannot borrow more than the cost of education at your school, minus any other financial aid you receive. The total Federal Stafford Loan debt you can have outstanding as a dependent undergraduate is $23,000; as an independent undergraduate, $46,000. The total debt allowed for graduate or professional study is $138,500 ($65,500 in Subsidized Federal Stafford Loans and $73,000 in Unsubsidized Stafford Loans). The graduate debt limit includes any Federal Stafford Loans you received as an undergraduate.

The current interest rate is variable based upon the interest rate of ninety-one day United States Treasury Bills plus 3.1%. It is adjusted July 1st of each year and is capped at eight-and-one quarter percent. From July 1, 1994 through June 30, 1995, the interest rate for a Federal Stafford Loan is 7.43%.

The amount of each monthly payment depends upon the size of your debt and the length of your repayment period. The minimum annual payment is $600 per year at $50 per month. Payments may be as much as $650 per month depending on the amount borrowed.

Repayment generally begins six months after you graduate, leave school, or drop below half-time enrollment. The loan must be repaid within ten years after repayment begins.

No later than six months before the date your first payment is due, your lender must offer you the option of repaying your loan based on a "graduated" or "income-sensitive" repayment. This means your financial situation is taken into account in determining your monthly payment.

Under certain conditions (in school, unemployment, economic hardship) you may be able to defer (postpone) repayment of your Federal Subsidized Stafford Loan. Check with your lender.

100% of your loan may be cancelled if you die or become totally and permanently disabled.

Although not a cancellation, if you serve as an enlisted person in certain selected specialties of the U.S. Army, the Army Reserves, the Army National Guard, or the Air National Guard, the Department of the Defense will , as an enlistment incentive, repay a portion of your Stafford Loan.

LOAN FEES

The PLUS Program charges a fee to help reduce the government's cost for these loans.

- An origination fee of three percent is deducted from the loan amount and paid to the federal government to help reduce the government's cost for these loans. This fee is subject to change.

- The California Student Aid Commission insures the loans and charges an insurance premium of one percent. This premium is deducted from the loan amount.

SUBSIDIZED

The federal government subsidizes the loan by paying loan interest while you are in school or in deferment. The government therefore subsidizes or supports these loans.

UNSUBSIDIZED

You are responsible for paying the interest while you are in school and until your repayments begin six months after you leave school. You may pay the interest or capitalize it — add it to the total loan amount, thereby spreading the interest accrued over the life of the loan.

PAYMENT OF LOAN MONEYS

Your lender sends your loan proceeds to your school, payable either to you or to both you and your school. Your school issues your loan proceeds to you in two or more payments after enrollment and satisfactory academic progress are verified. In your first year of college, your college may not release the first installment until thirty days after your first day of study. Do not plan to use this loan to pay pre-registration fees, housing deposits, or other early fees.

APPLICATION PROCEDURES AND DEADLINES

Application: Submit the FAFSA.

Deadline: Apply as soon as possible after January 1, 1995 but not later than March 2, 1995 if you apply for Cal Grant and institutional aid as well. Otherwise, you have until May 2, 1996 to apply.

Additional Application: After you have submitted your application for the Federal Pell Grant, and your eligibility for it is determined, ask your college financial aid office for their specific application materials for the Federal Stafford Loan.

Special applications/promissory notes are available in the financial aid offices of colleges, universities and postsecondary vocational schools, from participating lending institutions, and the California Student Aid Commission.

Fill out your part of this additional application and submit it to your college. The college is required to (a) certify your enrollment, your cost of education, your academic standing, the amount of your financial need, and (b) list other financial aid you will receive. You or your college must forward the certified application to a commercial lender to finalize the loan process.

The college financial aid office has a list of commercial lenders who have made student loans in the past, together with current lending policies for many of them.

PLUS — *Federal Parent Loans For Students*

The Federal PLUS program is designed for middle-income families who generally do not qualify for other financial assistance, and who are able to meet the additional burden of loan payments. PLUS is for parents who wish to borrow for the education of their dependents.

SOURCE

Loans are made by a lender such as a bank, credit union, or savings and loan association. These loans are insured by the California Student Aid Commission, the "Guarantee Agency" in California, and reinsured by the federal government. This means that both California and the United States government protect the lender from losses if you do not pay back your loan.

ELIGIBILITY REQUIREMENTS

You must meet federal eligibility requirements described on page 4--4. *Financial need is not a criteria for PLUS.*

PLUS is available to parent borrowers who want to borrow to help pay for their children's education. These are the requirements to qualify for a PLUS loan:

- Your parents must be California residents, or if residents of another state, you must be enrolled or accepted for enrollment on at least a halftime basis in a school in California that is approved by the United States Department of Education and the California Student Aid Commission.
- If both you and your parents are California residents, you must be enrolled or accepted on at least a halftime basis at an approved school in California, another state, or a foreign country.
- Your parents must complete a lender credit check. Lenders may deny a PLUS application because of bad credit.

LOAN AMOUNTS AND REPAYMENT PLANS

Although PLUS loans are not need-based, borrowing limits depend upon other aid received. When added to your other aid, the total cannot exceed your estimated total cost of attendance at your school. Consequently, your school determines the amount of money your parents are eligible to borrow. This loan amount can serve as a supplemental source of money to parents on behalf of dependent students who are borrowing under the Federal Stafford Loan program.

Your parents must begin repayment of principal and interest within sixty days after the final loan disbursement unless they receive a deferment. Under certain conditions (unemployment, protracted illness, service in a tax exempt organization, for example) your parents may be able to defer (postpone) repayment of their loan. Check with the lender.

The repayment schedule must be at least five years and not more than ten. Interest begins accruing immediately upon disbursement.

The current interest rate is variable based upon the interest rate of fifty-two day United States Treasury Bills plus 3.1%. It is adjusted July 1st of each year and is capped at nine percent. From July 1, 1994 to June 30, 1995 the rate for a PLUS 8.38 %.

LOAN FEES

The PLUS Program charges a fee to help reduce the government's cost for these loans.

- An origination fee of three percent is deducted from the loan amount and paid to the federal government to help reduce the government's cost of subsidizing the loan. This fee is subject to change.

- The California Student Aid Commission insures the loans and charges an insurance premium of one percent. This premium is deducted from the loan amount.

The minimum monthly payment of principal and interest is $50. The actual payment amount depends upon the size of the debt and the length of the repayment period.

Under certain conditions you may be able to defer (postpone) repayment of PLUS loans. Deferments apply only to loan principal, not interest. Check with your lender.

Up to 100% of PLUS loans may be cancelled in the case of the death or total and permanent disability of the borrower. This includes the death of the child for whom the parent borrowed.

PAYMENT OF LOAN MONEYS

The lender sends the full amount of the loan proceeds to the college electronically or through co-payable checks to the college and your parents. Your parents may receive payment as often as weekly or monthly. These payments must be in equal installments. If your parents are paid less frequently, no payment may exceed one-half of the loan amount.

APPLICATION PROCEDURES AND DEADLINES

Special applications/promissory notes for Federal PLUS loans are available in the financial aid offices of colleges, universities and postsecondary vocational schools and from participating lending institutions.

Application: You do not need to complete the FAFSA, but your parents must undergo a credit check in addition to filing a PLUS loan/promissory note application with the college financial aid office. Ask your college financial aid office for their specific application materials.

After your parents fill out their part of this application, the college must complete its section, certifying your enrollment, your cost of education, and your academic standing. The college must also list other financial aid, including amounts, you will receive. Once this is done, your parents or your college must forward the certified application to a commercial lender to complete the loan process.

The financial aid office has a list of lenders who have made student loans in the past, together with current lending policies for many of them.

Deadline: The deadline varies according to the lender.

FEDERAL CONSOLIDATION LOAN PROGRAM

The Federal Consolidation Loan Program makes repayment easier for you if you have large or unmanageable educational loan payments. Consolidation lenders, such as banks and savings and loan associations, pay off existing student loans and offer you a new loan with a single monthly payment and extended repayment terms of up to thirty years.

PAYING FOR COLLEGE

SOURCE

Loans are made by a lender such as a bank, credit union, or savings and loan association.

ELIGIBILITY REQUIREMENTS

You must have borrowed $7,500 or more in Federal Perkins and Stafford loans. Federal PLUS loans may not be consolidated. Spouses may combine eligible loans under a single consolidation.

You must be in a "grace period," the amount of time after you receive loan money during which you do not have to begin repaying your loan, or in repayment of each of the loans to be consolidated.

You must have no other consolidation application pending or in process at another lender.

You must not have been enrolled at least half-time at an eligible institution during the previous four months.

LOAN AMOUNTS AND REPAYMENT PLANS

There are no insurance or origination fees.

The interest rate is at least nine percent and not more than twelve percent per year, based upon the weighted average of all loans being consolidated.

Each lender offers its own repayment options and plans. Some plans may (a) have level payments for the life of the loan, (b) have interest-only payments for a period of time, (c) involve graduated payments, or (d) have income-sensitive payments, which begin low but increase later.

The benefits of loan consolidation are different for each borrower and depend upon the loan type, amount, interest rate, and repayment terms.

Advantages of consolidation:

- Monthly payments are significantly lower because the term of the loan is longer.
- You have one monthly payment rather than several.
- You can obtain extended repayment terms.
- You have a choice of repayment terms.
- Your chances of default are reduced.

Disadvantages of consolidation:

- Your total payback amount is significantly higher because you are paying interest on the principal for a longer period of time.
- Payment plans are graduated with little or no reduction of the loan principal amount in the early years of repayment because most of the monthly payment is applied to interest.
- Only that portion of monthly payments applied to principal can be deferred. The portion applied to interest cannot be deferred.
- There are no cancellation provisions for teaching or public or military service.

PAYMENT OF LOAN MONEYS

Your consolidation loan payments begin within sixty days after the consolidating lender pays off the full amount of your original loans. You must continue making regular loan payments until you receive a disclosure statement and a repayment schedule reflecting your new total indebtedness to the consolidating lender.

APPLICATION PROCEDURES AND DEADLINES

Special applications/promissory notes for the Federal Consolidation Loan Program are available in the financial aid offices of colleges, universities, or postsecondary vocational schools, and from participating lending institutions.

Application: You must complete a Federal Consolidation Loan Program application and submit it to a lender who holds one of your existing loans and participates in the program. If your lender does not participate, submit it to any other participating lender in the program.

Deadline: Your lender establishes the required deadlines.

APLE — Assumption Program Of Loans For Education

APLE will assume (pay off) your educational loans up to $8,000 if you are an outstanding student enrolled in a course of study or teacher preparation program leading to a teaching credential.

SOURCE

A State of California program with funds administered by the California Student Aid Commission.

ELIGIBILITY REQUIREMENTS

You must be a legal resident of California.

You must be enrolled in a program leading to a Bachelor's degree or in an approved professional teacher preparation program.

You must have completed at least sixty semester units — ninety quarter units — of undergraduate study and be enrolled for at least ten semester units or the equivalent.

You must not have completed the coursework necessary to obtain an initial teaching credential. You must commit yourself to three consecutive years of teaching in a California public school in a subject matter shortage area — mathematics, English, science, bilingual education, foreign language, or special education — or in a school serving a high proportion of low-income students. These areas may change from year to year.

You must have received or been approved to receive Federal Perkins, Stafford, or Consolidated, or private educational loans.

You must not be in default on a federal loan or owe a refund on a federal or state grant.

ADDITIONAL REQUIREMENTS AND INFORMATION

Participating colleges and universities distribute applications, assess academic ability, and select applicants. The California Student Aid Commission accepts up to five-hundred new APLE program applicants each year.

LOAN AMOUNTS AND REPAYMENT PLANS

After you have completed the first of three consecutive years of eligible teaching, the state will assume up to $2,000 of your student loan balances; after the second year, $3,000; after the third year, an additional $3,000 for a maximum of $8,000.

APPLICATION PROCEDURES AND DEADLINES

Application: Applications for the APLE program may be obtained after March 1, 1995 from any California college or university offering an approved teacher credentialing program.

Deadline: Your application must be submitted by your college to the Student Aid Commission by June 30, 1995.

Child Development Teacher Loan Assumption Program

This program will assume (pay off) your educational loan debt in return for your service as a teacher or supervisor in a California licensed children's center which serves low-income families.

SOURCE

A federal program with funds administered by the California Student Aid Commission.

ELIGIBILITY REQUIREMENTS

You must be a United States citizen or eligible noncitizen as described on page 4--4.

You must be a legal resident of California.

You must have received or been approved to receive Federal Perkins, Stafford, SLS, or Consolidated or private educational loans.

You must be enrolled in a course of study leading to a Regular Children's Center Instructional Permit *or* hold this permit and be enrolled in coursework leading to a Bachelor's degree and the Regular Children's Center Supervision Permit.

You must maintain enrollment in at least twelve semester units or the equivalent each term and maintain at least a C grade point average.

You must provide two consecutive years of full-time teaching or supervision service in the same children's center within three years of completing the coursework for your Instructional or Supervision permit.

You must not be in default on a federal loan or owe a refund on a federal or state grant.

ADDITIONAL REQUIREMENTS AND INFORMATION

The California Student Aid Commission selects up to one-hundred outstanding college students. Eighty percent of the selected participants are working toward an Instructional Permit; twenty percent are working toward a Supervisory Permit. Up to twenty-five percent of selected students within each category will be given priority consideration if they have bilingual skills.

LOAN AMOUNTS AND REPAYMENT PLANS

You must teach or supervise full-time in an eligible children's center for two consecutive years to receive full program benefits. The Commission will assume up to $1,000 of educational loans after each year of the two consecutive years in which you *teach* full-time for a maximum assumption of $2,000. It will assume up to $2,000 after each year of the two consecutive years in which you provide full-time *supervisory service* for a maximum assumption of $4,000.

APPLICATION PROCEDURES AND DEADLINES

Application: Applications for the 1995-96 program may be obtained from your college or the California Student Aid Commission during the spring term.

Deadline: Your application must be submitted to the California Student Aid Commission by the postmarked date of May 30, 1995.

Notification: The Commission will notify you if you are a recipient by November 1995.

OTHER LOANS

Other loans are available regardless of financial need and independent of government guarantees.

SOURCE

Private programs with funds provided and administered by banks, savings and loan associations, credit unions, and private lending organizations and institutions.

Check with your college financial aid office for information and a listing of specific banks and loan sources that have given their students and their families educational loans in the past.

The following information is presented to make you aware of the types of loan plans available. Ask about them at your college. Also, call major banks in your area and inquire about their programs for educational loans.

Research various options carefully. Have your parents consult with their accountant and/or financial planner to fully understand the impact of different options upon their financial situation.

ELIGIBILITY

Loan eligibility through these sources is determined by evaluating the credit worthiness of your parents who will be the primary borrower of these loans. If your parents have a good credit history, a stable income, and appear to be in a financial position to handle the loan payments required, they probably can qualify for these educational loans.

ADDITIONAL REQUIREMENTS AND INFORMATION

These loans are available in a variety of structures but are not guaranteed by the federal government or by the state. They may be one of the following types:

- Your parents may secure an educational loan with the equity in their home. Their home is collateral — the backup — subject to forfeiture if they cannot pay back the loan.

- Your parents may take out a new loan on their house and borrow from the bank using the house as security for the educational loan. The home mortgage interest may be eligible for a federal and/or California income tax deduction.

- Your parents may open a savings account and set up a loan for as much as two-and-one-half times their deposit. The interest earned on the deposit helps to offset the interest charges on the loan. This account serves as collateral for the loan.

- Collateral may not be needed at all; their signature may be enough, provided they have been evaluated as credit worthy by the bank.

- The loan may be in the form of a "line of credit." The bank provides a book of checks that your parents use to withdraw amounts against a loan account to pay your college expenses. Instead of owing interest on the total amount of the loan from the outset, the interest begins only as the funds are needed and used.

- Your parents may select a plan that allows them to extend their educational payments over a greater length of time, as long as ten years. The lender makes payments directly to the college for your educational expenses as they are billed and your parents pay back the lender in monthly payments over ten years.

- Your parents can sell stocks in their stock market investments, and use the proceeds to pay your educational expenses. They also can borrow against their stocks in a "margin account."

- You may be able to borrow against a whole life insurance policy of a family member. Unless it is repaid, the amount borrowed reduces the insurance benefit by an equal amount.

- A family member's retirement plan may allow up to a specified maximum to be borrowed without owing taxes or penalties.

LOAN AMOUNTS AND REPAYMENT PLANS

These loans can amount to substantially more money than those subsidized by the government. In fact, they can be taken out to cover as much as the full cost of a four-year education. How much your family borrows depends upon their financial circumstances.

Interest rates may be fixed or variable and vary widely from loan plan to loan plan.

Repayment plans vary. In some plans, your parents begin making interest and principal payments as soon as they receive the money; in others, interest payments begin immediately, but principal payments do not begin until you leave school or attend school less than halftime. In still others, both principal and interest payments may be deferred until you are out of school.

The number of years you have to pay off the loan varies with each lender.

PAYMENT OF LOAN MONEYS

Some plans disburse the money to your parents in large lump sums; others send the funds directly to the college when term bills are due. The latter approach can reduce your costs because you owe interest only on the amounts actually paid to the college. Some plans offer to insure your education by paying out the entire loan commitment if your parent dies.

APPLICATION PROCEDURES AND DEADLINES

Application: Application forms vary from lender to lender. Generally, the lender wants information that helps to determine the credit worthiness of your parents. This information might include all income information, bank account numbers, copies of income tax returns, credit card and other existing loan information, and listings of assets. Additionally, your college financial aid office may be asked to certify your college admission and satisfactory academic progress.

Deadline: Deadlines vary according to the lender.

WORK-STUDY

Many students work part time while attending college to help defray college expenses.

Your study skills, energy level, health, financial circumstances, family and personal commitments, course load, and extracurricular involvements, are some of the major factors to consider when planning how many hours a week you can work on a job. It is important that you carefully determine how many hours a week you can work and still do your best in your studies. Here is a general rule of thumb: *For every hour of class, plan for at least two hours of study.* During examination weeks, you probably need even more study time. You also need to plan time for recreation.

Your college financial aid office, placement office, advisor, or counselor can help you determine the number of working hours versus class hours you should realistically plan into your schedule. For financial planning purposes, calculate wages for no more than ten to fifteen hours of work per week.

As a freshman, you may prefer not to work at all until you have adjusted to the pace of college and have a sense of how much responsibility you can undertake.

FWS — FEDERAL WORK-STUDY PROGRAMS

SOURCE

A federal program with funds administered by the colleges.

ELIGIBILITY REQUIREMENTS

You must meet federal eligibility requirements described on page 4--4.

You must need financial aid.

You may attend school less than halftime and still be eligible to receive FWS aid.

How much aid you receive from the program depends upon your financial need, the amount of other aid you receive, and the availability of funds at your school.

ADDITIONAL REQUIREMENTS AND INFORMATION

Your job may be on campus or off campus. If you work on campus, you usually work for your school. Off-campus jobs generally involve work that is in the public interest; your employer is a public or private nonprofit organization, or a local, state, or federal agency. However, some schools may have agreements with private profit-making employers for FWS jobs.

To the maximum practical extent, you are placed in work relating to your studies or career plans.

You cannot work as many hours as you wish. Your school sets your work schedule. In arranging a job and assigning work hours, your financial aid administrator considers your class schedule, your health, and your academic progress.

Each year, your school receives a fixed amount of funds from the government to pay their portion of your wages. When that money is gone, no more awards are made from this program for the remainder of the school year. Your college must use ten percent of their Federal Work Study amount for Community Service.

ANNUAL AWARD AMOUNTS

The federal government and your employer jointly fund your wages.

Your FWS award amount is a part of your financial aid package and your earnings are limited to the amount of your FWS award.

Your pay is at least the current federal minimum wage, but it may also be related to the type of work you do, the skills required, and your level of responsibility.

As an undergraduate, you are paid by the hour.

No FWS student may be paid by commission or fee.

PAYMENT OF EARNINGS

Your school pays you at least once a month.

APPLICATION PROCEDURES AND DEADLINES

Application: Your college financial aid office has appropriate applications.

Deadline: Your college sets its own deadlines for submitting your application forms. However, because your college has a fixed amount of money for the program, apply early before all their funds have been allocated to other students.

NATIONAL SERVICE TRUST

The National Service Trust is a national service program begun in September 1994. It provides $4,725 a year for up to two years of community service in one of four priority areas: education, human needs, the environment, and public safety. This domestic Peace Corps is called AmeriCorps.

You must complete 1,700 hours of service work a year and can work before or after you go to college, graduate school, or trade school. The funds can be used to pay current educational expenses or to repay federal student loans. You receive a living allowance of at least $7,400 a year and, if necessary, health care and child care allowances. For application materials and information contact:

Corporation for National Service
P.O. Box 438
Beltsville, Maryland 20704-9977

AmeriCorps Hotline
(800) 942-2677
TDD (800) 833-3722

State Work-Study Program

SOURCE

A California state-funded program with funds administered by the colleges.

ELIGIBILITY REQUIREMENTS

You must be a legal California resident.

You must demonstrate financial need as determined by the financial aid office of the college in which you are enrolled.

You must be enrolled at least half time.

You must demonstrate satisfactory academic progress.

ADDITIONAL REQUIREMENTS AND INFORMATION

The following California postsecondary institutions participated in this program for 1994-95.

Butte College
California Lutheran University
California State University — Chico
California State University — San Bernardino
Fashion Institute of Design and Merchandising
Humboldt State University
Imperial Valley College
Pasadena City College
University of California — Berkeley
University of California — Davis
University of California — San Diego
University of the Pacific
University of Redlands

The program is designed to provide eligible students with an opportunity to earn money to help defray educational costs while gaining experience in educationally beneficial or career-related employment.

Your college assists you in selecting positions related to your course of study, career goal, or the exploration of career objectives. Jobs may be available with public institutions or nonprofit or profit-seeking enterprises.

Public schools may employ students as librarians, teacher aides, bilingual teacher aides, and tutors. Private and proprietary (for profit) postsecondary institutions are prohibited from employing students.

ANNUAL AWARD AMOUNTS

You are paid at rates comparable to those paid for similar positions within the employing organization.

APPLICATION PROCEDURES AND DEADLINES

Application: Contact the financial aid office of your college if it is listed on this page as a program participant. Because other schools might be added in the future, check with your college even if it is not listed above.

Deadline: Contact your college financial aid office for further information.

Working Your Way Through College

SOURCE

The employment marketplace.

ELIGIBILITY REQUIREMENTS

Your job skills and past work experience are important in finding a job during the academic year and during the summers while you are in college.

Financial need is not a factor. Your desire to work is the major criterion.

ADDITIONAL REQUIREMENTS AND INFORMATION

It is your responsibility to find a job to help you earn your way through college. Jobs may be on or off campus. A major source of job listings is the job placement office of your school. Employers contact this office with job needs for part-time employees and for summer needs. There is often a bulletin board near this office with postings of opportunities. Contact the job placement office as soon as possible when you enroll in college to become familiar with its operations and offerings.

The California State Employment Development Department, newspapers, friends, family contacts, and employment agencies are other resources that can help you discover employment opportunities.

Your college may offer college credit for work experience in a job related to your major. Ask if this opportunity is available at your school.

ANNUAL AWARD AMOUNTS

Amounts vary according to the number of hours worked, type of job, level of responsibility, and required skills.

APPLICATION PROCEDURES AND DEADLINES

Applications and deadlines vary according to the particular job opportunity.

COOPERATIVE EDUCATION

Cooperative education is an integrated program of classroom study and job experience. Colleges and employers cooperate to form a total educational program that interrelates your studies with work experience, thereby providing practical application of what you are learning in the classroom. Because the job is closely related to your major, you have the opportunity to work in your field, to get practical experience, and to evaluate your career choice. Numerous colleges in California offer a co-op program.

STRUCTURE OF CO-OP PROGRAMS

Most four-year colleges that offer co-op provide it on an optional basis — it is not a required program. Provisions are made for you to spend two or three semesters or quarters away from your classes in full-time work assignments over the course of your regular academic program. Community colleges participating in co-op generally offer parallel programs with part of the day spent in class and part on a work assignment.

Your work experience is supervised by a coordinator from the co-op program at your college. The coordinator helps you identify job openings that meet your interests and background and train you in job-seeking skills such as resume writing and interview techniques. The coordinator meets with you and your employer on a regular basis to evaluate your employment skills.

Advantages of co-op education:

- You can often earn enough money while working to pay for the next school year.
- The financial assistance provided in this program is available to you regardless of your family income level or other financial aid, and it decreases your need for loans.
- You gain a close-up look at a career field to determine if it is the right one for you.
- You can arrange for a series of assignments to provide for a wide variety of experiences if you are unsure of a career direction.
- You can grow in responsibility in your job so that you are ready for a more responsible position after college.
- When you graduate, you will have had work experience in your field that will help you to obtain a professional full-time employment position.
- When you graduate, you may begin working at a higher salary than you would without this experience.

QUESTIONS YOU NEED TO ASK

If a cooperative education program appeals to you as an approach to paying for your college education, consider the following questions. Find out if the colleges of interest to you offer the program. If so, call the cooperative education offices of the colleges to get the information you need.

- ❒ How is the program structured? Will you work full-time? For how many semesters? For how many quarters? Will you work part-time while attending college?
- ❒ A co-op college may not offer a co-op opportunity in every one of its academic areas. Is your academic major one that participates in the program at that campus?
- ❒ Will you get academic credit for your co-op job assignment?
- ❒ If credit is given, are the credits in addition to those already required for the degree, or do they replace classroom credit?
- ❒ In what college year can you begin your co-op job? In many programs, you must have had some college background before employers are willing to hire you.
- ❒ Does it take longer to complete your degree because you spend semesters or quarters working instead of taking classes?
- ❒ Do you have to pay tuition or fees during the terms you are on a co-op job?
- ❒ Can you live on campus during the terms that you are on a co-op job?
- ❒ How does the co-op program affect your participation in extracurricular activities and/or athletics?

APPLICATION PROCEDURES AND DEADLINES

Application: Apply through the cooperative education office of your college.

Deadline: Deadlines vary according to college.

COLLEGE COST REDUCTION PLANS

College cost reduction plans are methods of reducing your actual costs of attending college.

PUBLIC VERSUS INDEPENDENT COLLEGES

Fees and tuition costs are considerably higher at independent colleges than at public institutions. This does not necessarily mean that attending a public institution will cost you and your family less. Remember, the amount of your expected family contribution is the same regardless of the cost of the college. Your need will be higher at a more expensive college, and it is this need that financial aid packages are designed to meet. Independent schools tend to be more generous in their financial aid packages — they make every effort to meet your financial need. Further, because of class availability, you may be able to finish your degree sooner at an independent college rather than at a public institution.

Carefully evaluate your financial aid packages from the colleges before you decide that it will cost you less to attend California State University or the University of California. Compare amounts of awards from scholarships, grants, loans, and work-study offers. Use the worksheet, MY FINANCIAL PLAN, on page 4--26 to compare financial aid packages.

REDUCE THE NUMBER OF YEARS YOU ATTEND COLLEGE

You can reduce the number of years you are in college, thereby reducing the total cost of your education.

- Begin taking college courses at your local community college while you are still in high school. Use these credits toward your college education.

- If you are an academically strong student and your high school offers Advanced Placement Examinations and courses, take advantage of this opportunity. You can receive college credit for high scores on these examinations. Your college may even give you a year's credit and allow you to enter college in advanced standing — as a sophomore — if you pass three or more AP Examinations. See chapter 6: COLLEGE ENTRANCE TESTS, AP Program and Examinations, page 6--57.

- Plan to attend summer school while in college to build up additional credits.

Credits from these various options can add up to a term or two or more at college.

SPREAD OUT YOUR EDUCATION OVER MORE THAN FOUR YEARS

You can reduce the number of courses and the number of units you take each year and increase the number of hours you work on a job. This strategy can lower the total cost of your education by reducing the amount of loans you must take out and repay. It also stretches out your college expenses over more years, possibly making it easier for your parents and you to afford them. Many, many students are taking more than four years to finish their Bachelor's degrees.

ATTEND A COMMUNITY COLLEGE FOR YOUR FRESHMAN AND SOPHOMORE YEARS

You can complete all of the lower-division freshman and sophomore General Education/Breadth Requirements and Major Preparation Requirements at a relatively low-cost community college and transfer to the more costly four-year school for your junior and senior years. Transferring takes careful planning. See chapter 9: CALIFORNIA COMMUNITY COLLEGES.

REDUCE YOUR EXPENSES WHILE ATTENDING COLLEGE

- Buy used books. Sell the books you do not need to keep. Buy your stationary supplies at discount stores.

- Choose a college near home. Living at home is less expensive than living away at school.

- If you live at home, carpool, take public transportation if it is available, or bicycle to college.

- If you live away at college, find the least expensive living accommodations. You might live in an apartment or house with other students to share expenses.

- If you live in a dormitory, you may have a choice of a less expensive room accommodation. You may be able to choose a reduced-cost food plan, which allows you to cook for yourself on weekends, or participate in some other arrangement that reduces your cost of dormitory food.

- If you go away to school, carpool with others to get home for your vacations.

- Other ideas for reducing your college expenses will occur to you after you are in school. Watch your expenses and determine where to cut back.

CREATIVE FINANCIAL PLANNING

Creatively approaching your college expenses can reduce the negative impact upon your parents' cash flow and assets as they attempt to meet your college expenses. They should consult an accountant and/or financial planner for advice about managing their assets and income during the years they will be paying your college expenses. Strategies can be developed for saving and for earning the money for your expenses.

- Your parents can buy off-campus property for you to live in and to rent to other students.

  This is an especially appealing strategy if property values are rising. This investment can have favorable tax treatment because of deductions for mortgage interest, depreciation, and operating expenses.

- Perhaps your parents can reduce their income or assets during those years when you are applying for financial aid. Income and assets are important criteria for determining your family contribution.

  An accountant and/or financial planner may be able to make some suggestions to your parents about this strategy. Can your parent postpone taking a year-end bonus? Can assets be reduced?

INSTALLMENT/DEFERRED PAYMENTS OF TUITION/FEES

Contact the colleges you are considering to find out if they offer an installment or deferral program for paying your college expenses. These programs allow you to stage your payments throughout the school year instead of paying large lump sums at the beginning of each term. Will the college allow you to stretch your payments into the following year?

Chapter 5

ATHLETICS

ATHLETICS

ATHLETICS

A wide range of intercollegiate athletic programs are available at the colleges and universities in California. Would you like to actively participate in an intercollegiate athletic program at college? Would you like your athletic skills help you to get financial aid?

OVERVIEW

If you are among the few, truly outstanding athletes in your sport, college coaches will find you and attempt to woo you with outstanding scholarship offers. Colleges are always on the lookout for top talent. They subscribe to local newspapers, contact and visit high schools, and talk to alumni.

If you are above average in your sport, you must market yourself to the college coaches.

If you are above average in your sport, but perhaps are not one of the special few, there are certainly opportunities available for you, *if you market yourself.* You must bring yourself to the college coaches' attention and show them that you have a talent they want.

Your academic record is important. College coaches will review your high school transcript to evaluate your potential for success at their colleges. If you are on the borderline of admissibility, the coach who wants you might request that the admissions office be flexible in their standards. However, the admissions offices will adapt their standards only within limits. Their goal is to admit students who can be successful academically as well as athletically.

If you are admissible and the coaches have great interest in you, they will contact their admissions offices tó assure the smooth processing of your application. The coaches also will encourage their financial aid offices to meet your financial need either through athletic scholarships, regular financial aid resources, or both. See chapter 4: PAYING FOR COLLEGE.

If your record indicates you would not be admissible to their school, or that you would have severe academic difficulty, the coaches might recommend you attend a California Community College and transfer to their institution at a later time.

STEPS TO RECRUITMENT

- Begin the process of marketing yourself to the college coaches in your junior year of high school, so that by the time you are a senior they know about you and are keeping track of your athletic progress.

Begin marketing yourself to college coaches in your junior year of high school.

- Talk frankly with your high school coach to get an evaluation of your athletic skills. How competitive are your skills?

- Create a list of colleges to consider that offer your sport and compete at your skill level. To develop this list:

  Ask your coach for a list of California colleges with programs in your sport or sports and appropriate to your athletic skills. What is the quality of each program? Does your coach know anything about the college coach and his/her effectiveness with students? What are the reports of other students from your high school who attended this college and competed in your sport?

  If you are interested in a school not mentioned by your coach, look up athletics in the college catalogue to find out if the sport you want is offered and at what level it competes.

ATHLETICS

- Review your list of colleges. Consider:

  Your academic record. Your college-preparatory courses, your grades, your test scores. Can you qualify academically for admission?

  The level of athletic competition at which you wish to participate. Do many athletes from the school turn professional? Is that your goal? If so, look for a school with a strong record for sending athletes in your sport on to professional teams. However, if you do not intend to play professional sports, a school with this strong record might play at a level too intense for you.

  The academic programs they offer. Will the college prepare you in your major? Does the school offer tutoring or advising for athletes? Do their programs indicate they are as concerned about your academic progress as about your athletic success?

Develop an athletic resume including awards and points, times, or distances of significance.

- Once you have identified the colleges that fit your needs both athletically and academically, get the names of their college coaches from your high school coach or the *National Directory of College Athletics*. Your high school athletic department should have a copy.

- Develop an athletic resume which reviews your athletic career. On it include awards and points, times, and/or distances of significance. Give specific data about athletic records, athletic clubs outside of high school, newspaper articles, honors, and any other information that describes your athletic accomplishments.

- Write to the college coaches. Tell them about your academic qualifications and why you would like to attend their college. Describe in detail your athletic abilities. Send a copy of your athletic resume. Include a written recommendation from your coach. You might want to send copies of news items and a short videotape of yourself participating in your sport.

- If the college coach contacts you with some interest, ask your high school coach to contact the college coach to further support your qualifications.

QUESTIONS TO ASK RECRUITERS

The assistant coach generally makes initial recruitment contacts. The head coach becomes involved in the final stages of the process.

Ask recruiters about the athletic and academic programs at their schools.

- ❒ Does the recruiter have authority to make commitments for the college's athletic department? Verbal commitments are not binding. Only the National Letter Of Intent, described on page 5--6, is a binding agreement.

- ❒ What is the background and experience of the head coach? How many total years of coaching? How many years of coaching at the college?

- ❒ What are the head coach's expectations regarding time commitment, rules, academics, etc.? What is the coach's style of working with athletes?

- ❒ Should you submit your admissions application to the college admissions office or through the athletics department?
- ❒ How many athletes will be coming into the program?
- ❒ What happens if you sustain an injury that benches you? Does your athletic scholarship continue? Will it be renewed for the next year if you are unable to continue in the sport? NCAA rules state that you cannot lose an athletic scholarship because of injury.
- ❒ What are the criteria for you to remain academically eligible to participate in the sport? Unit requirement? GPA requirement?
- ❒ Will your scholarship continue if you are placed on academic probation?
- ❒ What happens if your eligibility expires? Will you continue to be on scholarship for the following year? NCAA and NAIA rules make you eligible to play four seasons in any one sport out of a five-year period. If it takes you five years to complete your degree, will the college give you scholarship money for the fifth year even though you are no longer eligible to participate in the sport?
- ❒ How much financial support does the athletic program receive from the college? Is the athletic program financially strong?
- ❒ What is the quality of the programs in majors you are considering? What is the number, variety, and scope of courses offered? Are these majors considered strong at this institution? What is the success rate of placing graduates in these majors in jobs?
- ❒ Will you have time to pursue your major and still participate in the sport?
- ❒ What academic support is available? Tutoring? Advisors? Are practices or games scheduled during finals?
- ❒ What percentage of athletes graduate in four years? In five years? How does this compare with the overall graduation rate at the college? Ask for the NCAA graduation report, which states the percentage of recruited athletes on athletic scholarships that graduated within five years from the college.

What happens if your eligibility expires? Will you continue to be on scholarship for the following year?

Colleges and universities with intercollegiate athletic programs join athletic associations. These associations have rules regarding eligibility requirements for college membership, academic eligibility for athletes, recruitment procedures, and financial assistance policies. The colleges compete in athletics with other schools in their association. The National Collegiate Athletic Association (NCAA) and the National Association of Intercollegiate Athletics (NAIA) are the two major athletic associations for four-year colleges in the United States. Several other associations exist in California. Some colleges may be members of more than one association.

Colleges and universities with athletic programs join athletic associations. The colleges compete in athletics with other schools in their association.

- ❒ To which associations does the college belong? Against which colleges does the school compete?
- ❒ Do you meet the academic eligibility requirements necessary to participate in your sport? Those established by the national association? Those established by the institution in addition to the national rules?

- ❒ What athletic scholarships are offered? Full or partial? Is additional institutional financial aid available? Ask for specific figures. Are there restrictions on other types of financial aid you may accept?
- ❒ What are the rules and regulations governing eligibility to participate in your sport?
- ❒ What are the recruitment procedures? What is your time-line for making decisions?

The National Letter of Intent is a form which commits you to enroll in a particular institution and play a specific sport.

ATHLETICS

NATIONAL LETTER OF INTENT

If you are an outstanding athlete in your sport, a college athletic director may ask you to sign a National Letter of Intent (NLI) administered by the Collegiate Commissioners Association. The National Letter of Intent is a form which commits you to enroll in a particular institution and play a specific sport. You, your parent or guardian, *and* the athletic director of the institution must sign the letter. To be valid, you must receive at the time of signing a written award or recommendation for athletics financial aid from the institution named in the NLI. This written offer or recommendation must list the type, amount, and duration of the financial aid.

For each sport there is a specific time period for signing the NLI.

For each sport, there is a specific time period for signing the NLI. It usually is at the end of that sport's season. Signing periods are clearly stated at the top of the NLI form. The 1994-95 National Letter of Intent signing dates are shown in this table.

1994-95
NATIONAL LETTER OF INTENT SIGNING DATES

Sport	Initial Date	Final Date
Basketball (Early Period)	November 9, 1994	November 16, 1994
Basketball (Late Period)	April 12, 1995	May 15, 1995
Football (Midyear JC Transfer)	December 21, 1994	January 15, 1995
Football (Regular)	February 8, 1995	April 1, 1995
Women's Volleyball, Field Hockey, Soccer, Water Polo	February 8, 1995	August 1, 1995
All Other Sports (Early Period)	November 9, 1994	November 16, 1994
All Other Sports (Late Period)	April 12, 1995	August 1, 1995

You and your parent or legal guardian have fourteen days to sign the NLI after it has been issued to you. Afterwards, it becomes invalid, although another NLI may be issued if the signing period has not closed. Do not sign any institutional or conference letter of intent or financial aid agreement before the NLI signing period. The National Letter of Intent describes regulations regarding obligations and restrictions to which you commit when you sign and the penalties for not meeting them. Read the entire document carefully before signing it.

You may sign only one NLI. It binds you to your decision and you cannot sign with any other college. The National Letter of Intent is not binding if you do not qualify for admission to the institution, or you do not qualify for financial aid under athletic association rules or college regulations for financial aid for athletes. Once you sign the NLI with an institution, other cooperating conferences and institutions will respect your decision and will not make further attempts to recruit you.

If you choose not to sign the NLI, you still may accept athletic scholarships, but only after the signing period for your sport. You are not bound to these college and athletic scholarships until after you report to the college to play.

Contact the conference office of the college you are planning to attend with any questions regarding signing dates or obligations and restrictions related to signing the NLI.

Members of the NCAA follow specific rules regarding eligibility, recruiting, playing season, and financial aid.

NCAA — NATIONAL COLLEGIATE ATHLETIC ASSOCIATION

ATHLETICS

The NCAA is the largest athletic association in the country. Its membership numbers almost 900 four-year colleges in the United States including the largest state universities and small, private- and church-affiliated colleges. The NCAA has legislated an extensive set of regulations regarding eligibility to participate, recruiting, playing seasons, and financial aid. The colleges and you are responsible for following these rules. Failure to do so may affect your eligibility for intercollegiate athletics. In addition to the national rules established by the NCAA, your college may have their own, more demanding requirements. Contact the NCAA office or the college of interest to you for an explanation of these regulations with regard to your particular circumstances.

Each year the NCAA publishes the *NCAA Guide for the College-Bound Student-Athlete* and the *NCAA Guide for the Two-Year College Student-Athlete.* NCAA eligibility requirements, appropriate recruiting practices, and financial aid opportunities are specifically described. Review the NCAA information early in your junior year of high school. The *NCAA Guides* should be available from your high school coach. If not, write or call:

National Collegiate Athletic Association (NCAA)
6201 College Boulevard
Overland Park, Kansas 66211-2422
(913) 339-1906

DIVISIONS

There are three Divisions in the NCAA.

There are three divisions in the NCAA. Generally, classification differences among them include sports sponsorship minimum criteria, football and basketball scheduling requirements, academic and eligibility standards, and financial aid limitations. In addition, Division I-A members are required to meet paid, football-attendance criteria.

Division I (301 schools) is made up of major colleges and universities with very competitive athletic programs. There are strict policies on recruitment and athletic scholarship procedures.

Division II (246 schools) is made up of schools smaller than those in Division I. Division II also has very competitive athletic programs. There are strict policies on recruitment and athletic scholarship procedures.

Division III (346 schools) also is made up of schools smaller than those in Division I, and their athletic programs are slightly less competitive. There are strict policies on recruitment procedures. There are no athletic scholarships.

INITIAL ACADEMIC ELIGIBILITY REQUIREMENTS

To practice and play during your freshman year at a Division I college, you must satisfy eligibility requirements.

ATHLETICS

FIRST-TIME FRESHMEN — DIVISION I

If you want to practice and play your freshman year at an NCAA Division I college, you must satisfy the following basic requirements (outlined in NCAA Bylaw 14.3, commonly known as Proposition 48).

DIVISION I REQUIREMENTS FOR ATHLETES FIRST ENTERING COLLEGE AFTER AUGUST 1, 1995

1. Graduate from high school.

2. Successfully complete a core curriculum of at least 13 academic courses which include:

   a. English .... 3 years.
   b. Mathematics .... 2 years.
   c. Social Science .... 2 years.
   d. Natural or Physical Science .... 2 years, including at least one laboratory class if offered by your high school.
   e. Additional courses .... 2 additional years in English, mathematics, or natural or physical science courses.
   f. Additional electives .... 2 years in any of the above or foreign language, computer science, philosophy, or nondoctrinal religion (such as comparative religion).

You must successfully complete a core curriculum of at least 13 academic courses.

3. Attain a GPA in the core curriculum (based upon a maximum of 4.000) and achieve a combined score on the SAT I verbal and mathematics sections or an ACT composite score based upon the index scale shown on the next page.

DIVISION I REQUIREMENTS FOR ATHLETES FIRST ENTERING COLLEGE AFTER AUGUST 1, 1996

1. Graduate from high school.

2. Successfully complete a core curriculum of at least 13 academic courses which include:

   a. English .... 4 years.
   b. Mathematics .... 2 years, comprised of one year of algebra and one year of geometry.
   c. Social Science .... 2 years.

d. Natural or Physical Science........ 2 years, including at least one laboratory class if offered by your high school.

e. Additional courses...................... 1 year in an additional course in English, mathematics or natural or physical science.

f. Additional electives .... 2 years in any of the above or foreign language, computer science, philosophy, or nondoctrinal religion (such as comparative religion).

Division I athletes must attain a GPA in the core curriculum (based upon a maximum of 4.000) and achieve a combined score on the SAT I verbal and mathematics sections or an ACT composite score based upon the NCAA Index Scale.

3. Attain a GPA in the core curriculum (based upon a maximum of 4.000) and achieve a combined score on the SAT I verbal and mathematics sections or an ACT composite score based upon the index scale shown below.

NCAA INDEX SCALE FOR DIVISION I

NCAA INDEX SCALE DIVISION I

Core GPA	Minimum Required SAT I Total Score	Minimum Required ACT Composite Score	Core GPA	Minimum Required SAT I Total Score	Minimum Required ACT Composite Score
Above 2.500	700	17	2.225	810	20
2.500	700	17	2.200	820	20
2.475	710	18	2.175	830	20
2.450	720	18	2.150	840	20
2.425	730	18	2.125	850	20
2.400	740	18	2.100	860	21
2.375	750	18	2.075	870	21
2.350	760	19	2.050	880	21
2.325	770	19	2.025	890	21
2.300	780	19	2.000	900	21
2.275	790	19	Below 2.000 Not Eligible	XX	XX
2.250	800	19			

The SAT I or ACT test scores must be achieved on a national testing date. You must achieve the minimum required SAT I or ACT score no later than the July 1 immediately before your first full-time college enrollment or by the end of your final term of high school.

The highest verbal and math scores from two different testing dates of the SAT I: Reasoning Test can be combined to meet the minimum test score requirement.

The highest verbal and math scores from two different testing dates of the SAT I: Reasoning Test can be combined to meet the minimum test score requirement. The highest scores taken from individual sub-tests of the ACT from more than one testing date may be combined to arrive at a composite score.

FIRST-TIME FRESHMEN — DIVISION II

If you want to practice and play your freshman year at an NCAA Division II college, you must satisfy the following basic requirements (outlined in NCAA Bylaw 14.3, commonly known as Proposition 48).

DIVISION II REQUIREMENTS FOR ATHLETES FIRST ENTERING COLLEGE AFTER AUGUST 1, 1995

1. Graduate from high school.

2. Attain a GPA of 2.000 (based upon a maximum of 4.000) in a successfully-completed core curriculum of at least 13 academic courses in the same areas listed for students first entering Division I institutions after August 1, 1995.

3. Achieve a combined score on the SAT I verbal and mathematics sections of 700 or a composite score on the ACT of 17. You must achieve the minimum required SAT I or ACT score on a national testing date before your first full-time college enrollment. The highest verbal and math scores from two different testing dates of the SAT I: Reasoning Test can be combined to meet the minimum test score requirement. The highest scores taken from individual sub-tests of the ACT from more than one testing date may be combined to arrive at a composite score.

You must satisfactorily complete all courses used to satisfy the core curriculum by achieving a non-failing grade of D or better.

CORE CURRICULUM

- You must satisfactorily complete all courses used to satisfy the core curriculum by achieving a non-failing grade of D or better in each.

- Eighth grade courses may be used to satisfy the core curriculum if they are considered to be equivalent to courses normally taken in the ninth grade or later.

- Effective with courses taken during the 1993-94 academic year, a course that is taken to prepare for a college-preparatory course may not be used to meet the core curriculum. For example, pre-algebra taken to prepare for algebra, cannot count towards meeting core curriculum requirements regardless of its course content.

- Division I does not count courses taken in the summer after grade twelve. Division II does count these courses.

- The thirteen best grades in the core curriculum are used to compute your GPA. Additional grades may be used to meet the GPA requirement provided the core curriculum requirements are met.

- Pass/fail grades may not be used.

- Honors-level courses may be given extra points in calculating the GPA if this practice is normal for your high school.

Effective with courses taken during the 1993-94 academic year, a course that is taken to prepare for a college-preparatory course may not be used to meet the core curriculum.

LEARNING-DISABLED OR HANDICAPPED STUDENTS

High school courses for the learning-disabled or handicapped may be used to meet the core course requirement if your high school principal provides a written statement indicating their equivalence to comparable core courses. Approval is on a case-by-case basis.

If you cannot take the SAT I: Reasoning Test or ACT under regular testing conditions, you may take nonstandard testing. See Chapter 8: EDUCATIONAL OPPORTUNITIES, Admissions Testing for Disabled Students, page 8--6. The NCAA requires that

a. you register for nonstandard testing in the manner outlined by the testing service, which requires that your handicap or learning disability be diagnosed professionally, properly documented, and confirmed,

b. the testing procedures followed must be those outlined by the testing service, and

c. the individuals administering the test may not be members of the high school's athletics department or a member institution's athletics department.

If you take a nonstandard test, you still must achieve the minimum required test score. However, the test does not have to be administered on a national testing date. The NCAA approves completion of the test score requirement on a case-by-case basis.

The NCAA may grant you an exemption to its eligibility requirements if you can present evidence that your overall academic record warrants it.

ELIGIBILITY WAIVERS

The NCAA may grant you an exception to its eligibility requirements if you can present evidence that your overall academic record warrants a waiver. The institution that has officially admitted you must initiate your appeal. Contact the college for information and assistance.

You also may be granted an exception if you leave high school after completion of your junior year or during your senior year to enter a Division I or II member institution. Your admission must be through an early admission program based solely upon outstanding academic performance and promise. You must have maintained a cumulative high school GPA of 3.500 and must have ranked in the top twenty percent of your class for the last four semesters of high school. In addition, all requirements — core curriculum grades and admissions test scores — must be met, except graduation from high school.

FIRST-TIME FRESHMEN — DIVISION III

To practice and play your freshman year at an NCAA Division III institution, you must meet the regular eligibility requirements for admission to that school. No national NCAA standards are established.

The NCAA Initial- Eligibility Clearinghouse compares your high school academic records and your SAT I and ACT test scores with NCAA eligibility requirements for Divisions I and II.

NCAA INITIAL-ELIGIBILITY CLEARINGHOUSE

In 1993 the institutional members of Divisions I and II of the NCAA approved the establishment of the NCAA Initial-Eligibility Clearinghouse to determine initial eligibility of applicants who wish to participate in college sports during their freshman year. The Clearinghouse compares your high school academic record and your SAT I and ACT test scores with NCAA eligibility requirements for Divisions I and II. If you meet the eligibility requirements, the NCAA Initial-Eligibility Clearinghouse certifies you as eligible to play.

If you are planning to enroll as a freshman and you wish to participate in Division I or Division II sports, you must be certified by the Clearinghouse to participate. For information contact:

NCAA Clearinghouse
P. O. Box 4044
Iowa City, Iowa 52244-4044
Phone: (319) 337-1492
Fax: (319) 337-1556

Call Monday through Friday between 8:30 A.M. and 4:30 P.M., Central time.

Register no later than the beginning of your senior year of high school if you want to participate in Division I or II sports as a freshman in college.

ATHLETICS

APPLYING FOR CERTIFICATION

- The NCAA Initial-Eligibility Clearinghouse publishes the brochure *Making Sure You Are Eligible to Participate in College Sports*. Obtain this brochure from your counselor, any NCAA member college offering Division I or Division II sports, or the NCAA Initial-Eligibility Clearinghouse. It contains a full explanation of the Clearinghouse process, the application for certification, and a mailing envelope. The application is a three copy form called the Student Release Form.

- Register with the NCAA Initial Eligibility Clearinghouse by submitting the white copy of the Student Release Form, the original, to the Clearinghouse. Register no later than the beginning of your senior year of high school if you want to participate in Division I or II sports as a freshman in college. It is best to register after your junior year grades appear on your high school transcript. This usually occurs during the summer after your junior year. Although you can register at anytime before participation, if you register late you may face delays that will prevent you from practice or competing.

  The white form gives the Clearinghouse permission to forward your academic, test score, and certification information to the colleges which you authorize on the form. The Clearinghouse will not send your eligibility information at your request; the college must make the request for this information.

You have two options for releasing your certification information to the colleges.

- You have two options for releasing your certification information to the colleges.

  Option 1 authorizes the NCAA Initial-Eligibility Clearinghouse to release your certification information to *any* Division I or II institution that requests it. Over ninety-five percent of students choose this option.

  Option 2 authorizes the NCAA Initial-Eligibility Clearinghouse to release your certification information *only* to the colleges you listed on the Student Release Form. You may list up to five college to receive this information.

  If you choose Option 2, and a college you did not list inquires about your eligibility, the Clearinghouse will write to you to ask if you want to release the information to that college. If you select Option 2 and want to add more colleges to your list, or want to switch to Option 1, you will need to fill out an Additional Certification Release (ACR) form. Call or write the NCAA Initial-Eligibility Clearinghouse for this form. There may be an additional fee for processing the ACR.

- Give the other two copies of your Student Release Form (pink and yellow) to your counselor or guidance administrator. This will authorize them to send your high school transcript, test scores, proof of graduation, and other academic information to the NCAA Initial-Eligibility Clearinghouse. Your high school will send the yellow copy along with an official copy of your high school transcript to the Clearinghouse and keep the pink copy for its files. If you have attended more than one high school, make photocopies of the pink and yellow forms and send them to each of your previous schools so they can send your records. If you attended ninth grade in a junior high school in the same school district as your high school, you do not need to send the form to that school.

- On your application, select a four-digit personal identification number (PIN). The PIN will serve as your private password if you call the Clearinghouse to request information about the status of your file or certification.

- Be sure to sign the authorization statement. If you are under eighteen, your parent or guardian must also sign.

Be sure to sign the authorization statement. If you are under eighteen, your parent or guardian must also sign.

ATHLETICS

FEES

The fee for processing your initial eligibility certification is $18.00. This fee covers the cost of evaluating your academic record and test scores and notifying the colleges of your certification status. Send your payment to the NCAA Initial-Eligibility Clearinghouse with your Student Release Form. If you have previously received a fee waiver for the SAT I: Reasoning Test or ACT, you are eligible for a waiver of the certification fee. To request a waiver, your counselor or guidance administrator must sign the fee waiver section of the Student Release Form.

SAT I OR ACT SCORES

If you have taken admissions tests more than once, have reports of all your SAT I and ACT scores sent to the NCAA Initial-Eligibility Clearinghouse as early as possible. Arrange to have the testing agency send an additional score report or reports to the Clearinghouse. Use code 9999 on the additional score report request. If you have not yet registered to take your entrance tests, mark code 9999 as one of your choices in the section that asks to which colleges do you wish your scores sent. See Chapter 6: COLLEGE ENTRANCE TESTS, Admissions Tests, pages 6--3.

If you have taken admissions tests more than once, have reports of all your SAT I and ACT scores sent to the NCAA Initial-Eligibility Clearinghouse as early as possible.

CERTIFICATION REPORTS

Your high school submits to the NCAA Initial-Eligibility Clearinghouse, on a form called the NCAA 48-H, a list of courses at your school that meet the core-curriculum standards established by the NCAA. The Clearinghouse will evaluate your transcript against your high school's list to determine whether you have successfully completed all academic work required for eligibility. They will also review your admission test scores.

The NCAA Initial-Eligibility Clearinghouse issues certification reports about your eligibility for both Division I and Division II. The reports are sent to you. Your certification information is forwarded to the colleges that request it and which you have authorized to receive it. The Clearinghouse may issue the following types of certification:

- Eligibility for an early expense-paid visit (*required* in all Division I sports except football, field hockey, water polo, soccer, or women's volleyball) based upon information available at the time of the request from the college.

- Preliminary certification based upon information available before graduation.
- Final certification based upon preliminary information plus proof of graduation (final transcript).

You may call the NCAA Initial-Eligibility Clearinghouse from a touchtone phone to check on your certification status.

If your report indicates that you currently do not meet the requirements of NCAA, the report will tell you why. If the NCAA Initial-Eligibility Clearinghouse subsequently receives additional information (such as new test scores or grades in additional core courses), your eligibility will be reevaluated based upon the new information. The Clearinghouse will issue a new certification report to you and to the institutions that received previous reports.

After you submit your Student Release Form and fee, you can check the status of your file, including information about missing documents and decisions, using a touch-tone phone. The telephone number for this 24-hour service is (319) 339-3003. When you call you must enter your Social Security number and your PIN.

TRANSFER REQUIREMENTS

TRANSFER FROM TWO-YEAR COLLEGES

If you transfer to an NCAA institution from a two-year college that conducts an intercollegiate athletics program, you must complete an academic year at the NCAA institution before you may practice, compete, or receive an athletic scholarship *unless* you meet the following eligibility requirements.

TRANSFER TO DIVISION I INSTITUTIONS — QUALIFIER

If you meet the initial academic eligibility requirements when you finish high school, you are considered a qualifier.

If you meet the NCAA initial academic eligibility requirements when you finish high school, you are considered a qualifier. You are eligible to practice, compete, and receive athletic scholarships in Division I institutions the first year of enrollment as a transfer if you meet *either* of these requirements:

1. You spent at least two semesters or three quarters at the two-year college (excluding summer session) and earned at least 24 semester/36 quarter transferable units with a cumulative GPA of 2.000. You must have completed an average of at least 12 semester or quarter transferable units for each term of attendance. Although summer school cannot be used to meet the two-semester/three-quarter requirement, summer school units can be counted toward the units requirement.

2. You graduated from the two-year college and completed a minimum of 48 semester/72 quarter transferable units and have a minimum cumulative GPA of 2.000.

TRANSFER TO DIVISION I INSTITUTIONS — NON-QUALIFIER OR PARTIAL QUALIFIER

If you do not meet the NCAA academic eligibility requirements when you finish high school, you are considered a non-qualifier or a partial qualifier. You are eligible to practice, compete, and receive athletic scholarships in Division I institutions the first year of enrollment as a transfer if you

a. have graduated from the two-year college with an Associate degree or equivalent in an academic curriculum,

b. have completed satisfactorily a minimum of 48 semester/72 quarters of transferable units,

c. have attended a two-year college as a full-time student for at least three semesters or four quarters (excluding summer terms), and

d. have earned a cumulative GPA of 2.000 in transferable units.

The requirements to practice and compete in Division II differ for qualifiers and non-qualifiers.

TRANSFER TO DIVISION II INSTITUTIONS — QUALIFIERS

You are eligible to compete in Division II institutions the first year of enrollment as a transfer only if you

a. graduated from a two-year college, or

b. present a minimum of 24 semester/36 quarter hours of transferable degree credit with a minimum cumulative college GPA of 2.000 and were enrolled at least two semesters or three quarters (excluding summer sessions) in the two year college.

TRANSFER TO DIVISION II INSTITUTIONS — NON-QUALIFIER OR PARTIAL QUALIFIER

If you are not a qualifier, you are eligible for practice and competition (and for nonqualifiers, for athletic scholarships) in Division II institutions during the first academic year of enrollment only if you have attended a two-year college as a full-time student for at least two semesters or three quarters and

a. graduated from the two-year college, or

b. present a minimum of 24 semester/36 quarter hours of transferable degree credit with a minimum cumulative college GPA of 2.000.

If you do not meet the NCAA academic eligibility requirements when you finish high school, you are considered a non-qualifier or a partial qualifier.

TRANSFER TO DIVISION III INSTITUTIONS

You are immediately eligible to compete in a Division III school upon transfer if you

a. have not previously participated in intercollegiate athletics, or

b. have previously participated in intercollegiate athletics and would have been academically eligible to participate had you remained at that institution.

TRANSFER FROM FOUR-YEAR COLLEGES

You are not eligible for intercollegiate competition at a Division I, II, or III institution until you attend one academic year (two full semesters, three full quarters) at the new school, unless you meet one of the applicable transfer exceptions or waivers. Contact the college for additional information and assistance.

Financial Aid

There are no guaranteed four-year athletic scholarships in Division I, II, or III. An athletic scholarship is awarded for no more than one academic year. It may be renewed each year for a maximum of five years within a six-year period. Some sports offer both full and partial scholarships. Sometimes the scholarship pays only for books. Football and basketball always offer full scholarships.

An athletic scholarship is awarded for no more than one academic year. It may be renewed each year for a maximum of five years within a six-year period.

ATHLETICS

DIVISION I

Student athletes who have met the NCAA academic eligibility requirements may receive athletic scholarships from the institution for up to five years. These scholarships may pay for tuition and fees, room and board, and books. Athletic scholarships are associated with athletic ability. There is a specified number of athletic scholarships that the institution can award for each sport. The institution may grant additional need-based financial assistance. In some cases, you may receive additional financial aid from government programs such as the Federal Pell Grant. Certain student-athletes who have not met initial academic eligibility requirements may receive need-based financial aid under specified conditions.

DIVISION II

Student athletes who have met the NCAA academic requirements may receive athletic scholarships from the institution for up to five years. These scholarships may pay for tuition and fees, room and board, and books. Athletic scholarships are associated with athletic ability. There is a specified number of athletic scholarships that the institution can award for each sport. The school may grant additional need-based financial assistance. In some cases, you may receive additional financial aid from government programs, such as the Federal Pell Grant. Certain student-athletes who have not met initial academic eligibility requirements may receive financial aid under specified conditions.

DIVISION III

There is a specified number of athletic scholarships that the institution can award for each sport.

Student athletes may receive financial aid up to the cost of attendance: Tuition and fees, room and board, books, transportation, and other expenses incidental to attendance. *However, this aid is based totally on financial need and not associated with athletic ability.* There is no limit to the number of financial-aid, need-based awards.

Recruiting Restrictions

NCAA coaches and athletic representatives must follow specific guidelines in their recruiting activities. These guidelines cover who can contact you, how many contacts can be made, the dates when these contacts can occur, limitations on high school campus visits by coaches, limitations on your college visits for the purpose of being recruited, and restrictions on benefits and inducements offered to you to attend an

NCAA school. The recruiting policies are different for each division. It is very important for you to know these guidelines. Failure to follow them can make you ineligible. The guidelines are described in detail in the *NCAA Guide for the College-Bound Athlete* and the *NCAA Guide for the Two-Year College Student Athlete.*

Recruiting guidelines are very specific and must be followed. They are described in detail in the NCAA Guides which are published each year.

CALIFORNIA NCAA MEMBERS

For 1994-95, forty-eight colleges and universities in California are members of NCAA. Membership is organized among the three divisions shown on the next page. Membership is based upon a college's ability to meet criteria established by the divisions. However, specific sports may be played in other divisions. Ask in which division your sport participates if you are interested in one of these colleges, or they recruit you. Division I is divided into I-A and I-AAA for football only.

DIVISION I-A

CSU Fresno
San Diego State University
San Jose State University
Stanford University
UC Berkeley
UC Los Angeles
University of Southern California
University of the Pacific

DIVISION I-AA

Cal Poly SLO
CSU Northridge
CSU Sacramento
St. Mary's College
University of San Diego

DIVISION I-AAA

CSU Fullerton
CSU Long Beach
Loyola Marymount University
Pepperdine University
Santa Clara University
UC Irvine
UC Santa Barbara
University of San Francisco

DIVISION II

Cal State Polytechnic University, Pomona
CSU Bakersfield
CSU Chico
CSU Dominguez Hills
CSU Hayward
CSU Los Angeles
CSU San Bernardino
CSU Stanislaus
College of Notre Dame
Humboldt State University
San Francisco State University
Sonoma State University
UC Davis
UC Riverside

DIVISION III

California Institute of Technology
California Lutheran University
Chapman University
Claremont McKenna-Harvey Mudd-Scripps Colleges
Menlo College
Mills College
Occidental College
Pomona-Pitzer Colleges
UC San Diego
UC Santa Cruz

For 1994-95, forty-eight colleges and universities in California are members of NCAA.

NAIA — NATIONAL ASSOCIATION OF INTERCOLLEGIATE ATHLETICS

Ask for the pamphlet, "A Guide For The College Bound Student," published by the NAIA.

ATHLETICS

NAIA is made up of approximately 400 accredited four-year colleges and universities throughout the United States and Canada, fifteen of them in California. A pamphlet, *A Guide For The College Bound Student*, describes basic NAIA eligibility regulations, financial assistance policies, tryout rules and recruitment policies. This pamphlet should be available from your high school coach. If not, write or call:

National Association of Intercollegiate Athletics (NAIA)
Two Warren Place
6120 South Yale Avenue, Suite 1450
Tulsa, Oklahoma 74136
(918) 494-8828
Fax: (918) 494-8841

ACADEMIC ELIGIBILITY REQUIREMENTS

FIRST-TIME FRESHMEN

You must be a graduate of an accredited high school or be accepted as a regular student in good standing as defined by the enrolling institution and must meet two of the three entry-level requirements.

A first-time freshman is a student who, upon becoming identified with an NAIA institution, has not previously been identified with another institution of higher learning for two semesters or three quarters (or equivalent). To be eligible to play for an NAIA institution, you must be a graduate of an accredited high school or be accepted as a regular student in good standing as defined by the enrolling institution. Further, you must meet two of the following three entry-level requirements:

1. An SAT I score of 740 or an ACT composite score of 18. Scores must be achieved on a single test, taken on a national or international testing date.

2. Achieve an overall high school GPA or 2.000 on a 4.000 scale.

3. Graduate in the top half of your high school graduating class.

If you do not meet two of these three standards, you may not participate in intercollegiate athletics at any NAIA member institution for the first full year of attendance (two semesters, three quarters, or equivalent) that you are identified with an institution. However, you may practice with the team and receive athletics-related financial aid.

TRANSFER REQUIREMENTS

You are considered a transfer student if you have been previously identified with another institution of higher learning. You become identified with an institution by (a) representing it in an intercollegiate contest, or (b) enrolling in nine or more institutional credit hours at any single institution (two- or four-year) in any term and attending any regularly-scheduled class, not including summer school.

Contact the institution to which you plan to transfer for specific rules on your eligibility to participate.

If you are transferring from a four-year institution at which you participated in intercollegiate competition, you may be required to meet a sixteen-week residency period before you become eligible. In any case, it is a good idea to contact the institution to which you plan to transfer for specific rules on your eligibility to participate.

ATHLETIC SCHOLARSHIPS

Athletes may receive no more institutionally-controlled financial aid than the actual cost of tuition, fees, books, supplies, room and board (based on the official board and room allowance listed in the institution's catalogue). In some cases, you may receive additional financial aid from government programs such as the Federal Pell Grant. There are specific limits of athletics-related financial aid that an institution may award per sport.

CALIFORNIA NAIA MEMBER

Azusa Pacific University
Bethany College
Biola University
California Baptist College
Christian Heritage College
Concordia University
Dominican College
Fresno Pacific College
Holy Names College
The Master's College
Mount Saint Mary's College
Point Loma Nazarene College
Southern California College
United States International University
Westmont College

Fifteen colleges in California are members of the NAIA.

ATHLETICS

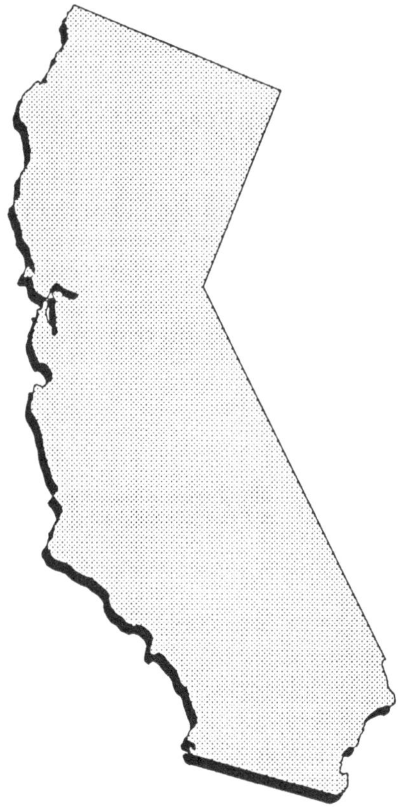

Chapter 6

COLLEGE ENTRANCE TESTS

Do not become overly anxious about college entrance testing. Colleges see you as much more than the sum of your scores.

Plan...

Prepare...

And do your best!

ADMISSIONS TESTS

Admissions test scores are one of several criteria admissions officers use to compare one student with another in preparation and ability to do college work. College applicants come from many high schools having courses, course content, and grading policies that differ from one another. Even within one high school, curriculum and grading approaches may vary widely among teachers of the same subject. Therefore, a review of your courses and your grades may not provide enough information for admissions personnel to determine your academic qualifications for their particular college. Test scores provide another standard by which they may assess you.

Colleges agree... Your scores on admissions tests are rarely the deciding criteria for acceptance.

Not every California college or university requires admissions test scores as a screening tool. This *GUIDE* contains information on which colleges do and do not require testing, which tests to take, and deadlines for taking them. You also can find this information in each college catalogue under admission information and in your admission application packet from the college.

COMMONLY ASKED QUESTIONS ABOUT ADMISSIONS TESTS

HOW IMPORTANT ARE ADMISSIONS TEST SCORES IN THE ADMISSIONS PROCESS

Test scores are one of several factors considered in reviewing your admission application. Colleges agree that your scores are rarely the deciding criteria for acceptance or rejection. They give tremendous weight in their admission decisions to your grades, the courses you have taken, evidence of your motivation, interests, energy, enthusiasm, and other qualities for successfully completing college. Do not feel that your test scores will make or break your college opportunities.

ARE THE ADMISSIONS TESTS GIVEN MORE THAN ONCE DURING THE SCHOOL YEAR?

The ACT Assessment, SAT I: Reasoning Test, SAT II: Subject Tests, and the TOEFL are given several times each school year during both the fall and spring semesters. You can take the PSAT/NMSQT only in October. See the test descriptions in this chapter, or check with your high school career center or college guidance source for testing dates and deadlines for applying. Pick up your test application materials at least eight weeks before the test date you want, so you have ample time to complete and submit your application.

Pick up your test application materials at least eight weeks before your preferred test date.

CAN I TAKE BOTH THE SAT I: REASONING TEST AND THE SAT II: SUBJECT TESTS ON THE SAME DAY?

Although the College Entrance Examination Board frequently administers both the SAT I: Reasoning Test and the SAT II: Subject Tests on the same dates, it does not allow you to take them on the same day. It really is not possible to do so because testing sessions for both begin at the same time, 8:00 A.M., and run until about 12:00 noon.

CAN I TAKE THE ADMISSIONS TESTS MORE THAN ONCE?

The colleges and universities differ in which scores they use to make their admission decisions.

You can take any of the tests more than once, and you probably should. Each time you retake a test you become more familiar with its format, type of test questions, and test content. While this strategy may improve your scores, do not overdo this retesting opportunity. Two to three retestings are probably enough to maximize your results. If you retake the tests too many times, you may get careless. Questions can look similar from test to test, but are not. Because of this, you may increase your wrong answers and your test scores will deteriorate. Also, you may get too stressed about taking the tests at the expense of your school work. According to College Board studies, low scores are most likely to improve, while high scores are most likely to decline.

The colleges and universities differ in which scores they use for admission. UC and CSU use your highest set of scores. The independent colleges may use your highest set of scores, your highest score on each sub-test, your most recent scores, or the average of your scores.

WHEN SHOULD I TAKE THE ADMISSIONS TESTS?

The most effective strategy is to take your admissions tests (ACT Assessment, SAT I: Reasoning Test, SAT II: Subject Tests, TOEFL) for the first time by the end of your junior year of high school. As a junior you take them in May and/or June of second semester. You may choose to test earlier than this for additional practice, or you may take the free practice tests that come with the test registration materials. You probably will want to take the tests again in your senior year, especially if you feel that retaking them can improve your scores.

Taking the tests by the end of your junior year gives you test score information that can help you determine how your scores match up to the requirements of the various colleges. The scores can guide you in choosing the colleges to visit and to which to apply.

The most effective strategy is to take your admissions tests for the first time by the end of your junior year.

If you miss junior-year testing, do not despair. While it is better to have tested for the first time as a junior, there are several testing dates each fall that allow you to complete your testing by the end of December of your senior year. This schedule permits you to meet the deadlines of most colleges to which you apply. A disadvantage of testing in your senior year is it conflicts with other demands for your time such as completing admission applications and writing your college application essays. Consequently, you have limited time to prepare for the tests and even less to take them more than once.

The best time to take the SAT II: Subject Tests in a subject is when you finish the course in that subject. This may occur at the end of your freshman, sophomore, or junior year.

SHOULD I TAKE THE ACT OR THE SAT I: REASONING TEST?

You might want to take both the ACT *and* the SAT I: Reasoning Test. Since the tests are somewhat different in purpose, content, and structure, you may find that you score better on one than the other. Many students find that they perform differently on the two tests. Review the descriptive information in this chapter and in the sample booklets that you receive with your testing application to determine which test might be better for you. If your grades are not strong enough to give you a good chance of admission at the college of your choice, test scores might make a difference. Therefore, it may be to your advantage to try both tests to maximize your admission opportunities.

Most colleges accept scores from either test. However, some institutions prefer one over the other and may not accept one or the other. Generally, the SAT I: Reasoning Test is more widely used. Check this *GUIDE* or the college itself for information about the admissions testing they require. California State University and the University of California accept scores from either test and provide tables that equate the scores from each. See chapter 10: CALIFORNIA STATE UNIVERSITY, Minimum Admission Requirements, page 10--5 and chapter 11: UNIVERSITY OF CALIFORNIA, Minimum Admission Requirements, page 11--5.

Most colleges require you to complete all admissions testing by the end of December of your senior year.

IS THERE A DEADLINE FOR COMPLETING ADMISSIONS TESTING?

Although you may apply to a particular college in November of your senior year, you do not need all of your testing completed by that time. The colleges take a few months to review student applications. They wait until your scores arrive before making their final admission decisions. Most colleges require you to complete all your admissions testing by the end of December of your senior year so that they have your scores on file by mid-January. If you apply for early decision at an independent college, the school probably expects all of your testing completed during your junior year or by the end of November of your senior year.

California State University allows you to keep resubmitting new test results throughout your senior year to help you qualify for admission. However, one campus, Cal Poly San Luis Obispo requires you to complete all testing by the end of November. The University of California requires that you complete all your testing by the end of December. The independent schools set their own deadlines, although the end of December is typical. Check this *GUIDE*, the college catalogues, or your college application packet for specific information.

I DO NOT KNOW TO WHICH COLLEGES I WILL APPLY. SHOULD I TAKE THE TESTS ANYWAY?

Apply for admissions tests even if you are not sure to which colleges you will apply.

Yes, you should. When you sign up for the tests, you may list the colleges to receive your test scores. Even if you are not sure of your choices at that time, list the ones you are considering. After you have taken the tests and even after you have received your results, you can have your scores sent to additional colleges for a small fee. If you retake the SAT I: Reasoning Test, a summary of your past scores is sent to the colleges you specify. You do not need to arrange for your scores from each separate testing to be submitted. Each time you take SAT II: Subject Tests, you decide whether to send individual test scores to the colleges of your choice. ACT does not send a summary, but reports only the test scores from a single test date. You must make a special request for other ACT Assessment scores to be sent.

HOW SOON AFTER I TAKE THE TESTS ARE MY TEST SCORES SENT TO THE COLLEGES AND TO ME?

It takes four to six weeks for your test scores to reach the colleges and you. It may be necessary to apply for retesting even though you do not yet have your scores. If the deadline for applying for the next set of tests comes before you receive your scores, you may have to decide if you need another retesting based upon your subjective feelings about how you did on the test, rather than upon actual results.

COLLEGE ENTRANCE TESTS

HOW SHOULD I PREPARE FOR THE TESTS? WHAT ABOUT COACHING?

Possibly the most important reason for you to do some preparation before you take any of the tests is to reduce your test anxiety.

Possibly the most important reason for you to do some preparation before you take any of the tests is to reduce your test anxiety. You will do your best work on the testing materials if you feel comfortable in the testing situation; are familiar with the procedures, the type of test questions, and the content to be covered; and are rested and not feeling too pressured. As a high school student you have been encouraged and taught to study and prepare yourself for class tests. This same approach applied to your admissions tests will help you feel more relaxed about them.

There are several books, computer software programs, and courses to help you prepare for admissions testing. They vary in cost and approach. Some help you with test content by giving you exercises to increase your mathematics and verbal skills. Others concentrate on developing your familiarity with the types and formats of the questions. Most present sample questions and test-taking strategies.

- The ACT Assessment, SAT I, and SAT II application packets come with booklets of sample practice tests. If you feel you need more experience, you can buy additional books from the testing companies or bookstores, or you can borrow them from the public library. Your high school career center and library also have study books.

- If you like to use a computer, you can buy test taking strategies and practice test exercises in software programs. Some may also be available at your high school.

- Many high schools offer test preparation workshops. They generally are taught by teachers and vary in material and format. Check with your school to find out if it holds these workshops. Some are free while others may charge a small fee.

- Several commercial companies offer "coaching" programs to train students to take the tests. These programs are often quite expensive and can cost several hundred dollars.

There really is no way to predict if and by how much you will profit from test preparation.

There is really no way to predict if and by how much you may profit from test preparation or which type of preparation might work best for you. You need to look at yourself and your opportunities. Will you prepare on your own by using practice materials? Does a computer motivate you to study? Will you be better motivated if you attend a test preparation workshop? Does your school offer a program? Can you afford a private program?

COACHING: The college entrance testing publishers have been reluctant to support the concept that coaching makes a big difference in your scores. The College Entrance Examination Board in its 1994-95 publication, Taking the SAT I: Reasoning Test, makes the following statement:

> "There is no simple answer. Anecdotal reports from individual students who had score increases, as well as claims made by many of the coaching schools, have led some to believe in extraordinary results from these programs. Rigorous research suggests the following: Short-duration programs (about 20 hours) improve scores an average of about 10 points on the verbal and about 15 points on the math. Longer-term programs (40 hours or so) improve scores an average of 15 to 20 points on the verbal and 20 to 30 points on the math. Math scores appear to benefit more from coaching than do verbal scores. Longer programs yield somewhat larger gains; however, beyond the first 20 or 30 hours of coaching, score gains are very minor.

A few words of caution about these conclusions: First, these results come from many different types of programs, ranging from basic familiarization to extensive programs that resemble full-time schooling. Second, many of the students enrolled in these programs may have also engaged in other preparation activities. And finally, these are averages and generalizations; keep in mind that some students experienced much larger score increases, while others may even have seen their scores go down.

Are these conclusions valid for the new SAT? Probably. Until there is carefully controlled research using data from the new SAT, nobody will know for sure."

If you do decide to take a commercial coaching program, look into it carefully. Ask for names of students who have gone through the program. Call them to evaluate the content and effectiveness of the program. What were the main benefits for them? Could you achieve the same advantages by studying on your own?

If you decide to take a commercial coaching program, look into it carefully.

THE PSAT/NMSQT

THE PRELIMINARY SAT/NATIONAL MERIT SCHOLARSHIP QUALIFYING TEST

PUBLISHER

The College Entrance Examination Board (CEEB), a nonprofit organization subcontracts PSAT test administration to Educational Testing Service (ETS).

National Office
PSAT/NMSQT Office
P.O. Box 6720
Princeton, NJ 08541-6720
(609) 771-7070
TDD (for hearing impaired): (609) 771-7150

WHAT IS THE PSAT/NMSQT?

The PSAT/NMSQT is a practice test to prepare for the SAT I: Reasoning Tests. Take it in your junior year and possibly in your sophomore year as well. Because it contains the same kinds of questions and produces similar scores, the PSAT/NMSQT is a preview of the SAT I: Reasoning Test. See this chapter: The SAT I: Reasoning Test, page 6--12.

The PSAT is a practice test to prepare for the SAT I: Reasoning Test. Take it in your junior year and possibly in your sophomore year as well.

The PSAT/NMSQT measures verbal and mathematics reasoning abilities important to doing college work. It assesses knowledge and skills that you develop through your classes and through your experiences outside the classroom. Measured are your ability to reason with facts and concepts rather than your ability to recall and recite them.

PSAT/NMSQT CONTENT

The PSAT/NMSQT has two thirty-minute verbal sections and two thirty-minute mathematics sections. The total testing session takes two hours plus twenty minutes for directions and completing the personal information section of the answer sheet.

The two verbal sections consist of...

58 questions that focus on your ability to read critically. Questions are of three types: 16 sentence completions; 12 analogies; and 30 critical reading questions. The sentence completion and analogy questions are selected from four broad content areas: humanities, social sciences, natural sciences, and human relations.

- Sentence completion questions measure the ability to recognize logical relationships between parts of a sentence.

The critical reading questions are designed to measure your ability to analyze and evaluate ideas, opinions, and arguments.

- Analogy questions test the ability to see a relationship between a pair of words and to recognize a similar or parallel relationship in another pair of words.

- Critical reading questions, based upon reading passages of 400 to 850 words, measure critical reading skills and knowledge of vocabulary in context. Reading selections are taken from a variety of fields including social sciences, natural sciences, and the humanities. In addition, narrative passages are included, either fiction or nonfiction. One set of reading questions is based upon a pair of related passages on a shared theme or issue. Most reading questions ask you to think about what is going on in the passage or the pair of related passages. The test is designed to measure your ability to analyze and evaluate ideas, opinions, and arguments.

- There are no antonyms.

The mathematics sections consist of...

50 questions with an increased emphasis in the mathematics reasoning sections on your ability to apply mathematical concepts and interpret data.

Mathematics questions of all types are from the areas of arithmetic reasoning, algebra, and geometry.

- Questions are presented in three formats: 25 standard multiple-choice questions; 15 quantitative comparisons (multiple-choice); 10 questions requiring you to produce your own answers rather than selecting from a set of multiple-choice alternatives. These 10 questions require you to fill in your answers on special grids on the answer sheet.

- Mathematics questions of all types are taken from the areas of arithmetic reasoning, algebra, and geometry. The tasks posed on the test are designed to assess how well you understand mathematics, how well you can apply what you already know to new situations, and how well you can use what you know to solve non-routine problems.

- The College Board recommends that you bring your calculator to the PSAT test. While no question requires a calculator to determine its answer, recent studies indicate that students who use calculators do slightly better on the test than those who do not. Most students will find a calculator useful for performing some of the incidental computations needed to solve some of the problems. Any four-function, scientific, or graphing calculator is permitted. Calculators will *not* be supplied at the test site.

WHEN YOU SHOULD TAKE THE PSAT/NMSQT

The PSAT/NMSQT is given only once a year during October on either a Tuesday or a Saturday. For fall 1994, the PSAT/NMSQT is given Tuesday, October 11, 1994 and Saturday, October 15, 1994. Your high school decides on which of these two dates it will administer the test to students in your school. Eighty percent of the high schools will test on Tuesday. If you cannot take the test on the day your school administers it, your school may be willing to help you arrange to take it at another school site on the alternate date.

The PSAT is given only once a year during October. Register for it at your high school.

You should take the PSAT/NMSQT in October of your sophomore and junior years to have two experiences with this test. Your junior year PSAT/NMSQT is the most important because it can qualify you for certain scholarship opportunities. See this chapter: PSAT/NMSQT, Additional Information, page 6--11. Sophomore testing is more of a practice and familiarization session. In October 1993, 1,159,578 juniors and over 506,942 sophomores took the test across the nation; 108,247 juniors and over 46,000 sophomores took it in California.

1994-95 PSAT/NMSQT FEES

The fee paid to the College Entrance Examination Board for the October 1994 administration of the PSAT/NMSQT is $8.00. Your high school collects this fee from you. Some high schools collect an additional amount to cover the cost of administering the test in your school. The teachers who administer the test are paid for this service and their payment is included in your total fee. The total fee amount differs from school to school depending upon how much each high school decides to charge for test administration.

You should take the PSAT/NMSQT in October of your sophomore and junior years to have two experiences with this test.

If you cannot afford to pay the fee for the test, ask your school about a fee waiver. If you qualify for one, you are allowed to take the test at no cost. Your school must request fee waivers by July 1st. Tell the PSAT coordinator at your high school in the spring that you need a fee waiver for the PSAT administered the following October.

HOW TO REGISTER FOR THE PSAT/NMSQT

Your high school registers you for the PSAT/NMSQT and gives you the *PSAT/NMSQT Student Bulletin*, which contains test-taking tips, sample questions with explanations of answers, and a complete practice test to take and score. It also describes scholarship opportunities that may be available based upon your scores on the PSAT/NMSQT when taken in your *junior* year.

PSAT/NMSQT SCORING

Your high school receives your scores in early to mid-December. They will distribute your Score Report with an explanation of the meaning of your scores and how you can use them for future planning.

PSAT/NMSQT 1993 SCORES		
Test	National Average	California Average
Verbal Score: (Range 20 - 80)		
Juniors (College bound)	41.1	40.3
Sophomores (College bound)	39.6	39.1
Math Score: (Range 20 - 80)		
Juniors (College bound)	45.8	46.2
Sophomores (College bound)	43.9	45.1

The PSAT/NMSQT is scored on a 20-80 scale. You receive two scores: A verbal score of 20-80 and a mathematics score of 20-80. No test can measure precisely what you know. If you had taken different editions of the test within a short time period your score would probably vary somewhat on the 20-80 scale. The best way to look at your score is as a range that extends from three or four points below your score to three or four points above it. For example, if your verbal score is 52, it might range from 49 to 55 if you took the test many times.

COLLEGE ENTRANCE TESTS

THE PSAT/NMSQT SCORE REPORT

You will receive a Score Report and your original test. Your Score Report reports your scores, your score range, your percentile score, your answers, and the correct answers. It identifies question difficulty level, and projects your likely SAT I scores based upon your PSAT/NMSQT scores. On the back of the report is a detailed explanation of all the information provided by the Score Report.

Your Score Report shows you the score range for each of your scores.

Your percentile rank allows you to compare your score with college-bound juniors who took the test. It shows the percent of students who scored lower than you did on the verbal or mathematics section.

The Score Report also indicates your percentile rank. Your percentile rank allows you to compare your score with college-bound juniors who took the test. It shows the percent of students who scored lower than you did on the verbal or mathematics section.

The PSAT/NMSQT score scale of 20 to 80 corresponds to the SAT I scale of 200 to 800. The Score Report estimates the verbal and mathematics scores you can expect on the SAT I based on your PSAT/NMSQT scores. This can be very helpful as you review the admissions requirements of the colleges which interest you. You have some idea whether your projected SAT I scores fit the profile of students admitted to a particular college.

Go through your original test analyzing which questions you answered correctly and which ones gave you problems. You can use this information to identify your areas of strength and weakness to prepare yourself for the SAT I: Reasoning Test. Your English and mathematics teachers may be able to suggest study materials or classes to help you improve in your areas of weakness.

The Score Report contains information about the major field of interest you indicated on the personal information section of the answer sheet. Included is a list of high school courses needed to pursue a particular field, a list of college courses required in that field of study, skills and interests associated with it, alternative majors, and careers likely to be chosen by people interested in that major.

RECENTERING PSAT/NMSQT SCORES

In April 1995, the SAT Program will recenter the SAT Program score scale. This change will place all SAT scores on new, recentered scales. Recentering will have the effect of reestablishing the average score on the SAT I at the midpoint of the 200-800 scale (about 500). It will redistribute the scores evenly over the scale and reestablish the average score at the middle of the scale as it was in 1941 when the College Board originally developed it. Recentering of the score scale will also affect the PSAT/NMSQT scores because this test is linked to the SAT I test. The October 1994 PSAT/NMSQT is the first test placed on the recentered SAT scale. Scores will still be reported on the 20-80 scale. See this chapter, page 6--21 for a full explanation of recentering of test scores.

Your PSAT scores do not affect your admission to college. The colleges do not ask for these scores when you apply for admission.

PSAT/NMSQT ADDITIONAL INFORMATION

- In scoring your PSAT/NMSQT, you lose a fraction of a point for each question you answer incorrectly. You neither gain nor lose credit for unanswered questions. Therefore, guess carefully. If you know that one or more answer choices for a question are definitely wrong, it is generally to your advantage to guess from the remaining choices. But with no knowledge of any of the choices, random guessing is unlikely to increase your score.

- In the mathematics section, ten questions require you to analyze and solve problems without the clues given by multiple-choice answers. The College Board believes that guessing is next to impossible on these items. There is no penalty for wrong answers to these questions.

- Your scores on this test do not affect your admission to college. The colleges do not ask for these scores when you apply for admission. The PSAT/NMSQT is your opportunity to get practice experience in college admissions testing with no jeopardy to you.

- When you take the test in your junior year, your scores, if they are high enough, may qualify you for consideration in three major scholarship opportunities: The **National Merit Scholarship Program**, and the **National Achievement Scholarship Program for Outstanding Negro Students** (for Black American students).

  These very competitive programs use PSAT/NMSQT scores to identify high-scoring candidates for scholarships. If your scores do qualify you for any of these opportunities, there are additional testing and application requirements to be completed in your senior year.

  The **National Merit Scholarship Program** uses a Selection Index based upon your *junior* PSAT scores to select participants in their competition. To compute the Selection Index double your verbal score and add your mathematics score to the product. For example, if you received 52 on your verbal score and 67 on your mathematics score, your Selection Index is $(2 \times 52) + 67 = 171$. 60 is the lowest Selection Index possible; 240 is the highest. Your Selection Index is stated on your Score Report.

  A Selection Index of at least 179 is usually required for recognition and possible participation in the **National Merit Scholarship Program**. The minimum Selection Index varies from state to state. In California, the minimum Selection Index for recognition and possible participation in the program has ranged from 196 to 198 over the past several years.

To compute your National Merit Scholarship Program Selection Index, double your verbal score and add your mathematics score to the product.

- The **National Hispanic Scholar Recognition Program** (for Hispanic American students) recognizes exceptional Hispanic high school students. Utilizing PSAT/NMSQT scores, the College Board identifies academically outstanding Hispanic students and furnishes their names to colleges and universities to encourage recruitment and financial support. To become eligible for consideration for this program , you must take the PSAT/NMSQT as a junior, indicate your interest in the program, and identify yourself as being of Hispanic descent.

Taking the PSAT/NMSQT gives you the opportunity to participate in the Student Search Service.

- Taking the PSAT/NMSQT gives you the opportunity to participate in the **Student Search Service**. If you give your approval on the personal information part of the test answer sheet, the College Entrance Examination Board gives your name — not your individual scores — to colleges throughout the country. You receive information about these colleges and their financial aid opportunities. You likely will be swamped with letters and brochures from colleges all over the country in the spring of your junior year. This can be fun or overwhelming! These materials can help you develop criteria for deciding upon colleges to which to apply.

- If you are a **disabled student**, arrangements can be made to accommodate your disability. The Tuesday edition is available in Braille and large type. Your school must order these special formats by mid-May of the prior school year. If you have other documented disabilities that require adjustment of the testing situation (such as extended time, special aids, and/or an alternate format), you may take the same edition of the PSAT/NMSQT on the same date as all other students in your school, but with special accommodations for you. You need to complete an eligibility form signed and authorized by your school. Speak to your counselor or assistant principal about these arrangements. See chapter 8: EDUCATIONAL OPPORTUNITIES, Admissions Testing For Disabled Students, page 8--6.

THE SAT I: REASONING TEST

THE SCHOLASTIC ASSESSMENT TEST

The SAT has been revised and renamed the SAT I: Reasoning Test. The Achievement Tests have been expanded and now are called the SAT II: Subject Tests.

PUBLISHER

The College Entrance Examination Board (CEEB), a nonprofit organization, subcontracts SAT I test administration to Educational Testing Service (ETS)

National Office

College Board ATP
P.O. Box 6200
Princeton, NJ 08541-6200
Phone: (609) 771-7600
TDD (for hearing impaired): (609) 882-4118

WHAT IS THE SAT I: REASONING TEST?

In March 1994 the College Entrance Examination Board introduced a new SAT Program. The SAT has been revised and renamed the SAT I: Reasoning Test. The Achievement Tests have been expanded and now are called the SAT II: Subject Tests.

Together the SAT I and the SAT II are known as the Scholastic Assessment Tests (SAT). With some additional services they constitute the SAT Program. See this chapter: SAT II: Subject Tests, page 6--30.

The SAT I: Reasoning Test measures general verbal and mathematics reasoning abilities important to doing college work. It assesses knowledge and skills that you develop through your classes and through your experiences outside the classroom. The test measures your ability to reason with facts and concepts rather than your ability to recall and recite them. SAT I scores are useful to college admissions officers in comparing your preparation and ability with applicants from different high schools having widely varying courses and grading standards.

The SAT I: Reasoning Test measures general verbal and mathematics reasoning abilities important to doing college work.

SAT I: REASONING TEST CONTENT

The College Board describes the SAT I: Reasoning Test as different from the "old" SAT but not harder. Its content includes old and new question types. The SAT I: Reasoning Test has seven sections: two thirty-minute and one fifteen-minute verbal sections, two thirty-minute and one fifteen-minute mathematics sections, and one thirty-minute section of equating questions. The College Board uses the equating section, which does not count in your score, to evaluate test questions. The seven sections are not in the same order in each test book.

The total test will take three hours plus an additional forty minutes or so for directions and completing the personal information section of the answer sheet.

The SAT I verbal sections consist of ...

78 questions that focus on your ability to read critically. They take a total of seventy-five minutes to answer. Questions are of three types: sentence completions; analogies; and critical reading questions. There are no antonyms. Critical reading questions make up fifty percent of the verbal test, and more than three-fourths of the verbal testing time is spent on reading passages and questions. The sentence completion and analogy questions are selected from four broad content areas: humanities, social sciences, natural sciences, and human relations.

The College Board describes the new SAT I: Reasoning Test as different from the "old" SAT but not harder. Its content includes old and new question types.

- Sentence completion: 19 questions. Sentence completion questions measure your knowledge of the meanings of words and your ability to understand how the different parts of a sentence logically fit together.
- Analogies: 19 questions. Analogy questions test your knowledge of the meaning of words, your ability to see a relationship in a pair of words, and your ability to recognize a similar or parallel relationship.
- Critical reading: 40 questions. These questions are based upon reading passages of 400 to 850 words. Reading questions measure critical reading skills and knowledge of vocabulary in context. Reading selections are taken from a variety of fields including social sciences, natural sciences, and the humanities. In addition, narrative passages are included, either fiction or nonfiction. One set of reading questions is based on a pair of related passages with a shared theme or issue. Most reading questions ask you to think about what is going on in the passage or the pair of related passages. The critical reading is designed to measure your ability to analyze and evaluate ideas, opinions, and arguments.

The SAT I mathematical sections consist of...

60 questions designed for the student who has had a year of algebra and some geometry. Most of the questions are classified as arithmetic, algebra, or geometry. There are approximately equal numbers of questions in each category. The test takes seventy-five minutes.

The mathematics reasoning sections include questions that require you to produce your own answers.

Arithmetic: Simple addition, subtraction, multiplication, and division; percent; data interpretation (including mean, median, and mode); odd and even numbers; prime numbers; divisibility.

Algebra: Negative numbers; substitution; simplifying algebraic expressions; simple factoring; linear equations; inequalities; simple quadratic equations; positive integer exponents; roots of numbers; sequences.

Geometry: Area and perimeter of a polygon; area and circumference of a circle; volume of a box, cube, and cylinder; Pythagorean Theorem and special properties of isosceles, equilateral, and right triangles; 30-60-90 degree and 45-45-90 degree triangles; properties of parallel and perpendicular lines; simple coordinate geometry; slope; similarity; geometric visualization.

Other: Logical reasoning; newly-defined symbols and operations that are based on commonly-used symbols and operation; probability and counting.

There is an emphasis in the mathematics reasoning sections upon your ability to apply mathematical concepts and interpret data.

The test is made up of:

Standard five-choice, multiple-choice questions: 35 questions.

Quantitative Comparison questions (Multiple-choice): 15 questions.

Student-Produced Response questions: 10 questions.

The College Board recommends that you bring your calculator to the SAT I: Reasoning Test.

In addition to multiple-choice and quantitative comparison questions, ten questions require you to produce your own answers, not just select one from a set of multiple-choice alternatives. You respond by filling in your own answers on special grids on the answer sheet.

The College Board recommends that you bring your calculator to the SAT I: Reasoning Test. While no question will require a calculator to determine its answer, recent studies indicate that students who use calculators do somewhat better on the test than those who do not. Any four-function, scientific or graphing calculator is permitted. Calculators will *not* be supplied at the test site.

WHEN YOU SHOULD TAKE THE SAT I: REASONING TEST

If you intend to take the SAT I: Reasoning Test, take it for the first time during the spring semester of your junior year. Some students choose to take it earlier than this for additional practice. You may want to retake it one or more times in your senior year. You can take the SAT I: Reasoning Test as many times as you wish; however, two to three times seems optimum. Beyond that, it becomes expensive and you probably will not see much change in your score. In fact, you may find that your scores do not differ much from testing to testing.

If you intend to take the SAT I, take it for the first time during the spring semester of your junior year. You may wish to take it again in your senior year.

According to the College Board...

"Students who take the SAT more than once almost always earn different scores. For the class of 1993, the average change between the spring of the junior year and the fall of the senior year was an increase of 18 points on the verbal and 18 points in math, for a total of 36 points. While the scores of nearly two-thirds of repeat test-takers rise, some decline. One out of every fifteen students sees increases of 100 or more points on either verbal or math, while one out of 70 students sees declines of 200 points or more, And, as a general rule, students with lower scores are more likely to see larger increases than students with higher scores."

SAT I: REASONING TEST
1994-95 TEST ADMINISTRATION & REGISTRATION DATES

Test Date	Regular Registration Postmark Date	Late Registration Postmark Date
October 8, 1994	September 9, 1994	September 10, 1994 to September 16, 1994
November 5, 1994	September 30, 1994	October 1, 1994 to October 12, 1994
December 3, 1994	October 28, 1994	October 29, 1994 to November 9, 1994
January 28, 1995	December 22, 1994	December 23, 1994 to January 4, 1995
April 1, 1995	February 24, 1995	February 25, 1995 to March 8, 1995
May 6, 1995	March 31, 1995	April 1, 1995 to April 12, 1995
June 3, 1995	April 28, 1995	April 29, 1995 to May 10, 1995

NOTES: 1. October testing takes place only in California, Florida, Georgia, Hawaii, Illinois, New Jersey, North Carolina, Pennsylvania, South Carolina, Texas, and Virginia.
2. No testing is offered in April outside the U. S. And Puerto Rico.
3. Registration Forms postmarked later than the Late Registration Dates will be returned.

If your Registration Form is postmarked later than the late registration date, it will be returned to you.

STANDBY TESTING

If you miss all the deadlines for registering, you may be able to take the test as a standby if the testing center has space and materials to accommodate you. You must take a completed Registration Form and a check or money order (no cash) for the appropriate test fee plus the additional standby fee to the testing center early the morning of the testing (by 8:00 A.M.). Ask the test administrator to accept you as a standby. This is an expensive way to go and may not work if the testing center is full. Call several nearby testing centers in advance to determine space availability.

A Question-and-Answer Service is available. You may review your own test and your own answers.

SUNDAY TESTING

Sunday testing is available only for students who cannot take the test on Saturday because of religious convictions. You must include with your Registration Form, a letter of explanation on your cleric's letterhead stationery and signed by your cleric. Sunday administrations take place after each Saturday test date. The Sunday test dates immediately follow each Saturday test date, except Saturday, June 3, 1995. The Sunday testing for June will take place on June 11, 1995. Testing on both Saturday and Sunday is not permitted, and scores from both days will not be reported.

QUESTION-AND-ANSWER SERVICE

A Question-and-Answer service is available for the SAT I: Reasoning Test. You can get a copy of the verbal and mathematics sections of the SAT I: Reasoning Test you took with a record of your answers, the correct answers, and scoring instructions. It will include information about the types of questions and the difficulty level of each question. This service is available for administrations of the SAT I on Saturday, November 5, 1994; Saturday, May 6, 1995; and Sunday, May 7, 1995. It takes eight weeks after your testing date to receive these materials.

Reviewing your own test and your answers can help you identify your strengths and weaknesses, determine areas needing extra study, and possibly improve your next set of scores. You may order this service when you register for the test or up to five months after the test date.

1994-95 SAT I FEES

TEST FEES

There is a two-part fee:

You pay a total of $21.00 in fees each time you take the SAT I.

$13.00 Basic Registration/Reporting Fee, *plus*

$8.00 SAT I: Reasoning Test Fee.

You pay a total of $21.00 in fees each time you take the SAT I. $17.00 of this total amount is a Nonrefundable Service Fee.

The test fees include Score Reports for as many as four colleges or scholarship programs when requested prior to the test date on the Registration Form or the Correction Form.

FEE WAIVER

If you cannot afford the test fee, ask your counselor or guidance administrator for a Fee Waiver Form. Enclose this form with your test application instead of a test fee. You may receive one fee waiver for the SAT I: Reasoning Test, and it may be used either during your junior or senior year. Students in other grades are not eligible for fee waivers. The waiver covers the fee for only one test date. Be sure to register by the regular deadline date since the waiver does not cover late registration fee, standby fee, or other service fees.

Number Of Dependents	Family Income
1	$20,210
2	$23,730
3	$26,770
4	$29,190
5	$30,830

Family income levels are based upon the Bureau of Labor Statistics low budget standard adjusted for inflation through December 1993.

Student eligibility for a fee waiver for 1994-95 is determined primarily by membership in a family whose annual income falls within the guidelines shown here.

Any of the following criteria can confirm eligibility for a fee waiver:

A fee waiver, good for one test date, is available if you qualify.

1. You are a member of a family receiving public assistance.
2. You are a resident in a federally-subsidized public housing project.
3. You are a resident of a foster home.
4. You are an enrollee in a program for the economically disadvantaged, such as Upward Bound.

NONREFUNDABLE SERVICE FEES

- $8.00 Reregister by telephone for each test date requested. (This fee is in addition to the test fee.)
- $15.00 Late registration fee. (This fee is in addition to the test fees.)
- $30.00 Standby fee. (This fee is in addition to the test fees.)
- $15.00 Test choice, test date, or test center change fee. You may make this change request by telephone.

You may reregister for the SAT I: Reasoning Test by phone.

- $6.50 Each Score Report to a college or scholarship program beyond the four included when you register or on the Correction Form).
- $20.00 Telephone Rush Reporting Service, plus $6.50 for each rush report. Use this service if you need your scores immediately sent to a college or scholarship to meet a deadline. The College Board sends your scores within two working days after your test has been scored — about three weeks after you take the test. If you are paying by credit card and are calling from a TouchTone phone within the U.S., Canada, the U.S. Virgin Islands, or Puerto Rico you may call this toll free number to rush scores (800) 728-7267. If you need to request additional services or speak to a customer service representative, call (609) 771-7600.
- $5.00 Per call for Additional Score Reports by telephone in addition to $6.50 for each report. If you order more than eight reports, you will have to place a second call.
- $10.00 SAT I Question-and-Answer Service.

HOW TO REGISTER FOR THE SAT I: REASONING TEST

The Student Descriptive Questionnaire is voluntary; you may answer all questions or skip some.

- Obtain the *1994-95 Registration Bulletin for the SAT Program* from your counselor, career center, or whoever is in charge of college information in your high school. The Registration Bulletin for the SAT Program contains an application, extensive information about registration procedures, a listing of test center locations and their code numbers, and a listing of college and scholarship code numbers. Decide upon your test date and test center location and mail in the Registration Form that includes the Student Descriptive Questionnaire by the deadlines shown on page 6--15. If you plan to take the test more than once, you must file a separate application for each test date.

- The Student Descriptive Questionnaire is voluntary; you may answer all questions or skip some. The questions ask for information regarding your educational background and plans. If you have already answered these questions on a prior test application — for the Achievement Tests, SAT II: Subject Tests, SAT, or SAT I: Reasoning Test — you do not have to answer these questions again. However, you can change those answers you wish updated. The information you give on most questions appears on your Score Report that is sent out to the colleges. The questionnaire indicates which answers are not included on these reports. Much of the information on the questionnaire is used for educational research.

- You make payment using check, money order, or credit card.

- If you are currently in high school and you have previously submitted a Registration Form for the SAT, SAT I: Reasoning Test, the Achievement Tests or the SAT II: Subject Tests, you may telephone to register for another date. You need not submit another Registration Form. In addition to the Basic Registration/Reporting Fee and the SAT I test fee, there is a fee for each date you request.

- Be sure to include your high school's code number — obtainable at your high school guidance office or career center — so that your scores come back to your school for inclusion in your official records.

You can request that the College Board send your scores to as many as four colleges and scholarship programs for the initial application fee.

- You have the opportunity to choose a first and a second choice testing center, ones that are convenient for you. The earlier you send in your Registration Form, the more likely you are to get your first choice. The College Board recommends sending it in at least six weeks before the test date.

- You can request that the College Board send your SAT I scores to as many as four colleges and scholarship programs for the Basic Registration/Reporting Fee. Additional colleges can be listed, but there is an extra fee for each. If you are not sure which colleges you wish to receive your scores, do not delay applying for the test. You have the opportunity when you receive your Admission Ticket/Correction Form to specify or change the colleges to receive your scores.

- You may add additional colleges or scholarships later, even after you have received your test scores. There is a fee for this service, but it allows you great flexibility; you can add schools and scholarship sources any time. Just send in the Additional Report Request Form — sent to you with your Admission Ticket — or request the form from your counselor or career center. You also can request additional reports by telephone. They will be mailed three to five weeks after you call.

- You receive an Admission Ticket/Correction Form at least one week before the test. If you do not receive it by this date, call the College Board at (609) 771-7600.

- To change your test choice, test date, test center, reregister, request additional Score Reports, or expedite scores, you may call (609) 771-7600 in Princeton, NJ or the TDD number for the deaf or hard of hearing (609) 882-4118. Services and information are available twenty-four hours a day, seven days a week, if you call from a TouchTone phone. To speak with a service representative, call between 8:30 A.M. and 9:30 P.M., New York time, Monday through Friday. When you call, have available your seven-digit registration number, the five-digit code of the test center you want, the four-digit number codes for your colleges and scholarship programs, and your credit card number and credit card expiration date.

- Check your ticket carefully for your identifying information, the test, the test date, the test center location, and the college and scholarship programs you indicated to receive your scores. If you find any errors send in the Correction Form immediately.

The best way to look at your score is as a range that extends from thirty or forty points below your score to thirty or forty points above

SAT I SCORING

The "old" SAT and SAT I: Reasoning Test test the same skills and developed abilities in similar ways and are scored on the same 200 to 800 scale. You receive two scores: A verbal score of 200 to 800 and a mathematics score of 200 to 800. No test can measure precisely what you know. If you had taken different editions of the test within a short time period your score would probably vary somewhat on the 200-800 scale. The best way to look at your score is as a range that extends from thirty or forty points below your score to thirty or forty points above it. For example, if your verbal score is 520, it might range from 490 to 550 if you took the test many times.

The College Board states that the "colleges and scholarship programs will use both the "old" and the "new" versions of the tests in the same ways when they make admission and placement decisions."

The College Board states that the "colleges and scholarship programs will use both the "old" and the "new" versions of the tests in the same ways when they make admission and placement decisions."

The following score data summarizes information for 1994 college-bound seniors who took the SAT/SAT I at any time during their high school years through March 1994. If a student took the test more than once, the most recent score is used. These average scores are based upon a total of 1,111,574 students nationwide and 135,862 California students.

1994 SAT SCORES

Test	Test Score Range	National Average Score	California Average Score
Verbal	200 - 800	423	413
Math	200 - 800	479	482

A score between 700 and 800 on the verbal or mathematics section indicates that the student was in the top one percent to two percent of those taking the test.

THE SAT I SCORE REPORT

Your Score Report reports your scores, your score range, your percentile scores, how your scores might change if you take the test again, how you did on each type of question, a summary of your scores, and characteristics of colleges to whom you sent a Score Report.

The Score Report indicates the percent of students with the same verbal or math scores who scored higher, lower, and the same on a second testing, as well as the average number of points gained or lost.

The Score Report indicates your percentile rank. The percentile rank allows you to compare your score with college-bound seniors who took the test. It shows the percent of students who scored lower than you did on the verbal or mathematics section.

To provide you with a good idea of how you might perform if you take the test again, the report indicates the percent of students with the same verbal or math scores who scored higher, lower, and the same on a second testing, as well as the average number of points gained or lost.

In addition to the verbal and mathematics scores, the SAT I Score Report identifies question types or content areas. The SAT I verbal score has three categories: Critical reading, analogies, and sentence completion. The SAT I mathematics score has two categories: Arithmetic/algebraic reasoning and geometric reasoning.

For each category, you are given the number of right, wrong, and omitted responses and a raw score. The number of questions in each category also is given. You are provided with comparative information regarding how your raw score compares to that of the average test-taker, and to those of test-takers with the same overall verbal and mathematics scores. This information will help you to understand your performance on the test in the context of all other test-takers, including those whose overall performance is equal or nearly equal to yours. Obtaining this specific information should help you to prepare for the next time you take the test by indicating areas of strength and weakness.

Your Score Report is mailed about five weeks after you take the test to you, your high school, and to the colleges and scholarship programs you requested. *Prior to October 1993*, the Score Report included *all your test scores* for your SAT and Achievement Tests, up to six scores for each. It was a summary of your SAT and Achievement Test score history.

UC and CSU use your highest total SAT I score (verbal plus mathematics) when reviewing admission eligibility.

Beginning with the 1993-94 testing program your Score Report reports all of your SAT (including the scores of those taken prior to October 1993) and SAT I scores, up to six, to the colleges, universities, and scholarship programs that you list on your Registration Form. However, you have the option to choose at the time of registration whether to release your SAT II: Subject Tests scores from that particular test administration to the colleges and scholarship programs. See this chapter: SAT II: Subject Tests, page 6--30.

If you have multiple scores, California State University and the University of California use your highest total score — SAT I verbal plus SAT I mathematics — from a single date. Private schools may also choose to do this. Alternatively, they may use your most recent score — nationally, eleven percent do — or your highest single verbal score and your highest single mathematics score — nationally, forty percent do. Some schools may average your scores. You may want to ask the private colleges to which you are applying about their policies to help you decide whether or not to retest.

RECENTERING THE SAT I SCORE SCALE

In April 1995, the SAT Program will recenter the SAT Program score scale. This change places all SAT scores on new, recentered scales. Over time, the average SAT I score has shifted away from 500. Recentering is a technical adjustment that moves the average score on the SAT I back to the center of the 200-800 scale (about 500). It will redistribute the scores evenly over the scale and reestablish the average score at the middle of the scale as it was in 1941 when the College Board originally developed it. Recentering will also affect the PSAT/NMSQT and SAT II: Subject Test scores because these tests are linked to the SAT I test.

Recentering is a technical adjustment that moves the average score on the SAT I back to the center of the 200-800 scale (about 500).

- The October 1994 PSAT/NMSQT is the first test placed on the new SAT scale. Most of the test takers are juniors who plan to graduate in 1996. Equivalence Tables will be available in December when you get your PSAT scores to compare "before" recentering scores with "after" recentering scores.
- The April 1, 1995 SAT I: Reasoning Test will be the first SAT I placed on the new scale. Most of the students who take this test will be juniors who plan to graduate in 1996. Equivalence Tables will be available in spring 1995 to compare "before" recentering scores with "after" recentering scores.
- The May 6, 1995 SAT II: Subject Tests will be the first SAT II to be converted to the new SAT scale. The scores of each Subject Test will be recentered and Equivalence Tables will be available in spring 1995 to compare "before" recentering scores with "after" recentering scores.

EFFECTS OF RECENTERING

- Scores will continue to range from 20-80 for the PSAT/NMSQT, and 200-800 for the SAT I: Reasoning Test and the SAT II: Subject Tests.
- With recentering, the SAT I verbal and math scores will be back in balance. On the current uncentered scale, identical verbal and mathematics scores do not indicate equal levels of skill. A student with 450 verbal and 450 mathematics scores currently may conclude that his or her verbal and mathematics skills are the same. However, the verbal score is above the current average (the national average for 1993-94 was 423) and the mathematics score is below the current average (the national average for 1993-94 was 479). On the recentered scale an original score of 450 on the verbal test will become 530, clearly above the average of about 500; an original score of 450 on the mathematics test will become 480, clearly below the average of about 500.
- Most students will receive scores that are higher than those they would have received prior to recentering. Because the average score is recentered to about 500 (higher than both the current verbal and mathematics average scores), nearly all students' scores will go up. If a student scored a verbal score of about 420 and a mathematics score of about 480 before recentering, the score would be about 500 for both verbal and mathematics when the test is recentered.
- Your percentile rank—your position in comparison to other students taking the test—*will remain the same* regardless of whether the current scale or the recentered scale is used. All students' scores remain stable relative to each other. A student who scored a 420 or 430 on the verbal section in 1993-94 (about the average verbal score for that year) would be at the 50th percentile. After recentering, that student's score would change to about 500 but would still be at the 50th percentile. *Even though the score changes, the percent of test takers who score higher and lower remains the same.*

Your percentile rank—your position in comparison to other students taking the test—will remain the same regardless of whether the current scale or the recentered scale is used.

- Recentering does not change the level of difficulty of the test.
- Until recentering, scores on the SAT I: Reasoning Test will be comparable to scores on the "old" SAT. After recentering occurs in April 1995, the scores will be comparable after scores from the old scale are translated to the new scale and vice versa. The College Board will provide Equivalence Tables in spring 1995 to compare test scores from tests taken before April 1, 1995 to scores from tests taken after recentering occurs.

The changes will not affect admission to college. Everyone's scores are readjusted. So even though the numerical value of a score increases, the value of the score as compared to others will remain the same.

- The changes will not affect admission to college. Everyone's scores are readjusted. So even though the numerical value of a score increases, the value of the score as compared to others will remain the same.
- The College Board will provide interpretive information to colleges, universities, and scholarship organizations to make comparisons of recentered scores and former scores easy to accomplish.

SAT I: REASONING TEST ADDITIONAL INFORMATION

- In scoring your SAT I: Reasoning Test, you lose a fraction of a point for each multiple-choice question you answer incorrectly. You neither gain nor lose credit for unanswered questions. Therefore, guess carefully on the multiple-choice questions. If you know that one or more answer choices for a question are definitely wrong, it is generally to your advantage to guess from the remaining choices. But with no knowledge of any of the choices, random guessing is unlikely to increase your score.

  In the SAT I mathematics section, ten questions require you to analyze and solve problems without the clues given by multiple-choice answers. The College Board believes that guessing will be next to impossible on these items. There is no penalty for wrong answers to these questions.

- When you pick up the *1994-95 Registration Bulletin for the SAT Program* at your school, be sure to get the booklet *Taking the SAT I: Reasoning Test.* The booklet contains important information about preparing for the tests, descriptions of each of the tests, and sample questions. An actual test that you can take and score is included. Reviewing this practice information gives you an idea of test content and format of the questions. The sample test has directions for scoring on either the old or the recentered scale.

The sample test has directions for scoring on either the old or the recentered scale.

- You need proper identification for admission to the testing center. This identification should have your picture on it or a written physical description of you by a school official, your name, and your signature. Your driver's license, a student body card, a passport, or a letter from your school will be acceptable.
- If you are a **disabled student** with a visual, hearing, physical, or learning disability, special arrangements can be made for administering the test to you. Your counselor or assistant principal must be able to verify your disability and can make special testing arrangements. These arrangements might include a special edition of the SAT I: Reasoning Test, an extended testing time, special aids such as a reader, and/or testing at your home school. See chapter 8: EDUCATIONAL OPPORTUNITIES, Admissions Testing For Disabled Students, page 8--6.
- The *Registration Bulletin* answers any questions you have about procedures (refunds, canceling scores, missing scores, telephone rush reporting, absence from the test ...) and should be reviewed carefully.

THE ACT ASSESSMENT

THE AMERICAN COLLEGE TESTING ASSESSMENT

PUBLISHER

American College Testing (ACT), an independent, nonprofit organization.

The ACT Assessment measures knowledge, understanding, and skills typically taught in high school.

National Office

ACT Test Administration
P.O. Box 168
Iowa City, Iowa 52243-0168
Registration: (319) 337-1270
Score Reports: (319) 337-1313
TDD (for hearing impaired): (319) 337-1524

Western Regional Office

ACT
10419 Old Placerville Road, Suite 262
Sacramento, CA 95827-2508
Phone: (916) 361-0656

Call between 8:30 A.M. and 4:30 P.M. Central time Monday through Friday.

WHAT IS THE ACT ASSESSMENT?

The ACT Assessment measures knowledge, understanding, and skills typically taught in high school that are important for successfully completing a college education. The scores are useful to college admissions officers in comparing applicants from different high schools with widely varying courses and grading standards.

ACT ASSESSMENT CONTENT

This test is a multiple-choice examination divided into four sections: English, mathematics, reading, and science reasoning. The total test takes about three hours plus an additional thirty minutes or so for directions and completing the personal information section of the answer sheet.

The ACT Assessment is a multiple-choice examination divided into four sections: English, mathematics, reading, and science reasoning.

The English section consists of...

A 75 question, forty-five minute test that measures your understanding of the conventions of standard written English, including 40 questions on punctuation, grammar and usage, and sentence structure; and 35 questions on rhetorical skills, including strategy, organization, and style. Spelling, vocabulary, and rote recall of rules of grammar are not tested.

The mathematics section consists of...

A 60 question, sixty minute test designed to assess the mathematical skills you have typically acquired in courses taken up to the beginning of grade twelve.

- Pre-algebra/elementary algebra: 24 questions.
  Pre-algebra: Operations with whole numbers, decimals, fractions, and integers; solutions of linear equations in one variable.
  Elementary algebra: Operations with algebraic expressions including the solution of quadratic equations by factoring.

You may not use a calculator on the mathematics section.

- Intermediate algebra/coordinate geometry: 18 questions.
  Intermediate algebra: Operations with integer exponents; radical expressions and rational expressions; the quadratic formula; linear inequalities in one variable; and systems of two linear equations in two variables.
  Coordinate geometry: Graphing on the coordinate line and in the coordinate plane; relationships between equations and graphs; and distance in a plane.

- Plane geometry/trigonometry: 18 questions.
  Plane geometry: Properties and relations of plane figures.
  Trigonometry: Right triangle trigonometry; graphs of the trigonometric functions; and basic trigonometric identities.

You may not use a calculator on the mathematics section.

The reading test consists of…

A 40 question, thirty-five minute test that measures your reading comprehension as a product of your skill in referring and reasoning. The test contains the following types of reading passages about which questions are asked.

- Social studies: 10 questions. History, political science, economics, anthropology, psychology, and sociology.

- Natural sciences: 10 questions. Biology, chemistry, physics, and physical sciences.

- Prose fiction: 10 questions. Intact short stories or excerpts from short stories or novels.

- Humanities: 10 questions. Art, music, philosophy, theater, architecture, and dance.

The science reasoning test consisting of…

The Science Reasoning Test presents scientific information in three different formats.

A 40 question, thirty-five minute test that measures the interpretation, analysis, evaluation, reasoning, and problem-solving skills required in the natural sciences. Test content is drawn from biology, chemistry, physics, and the physical sciences (e.g., geology, astronomy, and meteorology). The test presents scientific information in three different formats.

- Data representation: Graphic and tabular material similar to that in science journals and texts is presented. Test items measure skills such as graph reading, interpretation of scatter plots, and interpretation of information presented in tables.

- Research summaries: This format provides descriptions of one or more related experiments. Test items focus on the design of experiments and the interpretation of experimental results.

- Conflicting viewpoints: This format presents sets of hypotheses or views that, being based on differing premises or on incomplete data, are inconsistent with one another. Test items focus on the understanding, analysis, and comparison of alternative viewpoints or hypotheses.

WHEN YOU SHOULD TAKE THE ACT ASSESSMENT

If you intend to take the ACT Assessment, take it for the first time during the spring semester of your junior year. Some take it earlier for additional practice. You may want to retake it one or more times in your senior year. Take the ACT Assessment as many times as you wish; however, two to three times seems optimum. Beyond that, it becomes expensive and you probably will not see significant change in your subsequent scores.

If you intend to take the ACT Assessment, take it in the spring of your junior year. You may wish to retake it as a senior.

ACT ASSESSMENT
1994-95 TEST ADMINISTRATION & REGISTRATION DATES

Test Date	Regular Registration Postmark Deadline	Late Registration Postmark Deadline
October 22, 1994	September 23, 1994	October 7, 1994
December 10, 1994	November 10 1994	November 28, 1994
February 4, 1995	January 6, 1995	January 23, 1995
April 8, 1995	March 10, 1995	March 27, 1995
June 10, 1995	May 12, 1995	May 26, 1995

Due to the special requirements of legislation in effect in New York, a February 1995 test is not scheduled in that State.

STANDBY TESTING

ACT does not offer a walk-in or standby testing opportunity. If you miss the regular or late registration deadline, you must take the next available testing date.

NON-SATURDAY TESTING

If your religious beliefs prohibit Saturday testing, you may take the test on another day, typically Sunday. The testing dates and locations that offer this opportunity are detailed in the Registration Booklet in the section, ACT Test Centers, a listing of testing center locations by state.

ACT does not offer a walk-in or standby testing opportunity.

ACT ASSESSMENT INFORMATION RELEASE

For a fee you can get a copy of the test questions, the answer key, and scoring instructions. For an additional fee, you may obtain a copy of your actual answer sheet. This service is available only for administrations of the ACT Assessment on the following dates: Saturday, December 10, 1994; Thursday, April 6, 1995 through Monday, April 10, 1995; Saturday, June 10, 1995; and Saturday, October 22, 1994 only for students at a New York test center. The results are mailed to you ten to twelve weeks after the test date.

1994-95 ACT ASSESSMENT FEES

TEST FEES

$17.00 Basic Test Fee. Includes Score Reports for up to three college choices. Only $5.00 of this amount is refundable if you miss the test.

$2.00 Additional Test Fee. For testing in New York or Florida.

$5.50 Additional Score Report. Each additional college or scholarship listed on your application, not to exceed three beyond the three included in the Basic Test Fee.

If you cannot afford the ACT test fee, you may qualify for a fee waiver. Speak to your counselor or guidance administrator about requesting ACT to waive your application fee.

FEE WAIVER

If you cannot afford the ACT fee, speak to your counselor or guidance administrator about making a request to ACT to waive your application fee. Use the form provided by ACT; it must be signed by you and your counselor or administrator and mailed with your registration form. The waiver covers the cost of one test date and up to three college choices. You may use it *once* in either your junior or senior year. Be sure to register by the regular deadline; the waiver does not cover late registration fees or other service fees.

To qualify for a fee waiver during 1994-95, you must come from a family whose total family income is at or below the maximum amounts shown here.

Number In Family	1994 Total Income
1	$8,300
2	$13,600
3	$18,600
4	$23,000
5	$27,100
6	$31,700
Over 6	$31,700 plus $2,450 for each additional person in family.

Family income levels are based upon the Bureau of Labor Statistics Low Standard Budget for 1994.

You may also demonstrate your economic need by *any* of these means:

1. Your family receives public assistance.
2. You are a ward of the state.
3. You reside in a foster home.
4. You participate in the free- or reduced-price lunch program at your school.
5. You are currently enrolled in an Upward Bound project.

COLLEGE ENTRANCE TESTS

SERVICE FEES

$17.00 Late Registration Fee. A nonrefundable fee in addition to the Basic Test Fee of $17.00.

After testing, additional Score Reports may be sent to colleges by submitting the Additional Score Form.

$10.00 ACT Assessment Information Release. Copy of the test questions, your answers, the answer key, and scoring instructions. For an additional $5.00, you also may obtain a copy of your actual answer sheet.

After testing, the following additional Score Reports may be sent to colleges by submitting the Additional Score Form, in the booklet, *Using Your Assessment Results,* which you receive with your scores.

$6.50 Regular Report. A complete report. One test date per report. Processed within one week of receipt of your request. Delivered in the next processing cycle requested by the college or agency, but at least once a month.

$8.00 Priority Report. Includes only your identifying information and scores. One test date per report. Processed within one working day of your request and usually delivered in two to three business days. A complete report is sent later.

$10.00 Mailgram Report. Includes only your identifying information and scores. One test date per report. Processed within one working day of your request and delivered the next business day. A complete report is sent later.

Telephone Express Service. Call (319) 337-1313 instead of mailing the Additional Score Report Form. You must use Visa or Mastercard. $10.00 Service Fee, plus $8.00 for each Priority Report or $10.00 for each Mailgram Report. Use this service if you need your scores sent immediately to a college or scholarship to meet a deadline. You may order up to four Priority Reports or Mailgrams by telephone. Your scores are sent within two working days after your test has been scored.

If you plan to take the test more than once, you must file a separate application for each test date.

HOW TO REGISTER FOR THE ACT ASSESSMENT

- Obtain the *ACT Assessment Registration Packet* from your counselor, career center, or whoever is in charge of college information in your high school. This packet includes:

  1. *ACT Assessment National Registration Folder*, the computer form you must submit.
  2. *Registering For The ACT Assessment*, an information booklet, which contains extensive information about registration procedures, a listing of test centers and their code numbers, and a listing of college and scholarship code numbers.
  3. *Preparing for the ACT Assessment*, a booklet which contains important information about strategies for taking the test, descriptions of test content, and a practice test that you can take and score. Reviewing this information gives you an idea of test content and the format of its questions.

- Decide upon your test date and test center. Mail in the registration materials at least six weeks before the test date and by the deadlines shown on page 6--24. If you plan to take the test more than once, you must file a separate application for each test date.

- You make payment using check or money order.

- The application includes three sections of questions about you: Your course and grade information; an interest inventory; and a student profile requesting information about your background. Answering these questions is voluntary; you may answer all questions or skip some. The information you give on most questions appears on your Score Reports that the ACT sends to the colleges. The questionnaire indicates which answers are not included. If you retake the ACT Assessment, you must complete this section again since no information is transferred from a previous registration.

- Be sure to include your high school's code number, obtained at your high school guidance office or career center, so that your scores come back to your school for inclusion in your official records.

- You have the opportunity to choose a first and a second choice testing center, ones that are convenient for you. The earlier you send in your registration form, the more likely you are to get your first choice.

Obtain the ACT Assessment Registration Packet from your counselor, career center, or whoever is in charge of college information in your high school.

- You can request that ACT send your scores to as many as three colleges and scholarship programs for the initial application fee. Additional colleges, up to three, can be listed on your registration form, but there is an extra fee for each.

After testing, you may send scores to additional colleges. You must pay extra fees for this service.

- If you are not sure which colleges you wish to receive your scores, do not delay applying for the test. You may add additional colleges or scholarships later, even after you have received your test scores. Send in the Additional Score Report Form that is the last page of the student guide, *Using Your Assessment Results*, received with your scores. You also can get this form from your counselor or career center. Wait until you have taken the ACT Assessment before sending in a request. There is a fee for requesting additional results, but this service allows you great flexibility. You can add schools and scholarship sources to receive scores any time after four weeks from the testing date; do not feel locked in to your original choices.

- You receive a Test Center Admission Ticket within twelve working days before the scheduled test date if you registered by the regular registration deadline. If you registered after the regular deadline, but by the late deadline, you should receive your ticket by priority letter or mailgram by the Wednesday before the test date. If you do not receive your ticket by these dates, call ACT Registration at (319) 337-1270.

- Check your Test Center Admission Ticket carefully for your identifying information, the test, the test date, the test center location, and the college and scholarship programs you indicated to receive your scores. If you find any errors, call ACT immediately.

ACT ASSESSMENT SCORING

Copies of your Student Report are mailed about four weeks after you take the test to you, your high school, and to the colleges and scholarships you have requested. Some high schools may request ACT to send your copy to them for distribution to you. The Student Report shows only the results for the current test date; no prior test scores are included. Therefore, you control the release of your scores. You can request that previous scores be sent to the colleges in which you are now interested by sending in the Additional Score Form.

The Student Report shows only the results for the current test date; no prior test scores are included. Therefore, you control the release of your scores.

If you do submit multiple scores, the University of California and California State University use your best Composite Score. Private schools also may choose to do this. Alternatively, they may use your most recent Composite Score, an average of your Composite Scores, or your highest scores on particular parts of the test. You may wish to ask the independent colleges to which you are applying about their policies to help you decide whether or not to retest.

Scores range from 1 (low) to 36 (high) for each of the four sections — English, mathematics, reading, and science reasoning — and for the Composite Score. The Composite Score is an average of your four section scores, rounded to the nearest whole number. The seven sub-scores (two in English, three in mathematics, and two in reading) range from 1 (low) to 18 (high).

The average score information on the next page is a report of the performance of 1994 graduating seniors who took the ACT Assessment as juniors or seniors. The averages are based upon 891,714 students nationwide and 29,116 California students.

In addition to test scores, your Student Report gives you (a) comparison information of your Composite Score with the Composite Scores of students at the colleges you listed on your registration form, and (b) career information relating to answers on your Registration Form regarding your interests and plans.

ACT ASSESSMENT 1994 TEST SCORES

Test	Test Score Range	National Average	California Average
English	1 - 36	20.3	20.4
Usage/Mechanics	1 - 18	10.2	10.3
Rhetorical Skills	1 - 18	10.4	10.5
Mathematics	1 - 36	20.2	21.3
Pre-Algebra/Elementary Algebra	1 - 18	10.4	11.0
Algebra/Coordinate Geometry	1 - 18	10.1	10.8
Plane Geometry/Trigonometry	1 - 18	10.3	11.0
Reading	1 - 36	21.2	21.4
Social Studies/Sciences	1 - 18	10.5	10.4
Arts/Literature	1 - 18	11.2	11.3
Science Reasoning	1 - 36	20.9	20.9
Composite Score (Average of English, Mathematics, Reading, & Science Scores)	1 - 36	20.8	21.1

NOTE: The test scores in English, Mathematics, and Reading are not the sum of the sub-scores in those subject areas.

Scores range from 1 (low) to 36 (high) for each of the four sections — English, mathematics, reading, and science reasoning — and for the Composite Score.

COLLEGE ENTRANCE TESTS

ACT ASSESSMENT ADDITIONAL INFORMATION

- ACT does not penalize you for wrong answers when scoring your test. This may encourage you to guess on questions.

Act does not penalize you for wrong answers when scoring your test.

- You need proper identification for admission to the testing center. This identification should have your picture on it or a written physical description of you by a school official, your name, and your signature. Your driver's license, a student body card, a passport, or a letter from your school is acceptable.

- If you are a **disabled student** with a visual, hearing, physical, or learning disability, special arrangements can be made for administering the test to you. Your counselor or assistant principal must be able to verify your disability and can request special testing arrangements. These arrangements might include a special edition of the ACT Assessment, an extended testing time, and/or special physical arrangements. See chapter 8: EDUCATIONAL OPPORTUNITIES, Admissions Testing For Disabled Students, page 8--6.

- The booklet, *Registering for the ACT Assessment* can answer any questions you have about procedures (refunds, canceling scores, missing scores, absence from the test...) and should be reviewed carefully.

SAT II: Subject Tests

PUBLISHER

The College Entrance Examination Board (CEEB), a nonprofit organization, subcontracts the SAT II administration to Educational Testing Service (ETS)

The Achievement Tests have been expanded and are now called the SAT II: Subject Tests.

National Office
College Board ATP
P.O. Box 6200
Princeton, NJ 08541-6200
Phone: (609) 771-7600
TDD (for hearing impaired): (609) 882-4118

WHAT ARE THE SAT II: SUBJECT TESTS?

In March 1994, the College Entrance Examination Board introduced a revised testing program. The SAT has been revised and renamed the SAT I: Reasoning Test, and the Achievement Tests have been expanded and are now called the SAT II: Subject Tests. Together the SAT I and the SAT II are known as the Scholastic Assessment Tests (SAT). See this chapter: SAT I: Reasoning Tests, page 6--12.

The SAT II: Subject Tests measure a wide variety of skills and areas of knowledge essential to solid academic work in college. They measure your knowledge or skills in a particular subject and your ability to apply that knowledge. Not all colleges require them — those having more competitive admissions criteria often do. All campuses of the University of California require SAT II: Subject Tests. Some independent California colleges recommend that you submit your SAT II scores even though they are not required. They use them for placement purposes. You can find further information about the independent schools in chapter 12: CALIFORNIA INDEPENDENT COLLEGES, College Profiles, page 12--12 to 12--75. Contact colleges in which you are interested and/or review your admission applications carefully for testing requirements.

The SAT II: Subject Tests are offered in eighteen specific subjects in the following general areas: English, foreign languages, history and social studies, mathematics, and sciences.

SAT II CONTENT

The SAT II: Subject Tests are offered in eighteen specific subjects in the following general areas: English, foreign languages, history and social studies, mathematics, and sciences. Each takes one hour of testing time. You may take one, two, or three one-hour tests on each test date. If you take three of these one-hour tests on your testing date, the total testing takes three hours plus an additional forty minutes or so for directions and completing the personal information section on the answer sheet. All tests consist entirely of multiple-choice questions except the Writing Test, and the language tests with listening: Chinese, French, German, Japanese, and Spanish.

WRITING TEST

The SAT II: Writing Test was administered for the first time in May 1994. It replaced the English Composition Test. The Writing Test measures your ability to express ideas effectively in standard written English, to recognize faults in usage and structure, and to use language with sensitivity to meaning. The Writing Subject Test differs from the other Subject Tests in that it measures skills you have developed over many years.

The test includes (a) a twenty-minute essay in response to an assigned topic, and (b) forty minutes to answer 60 multiple-choice questions that require recognition of the conventions of standard written English, appropriate diction, and effective and logical expression. The multiple-choice questions include use of language, sentence correction, and revision in context.

The topic of the essay does not require specialized knowledge of any particular academic discipline but gives you an opportunity to use a broad range of knowledge and experiences in support of your discussion.

The topic of the essay does not require specialized knowledge of any particular academic discipline but gives you an opportunity to use a broad range of knowledge and experiences in support of your discussion. The essay is scored by two readers, experienced high school and college teachers who have reasonable expectations of the quality of writing done by students at the end of high school or the beginning of college. Your essay score is one-third of your total Writing Test Score. The essay is judged on its total impression and aspects of writing such as organization, choice of words, sentence structure, and punctuation. Appropriateness of examples, logical presentation, and development of ideas are also considered. The Writing Test must be taken during the first hour of testing.

Generally, colleges that require or recommend that you take the SAT II: Subject Tests specify that the Writing Test is one of them.

LITERATURE

The Literature Test contains approximately 60 multiple-choice questions based upon six to eight reading selections, about half of which are poetry and half prose. It is designed to measure how well you have learned to read literature. The questions on the test are based upon selections from works written in English from the Renaissance to the present.

FOREIGN LANGUAGES

The foreign language tests are appropriate if you have studied the language for three to four years in high school. If you are outstanding in a language, you may want to take the test after just two years of study. Through use of a variety of questions requiring a wide-ranging knowledge of the language, the tests measure your reading ability in three areas: precision of vocabulary, structure, and reading comprehension.

The Foreign Language Tests with Listening are administered only at participating high schools and not at test centers or on national test dates.

The College Board offers two types of one-hour French, German, and Spanish SAT II: Subject Tests. In addition to the multiple-choice reading test in each of these languages, a Foreign Language SAT II: Subject Test with Listening is also offered. There is a SAT II: Subject Test with Listening in Chinese and Japanese; however, no reading-only test is offered in these languages.

The Foreign Language Subject Tests with Listening consist of 85 to 90 multiple-choice listening and reading questions. There is a twenty-minute listening section and a forty-minute reading section. These tests measure your reading ability *and* your ability to understand the spoken language.

The Foreign Language Tests with Listening are administered in November only at participating high schools and not at test centers or on national test dates. A special registration form is required. You cannot register for them by phone or use the regular registration form in the 1994-95 Registration Bulletin for the SAT Program. Ask your counselor or guidance administrator for further information.

Chinese with Listening: 85 multiple-choice listening and reading questions.

French: 85 multiple-choice reading questions.

French with Listening: 85 to 90 multiple-choice listening and reading questions.

German: 80 to 85 multiple-choice reading questions.

German with Listening: 85 to 90 multiple-choice listening and reading questions.

Italian: 80 to 85 multiple-choice reading questions.

Japanese with Listening: 80 to 85 multiple-choice listening and reading questions.

Latin: 70 to 75 multiple-choice reading questions.

Modern Hebrew: 85 multiple-choice reading questions.

Spanish: 85 multiple-choice reading questions.

Spanish with Listening: 85 multiple-choice listening and reading questions.

HISTORY AND SOCIAL STUDIES

American History and Social Studies: 90 to 95 multiple-choice questions with an emphasis on American history from pre-Colombian times to the present. A lesser emphasis is placed upon basic social science concepts, methods, and generalizations. The questions cover political, economic, social, intellectual, and cultural history, and foreign policy.

World History: 95 multiple-choice questions measuring your understanding of the development of major world cultures and use of basic historical techniques. Approximately half the test questions deal with Europe; the remainder cover the Africa, Southwest Asia, South Asia, East Asia, and the Americas (excluding the United States).

In June 1995, a new version of Mathematics Level I (Mathematics IC) will require the use of a scientific or graphing calculator to solve some of its problems.

MATHEMATICS

Mathematics Level I: 50 multiple-choice questions that cover content typical of three years of college-preparatory mathematics: Two years of algebra and a year of geometry. The test contains questions in algebra; geometry (plane, coordinate, and solid); basic trigonometry; algebraic functions; elementary statistics, including counting problems, data interpretation, and measures of central tendency (mean, median, and mode); and other miscellaneous topics, including logic, elementary number theory and arithmetic and geometric sequences. You need not have studied every topic on the test. You *may not* use a calculator on any Mathematics Level I Subject Tests.

Mathematics Level IC: In June 1995, a new version of Mathematics Level I (Mathematics IC) will require the use of a scientific or graphing calculator to solve some of its problems. The preparation required and topics tested are the same as those for the Level I test. Only students who use a scientific or graphing calculator routinely in their mathematics classes should choose this test.

Mathematics Level I and Level IC will both be given during the 1995-96 academic year.

Mathematics Level IIC (Calculator): 50 multiple-choice questions, some of which require the use of a scientific calculator. It is intended for students who have taken college-preparatory mathematics for more than three years: Two years of algebra and a year of geometry, and elementary functions (precalculus) and/or trigonometry. The test contains questions in algebra; geometry (coordinate and solid), trigonometry; functions; statistics including probability, permutations, and combinations; and miscellaneous topics, including logic and proof; elementary number theory, sequences and limits. You need not have studied every topic. All Mathematics Level IIC Subject Tests *require the use of a scientific or graphing calculator.*

If you have had preparation in trigonometry and elementary functions and have attained grades of B or better in your mathematics courses, you should select the Level IIC test.

Open-ended or constructed-response questions in the Mathematics Level IC and IIC Subject Tests are under discussion by the College Board. These questions would require you to produce your own answers, not just select one from a set of multiple-choice alternatives.

Some tips on which mathematics test to take...

If you have had preparation in trigonometry and elementary functions and have attained grades of B or better in your mathematics courses, you should select the Level IIC test. If you are planning to major in mathematics, engineering, or a science requiring a strong foundation in mathematics, a score on the Level IIC test is more significant to the colleges to which you are applying. If you are really unsure of which test will give you a better score, you may take each level. You can take one or two on a single testing date or take a different one on each of two testing dates.

This table shows approximately how the questions in each test are distributed among the major curriculum areas. Although some questions may be appropriate for all three tests, the emphasis on the level IIC test is on more advanced content. Comparison of the percentages for the levels should help you decide which test you are better prepared to take.

MATHEMATICS SUBJECT TEST PERCENTAGE OF TEST BY TOPIC		
Test Topic	LEVEL I/IC	LEVEL IIC
Algebra	30%	18%
Geometry		
Plane Euclidean	20%	0%
Solid	6%	8%
Coordinate	12%	12%
Trigonometry	8%	20%
Functions	12%	24%
Statistics/Probability	6%	6%
Miscellaneous	6%	12%

Geometry: In Level I/IC a significant number of questions is devoted to plane geometry which is not tested directly on Level IIC. The geometry questions on Level IC cover topics such as coordinate geometry in two or three dimensions, transformations, and solid geometry.

Although some questions may be appropriate for all three tests, the emphasis on the Level IIC test is on more advanced content.

Trigonometry: Level I/IC questions are primarily limited to right triangle trigonometry and the fundamental relationships among the trigonometric ratios. The Level IIC test places more emphasis on the properties and graphs of the trigonometric functions, the inverse trigonometric functions, trigonometric equations and identities, and the laws of sines and cosines.

Functions: Level I/IC contains mainly algebraic functions, whereas the Level IIC test also contains more advanced functions, such as logarithmic and exponential functions.

Statistics: Level I/IC includes mean, median, mode, counting, and data interpretation. Level IIC also has questions on probability, permutations, and combinations.

SCIENCES

Biology: 95 multiple-choice questions based upon the assumption you have had a one-year course in general biology at a level suitable for college preparation. Topics covered include cellular and molecular biology; ecology; classical genetics; organismal biology; and evolution and diversity.

Chemistry: 85 multiple-choice questions based upon the assumption you have had a one-year introductory course in chemistry at a level suitable for college preparation. Topics covered include atomic and molecular structure, states of matter, reaction types, stoichiometry, equilibrium and reaction rates, thermodynamics, descriptive chemistry, laboratory. Every edition of the test includes approximately five questions on equation balancing and/or predicting products of chemical reactions. They are distributed among the various content categories.

The colleges that require or recommend SAT II scores generally expect you to test in three subjects.

Physics: 75 multiple-choice questions based on the assumption that you have completed a one-year introductory course in physics at a level suitable for college preparation. Topics covered include: mechanics; electricity and magnetism; waves; heat, kinetic theory, and thermodynamics; modern physics; and miscellaneous: measurement, mathematics skills, laboratory skills, history of physics, questions of a general nature that overlap several major topics.

WHEN YOU SHOULD TAKE THE SAT II: SUBJECT TESTS AND WHICH ONES YOU SHOULD TAKE

The colleges that require or recommend SAT II: Subject Tests scores generally expect you to test in three subjects. Your SAT II application registers you to take up to three subject tests on a particular date.

Most colleges that require SAT II scores expect you to take the SAT II: Writing Test and, most likely, one of the mathematics tests. Check carefully with the colleges in which you are interested to find out which SAT II: Subject Tests they require. If the school requires a particular subject test and you do not take it, you may seriously jeopardize your chances for admission.

Check carefully with the colleges in which you are interested to find out which SAT II: Subject Tests they require. The colleges will use your highest SAT II scores.

The colleges use your highest scores on the tests they require. If you take a particular test more than once, your strongest score is used as a factor in determining your qualifications for admission. You could take the SAT II: Subject Tests in several different subjects — for example, Writing, Mathematics Level I, and American History and Social Studies on one test date; and Writing, Mathematics Level IIC, and French on another test date. In this example, the college might consider your highest Writing score, your highest Mathematics score, and either your American History and Social Studies or French score. The latter selection depends upon which score is higher or which test better relates to your stated major. Whenever possible, the best strategy is to choose your third test in your strongest subject area.

The University of California requires SAT II: Subject Tests for admission: SAT II: Writing Test; Mathematics Level I or IIC; and a third one chosen by you. Take the examination in Writing, not Literature, to meet this requirement. If you take Writing more than once, your highest score will be considered. The same is true for your Mathematics Test. For the third test, any one, other than SAT II: Writing in which you scored your highest may be used. If you plan to be an engineering or science major, you may be expected to take your third examination in an appropriate science.

SAT II: SUBJECT TESTS 1994-95 ADMINISTRATION & REGISTRATION DATES		
Test Date	**Regular Registration Postmark Date**	**Late Registration Postmark Date**
November 5, 1994	September 30, 1994	October 1, 1994 to October 12, 1994
December 3, 1994	October 28, 1994	October 29, 1994 to November 9, 1994
January 28, 1995	December 22, 1994	December 23, 1994 to January 4,1995
May 6, 1995	March 31, 1995	April 1, 1995 to April 12, 1995
June 3, 1995	April 28, 1995	April 29, 1995 to May 10, 1995

Registration Forms postmarked later than the Late Registration Dates will be returned.

COLLEGE ENTRANCE TESTS

Not all SAT II: Subject Tests are given on each testing administration date. The following chart shows which subject tests are offered on each date.

SAT II: SUBJECT TESTS 1994-95 SUBJECT ADMINISTRATION SCHEDULE					
Test	**Nov 5, 1994**	**Dec 3, 1994**	**Jan 28, 1995**	**May 6, 1995**	**June 3, 1995**
Writing	✓	✓	✓	✓	✓
Literature	✓	✓	✓	✓	✓
American History and Social Studies	✓	✓	✓	✓	✓
World History		✓			✓
Mathematics Level I	✓	✓	✓	✓	✓
Mathematics Level IC					✓
Mathematics Level IIC	✓	✓	✓	✓	✓
Chinese with Listening	(See Note 1)				
French (reading only)		✓	✓	✓	✓
French with Listening	(See Note 1)				
German (reading only)		✓			✓
German with Listening	(See Note 1)				
Modern Hebrew					✓
Italian		✓			
Japanese with Listening	(See Note 1)				
Latin		✓			✓
Spanish (reading only)		✓	✓	✓	✓
Spanish with Listening	(See Note 1)				
Biology	✓	✓	✓	✓	✓
Chemistry	✓	✓	✓	✓	✓
Physics	✓	✓	✓	✓	✓

Note: 1. The Foreign Language Tests with Listening in Chinese, French, German, Japanese, and Spanish will be offered in November 1994 only at participating high schools. Contact your counselor or guidance administrator if you are interested in taking any of these tests.

Not all SAT II: Subject Tests are given on each testing administration date.

Take the SAT II: Subject Test when you finish the course and are most familiar with its content. This can occur at the end of the ninth, tenth, or eleventh grade.

A new policy, begun in 1993-94, allows you to hold your scores on the SAT II: Subject Tests you take until you have had a chance to review them. You may select the specific SAT II scores sent to the colleges and scholarship programs. This assures you that only your best test scores will be considered. All scores of Achievement Tests taken *prior to 1993-94*, up to six scores, are automatically sent to the colleges and scholarship programs. See this chapter: SAT II: Scoring, page 6--40.

You may take the SAT II: Subject Tests more than once, and you may take any particular SAT II: Subject Test more than once. Many students take them at the end of their junior year, and again, one or more times in the fall of their senior year. However, if you have (a) taken a year of biology, chemistry, or physics, or (b) finished your study of foreign language, or (c) had your United States history or world history by the end of your sophomore year, why not take the appropriate SAT II: Subject Tests at that time? The course material is fresh in your mind, and you have your best chance of scoring high on the test. A good rule of thumb to consider is take the SAT II: Subject Test when you finish the course and are most familiar with its content. This could occur at the end of ninth, tenth, or eleventh grade. Do not wait four to six months, or a year, to take it.

STANDBY TESTING

If you miss all the deadlines for registering, you may be able to take the test as a standby if the testing center has space and materials to accommodate you. You must take a completed Registration Form and a check or money order (no cash) for the appropriate test fee plus the additional standby fee to the testing center early the morning of the testing (before 8:00 A.M.). Ask the test administrator to accept you as a standby. This is an expensive way to go and may not work if the testing center is full. Call several nearby testing centers to determine which one is most likely to have space available.

SUNDAY TESTING

Sunday testing is available only for students who cannot take a test on Saturday because of religious convictions. You must include with your Registration Form, a letter of explanation on your cleric's letterhead stationery, signed by your cleric. Sunday administrations take place after each Saturday test date. The Sunday test dates immediately follow each Saturday test date, except Saturday, June 3, 1995. The Sunday testing for June will take place on June 11, 1995. Testing on both Saturday and Sunday is not permitted, and scores from both days will not be reported.

WRITING SAMPLE COPY SERVICE

You have the option of requesting copies of the timed essay you have written for the Writing Test.

You have the option of requesting copies of the timed essay you have written for Writing Test. The Writing Sample Copy Service will provide you with three copies of your essay with a seal showing that it is an official copy of your Writing Test essay. Your raw score for the essay will appear on the copy. You may submit these copies to colleges. An order form is included with your Score Report. There is a fee for this service.

QUESTION-AND-ANSWER SERVICE

The College Entrance Examination Board does not offer this service for the SAT II: Subject Tests.

1994-95 SAT II FEES

TEST FEES

There is a two-part fee:

1. $13.00 Basic Registration/Reporting Fee, plus

2. $4.00 for one SAT II: Subject Test, for a total of $17.00
   $8.00 for two SAT II: Subject Tests, for a total of $21.00
   $12.00 for three SAT II: Subject Tests, for a total of $25.00.

There is a two-part fee: a Basic Registration/ Reporting Fee and a fee for each test.

$17.00 of the total amount is a Nonrefundable Service Fee. The test fee includes Score Reports for as many as four colleges or scholarship programs when they are requested on the Registration Form or the Correction Form prior to the test date.

Additionally, if you take the Foreign Language SAT II: Subject Test with Listening, the fee is $12.00 and includes registration and reporting fees.

FEE WAIVER

If you cannot afford the test fee, ask your counselor for a Fee Waiver Form. Enclose this form with your test application instead of a test fee. You may receive only one fee waiver for the Subject Tests, and you may use it either during your junior or senior year. Students in other grades are not eligible for fee waivers. The waiver covers the fee for only one test date. Be sure to register by the regular deadline date as the waiver does not cover late registration fee, standby fee, or other service fees.

Student eligibility for a fee waiver for 1994-95 is primarily determined by membership in a family whose annual income falls within the guidelines shown here.

Number Of Dependents	Family Income
1	$20,210
2	$23,730
3	$26,770
4	$29,190
5	$30,830

Family income levels are based upon the Bureau of Labor Statistics low budget standard adjusted for inflation through December 1993.

The fee waiver does not cover late registration fee, standby fee, or other service fees.

Any of the following criteria can confirm eligibility for a fee waiver:

1. You are a member of a family receiving public assistance.
2. You are a resident in a federally-subsidized public housing project.
3. You are a resident of a foster home.
4. You are an enrollee in a program for the economically disadvantaged, such as Upward Bound.

NONREFUNDABLE SERVICE FEES

$8.00 Reregistration by telephone for each test date requested. (This fee is in addition to the test fee.)

$15.00 Late registration fee. (This fee is in addition to the test fee.)

$30.00 Standby fee. (This fee is in addition to the test fee.)

$15.00 Test choice, test date, or test center change fee. You may make this change request by telephone.

$6.50 Each Score Report to a college or scholarship program beyond the four included when you register or on the Correction Form.

$20.00 Telephone Rush Reporting Service, plus $6.00 for each rush report. Use this service if you need your scores immediately sent to a college or scholarship to meet a deadline. Your scores are sent within two working days after your test has been scored — about three weeks after you take the test.

You may take one, two, or three SAT II: Subject Tests on any given test date.

$5.00 Per call for Additional Score Reports by telephone in addition to $6.50 for each report. If you order more than eight reports, you will have to place a second call.

$10.00 Writing Sample Copy Service.

HOW TO REGISTER FOR THE SAT II: SUBJECT TESTS

- Obtain the *1994-95 Registration Bulletin for the SAT Program* from your counselor, career center, or whoever is in charge of college information in your high school. This bulletin includes extensive information about registration procedures, a listing of test center locations and their code numbers, and a listing of college and scholarship code numbers. Decide upon your test date and test center location and mail the Registration Form and Student Descriptive Questionnaire by the deadlines indicated on page 6--36. If you plan to take the test more than once, you must file a separate application for each test date.

- You may take one, two, or three SAT II: Subject Tests on any given test date. Your testing fee will vary accordingly.

- You must indicate on your Registration Form which SAT II: Subject Tests you plan to take. You can change your mind on the test day and select other tests offered on that day.

You must indicate on your Registration Form which SAT II: Subject Tests you plan to take.

- The Student Descriptive Questionnaire is voluntary: you may answer all questions or skip some. The questions ask for information regarding your educational background and plans. If you have already answered these questions on a previous test application (for the SAT, SAT I: Reasoning Test, other Achievement Tests, or SAT II: Subject Tests), you do not need to answer these questions again. However, you can change those answers you wish updated. The information you give on most questions appears on your Score Reports sent to the colleges. The questionnaire indicates which answers are not included on these reports. Much of the information on the questionnaire is used for educational research.

- You make payment using check, money order, Visa or Mastercard.

- If you are currently in high school and you have previously submitted a Registration Form for either the SAT or SAT I: Reasoning Test, the Achievement Tests, or SAT II: Subject Tests, you may telephone to register for another date. You need not submit another Registration Form. There is a fee for each date you request in addition to the test fee itself.

- Be sure to include your high school's code number, obtained at your high school guidance office or career center, so that your scores come back to your school for inclusion in your official records.

- You have the opportunity to select a first choice and a second choice testing center location, ones convenient for you. The earlier you send in your Registration Form the more likely you are to get your first choice. The College Board recommends submitting it at least six weeks before the test date.

- You can request that the College Board send your scores to as many as four colleges and scholarship programs for the Basic Registration/Reporting Fee. Additional colleges can be listed, but there is an extra fee for each one. If you wish to send your scores from that test date to colleges, but you are not sure of which ones, do not delay applying for the test. You have the opportunity when you receive your Admission Ticket/Correction Form to specify or change the colleges to receive your scores.

- **Score Choice** is a new option begun in 1993-94. It allows you to choose at the time of registration for your SAT II: Subject Tests to release your scores from that particular administration to colleges, universities, and scholarship programs. If you choose not to release your scores, you indicate your preference on your Registration Form. You do not list any colleges or scholarship programs to receive your scores. By using Score Choice, you have declined to send your scores to the four colleges or scholarship programs paid for in your Basic Registration/Reporting Fee. Although your test scores are not reported to colleges, universities, or scholarship programs, they are reported to you and your high school. They are kept on hold until you release them. All scores on hold are flagged with a "#" sign on your copy of the Score Report, indicating to you that the score has not been released.

Score Choice allows you to choose at the time of registration for your SAT II: Subject Tests whether to release your scores from that particular administration to colleges, universities, and scholarship programs.

After you have had an opportunity to review your test results, you may select the individual scores you want released. You may release *any or all* of your scores at any time up to one year after graduating from high school. There is no fee to take test scores out of hold. Your Registration Bulletin has An Authorization to Release SAT II: Subject Test Scores form. On it you indicate the specific test scores you wish released. You may either mail this form to the College Board or fax it to (609) 771-7681. You may not release scores by phone.

After you have had an opportunity to review your test results, you may select the scores you want released.

To have the released scores subsequently sent to the colleges, you have four options:

1. List the colleges to which you wish to release scores on the Authorization to Release SAT II: Subject Test Scores form. Three to five weeks after your scores are released from hold, a Score Report will be mailed to the institutions and programs you indicated. There is a fee of $6.50 for each Score Report you request. Make your request at least five weeks before the date you want colleges and scholarship programs to receive your Score Report.

2. Register for additional tests — SAT I: Reasoning Test or SAT II: Subject Tests. List the colleges to receive your scores on your Registration Form. Up to four colleges can be listed for the Basic Registration/Reporting Fee. Your released scores are reported along with any other scores you subsequently report to colleges or scholarship programs. This approach saves you the extra Score Report fee.

3. Call 609-771-7600 to have additional score reports sent.

4. Submit an Additional Report Request Form sent to you with your Admission Ticket, or request the form from your counselor or career center. You can request additional reports by telephone. Three to five weeks after your scores are released from hold, a Score Report will be mailed to the institutions and programs you indicated. There is a fee of $6.50 for each Score Report you request. Make your request at least five weeks before the date you want colleges and scholarship programs to receive your Score Report.

Once your scores are released from hold, they cannot be placed on hold again.

Once your scores are released from hold, they cannot be placed on hold again. They become an active part of your score record. From that time on, they appear whenever you request that test scores be reported to colleges or scholarship programs.

See the next page for a review of the advantages of utilizing the Score Choice option.

- If you do choose at the time of registration to release your scores and list the colleges to receive them on your Registration Form, you may add additional colleges or scholarships later, even after you have received your test scores. There is a fee for this service, but it allows you great flexibility; you can add schools and scholarship sources at any time. Do not feel locked in to your original choices. Just send in the Additional Report Request Form sent to you with your Admission Ticket, or request the form from your counselor or career center. You also can request additional reports by telephone. Make your request at least five weeks before the date you want colleges and scholarship programs to receive your report.

- You will receive an Admission Ticket/Correction Form at least one week before the test. If you do not receive it by this date, call the College Board at (609) 771-7600.

- To change your test choice, test date, test center, reregister, request additional Score Reports, or expedite scores, call Princeton, NJ. Services and information are available twenty-four hours a day, seven days a week, if you call from a TouchTone phone. To speak with a service representative, call between 8:30 A.M. and 9:30 P.M., New York time, Monday through Friday. When you call, have available your seven-digit registration number, the five-digit code of the test center you want, the four-digit number codes for your colleges and scholarship programs, and your credit card number and credit card expiration date.

You can change your mind about Score Choice between the time you register for the SAT II: Subject Tests and the test day by using the Correction Form.

- Check your ticket carefully for your identifying information, the test, the test date, the test center location, and the college and scholarship programs you indicated to receive your scores. If you find any errors send in the Correction Form immediately.

  You can change your mind about Score Choice between the time you register for the SAT II: Subject Tests and the test day by using the Correction Form. To reverse your decision to either hold or release your scores, mail in your Correction Form with your Score Choice indicated. There is no charge for changing your mind during this period. You may not place a hold on your scores after you have begun taking your SAT II: Subject Tests.

SAT II SCORING

The range of scores for each SAT II: Subject Test is 200 to 800. The data shown on the next page summarizes 1994 information for 201,744 college-bound seniors nationwide and 52,200 California seniors who took at least one Achievement Test/SAT II Subject Test any time during their high school years through March 1994.

If a student took the test more than once, the most recent score is used.

1994 ACHIEVEMENT/SAT II TEST SCORES		
Test	National Average Score	California Average Score
ALL ACHIEVEMENT/SAT II TESTS	548	515
English Composition	520	477
Literature	532	492
American History	526	496
World History	539	503
Math Level I	550	520
Math Level II	662	641
Math Level IIC	674	667
Chinese with Listening	(Note 1.)	(Note 1.)
French	549	533
French with Listening	516	542
German	566	545
German with Listening	519	517
Italian	577	622
Japanese with Listening	581	626
Modern Hebrew	632	628
Latin	556	546
Spanish	562	581
Spanish with Listening	539	588
Biology	555	518
Chemistry	582	547
Physics	604	570

Note 1. Scores for Chinese with Listening test, given in April 1994, are not reported and are not included in the all Achievement/SAT II Test Averages.

The range of scores for each SAT II: Subject Test is 200 to 800.

COLLEGE ENTRANCE TESTS

YOUR SAT II: SUBJECT TEST SCORE REPORT

After you receive your scores and have the opportunity to review them, you can release individual scores from SAT II: Subject Tests.

Your Score Report is mailed to you, your high school, and to the colleges and scholarships you requested about five weeks after you take the test. The Score Report reports all your test scores on the SAT/SAT I: Reasoning Test and Achievement Tests/ SAT II: Subject Tests, up to six scores for each. It is actually a summary of your SAT/SAT I and Achievement Tests/SAT II history.

Begun in the 1993-94 academic year the SAT II program offers you the opportunity to choose, at the time of registering for a particular test date, if you wish to submit your SAT II scores from *that test administration* to colleges, universities, and scholarship programs. The College Board calls this Score Choice.

After you receive your scores and have the opportunity to review them, you can release individual scores from SAT II: Subject Tests. To do this you must submit a request with your signature to the College Board. See this chapter: Registering for the SAT II: Subject Tests, page 6--39 for a description of the Score Choice option.

Utilizing the Score Choice option gives you greater control over the information that is forwarded to the colleges and scholarship programs. There are several advantages to you of holding your scores.

• You may take Subject Tests earlier in your high school years, free from the concern that your scores will jeopardize admission decisions.

• You may take Subject Tests in disciplines in which you are not as strong as you wish without the fear that your weaker score is automatically reported to the colleges.

Be sure to release your scores and arrange to have them sent early enough to meet college deadlines.

• You may select your highest score in a SAT II: Subject Test to submit to the colleges. For example, if you take the Writing Test three times, the college will see only the score, or scores, on this test that you choose for them to see.

• You may wait until the fall of your senior year, review all of your SAT II scores, and then select the specific ones you wish released to the colleges. Be sure to release your scores and arrange to have them sent early enough to meet college deadlines.

• Colleges not requiring or recommending SAT II: Subject Tests for admission will not receive your scores.

RECENTERING THE SAT II SCORE SCALE

In April 1995, the SAT Program will recenter the SAT Program score scale. This change places all SAT scores on new, recentered scales. Scores for all test dates on or after April 1, 1995 will be reported on the recentered scale. Over time, the average SAT I score has shifted away from 500. Recentering is a technical adjustment that moves the average score on the SAT I and each of the SAT II: Subject Tests back to the center of the 200-800 scale (about 500). It will redistribute the scores evenly over the scale and reestablish the average score at the middle of the scale as it was in 1941 when the College Board originally developed it. Recentering will also affect the PSAT/NMSQT. See this chapter, page 6--20 for further information on recentering SAT Program scores.

The scores of each Subject Test will be recentered and Equivalence Tables will be available in spring 1995 to compare "before" recentering scores with "after" recentering scores.

- The April 1, 1995 SAT I: Reasoning Test will be the first SAT I placed on the new scale. Most of the students who take this test will be juniors who plan to graduate in 1996.

- The May 6, 1995 SAT II: Subject Tests will be the first SAT II to be converted to the new SAT scale. The scores of each Subject Test will be recentered and Equivalence Tables will be available in spring 1995 to compare "before" recentering scores with "after" recentering scores.

SAT II: SUBJECT TESTS ADDITIONAL INFORMATION

- In scoring your SAT II: Subject Tests, you lose a fraction of a point for each question you answer incorrectly. You neither gain nor lose credit for unanswered questions. Therefore, guess carefully. If you know that one or more answer choices for a question are definitely wrong, then it is generally to your advantage to guess from the remaining choices. But with no knowledge of any of the choices, random guessing is unlikely to increase your score.

- When you pick up your *Registration Bulletin* at your school be sure to get the booklet *Taking the SAT II: Subject Tests*. It includes important information about preparing for the tests, descriptions of each of the tests, and sample questions. Reviewing the test content and question format can help you decide which tests to take.

- You need proper identification for admission to the testing center. This identification should have your picture on it or a written physical description of you by a school official, your name, and your signature. Your driver's license, a student body card, a passport, or a letter from your school is acceptable.

- If you are a **disabled student** with a visual, hearing, physical, or learning disability, special arrangements can be made for administering the test to you. Your counselor or assistant principal must be able to verify your disability and can make special testing arrangements for you. These arrangements might include a special edition of the SAT II, an extended testing time, and/or testing at your home school. See chapter 8: EDUCATIONAL OPPORTUNITIES, Admission Testing for Disabled Students, page 8--6.

- The Registration Bulletin can answer any questions you have about procedures (refunds, canceling scores, missing scores, telephone rush reporting, absence from the test ...) and should be reviewed carefully.

You need proper identification for admission to the testing center.

TOEFL

TEST OF ENGLISH AS A FOREIGN LANGUAGE

PUBLISHER

Educational Testing Service, a nonprofit organization affiliated with the College Entrance Examination Board.

National Office
TOEFL/TSE Services
P.O. Box 6151
Princeton, NJ 08541-6151
(609) 771-7760
Fax: (609) 771-7765
TDD (for hearing impaired): (609) 771-7150

The TOEFL is designed to measure if your English comprehension and usage are strong enough to handle the college curriculum.

WHAT IS THE TOEFL?

The TOEFL evaluates the English proficiency of those students whose native language is not English. The colleges to which you apply probably will require you to take the TOEFL if (a) you were born in a country in which English is not the official language, and you have been in the United States for a relatively short time, usually less than three years, or (b) you have not lived in the United States at all. Your score on this test demonstrates if your English comprehension and usage are strong enough to handle the college curriculum. Do not assume all colleges expect you to take this test. Contact the schools in which you are interested to find out if you are required to take it and, if so, by what date.

The TOEFL is not a substitute for the SAT I: Reasoning Test, ACT Assessment, or SAT II: Subject Tests. It does not measure your academic aptitude or subject matter competence. Colleges may require you to take the SAT I: Reasoning Test, the ACT Assessment, and/or the SAT II: Subject Tests *in addition* to the TOEFL.

TOEFL CONTENT

The Test of Written English (TWE) requires a short essay to demonstrate your ability to express yourself in written English.

The TOEFL consists of three separately-timed sections. The questions in each section are in multiple-choice format and designed to measure your ability to understand North American English. The total test time is approximately two-and-one-half hours plus an additional hour to distribute and collect materials and fill out identifying information on your answer sheet. If you take the Test of Written English (TWE) with the TOEFL, add thirty minutes to your testing time.

The three sections are...

- Listening Comprehension: Measures your ability to understand English as spoken in North America. A recording of sentences, short conversations, and longer talks and conversations in English is played for you. You must answer questions about what is spoken.

- Structure and Written Expression: Measures your ability to recognize language that is appropriate for standard written English. Written questions are used for this part of the test.

- Vocabulary and Reading Comprehension: Measures your comprehension of standard written English. Written questions are used for this part of the test.

THE TWE — THE TEST OF WRITTEN ENGLISH

If you take the TOEFL on the August, September, October, February, or May administration date, you also are required to write a short essay to demonstrate your ability to express yourself in written English. You are given the TWE to evaluate your ability to generate and organize ideas and to support those ideas with examples or evidence. You have thirty minutes to write about two-hundred to three-hundred words on one topic printed in your test booklet. You do not need special knowledge of the topic. This test must be taken on one of the combined TOEFL/TWE administrations. You cannot register for the TWE only.

WHEN YOU SHOULD TAKE THE TOEFL

You should be in at least the eleventh grade — a junior — to take the TOEFL.

You should be in at least the eleventh grade — a junior — to take the test. It may be taken more than once. You may want to take the test during the second semester of your junior year and again during the first semester of your senior year. Taking the test the first time familiarizes you with the types of questions asked and helps you understand areas of weakness you need to improve upon before retaking it.

Because this test is expensive, you may not be able to afford to take it more than once. Send for the *TOEFL Sample Test* or other study materials described in the *Bulletin of Information for the TOEFL, TWE and TSE.* These practice materials are not too costly. They can show you what to expect when you take the test and give you helpful practice on similar questions.

There are two testing programs, the Friday Testing Program and the Saturday Testing Program. The Friday tests are administered in the afternoon; the Saturday tests are administered in the morning. The format and length of the tests are the same for both programs.

These charts show testing schedules in the *United States.* If you are an international student living in another country, testing information and dates for Canada, Europe, Overseas, and Middle East/North Africa can be found in chapter 8: EDUCATIONAL OPPORTUNITIES, International Students, page 8--11.

TOEFL/TWE 1994-95 U.S. AND CANADA TEST ADMINISTRATION AND REGISTRATION DATES THE FRIDAY TESTING PROGRAM

TOEFL	TWE (Note 1)	Test Dates	Registration Deadline Dates (Note 2)	Approximate Score Report Mailing Dates
Yes(3)		July 8, 1994	June 6, 1994	August 10, 1994
Yes(3)	Yes	September 9, 1994	August 8, 1994	October 12, 1994
Yes		December 9, 1994	November 7, 1994	January 11, 1995
Yes		March 10, 1995	February 6, 1995	April 12, 1995
Yes		June 2, 1995	May 1, 1995	July 5, 1995

There is no late registration for the TOEFL. If you miss the deadline, you will have to test on the next test date or receive a refund.

COLLEGE ENTRANCE TESTS

TOEFL/TWE 1994-95 U.S. AND CANADA TEST ADMINISTRATION AND REGISTRATION DATES THE SATURDAY TESTING PROGRAM

TOEFL	TWE (Note 1)	Test Dates	Registration Deadline Dates (Note 2)	Approximate Score Report Mailing Dates
Yes(3)	Yes	August 6, 1994	July 5, 1994	September 7, 1994
Yes(3)	Yes	October 22, 1994	September 19, 1994	November 23, 1994
Yes		November 19, 1994	October 17, 1994	December 21, 1994
Yes		January 14, 1995	December 12, 1994	February 15, 1995
Yes	Yes	February 11, 1995	January 9, 1995	March 15, 1995
Yes		April 22, 1995	March 20, 1995	May 24, 1995
Yes(3)	Yes	May 13, 1995	April 10, 1995	June 14, 1995

Note 1. TWE is given with the TOEFL test at these administrations. Examinees are expected to write a TWE essay.

Note 2. If your Registration Form arrives after these deadline dates, it will be processed according to your instructions given on your Registration Form. You will be offered the options of the next Friday date, the next Saturday date, or a refund. There is no late registration permitted.

Note 3. Examinees who complete the TOEFL test given on these dates will be permitted to keep their test books.

1994-95 TOEFL FEES

TEST FEES

Your registration fee covers the cost of sending your TOEFL scores to three colleges. If you change your test date, or cancel your registration, you receive a credit of $10.00, which may be used toward another test registration. Cash refunds are not available.

Your registration fee covers the cost of sending your TOEFL scores to three colleges.

1994-95 TOEFL FEES	Friday Testing Program	Saturday Testing Program
Test Fee	$10.00	$10.00
Registration Processing Charge	$35.00	$28.00
Total Payment	$45.00	$38.00

To register, mail in the Registration Form. You cannot register by phone or at the test center on the day of the test.

SERVICE FEES

Additional Score Report Request:

Regular Service: Mailed two weeks after receipt of request or after scores become available. $11.00 per college.

Rush Service: Mailed four working days after receipt of request or after scores become available. $31.00 for the first college, $11.00 for each additional college.

COLLEGE ENTRANCE TESTS

HOW TO REGISTER FOR THE TOEFL

- Obtain the *1994-95 Bulletin of Information for the TOEFL, TWE, and TSE* from your counselor, career center, or whoever is in charge of college information in your high school. This bulletin includes extensive information about registration procedures, a listing of test centers and their code numbers, and a listing of college code numbers. Decide upon your test date and test center location and mail the Registration Form to arrive in time for the deadlines indicated on the opposite page. You cannot register by phone or at the test center on the day of the test. If you plan to take the test more than once, you must file a separate application for each test date.

NOTE: The TSE, Test of Spoken English, generally is taken by graduate students and research assistants and by individuals seeking licensing and certification in a professional or occupational field. As an applicant for undergraduate college admission, you are not required to take the TSE.

You can request that your TOEFL scores be sent to as many as three colleges by listing their code numbers on your answer sheet the day you take the test.

- You may choose a first choice and a second choice testing center, ones that are convenient for you. The earlier you send in your Registration Form, the more likely you are to get your first choice. Not all centers are open on all test dates. Check your bulletin carefully to make sure the center you want is open on the date you wish to test.

- You can request that TOEFL/TSE Services send your TOEFL scores to as many as three colleges or agencies by listing their college code numbers on your answer sheet on the day you take the test. List these code numbers on the back of your Admission Ticket before you go to the test so you have these numbers with you. Your initial application fee covers the cost of this service. Your test results are sent to you and the institutions you have requested about one month after you take the tests.

- If you need Score Reports sent to additional colleges, submit the Score Report Request Form in your *Bulletin of Information for the TOEFL, TWE, and TSE* with the appropriate fee for each one you request. You may add additional colleges up to two years after you have taken the tests. There is a fee for this service, but it allows you great flexibility. You need not feel locked in to your original choices.

- If you have not received your Admission Ticket five days before the test date, call TOEFL/TSE Services at (609) 771-7760 between 8:30 A.M. and 4:30 P.M. New York time (Monday-Friday), or, send a fax to (609) 771-7765.

- Check your ticket carefully for your identifying information, the test, the testing date, and the test center location. If you find any errors, follow the directions on the ticket, and give the corrections to the testing supervisor on the day of the test. Do not return the ticket; you need it at the test center.

- You receive a Photo File Record on the back of your Admission Ticket. Fill it out according to directions, and most importantly, attach a recent photograph of yourself (taken within the last six months) showing only your face and shoulders. You must give the testing supervisor this record with your picture, or your answer sheet will not be scored. You need additional official identification at the test center. Read your bulletin carefully to determine what documents you need to identify yourself.

You must give the testing supervisor the Photo File Record with your picture, or your answer sheet will not be scored.

TOEFL AND TWE SCORING

TOEFL

Your TOEFL scores are mailed to you about one month after you take the test.

The score range for each of the three sections — listening comprehension; structure and written expression; and vocabulary and reading comprehension — is 20 to 68. A score of 52 is about average. To obtain the total score for the TOEFL, add the scores of each section and multiply this total by ten thirds, ($^{10}/_{3}$). For example, if your scores for each of the three sections are 46, 54, and 50, your total score is (46 + 54 + 50) x ($^{10}/_{3}$) = 500. The total score range is 200 to 677. A score of 520 is about average.

In general, institutions consider a total score of 600 or above to be excellent and a score below 400 as inadequate. Most colleges are looking for a score between 500 and 600. However, an acceptable TOEFL score entirely depends upon the requirements of each institution. There is no specific passing or failing score. Contact the schools directly for information about how your scores will be used or interpreted and what scores, or range of scores, are acceptable. See chapter 10: CALIFORNIA STATE UNIVERSITY, TOEFL, page 10--8; chapter 11: UNIVERSITY OF CALIFORNIA, TOEFL, page 11--9; and chapter 12: CALIFORNIA INDEPENDENT COLLEGES, College Profiles, page 12--12 to 12--75 for minimum TOEFL score requirements.

An acceptable TOEFL score depends entirely upon the requirements of each college.

TWE

The TWE is reported on a scale of 1 to 6. A score of 4 is about average and indicates minimal competence in writing. The TWE score does not affect your total TOEFL test score.

TOEFL ADDITIONAL INFORMATION

- The TOEFL does not penalize you for wrong answers when scoring your test. This may encourage you to guess on questions.

- Your test application is contained in the *Bulletin of Information for the TOEFL, TWE, and TSE*. Read the bulletin carefully. It contains important information about preparing for the tests, descriptions of each of the tests, and sample questions. Practice tests for the TOEFL and the TWE are included. Reviewing this material gives you an idea of what you need to know and the format of the questions.

On the day of the test, bring your valid passport, which must contain your signature and a recognizable photograph.

- If, after you have completed your testing, you decide to apply to additional colleges, you may submit the appropriate fee as described on page 6--46 with the Additional Score Report Request Form located at the back of your *Bulletin of Information for the TOEFL, TWE and TSE*. For Regular Service, your Score Report is mailed to these colleges three weeks after receipt of your request. For Rush Service, it is mailed two working days after receipt of your request.

- On the day of the test, bring your valid passport, which must contain your signature and a recognizable photograph. Your *Bulletin of Information for the TOEFL, TWE, and TSE* describes exceptions to this requirement. Do not forget your Photo File Record.

- If you are a **disabled student** with a disability that you believe makes it impossible for you to test under standard conditions, ask the colleges to which you are applying to consider other ways of evaluating your English language proficiency. If you must take the test, special arrangements can be made for administering the test to you at the regular test center on a regular test date. Notify TOEFL/TSE Services in writing at least three months before the test date you prefer that you will need special arrangements. You will be sent a questionnaire to complete and return; the information you provide in the questionnaire will allow the TOEFL office to prepare appropriate special materials or aids and to contact your prospective center prior to the test date to arrange for the suitable accommodations. Your counselor or school administrator can help you with this request. See chapter 8: EDUCATIONAL OPPORTUNITIES, Disabled Students, page 8--6.

- The *Bulletin of Information for the TOEFL, TWE, and TSE* can answer any questions you have about procedures (refunds, canceling scores, missing scores, absence from the test ...) and should be reviewed carefully.

PLACEMENT TESTS

Placement tests should not affect your college admission status.

There are two categories of placement tests. In the first are those tests colleges use to determine the level of college course in which you will be successful. Your scores show if you are adequately prepared or if you need to enroll in skills development classes to prepare you for particular college level courses. Reading, writing, and mathematics skill levels are frequently assessed in these tests. The placement tests for California State University (the English Placement Test and the Entry-Level Mathematics Examination) and the University of California (Universitywide Subject A Examination) are of this type. The California Community Colleges and the independent colleges also administer their own selected placement tests to evaluate you for placement purposes.

The second category of placement tests is designed to measure your preparedness to enroll in more advanced college classes, those beyond typical freshman entry-level courses. High scores may allow you to waive taking specific courses, and possibly, receive college units in them to apply toward your degree requirements. The Advanced Placement Examinations fit this category.

THE UNIVERSITYWIDE SUBJECT A EXAMINATION

THE UNIVERSITY OF CALIFORNIA
INFORMS YOU OF
THE SUBJECT A EXAMINATION,
REGISTERS YOU FOR IT, AND
ASSIGNS YOU TO A TEST CENTER.

COORDINATOR

Educational Testing Service, a nonprofit organization affiliated with the College Entrance Examination Board.

Educational Testing Service
Subject A Administration
1707 64th Street
Emeryville, CA 94608
(510) 596-4385
TDD (for the hearing impaired): (510) 420-1737

For further information, contact the UC Subject A Office at any UC campus or University of California, Student Academic Services, (510)-987-9422.

WHAT IS THE UNIVERSITYWIDE SUBJECT A EXAMINATION?

After the University of California accepts you as an undergraduate, you must demonstrate proficiency in writing prior to enrolling. You must take the Universitywide Subject A Examination to meet this requirement, unless you have satisfied it by April 1st of your senior year of high school in any of the following ways:

You may be exempt from taking the Subject A Examination.

1. Score a 3 or higher on the College Board Advanced Placement Examination in English. See this chapter: The AP Program and Examinations, page 6--57.

2. Score 5 or higher on the International Baccalaureate Higher Level Examination (English A only).

3. Score 600 or higher on the College Board SAT II: Writing. See this chapter: The SAT II: Subject Tests, page 6--30.

4. Complete, with a grade of C or better, an acceptable college course in English Composition.

5. Complete an appropriate English course at the University of California.

If you must take the Subject A Examination, your score does not affect your admission to UC, but it does determine the entering level of English course for which you are qualified. See chapter 11: UNIVERSITY OF CALIFORNIA, Placement Tests, page 11--59.

SUBJECT A EXAMINATION CONTENT

Your Subject A Examination score does not affect your admission to the University of California.

You are presented with a prose passage of some seven-hundred to one-thousand words of a level of difficulty encountered in beginning University courses. After reading the passage, you will be given two hours to write an essay responding to a single topic based upon the passage's content. The topic is one of two general kinds: One focusing almost exclusively upon the reading passage itself; and the other encouraging you to draw upon your personal knowledge and experience. Both topics ask you to read thoughtfully and provide reasoned, concrete, and developed presentations of your points of view, not unsubstantiated statements of agreement or disagreement.

WHEN YOU SHOULD TAKE THE SUBJECT A EXAMINATION

The Universitywide Subject A Examination is given one day a year on the second Saturday in May. For California residents entering as Freshmen in the fall of 1995, the test will be administered on Saturday, May 13, 1995. It will be offered at test centers throughout the State.

If you are not from California, you may take the examination in the fall after you enroll at UC.

1994-95 SUBJECT A EXAMINATION FEES

A nonrefundable fee of $55.00 will be charged in May 1995 to cover the Subject A Examination administration. You make payment using check or money order. If you received a UC Admissions Application Fee Waiver, the University will automatically waive this test fee. See chapter 11: UNIVERSITY OF CALIFORNIA, Applying To The University Of California, page 11--49.

The Subject A Examination requires you to write an essay to demonstrate your proficiency in writing.

HOW TO REGISTER FOR THE SUBJECT A EXAMINATION

If you have been accepted for admission to UC for fall and have not met the Subject A requirement, you will receive detailed information from the University about the examination after April 1st. In addition, *An Information Booklet for the Universitywide Subject A Examination* will be sent to you in early April. This booklet contains previous Subject A passages and topics, the scoring guide, and student essays with comments explaining why they did or did not pass. Reviewing this booklet will help you prepare for the Subject A Examination.

UC mails these materials to every high school in California as well as to every admitted freshman. If you do not receive your material, contact the guidance administrator, counselor, or head of the English department in your high school.

SUBJECT A EXAMINATION SCORING

Each essay is scored independently by two readers on a scale of 1 to 6, 6 being the highest score. Essays whose scores by the two readers are more than two points apart are read a third time, as are those with reader scores of 3 and 4. The two scores are added together; those with a combined score of 8 or higher pass. Essays whose combined scores are 6 and below do not pass.

You will be notified in late June if you passed the Subject A Examination. You may not retake it. If you do not pass, you will need to take a preparatory writing course at UC and earn a grade of C or better. You must satisfy the Subject A Examination requirement as soon as possible in your freshman year. Remember, your score on the examination will have no effect upon your admission to UC.

47.4 percent of the 16,164 UC-admitted students taking the May 1994 Examination passed.

Some statistics ...

47.4 percent of the 16,164 UC-admitted students taking the May 1994 Examination passed. The number of admitted students who subsequently enroll in a UC campus and who satisfy the Subject A requirement by all methods — the examination or alternative methods described on page 6--49 — remains fairly stable from year to year, fluctuating between fifty-nine percent and sixty-two percent.

SUBJECT A EXAMINATION ADDITIONAL INFORMATION

- The deadline for waiving the Subject A Examination is April 1, 1995. The Advanced Placement Examination in English is given in May, too late to use it to waive taking the Subject A Examination. Of course, you could have your score on time if you took the Advanced Placement Examination in English a year earlier in your junior year. Your score on the International Baccalaureate Higher Level English A Examination also will arrive too late to meet the deadline for waiving the Subject A Examination.

  If you take and do not pass the Subject A Examination, you will pass the requirement when (a) your score of 3, 4, or 5 on your English Advanced Placement Examination taken in May of your senior year reaches your UC campus in July, or (b) your score of 5 on the International Baccalaureate Higher Level English A Examination arrives at your campus in the summer.

If you do not pass the Subject A Examination, you will need to take a preparatory writing course at UC and earn a grade of C or better.

- If you are a **disabled student** requiring extended time, special equipment, a large print test booklet, or assistance, you may take the regular May examination. Special accommodations will be made for you at the test site. You must submit a letter from your doctor certifying your disability and inform the Educational Testing Service in advance of your special needs.

- If the Saturday test date conflicts with your Sabbath observance, you should have an official of your Church or Synagogue write to the ETS and request a Sunday assignment for you.

THE EPT AND ELM TESTS

The EPT and ELM are designed to measure your college entry-level skills in English and mathematics. They do not affect your admission to California State University.

THE ENGLISH PLACEMENT TEST (EPT)
AND THE ENTRY LEVEL MATHEMATICS TEST (ELM)
AT CALIFORNIA STATE UNIVERSITY

CALIFORNIA STATE UNIVERSITY
INFORMS YOU OF
THE EPT AND ELM TESTS,
REGISTERS YOU FOR THEM, AND
ADMINISTERS THEM ON THEIR CAMPUSES.

For questions regarding the EPT/ELM Tests, contact your CSU campus or

CSU Office of Systemwide Testing
CSU Fresno
5241 N. Maple Avenue
Fresno, California 93740-0354
(209) 278-6951

WHAT ARE THE EPT AND ELM TESTS?

After your CSU campus admits you, it notifies you that you may be required to take diagnostic testing in basic reading, writing, and mathematics skills. These tests are called the English Placement Test (EPT) and the Entry Level Mathematics Test (ELM).

These tests do not affect your admission to CSU. They are used to determine the level of college English and mathematics courses for which you are prepared and for placement purposes. See chapter 10: CALIFORNIA STATE UNIVERSITY, Placement Tests, page 10--46.

If you are unable to demonstrate college entry-level skills in these knowledge areas, you may need to enroll in courses or programs early in your college career at your CSU campus to correct your deficiencies. These remedial courses and programs may not give you college credit toward your four-year college degree.

The EPT determines if you are prepared to undertake college-level work in reading and writing.

EPT AND ELM TEST CONTENT

EPT

The English Placement Test determines if you are prepared to undertake college-level work in reading and writing. It assesses your level of analytical reading and writing. The results of the test are used to place you in appropriate courses.

The English Placement Test requires one hour and forty-five minutes to administer. *It contains the following three sections:*

- Essay: Forty-five minutes, one assigned topic. This section indicates if you have the skills necessary to write in-class papers and examinations in college. The topic asks you to take and defend a position on some issue of general interest. You must draw upon your personal experience, observation, or reading.

- Reading Skills: Thirty minutes, 45 multiple-choice questions. This section indicates whether you are reading at a college-entry level or whether you should receive special instruction in reading. You must interpret ideas stated directly or indirectly in the text, determine the meaning of a word from the context in which it appears, and to identify the logical relationship between sentences.

The ELM is designed to determine if you have basic competency in first- and second-year algebra and geometry.

- Composing Skills: Thirty minutes, 45 multiple-choice questions. This section indicates your ability to select sentences that establish clear meaning, your knowledge of sentence structure according to the conventions of standard written English at the college-entry level, and your ability to recognize statements that support or help develop other expressed ideas. It examines your ability to revise and edit material accessible to and appropriate for college-bound students.

Because the test measures reading and writing skills developed through steady practice over a period of years, CSU recommends no special preparation for the EPT.

ELM

The ELM Test consists of sixty-five multiple-choice questions. Of these, sixty are counted in your score, and five are used only for field testing of future tests. The test is designed to determine if you possess basic competency in first and second year algebra and in geometry. Such skills generally are acquired in three years of rigorous college-preparatory mathematics courses in high school.

The ELM is a seventy-five minute test and may contain the following topics:

- Algebra: 48 questions.
  Elementary operations.
  Operations with polynomials (one or more variables).
  Operations with rational expressions (one or more variables).
  Operations with powers and roots.
  Solution of equations.
  Solution of inequalities.
  Graphing.
  Functions of one variable.

You may not use a calculator during the ELM Test.

- Geometry: 12 questions.
  Perimeter and area of squares, rectangles, parallelograms, and triangles.
  Properties of circles: radius, diameter, circumference, and area.
  Volume of rectangular solids, cylinders, and spheres.
  Properties of triangles: sum of interior angles, isosceles, equilateral, similar and congruent triangles.
  The Pythagorean theorem and its applications including distance formula, 45-45-90 degree, and 30-60-90 degree triangles.
  Parallelism.
  Perpendicularity.

Not all versions of the ELM will contain questions on all these topics.

You may *not* use a calculator during the examination. You may want to review the covered topics before taking the test. Use good high school second-year algebra and geometry texts.

WHEN YOU SHOULD TAKE THE EPT AND ELM TESTS

The EPT and ELM should be taken as soon as possible after CSU notifies you that you are admitted.

COLLEGE ENTRANCE TESTS

EPT AND ELM TEST DATES

Test Administration	Registration Deadline
October 15, 1994	September 30, 1994
November 5, 1994 through January 28, 1995	Variable by campus
May 6, 1995	April 21, 1995
July 8, 1995	June 23, 1995
October 14, 1995	September 29, 1995

Registration should be received by the indicated Registration Deadline.

The EPT and ELM Tests should be taken as soon as possible after CSU informs you that you are admitted and before you enroll. You cannot take either test until CSU officially accepts you for admission.

CSU offers the tests four times a year throughout the system. The tests are administered on the CSU campuses. The dates in October, May, and July are the same for every campus. Each CSU campus selects a fourth date, sometime in November through January. For this date, some campuses will offer only the ELM; others will offer both the EPT and the ELM. The ELM may be taken only once during the November to January period. The tests may be given at other times on some campuses to accommodate large numbers of students. The Testing Office of any CSU campus can provide information about testing dates.

1994-95 EPT AND ELM TEST FEES

There is no charge for the EPT. The fee for the ELM Test is $16.00. You pay for the ELM when you report for the test. You make payment using check or money order.

HOW TO REGISTER FOR THE EPT AND ELM TESTS

You may register for both the EPT and the ELM at one administration, for only the EPT, or for only the ELM test.

After you are admitted, CSU sends you an *Information Bulletin for the California State University EPT and ELM Test* and a Registration Form. The bulletin includes test dates, registration procedures, an overview of what is covered, and some sample questions.

You may register for both the EPT and the ELM at one administration, for only the EPT, or for only the ELM test. You do not have to take the tests at the CSU campus you will attend; every campus is a test center and forwards your scores to your chosen campus.

EPT AND ELM TESTS SCORING

CSU sends Score Reports to you and to the CSU campus you will attend. Your high school receives summary test information, but not individual student scores. In 1994, twenty to twenty-five percent of incoming freshmen were exempt from taking one or both tests. 23,000 to 24,000 incoming freshmen took the EPT. Sixty percent met the English proficiency requirement through exemption or by passing the English Placement Test. 34,000 to 35,000 incoming freshmen took the ELM. Sixty-five percent met the mathematics proficiency requirement through exemption or by passing the Entry Level Mathematics Test.

EPT

You receive a reading skills score, a composing skills score, an essay score, and a total score. CSU uses these scores to determine if you have the skills in English to perform successfully in college classes. Reading and/or writing skills improvement classes may be indicated. The total score shows how well you did on all sections of the test. The score range is 120 to 180. A score of 151 or above indicates that you are ready for a college English class that qualifies for credit toward your Bachelor's degree. Individual campuses may designate a slightly lower score based on school policy. A low total score indicates that you should enroll in a class or laboratory designed to improve your English skills.

A low total score on the EPT indicates that you should enroll in a class or laboratory designed to improve your English skills.

ELM

CSU reports scores on a scale of 100 to 700. The passing score is slightly higher than 550, corresponding to approximately thirty-nine correct answers to the sixty scored questions. Two sub-scores are reported: One for the algebra section and one for the geometry section.

The CSU campuses have individual policies regarding the use of your ELM Test scores. If you pass the ELM, you are eligible to enroll in a mathematics course that satisfies the General Education/Breadth Requirement in mathematics. This course is more advanced than intermediate algebra. If you do not pass the ELM test, your CSU campus may (a) refer you to appropriate coursework, (b) refer you to self-study, tutorial, or learning assistance, (c) permit you to retake the test, and/or (d) require you to retake the test. Coursework may be noncredit remedial classes to prepare you either to pass the ELM test or to enroll in the GE/Breadth Requirement in quantitative reasoning. Campuses have the option of requiring you to pass the ELM before enrolling in a mathematics course that gives credit toward a Bachelor's degree.

EPT AND ELM TEST EXEMPTIONS

You may be exempt from taking either or both examinations.

EPT EXEMPTIONS

You are required to complete the EPT unless you have taken one of the approved exemptions and scored at or above the indicated minimum levels.

If you pass the ELM, you are eligible to enroll in a mathematics course satisfying the CSU General Education/ Breadth Requirement in mathematics.

APPROVED EPT EXEMPTIONS

Test	Minimum Score
College Board AP Examination: Language & Composition, or Literature & Composition	3 or above
College Board SAT I: Verbal	470
College Board SAT II: Writing	600
ACT: English	25
Completion of an acceptable college-level English Composition course of 3 semester or 4 quarter units	Grade of C or better

In the Spring of 1995, CSU will publish new exemption score requirements for the SAT I: Verbal and SAT II: Writing examinations taken after March 1995.

Take heart! Based upon these criteria, about thirty percent of regularly admitted students are exempt from taking the EPT. About seventy percent of admitted students must take it.

ELM TEST EXEMPTIONS

You are required to complete the ELM Test unless you have taken one of the approved exemptions listed here and scored at or above the indicated minimum levels.

If you are exempt from one or both tests, be certain to provide your CSU campus with official transcripts or test scores to establish the basis for your exemption.

APPROVED ELM TEST EXEMPTIONS	
Test	Minimum Score
College Board AP Examination: Calculus (AB or BC)	3 or above
College Board SAT I: Mathematics	560
College Board SAT II: Mathematics Level I or IIC	560
ACT: Mathematics	25
Completion of an acceptable college-level mathematics course that satisfies the CSU General Education/Breadth Requirement in quantitative reasoning. To receive the Exemption, the course taken must be above the level of intermediate algebra with a grade of C or better.	Grade of C

In the Spring of 1995, CSU will publish new exemption score requirements for the SAT I: Mathematics and SAT II: Mathematics Level I, IC, or IIC examinations taken after March 1995.

If you are exempt from one or both tests, be certain to provide your CSU campus with official transcripts or test scores to establish the basis for your exemption. Your Advanced Placement Test scores are unavailable to you as EPT and ELM Test exemptions because the College Entrance Examination Board sends your Score Report to the college in July.

EPT AND ELM ADDITIONAL INFORMATION

The EPT should be taken only once and may not be repeated.

- The EPT should be taken only once and may not be repeated.
- Early registration is recommended. If a CSU test center is filled, you may be unable to take the EPT and/or the ELM Test until the next scheduled test administration.
- Walk-in registration is available on a first-come, first-served basis.
- You will receive an admission ticket one to two weeks prior to the test(s). If you do not receive your admission ticket before the test date, contact the CSU campus where you plan to take the test.
- You will need proper identification for admission to the test center. Your identification must bear your photograph and your signature. A driver's license, a student body card, or any other official identification is acceptable.
- The ELM Workbook is available for sale at all CSU bookstores. This workbook contains test items in elementary algebra, geometry, and intermediate algebra of the type appearing in the ELM Test.

• If religious convictions prevent you from taking either test on the scheduled test date, you must request special arrangements by including with your registration forms a letter from an appropriate religious authority.

• If you are a **disabled student** requiring special test arrangements for taking the test(s), contact the Testing Center or the Disabled Students Coordinator of the CSU campus where you will be taking the test by the published deadline for all students.

The ELM Workbook is available at all CSU bookstores. This workbook contains test items of the type appearing in the ELM Test.

THE AP PROGRAM AND EXAMINATIONS

THE ADVANCED PLACEMENT PROGRAM AND EXAMINATIONS

PUBLISHER

The College Entrance Examination Board (CEEB), a nonprofit organization.

National Office

Advanced Placement Program
P.O. Box 6671
Princeton, NJ 08541-6671
(609) 771-7300
TDD (for hearing impaired) (609) 771-7150

WHAT ARE THE AP PROGRAM AND EXAMINATIONS?

The AP Program and Examinations are your opportunity to take college-level courses and examinations while you are still in high school. You can receive Advanced Placement and/or college credit when you enter college.

If you score high enough on an AP Examination, the college you plan to attend may give you credit toward their related college-level course.

Your high school may be one of fifty percent of the nation's 21,000 secondary schools that offer college-level AP courses. Ask your counselor or assistant principal which courses meet this definition in your school. They may not be called AP courses in your high school; they may be honors classes, intensive regular courses, tutorials, or independent study.

In 1993, students sent their AP grades to more than twenty-eight hundred United States colleges and universities. Having completed your AP preparation and taken the AP Examination, if your score is high enough, the college you plan to attend may give you credit toward their related college level course. Nearly all colleges and universities in the United States grant credit or placement on the basis of AP Examination performance. Some colleges may not give you credit, but recognize that you have mastered the subject matter. In either case, you may be able to enroll in a higher level course, or skip the subject altogether and enroll in some other class of interest to you. If you are fluent in a language other than English, you may take advantage of this opportunity to gain AP credit.

CALIFORNIA COLLEGES OFFERING 1994 SOPHOMORE STANDING

Academy of Art College
Allan Hancock College
Antelope Valley College
Antelope Valley College
Antelope Valley College
California Lutheran University
California State Polytechnic University, Pomona
California State University: Bakersfield, Chico, Dominguez Hills, Fresno, Fullerton, Hayward, Long Beach, Los Angeles, Northridge, Sacramento, San Bernardino, Stanislaus
Cañada College
Chapman College
Citrus College
City College of San Francisco
Claremont McKenna College
Coastline Community College
College of the Canyons
College of Notre Dame
College of San Mateo
Concordia University
Diablo Valley College
Fresno City College
Fresno Pacific College
Fullerton College
Golden Gate University
Golden West College
Harvey Mudd College
Holy Names College
Humboldt State University
Lassen College
LIFE Bible College
Los Angeles Pierce College
Loyola Marymount University
Menlo College
Mills College
Mount St. Mary's College
New College of California
Occidental College
Orange Coast College
Otis College of Art and Design
Pacific Christian College
Pepperdine University
Pitzer College
Point Loma Nazarene College
San Bernardino Valley College
San Diego City College
San Diego State University
San Franciso State University
San Jose State University
Santa Clara University
Santa Monica College
Santa Rosa Junior College
Simpson College
Sonoma State University
Southern California College
Southern California Institute of Architecture
St. Mary's College of California
United States International University
University of California: Berkeley, Davis, Irvine, Los Angeles, San Diego, Santa Barbara, Santa Cruz
University of San Diego
University of San Francisco
University of Southern California
University of the Pacific
West Coast University
Whittier College
Woodbury University

COLLEGE ENTRANCE TESTS

If you earn the required grade on an AP Examination, you may receive the equivalent of credit for a one-year course, costing as much as $2,500 at a private college. Nationally, more than thirteen-hundred institutions consider three or more AP Examinations with acceptable grades as evidence that you have done work comparable to a year's academic program at college. If your college grants you a full year of college credit, the savings can be more than $18,000, the equivalent of a year's tuition, room, and board.

Contact the college you plan to attend for specific information about their AP credit procedures.

Some colleges in California award advanced standing to entering students who pass three or more Advanced Placement Examinations. The California colleges listed here have reported to the College Entrance Examination Board that they stand ready to grant a year's credit based upon Advanced Placement Examination performance. Many colleges consider your entire academic record as well as your AP Examination scores as criteria for granting advanced standing credit. Also, some institutions specify certain courses or other requirements as prerequisites for sophomore standing. The college catalogue usually has detailed information regarding policies. Call the college directly to clarify procedures.

A word of caution: If you attend a community college that gives you a year's academic credit based upon your Advanced Placement Examination scores, determine if the four-year college you may wish to attend later will also grant this credit to you.

Contact the college you plan to attend for specific information on their policies regarding giving credit for Advanced Placement Examination scores.

AP EXAMINATIONS CONTENT

The College Entrance Examination Board offers Advanced Placement Examinations in sixteen disciplines:

ADVANCED PLACEMENT EXAMINATIONS

ART	FRENCH	MATHEMATICS
History of Art	Language	Calculus AB
Studio Art	Literature	Calculus BC
Drawing	GERMAN	MUSIC THEORY
General Portfolio	Language	PHYSICS
BIOLOGY	GOVERNMENT & POLITICS	Physics B
CHEMISTRY	Comparative	Physics C
COMPUTER SCIENCE	United States	Mechanics
Computer Science A	HISTORY	Electricity & Magnetism
Computer Science AB	European	PSYCHOLOGY
ECONOMICS	United States	SPANISH
Macroeconomics	LATIN	Language
Microeconomics	Vergil	Literature
ENGLISH	Literature	
Language & Composition		
Literature &Composition		

The College Entrance Examination Board offers Advanced Placement Examinations in sixteen disciplines:

AP Examinations (except Studio Art) contain both multiple-choice and free-response questions. Free-response questions require essay writing, problem solving, and other skills. In Studio Art, you must submit portfolios of your work instead of taking an examination. History of Art contains questions based upon projected color slides. The foreign language examinations and Music Theory use tape recordings for certain portions.

The Calculus AB and Calculus BC Examinations contain some questions for which a scientific calculator (nongraphing, nonprogrammable) is necessary. You are expected to bring a scientific calculator to the examination.

A scientific, nonprogrammable calculator is allowed on the chemistry and physics examinations. A table of logarithms is not provided in the chemistry examination booklet. The College Board advises you to bring a scientific calculator to these examinations.

Most examinations are three hours long, but those for semester courses take only one-and-one-half or two hours. You can take as many AP Examinations in any one year as you wish. However, there are some limitations as described in the Advanced Placement Examination Bulletin For Students.

AP Examinations (except Studio Art) contain both multiple-choice and free-response questions. Free-response questions require essay writing, problem solving, and other skills.

WHEN YOU SHOULD TAKE THE AP EXAMINATIONS

You may take the AP Examinations after completing the Advanced Placement course material, typically in your junior or senior year, sometimes earlier.

All AP Examinations are given during the second and third weeks of May during morning or afternoon sessions. In 1995, they take place on the following dates: May 8th through May 12th, May 15th through May 19th.

1994-95 AP EXAMINATIONS FEES

The fee for each AP Examination in May 1995 is $72.00. In any one year, you may take both of the Economics, Government and Politics, Latin, or Physics C Examinations for a single $72.00 fee. Do not send the fee to the College Entrance Examination Board; your high school collects it. Your school receives $6.00 of the fee for administering the examination.

If you have financial need, fee reductions of about $17.00 are available and your high school forgoes the $6.00 fee it normally receives. See your AP Coordinator early in the year so he or she can submit your request for a fee reduction with your examination order.

HOW TO REGISTER FOR THE AP EXAMINATIONS

Scores on the AP Examinations are called grades and are reported on a five-point scale.

Your high school sets up a registration procedure for you at your school to take the examinations. Usually, a staff member at each high school, who is the AP Coordinator, makes all arrangements for registering students, collecting fees, and administering the examinations. Your AP course teachers inform you of the procedures to follow.

AP EXAMINATION SCORING

Scores on the Advanced Placement Examinations are called "grades" and are reported on a five-point scale.

The multiple-choice questions are sufficiently challenging that, on a typical examination, you need to answer about fifty percent of the questions correctly to earn a multiple-choice score comparable to a total grade of 3.

ADVANCED PLACEMENT EXAMINATION GRADE	
Extremely Well Qualified	5
Well Qualified	4
Qualified	3
Possibly Qualified	2
No Recommendation	1

Overall, two thirds of those taking AP Examinations receive an AP grade of 3 or higher. Most colleges consider this score an indicator of successful work.

According to the California Department of Education, the number of California high school students passing AP Examinations for college level courses more than doubled between 1984 and 1990.

You decide if your AP Examination scores should be sent to your colleges.

AP Grade Reports, including grades on previous AP Examinations, are sent in July to your home address, your high school, and, if you requested it, to your selected colleges. You can have your AP Examination grades sent to colleges by designating them on the identification portion of your Master Identification/Answer Sheet, or on your College Information Card that you complete at the AP Examination session. You also can request that your high school send to the college you will be attending an additional transcript containing your AP Examination grades.

For most colleges, you may request that one or more of your grades not be included in the report sent to a college. Make this request by June 15th. The University of California requires that the College Entrance Examination Board reports all AP Test results to them. Thus, you do not have the option of choosing which test scores you wish reported to UC.

ADDITIONAL AP EXAMINATION INFORMATION

- In scoring your Advanced Placement Examination, you lose a fraction of a point for each incorrect answer. You neither gain nor lose credit for unanswered questions. Therefore, guess carefully! If you know one or more answer choices for a question are definitely wrong, then it is generally to your advantage to guess from the remaining choices. But with no knowledge of any of the choices, random guessing is unlikely to increase your scores.

Each college decides which AP Examination grades it accepts for credit and/or Advanced Placement. Most colleges and universities accept grades of 3 and above.

- Each college decides which AP Examination grades it accepts for credit and/or Advanced Placement. Most colleges and universities accept grades of 3 and above. To find out which AP grades they consider acceptable and how they grant course credit, contact the admissions offices of the colleges of interest to you. See chapter 10: CALIFORNIA STATE UNIVERSITY, Placement Tests, page 10--47 and chapter 11: UNIVERSITY OF CALIFORNIA, Placement Tests, page 11--60.

- It is highly unlikely that high school grades you receive in AP courses or your AP Examination scores can hurt your chances for admission to college.

  Many high schools apply extra weighting to grades you receive in AP courses. For example, a B in an AP or honors course counts as an A in your grade point average. Even without this additional weighting, the colleges consider the greater rigor of AP courses when reviewing your grades for admission. That you are willing to challenge yourself by taking an AP course may be considered a positive factor by admissions officers.

  Your requested colleges receive your AP Grade Report in July well after you have been officially admitted.

It is highly unlikely that your grades in AP courses or your AP Examination grade will affect your college admission status.

- You do not have to take an AP Course to take an AP Examination. However you prepare for an Examination, be sure your study follows the corresponding AP Course Description written by and available from the Advanced Placement Program.

- If you are a **disabled student** and cannot test under standard conditions, your AP Coordinator can make special testing provisions for you. These provisions may involve testing in a different location, allowing extended time, or the use of a reader or amanuensis, or provide a written script for hearing impaired students. Photo-enlarged editions of all examinations and braille versions of nearly all exams are available upon request. Contact your high school's AP Coordinator before February 15th to make appropriate arrangements.

- Two brochures, *Some Questions and Answers About The Advanced Placement Program* and *Advanced Placement Examinations Bulletin For Students* are given to you by your high school in February or March. These publications contain further information about the Advanced Placement Examinations.

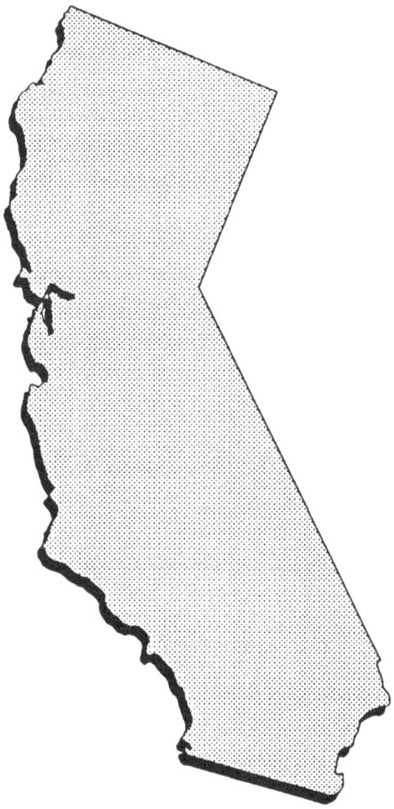

Chapter 7

STEPS IN THE APPLICATION PROCESS

Applying to college is a multiple-step process, and each step is important in reaching your goal of college admission. Knowing what to do, and when and how to do it are the tools to effectively complete the college application materials and procedures in a way that enhances your chances of admission.

GENERAL TIPS

SOCIAL SECURITY NUMBER

Get a social security number as soon as possible. This number is used to identify you on all your college, entrance testing, and financial aid applications.

YOUR NAME

Decide upon the exact name you want on your applications and use it for every application you complete.

Decide upon the exact name you want on your applications and use it for every application you complete. Preferably, use the same name which appears on your high school records. If you have a middle name, use it. The consistent use of one name simplifies procedures for you and reduces the possibility that an important item — like your transcript — might be misplaced in someone else's file with a name similar to yours.

YOUR HIGH SCHOOL RESOURCES

Research your high school's college and financial aid information resources. Where is college information found on your high school campus? In the career center? Guidance center? Counselor's office? Library? Administration office? Who gives out applications for college admission and financial aid? Who is knowledgeable and can answer your questions about college and financial aid application requirements and procedures? How are scholarship opportunities publicized? Who arranges for college representatives to visit your campus, and where do their presentations take place? Are written materials about college found in parent newsletters? Handed out in class presentations? Displayed on racks in a central location?

HOW TO GET YOUR TOUGH QUESTIONS ANSWERED

You may have specific questions about colleges, entrance tests, or financial aid for which you cannot find an answer. Perhaps you have found an error in the handling of your application. College, testing, and financial aid information can be complex and confusing. You may have a unique question. Errors are occasionally made in processing students. If you cannot get satisfactory answers from the resources in your school, do not hesitate to telephone the entrance testing service, financial aid sources, and/or the colleges of interest to you. Generally, you will find their personnel courteous and eager to help.

Before you call the college, testing, or financial aid offices, write down all your questions.

YOUR TELEPHONE STRATEGIES

- When you call college, testing, or financial aid offices for answers to your questions, have your social security number available together with any registration numbers you have been assigned. You will usually be asked for your date of birth as well.

- Write down all your questions before you make the call. Do not trust to memory. You may get nervous and forget one or more critical questions.

When calling for information get the name of the person to whom you are talking in case you need to call again.

- Write down the answers you receive to your questions for later review. Get the name of the person to whom you are talking. You may need to call again to verify information given to you or to obtain further information. Furthermore, by talking to the same person on subsequent calls you establish a connection which may be useful to you in the future.
- Correspondence from college admissions and financial aid offices is usually signed. Make a note of the individual's name, and direct any calls to that person specifically. He or she is most likely the one handling your file and is most familiar with it.
- It is often very difficult to connect with the college admissions and financial aid offices. Their telephone lines are frequently busy. Call when their offices just open early in the day, or at the end of the day. You probably will not have much luck on Mondays. Students are inclined to work on their applications on weekends and have burning questions at the beginning of the week.

INFORMATION/APPLICATION REQUEST LETTER

California State University, the University of California, and nearby California Community Colleges provide information and application packets to your high school to be distributed to students. You do not need to write to these institutions for these materials. On the other hand, you must contact independent colleges directly for their application information and materials. Use this sample letter for your request.

Your high school has application materials for CSU, UC, and nearby community colleges. You must contact the independent colleges directly for their applications.

{your complete street address}
{your city, state, zip code}
{date}

Director of Admissions
{full name of college or university}
{complete address of college or university}
{college or university city, state, zip code}

Dear Director:

I am a student at *{full name of your high school, city, and state}* and will graduate in June, *{fill in the date}*.

I am interested in your college and would appreciate receiving a freshman application, brochures, and any information which would be helpful to me in learning more about your school. I am also interested in financial aid and housing opportunities.

I am considering majors in *{fill in your preferred majors}* and would like information about your programs for these majors.

Thank you very much.

Sincerely,

{sign your letter here}

{type your full name here}

COMPLETING THE ADMISSIONS APPLICATION PROCESS

THE APPLICATION

The college application packet you receive *may* contain some or all of the following materials:

College application packets may contain several different forms.

- Specific deadlines for submitting all materials.
- Application fee information.
- Preliminary information form, which is a request for identifying information. Send this form, prior to submitting your application, to establish your file in the admissions office.
- The admissions application form. Most have two parts: Factual questions and one or more essay questions.
- A request for an official copy of your high school transcript.
- A Secondary School Report form from the independent colleges, which is a recommendation form usually completed by your counselor or school administrator. The request for your high school transcript may be included on this form.
- A 7th Semester Report form from the independent colleges, which is a follow-up recommendation form and a request for grades for the first semester of your senior year. This form is usually completed by a counselor or a school administrator.
- A request for an official copy of your entrance test scores.
- A request for recommendations from two or three of your teachers and from your counselor or other school official — assistant principal or principal. Recommendations from church officials, athletic coaches, employers, and/or club advisors also may be requested.
- The institution's own financial aid application.
- A housing application.
- A reference to supplementary application materials which are sent to you after your initial application is received.
- Directions about how to fill out the various forms.

GETTING STARTED

Set up a folder for each application and attach a cover sheet with deadline dates boldly printed on it.

- ❒ Set up a folder for each application. Keep all material relevant to each college in its own folder.

- ❒ Attach a cover sheet of paper to each application packet with deadline dates boldly printed on it for each item of the application materials. Also note due dates on your worksheet, MY APPLICATION CHECKLIST, found at the end of this chapter. If you resolve to submit all of your college applications in November — recommended in chapter 2: ACTION PLANS, Grade Twelve, page 1--15 to 1--24 — you will not miss application deadlines.

  If you apply to an independent college under an early application plan, you may have to submit your application prior to November. Look for this deadline information in your application packets. See chapter 12: CALIFORNIA INDEPENDENT COLLEGES, College Profile, page 12--12 to 12--75.

- ❒ Review all application materials as they arrive. Set up a schedule for completing them. Completing applications is not much fun, and you may be inclined to put off this task as long as you can. Procrastinating is risky. There is a lot to do, especially if you have several essays to write. You may not do the application (and yourself) justice if you leave it to the last minute. Remember: Leave enough time for correcting and revising.

- ❒ Make two or more copies of the blank application to use as rough drafts and extras in case you make a serious error and ruin the original.

COMPLETING THE APPLICATION PROCESS

Make two or more copies of the blank application to use as rough drafts.

- ❒ Review the application and its directions completely before you start to work on it.

- ❒ Work on your rough draft in pencil so that you can make changes easily.

- ❒ Be accurate, honest, and neat. Spell correctly and use good grammar.

- ❒ Although for neatness and legibility it may be better to type the factual sections of your application form, typing is not required. If you believe you can do a neat, legible, and accurate job completing it by hand, go ahead. Be sure to print legibly in ink. Black ink is often preferred because it copies clearly in copy machines.

- ❒ If possible, type your essay question responses.

- ❒ Give recommendation forms with addressed, stamped envelopes to those persons who must write them for you as soon as you receive your applications. If possible, give the recommendation writer at least two months notice. About two weeks before the deadline for recommendations, ask the writers if they need more information. Generally, a recommendation is sent directly to your college by the writer, separate from your application materials.

- ❐ If a college requires your official high school transcript, make a formal request to your high school to send it. For this purpose, most high schools use a transcript request form, which you give to the registrar, the person who maintains student records at your high school. If an independent college has sent you their own form, the Secondary School Report and/or the 7th Semester Report, submit it with your request. Make your transcript request at least two to three weeks before its due date. Remember, you are not the only senior asking for this service.

If a college requires your official high school transcript, make a formal request to your high school to send it.

- ❐ To be official, your transcript must be in an envelope which is sealed with the school seal or some other official designation. Only by breaking the seal can the envelope be opened. Generally, your high school sends your transcript directly to the college, separate from your application materials. If you are directed to include your official transcript with your application materials, *do not open the sealed transcript envelope. If you do, you may render it unofficial and unacceptable by the college.*

- ❐ At your request, the College Entrance Examination Board or American College Testing sends the official record of your entrance test scores directly to the colleges. Do not send a photocopy of your own test score report unless requested to do so. Sometimes, a college accepts a photocopy as a means of obtaining preliminary information, but it will require the official report to make an official offer of admission.

  Make your request to the testing company on your testing registration form. If you missed the opportunity to do this, there are several other ways to request that scores be sent. See chapter 6: COLLEGE ENTRANCE TESTS, Admissions Tests, pages 6--3 to 6--48.

- ❐ Be sure to sign your application in the appropriate spaces. Some applications require your name on every page.

- ❐ When you have completed your application, ask someone to review it and check it for errors. *Keep one extra blank copy on hand in case you need to redo it.*

Do not forget to enclose your application fee with your application. If you cannot afford the fee, determine if the colleges to which you are applying accept fee waivers.

- ❐ Do not forget to enclose your application fee with your application. Fees range from $20.00 to $60.00. If you believe you cannot afford the fee, determine if the colleges to which you are applying accept fee waivers. For more information about fee waivers for specific colleges, see chapter 10: CALIFORNIA STATE UNIVERSITY, Applying To California State University, page 10--36; chapter 11: UNIVERSITY OF CALIFORNIA, Applying To The University Of California, page 11--47; chapter 12: CALIFORNIA INDEPENDENT COLLEGES, College Profiles, pages 12--12 to 12--75. Obtain a fee waiver form or letter from your high school counselor or administrator and submit it with your application in lieu of your fee payment.

- ❐ Make a copy of all completed application materials before you mail them in case your application gets lost.

- ❐ Mail your application by the required deadline! Get a "Certificate of Mailing" at the post office. It costs about fifty cents and you receive a receipt verifying the date on which you mailed your forms. You will have proof that you mailed your application should it be lost. Do *not* send your application by "certified mail," "registered mail," or "overnight" mail. These methods require a signature by the recipient; the colleges receive too many applications to be able to sign for them.

Within four weeks of mailing your application, you should receive an acknowledgment from the college that they have received it.

- ❐ Within four weeks of mailing your application, you should receive an acknowledgment from the college that they have received it. If you do not, call the college admissions office and inquire.

- ❐ Use your worksheet, MY APPLICATION CHECKLIST, at the end of this chapter to monitor your progress through the steps of applying. When you have several applications in process at one time, you may lose track of what you have sent and when. Noting important dates on this form can help keep you organized and give you a feeling of accomplishment as you proceed through the steps.

One final thought ...

Most of the tips presented here are also useful for the scholarship application process.

EARLY APPLICATION PLANS

The independent colleges and universities may offer an early application plan as an option to their regular application procedures. Several, such as Stanford University, do not. California State University and the University of California do not. There are two basic types of plans: The Early Decision Plan and the Early Action Plan. Both are designed to inform you early in your senior year if you have been accepted. By accepting strong candidates early in their senior year, colleges offering these plans encourage well-qualified applicants to attend their schools. The advantage to you is that an early acceptance relieves your anxiety about college admission. It is great to know you are "in" and can focus your energies on high school and other goals and activities.

The Early Decision Plan and the Early Action Plan are designed to inform you early in your senior year if you have been accepted.

Under regular admission procedures, you are notified of admission by April 15th and have until May 1st to inform the college of your intent to enroll. Under early application plans, the deadline for your application is earlier, generally by mid-November. The colleges notify you within a short time after you have applied if you are admitted, usually by mid-December. Consequently, your first-semester senior-year grades are not a factor in assessing your academic potential. Specific dates may differ by college. Early admission can be withdrawn if your grades decline dramatically as evidenced on your final high school transcript.

EARLY DECISION PLAN

If a particular college is absolutely your first choice, and it offers an Early Decision Plan, you may want to seriously consider it. You have a chance of being accepted under this plan if you are strongly qualified for the college. The plan requires a commitment from you that if you are admitted to the college under Early Decision, you will enroll in the college. The college expects you to submit a commitment deposit once accepted. As soon as you accept the offer of admission, you must withdraw all of your other college applications. Some schools require you to wait until notified by them that you are not accepted before you may apply to other schools. This is highly risky and should be considered carefully. Read the early decision expectations of the colleges to which you apply before you choose the Early Decision Plan.

If you apply for Early Decision and do not get accepted, the colleges generally, but not necessarily, move your application to the regular admission cycle, and consider it again with regular decision candidates. In the regular admissions cycle, your first-semester senior year grades may be included in your admission evaluation. The colleges state that if you are not accepted through the Early Decision Plan, your chances of being admitted under the regular plan are not damaged.

EARLY ACTION PLAN

In this plan, you are notified early of the college's decision to accept you, but you do not have to make any enrollment commitment. You have until May 1st to decide which college to attend and to submit your commitment deposit. Acceptance through an Early Action Plan can reduce your anxiety about the college application process. You know you have one or more colleges "in the bag."

The colleges are interested in the quality and depth of your participation in activities.

ACTIVITIES

You may become involved in activities both in and outside of your high school. Activities can include school clubs, student government, athletics, jobs, volunteer work, church and community organizations and services, hobbies and interests, and travel. The colleges are interested in the quality and depth of your participation, not in a long list of organizations and activities in which you were active at one time or another. Your involvement gives evidence of maturity, leadership, energy, and motivation. Did you focus on one area and participate extensively in several related activities? What did you learn from your involvement? What are some accomplishments you are proud of? What were your goals, and did you attain them? Did you receive recognition for your accomplishments? Reflect on how your accomplishments and disappointments have helped shape your character and your development.

To help monitor your activities as you go through high school, fill in your worksheet, MY ACTIVITIES, at the end of this chapter. Be sure to note what you did, when you did it, what you accomplished, what you learned, and why the activity was important to you. If you fill in this worksheet as you go through your high school years, you will comment on the significance of the activities as you experience them when they are fresh in your mind. A copy of this worksheet can be given to your teachers, counselor, and administrator when you ask for recommendations. It also can be very useful when you complete application forms for college and financial aid, and when you write your college and financial aid application essays.

View your essay as your big chance to present your human side.

WRITING YOUR ESSAY

Your essay or personal statement is your opportunity to tell the admissions officer reading your file *who you are*. Admissions personnel already have information about your completed and planned high school courses, grades, and entrance test scores. In these areas, you probably resemble other applicants. Now, help the admissions committee see you as a thinking and feeling human being, rather than a set of impersonal statistics. View your essay as your big chance to present your human side.

What the admissions officer needs to know to make an admission decision about you is what makes you different from all other applicants. What makes you a special and unique human being who they would like to get to know? What do you have to offer which will be an asset to their student body?

No matter what the topic, the colleges design essay questions to find out about you.

What is your personality like? What is important to you? What are your strengths? Your weaknesses? How have the people and events of your life affected what you have become as a human being? Do you have a sense of humor? What do you worry about? How would you like to change? What are your opinions, feelings, likes, dislikes? What are your passions, commitments, dilemmas? What obstacles, if any, have you overcome?

What is the essence of you?

ESSAY TOPICS

To elicit information about you, to help you reveal your thoughts, personality, and opinions, college essay topics are typically of four different types. Generally, you must write one to three essays for an admission application. Remember, no matter what the topic type, the colleges design essay questions to find out about you. Who are you, really? How well do you express yourself? Will you be an asset to the school?

On the following pages are the four types of topics taken directly from the application forms of California colleges and universities with samples illustrating each.

TYPE ONE — "TELL US ABOUT YOURSELF"

This open-ended essay topic can be the most difficult type because it requires you to decide what to focus on about your life. The colleges are as interested in what you choose to write about as in what you actually write.

The " tell us about yourself " topic is open-ended and can be the most difficult type because it requires you to decide what to focus on about your life.

FROM THE UNIVERSITY OF CALIFORNIA ...

"The essay is an important part of your application for admission and scholarships. For admission purposes, the essay gives you the opportunity to discuss personal attributes that may not be evident through a review of your academic record. You may use the essay to discuss your achievements, school activities, employment, or volunteer work. Or, you may write about your interests and goals, significant experiences in your life, or unusual circumstances, challenges, or hardships you have faced.

Regardless of which of the above areas you choose to write about, remember that the University uses the essay to gain insight into applicants on a personal level. Do not simply list activities or accomplishments; rather, describe your level of effort and achievement, and elaborate on the personal qualities revealed by your involvement.

If you are applying for EOP (or AAP at UCLA) consideration, discuss your reasons for doing so.

If you have a disability, describe your disability and discuss its impact on your life, in particular on your education and goals.

If your are applying to a professional school or college (such as engineering or architecture), discuss your interest in your intended field of study.

If you are a transfer applicant, discuss your interest in your intended major, describing any related work or volunteer experience and explaining how your interest in the field developed.

Scholarship applicants: The University seeks information about exceptional achievements that qualify you as a candidate for scholarship awards. Elaborate on information presented in the application Section XI (Activities, Honors, Awards, and Employment) that demonstrates your motivation, achievement, leadership, and commitment."

FROM THE UNIVERSITY OF THE PACIFIC ...

"Please provide us a written statement (at least 250 words in length). Your essay may describe significant life experiences, career goals, your expectations of college life, or another topic of interest to you."

TYPE TWO — "REVEAL YOURSELF"

This topic asks you to write about a particular interest, idea, achievement, experience, or person. This is a more focused question to get at how you think and feel.

The "reveal yourself" topic is a more focused question to get at how you think and feel.

FROM SCRIPPS COLLEGE ...

"Discuss your thoughts on one of the following questions, or on a topic of your own. We are interested in your ideas and how well you express them.

a. Please tell us about an influential or unusual person. Explain how he or she is unique, and why you think that individual is inspirational.

b. What event in history has influenced your life the most?

c. Tell us about a conviction you hold so strongly you would support it even when confronted with significant opposition.

d. Please tell us something about yourself that is not otherwise apparent in your application."

TYPE THREE — "WHY DO YOU ...."

This topic asks you to answer the question, "Why do you want to come to this college?", or alternately, "Why do you want to go to college?"

FROM DOMINICAN COLLEGE ...

"Please state your reasons for wanting to attend Dominican College. If you feel your previous work does not accurately reflect your potential, please give us any additional information which would help in evaluating your application."

TYPE FOUR — "THE IMAGINARY SITUATION"

This topic is intended to excite your imagination and creativity.

The "imaginary situation" topic is intended to excite your imagination and creativity.

FROM HARVEY MUDD COLLEGE ...

"You have been invited to be one of the two keynote speakers at your Harvey Mudd College twentieth college reunion. The other speaker developed the vaccine for the prevention of Aids. Why have you been selected as a speaker?"

"If you could travel to any time in history where you could change the course of events, to what time period would you travel, what would you change, and why?"

MIXED TYPES

Some colleges present a mixture of all four types of topics for you to write about or choose from. As a result, you have some flexibility in how you can best tell about yourself.

FROM POMONA COLLEGE ...

"Pomona requires two essays:

Essay One — Choose one from the following topics:

1. What scientific discovery or development since 1960 has had or will have a significant impact upon humanity? Why do you think so? Please be as specific as you can.

2. Reflect upon ways in which you expect Pomona College's diverse student body will affect your experience inside and out of the classroom.

3. If you could introduce one new idea or material thing to a pre-industrial culture, what would it be and why? Discuss the implications.

4. Identify a real or fictional person or character who is a personal hero or heroine, and articulate the influence this person or character has had on you.

You have some flexibility in how you can best tell about yourself when presented with a mixture of topic types.

Essay Two — All applicants must write about this topic:

As a residential liberal arts institution, Pomona College places enormous value on the contributions of its individual members to the educational community. We are deeply interested in learning what we can about our prospective students and what they will bring to this community.

Please provide information that you feel will give a more complete and accurate picture of yourself, e.g., background, personal philosophy or traits, goals, etc. Be sure to describe the influence of these factors."

THE "ESSENCE OF YOU"

Regardless of the topic, the purpose of the essay is to provide you with the opportunity to differentiate yourself from other applicants, to demonstrate that you are a good fit, and to show that you will be successful at the college. Furthermore, you want to make the reader feel that you are a person worth knowing, and the college would gain from accepting you because you would add to the diversity of the student body in a positive way. To do this, you must have a clear vision of yourself. Who exactly are you? In order to convince the reader of who you are, you must be able to define yourself. You may learn something from this exercise. View the essay as an opportunity for self-exploration, not as just a device to get into college. Here are some strategies to get you started.

Regardless of the topic, the purpose of the essay is to provide you with the opportunity to differentiate yourself from other candidates.

- Ask your friends, parents, sisters, brothers, grandparents, aunts, uncles, cousins, and teachers to describe you. Pick the people with whom you are close and whom you think know and understand you. If they were telling someone who does not know you about you, what would they say? What are your outstanding qualities? What do they like best about you? About being with you? About teaching you? What improvements do they think you need to make?

  Ask your friends to jot down some thoughts about you. You can do the same for them to help with their essays.

  Ask your parents to write a few paragraphs about you. What qualities do they appreciate and respect in your personality? When they brag about you to their friends, what do they point out? What about you concerns them?

- Look at yourself.

  Make lists of the things you have done, the places you have gone, the people you do and do not admire, your favorite things, your special accomplishments and failures. What is important to you in your life now: The events, people, places and things in your life that really stand out to you and make significant impressions? Write down why these are the ones you have picked. How have they changed you? What did you learn? What are you learning? What would you do differently?

  What are your hobbies and special interests? Do you have an interest in an academic area which you pursued on your own? What jobs have you had or do you have now? In what clubs and activities do you choose to get involved? Why these particular ones? What is your role in them? How involved are you? Why are they important to you? How have you developed by participating in them?

  Do you have a particular major or career in mind? Why? Why not? What experiences have lead you to this major or career choice?

  Why do you want to go to college? What do you expect to gain from it? What are you looking for in a college? Review your worksheet, CHOOSING MY COLLEGE. See chapter 2: CHOOSING YOUR COLLEGE, page 2--18 to 2--19.

  Have any special factors in your life adversely affected your performance: Personal, emotional, financial, social, cultural problems, or physical or learning disabilities? Describe them. How have they affected you? What are you doing to overcome the difficulties they create?

In order to convince the reader of who you are, you must be able to define yourself.

Using a scale of one to five, five being the most positive, rank yourself in terms of the qualities listed here. Be honest. Ask someone who knows you well to do the same for you. This activity will provide valuable insights about yourself.

WHO AM I?

Quality	Rank	Quality	Rank	Quality	Rank
Intelligent		Generous		Studious	
Organized		React Well to Setbacks		Reflective	
Mature		Emotionally Stable		Observant	
Good Sense of Humor		Tolerant of Uncertainty		Patient	
Creative		High Integrity		Precise	
Compassionate		Sociable		Warm Personality	
Logical		Open-minded		Reserved	
Enthusiastic		Pursuasive		Make Friends Easily	
Intellectually Curious		Perceptive		Have Close Friends	
Take Initiative		Sensitive		Solitary	
Ambitious		Positive		Outgoing	
Energetic		Adventurous		Quiet	
Self-Confident		Analytical		Intellectual	
Independent		Articulate		Social	
Have Special Talents		Risk Taker		Emotional	
Leader		Flexible		Not Easily Angered	
Responsible		Decisive		Excitable	

Use a scale of 1 to 5, 5 being the highest ranking, to rank yourself in terms of these qualities.

COLLEGE IN CALIFORNIA: *The Inside Track*

STEPS IN THE APPLICATION PROCESS

What intrigues you? What is your outlook on life? What challenges have you already met, and how did they work out? How do you see yourself ten years from now? Twenty years from now?

Complete the worksheet, MY PERSONAL INFORMATION, at the end of this chapter before writing your essay. It will help you crystallize your thoughts.

Narrow the points you want to make to just one or two major themes, and then elaborate on them. Describe examples, facts, incidents.

NARROW YOUR FOCUS

Review what you have learned about yourself by having gone through the ranking activity and having answered the questions about yourself on the previous pages. What stands out? Do you see any linking threads? Narrow the points you want to make to just one or two major themes. Describe examples, facts, incidents. Make them real. Do not give just a list of your qualities or state generalities. Describe situations. Be vivid. Use details. Support your statements with evidence. Show "what makes you tick" by honestly revealing your personality in writing what you think and why.

Be vivid. Use details.

For instance, if you believe your concern for others is one of your finest qualities, describe a situation in which you exemplified this. If the college topic essay question asks about persons you most admire or learned from, support your affinity for compassion by describing a person who shows unusual sensitivity. Describe how this person's actions and qualities have affected you.

CONSIDER YOUR AUDIENCE

What are the admissions officers looking for? They know their schools — curriculum, social climate, strengths and weaknesses. They have in mind a general profile of the type of student that finds success there. They must find students who can successfully handle the college courses and become a part of the campus life. They want students who can feel emotionally comfortable with the intellectual and social climate of their school. They want students who can add to the diversity and character of their student body. They may be looking for geographic, cultural, ethnic, and socioeconomic diversity or for diversity in talents and interests. They seek students who know something about their college and have some clearly defined reasons for wanting to go there. They are generally looking for commitment, energy, and a positive attitude.

What you choose to say about yourself and your topic, and how you say it, will help the readers decide if you match their particular admission criteria.

What you choose to say about yourself and your topic, and how you say it, will help them decide if you match their particular criteria.

CATCH YOUR READER'S INTEREST

The reader may have fifty essays to read the day he or she reads yours. After a while the essays may begin to read like one another. Your essay must awaken their interest; it must be distinctive; it must be well-presented.

Your first paragraph is very important. Arouse the reader's interest with an anecdote, a quotation, or an unusual statement. Do not be afraid to be different. Grab the reader's attention, and tell him or her what is to come. Make essential points. Set the framework for your essay.

A unique approach to your topic can be refreshing and catch the reader's curiosity. Can you describe yourself through the eyes of your cocker spaniel? Do you have an ancestor of whom you are ashamed and to whom you do not want to be compared, or one that you greatly admire and want to pattern your life after? Can you analyze your name in a way that it shows who you are? Do you have an interest that you can write about in a way that tells about you? How does a particular color describe your personality? In what ways are you like a certain animal?

Have you had an experience that had an overwhelming effect upon the person you have become? Are there any family activities or routines that are especially significant in your life? Reveal the effects your experiences have had on you and what they mean to you. What do they mean to others?

Your essay must awaken the reader's interest. It must be distinctive; it must be well-presented.

If you have a choice, choose a topic that evokes an emotional reaction in you and let go. Be creative if you can, but do not be absurd or silly. Be careful not to let your style overcome your substance. What you say is just as important as how you say it!

If you do not take a unique approach, then be fully descriptive. By expressing and supporting your feelings honestly, you do not sound like everyone else. Your examples are different, and your opinions put a fresh perspective on what you are saying.

You might try, without sounding strained, to put some humor into your essay. But do this only if it is comfortable for you. Express enthusiasm, friendliness, and self-confidence. Avoid pleading, self-depreciation, and complaining.

STRATEGIES

Write not just the what. Tell the why. Bring yourself to life for your reader.

- Do not leave writing your essay to the last minute. Because the colleges require you to use different topics, you may find that you have five or six or seven separate essays to write. You must plan ample time to do them well. Hopefully, you can adapt the core of what you write about yourself to each of your essays — regardless of the essay topic — to avoid writing a totally different essay for each question.
- Write your first draft, leave it alone for a few days, and come back to it. You will find that a fresh perspective can help you evaluate what you have written. Read it out loud. Is it clear and well-organized? Is it interesting? Does the "essence of you" show through?
- Check your spelling, grammar, and sentence structure. You are evaluated on how well you use standard written English. Use the simple vocabulary of your everyday language. Do not try to impress with long words. Do not be flowery.
- Keep the length of your essay limited to the amount specified in the question. If the college wants the essay all on one page of your application, do not make it longer. Type it on a separate piece of paper and rework it until it fits in the allowed space. Even if the directions do not limit its length, try not to make your essay longer than two pages. If you have your points clearly in mind and have a well-planned framework, you should not need more than two pages to say what you want to say. Remember how many essays the admissions personnel have to read.
- When your essay is close to the way you want it, show it to your English teacher or anyone else whose judgement you trust, and who knows you well. Does the essay sound like you? Are its points well-presented? Is it clear and concise? Elicit their opinions, but rewrite it yourself. The style and vocabulary must remain yours.
- Show it to someone who does not know you very well — a neighbor, an acquaintance at school or work, a teacher you have heard good things about but have not had for a class. Ask him or her if they feel they know who you are now that they have read your essay. Are there any points they would like clarified or expanded upon? What is the impact of your essay on this relative stranger? Does it make the impression you want?

When you read the final draft of your essay, you should be able to say: "This sounds just like me."

THE FINAL DRAFT MUST SOUND LIKE YOU

When you reread your essay you should be able to say: "This sounds just like me. You and I are having a meaningful conversation, and I am openly expressing myself in a way that honestly lets you know who I am."

The worksheet, MY PERSONAL INFORMATION, at the end of this chapter can be used as a basis for your essays as well as an information sheet for your recommendation writers. You do not need to write an essay about each of these questions. Jot down some thoughts, phrases, a few sentences about each.

LETTERS OF RECOMMENDATION

Many colleges and scholarship opportunities ask for letters of recommendation to be written by your school counselor or administrator and by your teachers. When college admissions officers read recommendations, they look for information which convinces them that you can be successful in their school and an asset to their student body. They prefer to read recommendations which describe your attributes with concrete examples or anecdotes. They are impressed with letters from staff members of your high school who demonstrate a real sense of who you are and what you can bring to the college setting. Scholarship committees want to be convinced that you are a good investment with qualities which ensure successful completion of college. Thus, your recommendations are a very important part of your college and financial aid application process. You must handle them effectively.

College admissions officers prefer to read recommendations which describe your attributes with concrete examples or anecdotes.

The following guidelines can help you with this step.

- You may be tempted to add extra recommendations to support your application. It is usually best to send the number of recommendations requested and no more, although in some instances you might wish to send one extra if it provides a perspective about you which is different from the others. If a college requires three, the typical number, then they believe this number gives them the information they need to help make an admission decision. There is a saying among admissions personnel: "The thicker the application, the thicker the applicant." Do not overdo it!

- One of the first items you may notice on recommendation forms or on your application in the section regarding recommendations is the question of whether you waive your right to read recommendations written for you. The colleges generally believe the recommendation writers will be more honest in their appraisal of you, and the recommendations will be more credible, if you waive your right to read your recommendations. Consequently, the reader has more trust in what is said. Furthermore, the colleges become suspicious when students are unwilling to allow a recommendation to be sent without seeing it prior to mailing. For these reasons, it is probably best to waive your right to read your recommendations. Some writers of recommendations may offer you the opportunity to read the recommendation after it is submitted, so you may still see it.

It is probably best to waive your right to read your recommendations.

- Your counselor or school administrator writes the school's recommendation for you. The Secondary School Report form is usually used for this purpose by independent colleges and universities. It requests your grades, rank in class, and a recommendation evaluating your potential for success in college and your personal qualities. If needed by California State University, the University of California, or scholarship opportunities, a recommendation letter on your high school's letterhead may be used. Be ready with the names of three or four teachers with whom the counselor or administrator can confer about your qualifications.

- For your teacher recommendations, select teachers you believe know you well, with whom you have had success, and have the time and interest to do a good job. If you are planning on a particular major, a teacher in your area of interest would be especially appropriate. The teachers you choose can be from your prior school years or from your senior year if they know you well enough. Some colleges specify teachers in academic subjects only or from grades eleven and twelve. Read the instructions carefully.

- Plan to request recommendations well in advance of their due dates. Give the writers as much notice as possible so they can give serious thought to and feel positive about writing your recommendations. A month or more is optimum, two weeks is minimum. Popular teachers often have several recommendations due at the same time. Get yours to them first. A recommendation request that is made the week before it is due, or even worse, a few days beforehand, may be resented or rushed; it will not be completed in the most favorable way for you.

Request recommendations well in advance of due dates. A month or more is optimum.

- If a form is required, make extra copies to have on hand in case your teachers, administrator, or counselor misplace the ones you give them.

- Make an appointment to talk with the teachers you have selected. Do not leave a form or a note in the teacher's mailbox or on the teacher's desk. Remember, you are asking for a favor. Be polite. Give the teachers an addressed, stamped envelope with your request. If the college or scholarship requires a form, be sure to give it to the recommendation writer.

- Use the data from your worksheets, MY ACTIVITIES and MY PERSONAL INFORMATION, at the end of this chapter to prepare a resume about yourself to give to the counselor, administrator, and/or teachers who will write your recommendations. Your school may have a special form for you to complete for this purpose. Alternately, you may give them copies of MY ACTIVITIES and MY PERSONAL INFORMATION.

- About a week before the recommendation due date, ask the teachers, the counselor, and/or the administrator if they need any other information to write your recommendation letter. This is a polite way of finding out if they have already sent the recommendation, and it serves as a gentle reminder if they have not.

- If you have several colleges and/or scholarships which require recommendations, it is appropriate to ask the same teachers who have previously written ones for you to write them. Once a teacher has written a recommendation for you, he or she can generally make copies of it or adapt it for additional requests and will not mind doing this. This is a better strategy than asking a new teacher to write one or asking a teacher who does not know you very well to write one. Give your teachers an addressed, stamped envelope for each additional request.

If you have several colleges and/or scholarships which require recommendations, it is appropriate to ask the same teachers who have previously written ones for you to write them.

- Some requests for recommendations do not specify that a teacher must write them, just someone who can describe your qualifications. Your employer, your coach, a club advisor, or a church official can write one regarding your work habits, reliability, people skills, ability to learn, and talents.

- Write a thank you note to those people who have written recommendations for you.

- Be sure to let your recommendation writers know the outcome of your applications. They undoubtedly will be interested in your successes.

YOUR INTERVIEW

Independent colleges often require an interview. It may take place on the college campus with an admissions officer or near your home with an alumnus or an admissions officer. If the interview takes place on the college campus, combine it with a tour of the campus. Even if you have been there before, refresh your knowledge of it. Take the tour first to stimulate your thinking about the school and to generate questions. The visit should be invigorating and prime you for your meeting.

Here is your opportunity to express who you are, to differentiate yourself from other applicants, and to learn about the college to determine if it is a good choice for you. The interview should be viewed as an interaction between you and the interviewer to better understand what each has to offer.

Consider your first few college interviews as practice experiences. Interview last at the colleges which most interest you.

GENERAL TIPS

- Consider your first few college interviews as practice experiences. Interview last at the colleges which most interest you. You will have a better understanding of the type of questions to expect and be more experienced for the interviews which count the most. You can try out your answers and improve them. Use each interview as a learning experience to get ready for interviews at your first-priority colleges.

- Dress comfortably and appropriately. Be neat and well-groomed. What is appropriate? Women may wear a dress; men, a jacket and tie. Do not wear jeans or too casual an outfit.

- If your parents are with you and if you are comfortable with it, have them meet the interviewer. But after a few questions, they should leave. It is your interview, and the admissions officer wants to talk with you alone. Having your parents present during your entire interview could give the impression that you are not mature enough to meet by yourself, and possibly not ready to go to college.

- Do not bring along a list of your accomplishments to read off. The interviewer is interested in depth and quality of involvement, not a long list.

- If you are nervous — it is natural that you will be — take a deep breath and talk slowly.

- After each interview, jot down the questions you were asked and your answers. Evaluate your responses. Think about how you might answer similar questions at your next interview. Also note your impressions of the college as a result of the interview. This will help you later when deciding which college to attend.

- Many of the college interview suggestions in this section also are applicable to your scholarship interviews.

If you are nervous — it is natural that you will be — take a deep breath and talk slowly.

FORMAT OF THE INTERVIEW

A typical interview usually takes thirty to forty minutes and can be broken down into four stages:

Research shows that the first few minutes of the interview are crucial. They create the dominant impression that is hard to change.

1. The introductory stage. The interviewer attempts to make you feel at ease by chatting with you in a casual manner. It is all right to tell the admissions officer if you feel very nervous. You probably will feel better if you do.

2. The review of your academic background and interests stage. The interviewer may ask you questions about your high school courses, grades, possible majors, entrance test scores, hobbies, activities, travels, jobs, and family.

3. The discussion of the college and how it fits your needs and goals stage. This part of the interview should be an interactive discussion between you. You may ask questions.

4. The closing stage. Points are clarified and you are encouraged to ask additional questions.

PREPARING FOR YOUR INTERVIEW

The key to a successful interview is preparation. You have two areas to prepare:

1. Your knowledge of the college. Review all information available to you about the college so you understand the school as well as possible. You must be prepared to answer questions about why you are interested in the college and to ask for information in a way that shows you have done your research. The campus tour, college brochures and information sheets, college catalogues, and former and current students are resources to utilize to develop your knowledge of the school.

2. What you want to emphasize to the interviewer about yourself. Reread your application essays and think about what you learned about yourself when you wrote them. Make a list of the major points you want to make: Your interests and activities, your personality, your leadership roles, your educational goals, and/or your major and career goals. Narrow down the specific areas you want to talk about, and integrate these into your discussion.

If you do not understand a question, do not guess at an answer. Ask for clarification.

INTERVIEW QUESTIONS

Whatever questions you are asked, be prepared to explain, elaborate, and give examples. If you say you read a lot of books, be ready to describe a few of them. If you mention an activity, talk about your involvement in depth — what it meant to you and what role you took. Give examples of some things you did and why you feel good about them. Do not make statements which you cannot verify with facts. Be honest and sincere.

If you do not understand a question, do not guess at an answer. Ask for clarification. Remember, the interviewer is human, understands how you feel, and undoubtedly likes students. He or she is not trying to trick you or make you tense. The admissions representative wants to help you feel comfortable so that your personality and qualifications are revealed more fully than can be read in your file.

Think about the following questions and rehearse your answers. Practice with a parent or friend, or in front of a mirror.

Think about questions the interviewer might ask you and rehearse your answers. Practice with a parent or friend, or in front of a mirror.

- The interviewer wants to learn about your academic record from your point of view. Are you satisfied with the courses you have taken and your grades in them? What could you have done to improve those areas with which you are not pleased? What are your favorite subjects? What subjects do you like least? Do your grades accurately reflect your capabilities? How do you feel about your entrance test scores?

- In what activities and interests are you involved? What have you learned from them? Have you taken a leadership role? How involved are you? Which ones intrigue you? Will you continue these pursuits in college, or are there other areas in which you are looking forward to participating? How do you spend your free time?

- Talk about yourself as a person. What are your strengths and weaknesses? How would others describe you? What have you accomplished that you are most proud of? What do you hope to accomplish in your future? If you are asked about a weakness, talk about how you are working to improve it: "I have difficulties with science but spend extra time on homework to improve my test scores." If you have strengths, describe them. Do not brag, but do not be overly modest either. It is all right to be proud of yourself. Let your personality show.

- The interviewer is interested in your ambitions. What are your goals during both your years in college and beyond? What do you want to gain from your college education? Do you have a major selected? What careers interest you? If you do not have a major in mind, what types of classes would you like to explore to help you decide? What would you like to be doing ten years from now?

- How do you feel about this college as an appropriate choice for you? The admissions officer may ask to what other colleges you have applied and try to determine if their college is high on your list. Until you have visited the schools on your list and know to which ones you have been accepted, you really do not know which ones you prefer. It is all right to say so. Do show enthusiasm for their school if you are sincerely interested in it as a choice.

- You will be asked if you have any questions about the college. What do you need to know to help you understand if this college is appropriate to you? Your questions should show that you have read materials about this school and are seeking additional information which you have not been able to find in the written materials: "I read such and such in your brochure and would like to know if, what, where, when, who...." Ask sincere, searching questions to which you could not find answers elsewhere. For example:

Ask sincere, searching questions to which you could not find answers elsewhere.

  "I am interested in majoring in journalism and note that you offer specializations in newspaper journalism and broadcast journalism. What kind of internships do you offer in these areas?"

  "I could not find any statistics in your brochures or catalog which indicate what percentage of your student body is on scholarship." Can you tell me about this?

- Remember, the college is looking for enthusiasm, commitment, and purposefulness. They do not expect you to be a sophisticated adult with polished interview skills. Be prepared and be yourself.

THE THANK YOU NOTE

Write a thank you note to the interviewer. Include in it references to some major points which you made during your interview to help the interviewer remember you. If you forgot to mention something, or there are some facts or impressions about the school which you gained from the interview, state them in the note.

The colleges select from the wait list students who will meet the school's need for a diversified and well-balanced class.

THE WAIT LIST

Instead of an acceptance or rejection letter, a college may send you a letter informing you that you are on their wait list. Colleges establish an enrollment figure as a goal for the size of their incoming freshman class. Because not every student the college accepts will decide to enroll, the college places on a wait list some additional qualified applicants who were not accepted. The list is used to fill in the freshman class if too many accepted students decide to go elsewhere. This procedure protects the college from having too small a freshman class.

Usually, the wait list letter does not estimate your chances of eventually being admitted. The college itself does not know how many students it will admit from the list until all accepted students let them know if they plan to enroll. Students have until the generally accepted deadline of May 1st to do this. Until then the colleges are reluctant to give you any estimate of your chances.

The colleges select students from the wait list who meet the school's need for a diversified and well-balanced class. For example, if a higher number of men than women have committed to enroll, the colleges may select women from the wait-listed applicants to better balance the class.

Contact the admissions office with questions to help you to calibrate your chances for admission and to decide what to do.

Being put on a wait list can cause a dilemma for you, especially if the college at which you are wait-listed is your first choice. What should you do? If you have been accepted to other schools, should you commit yourself to one of them or wait until the wait-list decisions are made? You have deadlines for your decisions to accept or not accept admission. These deadlines are well before wait-list decisions are made. August 1st is the commonly accepted absolute deadline for the colleges to inform wait-listed students of their decisions. Many institutions inform students as soon after May 1st as possible and aim for a July 1st deadline.

ASK THESE QUESTIONS

Here are some questions to ask the admissions office to help you to calibrate your chances for admission and to decide what to do. You may call the admissions office yourself, or ask your counselor or administrator to call for you.

- ❒ How long is your wait list?
- ❒ Does your college rank your wait-list candidates? If so, what is my rank? (The college may not be willing to give you this information, but ask anyway.)

- ❒ Did your college accept students from your wait list last year, and if so, how many? Are the number of admits and the number on the wait list similar this year to last year? What has been the trend over the past five years in percentage of wait-list students who are eventually accepted?
- ❒ Can I give you any further information about myself to help my chances? Second semester grades? Special honors? Honors at graduation? Additional recommendations?
- ❒ Does your college have a deadline for making their final decisions for those students on the wait list? (The colleges generally try to make their decisions by July 1st.)
- ❒ If I am accepted, will I still be considered for financial aid?

You may find as time goes by that you become more excited about the college to which you have committed, and the wait-listed school becomes less important to you.

YOUR CHOICES

The answers to the previous questions may give you some sense of your chances, but you will not know for sure. You have some choices to make.

- You can let the wait-listed college know that you wish to remain on their list and are still very interested in attending. Write a letter indicating that the school is your first choice. List the other schools that have accepted you. Give some new information about yourself: Honors, awards, special recognitions.
- You can submit your deposit to reserve your space at another college while waiting for a final decision by the wait-listed school. You may find as time goes by that you become more excited about the college to which you have committed, and the wait-listed school becomes less important to you.
- You can eliminate the wait-listed college from consideration and commit yourself to enroll in one of the other colleges to which you have been accepted.

ORGANIZING YOUR INFORMATION

Use the worksheets on the next few pages to organize and track your activities, to review your personal characteristics and qualities, and to monitor your progress through the steps of the application process. Organizing yourself in this way can optimize your chances for successfully completing the steps to admission.

MY ACTIVITIES

Be Specific! List Dates, Year In School, Positions, etc.	*What I did. When I did it. What I accomplished. What I learned. Why it was important to me!*
HOBBIES, INTERESTS, TALENTS	
SCHOOL CLUBS AND ORGANIZATIONS	
ELECTED OFFICES	

COLLEGE IN CALIFORNIA: *The Inside Track*

MY ACTIVITIES	
Be Specific! List Dates, Year In School, Positions, etc.	*What I did.* *When I did it.* *What I accomplished.* *What I learned.* *Why it was important to me!*
ATHLETICS	
JOB EXPERIENCES	
CHURCH AND/OR COMMUNITY ACTIVITIES	
TRAVEL	
AWARDS AND HONORS	

STEPS IN THE APPLICATION PROCESS

STEPS IN THE APPLICATION PROCESS

MY PERSONAL INFORMATION

GPA	Highest SAT/SAT I Scores	Highest ACT Score	Highest Achievement Tests/SAT II Scores	
UC:________	Verbal:________	Composite:____	Test:_______ Score:____	Test:_______ Score:____
CSU:_______	Mathematics:____	Test Date:______	Test:_______ Score:____	Test:_______ Score:____
Overall:____	Test Date:_______		Test:_______ Score:____	Test:_______ Score:____

Why do I want to go to college?

Which colleges? Why?

Which majors? Why?

Which careers? Why?

How do I see myself in ten years? In twenty years?

What are my strongest school subjects? Why?

What are my weakest school subjects? Why?

Is my academic record indicative of my abilities? Why? Why not?

How do I rank in comparison with other students?

COLLEGE IN CALIFORNIA: *The Inside Track*

MY PERSONAL INFORMATION

What type of student am I?

Of what single accomplishment am I most proud?
What did I do? Why this particular accomplishment?

What challenges have I met? How did they work out?

What is unusual about my background? How has this impacted my life?

What do I want colleges to know about me? How am I unique?

What would those who know me well say are my qualities?

MY APPLICATION CHECKLIST

COLLEGE APPLICATIONS

College Name	Application	Tests		Transcript	Financial Aid Application
	Due Date / Date Mailed	Required	Must Be Taken By	Due Date / Date Mailed	Due Date / Date Mailed
	/			/	/
	/			/	/
	/			/	/
	/			/	/
	/			/	/
	/			/	/

RECOMMENDATIONS

College Or Scholarship	Due Date	Requested From/ Date Requested	Requested From/ Date Requested	Requested From/ Date Requested
		/	/	/
		/	/	/
		/	/	/
		/	/	/
		/	/	/
		/	/	/
		/	/	/
		/	/	/
		/	/	/
		/	/	/

FINANCIAL AID

Application	Due Date / Date Mailed
FAFSA/FAF	March 2 /
	/
	/
	/
	/
	/
	/
	/
	/
	/

COLLEGE TOURS/INTERVIEWS

College Or Scholarship	Tour Date	Interview Date

COLLEGE IN CALIFORNIA: *The Inside Track*

STEPS IN THE APPLICATION PROCESS

Chapter 8

EDUCATIONAL OPPORTUNITIES

Colleges and universities in California offer educational opportunities and services to underrepresented minority, educationally-disadvantaged, learning-disabled, and international students. Take advantage of these programs.

MINORITY AND/OR EDUCATIONALLY-DISADVANTAGED STUDENTS

California public and independent colleges and universities seek out students who bring to their campuses a mix of cultures, backgrounds, and talents. To enrich the composition of their schools and to encourage qualified students to attend college, who might not have otherwise done so, the institutions make a strong effort to recruit underrepresented minority students and educationally-disadvantaged students.

The colleges and universities of California make a strong effort to recruit underrepresented minority students and educationally-disadvantaged students.

Underrepresented minority students come from ethnic backgrounds that do not have the same percentage of representation in college as they do in the general population. Black, Mexican American, Latino, Native American, and Native Alaskan students are the ethnic groups generally identified as underrepresented in college. Educationally-disadvantaged students come from families which traditionally have not had family members attend college because of low income or lack of educational opportunity.

California Community Colleges, California State University, the University of California, and many independent colleges have developed programs to provide access to educational opportunities for underrepresented minorities and educationally-disadvantaged students. Programs may begin as early as eighth grade and extend through college. Ask if any of these programs provide services to students in your school.

Contact the admissions offices of the colleges of interest to you to determine if they offer special opportunities and support services. Be sure to describe your background — ethnic, financial, first member of your family to attend college ....

Programs and services have a variety of titles: UC AEP (Academic Enrichment Program), UC Partnership - Junior/Senior High School, UC Immediate Outreach, MESA (Mathematics, Engineering, Science Achievement), Community College EOPS (Educational Opportunity Programs and Services), CAL-SOAP, PDP (Professional Development Program), Minority Engineering Program, Upward Bound, Talent Search/EOC, FEP (Field Evaluation Program), Puente Program, SAA (Student Affirmative Action), EOP (Educational Opportunity Program). Some of these programs serve high school students, some serve college students, and most offer services at both educational levels.

Contact the admissions offices of the colleges of interest to you to determine if they offer special opportunities and support services.

These programs offer:

- High school services to guide and encourage your college plans: Academic program planning, college tours, application workshops.
- Summer programs at colleges, which acquaint you with the college and its programs while you are still in high school.
- Special admission opportunities with course, GPA, and test score admission requirements somewhat adjusted to support your application.
- Financial aid to assist you to afford the institution.
- Summer orientation and programs the summer before fall enrollment to build academic skills and familiarize you with the college environment.

- Assistance in adjusting to the college environment, curriculum, and expectations after you are enrolled. Services include academic planning, tutoring, programs for academic skill development, career planning, housing and financial aid advising, and peer counseling.

Take advantage of support services. Contact with college students and faculty enhance your chances for admission and successful completion of your education.

Take advantage of these support services. You meet college students and faculty who are committed to helping you reach your college goals. These contacts enhance your chances for admission and successful completion of your education.

Special admission opportunities are described in chapter 10: CALIFORNIA STATE UNIVERSITY, Special Admission Opportunities, page 10--32 and chapter 11: UNIVERSITY OF CALIFORNIA, Admission By Exception, page 11--22.

DISABLED STUDENTS

By law, a student who is otherwise qualified cannot be excluded from college solely because of a disability. If you are a disabled student who meets the academic qualifications of a college, you should apply for admission. All public colleges and many independent schools have disabled student services. Benefits may include counseling, tutoring, readers, interpreters, note takers, special parking zones, and loan of special equipment. You may request that a class be relocated to a more accessible place. For specific information about the benefits available, contact the college's disabled students' office or the national organizations serving your particular disability. Also, contact the nearest office of the California Department of Rehabilitation.

STUDENTS WITH LEARNING DISABILITIES

The goal of college services is to enable learning-disabled students to successfully participate in regular classes, activities, and programs offered by the college.

Many colleges in California offer special programs and services for students with identified learning disabilities. The goal of these services is to enable students with learning disabilities to participate successfully in regular classes, activities, and programs offered by the college. When inquiring about services, call the office for disabled students at the college. The type, extent, and quality of these services vary widely. When researching learning-disability programs, ask the following questions:

- ❒ Does the school offer programs and services to students with learning disabilities?
- ❒ Does the school have learning-disabilities specialists to provide these services? How many?
- ❒ What is the ratio of students to specialists?
- ❒ Are admission requirements modified to meet qualifications of learning-disabled students?
- ❒ Is individual counseling available?

- ❑ Is individual guidance in planning your educational program available?
- ❑ Is assistance with registration provided?
- ❑ Is there a special summer orientation or program for learning-disabled students?
- ❑ Are career planning services provided?
- ❑ Is there diagnostic assessment to determine your specific needs?
- ❑ Are individual programs designed for developing your specific skills in reading, spelling, writing, and mathematics?
- ❑ Is individual tutoring available in academic or vocational subjects?
- ❑ Is there communication and coordination with the faculty and other school personnel?
- ❑ Can you take adapted testing in your academic work: Oral or untimed examinations?
- ❑ Are computers with spell-checking available for your use?
- ❑ Is taping of lectures or textbooks available?
- ❑ Are notetakers available to accompany you to class?
- ❑ Are readers available if you have severe reading difficulties?
- ❑ If you have other physical disabilities, are services available to accommodate your needs? Braille or large text if you are visually impaired? Interpreter services if you are hearing impaired? Mobility assistance if you need help to and from classes?
- ❑ Are there fees for any of these services?
- ❑ What is the graduation rate of learning-disabled students compared with the graduation rate of students in general?

Inquire about specific services the college offers to learning-disabled students. Ask if learning-disabilities specialists are on staff.

COLLEGES WITH LEARNING-DISABILITIES PROGRAMS

All California Community Colleges, California State University campuses, and University of California campuses offer services to learning-disabled students. However, not all campuses have learning disabilities specialists on staff. The College Profiles in chapter 12: CALIFORNIA INDEPENDENT COLLEGES, pages 12--12 to 12--75 indicate for each of the independent schools if services are available. Contact the California Community Colleges, CSU campuses, UC campuses, and independent colleges of interest to you and inquire about the *specific services* available on their campuses. Ask if these services are provided by learning-disabilities specialists.

All California Community Colleges, California State University campuses, and University of California campuses offer services to learning-disabled students.

FINANCIAL AID FOR DISABLED STUDENTS

When the college calculates your student expense budget as a factor in determining your financial need, they should include all educational expenses necessary to accommodate your disability.

If you need assistance with paying for your college education, apply for financial aid. See chapter 4: PAYING FOR COLLEGE. When a college calculates your student expense budget as a factor in determining your financial need, they should include all educational expenses necessary to accommodate your disability. The United States Department of Education has free cassette recordings of financial aid information available for disabled students. For further information, write to:

Cassette
United States Department of Education
Office of Student Financial Assistance
Room 4051
ROB-3
400 Maryland Avenue, S.W.
Washington, D.C. 20202
(800) 4-FED Aid.

ADMISSIONS TESTING FOR DISABLED STUDENTS

You can make special arrangements to take the ACT, PSAT/NMSQT, SAT I: Reasoning Test, SAT II: Subject Tests, and the TOEFL if you have a documented or tested learning disability and/or physical disability. These arrangements can help to minimize the effects of your disability upon your test results. Your score report indicates that you took the test under nonstandard conditions. See chapter 6: COLLEGE ENTRANCE TESTS, Admissions Tests, pages 6--3 to 6--48 for a more detailed description of these tests.

You can make special arrangements to take the ACT, PSAT, SAT I: Reasoning Test, SAT II: Subject Tests, and the TOEFL if you have a learning and/or a physical disability.

ACT

If you can test under standard conditions (within standard time limits using a regular-print test booklet and answer sheet at a regularly-scheduled, national test center), register in the usual manner as explained in chapter 6: COLLEGE ENTRANCE TESTS. Enclose the Special Accommodations Request Form that comes with your registration packet to explain any special arrangements you need at the test center. An interpreter to sign verbal instructions and wheelchair access are examples of these arrangements. Only regular-print booklets are available on national test dates. Extended time is never allowed at a national test center.

If your disability

a. prevents you from testing under standard conditions, and

b. has been diagnosed or reconfirmed within the last three years, or your school has an Individualized Educational Plan (IEP) on file for you, ask your counselor or administrator about special testing, rather than send in a regular registration form. Special accommodations can include Braille, large-print, and audio-cassette editions of the test. Extended time for testing may also be available to you. Ask for a Request For ACT Assessment Special Testing form. Make your request at least four weeks prior to your proposed test date — six weeks preferred. Special testing may be administered at any time between September 1st and June 30th.

For further information contact:

ACT Universal Testing
P.O. Box 4028
Iowa City, Iowa 52243-4028
(319) 337-1332 or (319) 337-1448
Voice/TDD (for hearing impaired): (319) 337-1524

PSAT/NMSQT

The Tuesday edition of the PSAT/NMSQT is available in Braille and large type.

The Tuesday edition of the PSAT/NMSQT is available in Braille and large type. Your school must order these special formats by mid-May of the prior school year. If you have other documented disabilities that require adjustment of the testing situation (such as extended time, special aids, and/or an alternate format), you may take the same edition of the PSAT/NMSQT on the same date as all other students in your school, but with special accommodations for you. You need to complete an eligibility form signed and authorized by your school. Speak to your counselor or assistant principal about these arrangements.

SAT I: REASONING TEST AND SAT II: SUBJECT TESTS

To be eligible for special arrangements for the SAT Program you must be currently be receiving the same accommodations for tests in school that you will be requesting for the SAT Program tests.

Approximately twenty-one thousand students with disabilities take the SAT I each year, with generally eighty-five to ninety percent of them requiring only extended testing time. Ask your counselor or administrator about special testing if your disability

a. prevents you from testing under standard conditions, *and*

b. you have on file at your school either

   i. a current Individualized Educational Plan (IEP), or

   ii. two signed documents, based on 1992-95 test results, obtained from any two of the following: Physicians, psychologists, child-study teams, or learning-disability specialists. Both documents cannot be from the same individual or team and cannot be more than three years old, *and*

c. you receive regular special arrangements in your school for instruction and assessment. To be eligible you must be currently be receiving the same accommodations for tests in school that you will be requesting for the SAT Program tests.

TWO SPECIAL TESTING PLANS

The College Board provides special testing arrangements under two plans:

PLAN A (SPECIAL ACCOMMODATIONS):

The College Board provides special testing arrangements under two plans: Plan A (Special Accommodations) and Plan B (Extended Time Only).

This plan is available to students with documented hearing, learning, physical, and/or visual disabilities. The plan permits special testing editions of the SAT I and SAT II, large-block answer sheets, aids (including a reader, recorder, sign-language interpreter, or magnifying device), extended testing time, and administration in your high school. You may use a reader or someone to record your answers. If you are hearing impaired and do not need additional time to test, you may bring a sign-language interpreter to any national administration. The signer may interpret only the spoken instructions

SAT I: Reasoning Test: The SAT I is available in regular type, large type, braille, cassette, and script. If you take the SAT I on May 10, 1995, you may obtain test questions, correct answers, and your own responses by ordering the Question-and-Answer Service.

SAT II: Subject Tests: The SAT II: Subject Tests are available in regular and large type, and some are currently available in braille. A standard version of an SAT II: Subject Test has a time limit of one hour. If you are eligible, you may have extended time. Most students requiring extended time complete each test in one-and-one half to two hours. If you register for two or three tests, you may take the second and third test on consecutive days, but, for security reasons, you must complete each test the day it is started.

You may take *either* the SAT I: Reasoning Test *or* the SAT II: Subject Tests (one, two, or three), except for the Writing, within each of the two-week periods listed on the chart. Note that May 10, 1995 is for testing the SAT I only. If you wish to take the SAT II: Writing Test, you will be tested at a national test center on a national test date. You may have extended time to complete the test. Contact you school counselor for information about dates, locations, and procedures for taking the SAT II: Foreign Language Tests with Listening.

SAT I AND SAT II 1994-95 REGISTRATION AND TEST DATES FOR STUDENTS WITH DISABILITIES PLAN A

TEST	TESTING PERIOD	REGISTRATION DEADLINE
SAT I and SAT II	November 3-16, 1994	September 28, 1994
SAT I and SAT II	December 1-14, 1994	October 26, 1994
SAT I and SAT II	March 9-22, 1995	February 1, 1995
SAT I and SAT II	May 4-17, 1995 (except May 10)	March 29, 1995
SAT I only	May 10, 1995	March 31, 1995
SAT I and SAT II	June 1-14, 1995	April 26, 1995

You have two opportunities to take the SAT I test in 1994-95, May 10, 1995 or within one of the two-week testing periods.

You have two opportunities to take the SAT I test in 1994-95, May 10, 1995 *or* within *one* of the two-week testing periods. These periods permit you to take the SAT I once as a junior and again as a senior. If you register for Plan A more than once per academic year, you may have to take the "old SAT".

PLAN B (EXTENDED TIME ONLY)

This plan is available only to students with documented learning disabilities. It permits no accommodation except ninety minutes of additional testing time for the SAT I: Reasoning Test. Plan B is available only at a national testing center on two dates: November 5, 1994 and May 6, 1995 for the SAT I: Reasoning Test. You must be able to use a regular-type test and machine-scannable answer sheet.

REGISTERING FOR PLAN A OR PLAN B

Plan B permits no accommodation except ninety minutes of additional testing time for the SAT I: Reasoning Test.

To test under plan A or plan B, submit with your Registration Form for the SAT Program, a special Plan A or Plan B registration form, completed by both you and your high school. Your counselor or school administrator must submit all materials at least five weeks prior to the test date for Plan A and by regular registration deadlines for Plan B. See Chapter 6: COLLEGE ENTRANCE TESTS, Admissions Tests, pages 6--3 to 6--43 for information about SAT I: Reasoning Test and SAT II: Subject Tests. A brochure describing special testing services for the new SAT I: Reasoning Test and SAT II: Subject Tests is available. For further information contact:

SAT Services for Students with Disabilities
P.O. Box 6226
Princeton, New Jersey 08541-6226
(609) 771-7137
TDD (609) 882-4118

TOEFL

If you have a disability that you believe would make it impossible for you to test under standard conditions, ask the colleges to which you are applying to consider other ways of evaluating your English language proficiency. If you must take the TOEFL, special arrangements can be made for administering the test to you at the regular test center on a regular test date. Register at least three months before the test date you prefer and notify TOEFL/TSE Services that you need special arrangements. You will be asked to complete a questionnaire to identify your special needs and to provide documentation of your disability. Your counselor or school administrator can help you with this request.

Nonstandard testing on the TOEFL takes place at a regular test center on a regular test date.

Nonstandard TOEFL testing arrangements may include large-type test books, the use of a reader and/or an amanuensis, a separate testing room, a typewriter, and extended time and/or rest breaks during the test administration. If you have a hearing problem, you are not scored on the listening comprehension section of the test and no total score will be reported.

INTERNATIONAL STUDENTS

Many students from countries around the world come to California to attend college. Colleges and universities welcome you, the international student, for the enrichment and diversity that your social and cultural background bring to their campuses. This opportunity to attend college in California can be a very exciting one. Follow the steps to making you a California college student very carefully.

Deadlines are particularly critical. Overseas mail may take several weeks to arrive in the United States. Because of the distances involved and possible delays, mail letters, admission, testing, and financial aid applications, and other forms and papers well ahead of due dates to assure arrival on time. The colleges and testing companies usually recommend mailing materials from overseas at least one month in advance of deadlines. You may fax materials and correspondence. Accuracy and following directions are also important. Questions from institutions and programs about your materials are usually handled by mail and can cause further delays in processing.

Deadlines are particularly critical for international students. Mail all materials well ahead of deadlines — at least one month or more.

Many institutions in California have international student advisors to help you through the process of applying to their college and adjusting to school after enrollment. When you send for applications and information, ask if this advisement is available. Those colleges that do offer this service frequently have a large number of international students on campus and have programs in place to provide support to them.

Financial Requirements

The United States Immigration and Naturalization Service (INS) requires that international students have sufficient financial resources for their stay in the United States. Colleges require that you submit proof that you can pay your tuition, fees, and living expenses for the first academic year at the college. Some institutions require proof of financial resources — a financial guarantee — for the duration of your college program. The foundation of this financial guarantee can be your personal resources or support from family members such as parents, brothers or sisters, or support from unrelated sponsors.

Colleges generally have official forms for you or your sponsors to complete. Most schools require the CSS Certificate of Finances (COF). The form requests detailed information about amounts and sources of your financial support. Information on the form must be verified by a bank, a United States Consul, a notary, or other official agency. If your financial support is personal or from a family member, you must send a bank statement verifying the resources to pay first-year expenses. If your sponsor is a government agency, it too must file appropriate documentation. Your college requires these statements before formally admitting you and before it issues the forms necessary for you to obtain a visa to enter this country as a student.

Colleges require that you submit proof that you can pay your tuition, fees, and living expenses for the first academic year.

Some of the more selective independent colleges may offer limited financial aid to international students — public colleges and universities do not. However, your need for financial aid may adversely affect your chances for admission. Colleges may prefer to admit international students with sufficient financial resources to attend without college aid.

When you apply for financial aid, a college may require you to complete the Foreign Student Financial Aid Application (FSFAA) prepared by the College Scholarship Service of the College Board. This form is widely available in many countries, or you may obtain it from the financial aid office at the college or the College Scholarship Service in Princeton, New Jersey.

Do not plan to meet educational expenses by working while attending college, especially during the first year. The United States Immigration and Naturalization Service requires you to be a full-time student during your first year of college, leaving little employment time. Furthermore, the INS must approve any off-campus jobs. Permission is granted during the first year of study only under special circumstances.

International students also are required to show proof of medical insurance.

YOUR UNITED STATES VISA

The I-20 is a certificate of eligibility for the F-1 student visa, which you need to enter the United States.

When you are officially admitted to a college in the United States, the college sends you extensive information on procedures to follow, papers required, and deadlines to meet. After you have submitted a commitment deposit and your guarantee of financial support indicating the amount and sources, the college issues you a form known as an I-20. The I-20 is a certificate of eligibility for the student visa, which is required for you to enter the United States.

You must take the I-20 to the American Consulate or Embassy in your country for further processing. The Consulate or Embassy then issues a nonimmigrant student visa, known as an F-1 Visa, which allows you to enter the United States as a full-time student. The majority of foreign students in the United States are studying here as F-1 visa students.

ADMISSION REQUIREMENTS

Admission requirements for international students may be different than those for American students, particularly regarding GPA, test, and test score requirements. Higher GPA's and test scores may be expected. Admissions and test criteria are described in chapter 10: CALIFORNIA STATE UNIVERSITY, chapter 11: UNIVERSITY OF CALIFORNIA, and chapter 12: CALIFORNIA INDEPENDENT COLLEGES. Write to your colleges of interest as soon as possible for their specific guidelines.

Some colleges admit international students for the fall term only.

COLLEGE ADMISSIONS TESTS

You probably must take the same tests for admission as do students from the United States. Additionally, the college may require you to take the TOEFL.

You probably must take the same tests for admission as do students from the United States. Additionally, if you come from a country in which English is not the primary language, the college will likely require you to take the TOEFL.

Detailed information about the ACT, SAT I: Reasoning Test, SAT II: Subject Tests and the TOEFL is presented in chapter 6: COLLEGE ENTRANCE TESTS, Admissions Tests, pages 6--3 to 6--48.

Test content, when in your high school years to take the tests, and scoring procedures are the same for international and United States students. The following test dates, application deadlines, and special costs are specifically for international testing.

ACT

If you want to test outside of the fifty United States, do not complete a registration folder. Contact:

ACT Universal Testing
P.O. Box 4028
Iowa City, Iowa 52243-4028
(319) 337-1332 or (319) 337-1448

SAT I: REASONING TEST AND SAT II: SUBJECT TESTS

You must take a photo identification to the test center in order to test. This identification can be a passport, photo ID, or another document bearing your name, your signature, and a recognizable photograph.

Obtain the *1994-95 Registration Bulletin for the SAT Program, International Edition,* if you are testing outside the United States, Puerto Rico, or United States territories. This bulletin has detailed information regarding registration procedures. Review it carefully.

REGISTRATION INFORMATION

- To change your test choice, test date, test center, reregister, request additional Score Reports, or expedite scores, you may call (609) 771-7600 in Princeton, NJ or the TDD number for the deaf or hard of hearing (609) 882-4118. Services and information are available twenty-four hours a day, seven days a week, if you call from a TouchTone phone.

- If you live more than seventy-five miles from the nearest test center, it may be possible to test closer to your home. A request in writing must accompany your Registration Form. This service is not available for test centers outside the United States for the June test date, nor for any test date in India.

- If you are requesting special arrangements — for example, to test on Sunday or closer to home — send your completed Registration Form and fees (including the overseas processing fee), together with a letter of request, in time to be received by the special requests deadline noted here. The regular registration deadline is not soon enough.

- There are no Sunday administrations for any test date in India.

- You must take a photo identification to the test center in order to test. This identification can be a passport, photo ID, or other document bearing your name, your signature, and a recognizable photograph.

Because of mail delivery delays in many parts of the world, mail your Registration Form at least three to four weeks before the registration deadline.

- Because of mail delivery delays in many parts of the world, mail your Registration Form at least three to four weeks before the registration deadline. Use the airmail envelope provided. Use sufficient postage.

- If you registered but have not received an Admission Ticket by the test date, you can take the test if the test center supervisor has a record of your registration. If the supervisor has no record of your registration, you may be admitted to the test center as a standby provided you pay a standby fee of $30.00 at the time, and space, materials, and staff are available. After the test, you can get a refund of the standby fee if you request it, and if your advance registration can be confirmed.

- If you live far from the test center, call a few days before your test date to confirm that the tests will be given on the scheduled date.
- Answer sheets returned from overseas usually take longer to arrive; therefore, it takes longer than usual for you to receive your score report.

SAT I AND SAT II ADMINISTRATION

This chart indicates test dates and registration deadlines for the international administration of the SAT I: Reasoning Test and the SAT II: Subject Tests. *Because there is no late registration, it is imperative that you mail your application early enough to be received by the regular registration deadline.* If you miss this deadline, you must contact the test center to determine if there is room for you to test as a standby. Standby testing is not permitted for students in Ghana and Nigeria.

SAT I & SAT II 1994-95 INTERNATIONAL REGISTRATION & TEST DATES

Test Date	Regular Registration Receipt Date	Receipt Date For Special Requests
November 5, 1994	September 30, 1994	September 7, 1994
December 3, 1994	October 28, 1994	October 5, 1994
January 28, 1995	December 22, 1994	November 30, 1994
May 6, 1995	March 31, 1995	March 8, 1995
June 3, 1995	April 28, 1995	April 5, 1995

The SAT I: Reasoning Test and the SAT II: Subject Tests cannot be taken on the same day. You must register separately for each test date. You may reregister by telephone unless making a special request.

If you live far from the test center, call a few days before your test date to confirm that the tests will be given on the scheduled date.

EDUCATIONAL OPPORTUNITIES

SAT I AND SAT II TEST CENTERS OUTSIDE OF THE UNITED STATES

United States Territories

American Samoa, Guam, Mariana Islands, Marshall Islands, Virgin Islands.

Countries other than the United States

Antigua, Argentina, Aruba, Australia, Austria, Azerbaijan, Azores, Bahamas, Bahrain, Bangladesh, Barbados, Belarus, Belgium, Belize, Bermuda, Bolivia, Botswana, Brazil, Brunei, Bulgaria, Cameroon, Canada, Cayman Islands, Chile, Colombia, Costa Rica, Croatia, Cuba, Cyprus, Czech Republic, Denmark, Dominica, Dominican Republic, Ecuador, Egypt, El Salvador, England, Estonia, Ethiopia, Fiji, Finland, France, Gambia, Georgia, Germany, Ghana, Greece, Grenada, Guatemala, Guyana, Haiti, Honduras, Hong Kong, Hungary, Iceland, India, Indonesia, Ireland, Israel, Italy, Ivory Coast, Jamaica, Japan, Jordan, Kazakhstan, Kenya, Korea, Kuwait, Kyrgyzstan, Latvia, Lebanon, Lesotho, Lithuania, Luxembourg, Macau, Malawi, Malaysia, Mali, Malta, Mauritius, Mexico, Micronesia (Federated States of), Morocco, Myanmar, Nepal, Netherlands, Netherlands Antilles, New Zealand, Nicaragua, Niger, Nigeria, Northern Ireland, Norway, Oman, Pakistan, Palau (Rep. of), Panama, Papua New Guinea, Paraguay, Peru, Philippines, Poland, Portugal, Qatar, Romania, Russia, St. Kitts, St. Lucia, St. Vincent, Saudi Arabia, Scotland, Senegal, Sierra Leone, Singapore, South Africa, Spain, Sri Lanka (Rep. of), Suriname, Swaziland, Sweden, Switzerland, Syria, Taiwan, Tanzania, Thailand, Togo, Tortola, Trinidad and Tobago, Tunisia, Turkey, Uganda, Ukraine, United Arab Emirates, Uruguay, Uzbekistan, Venezuela, Wales, West Bank (Via Israel), Yemen, Zaire, Zambia, Zimbabwe.

The SAT I: Reasoning Test and SAT II: Subject Tests are administered in numerous test centers throughout the world.

FEES FOR 1994-95 SAT I AND SAT II

All fees are the same as those for testing in the United States with the following exception:

Nonrefundable Service Fees

$10.00 international processing fee for students testing in countries other than the United States, Puerto Rico, and United States territories.

$10.00 surcharge for students in India to pay for extraordinary security measures.

Your scores on the TOEFL demonstrate if your English skills are sufficiently developed for you to successfully attend college in the United States.

Test fee waivers are available only to candidates tested in the United States, Puerto Rico, or U.S. territories and to American citizens attending U.S. Department of Defense and State Department schools abroad.

TOEFL/TWE

The Test of English as a Foreign Language, the TOEFL, is administered in many countries throughout the world. If you come from a country where English is not the major language, you undoubtedly will be expected to take the TOEFL. Your scores on this test demonstrate if your English skills are sufficiently developed for you to successfully attend college in the United States. Obtain the *1994-95 Bulletin Of Information For TOEFL, TWE and TSE, Canada, Europe, Overseas, or Middle East / North Africa (except Israel) Edition,* depending on where you take the test. It contains detailed information regarding registration procedures.

REGISTRATION INFORMATION

- You cannot register at the test center or by personal letter, telephone, fax, or cable. You must complete and mail the Registration Form in the envelope provided in the *1994-95 Bulletin Of Information For TOEFL, TWE and TSE*
- You may obtain the Bulletin, but not register, by contacting:

You cannot register at the test center or by personal letter, telephone, fax, or cable. You must complete and mail the Registration Form.

TOEFL/TSE Services	Telephone: (609) 771-7760
P.O. Box 6151	Fax: (609) 771-7765
Princeton, NJ 08541-6151	Cable: EDUCTESTSVC, Princeton, NJ, USA
USA	Telex: 5106859596 ETSSCHO A PRIN

Call Monday through Friday between 8:30 A.M. and 4:30 P.M., Eastern time.

TOEFL/TWE TEST CENTERS OUTSIDE OF THE UNITED STATES

CANADA: Alberta, British Columbia, Manitoba, New Brunswick, Newfoundland, Northwest Territories, Nova Scotia, Ontario, Prince Edward Island, Quebec, Saskatchewan, Yukon Territory.

EUROPE: Albania, Armenia, Austria, Azerbaijan, Belarus, Belgium, Bulgaria, Croatia, Cyprus, Czech Republic, Denmark, England, Estonia, Finland, France, Georgia, Germany, Greece, Hungary, Iceland, Ireland, Italy, Kazakhstan, Kyrgystan, Latvia, Lithuania, Luxembourg, Malta, Moldova, Netherlands, Norway, Poland, Portugal, Romania, Russia, Scotland, Slovak Republic, Spain, Sweden, Switzerland, Turkey, Turkmenistan, Ukraine, United Kingdom, Uzbekistan, Wales, FMR. Yugoslav Rep. of Macedonia.

OVERSEAS: Antigua, Argentina, Aruba, Bahamas, Bangladesh, Barbados, Belize, Benin, Bermuda, Bolivia, Botswana, Brunei (State of), Burkina Faso, Burma, Burundi, Cameroon, Cape Verde, Central African Republic, Chad, Chile, Colombia, Congo, Costa Rica, Djibouti, Dominican Republic, Ecuador, Equatorial Guinea, El Salvador, Eritrea, Ethiopia, Fiji, Gabon, Gambia, Gaza Strip, Ghana, Grenada, Guadeloupe, Guatemala, Guinea, Guinea-Bissau, Guyana, Haiti, Honduras, Israel, Ivory Coast, Jamaica, Kenya, Lesotho, Macao, Madagascar, Malawi, Maldives, Mali, Martinique, Mauritius, Mozambique, Namibia, Nepal, Netherlands Antilles, New Caledonia, Nicaragua, Niger, Nigeria, Panama, Paraguay, Peru, Philippines, Reunion, Rwanda, St. Kitts, St. Lucia, St. Vincent, Sao Tome & Principe, Senegal, Seychelles, Sierra Leone, Solomon Islands, South Africa, Sri Lanka, Suriname, Swaziland, Tahiti, Tanzania, Togo, Tonga, Trinidad and Tobago, Uganda, Uruguay, Venezuela, West Bank, Zaire, Zambia, Zimbabwe.

The TOEFL is administered in numerous test centers throughout the world.

MIDDLE EAST/NORTH AFRICA: Algeria, Bahrain, Egypt, Jordan, Kuwait, Lebanon, Morocco, Oman, Oatar, Saudi Arabia, Sudan, Syria, Tunisia, United Arab Emirates, Yemen.

FEES FOR 1994-95 INTERNATIONAL TOEFL/TWE

FEES FOR 1994-95 INTERNATIONAL TOEFL/TWE				
TESTING PROGRAM	CANADA	EUROPE	OVERSEAS	MIDDLE EAST/ NORTH AFRICA
FRIDAY	CDN$63	US$53	US$45	US$61
SATURDAY	CDN$53	US$46	US$38	US$54

If you change your test date or do not take the test, you receive a credit of $10.00, which may be used toward another test registration. Cash refunds are not available.

TOEFL/TSE Services mails Score Reports to the institutions after the score reporting date listed on the previous page. To send scores to additional institutions, you must pay the following service fees.

Regular Service: Mailed three weeks after receipt of request or after scores become available. $11.00 per college.
Rush Service: Mailed two working days after receipt of request or after scores become available. $31.00 for the first college, $11.00 for each additional college.

If you come from a country where currency exchange regulations make it difficult to obtain U.S. dollars, TOEFL offers a Registration Fee Certificate program.

If you come from a country where currency exchange regulations make it difficult to obtain U.S. dollars, TOEFL offers a Registration Fee Certificate Service. This program allows family or friends in the United States, Canada, and other countries where U.S. dollars are available to purchase certificates from the TOEFL program for US $55.00. The purchaser can then send the certificate to you as proof of payment for the test fee. The certificate is accepted as a valid form of TOEFL registration fee payment anywhere in the world (except Japan, Taiwan, and the People's Republic of China). Submit the certificate as payment when you register for the TOEFL. For a certificate application and further information contact:

TOEFL Registration Fee Certificate Service
P.O. Box 6155
Princeton, NJ 08541-6155, USA

TWO TESTING PROGRAMS

There are two international testing programs, the Friday Testing Program and the Saturday Testing Program. The form and length of the tests are the same for both programs. Not every country listed on page 8--14 to 8--15 tests on both days. A limited number test on Friday. You must check your registration bulletin for the listing of countries where testing takes place on Friday. The testing schedule shown is for Overseas, Europe, and the Middle East/North Africa. The schedule for Canada is the same as for the United States, see chapter 6: COLLEGE ENTRANCE TESTS, Admissions Tests, page 6--3 to 6--48.

There are two overseas testing programs, the Friday Testing Program and the Saturday Testing Program. The form and length of the tests are the same for both programs.

TOEFL/TWE 1994-95 INTERNATIONAL TEST ADMINISTRATION AND REGISTRATION DATES
THE FRIDAY TESTING PROGRAM

TOEFL	TWE (Note 1)	Test Dates	Registration Deadline Dates (Note 2)	Approximate Score Report Mailing Dates
Yes(3)		July 8, 1994	May 23, 1994	August 17, 1994
Yes(3)	Yes	September 9, 1994	July 25, 1994	October 19, 1994
Yes		December 9, 1994	October 24, 1994	January 18, 1995
Yes		March 10, 1995	January 23, 1995	April 19, 1995
Yes		June 2, 1995	April 17, 1995	July 12, 1995

TOEFL/TWE 1994-95 INTERNATIONAL TEST ADMINISTRATION AND REGISTRATION DATES
THE SATURDAY TESTING PROGRAM

TOEFL	TWE (Note 1)	Test Dates	Registration Deadline Dates (Note 2)	Approximate Score Report Mailing Dates
Yes(3)	Yes	August 6, 1994	June 20, 1994	September 14, 1994
Yes(3)	Yes	October 22, 1994	September 5, 1994	November 30, 1994
Yes		November 19, 1994	October 3, 1994	December 28, 1994
Yes		January 14, 1995	November 28, 1994	February 22, 1995
Yes	Yes	February 11, 1995	December 27, 1994	March 22, 1995
Yes		April 22, 1995	March 6, 1995	May 31, 1995
Yes(3)	Yes	May 13, 1995	March 27, 1995	June 21, 1995

Late registration is not permitted.

Note 1: TWE is given with the TOEFL test at these administrations. Examinees are expected to write a TWE essay.
Note 2: If your Registration Form arrives after these deadline dates, it is processed according to your instructions given on your Registration Form. You are offered the options of the next Friday date, the next Saturday date, or a refund. There is no late registration permitted.
Note 3: Examinees who complete the TOEFL test given on these dates are permitted to keep their test books.

Chapter 9

CALIFORNIA COMMUNITY COLLEGES

Three out of four college-bound California high school graduates continue their education at a California Community College. They enroll to prepare for transfer to a four-year institution or to develop career skills. The California Community Colleges' open admission policies and low costs offer every student an opportunity to receive a college education.

OVERVIEW

There are one-hundred seven publicly-supported California Community Colleges located throughout the state. They offer low-cost education to more than 1.3 million students annually. Projections indicate that enrollment will reach 1.9 million by the year 2005.

Seventy-six percent of students attend part-time, eighty percent work, and at least forty percent work full time. The ethnic and gender enrollment of the community colleges reflects the state's diversity.

Hispanic	21%
Black	8%
Asian	12%
White	54%
Men	45%
Women	55%

There are one-hundred seven California Community Colleges located throughout the state.

CURRICULAR PROGRAMS

Community colleges offer two curricular programs:

1. Transfer programs to prepare students for transfer to four-year institutions.

2. Occupational programs to prepare students for immediate employment. Depending upon the particular program that is successfully completed, students receive either a Certificate of Proficiency/Completion or an Associates degree.

In addition, the community colleges offer classes for basic skills development, self-enrichment, and professional growth. Classes take place in the daytime and in the late afternoon and evening to accommodate the working adult. Several community colleges offer study-abroad programs. Honors programs provide enriched academic opportunities.

ACADEMIC CALENDAR

The following seven campuses operate on a quarter system. The remaining one-hundred campuses operate on a semester system.

Chabot College
Chaffey College
College of Alameda
De Anza College
Foothill College
Lake Tahoe Community College
Las Positas College

Thirteen community colleges provide campus housing.

HOUSING

Most California Community Colleges are designed to serve commuting students. However, the following schools provide campus housing.

Bakersfield College
College of the Redwoods
College of the Siskiyous
Columbia College
Cuesta College
Feather River College
Kings River Community College
Lassen College
Santa Rosa Junior College
Shasta College
Sierra College
Taft College
Yuba College

The community colleges have bulletin board listings of available off-campus housing.

CALIFORNIA COMMUNITY COLLEGES

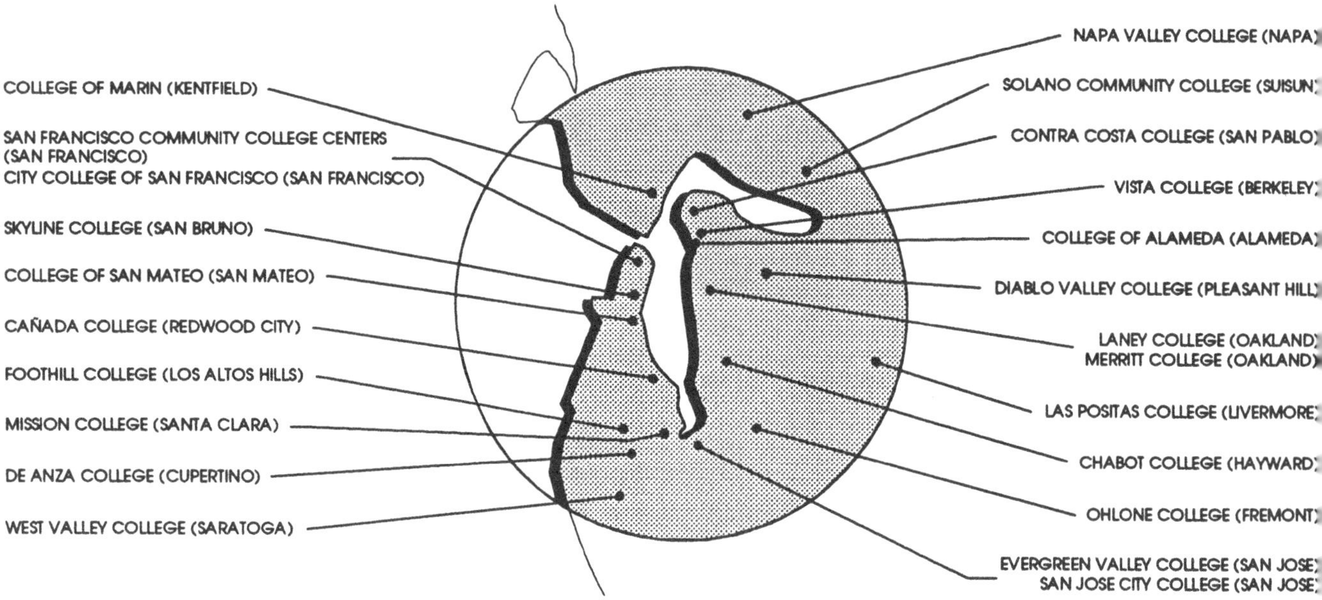

SAN FRANCISCO BAY AREA

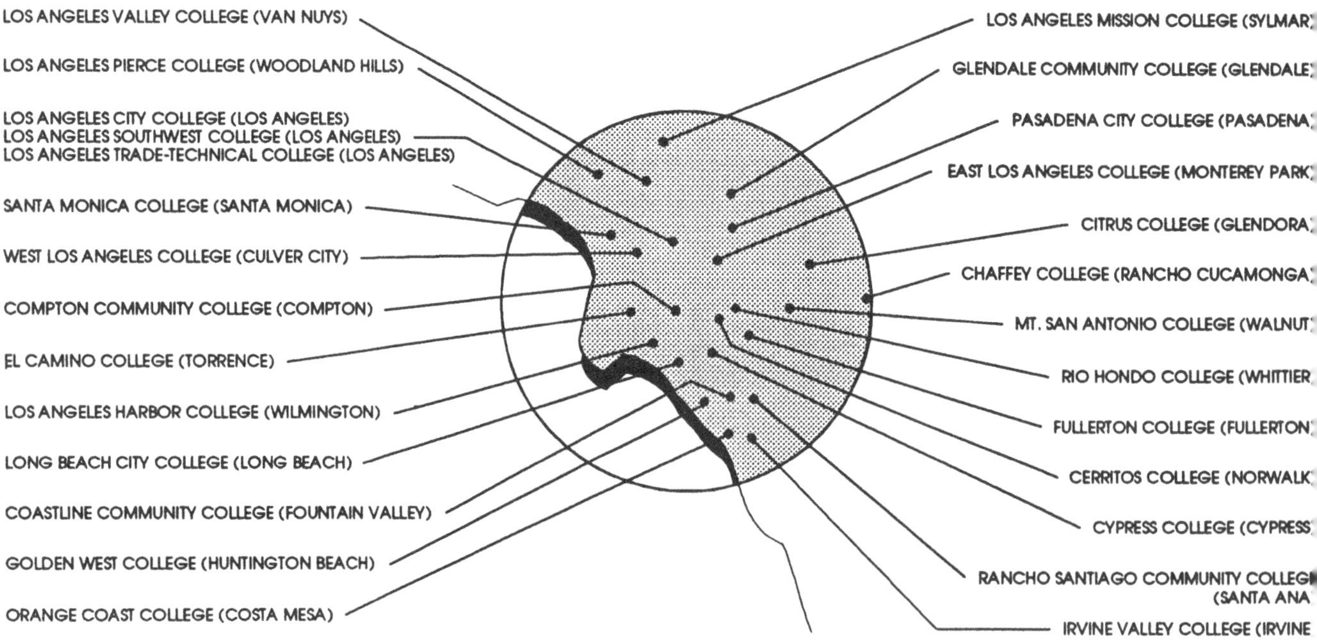

GREATER LOS ANGELES AREA

CALIFORNIA COMMUNITY COLLEGES

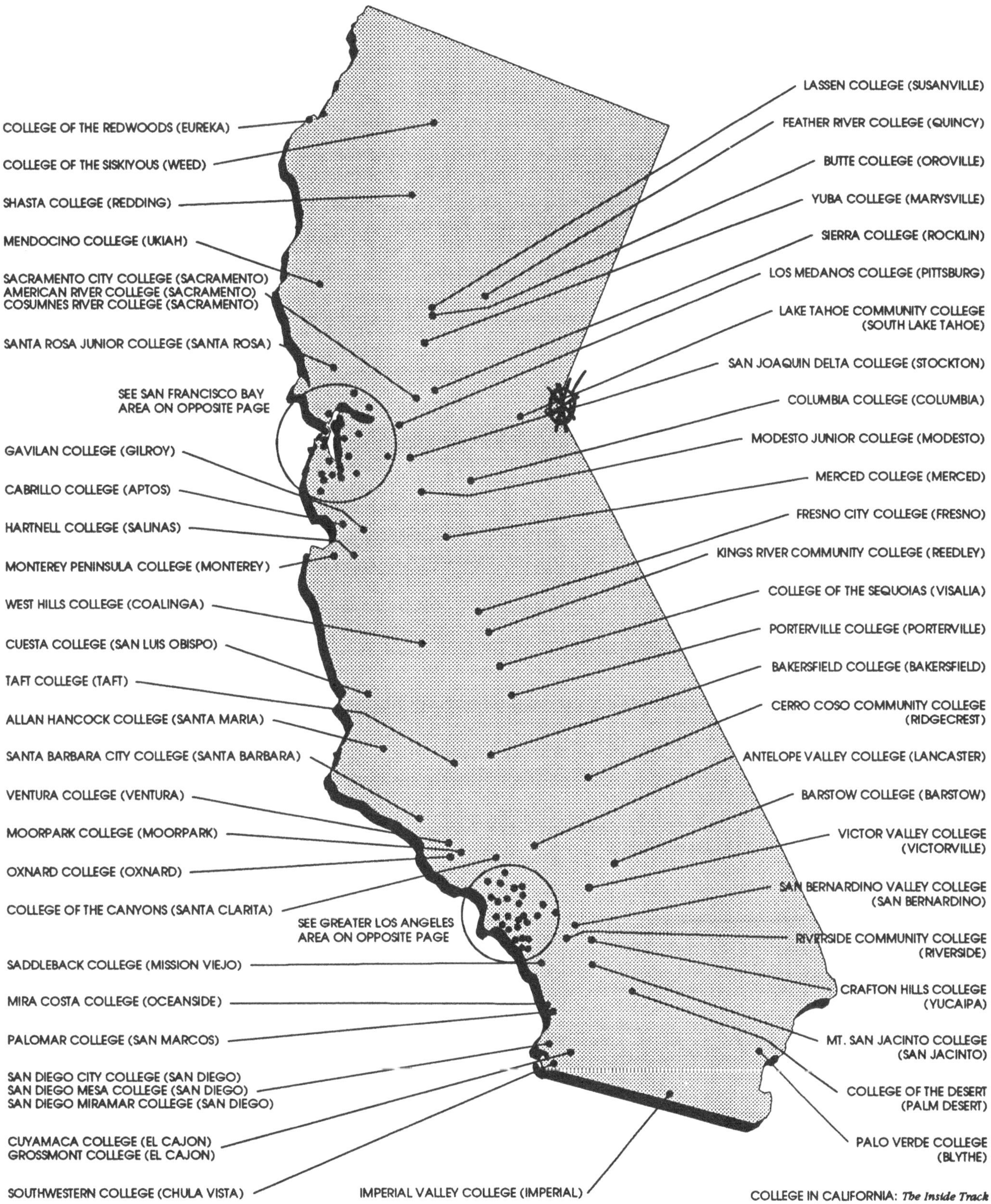

COLLEGE IN CALIFORNIA: *The Inside Track*

CAMPUS LIFE

Community colleges offer numerous extracurricular opportunities: Clubs, student government, and intercollegiate and intramural sports competition. Many clubs are related to occupational majors.

STUDENT SERVICES

EOPS provides special counseling, tutoring, and financial aid for students with economic, cultural, and/or language needs.

The California Community Colleges offer a full complement of student services including educational and career planning, tutoring, personal counseling, job placement, child care, programs for the learning- and physically-disabled, reentry counseling for the older returning student, services for welfare-dependent single heads of households, financial aid, and veteran advising.

Several programs recruit and encourage educationally-disadvantaged and underrepresented minority students. Extended Opportunity Programs and Services (EOPS) provides special counseling, tutoring, and financial aid for students with economic, cultural, and/or language needs.

ADMISSION REQUIREMENTS

CALIFORNIA COMMUNITY COLLEGES HAVE AN OPEN ADMISSIONS POLICY

You may attend any California Community College in the state.
If you have a high school diploma, you are admitted regardless of your age, prior course work, or grades.

If you do not have a high school diploma, you are admitted if

a. you are eighteen years of age or older, or
b. you have successfully passed the California High School Proficiency Examination, or
c. you have successfully passed the GED (General Education Development) Examination.

Most community colleges require placement testing of incoming students.

If you are currently attending high school and would like to take classes at the community college for enrichment or to make up credit, you may attend with written permission from your parents and your high school.

PLACEMENT TESTING

To assess your basic skill levels and help you select courses that are appropriate to these skills, most community colleges require placement testing of incoming students. These tests generally are in English, reading, and mathematics and are administered for advisory purposes. Test scores are not admission criteria.

Each community college has its own policies regarding placement assessment procedures, specific tests to administer, and use of test scores to establish course eligibility. Some community colleges use SAT I: Reasoning Test and ACT test scores for placement purposes. Several community colleges have developed self-assessment procedures instead of tests to help you determine for yourself the course level appropriate to your academic skills. If your community college requires or recommends their own tests or self-assessment activities, they usually take place prior to your registration for classes. No special preparation is needed.

Each community college has its own policies regarding placement assessment procedures, specific tests to administer, and the use of test scores to establish course eligibility.

You may feel your placement test scores do not accurately portray your skill level, and you would like to take a course for which you do not appear to be qualified. The colleges have a variety of procedures by which you can request a waiver of test results and enroll in the classes you want. These procedures may include meeting with a counselor, a dean, a department head, retaking the test, and/or signing a waiver form. Be sure to inquire at your community college about their particular policies, but consider carefully before you pursue this option. College-level courses are much more difficult and demanding than high school classes. You do not want to overextend yourself, especially during your first semester or quarter at college.

APPLICATION PROCEDURES

Pick up an application at your high school career center or guidance center, or request it directly from the California Community College you wish to attend. Applications for the following fall may be available as early as September of your senior year. The community colleges encourage you to apply during your senior year for fall admission. There is no fee for applying. Ask your high school to send a copy of your final high school transcript as soon as you have graduated to complete your application process.

Most California Community Colleges require you to attend an Orientation to College program which presents an overview of their school, and reviews major, Certificate, Associates degree, and transfer requirements. It also guides you in creating an educational plan of the courses needed to meet your educational goals. Your test scores probably will be used in this planning process.

Most California Community Colleges require you to attend an Orientation to College program.

Each community college which offers one, develops its own Orientation to College program. The college usually notifies you about it when you apply for admission. These programs vary from a few hours to a full day or more and range from individual conferences to class presentations.

Orientation is very beneficial to you in planning your course selections, and you should complete it as soon as possible after submitting your admission application and before enrolling in classes. The earlier you select your classes the better are your chances of getting the courses you need at the times you want them. Classes do fill up. Do not wait until late July or August to apply and register for fall unless the community college requires this.

If your community college does not offer orientation, arrange an appointment with a college counselor to explain program requirements and to help you develop your educational plan.

1994-95 COSTS

Each community college course you sign up for is worth a particular number of units (called credits in high school). The college catalogue and the class schedule present course and unit information. All California Community Colleges charge enrollment fees based upon the total course units in which you enroll as shown here:

CALIFORNIA COMMUNITY COLLEGE 1994-95 ENROLLMENT FEES		
	Per Semester at a Semester System Campus	Per Quarter at a Quarter System Campus
For students without a Bachelor' s degree	$13.00/Unit	Fall, winter terms.........$9.00/Unit Spring term..................$8.00/Unit
For students with a Bachelor' s degree	$50.00/Unit	Fall, winter terms.......$34.00/Unit Spring term.................$33.00/Unit

All California Community Colleges charge enrollment fees based upon the total course units in which you enroll.

The maximum amount for enrollment fees for the 1994-95 academic year of two semesters or three quarters depends upon the number of units in which you enroll. These fees are effective for students enrolling in classes which begin fall 1994. All fees may change annually.

You may be exempt from paying the higher fees for those with Bachelor's degrees if you are (a) a Dislocated Worker, (b) a Displaced Homemaker, or (c) a recipient of public assistance. Contact the financial aid office at the community college.

CALIFORNIA COMMUNITY COLLEGES

GENERAL FEES

Living at Home and Commuting *$5,226*
Living Off-Campus *$8,760*
Living On-Campus *$6,700*

In addition to these enrollment fees, the community college may charge you other general fees for such items as parking, health services, student body activities, and campus-center usage. You must also pay for your own textbooks and supplies. This table shows the estimated average expenses for a California resident attending California Community College during the 1994-95 academic year.

Nonresidents of California are required to pay tuition in addition to enrollment fees.

These estimated figures include fees, room and board expenses, books, supplies, transportation, and personal expenses such as laundry, clothing, and entertainment. Nonresidents must add tuition costs to these figures.

NONRESIDENT COSTS

In addition to enrollment and other general fees, nonresidents of California are required to pay tuition of $112.00 per semester unit/$75.00 per quarter unit plus fees. See appendix A: CALIFORNIA RESIDENCY REQUIREMENTS. Undocumented alien students are considered nonresidents of California and must pay nonresident tuition plus fees.

Financial Aid

One in ten community college students receives financial aid. A variety of scholarships, grants, loans, and work-study opportunities are available. The Board of Governors Grants is a special program for California Community College students which pays enrollment fees for students needing financial assistance. See chapter 4: PAYING FOR COLLEGE for a description of financial aid opportunities.

One in ten community college students receives financial aid.

TRANSFER PROGRAMS

Forty-five percent of all community college students plan to transfer to four-year colleges or universities. More than 70,000 students transfer each year and complete their Bachelor's degree programs with the same success as those students who began their college educations at four-year institutions. More than fifty percent of California State University graduates and twenty percent of University of California graduates have transferred from California Community Colleges. Of every ten community college students who transfer, seven go to a CSU campus, one to a UC campus, one to an independent college, and one goes to an out-of-state school.

If, upon graduation from high school, you enroll in a regular session at a California Community College (not including the summer session immediately after graduation), you are considered a transfer student. Once classified as a transfer student, you cannot disregard your college record and apply for freshman admission to a four-year institution. You must apply as a transfer student and meet whatever transfer requirements the four-year college has established.

California State University and the University of California give priority consideration to California Community College transfers over transfers from four-year institutions. The independent colleges in California have individually established criteria for admitting transfer students.

You may choose to enroll in a transfer program for a number of reasons:

- Your academic record does not qualify you for the four-year college in which you are most interested because of inappropriate courses, grades below acceptable levels, or non-qualifying entrance test scores.
- Your academic record qualifies you for a four-year college, but you are not accepted into the college or the major you prefer because of intense competition for admission.
- You may not feel ready to go directly to a four-year institution immediately out of high school — you prefer to stay close to home a while longer.
- Smaller class sizes, more personal attention, and special services provided by most California Community Colleges may better meet your needs.
- Money may be an issue in your decision. Community college fees are considerably less than the fees and/or tuition at four-year institutions, whether they are public or independent. Students usually attend community colleges close to home to keep living costs and transportation expenses as low as possible.

CSU and UC give priority consideration to California Community College transfers over transfers from four-year colleges.

- Friends, family commitments, location, and a job are some other reasons students choose the community college.

General Tips For Planning Your Transfer Program

The minimum course and unit requirements to transfer vary depending upon the college or university to which you plan to transfer and the major you select.

When planning your transfer program, you must consider:

a. Minimum admission requirements (total units and college GPA) you must satisfy to transfer to the four-year school and program of interest to you.

b. The courses you must take to earn these units and this GPA.

The remainder of this section, Transfer Programs, describes these considerations for CSU, UC and the California independent colleges.

Planning your transfer program can be difficult and confusing. The minimum course and unit requirements to transfer vary depending upon the college or university to which you plan to transfer and the major you select.

Every California Community College has its own course titles and course identification numbers. It is very hard to know which courses at your community college are equivalent to the courses required for transfer and listed in the four-year college catalogue. "Beginning psychology" might be called "intro to psychology" or "general psychology," or some other title variation. It may be identified numerically as "psychology 1" or "psychology 101." You need to investigate and plan very carefully to complete appropriate courses needed to reach your transfer goals.

There are several sources of information to explore when you have questions regarding your transfer plans.

- Attend your community college orientation if it is offered. The instructor will likely review transfer requirements.

The four-year institution to which you plan to transfer is a key source of information.

- Contact the counseling staff at your community college. They have most of the information you need to make well-informed choices and plans. Make an individual appointment, either before you enroll or shortly thereafter, to develop your schedule. Once you have established this connection with a counselor, meet with him or her on a regular basis as you progress through your program.
- Research the general catalogue of the four-year college to which you plan to transfer.
- If your community college has a transfer center, it can provide extensive four-year college information. It probably has a program for four-year college representatives to make presentations and meet with students.
- If you have unanswered questions, contact the admissions office of the four-year institution to which you are interested in transferring. This is particularly important if you plan to transfer to an independent college.

- If you meet with an admissions officer, counselor, or advisor, bring your community college catalogue with you so the advisor can give you specific course suggestions for planning your program. Make an educational plan for at least one academic year.

As you develop your California Community College educational plan, check each course carefully to make sure it is transferable. Determine if it can transfer to California State University and/or the University of California. Your community college catalogue should indicate this information. Generally, if a course is acceptable for transfer to these institutions, it also qualifies for transfer to independent colleges. To be certain, contact the independent institution in which you are interested and inquire.

Check each community college course to make sure it is transferable.

Your skill level, as indicated by your placement testing, may need further development for you to be successful in a transferable course. You may need to enroll in developmental courses to better prepare you. For example, at least one semester of English composition generally is required to transfer to California State University, the University of California, and most independent colleges. If you do not appear to be qualified for the community college English composition course (indeed, many students do not score high enough on the community college placement tests to qualify), you will need to take preparatory, developmental classes in writing, and possibly reading, to prepare you. Generally, these developmental classes are not transferable. You cannot use their units toward your total units needed to transfer or toward a Bachelor's degree. Do not get discouraged. Students directly entering a four-year college often do not qualify for English composition and must take noncredit preparatory courses at the four-year institution.

Completing your freshman and sophomore coursework at a community college before transferring as a junior (if this is your plan) may take you more than two years. The length of time depends upon how many nontransferable developmental courses you must take, the transfer requirements of the particular college and major to which you will transfer, and how many units you carry each semester or quarter. For example, 56 semester/84 quarter transferable units are required to transfer as a junior to California State University or the University of California. To complete your transfer program in two years, you must carry approximately 15 transferable units each semester or quarter. You could carry fewer units during the school year by attending summer school. If you have a job, the number of hours you work may affect the number of units you can successfully complete each term.

Completing your freshman and sophomore coursework at a community college before transferring may take you more than two years.

Colleges set a limit on the total number of transfer units they accept. Additional units can count toward fulfilling specific subject requirements, but they cannot be used for credit toward the Bachelor's degree. Check this out early to avoid taking excess units that the college will not credit toward your four-year degree.

You can transfer between a semester system and a quarter system. Before you transfer, it is important that you try to complete series courses (such as chemistry 1A-1B) to avoid duplicating coursework. All transferable units are converted if necessary. To convert semester units to quarter units, multiply semester units by $^3/_2$; to convert quarter units to semester units, multiply quarter units by $^2/_3$.

COMPONENTS OF A TRANSFER PROGRAM

To receive your Bachelor's degree from a four-year college, you must fulfill both the requirements of your major *and* the General Education/Breadth Requirement specified by the four-year institution. See chapter 3: CHOOSING YOUR MAJOR, College Degrees, page 3--3. You may complete the freshman and sophomore levels (lower-division) of these requirements at the California Community College. However, no junior- or senior-level (upper-division) courses are available at community colleges.

To receive your Bachelor's degree from a four-year college, you must fulfill both the requirements of your major and the General Education/ Breadth Requirement specified by the four-year institution.

MAJOR PREPARATION REQUIREMENTS

Major Preparation Requirements are those courses you must take during your first two years of college to prepare for advanced study in your major during your junior and senior years. They may be required to gain admission to your major, they may be a part of your major, or they may be prerequisites for more advanced courses in your major. Four-year colleges differ in their course requirements for majors. If you have a particular four-year school in mind, find out about the lower-division courses needed to prepare for your major. Include these courses in your community college educational planning. If your major requires mathematics and science, it is particularly important that you complete all of the prerequisites for these subject areas before you transfer.

GENERAL EDUCATION (GE)/ BREADTH REQUIREMENT

California colleges and universities have designed the General Education (GE) Requirement to give undergraduates a broad background in the arts and sciences regardless of major. This requirement is the foundation for the undergraduate Associates and Bachelor's degrees. The General Education Requirement, sometimes called the Breadth Requirement, identifies the academic areas you must study, specific courses you must take, and units you must complete in each academic area.

The General Education/Breadth Requirement is not an admission requirement. It can be compared to high school graduation requirements. To graduate from high school, you must take and earn so many credits in certain courses: English, mathematics, science, history .... Similarly, colleges also expect their students to complete and earn so many units in certain courses from various academic areas to graduate and receive a degree.

General Education/ Breadth Requirement courses give you a broad background in the arts and sciences regardless of your major.

The following list of academic areas is fairly typical of those which are included in the General Education/Breadth Requirement.

GENERAL EDUCATION/BREADTH REQUIREMENT
ACADEMIC AREAS

English Communication/Critical Thinking
Social and Behavioral Sciences
The Arts
Humanities
Mathematics
Physical and Biological Sciences

Lower division: Lower-division (freshman/sophomore) General Education/Breadth Requirement courses may be taken at a community college.

Upper division: The upper-division (junior/senior) General Education/Breadth Requirement is fulfilled as part of your junior and senior year curriculum after you transfer to a four-year institution.

The majority of General Education/Breadth Requirement courses needed for a four-year degree are lower-division courses. The last two years of college focus more upon your major. The four-year college catalogue can provide you with information about particular lower-division and upper-division GE/Breadth Requirements and the courses to meet them.

The GE/Breadth Requirement is not the same at each four-year college and university.

SATISFYING THE GENERAL EDUCATION/BREADTH REQUIREMENT

The GE/Breadth Requirement is not the same at each four-year college and university. It can differ in the type and number of academic areas, the specific courses within an academic area, and/or the number of units necessary to satisfy the requirements of an academic area.

While there has been progress in standardizing the GE/Breadth Requirement among schools, institutions have their own campus-specific versions of the GE/Breadth Requirement. There is considerable but not total commonality among these various versions. The absence of a truly common set of academic areas, courses, and required units can have unfortunate consequences for the unwary transfer student who does not have a well-developed transfer plan. Although no common requirements have been developed for independent institutions, there are two programs of common lower-division GE/Breadth Requirement courses within the California public university systems. The two programs are:

1. The CSU GE/Breadth Certification Program for lower-division transfer to any one of the twenty CSU campuses.
2. IGETC for lower-division transfer to any one of the twenty CSU campuses or any one of the nine UC campuses.

There are two programs of common lower-division GE/Breadth Requirement courses within the California public university systems.

These programs are described fully on the next several pages. Depending upon your particular transfer plans, following one of these programs may offer you the assurance of completing all of your lower-division GE/Breadth Requirement courses at a community college in anticipation of transferring. These are the principal advantages of successfully participating in one of these programs:

1. If you complete one of these programs, you will not find yourself in the situation of having to take lower-division GE/Breadth Requirement courses after you transfer. Also, completion will improve your chances for admission to impacted programs.

2. If you pursuing either of these programs while attending a community college, you need not select the specific CSU campus to which you will transfer.

3. If you elect the IGETC program while attending a community college, you may keep open both your decision to transfer to either the CSU system or the UC system and your choice of specific campus in either system.

You are not obliged to participate in either the CSU GE/Breadth Certification Program or IGETC. Instead, you may elect to satisfy the GE/Breadth Requirement of a *particular* CSU or UC campus.

Although you may concentrate on satisfying the General Education/ Breadth Requirement at the community college, you should also begin preparing for your major as soon as you have selected one.

Although you may concentrate on satisfying the General Education/Breadth Requirement at the community college, you should also begin preparing for your major as soon as you have selected one. Lack of pre-major work may affect your eligibility for transfer to your major, particularly if the major at a specific college has many applicants and a limited number of spaces. A major such as Engineering, which requires a great number of lower-division courses and units to prepare for upper-division courses, may force you to concentrate on your Major Preparation Requirements, postponing some of your lower-division General Education/Breadth Requirement courses until after you have transferred. The following table summarizes the options available to meet lower-division transfer requirements.

<table>
<tr><th colspan="4">CALIFORNIA COMMUNITY COLLEGE
LOWER-DIVISION TRANSFER PROGRAM OPTIONS</th></tr>
<tr><th></th><th>California State University</th><th>University of California</th><th>Independent Colleges and Universities</th></tr>
<tr><td>Major Preparation Requirements met by ...</td><td>Campus-Specific Major Preparation Requirements</td><td>Campus-Specific Major Preparation Requirements</td><td>Campus-Specific Major Preparation Requirements</td></tr>
<tr><td rowspan="2">General Education/Breadth Requirements met by ...</td><td colspan="2">IGETC</td><td rowspan="2">Campus-Specific GE/Breadth Requirements</td></tr>
<tr><td>or . . .
CSU GE/Breadth Requirements Certification Program</td><td>or . . .
UC Campus-Specific GE/Breadth Requirements</td></tr>
</table>

Articulation Agreements identify specific community college courses that participating four-year colleges have agreed are equivalent to their courses and acceptable for transfer.

ADDITIONAL INFORMATION ABOUT TRANSFERRING

- You must plan carefully for the completion of both Major Preparation Requirements and the GE/Breadth Requirement. Try to decide upon and then research the four-year college and the major you want as early as possible to determine the Major Preparation Requirements courses and the GE/Breadth Requirement courses that are expected of transfer students. Careful planning will minimize the loss of credit and/or time in your progress toward your Bachelor's degree.

- **Articulation Agreements:** California Community Colleges have Articulation Agreements with four-year institutions. These agreements identify specific community college courses that participating four-year institutions have agreed are equivalent to their courses, and acceptable for transfer. These agreements also state which courses meet General Education/Breadth Requirement and Major Preparation Requirements — information essential to planning your transfer program.

All California Community Colleges do not have Articulation Agreements with all four-year institutions in California. Agreements regarding transferable courses and the GE/Breadth Requirement are often developed. However, agreements regarding Major Preparation Requirements usually exist only with those four-year schools to which a particular community college's students most frequently transfer. More information about transferable courses and programs is available in your California Community College counseling and/or transfer center.

If you have not decided upon a major, you can transfer as a liberal arts student or Undeclared.

- If you are unsure of your college goals but plan to continue your education at a California State University or University of California campus, you can meet your GE/Breadth Requirement for both systems simultaneously as described below in the section: IGETC.
- If you have not decided upon a major, you can transfer as a liberal arts student or Undeclared.
- Independent colleges have their own General Education/Breadth Requirement and Major Preparation Requirements course expectations of transfers.
- Do you plan to transfer before your junior year? As a junior? Your four-year school specifies the minimum number of units you need as well as the particular subject areas and courses you must complete for either plan. Further, the college probably requires a minimum GPA in transferable units.
- You may or may not need to complete your entire General Education/Breadth Requirement and/or all of your Major Preparation Requirements before transferring. Research the minimum required for the particular school and also the major you have in mind.
- The maximum number of units that can be transferred differs among four-year schools. CSU and UC have set 70 semester/105 quarter units as the maximum number. The independent colleges have individually-determined limits.

IGETC — Intersegmental General Education Transfer Curriculum

IGETC is particularly helpful if you have not decided if you wish to transfer to a CSU or a UC campus.

The IGETC (pronounced eye-GET-see) is a transfer curriculum which allows California Community College students to meet simultaneously the lower-division (freshman/sophomore) General Education/Breadth Requirement at both California State University and the University of California. The IGETC was developed to simplify the transfer process for students. It is *one* option you can choose to complete your General Education/Breadth Requirement in preparation for transfer. It allows you to work toward meeting the lower-division General Education/Breadth Requirement at California State University or the University of California beginning in your first term at a community college. IGETC is especially helpful if you have not decided if you wish to transfer to a CSU or UC campus. *You can remain undecided and fulfill the GE/Breadth Requirement for both systems with the same coursework.*

IGETC SUBJECT AND UNIT REQUIREMENTS		
Subject Area	**Required Courses**	**Units Required**
1. ENGLISH COMMUNICATION One course in English composition and one course in critical thinking/English composition. Students transferring to CSU must take an additional course in oral communication.	2 Courses	6 Semester Units or 8 to 10 Quarter Units
2. MATHEMATICS CONCEPTS AND QUANTITATIVE REASONING	1 Course	3 Semester Units or 4 to 5 Quarter Units
3. ARTS AND HUMANITIES Three courses with at least one from the arts and one from the humanities.	3 Courses	9 Semester Units or 12 to 15 Quarter Units
4. SOCIAL AND BEHAVIORAL SCIENCES Three courses from at least two disciplines or an interdisciplinary sequence.(1)	3 Courses	9 Semester Units or 12 to 15 Quarter Units
5. PHYSICAL AND BIOLOGICAL SCIENCES One physical science course and one biological science course, at least one of which includes a laboratory.	2 Courses	7 to 9 Semester Units or 9 to 12 Quarter Units
6. LANGUAGE OTHER THAN ENGLISH Proficiency equivalent to two years of high school in the same language. Not required of students transferring to CSU.	Proficiency	Proficiency
TOTAL	11 Courses	**34 Semester Units or 49 Quarter Units**

Note 1. Disciplines in the Social and Behavioral Sciences are courses such as anthropology, geography, psychology, economics, political science, and sociology.

IGETC is a transfer curriculum which allows community college students to meet simultaneously the lower-division GE/Breadth Requirements of both CSU and UC.

CALIFORNIA COMMUNITY COLLEGES

ADDITIONAL INFORMATION

To transfer to California State University ...

a. You must take an additional 3 semester/4 quarter unit course in oral communications, raising the unit requirement in the English Communication Subject Area to 9 semester/13 quarter units and the total IGETC unit requirement to 37 semester/49 quarter units.

b. You do not need to demonstrate proficiency in a language other than English.

To transfer to the University of California ...

You must demonstrate a proficiency in a language other than English equivalent to two years of high school study in the same language. This requirement may be fulfilled by completion of two years of foreign language in high school with a C or better, or equivalent proficiency demonstrated by college courses. A minimum score of 550 on an SAT II: Subject Test in a foreign language, or a score of 3 or higher on an Advanced Placement Examination in a foreign language also meets this requirement.

After you complete the IGETC pattern, you may apply to your community college for Certification of Completion of IGETC. A record of this certification is sent on your transcript to the California State University or the University of California campus to which you transfer. This certification assures you that after transfer, you will not be required to take additional *lower-division* General Education/Breadth Requirement courses at CSU or UC.

Completion and certification of IGETC assures you that you will not be required to take additional lower-division General Education/ Breadth Requirement courses at CSU or UC.

COMMONLY ASKED QUESTIONS ABOUT IGETC

HOW DO I KNOW WHICH COURSES TO TAKE AT THE CALIFORNIA COMMUNITY COLLEGE TO FULFILL EACH OF THE IGETC AREAS?

California State University and the University of California have coordinated with the California Community Colleges to develop agreements that identify the community college courses that may be applied to each academic area of the IGETC. Your community college can provide you with an approved IGETC course list.

IS THE IGETC AN ADMISSION REQUIREMENT?

No, the IGETC is not an admission requirement. It is one of your options for satisfying your lower-division General Education/Breadth Requirement. Completing the IGETC does not guarantee admission to California State University or the University of California. However, completing the lower-division General Education/Breadth Requirement through the IGETC may improve your chances of admission to a competitive campus and/or major.

Completing the IGETC does not guarantee admission to CSU or UC, although it may improve your chances of admission to a competitive campus and/or major.

IF I DO NOT COMPLETE THE ENTIRE IGETC BEFORE TRANSFERRING, CAN I COMPLETE MY REMAINING IGETC COURSES AT CALIFORNIA STATE UNIVERSITY OR THE UNIVERSITY OF CALIFORNIA?

No, you cannot. If you select IGETC as your option for meeting your lower-division General Education/Breadth Requirement, you must complete it entirely in all subject and unit categories, prior to transfer. If you do not, you will be required to complete the Campus-Specific Requirements at the UC college or school to which you transfer or the CSU General Education/Breadth Requirement at the CSU campus. The IGETC courses you have completed at your community college may be applied toward your Bachelor's degree. You may find that to a great extent the IGETC courses satisfy the General Education/Breadth Requirement for transfer to CSU or Campus-Specific Requirements for transfer to UC. UC Campus-Specific and the CSU General Education/ Breadth Requirement are further described later in this chapter.

IS THERE A GPA REQUIREMENT FOR IGETC COURSEWORK?

IGETC courses must be completed with a grade of C or better. A grade of Credit or Pass may be used if the community college's policy states that it is equivalent to a grade of C or better. C-minus is not acceptable.

IGETC courses must be completed with a grade of C or better. C-minus is not acceptable.

MUST I COMPLETE ALL IGETC COURSEWORK AT THE SAME CALIFORNIA COMMUNITY COLLEGE?

Courses may be taken at more than one community college to fulfill the IGETC requirement. However, the application of courses to satisfy IGETC subject areas may vary from one community college to another. A particular course might count in an IGETC area at one community college, but at another it might count in a different IGETC area, or perhaps not count at all. Meet with a counselor if you change community colleges to understand just how courses you have taken elsewhere satisfy to the IGETC areas of your present community college.

CAN COURSEWORK COMPLETED AT OUT-OF-STATE AND INDEPENDENT COLLEGES BE APPLIED TO THE IGETC?

Yes, but only if the California Community College determines that it is equivalent to coursework on its approved IGETC course list. Find out who on your community college campus officially evaluates transcripts, and submit your records for evaluation.

CAN A COURSE BE USED TO SATISFY MORE THAN ONE IGETC SUBJECT AREA?

No. Although a particular course may be listed in more than one subject area, it can be credited to only one.

CAN THE SAME COURSES BE APPLIED TO BOTH THE IGETC AND A MAJOR PREPARATION COURSE REQUIREMENT?

CSU and UC generally allow "double-counting" of courses toward the IGETC and Major Preparation Requirements.

Yes, California State University and the University of California generally allow "double-counting" of courses toward the IGETC and Major Preparation Requirements. Individual campuses or programs may have their own policies regarding double-counting. For example, some campuses allow double-counting of only one course.

CAN ADVANCED PLACEMENT EXAMINATION SCORES BE USED TO SATISFY ANY AREAS OF THE IGETC?

Yes, IGETC course credit may be earned for acceptable scores on Advanced Placement Examinations that the California Community College faculty recognizes as equivalent to its IGETC-approved courses. See chapter 6: COLLEGE ENTRANCE TESTS, AP Program And Examinations, page 6—57.

IS IT TRUE THAT TWO COLLEGES AT THE UNIVERSITY OF CALIFORNIA SAN DIEGO DO NOT ACCEPT THE IGETC?

Yes. Although all other California State University and University of California campuses accept the IGETC, Eleanor Roosevelt and Revelle Colleges at University of California San Diego do not. If you complete the IGETC and plan to attend the University of California San Diego, you must enroll in Muir, Marshall, or Warren College. However, because all majors are offered to students in each of these colleges, eliminating Roosevelt and Revelle as options does not restrict your choice of major. See chapter 11: UNIVERSITY OF CALIFORNIA, Campus Profiles, UC San Diego, page 11--81.

Community college transfer students receive priority consideration for admission to impacted programs at UC.

TRANSFER TO THE UNIVERSITY OF CALIFORNIA

In 1993, almost 8,800 students transferred from California Community Colleges to the University of California. Nearly one-quarter of UC Bachelor's degrees were awarded to students who started their four-year education at a California Community College. Community college transfer students receive priority consideration for admission to impacted programs — programs for which there are more qualified candidates than can be accommodated.

WHEN CAN YOU TRANSFER TO UC?

Are you planning to take a limited number of classes and transfer before all of your freshman and sophomore classes are completed (a lower-division transfer)?

Would you like to complete your freshman and sophomore years at a California Community College and transfer to the University of California as a junior (upper-division transfer)? You must complete 56 semester/84 quarter transferable units to transfer as a junior.

Availability of either of these choices depends upon

a. your eligibility status for freshman admission when you complete high school, and

b. whether or not the college and/or the major you want is accepting lower-division transfers or is requiring students to transfer as juniors with 56 semester/84 quarter transferable units completed.

Minimum admission requirements for transfer to the University of California vary depending upon your eligibility for admission to UC when you graduate from high school.

MINIMUM ADMISSION REQUIREMENTS FOR TRANSFER TO UC

Minimum admission requirements for transfer to the University of California vary depending upon your eligibility for admission to UC when you graduate from high school. Your high school eligibility determines the total units and GPA which you must earn at the California Community College to transfer.

To qualify for admission to the University of California as a transfer student, you must meet one of the three following sets of requirements. In all cases, if you are a California resident, you must have at least a C (2.00) average in all transferable coursework. A nonresident student must satisfy the same requirements, but with a minimum grade point average of 2.80 for all transferable college courses. See appendix A: CALIFORNIA RESIDENCY REQUIREMENTS.

If you were not eligible for admission to UC when you graduated from high school, you must transfer as an upper-division (junior) student.

Before you read the following information, review the Subject, Examination, and Scholarship Requirements for freshman admission to the University of California. See chapter 11: UNIVERSITY OF CALIFORNIA, Minimum Admission Requirements, page 11--5.

IF YOU WERE NOT ELIGIBLE FOR ADMISSION TO THE UNIVERSITY OF CALIFORNIA WHEN YOU GRADUATED FROM HIGH SCHOOL ...

If you were not eligible for admission to the University of California when you graduated from high school because

a. you did not meet the Scholarship Requirement, ***or***

b. you did not meet the Scholarship Requirement, and you did not complete the "a-f" Subject Requirement, ***then***

you must complete 56 semester units/84 quarter units of transferable college credit and be an upper-division transfer. You must earn a GPA of at least a 2.40, ***and satisfy either*** (a) ***or*** (b) below:

a. Take college courses in the subjects you are lacking and earn a grade of C or better in each one. The University of California will waive up to two units of the required high school coursework except in mathematics and English. A high school unit equals one academic year (or two semesters) of study.

b. Complete one college course in mathematics, one in English, and one selected from either United States history, laboratory science, or languages other than English. You must earn a grade of C or better in each course. The course in mathematics must assume a proficiency level equivalent to three years of high school mathematics (i.e., elementary algebra, intermediate algebra, and geometry). It must be at a level beyond intermediate algebra. The course may be trigonometry or a more advanced course in mathematics or statistics for which intermediate algebra is a prerequisite. All courses, with the exception of mathematics, must be transferable to the University.

If you were eligible for admission to the University of California when you graduated from high school, you are eligible to transfer as either a lower-division or upper-division transfer, provided space is available.

IF YOU WERE ELIGIBLE FOR ADMISSION TO THE UNIVERSITY OF CALIFORNIA WHEN YOU GRADUATED FROM HIGH SCHOOL ...

If you were eligible for admission to the University of California when you graduated from high school — you satisfied the "a-f" Subject Requirement, the Examination Requirement, and the Scholarship Requirement — you are eligible to transfer at any time as either a lower-division or upper-division transfer, provided space is available. You must have at least a C (2.00) average in your transferable college courses. Most campuses rarely accept lower-division transfers. Riverside and Santa Cruz will accept lower-division students.

IF YOU MET THE SCHOLARSHIP REQUIREMENT,
BUT DID NOT SATISFY THE "a-f" SUBJECT REQUIREMENT
WHEN YOU GRADUATED FROM HIGH SCHOOL ...

If you met the Scholarship Requirement, but did not satisfy the "a-f" Subject Requirement, you must take college courses in the subjects you are missing to be eligible to transfer as a lower- or upper-division student. One college-level course of at least three semester units/four quarter units is usually considered equivalent to one year of high school study.

If you did not satisfy the "a-f" Subject Requirement when you graduated from high school, you must take college courses in the subjects you are missing to be eligible to transfer.

You must earn a grade of C or better in each of these required courses and an overall C (2.00) average in all transferable college coursework. If you complete less than twelve quarter or semester units of transferable college coursework, you also must satisfy the Examination Requirement (SAT I or ACT and SAT II: Subject tests) for freshman applicants.

CLEARING DEFICIENCIES IN THE UC "a-f" SUBJECT REQUIREMENT

The table on the next page indicates which courses to take at the community college to clear subjects you did not satisfy in high school. This information is valid for high school graduates in 1994 and thereafter. See chapter 11: UNIVERSITY OF CALIFORNIA, Minimum Admission Requirements, page 11--5.

ADDITIONAL INFORMATION ABOUT TRANSFERRING TO UC

- A grade of D in a transferable course is acceptable toward the 56 semester/84 quarter units for transfer, and the course will receive graduation credit at the University. However, any D grade you earn in transferable coursework lowers your GPA for admission. In addition, courses in which you earn a D cannot be used to clear high school "a-f" Subject Requirement deficiencies, and they may not satisfy Major Preparation or General Education/Breadth Requirements. For example, you must receive a grade of C or better in each IGETC course.

A grade of D in a transferable course is acceptable toward the 56 semester/84 quarter units for transfer.

- Each campus of the University of California makes every effort to provide a place for all California-resident applicants who meet the minimum admission requirements described earlier, and who file an application during the appropriate filing period. Further, the campuses are committed to achieving a student body that meets the University's high academic standards and reflects the cultural, racial, geographic, economic, and social diversity of California itself.

- If the number of applicants exceeds the spaces available for a particular campus or major — as is often the case — criteria which exceed the minimum requirements are used to select students.

Meeting the minimum requirements is not enough to gain admission to many University of California campuses and programs.

REQUIREMENTS TO CLEAR SUBJECT REQUIREMENT DEFICIENCIES FOR TRANSFER TO THE UNIVERSITY OF CALIFORNIA

Subject ("a-f") Requirement	High School Requirement	College
a. HISTORY/ SOCIAL SCIENCE	Two Years Two years of history/social science, including one year of U.S. History or one-half year of U.S. History and one-half year of civics or American government; and one year of world history, cultures, and geography.	For a deficiency in U.S. History/civics/American government, a transferable college course of three or more quarter units in U.S. History, civics, or American government. For a deficiency in world history/cultures/geography, a transferable college course of three or more quarter units in world history, cultures, and geography.
b. ENGLISH	Four Years Four years of college-preparatory English that include frequent and regular writing and reading of classic and modern literature, poetry, and drama. Not more than two semesters of ninth grade English can be used to meet this requirement.	For each year of deficiency, one course of four or more quarter units in English composition, literature (American or English), speech, foreign literature in translation, public speaking, or oral interpretation of literature. Literature and speech courses must have substantial composition.
c. MATHEMATICS	Three Years Three years of college-preparatory mathematics that include the topics covered in elementary and advanced algebra and two and three dimensional geometry. Mathematics courses taken in the seventh and eighth grades may be used to fulfill part of this requirement if your high school accepts them as equivalent to its own courses.	For each year of deficiency, one course in mathematics, such as elementary algebra, intermediate algebra, or plane or solid geometry; courses need not be transferable. To clear the entire deficiency, complete one of the following: a nontransferable two semester (or three quarter) unit course in trigonometry; or a transferable mathematics course that employs the topics of intermediate algebra; or a transferable statistics course that has intermediate algebra as a prerequisite.
d. LABORATORY SCIENCE	Two Years Two years of laboratory science providing fundamental knowledge in at least two of these three areas: biology, chemistry, and physics. Laboratory courses in earth/space sciences are acceptable if they have as prerequisites or provide basic knowledge in biology, chemistry, or physics. Not more than one year of laboratory science completed in the ninth grade can be used to meet this requirement.	For each year of deficiency, a course in a natural (physical or biological) science with at least 30 hours of laboratory (not "demonstration"). Applied or vocationally slanted courses are not acceptable, nor are narrowly defined disciplines, e.g., electronics.
e. LANGUAGES OTHER THAN ENGLISH	Two Years Two years of the same language other than English. Courses should emphasize speaking and understanding and include instruction in grammar, vocabulary, reading, and composition.	Any course(s) (excluding conversation) held by your college to be equivalent to two years of high school language. Many colleges list the prerequisites for their second course in language as "Language 1 at this college or two years of high school language." In this case, Language 1 clears both years of the requirement.
f. COLLEGE PREPARATORY ELECTIVES	Two Years Two units (4 semesters), in addition to those required in "a-e" above, chosen from the following areas: visual and performing arts, history, social science, English, advanced mathematics, laboratory science, and language other than English.	For each year of deficiency, any one course beyond those listed above in "a-e", or having courses equivalent to (c), (d), and (e) as prerequisites, or the equivalent of two high school years in a second language. In addition, any transferable course of four or more quarter units in history, social science, or, visual and performing arts.

- Although some University of California campuses are able to admit all eligible transfer applicants, others can accommodate only a limited number each year. Some campuses accept transfer students who have completed a minimum of 56 transferable semester units/84 transferable quarter units. Other campuses and majors accept or give priority consideration only to students who are fully qualified as juniors. To be fully qualified as a junior, a student must have completed a minimum of 60 transferable semester units/90 transferable quarter units prior to transfer. The Berkeley and San Diego campuses, and the business administration major at Riverside accept *only* students who will complete 60 semester/90 quarter units prior to transfer. Davis and Los Angeles *give admission preference* to applicants who have completed these units.

The Berkeley and San Diego campuses, and the Business Administration major at Riverside accept only students who will complete 60 semester/90 quarter units prior to transfer; Davis and Los Angeles give admission preference to applicants who have completed these units.

- Oversubscription (more qualified applicants than can be accommodated) may occur in specific majors as well as on a campuswide basis for applicants at various levels. Some undergraduate programs, such as Engineering, Computer Science, and Business Administration are oversubscribed at most campuses where they are offered. In general, students admitted to oversubscribed programs have demonstrated high levels of scholarship in preparing for University work. Their qualifications usually exceed the minimum eligibility requirements. Most have taken specific courses in preparation for their intended major at the University.

- The following Transfer Profile summarizes by UC campus the average GPA of California resident California Community College transfer applicants with at least 56 semester units who were regularly admitted for fall 1993. The profile is most useful as a guide to selection, rather than as a predictor of an individual student's chances for admission to specific academic programs. The GPA shown is for all college coursework completed as self-reported on the application for undergraduate admission. This self-reported GPA includes grades earned in nontransferable courses; it may differ from a GPA calculated using only transferable coursework.

In each block, the first figure represents the average GPA of fall 1993 community college transfers in the discipline. The second figure is the total number of transfers admitted in the discipline.

1993 COMMUNITY COLLEGE TRANSFER PROFILE

Campus	Engineering	Physical Science	Natural Science	Humanities	Social Science	Other/ Undecided	Total
Berkeley	3.78/178	3.67/135	3.43/145	3.48/403	3.49/399	3.54/281	3.54/1541
Davis	3.53/271	3.40/168	3.37/498	3.38/261	3.32/598	3.24/227	3.37/2023
Irvine	3.45/125	3.25/379	3.28/344	3.05/378	3.20/517	2.89/312	3.16/2055
Los Angeles	3.75/173	3.45/nd	3.42/515	3.29/671	3.34/nd	3.37/258	3.38/2735
Riverside	3.21/23	3.20/53	3.18/298	3.13/135	3.04/250	3.15/227	3.13/987
San Diego	3.45/319	3.41/165	3.37/316	3.35/208	3.28/585	3.28/98	3.35/1691
Santa Barbara	3.58/104	3.30/154	3.22/319	3.22/373	3.18/615	3.19/533	3.22/2098
Santa Cruz	3.37/47	3.27/178	3.23/252	3.27/450	3.24/615	3.23/324	3.25/1866

- Each June the University of California publishes *Answers For Transfers*, a planning guide for prospective transfer students from California Community Colleges as well as four-year colleges and universities. It includes important information about admission and selection procedures. Obtain this guide from your nearest community college.

ADVANCED STANDING SELECTION CRITERIA

In addition to college GPA, the campuses consider other factors such as course pattern and personal qualifications.

In addition to college GPA, the campuses consider other factors such as course pattern and personal qualifications. Completion of specific courses in preparation for your intended major at the University is an important criterion. These other factors identify those students who have demonstrated the capacity for high academic achievement, and who have a variety of other qualities that can contribute to the strength and diversity of the campus community. While the campuses use similar indicators of academic and personal qualifications to evaluate applicants, the specific evaluation process and weight of factors do differ from campus to campus depending upon enrollment targets and the number and qualifications of applicants.

The campuses use the academic criteria described on the following page as the primary means of evaluating advanced standing applicants. Supplemental criteria are used to assess overall likelihood of success at the campus or potential to contribute to the strength and diversity of the student population. The highest priority for advanced standing admission is given to junior-level transfers from California Community Colleges.

ACADEMIC CRITERIA

1. Completion of a specified pattern or number of courses that meet the General Education/Breadth Requirement.

2. Completion of a specified pattern or number of courses that provide continuity with upper-division courses in the selected major.

3. GPA in all transferable courses.

4. Participation in academically-selective honors courses or programs.

The campuses use academic and supplemental criteria to evaluate advanced standing applicants.

SUPPLEMENTAL CRITERIA

1. Special talents, interests, or experiences beyond those indicated by the academic criteria, which demonstrate unusual promise of leadership, achievement, and service in a particular field such as civic life or the arts.

2. Special circumstances that have adversely affected the applicant's life experiences. These circumstances may include, for example, disabilities, personal difficulties, low family income, refugee status, or veteran status.

3. Ethnic identity, gender, and location of residence. These factors are considered to provide cultural, racial, geographic, and socioeconomic diversity in the student population.

MAJOR PREPARATION REQUIREMENTS FOR TRANSFER TO UC

UC encourages you to complete the minimum coursework required to prepare for your major, even at the expense of completing your GE/Breadth Requirement or IGETC coursework.

The University of California encourages you, while attending your California Community College, to complete the minimum coursework required to prepare you for your major even at the expense of completing your General Education/Breadth Requirement or IGETC coursework. In many cases, completing a portion or all of the lower-division major requirements is essential to gain admission to the major at the junior level. Thus, UC places more emphasis upon preparation for your major than upon satisfaction of the GE/Breadth Requirement or IGETC while at the community college. This is particularly important in those professional or "high unit" majors that select applicants on the basis of satisfaction of lower-division Major Preparation requirements.

Research the exact Major Preparation Requirements of the campus to which you plan to apply. Does your community college have an Articulation Agreement with the campus you are planning to attend? What courses does this agreement specify for your intended major? Confer with your community college counselor, read the University of California campus catalogue, and call the University of California campus, if necessary, to clarify any ambiguities. Begin your courses in your major as soon as you have selected it. Lack of pre-major work may affect your eligibility for your major choice when you transfer.

GENERAL EDUCATION/BREADTH REQUIREMENT FOR TRANSFER TO UC

You have two options for fulfilling the lower-division General Education/Breadth Requirement for the University of California.

OPTION 1: IGETC

The IGETC program requires the completion of a minimum of 34 semester/45 quarter units of lower-division coursework with a grade of C or better in each course. The IGETC is most advantageous if you have not yet decided on a major or a campus. In general, it is not advisable for transfers to Engineering majors at any UC campus to use IGETC. If you are entering a "high unit" major, such as science, you can follow the IGETC, but you must be careful to complete the substantial number of science and mathematics lower-division, Major Preparation requirement courses.

A detailed explanation of the IGETC appears earlier in this chapter on page 9--15.

Each school and college at every UC campus has its own particular set of GE/Breadth Requirement courses. They may differ from one another.

OPTION 2: CAMPUS-SPECIFIC GENERAL EDUCATION/BREADTH REQUIREMENT

Each school and college at every University of California campus has its own particular set of General Education/Breadth Requirement courses. These may differ from one another. If you choose the Campus-Specific GE/Breadth Requirement option rather than the IGETC as the means to satisfy this General Education/Breadth Requirement, you must

a. decide upon the specific University of California campus and the school or college on that campus you expect to attend as soon as possible — and certainly by the end of your first year at community college,

b. check the catalogue of that campus and review the lower-division General Education/Breadth Requirement of the school or college at that campus, and

c. develop an educational plan to meet the specific course requirements for the General Education/Breadth Requirement areas described. Do this with your community college counselor just as soon as you make your campus and major decisions.

Develop an educational plan to meet the specific course requirements of the campus-specific General Education/Breadth Requirement.

The Campus-Specific GE/Breadth Requirement option can be complex because of the individuality of each campus and the schools and colleges within it. It is particularly suited to those students who are transferring into high-unit majors such as Engineering and sciences. High-unit majors require extensive lower-division major preparation. Concentrate on completing the many major prerequisites that the campus screens to determine eligibility for admission to these majors. You can complete at the UC campus any part of the General Education/Breadth Requirement not satisfied at the community college. Thus, it is best to follow the specific course requirements of the school or college at that campus for meeting the GE/Breadth Requirement and Major Preparation Requirements.

If you pursue the Campus-Specific GE/Breadth Requirement option for a particular campus and subsequently enroll in a different campus or program, you may need to complete additional courses to meet the Campus-Specific GE/Breadth Requirement of the campus you do attend. Do not be overly concerned. There is considerable similarity and overlap of these requirements from campus to campus.

Completing the lower-division General Education/Breadth Requirement does not guarantee admission to the campus or program of choice. However, completing this requirement, whether through the IGETC or the Campus-Specific GE/Breadth Requirement option, may improve your chances for admission to a competitive campus and/or program.

The University of California has an American history and institutions requirement for graduation.

AMERICAN HISTORY AND INSTITUTIONS REQUIREMENT

The University of California has an American history and institutions requirement for graduation. It is satisfied by completion in high school of a one-year course in United States history, or a half-year course in United States history and a half-year course in American government. The University of California Los Angeles requires you to have earned a B average in these courses. The University of California Santa Barbara does not accept your high school courses for completing this requirement and requires you to complete a college-level course. Satisfaction of your community college American history and institutions requirement for your Associates degree also will meet the requirement at most UC campuses.

Transfer To California State University

California Community College transfers comprise the majority of California State University students in all majors and well over half the Bachelor's degrees awarded each year.

California Community College transfers comprise the majority of California State University students in all majors and well over half the Bachelor's degrees awarded each year. Each year CSU admits approximately 36,000 transfers. Over 28,000 (80%) of these students transfer from a California Community College. About one third of community college transfers are lower-division transfers; two thirds are upper-division transfers.

WHEN CAN YOU TRANSFER?

Are you planning to take a limited number of courses at a California Community College and transfer before all of your freshman and sophomore classes are completed (lower-division transfer)?

Would you like to complete your freshman and sophomore years at a California Community College and transfer to CSU as a junior (upper-division transfer)? You must complete 56 semester/84 quarter transferable units to do so.

Availability of either of these choices depends upon

a. your eligibility status for freshman admission when you complete high school, and

b. whether or not the college and/or the major you want is accepting lower-division transfers or requiring students to transfer as juniors with a minimum of 56 semester/84 quarter transferable units completed.

CALIFORNIA COMMUNITY COLLEGES

MINIMUM ADMISSION REQUIREMENTS FOR TRANSFER TO CSU

The following requirements are applicable to students graduating from high school in 1988 or later.

If you have less than 56 transferable semester/84 transferable quarter units, you are a lower-division transfer student (freshman or sophomore).

LOWER-DIVISION TRANSFER

TO TRANSFER WITH LESS THAN 56 TRANSFERABLE SEMESTER UNITS/84 TRANSFERABLE QUARTER UNITS ...

If you have ***less than 56 transferable semester/84 transferable quarter units***, you are a lower-division transfer student (freshman or sophomore) and you must

a. have a grade point average of C (2.00) or better in all transferable units attempted, and

b. be in good standing at the last college attended (not under disciplinary or academic suspension, dismissal, expulsion, or similar action).

In addition to satisfying both of the previous requirements (a) ***and*** (b), you must also meet ***any*** of the following three standards:

1. You were eligible for admission as a first-time freshman when you graduated from high school (you met California State University admission standards in the Subject, Examination, and Scholarship Requirements and have been in continuous attendance in college since high school graduation.) See chapter 10: CALIFORNIA STATE UNIVERSITY: Minimum Admission Requirements, page 10--5.

Any student applying for lower-division transfer must meet the same requirements as first-time freshmen.

2. You were eligible as a freshman at the time of high school graduation, except for completing the CSU Subject Requirement, have made up the missing courses, and have been in continuous attendance in an accredited college since high school graduation.

3. You will meet the freshman admission requirements in effect for the term to which you are applying.

"Continuous attendance" means that you attended at least one course for at least one term (one regular semester or two regular quarters) in each calendar year.

Any student applying for lower-division transfer must meet the same requirements as first-time freshmen.

If your high school GPA for admission to CSU (all courses for the last three years of high school except physical education and military science) is below 3.00, CSU requires you to take the SAT I: Reasoning Test or ACT for admission.

MAKING UP MISSING CSU SUBJECT REQUIREMENT COURSES

If you did not complete the required fifteen units of the CSU Subject Requirement in high school with at least a C or better, you may use ***any*** of the following ways to makeup subjects:

You must make up missing CSU Subject Requirement courses that you did not complete with a C or better in high school.

1. For each missing Subject Requirement course, complete a college course with a grade of C or better. For example, take intermediate algebra in college if you did not complete it in high school. One college course of at least three semester or four quarter units is considered equivalent to one year of high school study.

2. For each missing CSU Subject Requirement course, complete a General Education course with a C or better in the subject that you are missing. For example, if you did not complete the fourth year of college-preparatory English in high school, you can complete the college English composition course (usually called English 1A). Your community college approves this same course to meet the CSU General Education/Breadth Requirement and the IGETC Requirement area in communication in English.

3. Earn acceptable scores on specified examinations, such as the SAT II: Subject Tests and Advanced Placement Examinations. See chapter 6: COLLEGE ENTRANCE TESTS, page 6--30 and page 6--57.

Meet with a community college counselor about courses and examination scores to satisfy CSU Subject Requirement courses not completed in high school.

UPPER DIVISION TRANSFER

TO TRANSFER WITH AT LEAST 56 TRANSFERABLE SEMESTER UNITS/84 TRANSFERABLE QUARTER UNITS ...

If you have ***at least 56 transferable semester/84 transferable quarter units***, you are an upper-division transfer student (junior or senior) and you must

a. have an overall grade point average of C (2.00) or better (2.40 for nonresidents of California) in transferable units attempted,

b. be in good standing at the last college attended, and

c. have completed or made up any subject deficiencies.

You do not have to have maintained continuous attendance.

If you have at least 56 transferable semester/84 transferable quarter units, you are an upper-division transfer student (junior or senior).

MAKING UP MISSING CSU SUBJECT REQUIREMENT COURSES

The best alternative available for *most* upper-division transfers (to make up CSU Subject Requirement courses not completed with a C or better in high school) is to complete a minimum of 30 semester/45 quarter units in the CSU General Education/ Breadth Requirement with a C grade or better in *each* course. These units may be chosen from courses in English, arts, humanities, social sciences, science, and mathematics that meet the GE/Breadth Requirement or are at least at an equivalent level to courses that meet this requirement.

These 30 semester/45 quarter units must include all CSU General Education/Breadth Certification or IGETC Requirements in communication in the English language (at least 9 semester units) and mathematics/quantitative reasoning (usually 3 semester units). CSU will accept D's in General Education units completed in excess of these 30 semester/45 quarter units, except in English language and mathematics/quantitative reasoning.

If foreign language was a course missing in your high school record, you do not necessarily need to take it in college for transfer or for your Bachelor's degree. However, depending upon your major or CSU campus, you may be required to complete foreign language coursework as a CSU graduation requirement. Courses in American sign language are acceptable for transfer as a foreign language.

If foreign language was a course missing in your high school record, you do not necessarily need to take it in college for transfer or for your Bachelor's degree.

Meet with a community college counselor for further information about courses and examinations to satisfy the CSU Subject Requirement not completed in high school.

MAJOR PREPARATION REQUIREMENTS FOR TRANSFER TO CSU

California State University encourages you to complete the minimum coursework required to prepare you for your major while attending a California Community College. You are evaluated, in part, on the basis of your performance in your major preparation courses. If your major requires mathematics and science, it is especially important that you complete the prerequisites for these subject areas before you transfer.

Research the exact Major Preparation Requirements you need. Confer with your community college counselor, read the California State University campus catalogue, and if necessary, contact the campus to clarify any ambiguities. Begin your courses in your major as soon as you have selected it. Lack of pre-major work may affect your eligibility for your major, particularly if it has many applicants and a limited number of spaces.

The CSU GE/ Breadth Requirement specifies a program of coursework to be completed as a condition for earning a Bachelor's degree at a CSU campus.

GENERAL EDUCATION/BREADTH REQUIREMENT FOR TRANSFER TO CSU

There are two options for completing the lower-division General Education/Breadth Requirement for California State University.

OPTION 1: IGETC

The IGETC program requires the completion of a minimum of 37 semester/49 quarter units of lower-division coursework with a C or better in each course. The program is explained in detail earlier in this chapter on page 9--15.

OPTION 2: CSU GENERAL EDUCATION/BREADTH REQUIREMENT CERTIFICATION PROGRAM

The General Education/Breadth Requirement of CSU specifies a program of coursework to be fulfilled as a condition for earning a Bachelor's degree from a California State University campus. You must complete a *minimum* of 48 semester/72 quarter units of General Education courses to receive your degree. This requirement is applicable to both CSU native students and transfer students.

You may complete as many as thirty-nine lower-division semester units of this General Education/ Breadth Requirement coursework at the community college.

CSU GENERAL EDUCATION/BREADTH REQUIREMENTS			
	Subject Area	Course Requirement	Semester Unit Requirement
A.	Communication in the English Language and Critical Thinking (Basic Subjects)	Written communication, critical thinking, and oral communication	At least 9 units
B.	Physical Universe and Its Life Forms	Natural sciences and mathematics. Includes a quantitative reasoning requirement which must be satisfied with a mathematics course at a level beyond intermediate algebra	At least 12 units
C.	Arts, Literature, Philosophy, and Foreign Language	At least one course in the arts and one course in the humanities	At least 12 units
D.	Social, Political, and Economic Institutions		At least 12 units
E.	Lifelong Understanding and Self- Development		At least 3 units
	Total		At least 48 units

You may complete as many as thirty-nine lower-division semester units of this General Education/Breadth Requirement coursework at the community college. You must compete the remaining minimum of nine upper-division semester units (junior/senior) after you transfer to CSU.

The CSU system delegates authority to each community college to identify and certify the specific lower-division courses in the community college catalogue that (a) fulfill this General Education/Breadth Requirement, (b) transfer for Bachelor's degree credit, and (c) meet the American Constitution requirement described below.

The California Community Colleges have established Full Certification and Subject Area Certification of General Education/ Breadth Requirement programs with the CSU system.

CERTIFICATION

The California Community Colleges have established Full Certification and Subject Area Certification of General Education/Breadth Requirement programs with the CSU system. These certification programs are tailored to California State University and cannot be used for admission to the University of California.

Full Certification of All Areas: When you complete the thirty-nine semester, lower-division General Education/Breadth Requirement units in the appropriate courses for each subject area listed above, you may apply to your community college for a Certification of Completion of all areas of the CSU lower-division General Education/Breadth Requirement. Your community college will certify on your college transcript that you have fully satisfied your California State University lower-division General Education/Breadth Requirement.

Subject Area Certification: CSU defines Subject Area Certification as certification of a complete subject area; e.g., no less than nine semester units for Basic Subjects. The minimum unit requirements for certifying each subject area are nine semester units in areas A, B, C, and D and at least three semester units in area E. Certification for area C must include at least one course in the arts and one course in the humanities. You can be certified as having completed one or more subject areas. Any subject areas not completed at the community college must be satisfied after you transfer.

The community college can report certified coursework completed at other certifying institutions (other community colleges) and nominate coursework from nonparticipating accredited universities (including accredited out-of-state universities) for the CSU campus to consider for certification. Nominated courses should be equivalent to courses the community college currently certifies as meeting CSU's General Education/Breadth Requirement.

If you receive Full or Subject Area Certification, the CSU campus will not require you to take any additional lower-division General Education requirements in the areas certified.

If you receive Full or Subject Area Certification, the CSU campus will not require you to take any additional lower-division General Education requirements in the areas certified.

AMERICAN INSTITUTIONS REQUIREMENT

CSU has a graduation requirement in American Institutions. You can complete this requirement either by passing a comprehensive examination or by completing the required courses, generally two. You may complete this requirement before or after transfer. If you choose to complete it before transfer, the California Community Colleges have identified courses that can be completed at the lower-division level to meet this requirement. Upon completion, your community college certifies that you have satisfied the American Institutions Requirement.

Most, but not all, CSU campuses permit courses that meet the American Institutions requirement to be used toward satisfying the CSU General Education/Breadth Certification Program Requirement of Social, Political, and Economic Institutions. The units earned can be used toward the thirty-nine semester units needed for certification if the CSU campus allows it. Check with the CSU campus to determine its policy.

Courses used to meet the American Institutions Requirement may not be used to fulfill IGETC. You need 37 semester/49 quarter units in IGETC to transfer to CSU plus additional lower-division units in American Institutions.

For admission, CSU requires of California residents a GPA of 2.00 or better in all transferable units attempted and a minimum grade of C in certain courses.

ADDITIONAL INFORMATION ABOUT TRANSFERRING TO CSU

- For admission, CSU requires of California residents a GPA of 2.00 or better in all transferable units attempted and a minimum grade of C in certain courses. The option you use for making up deficiencies in the CSU Subject Requirement for freshman admission determines the coursework requiring at least a C grade. There is no CSU systemwide policy that requires a particular course grade or GPA for General Education/Breadth Requirement coursework accepted in transferring. However, individual CSU campuses may require a minimum GPA or a minimum grade in courses taken.

- If you use IGETC to meet the lower-division General Education/Breadth Requirement, you must have a grade of C or better in each course used to meet this requirement.

- Elective courses count toward total transfer units needed for admission but are not used to fulfill lower-division Major Preparation Requirements or the General Education/Breadth Requirement. Check your community college catalog to make sure your electives are transferable to CSU.

- A major difference between the California State University General Education/Breadth Requirement Certification Program and IGETC is that you can partially complete the California State University Certification Program. You can receive Subject Area Certification on your transcript identifying the subject areas you have fulfilled.

You can partially fulfill the CSU General Education/ Breadth Requirement Certification Program. There is no Subject Area Certification of IGETC.

- By contrast, if you do not complete IGETC at the community college, you cannot finish it at California State University. There is no Subject Area Certification of IGETC. At the time of your transfer, you must meet course requirements in all five IGETC areas. If you do not, you can still transfer provided you have enough transfer units. However, you will be required to meet the General Education/Breadth Requirement of the campus you attend.

- Although you do not need to complete all CSU General Education/Breadth Requirement courses before transferring, it is strongly recommended that you do. All CSU campuses follow the same definition of the General Education/Breadth Requirement areas shown in the chart on page 9--30. However, each CSU campus establishes how individual General Education/Breadth Requirement subject areas are satisfied and the courses in the CSU campus catalogue that fulfill each subject area requirement. The Articulation Agreement then defines which community college courses are equivalent to the CSU campus courses. See page 9--14.

Without Full Certification, or with Subject Area Certification, the California State University campus you attend may question if some of your courses in non-certified subject areas fulfill their General Education/Breadth Requirement subject areas according to their campus definition. To your dismay, you could be required to take additional courses to fully complete the campus General Education/Breadth Requirement.

- All CSU campuses except Los Angeles require all candidates for the bachelor's degree to complete one course in multicultural/ethnic studies as a condition for graduation. Most campuses allow you to complete the course at the lower division level prior to transfer and have identified several courses that meet this requirement. Dominguez Hills, Long Beach, San Bernardino, San Diego, San Francisco, and San Jose require you to complete this course at the upper-division level after you transfer.

- When planning your program to meet the California State University General Education/Breadth Requirement, note that some majors (for example Engineering) require many Major Preparation Requirement courses. You may need to take more than 56 semester/84 quarter units to satisfy your entire General Education/Breadth Requirement *and* Major Preparation Requirement prior to transfer.

- Completing the lower-division General Education/Breadth Requirement does not guarantee admission to the California State University campus or program of choice. However, completing this requirement through the IGETC or the California State University General Education/Breadth Requirement Certification Program may improve your chances for admission to a competitive campus and/or program.

- Many CSU campuses are experiencing enrollment pressures. If you apply after the first month of the filing period, you may find it difficult to gain admission to certain majors or particular campuses. See chapter 10: CALIFORNIA STATE UNIVERSITY, Applying to California State University, page 10--36. When a campus finds it necessary to limit enrollment, it gives first priority in admission to *upper-division* California Community College transfers.

When a CSU campus finds it necessary to limit enrollment, it gives first priority in admission to upper-division California Community College transfers.

In fact, some campuses do not accept lower-division applications. They give enrollment priority to upper-division transfers because upper-division students have exhausted their options at the community college and cannot continue progress toward meeting Bachelor's degree requirements. If a campus in which you are interested does not accept lower-division applications, you will not lose time or credits by continuing to complete your lower-division coursework at the community college.

As a first step in planning your California Community College course selections, identify the admission requirements you must meet at CSU and/or UC.

Strategies For Transferring To CSU And UC

- As a first step in planning your California Community College course selections, identify the admission requirements you must meet at CSU and/or UC. Do you qualify to transfer as a lower-division student, or must you complete your freshman and sophomore years at a California Community College and transfer as a junior, upper-division student? To determine your admission eligibility status at the time of your high school graduation, get a copy of your final high school transcript and meet with your community college counselor to review your record. You might also contact a CSU or UC admissions office for further evaluation.

- Does the campus in which you are interested accept lower-division transfers? Does your intended major at that campus accept lower-division transfers?

- Set up an appointment with your community college counselor who has much of the information you need to start planning.

- Give top priority to those courses that clear high school subject deficiencies in the CSU Subject Requirement and the UC "a-f" Subject Requirement for freshman admission.

A maximum of 70 semester/ 105 quarter units of transferable coursework from a California Community College can be applied to your graduation credit requirements at CSU or UC.

- Research your campus and major. Meet with a community college counselor. Review college catalogs. Determine specific Major Preparation Requirements for the program you plan to enter. Include required courses in your educational planning.

- If you choose not to transfer until your junior year and you expect to take 56 semester/84 quarter units, plan your courses to meet both the General Education/Breadth Requirement and lower-division Major Preparation Requirements.

- A maximum of 70 semester/105 quarter units of transferable coursework from a California Community College can be applied to your graduation credit requirements at California State University or the University of California. While they cannot count toward the total units needed for your four-year degree, courses in excess of this maximum can receive subject credit to satisfy the General Education/Breadth Requirement or major requirements. You do not need to repeat these courses.

- Transfer Admission Agreements, which guarantee an advanced reserved space if you meet transfer requirements to CSU or UC, can assist you with the transfer process. See the following page for more information about them.

Transfer To An Independent College

Planning your transfer to an independent college requires that you contact the four-year institution directly to determine its exact policies regarding course, unit, and GPA requirements. Try to meet with an admissions officer from the independent school. Bring your high school and college transcripts, college entrance test scores, California Community College placement test scores, your community college catalogue, and any other information about you that will be helpful at this conference. If you cannot meet, make the contact by telephone.

Try to meet with an admissions officer from the independent school.

WHEN CAN YOU TRANSFER TO AN INDEPENDENT COLLEGE?

The policies of the particular independent college will determine when you can transfer. Course, unit, and GPA requirements differ from school to school. See chapter 12: CALIFORNIA INDEPENDENT COLLEGES, College Profiles, pages 12--12 to 12--75. For out-of-state colleges, contact the institution directly for information about their transfer policies.

MAJOR PREPARATION REQUIREMENTS AND GENERAL EDUCATION/BREADTH REQUIREMENT FOR TRANSFERRING TO AN INDEPENDENT COLLEGE

The independent colleges have their own criteria for satisfying Major Preparation and General Education/Breadth Requirements prior to transfer. Check the independent college catalogue carefully and contact the admissions office for exact policies.

TAA's — Transfer Admission Agreements

Transfer Admission Agreements is a program that guarantees *qualifying* students admission to several campuses of California State University and the University of California as well as a limited number of independent colleges. The Transfer Admission Agreement is a contract made between the California Community College and the four-year institution guaranteeing, that upon completion of the conditions of the agreement, the student will be admitted for a specific term at the four-year college.

The TAA is a contract made between the California Community College and the four-year institution. It guarantees that, upon completion of the conditions of the agreement, the student will be admitted for a specific term at the four-year college.

At this time, not all California State University, University of California, or independent college campuses and programs offer TAA's. Further, not all California Community Colleges have established TAA's with four-year institutions. Inquire at your community college to learn with which four-year colleges they have set up TAA's and the procedures you must follow.

HOW THE TAA WORKS

After you have

a. earned a minimum number of transferable units (usually 30 semester/48 quarter units),

b. achieved a GPA in transferable courses that is acceptable for admission (The minimum is 2.00 for California State University and 2.40 for the University of California. Some campuses of CSU and UC and some programs may require a higher minimum GPA. The GPA minimum varies for independent colleges.), and

c. at least one year in advance of your anticipated transfer,

meet with a community college counselor and draft a Transfer Admission Agreement application or request. On this application, list those courses you have already completed and those you plan to complete at your community college. Your TAA application should include your GPA and those courses which satisfy the General Education/ Breadth Requirement, Major Preparation Requirements, and admission requirements of the college to which you are applying. Your GPA calculation is based upon your grades in transferable courses.

Your GPA calculation is based upon your grades in transferable courses.

Submit this agreement to the admissions office at the particular California State University, University of California, or independent college campus in which you are interested. The colleges have established deadlines for receiving the TAA application. Deadlines vary according to the term in which you plan to enroll. Within approximately three weeks after you have mailed your request, you will receive an evaluation of your record, and if you have qualified, a guarantee of admission. This guarantee is conditioned upon your completion of the course pattern described in the TAA with an acceptable GPA.

Even if you are accepted with a TAA, you must still submit an admission application during the regular filing period.

ADVANTAGES OF TAA'S

- Under regular admission procedures you must wait several months to be notified if you have been admitted. With a TAA, you are notified within approximately three weeks. This provides you with the opportunity for early planning for financial assistance and housing away from home.
- The college or university gives you immediate feedback of any additional requirements to be completed before acceptance. This information can guide you to correct any errors you have made in course planning. They also inform you if your GPA needs improvement.
- The guarantee reserves the admission opening for you for the term you requested on the TAA, and you are admitted if you fulfill the course and grade commitments you stated in your agreement.

ADDITIONAL INFORMATION ABOUT TAA'S

- Even if you are accepted with a Transfer Admission Agreement, you must still submit an admission application during the regular filing period.
- Most California State University and University of California campuses do not offer TAA's for impacted majors.
- You can transfer without a TAA. The TAA can provide a level of comfort to you, but you do *not* need to submit a TAA to transfer. You may apply for admission in the usual manner. Your qualifications receive full consideration, although you wait several months before you know whether or not you have been admitted.
- Meet with a counselor early in your California Community College program to start the process of developing your educational plan to fulfill transfer requirements.

You can transfer without a TAA. Apply for admission in the usual manner.

UNIVERSITY OF CALIFORNIA TRANSFER ADMISSION PROGRAMS

University of California campuses offer a variety of programs in support of transfer admission, particularly for community college students. Under some programs, students at specified community colleges are guaranteed admission to a University of California campus if they meet specific requirements. Other programs provide extensive academic and admission support services to transfer applicants, but do not guarantee admission.

Presented here is a list of University of California campus Transfer Admission Agreement programs. Each University of California campus arranges its own program with individual California Community Colleges. You must determine if a particular community college and University of California campus jointly offer a program. Inquire at your community college, or contact the admissions offices of the University of California campuses. Note that the campuses have their own titles for the programs and that the requirements and the program definitions and benefits vary.

As you read about the various campus programs, note that several of them are really Transfer Admission Agreement programs that are given a different title by the campuses.

You must determine if a particular community college and UC campus jointly offer a program.

BERKELEY

Cooperative Admissions Program (CAP): CAP gives you the opportunity to combine lower-division study at a community college with a guarantee of admission to Berkeley as a junior. *The program is specifically for students who apply to Berkeley for freshman admission and are UC-eligible (meet the minimum admission requirements for freshmen), but are not admitted as freshmen.* These four colleges at Berkeley participate in CAP:

College of Letters and Science: All UC-eligible freshman applicants to the College of Letters and Science who are not admitted may gain admission to the College through CAP. You must complete a minimum of 60 semester/90 quarter units, including the College's basic General Education/Breadth Requirement (foreign language, quantitative reasoning, and reading and composition) and prerequisites in your major, if appropriate. You must earn at least a 3.00 GPA. You are not guaranteed admission to specific majors. Acceptance into a specific major takes place after enrollment and is subject to completion of departmental prerequisites and conditions.

UC Berkeley's Cooperative Admissions Program is specifically for students who apply to Berkeley for freshman admission and are UC-eligible, but are not admitted as freshmen.

CALIFORNIA COMMUNITY COLLEGES

College of Environmental Design: The faculty of the College of Environmental Design select the freshman applicants for the CAP option. You must complete a minimum of 60 semester/90 quarter units with a GPA of at least 3.00. Courses completed must include all prerequisites for your intended major.

College of Engineering: The CAP option is available in all majors. You must complete a minimum of 60 semester/90 quarter units, including lower-division prerequisites, and earn a GPA of at least 3.50.

College of Natural Resources: All UC-eligible freshman applicants to the College of Natural Resources who are not admitted are eligible to participate. You are required to complete a minimum of 60 semester/90 quarter units and earn a GPA of at least 3.00.

Community College Transfer Center Program: This program provides a variety of services to facilitate the transfer process for community college students, particularly underrepresented students. The program offers individual academic counseling and group advising.

DAVIS

Transfer Opportunity Program: TOP is a program which provides support services such as pre-admission transcript evaluation, admission counseling and workshops, and guidance in developing individual Transfer Admission Agreements. TOP advisors visit participating community college campuses to provide guidance. The advisor evaluates your transcript to assure that admission requirements are met and that community college courses taken are transferable to the University.

Transfer Admission Agreements: UC Davis has developed TAA's with a number of community colleges. If you comply with the TAA and apply for admission on time during the appropriate filing period, you are guaranteed, in advance, admission to a specific quarter. This option is available to students in all majors.

Some UC campuses have programs that give priority consideration for admission but do not guarantee admission.

IRVINE

Zero in On Transferring (ZOT!): ZOT! is UC Irvine's transfer admission assurance program for junior-level transfers from participating community colleges. To participate in ZOT! you must complete 24 transferable semester units with a competitive GPA. You will receive individual advising to determine your admission status and to identify specific community college courses you must complete. You receive a written admission agreement. Some majors may not be available to ZOT! participants, depending upon space availability.

LOS ANGELES

Community College Transfer Program: This program provides pre-admission evaluations, admission counseling, and workshops. Program staff visit participating community colleges several times a month. Particular emphasis is placed upon supporting underrepresented students.

Transfer Alliance Program (TAP): The TAP program prepares students at participating community colleges to transfer to UC Los Angeles as juniors. You must complete a rigorous academic program at the community college. Students who complete the program are given priority consideration for admission to the College of Letters and Science (except for the Communication Studies major).

RIVERSIDE

Memorandum of Understanding (MOA): Through the MOA program, qualified students at participating community colleges develop contracts with UCR specifying coursework and other requirements to complete while at the community college. You are assured priority consideration for admission to UCR when you fulfill your contract. This program includes advising sessions, articulation agreements, and individual student progress reviews.

SAN DIEGO

Transfer Admission Guarantee (TAG): TAG students enter into a contract that specifies requirements to be satisfied at a community college and guarantees admission to the college of choice at UC San Diego. Admission to impacted majors, such as Computer Science and Electrical Engineering, is not guaranteed.

You must meet minimum eligibility requirements for transfer students, including completion of at least 60 transferable semester/90 quarter units; earn a specified minimum GPA and be in good academic standing; clear all subject omissions/deficiencies in English and mathematics; complete all TAG core courses (transferable courses which help satisfy a portion of the General Education/Breadth Requirement) with a C or better; and complete additional courses as recommended by the specific UC San Diego college you plan to enter.

SANTA BARBARA

Transfer Support Services: This program offers a variety of support services to assist community college students to transfer to UCSB. Transfer advising sessions take place at 2:00 P.M. on Fridays on the UCSB campus. Advisors also make regularly scheduled visits to community colleges in nearby counties to offer transfer advising, application and financial aid workshops, and individual academic advising.

SBCC/UCSB Transition Program: This program helps Santa Barbara City College (SBCC) students transfer to UC Santa Barbara. Academic advising is provided. An admission agreement is in place that designates specific criteria that, when satisfied, ensure transfer to UC Santa Barbara. SBCC students admitted to UCSB are also eligible for special scholarships.

Transfer Achievement Program (TAP): TAP provides Student Affirmative Action, low-income, and disabled students at Santa Barbara City College with individual services to assist in transferring to UC Santa Barbara.

SANTA CRUZ

Guaranteed Admission for Transfer Entry (GATE): The GATE program at UC Santa Cruz offers guaranteed admission to qualified junior-level transfers from participating California Community Colleges. You must have a minimum of 30 transferable semester/45 quarter units and less than 90 semester units/135 quarter units of coursework; have a GPA of at least 3.00; and be registered at one of the participating community colleges. Prior to transfer, you must complete at the participating community college at least 30 of the 56 semester units (45 of the 84 quarter units) required to be eligible for admission. The GATE program offers guaranteed admission for the fall quarter only.

Transfer Program: The transfer program provides services to students interested in transferring, including admission guidance and workshops. Admission outreach counselors regularly visit many of the community colleges in central California providing guidance services as well as workshops for reentry, EOPS, and disabled students.

CSU TRANSFER ADMISSION PROGRAMS

Most CSU campuses have developed TAA programs with community colleges in their immediate service area located near their campuses. However, some CSU campuses are not developing Transfer Admission Agreements with community colleges because of pressures of increased enrollment and reduced fund support. Their departments and schools are finding it difficult to honor transfer agreements that *guarantee* admission to certain programs for all upper-division transfer students completing lower-division requirements. This is especially true if applications are not received during the initial filing period.

Some CSU campuses are not developing TAA's with community colleges because of pressures of increased enrollment and reduced fund support.

OCCUPATIONAL PROGRAMS

Community colleges differ somewhat from one another in the occupational programs which they offer.

California Community Colleges offer more than three-hundred forty career and vocational programs. Programs are available in the areas of agriculture, business, health, home economics, office occupations, public safety, trade and industry, and technical fields. You may prepare for entry-level jobs, advancement in your current position, or for a new career.

Programs are offered in occupations such as nursing, drafting, auto mechanics, engineering technology, criminal justice, manufacturing technology, paralegal, fire fighting, cosmetology, fashion merchandising, welding, and more than three-hundred thirty others.

Community colleges differ somewhat from one another in the occupational programs which they offer. If you have a particular field in mind, do not assume that the community college close to home has a program for you, or that it is the best one available. If it does have the program, determine if it has the range of courses and the career emphasis you are seeking. You may find that you need to research several community colleges to find the program you have in mind. Shop for your community college as you would for a four-year school. Consider your major and the criteria in chapter 2: CHOOSING YOUR COLLEGE.

The community colleges identify the courses in their curriculum and the program for you to follow to train for your career. You may prepare for your occupation by completing an Associates degree or by satisfying the requirements for a Certificate of Proficiency/Completion. Meet with a community college counselor as soon as possible after you enroll to plan your educational program to meet your goals.

ASSOCIATES DEGREE PROGRAMS

To receive an Associates degree you must complete the General Education/Breadth Requirement and Career Preparation courses of the community college campus.

A total of 60 semester units/90 quarter units are required to complete the Associates degree. These units are made up of a combination of the General Education/Breadth Requirement courses and the Career Preparation Courses required at the community college. The community college determines the General Education/Breadth Requirement subject areas, the Career Preparation curriculum, and the units and courses to fulfill them. Associates degree programs are intended primarily to develop personal and technical competencies for employment purposes. However, many of the units earned in the curriculum may be transferable and acceptable to four-year colleges to meet the lower-division (freshman and sophomore) General Education/Breadth Requirement and Major Preparation Requirements.

In fact, with careful educational planning, you may be able to complete the General Education/Breadth Requirement and Major Preparation Requirements with the same courses for both transfer to the four-year institution and the Associates degree. Having an Associates degree when you transfer can be beneficial to you. You are more competitive for part-time or summer jobs during your college years, and if you do not complete your Bachelor's degree, you have the Associates degree to your credit.

CERTIFICATE OF PROFICIENCY/ COMPLETION PROGRAMS

You may receive a Certificate of Proficiency/Completion if you complete all the occupational education courses of a particular career major. This option is particularly suited to those students wanting career training and who wish to seek employment as soon as possible. Many, but not all, Certificate programs can be completed in one school year or less. You take only those courses which relate directly to your career major. You do not include any General Education/Breadth Requirement courses. The number of units required to complete the Certificate varies according to the field you are studying and the California Community College you are attending.

Many students become employed after achieving their certificate and continue their studies on a part-time basis, taking the General Education/Breadth Requirement courses required for the Associates degree, or the General Education/Breadth Requirement and additional major preparation courses for fulfilling transfer requirements.

Many students become employed after achieving their certificate and continue their studies on a part-time basis to complete an Associates degree and/or a transfer program.

CAMPUSES

ALLAN HANCOCK COLLEGE
800 South College Drive
Santa Maria, California 93454
Santa Barbara County
(805) 922-6966
Location: Serves most of Santa Barbara County with campuses in Santa Maria and Lompoc.
Total Enrollment: 15,395

AMERICAN RIVER COLLEGE
4700 College Oak Drive
Sacramento, California 95841
Sacramento County
(916) 484-8011
Location: Northeast side of Sacramento.
Total Enrollment: 21,815

ANTELOPE VALLEY COLLEGE
3041 West Avenue K
Lancaster, California 93536
Los Angeles County
(805) 943-3241
Location: In the high desert fifty-five miles northeast of Los Angeles in the heart of Aerospace Valley.
Total Enrollment: 10,401

BAKERSFIELD COLLEGE
1801 Panorama Drive
Bakersfield, California 93305
Kern County
(805) 395-4011
Location: In the rich agricultural and oil field center of the San Joaquin Valley.
Total Enrollment: 13,294

BARSTOW COLLEGE
2700 Barstow Road
Barstow, California 92311
San Bernardino County
(619) 252-2411
Location: In the Mojave Desert midway between Los Angeles and Las Vegas.
Total Enrollment: 2,517

BUTTE COMMUNITY COLLEGE
3536 Butte Campus Drive
Oroville, California 95965
Butte County
(916) 895-2511
Location: Midway between Chico and Oroville, in northern California at the base of the Sierra Nevada range.
Total Enrollment: 11,313

CABRILLO COLLEGE
6500 Soquel Drive
Aptos, California 95003
Santa Cruz County
(408) 479-6100
Location: In the hills above Aptos overlooking Monterey Bay.
Total Enrollment: 12,328

CAÑADA COLLEGE
4200 Farm Hill Boulevard
Redwood City, California 94061
San Mateo County
(415) 306-3100
Location: In the western foothills of Redwood City overlooking San Francisco Bay.
Total Enrollment: 5,681

CERRITOS COLLEGE
11110 Alondra Boulevard
Norwalk, California 90650
Los Angeles County
(310) 860-2451
Location: Serving the suburban cities of southeast Los Angeles County.
Total Enrollment: 20,889

CERRO COSO COMMUNITY COLLEGE
3000 College Heights Boulevard
Ridgecrest, California 93555
Kern County
(619) 375-5001
Location: In the upper Mojave Desert at an elevation of 2,800 feet.
Total Enrollment: 4,854

CHABOT COLLEGE
25555 Hesperian Boulevard
Post Office Box 5001
Hayward, California 94540
Alameda County
(510) 786-6600
Location: In a metropolitan location close to events and activities offered throughout the greater San Francisco Bay Area.
Total Enrollment: 14,179

CHAFFEY COLLEGE
5885 Haven Avenue
Rancho Cucamonga, California 91737
San Bernardino County
(909) 987-1737
Location: At the west end of San Bernardino County high above a rapidly growing suburban valley.
Total Enrollment: 14,970

CITRUS COLLEGE
1000 West Foothill Boulevard
Glendora, California 91741
Los Angeles County
(818) 963-0323
Location: Nestled near the foothills of the San Gabriel Mountains.
Total Enrollment: 12,374

CITY COLLEGE OF SAN FRANCISCO
50 Phelan Avenue
San Francisco, California 94112
San Francisco County
(415) 239-3000
Location: On a hilltop overlooking San Francisco.
Total Enrollment: 66,077

COASTLINE COMMUNITY COLLEGE
11460 Warner Avenue
Fountain Valley, California 92708
Orange County
(714) 432-5600
Location: In north-coastal Orange County.
Total Enrollment: 12,953

COLLEGE OF ALAMEDA
555 Atlantic Avenue
Alameda, California 94501
Alameda County
(510) 522-7221
Location: Five minutes by automobile or public transportation from downtown Oakland.
Total Enrollment: 5,679

COLLEGE OF MARIN
885 College Avenue
Kentfield, California 94904
Marin County
(415) 457-8811
Location: Across the Golden Gate Bridge from San Francisco.
Total Enrollment: 13,197

COLLEGE OF SAN MATEO
1700 West Hillsdale Boulevard
San Mateo, California 94402
San Mateo County
(415) 574-6161
Location: In the San Mateo hills with a panoramic view of the north San Francisco Bay Area.
Total Enrollment: 14,485

COLLEGE OF THE CANYONS
26455 North Rockwell Canyon Road
Santa Clarita, California 91355
Los Angeles County
(805) 259-7800
Location: In the northwestern section of Los Angeles County.
Total Enrollment: 6,485

COLLEGE OF THE DESERT
43-500 Monterey Avenue
Palm Desert, California 92260
Riverside County
(619) 346-8041
Location: In the Coachella Valley whose burgeoning economy is primarily supported by tourism and agriculture.
Total Enrollment: 9,549

COLLEGE OF THE REDWOODS
7351 Tompkins Hill Road
Eureka, California 95501
Humboldt County
(707) 445-6700
Location: On coastal land near Eureka and Humboldt State University.
Total Enrollment: 3,303

COLLEGE OF THE SEQUOIAS
915 South Mooney Boulevard
Visalia, California 93277
Tulare County
(209) 730-3700
Location: In the heart of the fertile San Joaquin Valley, an hour from the Sierra Nevada range
Total Enrollment: 8,626

COLLEGE OF THE SISKIYOUS
800 College Avenue
Weed, California 96094
Siskiyou County
(916) 938-4462
Location: At the base of majestic Mount Shasta in a beautiful alpine setting.
Total Enrollment: 2,849

COLUMBIA COLLEGE
11600 Columbia College Drive
Sonora, California 95370
Tuolumne County
(209) 533-5100
Location: In the foothills of the Sierra Nevada Mountains
Total Enrollment: 2,353

COMPTON COMMUNITY COLLEGE
1111 East Artesia Boulevard
Compton, California 90221
Los Angeles County
(310) 637-2660
Location: Serves the residents of Compton, Enterprise, Lynwood, Paramount, and Willowbrook.
Total Enrollment: 5,696

CONTRA COSTA COLLEGE
2600 Mission Bell Drive
San Pablo, California 94806
Contra Costa County
(510) 235-7800
Location: In west Contra Costa County on acreage adjoining the cities of San Pablo and Richmond.
Total Enrollment: 8,454

COSUMNES RIVER COLLEGE
8401 Center Parkway
Sacramento, California 95823
Sacramento County
(916) 688-7451
Location: An expanded campus in South Sacramento.
Total Enrollment: 11,639

CRAFTON HILLS COLLEGE
11711 Sand Canyon Road
Yucaipa, California 92399
San Bernardino County
(909) 794-2161
Location: Two miles from busy interstate 10 and major cultural centers.
Total Enrollment: 5,048

CUESTA COLLEGE
Post Office Box 8106
San Luis Obispo, California 93403
San Luis Obispo County
(805) 546-3100
Location: Between the cities of San Luis Obispo and Morro Bay on State Highway 1.
Total Enrollment: 7,408

CUYAMACA COLLEGE
2950 Jamacha Road
El Cajon, California 92019
San Diego County
(619) 670-1980
Location: twelve miles east of the city of San Diego among gently rolling hills and valleys.
Total Enrollment: 4,591

CYPRESS COLLEGE
9200 Valley View Street
Cypress, California 90630
Orange County
(714) 826-2220
Location: Western Orange County.
Total Enrollment: 13,876

DE ANZA COLLEGE
21250 Stevens Creek Boulevard
Cupertino, California 95014
Santa Clara County
(408) 864-5678
Location: In the heart of Silicon Valley near San Jose.
Total Enrollment: 25,002

DIABLO VALLEY COLLEGE
321 Golf Club Road
Pleasant Hill, California 94523
Contra Costa County
(510) 685-1230
Location: In the East Bay of the San Francisco Bay Area west of Mt. Diablo.
Total Enrollment: 20,783

EAST LOS ANGELES COLLEGE
1301 Avenida Cesar Chavez
Monterey Park, California 91754
Los Angeles County
(213) 265-8650
Location: At the easterly extreme of the Los Angeles Community College District near the largest high-technology industrial complex in Southern California.
Total Enrollment: 14,738

EL CAMINO COLLEGE
16007 Crenshaw Boulevard
Torrance, California 90506
Los Angeles County
(310) 532-3670
Location: In the South Bay area of Los Angeles County.
Total Enrollment: 23,448

EVERGREEN VALLEY COLLEGE
3095 Yerba Buena Road
San Jose, California 95135
Santa Clara County
(408) 274-7900
Location: Nestled in the rolling hills of southeast San Jose.
Total Enrollment: 9,228

FEATHER RIVER COLLEGE
570 Golden Eagle Avenue
Post Office Box 11110
Quincy, California 95971
Plumas County
(916) 283-0202
Location: In northeastern California.
Total Enrollment: 1,043

FOOTHILL COLLEGE
12345 El Monte Road
Los Altos Hills, California 94022
Santa Clara County
(415) 949-7777
Location: In the foothills south of San Francisco.
Total Enrollment: 15,465

FRESNO CITY COLLEGE
1101 East University Avenue
Fresno, California 93741
Fresno County
(209) 442-4600
Location: In the city of Fresno.
Total Enrollment: 17,985

FULLERTON COLLEGE
321 East Chapman Avenue
Fullerton, California 92632
Orange County
(714) 992-7000
Location: In north Orange County.
Total Enrollment: 18,699

GAVILAN COLLEGE
5055 Santa Teresa Boulevard
Gilroy, California 95020
Santa Clara County
(408) 847-1400
Location: In the southern portion of Santa Clara County and nestled against the coastal foothills.
Total Enrollment: 1,731

GLENDALE COMMUNITY COLLEGE
1500 North Verdugo Road
Glendale, California 91208
Los Angeles County
(818) 240-1000
Location: Hillside campus, nestled in the crown of rustic mountains of the "Jewel City."
Total Enrollment: 1,618

GOLDEN WEST COLLEGE
15744 Golden West Street
Huntington Beach, California 92647
Orange County
(714) 892-7711
Location: In the city of Huntington Beach.
Total Enrollment: 13,969

GROSSMONT COLLEGE
8800 Grossmont College Drive
El Cajon, California 92020
San Diego County
(619) 465-1700
Location: On a mesa fifteen miles east of San Diego.
Total Enrollment: 15,197

HARTNELL COLLEGE
156 Homestead Avenue
Salinas, California 93901
Monterey County
(408) 755-6900
Location: In the Gabilan foothills of the Salinas Valley.
Total Enrollment: 6,765

IMPERIAL VALLEY COLLEGE
380 East Aten Road
Imperial, California 92251
Imperial County
(619) 352-8320
Location: Near the Mexican border. Reflects the agricultural and Hispanic influence in its service area.
Total Enrollment: 6,445

IRVINE VALLEY COLLEGE
5500 Irvine Center Drive
Irvine, California 92720
Orange County
(714) 559-9300
Location: In a rapid growth area in southern Orange County.
Total Enrollment: 9,855

KINGS RIVER COMMUNITY COLLEGE
995 North Reed Avenue
Reedley, California 93654
Fresno County
(209) 638-3641
Location: Spacious campus near Fresno.
Total Enrollment: 6,222

LAKE TAHOE COMMUNITY COLLEGE
One College Drive
South Lake Tahoe, California 96150
El Dorado County
(916) 541-4660
Location: In the scenic Lake Tahoe basin of the Sierra Nevada.
Total Enrollment: 2,441

LANEY COLLEGE
900 Fallon Street
Oakland, California 94607
Alameda County
(510) 834-5740
Location: In the city of Oakland.
Total Enrollment: 11,143

LAS POSITAS COLLEGE
3033 Collier Canyon Road
Livermore, California 94550
Alameda County
(510) 373-5800
Location: In the Livermore-Amador Valley.
Total Enrollment: 5,535

LASSEN COLLEGE
Highway 139
Post Office Box 3000
Susanville, California 96130
Lassen County
(916) 257-6181
Location: Nestled in the Sierra Nevada Mountains of northeastern California some one-hundred miles northeast of Chico and ninety miles northwest of Reno.
Total Enrollment: 3,368

LONG BEACH CITY COLLEGE
4901 East Carson Street
Long Beach, California 90808
Los Angeles County
(310) 420-4111
Location: In the city of Long Beach.
Total Enrollment: 23,646

LOS ANGELES CITY COLLEGE
855 North Vermont Avenue
Los Angeles, California 90029
Los Angeles County
(213) 953-4000
Location: In the heart of Hollywood
Total Enrollment: 15,873

LOS ANGELES HARBOR COLLEGE
1111 Figueroa Place
Wilmington, California 90744
Los Angeles County
(310) 522-8200
Location: At the foot of the Palos Verdes Hills on the outskirts of Los Angeles.
Total Enrollment: 8,323

LOS ANGELES MISSION COLLEGE
13356 Eldridge Avenue
Sylmar, California 91342
Los Angeles County
(818) 364-7600
Location: In the northeast sector of the San Fernando Valley.
Total Enrollment: 6,429

LOS ANGELES PIERCE COLLEGE
6201 Winnetka Avenue
Woodland Hills, California 91371
Los Angeles County
(818) 347-0551
Location: In the western San Fernando Valley.
Total Enrollment: 15,865

LOS ANGELES SOUTHWEST COLLEGE
1600 West Imperial Highway
Los Angeles, California 90047
Los Angeles County
(213) 241-5225
Location: In south-central Los Angeles.
Total Enrollment: 5,831

LOS ANGELES TRADE-TECHNICAL COLLEGE
400 West Washington Boulevard
Los Angeles, California 90015
Los Angeles County
(213) 744-9058
Location: Near the downtown business district of Los Angeles.
Total Enrollment: 13,304

LOS ANGELES VALLEY COLLEGE
5800 Fulton Avenue
Van Nuys, California 91401
Los Angeles County
(818) 781-1200
Location: In the eastern San Fernando Valley.
Total Enrollment: 17,389

LOS MEDANOS COLLEGE
2700 East Leland Road
Pittsburg, California 94565
Contra Costa County
(510) 439-2181
Location: In a rapidly growing area of northern Contra Costa County.
Total Enrollment: 7,481

MENDOCINO COLLEGE
1000 Hensley Creek Road
Post Office Box 3000
Ukiah, California 95482
Mendocino County
(707) 468-3100
Location: In Ukiah, one-hundred seventeen miles north of San Francisco and one-hundred fifty-five miles due west of Sacramento.
Total Enrollment: 4,816

MERCED COLLEGE
3600 M Street
Merced, California 95348
Merced County
(209) 384-6000
Location: In the center of the San Joaquin Valley.
Total Enrollment: 10,458

MERRITT COLLEGE
12500 Campus Drive
Oakland, California 94619
Alameda County
(510) 531-4911
Location: In the hills of East Oakland.
Total Enrollment: 5,460

MIRA COSTA COLLEGE
One Barnard Drive
Oceanside, California 92056
San Diego County
(619) 757-2121
Location: In the northern part of San Diego County.
Total Enrollment: 12,816

MISSION COLLEGE
3000 Mission Boulevard
Santa Clara, California 95054
Santa Clara County
(408) 988-2200
Location: In the heart of Santa Clara Valley.
Total Enrollment: 10.655

MODESTO JUNIOR COLLEGE
435 College Avenue
Modesto, California 95350
Stanislaus County
(209) 575-6094
Location: In Modesto, a fast-growing Central Valley City.
Total Enrollment: 15,480

MONTEREY PENINSULA COLLEGE
980 Fremont Street
Monterey, California 93940
Monterey County
(408) 646-4000
Location: In a semi-rural area whose principal industries relate to the military and tourism.
Total Enrollment: 10,500

MOORPARK COLLEGE
7075 Campus Road
Moorpark, California 93021
Ventura County
(805) 378-1400
Location: In the hills above Moorpark, it offers easy access to both Los Angeles and Santa Barbara as well as the southern California coast.
Total Enrollment: 10,975

MT. SAN ANTONIO COLLEGE
1100 North Grand Avenue
Walnut, California 91789
Los Angeles County
(909) 594-5611
Location: Easily accessible from the major metropolitan areas of Los Angeles, Orange, and San Bernardino Counties.
Total Enrollment: 23,615

MT. SAN JACINTO COLLEGE
1499 North State Street
San Jacinto, California 92583
Riverside County
(909) 654-8011
Location: At the northern edge of San Jacinto Valley.
Total Enrollment: 7,022

NAPA VALLEY COLLEGE
2277 Napa-Vallejo Highway
Napa, California 94558
Napa County
(707) 253-3000
Location: In the heart of California's premium wine country.
Total Enrollment: 7,102

OHLONE COLLEGE
43600 Mission Boulevard
Fremont, California 94539
Alameda County
(510) 659-6000
Location: In the foothills overlooking San Francisco Bay.
Total Enrollment: 9,827

ORANGE COAST COLLEGE
2701 Fairview Road
Post Office Box 5005
Costa Mesa, California 92628
Orange County
(714) 432-0202
Location: Situated on Southern California's beautiful Orange Coast, just four miles from the Pacific.
Total Enrollment: 25,465

OXNARD COLLEGE
4000 South Rose Avenue
Oxnard, California 93033
Ventura County
(805) 986-5800
Location: Between Los Angeles and Santa Barbara on the Pacific Ocean along California's Gold Coast.
Total Enrollment: 6,342

PALO VERDE COLLEGE
811 West Chanslorway
Blythe, California 92225
Riverside County
(619) 922-6168
Location: Rural area in the southeastern desert next to the Colorado River.
Total Enrollment: 1,386

PALOMAR COLLEGE
1140 West Mission Road
San Marcos, California 92069
San Diego County
(619) 744-1150
Location: In a small rural community in Northern San Diego County.
Total Enrollment: 21,264

PASADENA CITY COLLEGE
1570 East Colorado Boulevard
Pasadena, California 91106
Los Angeles County
(818) 585-7123
Location: In the city of Pasadena.
Total Enrollment: 28,000

PORTERVILLE COLLEGE
100 East College Avenue
Porterville, California 93257
Tulare County
(209) 781-3130
Location: In the scenic foothills of the Sierras in southeastern Tulare County in central California.
Total Enrollment: 2,780

RANCHO SANTIAGO COMMUNITY COLLEGE
1530 West 17th Street
Santa Ana, California 92706
Orange County
(714) 564-6000
Location: In central Orange County.
Total Enrollment: 26,379

RIO HONDO COLLEGE
3600 Workman Mill Road
Whittier, California 90601
Los Angeles County
(310) 692-0921
Location: In the eastern part of Los Angeles County.
Total Enrollment: 18,400

RIVERSIDE COMMUNITY COLLEGE
4800 Magnolia Avenue
Riverside, California 92506
Riverside County
(909) 684-3240
Location: In the heart of Riverside, only sixty-five miles east of Los Angeles.
Total Enrollment: 21,,684

SACRAMENTO CITY COLLEGE
3835 Freeport Boulevard
Sacramento, California 95822
Sacramento County
(916) 558-2111
Location: Three miles south of the State Capitol building.
Total Enrollment: 17,737

SADDLEBACK COLLEGE
28000 Marguerite Parkway
Mission Viejo, California 92692
Orange County
(714) 582-4500
Location: In South Orange County.
Total Enrollment: 23,316

SAN BERNARDINO VALLEY COLLEGE
701 South Mount Vernon Avenue
San Bernardino, California 92410
San Bernardino County
(909) 888-6511
Location: In the rapidly growing urban area of southern California's Inland Empire.
Total Enrollment: 12,651

SAN DIEGO CITY COLLEGE
1313 Twelfth Avenue
San Diego, California 92101
San Diego County
(619) 230-2400
Location: Within walking distance or a short trolley ride to downtown San Diego, Balboa Park, and oceanfront areas.
Total Enrollment: 13,000

SAN DIEGO COMMUNITY COLLEGE EDUCATION CENTERS
4343 Ocean View Boulevard
San Diego, California 92113
San Diego County
(619) 536-7800
Location: No data
Total Enrollment: No data

SAN DIEGO MESA COLLEGE
7250 Mesa College Drive
San Diego, California 92111
San Diego County
(619) 627-2600
Location: The largest community college in the city of San Diego.
Total Enrollment: 24,401

SAN DIEGO MIRAMAR COLLEGE
10440 Black Mountain Road
San Diego, California 92126
San Diego County
(619) 536-7800
Location: Serves the rapidly growing northern suburbs of San Diego County.
Total Enrollment: 7,723

SAN JOAQUIN DELTA COLLEGE
5151 Pacific Avenue
Stockton, California 95207
San Joaquin County
(209) 474-5151
Location: Main campus in Stockton with several other centers located throughout the College district.
Total Enrollment: 18,014

SAN JOSE CITY COLLEGE
2100 Moorpark Avenue
San Jose, California 95128
Santa Clara County
(408) 298-2181
Location: In the city of San Jose.
Total Enrollment: 10,048

SANTA BARBARA CITY COLLEGE
721 Cliff Drive
Santa Barbara, California 93109
Santa Barbara County
(805) 965-0581
Location: On a bluff overlooking the beaches and resort community of Santa Barbara.
Total Enrollment: 11,157

SANTA MONICA COLLEGE
1900 Pico Boulevard
Santa Monica, California 90405
Los Angeles County
(310) 450-5150
Location: Just over a mile from the Pacific Ocean.
Total Enrollment: 24,209

SANTA ROSA JUNIOR COLLEGE
1501 Mendocino Avenue
Santa Rosa, California 95401
Sonoma County
(707) 527-4431
Location: In the California wine country.
Total Enrollment: 26,518

SHASTA COLLEGE
P.O. Box 496006
Redding, California 96049
Shasta County
(916) 225-4600
Location: In the heart of the Shasta Cascade wonderland of recreation.
Total Enrollment: 10,250

SIERRA COLLEGE
5000 Rocklin Road
Rocklin, California 95677
Placer County
(916) 624-3333
Location: Serves rural and mountain communities from Roseville to Lake Tahoe.
Total Enrollment: 13,729

SKYLINE COLLEGE
3300 College Drive
San Bruno, California 94066
San Mateo County
(415) 355-7000
Location: In northern San Mateo County on a bluff overlooking the Pacific Ocean.
Total Enrollment: 7,850

SOLANO COMMUNITY COLLEGE
4000 Suisun Valley Road
Suisun, California 94585
Solano County
(707) 864-7000
Location: Halfway between San Francisco and Sacramento in the Suisun Valley.
Total Enrollment: 10,457

SOUTHWESTERN COLLEGE
900 Otay Lakes Road
Chula Vista, California 91910
San Diego County
(619) 421-6700
Location: Seven miles south of San Diego.
Total Enrollment: 15,980

TAFT COLLEGE
29 Emmons Park Drive
Taft, California 93268
Kern County
(805) 763-4282
Location: In the San Joaquin Valley.
Total Enrollment: 1,102

VENTURA COLLEGE
4667 Telegraph Road
Ventura, California 93003
Ventura County
(805) 654-6400
Location: In the foothills of Ventura about sixty miles north of Los Angeles.
Total Enrollment: 10,451

VICTOR VALLEY COLLEGE
18422 Bear Valley Road
Victorville, California 92392
San Bernardino County
(619) 245-4271
Location: On the high Mojave Desert Plateau, approximately ninety miles from Los Angeles.
Total Enrollment: 9,186

VISTA COLLEGE
2020 Milvia Street
Berkeley, California 94704
Alameda County
(510) 841-8431
Location: In more than two-hundred Alameda County locations.
Total Enrollment: 3,165

WEST HILLS COLLEGE
300 Cherry Lane
Coalinga, California 93210
Fresno County
(209) 935-0801
Location: Western side of the San Joaquin Valley.
Total Enrollment: 2,716

WEST LOS ANGELES COLLEGE
4800 Freshman Drive
Culver City, California 90230
Los Angeles County
(310) 287-4200
Location: In the hills above Culver City, part of Los Angeles' west side.
Total Enrollment: 7,823

WEST VALLEY COLLEGE
14000 Fruitvale Avenue
Saratoga, California 95070
Santa Clara County
(408) 867-2200
Location: In the heart of Silicon Valley.
Total Enrollment: 12,771

YUBA COLLEGE
2088 North Beale Road
Marysville, California 95901
Yuba County
(916) 741-6700
Location: Service area stretches from high in the Coast Range across California's central valley to the foothills of the Sierra Nevada.
Total Enrollment: 9,017

Chapter 10

CALIFORNIA STATE UNIVERSITY

The primary function of California State University is the instruction of undergraduate and Master's degree students in the liberal arts and sciences, applied fields, and professions, including teaching. Twenty campuses are located throughout the state varying in enrollment size from San Diego with about 31,000 students to Bakersfield, San Marcos, and Stanislaus each with less than 6,000 students. Each campus has its own unique geographic location and distinctive character.

CALIFORNIA STATE UNIVERSITY

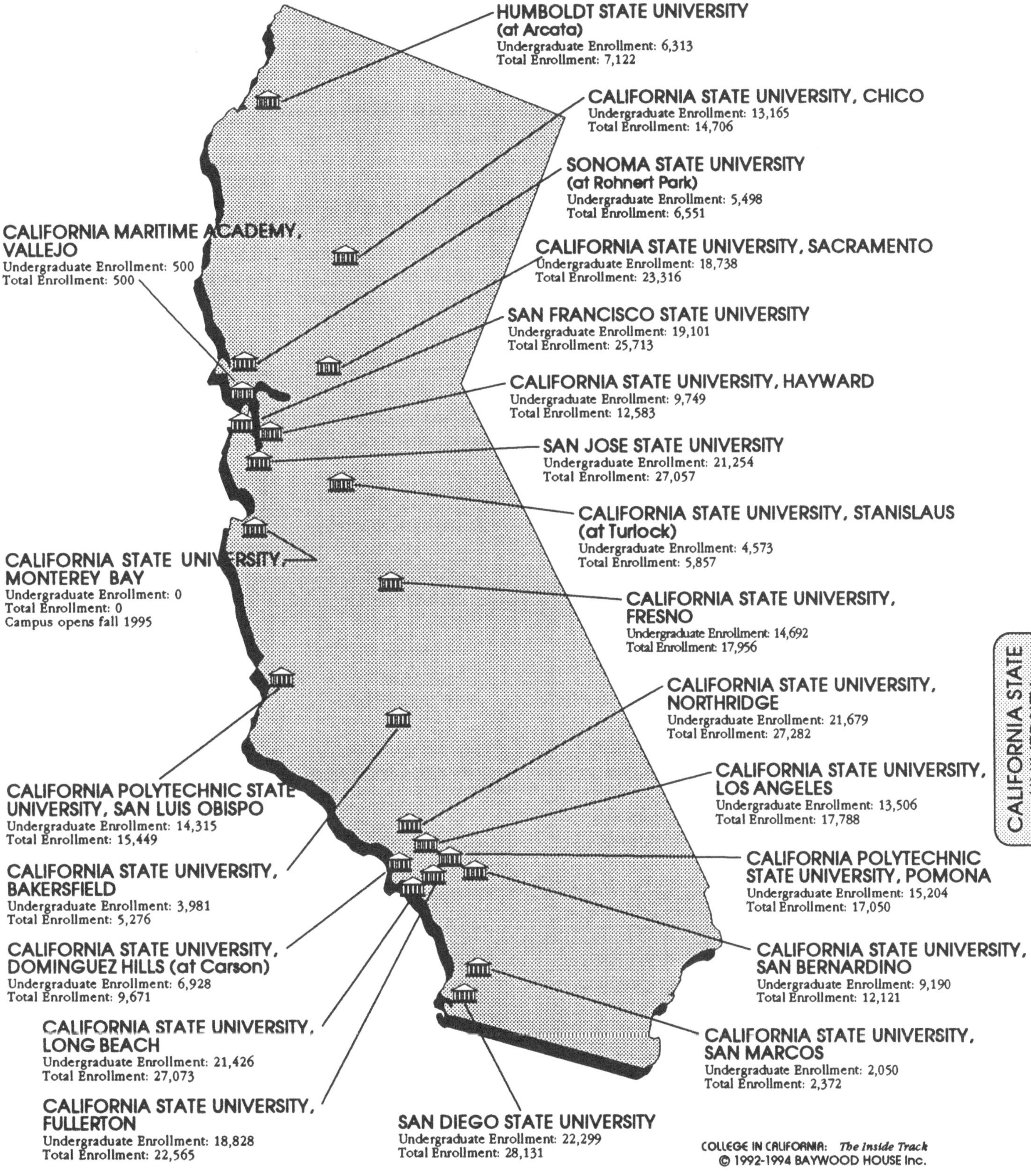

CALIFORNIA STATE UNIVERSITY

OVERVIEW

The California State University system enrolls approximately 325,000 students who are taught by some 16,000 faculty. Last year the system awarded over fifty percent of the Bachelor's degrees and thirty percent of the Master's degrees granted in California. More than 1.3 million students have been graduated from the nineteen campuses since 1960.

Last year the system awarded over fifty percent of the Bachelor's degrees and thirty percent of the Master's degrees granted in California.

Each campus in the system has its own unique geographic and curricular character. All campuses, as multipurpose institutions, offer undergraduate and graduate instruction for professional and occupational goals as well as broad liberal education. CSU offers more than fifteen-hundred Bachelor's and Master's degree programs in some two-hundred subject areas. In addition, a variety of teaching and school service credential programs are available. Many of these programs are offered in the late afternoon and evening, allowing students to complete their upper-division (junior/senior) and graduate requirements while attending part-time. A limited number of Doctoral degrees are offered jointly with the University of California and with private institutions in California.

Currently, there are twenty-two campuses in the CSU system: San Jose, the oldest, opened in 1857; Monterey Bay, the newest, will open to freshmen in September 1995. San Marcos opened to upper-division students in September 1990 and will open to freshmen in fall 1995. The California Maritime Academy will become part of the CSU system effective July 1, 1995.

There are twenty-two campuses in the CSU system.

These campuses are on a SEMESTER SYSTEM.

Cal Maritime
Chico
Dominguez Hills
Fresno
Fullerton
Humboldt
Long Beach
Monterey Bay
Northridge
Sacramento
San Diego
San Francisco
San Jose
San Marcos
Sonoma

These campuses are on a QUARTER SYSTEM.

Bakersfield
Hayward
Los Angeles
Pomona
San Bernardino
San Luis Obispo

Stanislaus is on a 4—1—4 CALENDAR of two semesters and a one-month winter term in January.

These campuses offer YEAR-ROUND INSTRUCTION including a full summer quarter.

Hayward
Los Angeles
Pomona
San Luis Obispo

Others offer limited summer programs.

MINIMUM ADMISSION REQUIREMENTS

Regularly-admitted freshmen to CSU must be academically among the top third of California high school graduates. All campuses adhere to the same minimum admission requirements for freshmen. You are a freshman applicant if after you have graduated from high school, you have not enrolled in a regular session between September and June at *any* college or university. If you have attended a summer college session immediately after graduation from high school, you still are considered a freshman applicant.

Meeting these minimum requirements does not necessarily guarantee to you a place at one of the campuses or the major of your choice.

To be eligible for admission as a first-time freshman you must be a high school graduate, meet the CSU Subject Requirement, the Examination Requirement, and the Scholarship Requirement. Meeting these minimum requirements does *not necessarily guarantee* to you a place at one of the campuses or the major of your choice. However, you must have an understanding of these minimum requirements as a basis for designing your high school program and setting your goals.

CSU SUBJECT REQUIREMENT

To satisfy the CSU Subject Requirement you must successfully complete the specific pattern of college-preparatory high school courses — described on the next page — by achieving *at least a C grade in each semester for each listed course.* CSU considers courses in which you receive a D, F, or Incomplete to be subject omissions which must be made up. See this chapter: Commonly Asked Questions About Admissions, page 10--13 to 10--16.

Each year, your California high school submits to the University of California a list of courses that it certifies as meeting the college-preparatory course criteria established by UC. To be accepted by UC, the courses you take to satisfy the UC "a-f" Subject Requirement must appear on the Official University of California Certified Course List of the high school you attend for the year you took the course. See chapter 11: UNIVERSITY OF CALIFORNIA, Minimum Admission Requirements, page 11--5.

For their admission evaluations, CSU uses this same Official University of California Certified Course List. Course titles must appear on your transcript exactly as they appear on this list. In addition, California State University accepts other courses in the visual and performing arts if they meet guidelines established by CSU. See this chapter: Commonly Asked Questions About Admissions, page 10--17. CSU also accepts courses in agriculture to meet the CSU Subject Requirement.

Courses in mathematics and foreign language completed in the seventh and eighth grades with at least a C grade may be counted toward the CSU Subject Requirement.

Ask your high school for copies of the Official University of California Certified Course List for each school year you attended the high school to make sure you are enrolling in the appropriate certified courses. CSU may count courses in mathematics and foreign language *completed* in the seventh and eighth grades with at least a C grade toward the CSU Subject Requirement. However, the principal of your high school must certify on your high school transcript that these seventh and eighth grade courses are comparable to those offered at your high school and are on the UC Certified Course List.

You must take a minimum of fifteen units of college prep courses to fulfill the CSU Subject Requirement. A unit is a course taken for one academic year or two semesters.

CALIFORNIA STATE UNIVERSITY SUBJECT REQUIREMENT

(Grades of C or better are required)	REQUIREMENT
English: 4 Years Required	Four years of college-preparatory English: Composition and literature. All English courses must require frequent and regular practice in writing expository prose compositions of some length.
Mathematics: 3 Years Required	Three years of college-preparatory mathematics: Algebra, geometry, intermediate algebra, trigonometry, analytical geometry, pre-calculus, calculus, or other approved courses.
U.S. History or U.S. History and Government: 1 Year Required	One year of United States history, or one-half year of United States history and one-half year of civics or American government.
Laboratory Science: 1 Year Required	One year of biology, chemistry, physics, or other acceptable laboratory science. Agriculture courses do not meet the laboratory science requirement.
Foreign Language: 2 Years Required	Both years must be in the same language. A waiver is available if you can show that you have equivalent foreign language competence. See this chapter: Commonly Asked Questions About Admissions, page 10--14.
Visual and Performing Arts 1 Year Required	One year of art, dance, music, or drama/theater. For examples of courses that meet this requirement see this chapter: Commonly Asked Questions About Admissions, page 10--14.
Electives: 3 Years Required	College-preparatory courses selected from the above categories, or agriculture, or social sciences.

This pattern of courses represents the minimum requirement. You present a stronger record for admission and are more prepared for college if you complete classes beyond this minimum.

Although not an admissions requirement, you are encouraged to complete four years of college-preparatory work in mathematics if you are planning to major in mathematics, the sciences — including computer science — engineering, pre-medicine, other science-related fields, business, or economics.

The courses listed here add up to fifteen one-year courses — units — the minimum number required for admission.

WORKSHEET

Use the worksheet, MY COURSE PLAN, below to monitor your progress towards meeting CSU admission requirements. Enter your grades as you complete your courses. Courses completed in the ninth grade or earlier with at least at grade of C should be marked X.

MY COURSE PLAN: CSU SUBJECT REQUIREMENT

California State University

ACADEMIC SUBJECTS	GRADES 7 OR 8	9TH GRADE			USE ALL GRADES ON THIS WORKSHEET & THOSE RECEIVED IN NON-COLLEGE-PREPARATORY COURSES (EXCEPT PE & MILITARY SCIENCE) EARNED IN THE 10TH THROUGH 12TH GRADES TO CALCULATE YOUR GPA. 10TH GRADE			11TH GRADE			12TH GRADE		
(Grades of C or better are required)	Course Title	Course Title	Fall Grade	Spring Grade	Course Title	Fall Grade	Spring Grade	Course Title	Fall Grade	Spring Grade	Course Title	Fall Grade	Spring Grade
English: 4 Years Required													
Mathematics: 3 Years Required													
U.S. History or U.S. History and Government: 1 Year Required													
Laboratory Science: 1 Year Required													
Foreign Language: 2 Years Required													
Visual and Performing Arts: 1 Year Required													
Electives: 3 Years Required													

COLLEGE IN CALIFORNIA: *The Inside Track*

CALIFORNIA STATE UNIVERSITY

EXAMINATION REQUIREMENT

In addition to successfully completing the CSU Subject Requirement, CSU may require you to take college admissions tests. Your scores on these tests can be important admission criteria.

Cal Poly San Luis Obispo requires test scores from all applicants and from a test date no later than November of the senior year of high school.

SAT I: REASONING TEST AND/OR ACT TESTS

If your high school GPA for CSU admission is less than 3.00 — 3.61 for nonresidents of California — or if you are applying to an impacted program that requires test scores, you *must* submit the test results of one college admissions test, *either* (1) *or* (2):

1. Scholastic Assessment Test (SAT I: Reasoning Test). The verbal and mathematics scores on this test must be received from one test sitting.
2. American College Test (ACT). The ACT composite score must be submitted.

SAT II: Subject Tests are not required or recommended for admission to CSU. See chapter 6: COLLEGE ENTRANCE TESTS, SAT II: Subject Tests, page 6--30.

If your *high school GPA for CSU admission* is above 3.00 — 3.61 for nonresidents — or you are not applying to an impacted major that requires them, you are still encouraged to take the admissions tests. CSU may use your scores for advising and placement purposes when you enroll. Impacted majors are those that receive more applications during the first month of the filing period than can be accommodated. See this chapter: Impacted Programs For 1994-95, page 10--24.

If you have not *attended a high school full-time for at least three years, where English is the principal language of instruction, you must take the TOEFL, the Test of English as a Foreign Language.*

CALIFORNIA STATE UNIVERSITY

California Polytechnic State University, San Luis Obispo requires test scores from *all* applicants. The campus requires you to take the SAT I: Reasoning Test or the ACT by either the *October or November* testing date of your senior year for fall admission. For fall admission to other CSU campuses in any impacted majors that require testing, plan to take the tests no later than *December* of your senior year.

TOEFL

If your preparatory education was principally in a language other than English, you must demonstrate competence in the use of the English language to be admitted to CSU. If you have *not* attended a high school full-time for at least three years, where English is the principal language of instruction, you must take the TOEFL, the Test of English as a Foreign Language. See chapter 6: COLLEGE ENTRANCE TESTS, TOEFL, page 6--43. CSU requires this testing regardless of your citizenship. You must obtain a minimum score of 500 on the TOEFL to be admitted to most CSU campuses. Some campuses require a higher score. You must take the TOEFL in addition to the SAT I: Reasoning Test or ACT. Plan to take it no later than April of your senior year.

Individual campuses establish TOEFL score minimums based upon campus-specific factors such as the nature of instruction offered, the availability of instruction in English as a second language, and student enrollment demand. For fall 1995 admission, CSU campuses required the minimum TOEFL scores shown here.

MINIMUM TOEFL SCORE REQUIREMENTS AT CALIFORNIA STATE UNIVERSITY CAMPUSES

CSU Campus	TOEFL Score	CSU Campus	TOEFL Score
Bakersfield	500	Maritime Academy	500
Chico [1]	500	Monterey Bay	---
Dominguez	550	Northridge	500
Fresno	500	Pomona	525
Fullerton	500	Sacramento	510
Hayward	525	San Bernardino	500
Humboldt State	550	San Diego State	550
Long Beach	500	San Francisco State	500
Except for majors in:		San Jose State	500
Business	550	San Luis Obispo	550
Engineering	525		
Journalism	600	San Marcos	550
Math, Comp Science	525		
Radio, TV	550	Sonoma State	500
Los Angeles	550	Stanislaus [2]	500

Note 1. Except for an unrestricted program of study — 550.
Note 2. Including part-scores of at least 50.

You must obtain a minimum score of 500 on the TOEFL to be admitted to most CSU campuses. Some campuses require higher scores.

SCHOLARSHIP REQUIREMENT

Eligibility for admission to CSU is based upon a combination of your high school grade point average and your SAT I: Reasoning Test or ACT admissions test scores.

COMPUTING YOUR GPA FOR CSU ADMISSION

Your high school GPA for CSU admission is based upon grades earned during your final three years of high school— grades ten through twelve. CSU uses all courses in your high school curriculum for these years with the exception of physical education and military science. They do not use just the CSU Subject Requirement college-preparatory courses on the Official University of California Certified Course List for your GPA calculation.

You may include in your high school GPA for CSU admission calculation *all* your course grades in shop, homemaking, business, art, music, drama, social studies, mathematics, science, English, and foreign language. You may do so even though some of these courses *may not be designated* as college-preparatory courses and do not appear on the Official University of California Certified Course List. Because CSU allows you to use these non-college-preparatory courses, which may be less rigorous, your high school GPA for CSU admission may be higher than that calculated for UC. See chapter 11: UNIVERSITY OF CALIFORNIA, Scholarship Requirement, page 11--9.

When calculating your GPA for CSU admission, include grades in courses taken in the tenth, eleventh, and twelfth grades. Use both college-preparatory and non-college-preparatory courses, except those in physical education and military science.

Do not misunderstand! *You must complete the CSU Subject Requirement* for admission as previously outlined. However, your grades for courses that meet the CSU Subject Requirement *and* your grades for those that do not (excluding physical education and military science) are used for your high school GPA for CSU admission calculation.

Grades earned in courses in the ninth grade or earlier are not used to calculate your high school GPA for CSU admission. However, these courses may be used to meet the CSU Subject Requirement if they are completed with at least a C grade.

You must submit your high school GPA for CSU admission in November of your senior year when you apply for admission and your senior grades are not yet available. Therefore, only your sophomore and junior grades are used to calculate your *preliminary* high school GPA for CSU admission. CSU does allow you to submit senior year grades to improve your high school GPA for CSU admission and will reassess your eligibility throughout your senior year. While this practice is CSU policy, it is not likely that impacted majors will use this flexibility.

- Grades earned in courses in the ninth grade or earlier are not used to calculate your high school GPA for CSU admission. However, these courses may be used to meet the CSU Subject Requirement if they are completed with at least a C grade. For example, CSU may count courses in foreign language and mathematics completed in grades seven and eight with grades of C or higher toward meeting the CSU Subject Requirement, but their grades are not calculated in your high school GPA for CSU admission. As another example, an English class completed in grade nine counts toward meeting the CSU Subject Requirement of four years of English; however the grade earned is not included in the calculation of your high school GPA for CSU admission.

- Each honors-level course taken in your *junior* and *senior* years in which you earn a grade of C or better is given an extra point when calculating your high school GPA for CSU admission. Honors-level courses include those designated as honors courses by your high school, Advanced Placement courses, and transferable college courses. See this chapter: Commonly Asked Questions About Admissions, pages 10--13 to 10--14 for a more detailed definition of honors-level courses. Up to eight semesters (four one-year courses) of honors-level courses and Advanced Placement courses can be used in your high school GPA for CSU admission calculation.

- If you repeat a course, use only the highest grade received in it. *Any* course grade may be repeated.

Any course grade may be repeated. When calculating your GPA for CSU admission, use only the highest course grade you received.

- Grades you receive in summer-session courses following grade nine are included in your high school GPA for CSU admission calculation. However, summer-session course grades after grade twelve, except when necessary for graduation, are not included.

Follow these seven steps to calculate your grade point average for CSU admission:

Step 1. Count the number of one-semester courses you have taken in grades ten, eleven, and twelve (except for PE and military science) for which you received a grade of A. Enter this number on line (1) in column (a).

Step 2. Repeat Step (1) for each grade received of B, C, D, and F and enter the corresponding counts on lines (2), (3), (4), and (5) in column (a).

Step 3. For each grade on lines (1) through (5), multiply the number of courses you entered in column (a) by the grade points per grade shown in column (b). Enter the result on the corresponding line in column (c).

Step 4. Total column (a) and enter the result on line (7) and at the bottom of the chart in the box marked TOTAL1.

Step 5. Count the number of one-semester honors-level courses you have taken in grades *eleven and twelve*. Enter this number to a maximum of eight semester courses on line (8) in column (c).

Step 6. Total column (c) and enter the result on line (9) and at the bottom of the chart in the box marked TOTAL2.

Step 7. At the bottom of the chart, divide TOTAL2 by TOTAL1 and enter the result to two decimal places in the box marked GPA. This number is YOUR PRELIMINARY HIGH SCHOOL GPA FOR CSU ADMISSION.

MY GPA COMPUTATION

CSU Admission Grade Point Average

		column (a)	column (b)	column (c)
	Letter Grade	Number of Semester Courses	Grade Points per Grade	Total Grade Points Earned column (a) x column (b)
line (1)	A		x 4	
line (2)	B		x 3	
line (3)	C		x 2	
line (4)	D		x 1	
line (5)	F		x 0	
line (7)	TOTAL1			
line (8)	No. of Semester Honors Courses			
line (9)			TOTAL2	

YOUR PRELIMINARY HIGH SCHOOL GPA FOR CSU ADMISSION

TOTAL2 ÷ TOTAL1 = .

COLLEGE IN CALIFORNIA: *The Inside Track* © 1992 BAYWOOD HOUSE Inc.

ELIGIBILITY INDEX

California high school graduates or residents of California must place on the eligibility index to meet minimum admission requirements for CSU. The eligibility index is a combination of (a) your high school GPA for CSU admission — calculated as described here — and (b) either your SAT I total, *before recentering*, or ACT composite college admissions test score. CSU will publish Equivalence Tables for comparing "before" recentering SAT I total scores with "after" recentering total scores in spring 1995. Students who plan to graduate in June 1996 or after will need to use recentered scores to determine their eligibility. See chapter 6: College Entrance Tests, page 10--21 for information on recentering of SAT I scores.

California high school graduates or residents of California must place on the eligibility index to meet minimum admission requirements for CSU.

Determine your own eligibility index by one of these calculations:

1. If you use your SAT I: Reasoning Test score, multiply your GPA by 800 and add your total SAT I score (verbal plus mathematics).

Your Eligibility Index = (Your GPA x 800) + (Your SAT I total score)

2. If you use your ACT score, multiply your GPA by 200 and add 10 times your ACT composite score.

If you have a 3.00 or higher high school GPA for CSU admission, you qualify for admission to CSU regardless of your test scores.

Your Eligibility Index = (200 x Your GPA) + (10 x Your ACT composite score)

If you are a California high school graduate or a resident of California for tuition purposes, you need a minimum eligibility index of 2800 using the SAT I: Reasoning Test or 694 using the ACT. If you neither graduated from a California high school nor are a resident of California for tuition purposes, you need a minimum eligibility index of 3402 using the SAT I: Reasoning Test or 842 using the ACT. See appendix A: CALIFORNIA RESIDENCY REQUIREMENTS.

The table on the following page shows the combinations of grade point average and test score that satisfy the eligibility index requirement for California high school graduates or residents of California. If you have a 3.00 or higher high school GPA for CSU admission, you qualify for admission to CSU regardless of your test scores. If you have a high school GPA for CSU admission below 2.00 you do not qualify for regular admission. If your high school GPA for CSU admission is above 1.99 but below 3.00, you have met the minimum requirement if you achieve the necessary college admissions test score. For example, if you have a GPA for CSU admission of 2.72, you need an SAT I total score of 630 or an ACT composite score of 15 to qualify for admission.

If you have taken the tests more than once and submit multiple score reports, CSU uses the highest total score from a single sitting of the test.

If you have taken the tests more than once and submit multiple score reports, CSU uses the highest total score from a single sitting of the test. If you take both the SAT I: Reasoning Test and the ACT, CSU uses whichever scores are higher.

If your eligibility index is too low to qualify for admission in November, you may have your senior year to improve it. CSU may recalculate your eligibility index using your senior year grades in addition to those in grades ten and eleven, and any additional test scores that improve your qualifications. You can try to improve your senior year grades to raise your GPA. You may retake the SAT I: Reasoning Test and/or the ACT several times if necessary. Impacted majors and campuses may not be willing to review your senior year record and later test scores. They may base their admission decisions upon the information you present on your admission application and any supplemental information they request from you. See this chapter: Impacted Campuses For 1994-95, page 10--21.

The eligibility index is in effect at this time. It has been set such that the upper one-third of California high school graduates are eligible for admission.

ELIGIBILITY INDEX TABLE
For California High School Graduates or Residents of California

GPA	ACT Score	SAT I Score	GPA	ACT Score	SAT I Score	GPA	ACT Score	SAT I Score	GPA	ACT Score	SAT I Score	GPA	ACT Score	SAT I Score
3.00 and above qualifies with any score			2.80	14	560	2.59	18	730	2.38	22	900	2.17	26	1070
			2.79	14	570	2.58	18	740	2.37	22	910	2.16	27	1080
2.99	10	410	2.78	14	580	2.57	18	750	2.36	23	920	2.15	27	1080
2.98	10	420	2.77	14	590	2.56	19	760	2.35	23	920	2.14	27	1090
2.97	10	430	2.76	15	600	2.55	19	760	2.34	23	930	2.13	27	1100
2.96	11	440	2.75	15	600	2.54	19	770	2.33	23	940	2.12	27	1110
2.95	11	440	2.74	15	610	2.53	19	780	2.32	23	950	2.11	28	1120
2.94	11	450	2.73	15	620	2.52	19	790	2.31	24	960	2.10	28	1120
2.93	11	460	2.72	15	630	2.51	20	800	2.30	24	960	2.09	28	1130
2.92	11	470	2.71	16	640	2.50	20	800	2.29	24	970	2.08	28	1140
2.91	12	480	2.70	16	640	2.49	20	810	2.28	24	980	2.07	28	1150
2.90	12	480	2.69	16	650	2.48	20	820	2.27	24	990	2.06	29	1160
2.89	12	490	2.68	16	660	2.47	20	830	2.26	25	1000	2.05	29	1160
2.88	12	500	2.67	16	670	2.46	21	840	2.25	25	1000	2.04	29	1170
2.87	12	510	2.66	17	680	2.45	21	840	2.24	25	1010	2.03	29	1180
2.86	13	520	2.65	17	680	2.44	21	850	2.23	25	1020	2.02	29	1190
2.85	13	520	2.64	17	690	2.43	21	860	2.22	25	1030	2.01	30	1200
2.84	13	530	2.63	17	700	2.42	21	870	2.21	26	1040	2.00	30	1200
2.83	13	540	2.62	17	710	2.41	22	880	2.20	26	1040	Below 2.00 does not qualify for regular admission		
2.82	13	550	2.61	18	720	2.40	22	880	2.19	26	1050			
2.81	14	560	2.60	18	720	2.39	22	890	2.18	26	1060			

The eligibility index has been set such that the upper one-third of California high school graduates are eligible for admission.

CALIFORNIA STATE UNIVERSITY

COMMONLY ASKED QUESTIONS ABOUT ADMISSIONS

WHAT ARE HONORS-LEVEL COURSES?

These are honors-level courses:

1. High school courses in English, foreign language, history, laboratory science, and advanced mathematics (advanced algebra, mathematics analysis, trigonometry, pre-calculus, calculus) that your high school may certify as being taught at the honors level. They are the same as those designated as honors courses for the University of California system and are listed on your high school's Official University of California Certified Course List of "a-f" Subject Requirement courses.

2. Advanced Placement courses in college-preparatory subjects that prepare you for an Advanced Placement Examination of the College Entrance Examination Board. See chapter 6: COLLEGE ENTRANCE TESTS, The AP Program And Examination, page 6--57.

Honors-level courses, to a maximum of four one-year courses (eight semester courses), taken in your junior and senior years *receive an extra point when calculating your high school GPA*

3. College courses in college-preparatory subjects (listed in item one on the previous page) that qualify as transferrable to CSU and appear on your high school transcript for high school credit. California Community College and four-year college courses fit this category. These are courses that you take at a college and transfer back to your high school for high school credit. A course and its credits that are transferred back to your high school become part of your high school record. Once transferred, you may use them as part of that record to meet college admission requirements, but they cannot be used for both high school credit and credit towards your college degree at CSU.

   Some community colleges do allow the course to remain on your college record even though you are also receiving high school credit for it. You receive both high school and community college credit for the same class, a practice called "double counting". Check with your local community college to find out what their policy is regarding course credit.

   If you need to use the course for honors credit to raise your high school GPA for CSU admission, transfer it back to your high school record even if it cannot be double-counted. On the other hand, if it cannot be double-counted, and you do not need it to improve your high school GPA for CSU admission, leave the course on your college record to be used later toward your college graduation requirements.

Honors-level courses, to a maximum of four one-year courses (eight semester courses), taken in your *junior and senior years* receive an extra point when calculating your high school GPA for CSU admission. Intensive or accelerated courses are not considered honors-level courses.

WHAT ARE THE ADVANTAGES OF TAKING TENTH GRADE HONORS COURSES IF I DO NOT EARN EXTRA GRADE POINTS IN CALCULATING MY HIGH SCHOOL GPA FOR CSU ADMISSION?

One of the primary benefits is preparation for more advanced high school classes and University work. In addition, the quality of your high school program is a consideration when your record is reviewed for admission. A challenging high school program including Advanced Placement and honors-level courses is one of the academic criteria CSU campuses use to admit freshman applicants to impacted campuses and programs.

Regardless of the grade you received in it, any course may be repeated.

WHAT ARE THE RULES REGARDING REPEATING COURSES?

If you need to repeat a course to satisfy the CSU Subject Requirement, only the highest grade you receive in the course is used to calculate your high school GPA for CSU admission. Regardless of the grade you received in it, any course may be repeated. For example, if you receive a C in a course, but believe you would like to repeat it to improve your high school GPA for CSU admission, you may do so. Be careful. Your high school may not give you high school credit for repeating a course that you have already passed.

HOW DOES CSU DEAL WITH D'S, F'S, OR INCOMPLETES IN CSU SUBJECT REQUIREMENT COURSES?

1. A full-year course is considered a successful completion of the CSU Subject Requirement if your final grade at the end of the year is C or better. It does not need to be repeated, even if your first semester grade in it was D, F, or Incomplete.

An example:

Course	Biology
First-Semester Grade	D
Second-Semester Grade	C
Result	Successful completion of the CSU Subject Requirement. The course does not need to be repeated.

A full-year course is a successful completion of the CSU Subject Requirement if your final grade at the end of the year is a C or better.

2. A full-year course is *not* considered a successful completion of the CSU Subject Requirement if your final grade at the end of the year is D, F, or Incomplete, even if you earned a C or higher in it for the first semester. You have met the first-semester CSU Subject Requirement, but you are lacking in the second semester of the course. You do receive credit toward meeting the CSU Subject Requirement for completing the first half of the course. However, you must repeat the second semester of the course.

An example:

Course	Biology
First-Semester Grade	C
Second-Semester Grade	D
Result	Unsuccessful completion of the CSU Subject Requirement. Credit received for completing the first semester. The second-semester course must be repeated.

If the course is part of a course sequence continuing into the following year, see item (3) below.

If you enroll in the second year of a course and complete it with at least a C grade, you are credited with two years toward the CSU Subject Requirement.

3. If you enroll in the second year of a course — doing so presumes you have knowledge of the first year's course material — and complete it with at least a C grade, you are credited with two years toward the CSU Subject Requirement. You do not need to make up the first year of the course, even if you received a final grade of D, F, or Incomplete at the end of the first year. Typically, mathematics and foreign language are sequential courses that fit this situation.

For instance, completing the second year of a foreign language with a C or better validates the first year regardless of your first-year grades in the language. You are credited with two years of that language toward your CSU Subject Requirement.

An example:

Course	Spanish I, Spanish II
Spanish I, first-semester grade	D
Spanish I, second-semester grade	D
Spanish II, first-semester grade	D
Spanish II, second-semester grade	C
Result	The C grade at the end of the second year validates the first year. You receive credit for two years of a foreign language toward your CSU Subject Requirement.

In examples (1) and (3), all of your semester grades for grades ten, eleven, and twelve, except those for physical education and military science, are included in calculating your high school GPA for CSU admission. In example (2), for which you must repeat a course, only the higher grade must be used in your GPA calculation.

HOW CAN I MAKE UP MISSING CSU SUBJECT REQUIREMENT COURSES?

You may make up missing CSU Subject Requirement courses in your regular high school program, or you can use either or both of the following alternatives:

You may make up missing CSU Subject Requirement courses through adult school, high school summer sessions, or college courses.

1. You may complete appropriate high school courses with a grade of C or better in adult school or high school summer sessions. Be certain the courses are on your high school's Official University of California Certified Course List or meet the visual and performing arts guidelines set forth by CSU as described at the bottom of this page.

2. You may complete appropriate courses in college with a C or better. One college course of three semester units (four quarter units) is usually considered equivalent to one year of high school study.

CAN I CLEAR UP DEFICIENCIES IN SUMMER SCHOOL AFTER GRADUATION?

You may clear deficiencies in summer school (but not necessarily for fall admission) at either a high school or community college. The courses you take must be on the approved Official University of California Certified Course List or meet the visual and performing arts guidelines set forth by CSU as described in the next question/answer.

HOW CAN I MEET THE VISUAL AND PERFORMING ARTS REQUIREMENT?

A broad array of courses may satisfy this requirement. CSU accepts all visual and performing arts courses on your high school's Official University of California Certified Course List. Additionally, CSU accepts other courses on your high school transcript that meet guidelines established by CSU but are not acceptable to UC. These courses are not listed on the Official University of California Certified Course List.

Here are examples of courses that meet the CSU visual and performing arts CSU Subject Requirement:

Art: Introduction to art, art appreciation, art history, art theory, art design (three dimensional), drawing, painting, ceramics, sculpture, studio art, life drawing, printmaking, museum studies, photography, art production, architectural design, ethnic art.

Dance: Ballet, modern dance, dance performance, dance history, choreography and production, jazz dance, ethnic dance, dance improvisation.

A broad array of visual and performing arts courses may meet the CSU one-year requirement.

Music: Music appreciation, music history, band (beginning, advanced, marching), jazz ensemble, percussion ensemble, orchestra, choir (beginning, concert), voice, music theory/harmony, instrument training (guitar, strings, winds, piano), glee, vocal ensemble, music laboratory.

Theater/Drama: Drama, acting, directing, theater arts, history of theater, dramatic productions.

Here are examples of courses that do not meet the CSU visual and performing arts CSU Subject Requirement:

Art: Graphic art, yearbook, mechanical drafting, architectural drafting/drawing, computer graphics, calligraphy, cartooning, basic crafts (jewelry, knitting, weaving, needlepoint, macrame, stitchery, cake decorating, sewing), stained glass, advertising/fashion/interior design, furniture design, basic wood, plastics, silk screening, design crafts.

Dance: Aerobic dance, drill team/marching dynamics/cheerleading, recreation dance (folk, square, social), banner/flag/baton, other dance courses in which the primary intent is physical fitness or exercise.

Music: Activities, such as pep band, that may not be part of a regular music or band course.

Theater/Drama: Stage craft, costume design, lighting design, playwriting, speech debate, TV/video/radio production, courses in other disciplines that require performance in occasional skits.

You may fulfill the visual and performing arts CSU Subject Requirement by taking two semester courses in two different subjects (e.g., one semester of dance and one semester of art appreciation), or you may complete one year of study in the same field (e.g., one year of drama). Visual or performing arts courses taken in the seventh or eighth grade do not fulfill the visual and performing arts requirement.

You may fulfill the visual and performing arts CSU Subject Requirement by taking two semester courses in two different subjects, or you may complete one year of study in the same field .

HOW CAN I WAIVE THE FOREIGN LANGUAGE CSU SUBJECT REQUIREMENT?

You may qualify for a waiver and not take foreign language courses, if you can show that you have had foreign language experiences equivalent to two years of high school courses.

If you are a newcomer to the United States, having come from a country where English is not the native language, or you are raised in a household where a language other than English is spoken, it is likely you qualify for a waiver.

There are two ways to establish your foreign language competency and eligibility for a waiver:

You may qualify for a waiver and not take foreign language courses if you can show that you have had foreign language experiences equivalent to two years of high school language.

1. Documentation: If you are a native speaker of a foreign language, you most likely qualify for a waiver. You need a school record in your school files verifying any of the following:

   a. No earlier than the age of seven you completed at least three years of formal instruction in a school where a language other than English was used as a medium of instruction at least one-third of the time. This includes bilingual or immersion language programs in the United States.

   b. At the age of ten or older you were identified by a United States school as having limited English proficiency and/or you were enrolled in programs such as English as a second language or bilingual education courses that are designed for limited English-proficiency students.

   c. At any time during your high school years, you were a tutor or interpreter for students or adults in a school or community setting.

2. Assessment: You demonstrate by testing that you have a competence level in a foreign language equal to two years of high school study in the same language. This testing may take place in your high school or at a CSU campus. Check with your counselor or guidance administrator to determine if your high school can administer the appropriate test to you. If you need to test at CSU, indicate this in the Foreign Language section on the High School Preparation form in your application. See this chapter: Completing Your CSU Application, page 10--42.

Documentation is preferred. Assessment may be used to obtain a waiver only if you cannot prove your foreign language competence through documents in your school files.

CALIFORNIA STATE UNIVERSITY

There are two ways to establish your foreign language competency and eligibility for a waiver: documentation and assessment.

Ask your counselor or a high school administrator for assistance with either of these alternatives. Your high school does not need to send the actual documents for your files. They should note on your high school transcript that the CSU Subject Requirement in foreign language is waived because of documentation or assessment. The notation should state specifically the basis for your waiver. For example, it might read, "CSU foreign language requirement met by formal schooling in Chinese." The CSU admissions office also will accept a letter from your counselor or administrator verifying your waiver qualifications.

DOES AMERICAN SIGN LANGUAGE (AMESLAN) SATISFY CSU'S FOREIGN LANGUAGE REQUIREMENT?

CSU will accept American Sign Language (Ameslan) courses on the Official University of California Certified Course List as meeting their foreign language admission requirement.

HOW DO ESL — ENGLISH AS A SECOND LANGUAGE — COURSES COUNT TOWARD MEETING THE ENGLISH CSU SUBJECT REQUIREMENT FOR ADMISSION?

If you are a student new to the United States and English is not your native language, your high school is likely to schedule you into ESL classes to develop your English skills. You may substitute two consecutive semesters of advanced ESL for the first year of the required four years of college-preparatory English, if they are listed on the Official University Of California Certified Course List. Elementary and intermediate courses in ESL do not meet the CSU Subject Requirement in English.

CAN I RECEIVE CREDIT FOR A COURSE NOT TAKEN BY TAKING AN ADVANCED COURSE IN THE SUBJECT?

If you complete with a grade of C or better the second year of a course sequence that presupposes knowledge of the first year, you have met a two-year CSU Subject Requirement. For example, satisfactory completion of the second year of a foreign language validates that you have successfully mastered the first year. The second year of algebra will validate first-year algebra but will not validate geometry. Typically, of the fifteen-unit CSU Subject Requirement, only mathematics and foreign language are presented in a sequential manner.

CAN I BE ADMITTED BY EXAMINATION ALONE IF I DO NOT MEET THE SUBJECT AND SCHOLARSHIP REQUIREMENTS?

CSU has no provision for admission by examination alone.

DO I NEED A HIGH SCHOOL DIPLOMA TO BE ADMITTED TO CSU?

Yes, high school graduation is a requirement for admission to CSU. If you do not have a high school diploma, you can meet this requirement by

a) passing the California High School Proficiency Examination, *or*

b) establishing high school graduation equivalence on the GED, the General Educational Development Tests, by achieving an average score for the five GED tests of 45 or better and a score on each test of at least 40.

If you meet the high school graduation requirement by either of these two alternatives, you are still expected to meet the fifteen-unit CSU Subject Requirement, Examination Requirement, and Scholarship Requirement.

If you do not have a high school diploma, you may meet the high school graduation requirement for admission to CSU by passing the California High School Proficiency Examination or the GED.

I HAVE TAKEN PART OF MY HIGH SCHOOL WORK IN A FOREIGN COUNTRY. CAN I USE MY FOREIGN SCHOOL COURSES TO QUALIFY FOR ADMISSION?

As long as your high school recognizes the courses you have taken in the foreign country as meeting the level of work required in the high school, CSU accepts them as meeting entrance requirements.

I LIVE OUT OF STATE, BUT I AM THE DEPENDENT OF A GRADUATE OF CSU. AM I CONSIDERED A CALIFORNIA RESIDENT FOR ADMISSION PURPOSES?

No, CSU does not consider you a resident for admission or tuition purposes.

I LIVE OUT OF STATE, BUT I AM THE DEPENDENT OF A CSU EMPLOYEE. AM I CONSIDERED A CALIFORNIA RESIDENT FOR ADMISSION PURPOSES?

If you are the dependent of a full-time employee of CSU, you are considered a resident for admission and tuition purposes.

If you are the dependent of a full-time employee of CSU, you are considered a resident for admission and tuition purposes.

I DO NOT QUALIFY AS A RESIDENT OF CALIFORNIA FOR ADMISSION PURPOSES. WHAT ARE THE MINIMUM FRESHMAN ADMISSION REQUIREMENTS FOR ME?

If you neither graduated from a California high school nor are a resident of California for tuition purposes, the admission requirements are the same as those for residents, except for the following:

You must have a minimum eligibility index of 3402 based upon your SAT I test scores or 842 based upon your ACT composite test score. See this chapter: Scholarship Requirement, page 10--9. If your high school GPA for CSU admission is 3.61 or higher, you are not required to submit test scores. However, you are urged to take the SAT I: Reasoning Test or ACT because campuses may use your test results for advising and placement purposes.

IMPACTED CAMPUSES FOR 1994-95

An undergraduate campus is designated as "impacted" if the number of applications received for it in the first month of the filing period is *expected* to be larger than the number of spaces available. The campuses use supplemental admission criteria to determine admission when this occurs. Cal Poly San Luis Obispo is impacted year after year. Other campuses may or may not be impacted from year to year, depending upon demand for and availability of spaces.

Each fall, usually in November, CSU publishes a list of expected impacted campuses for the following school year. This information appears in the CSU monthly publication for counselors, *CSU Review*. This newsletter also reviews the latest supplemental criteria for admission to these campuses. Ask to see this newsletter at your high school. The information presented on the following pages is extracted from the November 1993 issue.

Humboldt State University has become very popular in recent years. It has defined supplemental admission criteria to be used to select first-time freshmen should applications received during the first month of the filing period — the initial filing period — exceed the number which can be accommodated. The Cal Poly San Luis Obispo campus has been impacted consistently for several years and uses a procedure known as the Multi-Criteria Admission Plan (MCA) to screen applicants.

It is essential that you apply during the initial month of the application period indicated here. New applications may not be considered later.

SEMESTER CAMPUSES

Fall	November
Spring	August

QUARTER CAMPUSES

Fall	November
Winter	June
Spring	August
Summer	February

HUMBOLDT STATE UNIVERSITY

SUPPLEMENTAL CRITERIA

When more applications are received during the first month of the filing period than can be accommodated, Humboldt uses supplemental criteria to screen applicants. First-time freshmen are required to have completed all fifteen-units of CSU's college-preparatory CSU Subject Requirement. Upper division transfer applicants who have completed the full 39 units of General Education courses will receive priority. Completion of IGETC also will be recognized. Applicants will be evaluated on the basis of academic performance with consideration given to factors contributing to campus diversity.

SONOMA STATE

Sonoma State is conducting a three year experiment to address retention and graduation of students and enrollment of underrepresented students. To help achieve this goal, Sonoma will extend the initial filing period to three months. All applications received prior to February 1, 1995 will be evaluated on the basis of academic accomplishment with consideration given to factors contributing to campus diversity.

CALIFORNIA POLYTECHNIC STATE UNIVERSITY SAN LUIS OBISPO

Cal Poly continues to receive more applications than can be accommodated in most programs. Qualified prospective applicants interested in agriculture programs are encouraged to apply. Qualified upper division community college transfers will find opportunities for admission to all programs.

AVERAGES OF ADMITTED FRESHMAN CAL POLY SAN LUIS OBISPO FALL 1994					
COLLEGE	APPLICANTS/ ADMITS	COLLEGE PREP GPA	SAT VERBAL	SAT MATH	SAT TOTAL
Agriculture	926/730	3.31	440	509	949
Architecture and Environmental Design	1041/286	3.75	502	603	1106
Business	1373/664	3.64	467	576	1044
Engineering	2,516/1492	3.72	494	623	1118
Liberal Arts	1,948/616	3.59	497	549	1046
Science and Mathematics	1,640/789	3.74	503	599	1103
TOTAL	9,470/4,577	3.63	484	583	1068

Regardless of your major, apply to Cal Poly during the first month of the filing period. Also, take your SAT I: Reasoning Test or ACT by October or November of your senior year to receive maximum consideration for available space for the fall term. If you take your tests for the first time in December of your senior year or later, you are evaluated for admission without test scores. If you are not admitted based upon this evaluation, you may apply for admission for either the summer or winter term.

SAT I: Reasoning Test and/or ACT scores are an important part of the selection criteria. *San Luis Obispo uses your highest SAT I verbal and mathematics scores. These scores need not be from the same test date.* Alternatively, if ACT scores are submitted, English and mathematics scores are used, rather than your ACT Composite score. These scores also need not be from the same test date.

The following majors accept new students only in the fall: Applied Art and Design, Architectural/Engineering, Architecture, City and Regional Planning, Construction Management, Landscape Architecture, and Music.

Cal Poly is particularly competitive to get into as a freshman. For fall 1994, new freshmen had an average high school GPA in college-preparatory courses of 3.63 and an average SAT total score of 1068. Upper-division transfers had an average GPA of 3.16 in transferable college classes.

Cal Poly received 9,470 freshman applications during the 1994 fall filing period and admitted 4,577 students. The campus received 4,407 upper-division transfer applicants and admitted 1,774 students.

MULTI-CRITERIA ADMISSION SELECTION PROCESS

The campus has developed the Multi-Criteria Admission Plan (MCA) to assist in making selections from a large number of freshman applicants. A questionnaire called the Admissions Supplemental Questionnaire (ASQ) is mailed to you, generally in early December, after you have filed for fall admission during the November filing period. Use your high school transcript to complete this form, and submit it by the deadline, sometime in the second week of January. Failure to return this questionnaire may eliminate you from consideration for admission. If you filed an Electronic Admission Application, the Admissions Supplemental Questionnaire information is requested on the disc. You do not have to submit a separate written form in January.

The questionnaire is the device used to implement the Multi-Criteria Admission Plan and to gather information for the selection of applicants to all majors. It asks you for the following information: your college-preparatory classes, your grades in your college-preparatory classes, your honors courses, your

SAT I and ACT scores, and your extracurricular activities (employment while in school and involvement and leadership roles in clubs). In addition to your responses on the questionnaire, the Applied Art and Design major requires a portfolio, and the Music major requires an audition or tape.

Cal Poly utilizes two rankings to determine which students to admit:

1. The academic ranking. This is an initial ranking to establish points for your academic portfolio. Your academic portfolio consists of your GPA in specific CSU college-preparatory courses, overall GPA for CSU admission, electives in the CSU Subject Requirement, admissions test scores, work experience, and extracurricular activities. See this chapter, page 10–9.

   Part-time jobs and extracurricular activities are considered indicators of commitment and ability. The admissions office is particularly interested in whether your job and/or activities relate to the career you plan to study and if you held a leadership position. The campus looks for students who are not only bright, but who also are willing to experiment, seek challenge, and commit time and effort to activities outside the classroom.

   Sixty percent of all freshman admits are based solely on earned academic points.

2. The secondary ranking: This evaluation *adds* additional points to your academic ranking. Factors considered are those that provide cultural, ethnic, and geographic diversity to the campus and balance underrepresentation within a major.

   Forty percent of the admits are based on both academic ranking and any additional points earned in secondary ranking.

CAL POLY SAN LUIS OBISPO MOST COMPETITIVE MAJORS
1993 FRESHMAN APPLICANTS

MAJOR	APPLICANTS/ADMITS % ADMITTED
Applied Art and Design	183/28 15%
Liberal Studies	231/38 16%
Architecture	629/126 20%
Ecology and Systematic Biology	120/29 24%
Construction Management	38/10 26%
Political Science	217/60 28%

Each academic department hopes to find a slightly different kind of student. The Electrical Engineering department, for example, looks for students who are talented and proficient in mathematics and physical sciences as shown by grades and test scores in those areas. High school courses in advanced mathematics — at least through precalculus — and physics are particularly important if you plan to major in Business Administration or any of the engineering, architecture, or physical science fields. The English department wants students with a solid background in mathematics, but it is even more interested in whether applicants have any aptitude for literature and communication.

Your responses on the questionnaire are scored and ranked according to the emphasis of the academic department to which you are applying. You compete for admission only with other freshman applicants in your major. If you have not completed all fifteen units of the CSU Subject Requirement, you receive fewer points and are at a serious disadvantage when competing for a space in one of Cal Poly's impacted majors.

IMPACTED PROGRAMS FOR 1994-95

An undergraduate program is designated as "impacted" when the number of applications received for it in the first month of the filing period is *expected* to be larger than the number of spaces available. Supplemental admission criteria are used to determine admission when this occurs. Many programs are impacted year after year. Others may or may not be impacted from year to year depending upon demand for and availability of spaces.

Each fall, usually in November, CSU publishes a list of expected impacted programs for the following school year. This information appears in the CSU monthly publication for counselors, *CSU Review*. This newsletter also reviews the latest supplemental criteria for admission to these programs. Ask to see this newsletter at your high school. The information presented on the following pages is extracted from the November 1993 issue.

The following information is for students who applied for freshman admission for the 1994-95 school year. *As you review this information, remember that there may be changes for the 1995-96 academic year in both impacted majors and supplemental criteria for screening applicants. Information about these changes will not be available until November, 1994.*

To be considered for freshman admission to any impacted program you must first meet regular admission requirements to CSU: Subject, Examination, and Scholarship Requirements. Supplemental admission criteria beyond those for regular admission are used to screen for impacted programs.

As you review the supplemental criteria described for each impacted program keep the following items in mind:

- This information is a general overview of criteria for first-time freshmen — students who have not previously enrolled at CSU as regularly-admitted students. Consult the campuses directly for further details, clarification, or explanation.
- You receive more detailed information about supplemental criteria from the campus after you apply to impacted programs.
- The number and quality of courses you have completed in the fifteen-unit CSU Subject Requirement can be important criteria. Some majors at some campuses require specific courses to meet the CSU Subject Requirement.
- Your eligibility index is an important criterion. Even though you are admissible to CSU because you have a qualifying eligibility index, you are nonetheless ranked with other applicants. The higher your index, the better are your chances.
- Some programs do not accept applicants for every term. Some accept new freshmen in the major only for fall semester/quarter. Others accept freshmen for any term.
- Many programs do not accept you as a freshman. Instead, the campus accepts you into a pre-major. *After* you have accumulated a certain number of units in specific major-preparation courses at the college, you may apply for admission to the major. Usually, you must also have a particular grade point average and fulfill other supplemental criteria. In most cases, you must complete fifty-six semester/eighty-four quarter college units before entering the major as an upper division (junior/senior) student. These requirements are indicated in the following supplemental criteria by the words, "... must complete certain college coursework for later admission to this major." When you enroll, inquire about the specifics for later admission to your major.
- *Apply for admission to impacted programs during the first month of the admission application filing period, the initial filing period, as indicated here:*

CSU IMPACTED UNDERGRADUATE PROGRAMS 1994-95

	Bakersfield	Chico	Dominguez Hills	Fresno	Fullerton	Hayward	Humboldt	Long Beach	Los Angeles	Northridge	Pomona	Sacramento	San Bernardino	San Diego	San Francisco	San Jose	San Luis Obispo	San Marcos	Sonoma	Stanislaus
Architecture											I						I			
Business Administration	O	O	O	O	O	O	O	I	O	O	O	O	O	I	O	O	I	O	O	O
Criminal Justice/Administration	O	O	O	O	O	O		O	O			O	O	I		O	N		O	O
Economics	O	O	O	O	O	O	O	O	O	I	O	O	O	O	O	O	I	O	O	O
Graphic Design		O	O	O	O			I	O	O	O		O	O		O	I			
Health Science	O	O	N	O		O		N	N	O	O		O	O	O	O				
Interior Design		O		O				N	O			O		O	O	O	N			
International Business					O									I						
Journalism		O	O	O	O	O	O	O	O	O	O	O		I	O	O	I			
Medical Technology	O	O	N		O	O	O	O	O	O	O	O		O	O	O	N		O	
Nursing	I	I	R	I	R	I	I	I	I	R		I		R	I	I	O		R	R
Physical Education	O	O	O	N	O	O	O	O	O	O	O	O			O	O	I		O	O
Physical Therapy				I				I		I										
Psychology	O	O	O	O	O	O	O	I	O	O	O	O	O	O	O	O	I	O	O	O
Public Administration	O	O	O	O	O	O		O	O	O	O		O	I		O	N	O		O
Radio-Television		O	O	O	O	O		I	O	O	O			I	O	O	N			
Social Work		I		O		O	O	I	O	O	O	O		O	O	O				

KEY:

I — Program impacted at this campus
O — Program offered at this campus but not impacted.
R — Program open only to upper-division students possessing the R.N.
— A blank space indicates the program is not offered at this campus.
N — See note for the campus.

CAMPUS NOTES:

Dominguez Hills: Health science — physician assistant and orthotics and prosthetics options impacted. Medical technology — clinical science-cytotechnology, human cytogenic technology, medical technology, and nuclear medicine technology options impacted.

Fresno: Training option impacted.

Long Beach: Health science: radiation therapy option impacted.

San Luis Obispo: Concentrations within impacted majors.

SEMESTER CAMPUSES

Fall .... November
Spring .... August

QUARTER CAMPUSES

Fall .... November
Winter .... June
Spring .... August
Summer .... February

- When applying for admission, the campus may require that you submit your high school transcript after your first-semester senior year grades become available. However, a particular impacted major may require that you submit it by a specific deadline. These dates are shown on the following pages.
- Nonresident applicants, including international students, are rarely admitted to impacted programs.
- If you meet minimum CSU admission requirements and are not admitted to an impacted program on your first-choice campus, your application may be redirected.
- Redirected application materials are subject to one of two options:

1. Your application materials are submitted for consideration in an alternative major on the campus to which you applied. Most campuses follow this option. However, Cal Poly San Luis Obispo does not redirect to another major on their campus. If you are not accepted to the major to which you apply at Cal Poly, your application is redirected to another campus.

2. Your application and files, including your test scores and high school grade transcript, are forwarded to a campus which you indicated as an alternative campus on your application, but only if your first-choice major is not impacted on that campus.

- If you apply to a major which is *impacted at every campus* at which it is offered, and your first-choice campus does not accept you in the major, they redirect your application to *an alternative major* which is not impacted on their campus. *Your application materials are not redirected to any other campus for that major.*

  The chart at the bottom of the previous page indicates specific majors at each CSU campus which are impacted.

- CSU expects that most programs impacted in 1994-95 will continue to be impacted in 1995-96. Additional programs may be added.

- Newly impacted programs for 1994-95 include Social Work at Chico, and Psychology and the Radiation Therapy option in Health Science at Long Beach.

- Only two majors are impacted at every campus at which they are offered: Architecture and Physical Therapy. All other majors are offered at campuses where they are not impacted.

- Most majors are impacted at Cal Poly San Luis Obispo.

ARCHITECTURE

POMONA

APPLICATIONS ACCEPTED

Fall quarter only.

SUPPLEMENTAL CRITERIA

Freshmen applicants are ranked on the eligibility index. After determination of eligibility, a portfolio will be requested and reviewed for placement in design.

CRITICAL DATES

March 6th: Transcripts must be on file in the Pomona admissions office.

SAN LUIS OBISPO

APPLICATIONS ACCEPTED

Fall quarter only.

SUPPLEMENTAL CRITERIA

The Multi-Criteria Admission Plan (MCA) is used. See this chapter: Multi-Criteria Admission Selection Process, page 10--22.

BUSINESS ADMINISTRATION

LONG BEACH

APPLICATIONS ACCEPTED

Freshmen are not admitted.

SUPPLEMENTAL CRITERIA

You must complete certain college coursework for later admission to this major.
at Northridge for spring admission.

SAN DIEGO

APPLICATIONS ACCEPTED

Fall and spring semesters.

SUPPLEMENTAL CRITERIA

All applicants apply to the pre-Business major and must complete certain college coursework for later admission to the major.

SAN LUIS OBISPO

APPLICATIONS ACCEPTED

All quarters.

SUPPLEMENTAL CRITERIA

The Multi-Criteria Admission Plan (MCA) is used. See this chapter: Multi-Criteria Admission Selection Process, page 10--22.

CRIMINAL JUSTICE/ ADMINISTRATION

SAN DIEGO

APPLICATIONS ACCEPTED

Fall and spring semesters.

SUPPLEMENTAL CRITERIA

Freshmen applicants apply to the pre-Criminal Justice major and must complete certain college coursework for later admission to the major.

ECONOMICS

NORTHRIDGE

APPLICATIONS ACCEPTED

Fall and spring semesters.

SUPPLEMENTAL CRITERIA

Freshmen applicants apply to the pre-Economics major and are ranked on the eligibility index. Selection is made on a space-available basis. You must complete certain college coursework for later admission to the major.

SAN LUIS OBISPO

APPLICATIONS ACCEPTED

All quarters.

SUPPLEMENTAL CRITERIA

The Multi-Criteria Admission Plan (MCA) is used. See this chapter: Multi-Criteria Admission Selection Process, page 10--22.

GRAPHIC DESIGN/ APPLIED ART

LONG BEACH

APPLICATIONS ACCEPTED

Freshmen are not admitted.

SUPPLEMENTAL CRITERIA

You must complete certain college coursework and a portfolio of representative creative work for later admission to this major.

SAN LUIS OBISPO

APPLICATIONS ACCEPTED

Fall quarter only.

SUPPLEMENTAL CRITERIA

The Multi-Criteria Admission Plan (MCA) is used. In addition, freshmen applicants must submit a portfolio of creative work. See this chapter: Multi-Criteria Admission Selection Process, page 10--22.

HEALTH SCIENCES

DOMINGUEZ HILLS

Orthotics and Prosthetics, and Physician Assistant options are impacted.

APPLICATIONS ACCEPTED

Freshmen are not admitted.

SUPPLEMENTAL CRITERIA

You must complete certain college coursework and have direct patient experience for later admission to this major.

LONG BEACH

Radiation Therapy

APPLICATIONS ACCEPTED

Freshmen not admitted.

SUPPLEMENTAL CRITERIA

You must complete certain college coursework and have direct patient experience for later admission to this major. You must show proof of CPR certification and complete forty hours of observation in a radiation therapy department for later admission to this major.

INTERNATIONAL BUSINESS

SAN DIEGO

APPLICATIONS ACCEPTED

Fall and spring semesters.

SUPPLEMENTAL CRITERIA

Freshmen are admitted as pre-International Business majors and must complete certain college coursework for later admission to this major.

JOURNALISM

SAN DIEGO

APPLICATIONS ACCEPTED

Fall and spring semesters.

SUPPLEMENTAL CRITERIA

Freshmen are admitted as pre-Journalism majors and must complete certain college coursework for later admission to this major.

SAN LUIS OBISPO

APPLICATIONS ACCEPTED

All quarters.

SUPPLEMENTAL CRITERIA

The Multi-Criteria Admission Plan (MCA) is used. See this chapter: Multi-Criteria Admission Selection Process, page 10--22.

MEDICAL TECHNOLOGY — CLINICAL PROGRAM

Human Cytogenetic Technology, Cytotechnology, Nuclear Medicine Technology and Medical Technology options are impacted for admission to the clinical year.

DOMINGUEZ HILLS

APPLICATIONS ACCEPTED

Freshmen are not admitted.

SUPPLEMENTAL CRITERIA

You must complete certain college coursework for later admission to this major.

NURSING — BASIC/GENERIC

BAKERSFIELD

APPLICATIONS ACCEPTED

Freshmen are not admitted.

SUPPLEMENTAL CRITERIA

You must complete certain college coursework for later admission to this major.

CHICO

APPLICATIONS ACCEPTED

Freshmen are not admitted.

SUPPLEMENTAL CRITERIA

You must complete certain coursework for later admission to this major.

FRESNO

APPLICATIONS ACCEPTED

Fall and spring semesters.

SUPPLEMENTAL CRITERIA

Freshmen may enroll in a pre-Nursing, Undeclared, or alternative major and complete certain coursework for later admission to this major.

HAYWARD

APPLICATIONS ACCEPTED

Freshmen are not admitted.

SUPPLEMENTAL CRITERIA

You must complete certain coursework for later admission to this major.

HUMBOLDT

APPLICATIONS ACCEPTED

Fall semester.

SUPPLEMENTAL CRITERIA

Freshmen are admitted as pre-Nursing majors and must complete certain coursework for later admission to this major.

LONG BEACH

APPLICATIONS ACCEPTED

Fall and spring semesters.

SUPPLEMENTAL CRITERIA

Freshmen may enroll in a pre-Nursing, Undeclared, or alternative major and complete certain coursework for later admission to this major.

LOS ANGELES

APPLICATIONS ACCEPTED

Freshmen are not admitted.

SUPPLEMENTAL CRITERIA

You must complete certain coursework for later admission to this major.

SACRAMENTO

APPLICATIONS ACCEPTED

Freshmen are not admitted.

SUPPLEMENTAL CRITERIA

You must complete certain college coursework for later admission to this major.

SAN DIEGO

APPLICATIONS ACCEPTED

Fall and spring semesters.

SUPPLEMENTAL CRITERIA

First-time freshmen must have completed one year of high school advanced algebra, biology, and chemistry with laboratory. Applicants must complete one of this campus' required writing tests with an appropriate score. Healthcare experience, bilingual ability, and leadership/achievement experience are also considered.

SAN FRANCISCO

APPLICATIONS ACCEPTED

Fall semester only.

SUPPLEMENTAL CRITERIA

First-time freshmen should apply to an alternate major or as undeclared. You must complete certain coursework for later admission to this major.

PHYSICAL EDUCATION

FRESNO

Only the emphasis in athletic training is impacted at this time.

APPLICATIONS ACCEPTED

Freshmen are not admitted.

SUPPLEMENTAL CRITERIA

You must complete certain college coursework for later admission to this major.

SAN LUIS OBISPO

APPLICATIONS ACCEPTED

All quarters.

SUPPLEMENTAL CRITERIA

The Multi-Criteria Admission Plan (MCA) is used. See this chapter: Multi-Criteria Admission Selection Process, page 10--22.

PHYSICAL THERAPY

FRESNO

APPLICATIONS ACCEPTED

Fall semester only.

SUPPLEMENTAL CRITERIA

Freshmen are admitted as pre-Physical Therapy majors and must complete certain college coursework for later admission to this major.

LONG BEACH

APPLICATIONS ACCEPTED

Fall and spring semesters.

SUPPLEMENTAL CRITERIA

Freshmen are admitted as pre-Physical Therapy majors and must complete certain college coursework for later admission to this major.

NORTHRIDGE

APPLICATIONS ACCEPTED

Freshmen are not admitted.

SUPPLEMENTAL CRITERIA

You must complete certain college coursework for later admission to this major.

PSYCHOLOGY

LONG BEACH

APPLICATIONS ACCEPTED

Freshmen are admitted as pre-Physical Therapy majors and must complete certain coursework for later admission to this major.

SUPPLEMENTAL CRITERIA

You must complete certain college coursework for later admission to this major.

PUBLIC ADMINISTRATION

AN DIEGO

APPLICATIONS ACCEPTED

Fall and spring semesters.

SUPPLEMENTAL CRITERIA

Freshmen are admitted as pre-Public Administration majors and must complete certain college coursework for later admission to this major.

RADIO-TELEVISION

LONG BEACH

The major is named Radio-Television and Film at Long Beach.

APPLICATIONS ACCEPTED

Freshmen are not admitted.

SUPPLEMENTAL CRITERIA

You must complete certain college coursework for later admission to this major.

SOCIAL WORK

CHICO

APPLICATIONS ACCEPTED

Freshmen are not admitted.

SUPPLEMENTAL CRITERIA

You must complete certain college coursework for later admission to this major.

LONG BEACH

APPLICATIONS ACCEPTED

Freshmen are admitted as pre-Social Work majors.

SUPPLEMENTAL CRITERIA

You must complete certain college coursework for later admission to this major.

HIGH DEMAND PROGRAMS

Every fall each campus publishes in *Campus Highlights* a list of undergraduate programs which *are not expected to be impacted but are in high demand*. Although these majors are very popular, the campuses expect to accommodate all qualified applicants to them. Occasionally, the number of applications received in November for a high-demand program is larger than anticipated, and the program is reclassified as impacted for fall admission.

Listed here, by campus, are those programs which were in high demand for the 1994-95 academic year. CSU expects that most programs in high demand for 1994-95 will continue to be in high demand in 1995-96. Apply during the first month of the filing period — the initial filing period — in all cases.

BAKERSFIELD

Business Administration, Criminal Justice, English, Liberal Studies, Nursing, Psychology, Public Administration

CHICO

Business Administration, Liberal Studies, Psychology, Information and Communication Studies

DOMINGUEZ HILLS

Business Administration, Communications, Human Services, Liberal Studies, Music Performance, Music Audio Recording and Electronic Synthesis, Nursing, Pre-Medical, Psychology, Public Administration, Theatre Arts Performance

HAYWARD

Biological Sciences, Business Administration, Computer Science, Criminal Justice Administration, Liberal Studies, Mass Communication, Nursing, Psychology

HUMBOLDT

Biology, Wildlife, Natural Resources Planning and Interpretation

LONG BEACH

Art, Business Administration, Graphic Design, Industrial Design, Interior Design, Journalism, Nursing, Physical Therapy, Political Science, Psychology, Radio, Television and Film, Speech Communication

LOS ANGELES

Business Administration, Engineering — Civil Option, Computer Information Science, Criminal Justice

NORTHRIDGE

Business Administration, Physical Therapy, Psychology, Radio-Television-Broadcasting, Speech Communication

SACRAMENTO

Communication Studies, Criminal Justice, Environmental Studies, Interior Design, Liberal Studies, Nursing (Pre-Clinical), Psychology

SAN BERNARDINO

Business, Education, Nursing

SAN DIEGO

Art (Graphic Design emphasis), Psychology, Speech Communication

SAN FRANCISCO

Radio/TV

SAN JOSE

Business, Engineering (particularly Electrical Engineering), Graphic Design, Industrial Design, Interior Design, Nursing, Occupational Therapy

SONOMA

Business, Communications, Criminal Justice Administration, Environmental Studies and Planning, Hutchins School of Liberal Studies, Psychology

STANISLAUS

Business Administration, Music

SPECIAL ADMISSION OPPORTUNITIES

Each campus offers special admission opportunities to a limited number of applicants who do not meet all admission requirements of CSU. There are two categories of special admission: Regular Exceptional Admission and EOP Admission.

Regular Exceptional Admission

Regular Exceptional Admission may be offered to you if you are not eligible for regular admission, but have extenuating circumstances which suggest you would succeed at CSU. Each campus establishes its own criteria. Factors which might be considered are variety and pattern of courses taken, recent improvement in academic record, admissions test scores, life experiences, maturity, athletic skills, special abilities and talents, special majors, extra-curricular activities, family responsibilities, work experience, and career and personal goals.

To be considered for Regular Exceptional Admission you must write a letter of appeal to the admissions office of the campus to which you were not admitted. If possible, meet with an admissions officer at the CSU campus. Describe your special circumstances, your motivations, and your reasons why you should be admitted. Explain your academic record: Did you involve yourself in too many extracurricular activities at the expense of your grades? Are your test scores an accurate indication of your capabilities? Do you have special family circumstances which have affected your record? A letter of support and verification of your circumstances from your counselor, administrator, or one of your teachers can be very effective. Do not hesitate to ask for it. Include it with your letter of appeal or bring it with you to your appointment at the CSU campus.

Regular Exceptional Admission may be offered to you if you are not eligible for regular admission, but have extenuating circumstances that suggest you will succeed at CSU.

Adults over twenty-five and veterans also may be eligible for Exceptional Admission.

EOP — Educational Opportunity Program

Each CSU campus has an Educational Opportunity Program for low-income and underrepresented ethnic students disadvantaged because of their economic and educational backgrounds. Through its special admissions program, the EOP assists California residents who do not meet regular admission standards to gain admission to CSU. Once admitted, the EOP provides a wide array of support services to assist you with adjusting to college and succeeding in your academic and career goals.

If you qualify for regular admission but are disadvantaged because of low income, you may still take advantage of the support services offered through the program. Contact the campus EOP office after you enroll to initiate these services.

California State University is committed to encouraging low-income and underrepresented students to attend its campuses. Hispanic and black students remain the most underrepresented in the CSU system. If you (a) are a minority student from a group historically underrepresented in higher education, (b) have a low-income background, and (c) have the potential and motivation to succeed in college, you probably qualify for the EOP. Because low income and potential for success in college are the primary requirements for program participation, you are eligible for the EOP, even if you are not a minority student but do meet the low-income criteria described here. Undocumented alien students are also eligible for admission to the EOP.

California State University is committed to encouraging low-income and underrepresented students to attend its campuses.

SUPPORT SERVICES

The EOP provides admission, academic and financial assistance.

- The EOP provides information to help you select a campus and may admit you to the campus of your choice.
- Before you enter college, you can enroll in an EOP Summer Bridge Program to help you make a smoother transition to college life. In this program you may brush up on mathematics, reading, or other subjects, and you may live and study on campus.

EOP provides a wide array of support services to assist you with adjusting to college and succeeding in your academic and career goals.

- Orientation sessions are offered to help you learn about campus services and procedures.
- After you are enrolled in college you can receive counseling and tutoring.
- EOP students who qualify for financial aid may receive an EOP grant up to $1,000 per year. See chapter 4: PAYING FOR COLLEGE, EOP Program and Grant, page 4--37.
- The EOP can also help you apply to graduate school or a job relating to your major.

EOP FAMILY INCOME GUIDELINES FOR 1995-96

For fall 1995, you qualify as an EOP candidate if your family meets the low-income guidelines presented here, and (b) demonstrates an inability to annually contribute more than $1,500 toward your college expenses as calculated on the FAFSA and supplementary application. See chapter 4: PAYING FOR COLLEGE, Applying For Financial Aid, page 4--9. If your total family income exceeds these guidelines, you still may be considered if your parental contribution does not exceed $1,500. These guidelines are not intended to exclude disadvantaged students, but to identify and give priority to the most financially-needy applicants.

You must meet low-income guidelines to qualify as an EOP candidate.

EOP FAMILY INCOME GUIDELINES FOR 1995-1996

Dependent Students		Independent Students	
Family Size	Parental Income	Family Size	Student/Spouse Income
2	$23,350	1	$6,950 Single, no dependents
3	$26,400		
4	$29,750		
5	$33,150		
6	$37,000	2	$13,350 Married, no dependents other than spouse
7	$39,950		
8	$42,950		
9	$45,950		
10	$48,900		

1. For independent students with dependents other than, or in addition to, a spouse, use the income for the appropriate family size in the Dependent Student category.
2. This table is based on the 1994-95 Expected Family Contribution (EFC) formulas for federal student aid.

CALIFORNIA STATE UNIVERSITY

APPLYING FOR EOP

APPLICATION

You must file a supplemental EOP application form in addition to the regular CSU admission application to be considered for admission to the Educational Opportunity Program.

The EOP application is usually available from your high school counselor, guidance office, or career center. If it is not, contact any California State University EOP office. The EOP application consists of four parts:

1. An Applicant Information Form, which requests your biographical, economic, and financial information.

2. An Autobiographical Statement in which you describe your motivation and preparation to undertake college work. Explain your background, your personal and career goals, and any family circumstances — extended unemployment, disability, financial hardships — which can help the review committee understand your academic preparation and motivation.

3. A Nomination Form completed by a counselor or a teacher who recommends you for consideration for the program.

4. A Recommendation Form completed by a counselor, teacher, community member, employer, or any individual who can comment about your potential to succeed in college.

The EOP application consists of four parts.

All EOP application materials should be submitted to the EOP office of the CSU campus you wish to attend.

SELECTION PROCEDURE

Each campus has an admissions review committee which considers such factors as disadvantaged background, financial need, academic performance, and motivation and potential for success in a four-year college. The committee may also look for any contribution you might make to society as a result of cultural background, work experience, or the career you wish to pursue.

Some campuses use interviews and/or skills-assessment testing to help determine the types of services you may need if admitted. The EOP office notifies you if either of these is required during the selection process.

DEADLINES

EOP application deadlines vary from campus to campus; however, to receive priority consideration, submit all four parts of the EOP application to the EOP office of the CSU campus you wish to attend by March 2nd. The EOP office normally sends admission notices to fall applicants in May or June to those who submit completed application materials by March 2nd.

Submit all four parts of your EOP application by March 2nd to receive priority consideration for fall admission to the program.

FINANCIAL AID

The award of financial aid is not part of the EOP admission process. You must apply for financial aid; submit the FAFSA which is used to determine your financial need. See chapter 4: PAYING FOR COLLEGE, Applying For Financial Aid, page 4--9. Apply as soon as possible after January 1, 1995 and before March 2, 1995. EOP grants are awarded only as long as funds are available. Call the EOP office to verify this deadline; some campuses may have an earlier filing period.

SAA — STUDENT AFFIRMATIVE ACTION

SAA is a special program of support services for students from underrepresented minority groups.

Student Affirmative Action (SAA) is a special program of support services for students from underrepresented minority groups: Black, Hispanic, and Native American. This program works closely with the EOP on CSU campuses. SAA has as its goal the recruitment of underrepresented students to California State University. Income is not a factor in qualifying for SAA support. In one of its programs, Outreach, college representatives meet with minority students at their high schools to encourage them to attend college. Several CSU campuses provide Outreach services, but they are not available at all high schools. Check with your high school to see if these recruitment services are offered.

APPLYING TO CALIFORNIA STATE UNIVERSITY

The guidelines presented here are important and worth remembering as you go through the process of applying to California State University. In addition to these guidelines, read the directions in the CSU application booklet. Follow the specifics of every step to successfully complete the application process.

WHEN TO APPLY

CSU strongly urges you to apply during the initial filing period, regardless of campus or major, to assure yourself that you have applied in time for your desired campus and/or program.

CSU urges you to file your application during the first month of the filing period, called the "initial filing period."

The campuses use the postmark date of your application to determine your filing date.

Except for applications to impacted campuses and majors, your application will likely be accepted for consideration after the initial filing period until enrollment spaces are filled. As long as the campus has space available, it will accept your application up to the term in which you intend to enroll.

CSU strongly urges you to apply during the initial filing period, regardless of campus and major, to assure yourself that you have applied in time for your desired campus and/or program. If you need to file an application after the initial filing period, contact the admissions office of the campus for up-to-date information about whether they are still accepting applications for the major and term of interest to you.

If you apply to an impacted campus or major, you have no choice. You must file your application during the first month of the filing period.

Apply during the initial filing period to Humboldt State University and/or Cal Poly San Luis Obispo to assure consideration of your application. These campuses are extremely popular and in high demand. Humboldt State University may be closed to applications after the initial filing period; Cal Poly San Luis Obispo *definitely* will be closed. See this chapter: Impacted Campuses For 1994-95, page 10--21 and Impacted Programs For 1994-95, page 10--24.

APPLICATION FILING PERIODS
1995-96 ACADEMIC YEAR

Academic Term	Applications First Accepted On	Initial Filing Period
Summer Quarter 1995	February 1, 1995	February 1, 1995 through February 28, 1995
Fall Semester or Quarter 1995	November 1, 1994	November 1, 1994 through November 30, 1994
Winter Quarter 1996	June 1, 1995	June 1, 1995 through June 30, 1995
Spring Semester or Quarter 1996	August 1, 1995	August 1, 1995 through August 31, 1995

During periods of high demand and limited resources, some campuses may not accept applications for winter, spring, or summer.

During periods of high demand and limited resources, some campuses may not accept applications for winter, spring, or summer.

If you qualify for special admission through EOP or SAA, you may be able to file a later admission application, even after a campus or program declares itself closed to applications. Contact the CSU campus EOP office or the SAA office to determine if they will consider your application. See this chapter: Special Admission Opportunities, page 10--32.

HOW TO APPLY

YOUR APPLICATION

California State University offers you the opportunity to apply either on a written application or electronically on a diskette.

California State University offers you the opportunity to apply either on a written application or electronically on a diskette.

WRITTEN APPLICATION: At the end of September or in early October, obtain a copy of the application booklet, *The California State University, 1995-96 Undergraduate Admission* from your high school counselor, guidance administrator, or career center. This booklet contains a review of important dates and deadlines, an information section with detailed directions for completing the application, information about majors and financial aid, and the admission application itself.

Make a copy of the application to use as your worksheet. After you are satisfied that you have completed the worksheet accurately, copy the information onto your application. You may type it or print it in black ink.

ELECTRONIC APPLICATION: You may use personal computers (IBM®-compatible, Macintosh®, etc.) to prepare and submit your application for admission. At the end of September or in early October, obtain a diskette from your high school counselor, guidance administrator, or career center. You need no previous computer experience or special computer skills to use this program. Your electronic application may be competed in your school computer lab, career center, at home, or wherever you can gain access to a computer. The electronic application includes many editing features to help you fill out the application completely and correctly. In field testing, average completion time for the electronic application was twenty minutes.

Cal Poly San Luis Obispo prefers that you apply electronically. It supplies a disk (XAP) tailored to the specific information they need to make admission decisions.

Cal Poly San Luis Obispo prefers that you apply electronically. It supplies a disk (XAP) tailored to the specific information they need to make admission decisions. In addition to the common application questions the disk includes all questions on the Admissions Supplemental Questionnaire (ASQ); see this chapter, page 10--22. To receive the Cal Poly San Luis Obispo disk, call or write to the admission office of the campus early in September. Be sure to indicate which version, IBM®-compatible or Macintosh®, you need. The disk will be mailed directly to your home. It may also be available in your high school counseling office or career center.

FILING YOUR APPLICATION

Application materials you submit consist of the completed application form, the Residency Questionnaire, and application fees. An essay is not required as part of your application materials.

RESIDENCY QUESTIONNAIRE

If you do not claim California residency, or if you have not lived in California continuously since birth, you must complete the Residency Questionnaire, a one-page form in the application booklet and submit it with your admission application. The questionnaire asks for information necessary to determine your residency status for tuition purposes. See appendix A: CALIFORNIA RESIDENCY REQUIREMENTS. The Residency Questionnaire is also contained on the electronic disk.

You must mail separate application materials to each CSU campus to which you apply.

HOW MANY CAMPUSES?

You must mail separate application materials to each CSU campus to which you apply. Generally, decide upon your first-choice campus and major and mail an application or disk to that campus stating that major. If you apply to more than one campus, and you are using a paper application , you may send copies of the original application to other campuses. The campuses accept duplicates, saving you the effort of completing an original written application for each. Be sure to sign each copy. If you are applying electronically, send duplicate disks to the other campuses.

You probably will be accepted and need not apply to more than one campus if you

a) meet *minimum* admission requirements — Subject, Examination, and Scholarship Requirements,
b) apply during the initial filing period,
c) are not applying to an impacted major, and
d) are not applying to San Luis Obispo.

Most qualified applicants are accepted at their first-choice campus in their first-choice major. If you apply to San Luis Obispo, apply to one or more other campuses as a backup; admission to SLO is very competitive. Here are some reasons you might prefer to file multiple applications:

1. You have not yet decided upon your first-choice campus and wish to be considered for admission to several.

2. Your first-choice major is impacted at every campus where it is offered, and there is no acceptable alternative major at your first-choice campus. In this case, apply to every campus where your desired major is offered even though it is impacted at each one. *Supplemental admission criteria differ from campus to campus. You might have a better chance of admission at one campus rather than another.* See this chapter: Impacted Campuses For 1994-95, page 10--22 and Impacted Programs For 1994-95, page 10--24.

3. You are applying to an impacted major at your first-choice campus. Your second-choice campus is one that expects to close to applications for the major before processing for your first-choice campus is completed.

If you are applying to Cal Poly San Luis Obispo, apply to one or more other campuses as a backup strategy.

ALTERNATIVE CAMPUS

On your admission application you have the option of listing an alternative campus to receive your application if your major and/or first-choice campus does not admit you. Designating an alternative campus does not reduce your prospects for being accepted to your first-choice campus or your first-choice major, but does expedite sending your application on to another campus, if needed.

If you are applying for a major which is impacted at one or more, *but not at all,* campuses at which it is offered, save yourself the expense and effort of submitting unnecessary applications by choosing an alternative campus at which this major is not impacted. If you are not admitted to the program at your first-choice campus, this campus will either

a) consider you for an alternative major on their campus, or

b) redirect your application materials to your alternative campus in your first-choice major, as you requested on your application. See this chapter: Impacted Programs For 1994-95, page 10--24.

Most campuses consider applications for alternative majors on their campuses before forwarding them to the alternative campuses. However, if you apply to San Luis Obispo, which has very selective admission standards, and they do not admit you, your application is not considered for an alternative major; it is redirected to your alternative campus. Be sure to choose an alternative campus which is not likely to close to applicants early in the application cycle. Do not, for example, choose Humboldt State University. This campus will likely be closed by the time San Luis Obispo redirects your application to it.

There is always the risk that your redirected application might get to your alternative campus and major too late, after they have closed to applicants. As a safeguard, CSU strongly recommends that you apply to more than one campus rather than take the chance this could happen. This is especially true when applying to Cal Poly San Luis Obispo as your first choice. Also, because of limited living facilities on the campuses, you may not obtain housing if you wait for redirection.

If you are not admitted to your first-choice campus, most CSU campuses will consider you for an alternative major on their campus. However, Cal Poly San Luis Obispo will redirect you application to an alternative campus.

MAILING YOUR APPLICATION

Before mailing your paper or disk application, duplicate it for future reference and to have as a backup should it get lost in the mail.

For those impacted campuses or programs for which it is recommended that you apply during the initial filing period, get a Certificate of Mailing from the post office. It is dated and is your proof of having sent your application during the critical initial filing period. *Do not send your application by* registered mail, certified mail, or by an express mail service which requires the recipient's signature. If your application is lost in the system and you have your proof of mailing, CSU accepts a duplicate application.

Mail your applications directly to the campuses. Enclose the application fee of $55.00 with your application to each campus to which you apply.

Mail your applications directly to the campuses. You are not required to use the official envelope that comes with your application. It is available as a convenience only.

APPLICATION FEES

The application fee for the 1995-96 school year is $55.00 per campus. Enclose this amount with each application. This fee is nonrefundable and may not be transferred to another admission application for a different term at any campus.

APPLICATION FEE WAIVER PROGRAM

A fee waiver is available. If you are from a low-income family for whom payment would be an undue hardship, your application fee may be waived. If you believe you qualify, obtain a Request To Waive Admission Application Fee form from the admissions office of any CSU campus. Submit it with your admission application instead of submitting your fee. CSU has been able to grant waivers to sixty-five percent of applicants requesting them.

The CSU campus reviews information about your family income which you provide on the Request for Waiver of Admission Application Fee form. If it determines you are not qualified for the waiver, you are informed and required to submit your fee.

CALIFORNIA STATE UNIVERSITY

Number of Persons in Parents' Household	Parents' Total Income (Taxable & Nontaxable)
2	$15,450
3	$18,500
4	$21,950
5	$25,350
6	$29,200
7	$32,150
8	$35,150

Add $2,600 for each additional family member when there are more than eight in the household.

When you call the CSU campus for the Request To Waive Admission Application Fee form, ask how they handle your admission application if they deny your fee waiver request. Does the campus retain your admission application and inform you that your fee waiver request is denied? Is the processing of your admission application delayed until the campus receives your fee or your appeal to reconsider their decision? Do they return your admission application to you and ask you to resubmit it with your fee? How does their procedure affect the filing date of your admission application? Do they use the date you first filed your admission application, the date they receive your application fee, or the date they receive your returned admission application with your fee? These questions are particularly important if you apply to impacted majors or high-demand campuses for which filing during the initial filing period is critical.

This table shows the criteria for awarding fee waivers to dependent applicants for the 1995-96 academic year. If your parents' income does not exceed the indicated amount, your fee waiver request may be approved.

CHANGE OF CAMPUS CHOICE

If you wish to change your campus choice after you have filed your application, contact the campus you wish to attend to determine if they still are accepting applications. If so, send them a Request For Transfer Of Admission Application To Alternative Campus Choice form obtainable from either CSU or your high school. The campus you are requesting completes their portion of the form and forwards it to the campus which has your application materials. The original campus then sends your application file — application, Residency Questionnaire, admissions test scores, transcript, and any other materials in your file — to the new campus. Using this process you avoid paying an additional application fee and completing another application. However, if the campus in which you are now interested is closing soon to new applicants, you may choose to submit a new application rather than wait for the first campus to transfer your files.

For fall admission, try to complete your testing by the end of December, if not sooner, so that your test scores arrive at the campuses by mid-January.

If you apply for financial aid and (a) change your choice of campus, or (b) your admission application is redirected to another CSU campus, you must send written notification to the financial aid office of the campus to which you originally sent your application. This notification is an authorization to transfer your financial aid files to the alternative campus. Also send a copy of this notification to the financial aid office of your alternative campus.

ADMISSIONS TESTS

If you take admissions tests, you may list on your testing application form to which campuses you want an official score report sent. Be sure to list the correct campus code numbers.

For fall admission, try to complete your testing by the end of December, if not sooner, so that your test scores arrive at the campuses by mid-January. Remember, you can take the tests more than once, and you can take both the SAT I: Reasoning Test and ACT for admission. Most campuses and majors allow you to retake tests throughout your senior year to improve your scores and your eligibility index. Impacted campuses and/or majors may not be willing to review later scores. Cal Poly San Luis Obispo does not consider for fall the admission scores of tests taken later than November of your senior year. See this chapter: Impacted Campuses For 1994-95, page 10--22.

The campuses differ as to whether they require a sixth semester, a seventh semester, or only a final transcript of your grades. They will inform you of their requirement.

TRANSCRIPTS

The campuses to which you apply will write to you to request your official high school transcripts. The campuses differ as to whether they want a sixth-semester record — through the end of the junior year, a seventh semester record — through the end of the first semester of the senior year, or only a final transcript after graduation. Therefore, wait until the campus informs you of which record they want.

It is your responsibility to request that your high school send an official copy of your record. Usually the high school prefers a written request from you; you may pay a small fee for this service. A final transcript *must* be sent after you have graduated. It states your courses and grades for all of your high school years and confirms your high school graduation.

28. **High School Preparation** (all first-time applicants). Enter in the appropriate section all **college preparatory** courses that you have completed, that you are currently enrolled in, or plan to complete by the time of your entrance to the CSU, including summer session. If the course has been completed, enter the grade earned; if in progress or planned, enter "IP" instead of grade. List only those courses that can be verified by your final transcript. List college preparatory elective courses in applicable subject area (e.g., fifth year of college preparatory English in English section). If you are listing courses at a high school other than the one you will graduate from, please write the high school name next to those courses.

College Preparatory Subjects	Grade Level Taken	Title of Courses Completed, in Progress, or Planned	Semester/Summer Grade Earned		
			Fall	Spring	Summer
(example)	9	ENGLISH 9A / 9B	B	A	—
English – 4 years Composition and literature and any other English courses designated as college preparatory.					
		Total number of English units ( )			
Mathematics – 3 years Algebra, geometry, intermediate algebra, trigonometry, and pre-calculus. Course taken in 7th & 8th grades may be considered. Do not include pre-algebra.					
		Total number of mathematics units ( )			
U.S. History/Government – 1 year One year of U.S. history or 1/2 year of U.S. history and 1/2 year of civics or American government.					
		Total number of U.S. history/government units ( )			
Laboratory Science – 1 year with laboratory Biology, chemistry, physics, etc.					
		Total number of science units ( )			
Foreign Language – 2 years In the same language. Subject to waiver for applicants who demonstrate equivalent competence.					
		Total number of foreign language units ( )			
Visual & Performing Arts – 1 year Art, dance, drama, music.					
		Total number of visual and performing arts units ( )			
College Preparatory Electives – 3 years Agriculture, social science (e.g., economics, geography, psychology, world cultures).					
		Total number of college-preparatory elective units ( )			

RECOMMENDATIONS

CSU does not typically require recommendations as a part of the application process, and they are not reviewed as part of your application file. However, some impacted programs may require recommendations; you are notified of this requirement after you have submitted your admission application.

COMPLETING YOUR CSU APPLICATION

You may be admitted as a freshman with an Undeclared major at all campuses except Cal Poly San Luis Obispo.

Read the application booklet carefully and follow the directions exactly. Be honest. If you falsify critical information and are found out, you may seriously impact your admission status.

MAJOR CHOICES

All undergraduate majors offered at CSU and the specific campuses at which they are available are listed at the back of your application booklet or on the electronic disk. Review program descriptions in campus catalogues before filing your application. Similar programs may have different names on different campuses. Accurately fill in the major title and code number for your major and alternative major. You may be admitted as a freshman with an Undeclared major at all campuses except Cal Poly San Luis Obispo. San Luis Obispo requires you to state a major on your application.

HIGH SCHOOL PREPARATION FORM

The High School Preparation form in the CSU admission application (and shown on page 10--42) requires you to list the college-preparatory courses — CSU Subject Requirement courses — you have taken, are currently taking, and will complete by the time you enter CSU. CSU reviews this information to determine if you have met the CSU Subject Requirement. See this chapter: CSU Subject Requirement, page 10--5.

Compute your high school GPA for CSU admission for all work you complete after ninth grade not including PE or Military Science.

List all grades earned, including those earned in the ninth grade. Refer to your high school's Official University of California Certified Course List for courses which you may include. Visual and performing arts courses must meet CSU criteria. Also include courses completed in summer school and courses completed at a college for high school credit. If you qualify for a foreign language waiver, indicate the specific language in which you are proficient and note "plan to waive" on the Foreign Language section of the High School Preparation form. For further information about visual and performing arts course criteria and the foreign language waiver procedure, see this chapter: Commonly Asked Questions About Admissions, pages 10--16 to 10--18.

HIGH SCHOOL GRADE POINT AVERAGE

The admission application requires you to compute your high school GPA for CSU admission for all work you complete *after* the ninth grade (college-preparatory and non-college-preparatory) not including physical education and military science. See this chapter: Scholarship Requirement, page 10--10.

Your semester grades in the sophomore and junior years are most critical. However, if you are not eligible for admission based upon your eligibility index, CSU includes in the GPA for CSU admission your fifth-semester grades — the first semester of your senior year — and if necessary, your sixth-semester grades — the second semester of your senior year. You may submit additional test scores through the last semester of your senior year. The campuses are willing to recalculate your eligibility index placement based upon additional course grades and test scores. Impacted campuses and majors may not follow this policy.

Within eight weeks after you have submitted your application, most campuses acknowledge receipt of your application with a space reservation letter.

If your final-semester grades or late test scores are needed to improve your eligibility index, you will not know if the campus has officially admitted you until your final grades and/or scores reach the campus, probably sometime during July.

CSU Admission Procedures

APPLICATION ACKNOWLEDGMENT

Within eight weeks after you have submitted your application, most campuses acknowledge receipt of your application with a "space reservation letter." *It is not a confirmation of admission.* The space reservation letter states that a place has been reserved for the term for which you applied if you meet the CSU campus and major admission requirements. This letter also specifies when to send the campus copies of your high school transcript and any college transcripts of courses you took while still in high school. If you do not receive the space reservation letter, call the campus admissions office to determine if it has received your application. When you call, have your social security number handy. Note the name of the person to whom you are speaking. If any further questions arise about your application, ask for the same person by name.

If you are not eligible for admission because you do not qualify on the eligibility index, the campus may inform you to submit additional senior year grades and SAT I: Reasoning Test or ACT test scores.

NOTIFICATION OF ADMISSION

Using the information on your High School Preparation form, your high school GPA for CSU admission which you entered on your admission application, your test scores, and your sixth or seventh-semester transcript (if required), the CSU campus determines whether you are admissible. Based upon this review of your qualifications, you may receive a "letter of provisional admission."

If you are not eligible for admission because you do not qualify on the eligibility index, the campus may inform you to submit additional senior year grades and SAT I: Reasoning Test or ACT test scores to establish your eligibility. The campus gives you the opportunity to improve your high school GPA for CSU admission and your admission test scores so that you may qualify on the eligibility index. If you are denied admission because you do not meet the CSU Subject Requirement, contact the campus to determine your options for completing the required courses. There may be courses you can take in the summer at your high school or community college to make up your deficiencies.

PROVISIONAL ADMISSION

Your letter of provisional admission states that based upon the information submitted, you are admitted to the CSU campus provided (a) you successfully complete your senior year, and (b) you maintain admissibility on the eligibility index. To clear your provisional status you must submit your final high school transcript indicating your grades through your senior year and your date of graduation.

CSU reviews your final transcript to verify information you provided on your application about courses completed and grades earned.

CSU reviews your final transcript to verify information you provided on your application about courses completed and grades earned. It is also checked to see if you completed in good standing the senior year courses indicated on the High School Preparation form of your admission application. A sample of this form is shown on page 10--43. This form lists your courses in progress during the fall of your senior year and planned for the second half of your senior year.

The admissions office of your chosen campus may reconsider your offer of admission if your transcript reveals that you provided inaccurate information on your High School Preparation form, did not complete the courses you wrote down as in progress or planned in your senior year, or failed to maintain a high level of scholarship. It is important that you fulfill your course commitments and maintain a strong record during your senior year.

APPEALS

If you are not admitted, and you believe you have special circumstances which warrant another review of your qualifications, you may write a letter of appeal or meet with an admissions officer at the CSU campus to request Regular Exceptional Admission. See this chapter: Regular Exceptional Admission, page 10--33.

If you are not admitted, but believe you have special circumstances which would warrant a review of your qualifications, you may write and appeal for Regular Exceptional Admission.

If you have any questions about your special circumstances, call the campus admissions office directly to discuss your unique situation.

ACCEPTANCE OF ADMISSION

For most CSU campuses there is no particular form which you must return to indicate your acceptance of admission. The campus learns that you are enrolling at the campus when you register for classes. Registration materials and information are mailed to you within a few months of your notification of admission.

Some campuses require you to indicate your intent to enroll. For example, Cal Poly San Luis Obispo requires you to submit the SIR (Student Intent To Register) form. Cal Poly SLO guarantees to you the opportunity to register only if you submit the SIR by May 1st for fall enrollment.

PLACEMENT TESTS

EPT — English Placement Test

ELM — Entry-Level Mathematics Test

The EPT and ELM are used for course placement purposes and do not affect your admission.

After CSU admits you, they may require you to take diagnostic testing in basic reading, writing, and mathematics skills. These tests are the English Placement Test (EPT) and the Entry-Level Mathematics Test (ELM) and are used to determine the level of college English and mathematics courses for which you are prepared. They are used for course placement purposes and do not affect your admission to CSU.

If you are unable to demonstrate college entry-level skills in these knowledge areas, you must enroll in courses or programs early in your college career at your CSU campus to correct your deficiencies. You do not receive credit for these remedial courses and programs toward your four-year college degree.

The EPT and ELM Test should be taken as soon as possible after CSU informs you that you are admitted and before you enroll at CSU. You cannot take either test until you have been officially accepted for admission. CSU sends you a choice of test dates and a registration form if you are required to take either test. You may be exempt from taking either or both. See chapter 6: COLLEGE ENTRANCE TESTS, The EPT And ELM Tests, page 6--52 for a full description of these tests, including test dates, fees, and exemption information.

Some statistics ...

In 1994, twenty to twenty-five percent of incoming freshmen were exempt from taking one or both tests. 23,000 to 24,000 incoming freshmen took the EPT. Sixty percent met the English proficiency requirement through exemption or by passing the English Placement Test. 34,000 to 35,000 incoming freshmen took the ELM. Sixty-five percent met the mathematics proficiency requirement through exemption or by passing the Entry Level Mathematics Test.

Advanced Placement Examinations

You may earn up to six semester units of baccalaureate credit for each Advanced Placement Examination of the College Entrance Examination Board (CEEB) for which you receive a score of 3, 4, or 5. Campuses award the amount of credit recommended by the College Entrance Examination Board. See chapter 6: COLLEGE ENTRANCE TESTS, The AP Program And Examinations, page 6--57.

INTERNATIONAL BACCALAUREATE

The International Baccalaureate, IB, is an internationally recognized two-year curriculum and examination for students between sixteen and nineteen years of age. Four-hundred schools in fifty-five countries throughout the world, including about 160 high schools in the United States and Canada have adopted the program. Many CSU campuses grant college units for each IB Higher Level Examination on which you score 5 or higher. IB Higher Level Examinations are considered honors-level courses which receive an extra point when calculating your CSU Subject Requirement GPA if they are listed on the Official University of California Certified Course List.

The CSU educational fee is the same at all campuses. Other fees and living expenses vary from campus to campus.

1994-95 COSTS

Because California State University is funded from state revenues, no tuition is charged to state residents. However, California students must pay educational fees. These fees are substantially less than tuition costs at independent colleges or those paid by out-of-state students attending CSU. See appendix A: CALIFORNIA RESIDENCY REQUIREMENTS. The CSU educational fee is the same at all campuses. Other fees and living expenses vary from campus to campus. Campus fees and living expenses have increased yearly and are likely to continue to increase in the future. For the 1994-95 academic year, the student fee for 2 semesters/3 quarters is $1,584 for a student enrolling in more than six units each term. The fee for enrolling in six or less units each term is $918 for the year.

CALIFORNIA STATE UNIVERSITY ESTIMATED AVERAGE EXPENSES FOR 1994-95

	Commuting From Parents'/ Relatives' Home	Living In Campus Housing	Living Away From Home & Off-Campus
CSU Fees For One Academic Year	$1,584	$1,584	$1,584
Miscellaneous Campus Fees	$240	$240	$240
Books/Supplies	$630	$630	$630
Meals/Housing	(Note 1.)	$5,140	$5,610
Miscellaneous Personal	(Note 1.)	$1,510	$1,565
Transportation	(Note 2.)	$538	$662
Total Costs		$9,642	$10,291

NOTES:
1. Costs for meals/housing and miscellaneous personal expenses for students who continue to live with parents or relatives are not expected to increase because of college attendance.
2. Transportation expenses for commuting students will vary depending upon the type of transportation used and the distance traveled.
3. All fees are subject to change.

Other CSU fees which may be applicable include those for filing your application, parking, attending summer session and extension courses, obtaining an I.D. card, miscellaneous fees for courses (e.g., laboratory, field trips, art materials, and instrument fees), and dormitory fees.

CALIFORNIA STATE UNIVERSITY

In addition to these fees, you can expect further costs for a variety of expenses such as books, meals, and housing. The table on the previous page shows these additional expenses and estimates of your total costs for one academic year. These expenses are estimates for the 1994-95 school year. Included on the personal/miscellaneous expense line are expenses for items such as recreation, clothes, personal items, and laundry. An estimate of transportation expenses is also included. All expenses vary considerably depending upon your tastes and life styles, and if you live on or off campus or with your family.

Student fees, campus fees, and living expenses have increased yearly and are likely to continue to increase in the future.

NONRESIDENT COSTS

In addition to the regular CSU fee, all out-of-state and foreign students must pay nonresident tuition: $164 per quarter unit, or $246 per semester unit. These amounts are subject to change. A nonresident student taking fifteen units per term pays nonresident tuition of $7,380 for a full academic year of forty-five quarter units/thirty semester units, the CSU fee, and miscellaneous campus fees.

UNDOCUMENTED ALIEN STUDENTS

CSU has made no final decision at this time whether undocumented alien students must pay nonresident tuition. Contact the residency specialist at the CSU campus of interest to you for the latest information.

Financial Aid

Apply for CSU financial aid by submitting the FAFSA application by March 2nd.

Approximately 200,000 students applied to California State University for student financial aid for the 1993-94 academic year. You may apply by submitting your FAFSA during the systemwide financial aid application priority filing period of January 1st through March 2nd. If you miss this priority filing period, you may not receive sufficient funds to meet one-hundred percent of your calculated financial need. Even if you miss the March 2nd date, you are encouraged to apply; the ability of each campus to meet your financial need depends upon the amount of financial aid funding it receives. See chapter 4: PAYING FOR COLLEGE, Applying For Financial Aid, page 4--9.

California residents who do not qualify for a Cal Grant, see Chapter 4: Paying for College, The Cal Program, page 4--29, may be eligible for the CSU State University Grant (SUG) program. According to the awarding policy, only students with an expected family contribution of $5,000 or less (approximately half of the total cost of attendance for students living on campus or in on-campus apartments) qualify for SUG. SUG provides funds to cover a portion of the State University Fee according to a sliding scale based on the level of a student's expected family contribution.

The most needy students, those with an EFC of $1,000 or less, receive one-hundred percent of the maximum State University grant which covers the entire State University fee. Students with a family contribution of $2,001 to $3,000 receive a grant of sixty percent. The remaining forty percent of the fee may be covered with funds from a student loan, and/or employment. While students with a family contribution of more than $5,000 will not receive a State University Grant to offset the fee, those students may receive student loans and/or employment awards to cover the fee as well as other educational expenses.

Financial aid awards cannot be transferred from one CSU campus to another.

The campuses also offer a variety of scholarships awarded on the basis of merit and financial need as well as donor-specified criteria. Contact the campus financial aid office for information on application procedures for these awards.

Financial aid awards cannot be transferred from one CSU campus to another. If you change your choice of CSU campuses, or if your admission application is redirected to another CSU campus, you must send written notification to the financial aid office at your first-choice campus — the original one to which you sent your application for admission — with a copy to the financial aid office of your alternative campus. This notification is an authorization to transfer your financial aid application files to the alternative campus.

FEE INSTALLMENT PLAN

CSU has established a fee installment plan for collecting the California State University Fee and nonresident tuition in installment payments. The plan allows students at semester-system campuses to pay their fees in three equal installments during the term. Students at quarter system campuses pay in two equal installments during the term. In both cases one payment is due at the time of registration. The campus collects a fee of $66.00 per year for the administration of the program. You may also pay for on-campus housing and meals on an installment program.

CSU has established a fee installment plan for collecting the California State University Fee and nonresident tuition in installment payments.

UNDOCUMENTED ALIEN STUDENTS

Undocumented alien students continue to be eligible for financial aid under the State University Grant Program — a program funded by CSU — and the EOP Grant Program. However, if you submit your FAFSA in the regular manner to the Need Analysis Processor, your financial information is sent automatically to the United States Department of Education. See chapter 4: PAYING FOR COLLEGE, Applying For Financial Aid, page 4--9. This department verifies your eligible noncitizen status with the Immigration and Naturalization Service (INS). Your status as an undocumented alien makes you ineligible for federal and state aid.

CSU recommends that instead of submitting your FAFSA to the Need Analysis Processor, submit it to your counselor or high school administrator. Your counselor or administrator will mail the completed FAFSA to the CSU campus financial aid director with a short cover letter of explanation. Following this procedure allows you to apply directly to CSU for the State University Grant and EOP Grant Programs.

For the question on the 1995-96 FAFSA regarding your citizenship, check "no, neither of the above." For the section titled Federal Student Aid Releases and Certification, leave all questions blank except for the required signatures and date.

GRADUATING IN FOUR YEARS

You must successfully complete an average of 16 semester units during each of eight academic terms to graduate in four years.

Depending upon your academic major, CSU requires you to complete between 124 and 140 semester units to complete a Bachelor's degree. You must successfully complete an average of 16 semester units during each of eight academic terms to graduate in four years. CSU undergraduates typically complete an average of 12 semester units or four, three-unit courses per term. At this rate, it takes between 10.3 and 11.6 semesters (five to six years) to earn a degree, unless you attend summer school. You will further extend your time to graduation if you take any courses beyond those needed to meet the requirements of your major or the GE/Breadth Requirement, or if you change your major. You can graduate in four years if you are a full time student and take 15 semester units every term except one in which 19 are required. The average time to graduate for first-time freshmen is 4.9 years.

The current fiscal crisis has reduced the number of sections offered; in many instances, classes are full. However, it is possible to get the classes you need. You must be flexible:

- You may have to take a second or third choice course to meet specific major, General Education, or graduation requirements if your first choice course is not available.
- You may have to take a class from a less preferred instructor.
- You need to be willing to take classes any time during the day or evening, including Saturday classes.

In 1993, 30% of students attending CSU attended on a part-time basis, taking less than twelve semester units a term.

Seventy-three percent of CSU students are employed while attending classes, fifty-four percent are employed twenty or more hours per week, and thirty-three percent work more than thirty hours a week. This not only limits time for classes and for studying, but it also affects when students are available to take courses. In 1993, 30% of CSU students attended on a part-time basis, taking less than twelve semester units a term.

If you are determined to graduate in four years make college your first priority and remain strongly focused. Decide on your major reasonable early in your undergraduate program. Develop an educational plan that includes courses to meet the General Education/Breadth Requirement as well as classes to complete your major. Select your courses with the assistance of instructors, CSU counselors, and academic advisors to avoid mistakes. Plan to earn fifteen to eighteen units of academic credit each semester. Consider taking classes in summer school. Expect to adjust your course selections, choice of instructors, and time schedule to take required classes. Limit your work hours so that you have ample time to carry a full load and take the courses you need when class space is available. Think carefully about taking time off for exchange programs, internships, or travel.

HOUSING

CSU campuses provide various forms of on-campus housing, including traditional residence hall, double occupancy rooms and high-rise apartments with full kitchens. The application process and the availability of housing facilities varies from campus to campus.

Although CSU gives first-time freshmen and transfer students priority in allocating on-campus housing spaces, waiting lists for on-campus housing at many campuses make it important to get your applications in early.

These campuses have high demand for student housing:

Chico	Pomona
Dominguez Hills	Sacramento
Fullerton	San Bernardino
Hayward	San Diego
Humboldt	San Jose
Long Beach	San Luis Obispo
Northridge	Sonoma

The new campus at San Marcos does not yet have on-campus housing available.

In 1993-94 the cost for a double occupancy room fee for the academic year ranged from $2,310 to $3,890 for an on campus apartment to $1,884 to $3,348 for an on campus residence hall. Board fees range from $1,611 to $2,418 for a standard nineteen meals per week plan. These figures may increase for 1994-95. The campuses provide several payment plans to choose from. You may pay for housing in a single payment or an installment program, which spreads your payments throughout the academic year. Installment programs differ from campus to campus and vary from plans with two payments to as many as six.

Single occupancy rooms are available on most campuses, although availability is limited and the cost is substantially higher than double occupancy. The campuses provide several food service plans offering from ten to nineteen meals per week and can accommodate special dietary needs by prior arrangement.

If the housing office does not assign you on-campus housing, the off-campus or community housing office can help you find a suitable place to live. Alternative housing can consist of student cooperatives, apartments or house rentals in the community. Lists of students seeking roommates are available. Some campuses offer off-campus students the option of buying a food service plan and eating with on-campus students. Several campuses are experiencing severe housing shortages in neighboring communities, most notably Humboldt, Long Beach, Dominguez Hills, and San Luis Obispo. If you are applying to these campuses, make your off-campus housing arrangements as early as possible.

HOUSING INFORMATION BY CAMPUS

As you read through the specific campus information note the following:

- The housing application process is separate from the process of admission to CSU. The campuses typically mail housing applications only upon request, although some will send one to you automatically when they receive your application for admission or after you are admitted. The campuses that provide housing information automatically are Bakersfield, California Maritime Academy, Fresno, Humboldt, Los Angeles, Long Beach, and Sonoma. San Luis Obispo sends housing information with your notice of admission. At all other campuses, write or call the housing office at the campus to obtain information and application materials. It is not necessary to wait until you are admitted to send for these materials.

- Campus housing offices have different names on each campus. The name for each is noted in the housing information on the following pages.

- If you plan to live on campus, apply for housing as early as possible after you receive your housing application. If you apply to a campus which sends housing applications only upon your request, send for your housing application as soon as possible. Note the critical dates. Space is very limited.

- Campuses admit students to the residence halls on a first-come, first-served basis. Most campuses do not charge a fee for submitting a housing application, although some do.

- On most campuses it is not necessary to wait until you are formally admitted to CSU before submitting your housing application. However, it is necessary to be admitted to the university before moving into the residence halls.

- If the campus offers you on-campus housing after you submit your housing application, you receive a housing License Agreement (a contract) to sign and a request for a deposit. The deposit is generally the first installment of your housing payment. Respond as quickly as possible. Many campuses use the date of the receipt of these materials as a priority date for assigning accommodations.

- The License Agreement specifies the conditions under which you may occupy the accommodations. You state the meal service plan and payment program you prefer. Each campus has their own License Agreement. On some you may have the opportunity to request a particular housing accommodation and/or roommate.

- The campus sends you a confirmation notice if they have assigned on-campus space to you.

- The housing office guarantees that you have housing when they *accept* your signed contract and first payment.

- Acceptance for on-campus housing does not mean you have been accepted for admission. If you make your housing payment before being admitted, and the campus denies you admission, the housing office refunds your payment.

- None of the campuses have extensive on-campus housing facilities, and most likely, you will need to consider off-campus housing. Request that off-campus housing information be sent with your housing application so that you can learn about alternatives.

- Some campuses give special housing consideration to disabled students, students with hardship situations, and other special need categories. Most campuses offer special facilities for disabled students. Campuses reserve a substantial number of spaces for returning students.

- The following on-campus housing information for each campus is for the 1994-95 school year and can change from year to year. For further details look up housing information in the campus catalogues and/or contact the housing office at the campuses of interest.

BAKERSFIELD

Space: There are 285 bed spaces in five, three-story residence halls. Most are double and triple rooms; a few singles are available.

Application: The Office of Residential Life automatically mails a housing application to you after the campus admits you.

CHICO

Space: There are 1,216 spaces in residence halls. Most are double rooms; the few singles available are generally offered to returning residents, not freshmen. Chico has a Thematic Living Program of apartment-style units with common kitchen and living areas. Each Thematic unit houses fourteen students who share the same major or common academic program. University Village, apartment style living a mile from campus, houses 224 students and is an alternative to residence halls.

Application: The University Housing and Food Service Office mails a housing application to you upon request. Applications for housing are accepted in the housing office as early as *a year-and-a-half* prior to occupancy. For fall 1995, housing applications were accepted beginning January 1993. For spring 1996, housing applications were accepted beginning August 1994. Early application is suggested.

DOMINGUEZ HILLS

Space: One, two, and three bedroom apartments accommodate 700 students. There are no traditional residence halls. The campus guarantees housing for four years.

Application: The Student Housing Office mails a housing application to you upon request.

FRESNO

On-Campus Space: Eleven residence halls have bed spaces for 1,124 students. Rooms are mostly doubles. There are some suites and a limited number of singles are available.

Application: The University Housing Office mails fall on-campus housing applications and License Agreements to all new students in late March.

Off-Campus Space: Off-campus spaces are abundant and affordable.

FULLERTON

On-Campus Space: At present, 396 students can be housed in 66 three bedroom apartments.

Application: The Housing Services and Residential Life Office mails a housing application to you upon request.

Off-Campus Space: Numerous apartment facilities are located nearby.

HAYWARD

On-Campus Space: 100 two-bedroom, self-contained apartments are available for 400 students.

Application: The Housing and Residential Life Office mails a housing application to you upon request.

Off-Campus Space: A privately owned and managed residence hall, providing both room and board, is available for 300 students.

HUMBOLDT

Space: There are five different living areas on campus housing 1,353 students. Double rooms and apartments are available.

Application: The Housing and Dining Services Office automatically sends you a housing application upon receipt of your application for admission. You are advised to make your housing arrangements well in advance; on-campus housing and housing in the immediate area of campus fills quickly. While most new students are accommodated, there have been waiting lists in the past.

LONG BEACH

Space: There are eighteen residence halls accommodating 1,844 students in suites, doubles, and a few singles. Two International Houses, accommodating 84 students, are dedicated to the interaction of American and international students. An American student is placed with an international student in these facilities. To apply for International House living send a brief statement with your housing application.

Application: All applicants for admission are automatically sent a housing application in March, but you may request an application earlier by phoning or writing to the Housing Office.

LOS ANGELES

Space: 908 students are accommodated in two- and four-bedroom Resident Apartments. A limited number of singles are available.

Application: The Office of Residence Life and Housing Services mails housing applications to all who apply for admission.

MONTEREY BAY

Information not available at this time.

NORTHRIDGE

Space: One-and two-bedroom apartments house 1,372 students and a residence hall has 870 spaces.

Application: Housing Services mails a housing application to you upon request.

POMONA

Space: Six on-campus residence halls accommodate 1,160 students in mostly double occupancy rooms. Pomona also offers 800 spaces in the University Village apartments, at the edge of the campus, to students with junior or senior standing.

Application: The Housing and Residential Life Office mails a housing application to you upon request.

SACRAMENTO

On-Campus Space: Approximately 1,225 students can be accommodated, primarily in double occupancy rooms, in six on-campus residence halls. A limited number of single rooms are available.

Application: The Housing and Residential Life Office mails a residence hall application to you upon request.

Off-Campus Space: Ample off-campus housing is available at reasonable rental costs within five miles of the campus.

SAN BERNARDINO

Space: Double and single rooms arranged in ten-person suites accommodate 397 residents.

Application: University Housing Services mails a housing application to you upon request any time during the year.

SAN DIEGO

Space: Nine on-campus residence halls house 2,241 students in single and double rooms. Two-bedroom apartments house an additional 15 students.

Application: Call or write the Housing and Residential Life Office to request an application.

SAN FRANCISCO

Space: San Francisco State has 767 spaces in three residence halls. Doubles and a limited number of suites and single rooms are available. One seventeen-story, high-rise residence apartment building with one-and two-bedroom units houses 576 residents.

Application: The Housing and Residential Services Office mails a housing application to you upon request.

SAN JOSE

On-Campus Space: Seven on-campus coeducational residence halls accommodate approximately 1,800 students. Apartment-style living for 220 students is available one mile south of the campus. An International Center houses 77 students.

Application: The University Housing Services Office mails a housing application to you upon request.

Off-Campus Space: Numerous off-campus houses and apartments are near the campus.

SAN LUIS OBISPO

Space: 2,750 students are housed in double occupancy rooms in six Living-Learning Centers. Each center is affiliated with one of the University's six Colleges and is dedicated to the promotion of the concerns and interests that compliment the academic studies of that College.

Application: The Department of Residential life and Education mails housing applications with the notice of admission. On-campus residence hall space is more than adequate for summer and fall 1993 students.

SAN MARCOS

No on-campus housing is available at this time. There are several apartment complexes near the campus that welcome students.

SONOMA

On-Campus Space: The residence halls are townhouses with double and single suite accommodations for 694 students. An additional 196 students are housed in two-bedroom apartments.

Application: The Housing Services Office mails a housing application to you upon receipt of an admissions application.

Off-Campus Space: A wide variety of housing choices is available.

STANISLAUS

On-Campus Space: The residence hall consists of double rooms for 163 students. Residential Life Village opened in the fall of 1993 and houses 260 students in apartments and suites.

Application: The Housing Office mails a housing application to you upon request.

Off-Campus Space: Reasonably priced apartments are near the campus.

STUDENT SERVICES

STUDENT SUPPORT

The California State University campuses offer many student services to assist you with your adjustment to college, course and program selection, career choice and job placement. Although their implementation may differ among the campuses, the following support services are available throughout the CSU system:

Orientation .... to college programs for new students to provide information on academic procedures, registration for classes, co-curricular and extracurricular activities, housing, part-time employment, and health services.

Academic advising .... to assist students in selecting courses of study and specific classes to meet academic goals.

Counseling services .... to assist students with personal adjustment problems.

Learning assistance programs............... to assist students with academic and study skills and specific course understanding.

Career planning .... to assist students with career decision-making.

Job placement services......... to assist students in developing the strategies for obtaining a job — for example, resume writing and interview techniques — and to help students with job placement.

The campuses offer many student services to assist you with your adjustment to college and your future planning.

Reentry services .... to assist students who are returning to school after several years of life and work experience.

Child care .... for infants, toddlers, and preschool children of students.

If you are unable to fulfill a specific course requirement because of your disability, alternative college-preparatory courses may be substituted for specific CSU Subject Requirement courses.

Other programs include health services, financial aid, housing, and international student advisement.

DISABLED STUDENTS

If you are a disabled high school student, CSU encourages you to complete the CSU Subject Requirement if at all possible. If you are unable to fulfill a specific course requirement because of your disability, alternative college-preparatory courses may be substituted for specific CSU Subject Requirement courses. If you are deaf and hearing impaired, or blind and visually impaired, or have learning disabilities, you may, in certain circumstances, qualify for substitutions of the foreign language, laboratory science, and mathematics courses of the CSU Subject Requirement.

Although your course pattern may differ from that of other students, you must still achieve fifteen units of college-preparatory study. Your course substitutions may limit later enrollment in certain majors. Have your guidance counselor or a high school administrator contact the disabled student services office at the CSU campuses of interest to you. They can confer about appropriate CSU Subject Requirement course substitutions.

Once you enroll at a CSU campus, you may receive special assistance to enable you to pursue your studies. During fall 1990, more than 7,800 students with physical disabilities received this support, which is offered at all twenty campuses of the CSU system. Each campus has a disabled student services office and staff to discuss your particular needs and the services available to you.

The campus you attend can provide you with readers, notetakers, and manual or oral interpreters. Special arrangements can be made for test-taking. Disability-related advising and counseling are available, as are registration, mobility assistance, and on-campus transportation. Adaptive equipment such as tape recorders, visual enlargers, braillers, and specialized computer equipment are available for your use. See chapter 8: EDUCATIONAL OPPORTUNITIES, Disabled Students, page 8--4.

All CSU campuses offer you the opportunity to study abroad for a full academic year.

INTERNATIONAL PROGRAMS

All California State University campuses offer you the opportunity to study abroad for a full academic year while remaining co-enrolled at your home campus. The program is called "California State University International Programs." Foreign universities in sixteen countries around the world, in cooperation with California State University International Programs, can accommodate a wide variety of academic majors.

Because you remain enrolled at your home campus while studying overseas, you earn full credit for all academic work completed abroad. All majors are available, although not in every country. Contact the International Programs Coordinator at your CSU campus to obtain the brochure, *Study Abroad* and learn more about this opportunity and the programs offered in each country.

SELECTION CRITERIA

You must pay current home-campus fees, round-trip transportation, living expenses, and incidentals.

To participate in California State University International Programs for the academic year beginning the following fall, you must meet these selection criteria:

1. You must be enrolled as (a) a CSU student not later than spring 1995, or (b) a California Community College student eligible to enter CSU by fall 1995.

2. You must be a CSU junior, senior or graduate student during the year abroad. If you are in an intensive language learning program in France, Germany, or Mexico, you may be a sophomore.

3. You must have a GPA of 2.75 or 3.00 depending upon the program. In certain instances, students who do not meet these standards may be considered for admission.

Most programs have prerequisites such as prior language study or specific coursework requirements. When there are more applicants than places at a particular study center, factors such as overall academic performance, depth of preparation, and aptness of academic/career objectives to programs applied for are considered.

COSTS

You must pay current home-campus fees, round-trip transportation, living expenses, and incidentals. There are no special tuition fees. Estimated total costs vary by country but range from approximately $9,000 to $16,000.

Financial aid, except work-study, may be applied toward your overseas study.

Financial aid — except work-study — available through CSU campuses, may be applied toward your overseas study. Each year more than half of all participants receive some kind of financial aid.

PARTICIPATING COUNTRIES

Thirty-seven foreign universities in sixteen countries participate in CSU International Programs.

Australia	Germany	New Zealand
Brazil	Israel	Spain
Canada	Italy	Sweden
Denmark	Japan	Taiwan
France	Mexico	United Kingdom
		Zimbabwe

SUMMER SESSIONS

Check with your career center or guidance office in early March and throughout the spring for the latest listing of CSU summer study opportunities.

The CSU campuses offer a wide range of summer courses. If you have completed your junior year in high school or have graduated, you may be able to attend a summer session on a CSU campus. Several campuses offer this opportunity. The campuses usually require a written recommendation from your counselor, guidance administrator, or principal. This recommendation should accompany your registration form and fees. A transcript may or may not be required.

There is no formal application process. Simply register for the courses of interest to you. Courses may have prerequisites, including test scores, or special qualifications, which are noted with the course descriptions.

Cal Poly San Luis Obispo offers a four-week Summer Architecture Career Workshop for high school students considering architecture as a career. You gain firsthand experience in studio design through a series of lectures, projects, and exercises. You live in a university residence hall during the program. Contact the Cal Poly Summer Architecture Career Workshop in the architecture department for application and fee information. Other campuses also may offer special summer programs for high school students.

Check with your career center or guidance office in early March and throughout the spring for the latest listing of CSU summer study opportunities. Contact the summer session office of the campus for registration and fee information.

CAMPUS PROFILES

ENROLLMENT HIGHLIGHTS FOR FALL 1993

- 325,639 students were enrolled in the CSU system. Of these, 262,492 were undergraduate students and 63,147 were graduate students.
- 97.7% of students enrolled in CSU were California residents.
- Most California residents (79.0%) attend campuses in the regions from which they originated.
- 0.3% of students enrolled on CSU campuses were from out-of-state.
- 2% of CSU total enrollment were from other countries.
- Nearly 38.6% of undergraduate enrollment is minority.

UNDERGRADUATE ENROLLMENT BY RACE AND ETHNICITY FALL 1993

Native American	1.0%
Asian/Pacific Islander	18.1%
Black	6.1%
Hispanic	15.9%
White	47.2%
Unknown	11.7%

FACULTY HIGHLIGHTS FOR FALL 1993

- Full-time faculty: 10,766
- Part-time faculty: 5,765
- Full-time faculty with Ph.D.'s: 78.7%

Profiles of the twenty-two CSU campuses present data for the 1993-94 academic year.

BAKERSFIELD

California State University, Bakersfield
9001 Stockdale Highway
Bakersfield, CA 93311-1099
(805) 664-2011
Admissions: (805) 664-3036
Financial Aid: (805) 664-3016
Housing: (805) 664-3014

DISTINGUISHING FEATURES: Cal State Bakersfield is the only four-year college within a one-hundred mile radius of the Bakersfield area. It has a strong base of regional interest and support for its programs. The campus prides itself on the extensive student/faculty interaction and advising which take place. The student/faculty ratio of 16/1 is the lowest in the CSU system and promotes a personalized atmosphere. The average class size is twenty-five students. The curriculum emphasis is on a liberal education. Bakersfield offers a broad range of programs in the arts, humanities, natural and health sciences, and applied programs in fields such as business and education. For a university of its size, the Cal State Bakersfield faculty has one of the highest percentages of research grants and fellowships among all the faculties of CSU campuses.

DEGREES OFFERED: Bachelor's, Master's.
COLLEGES: Schools of Arts and Sciences, Business and Public Administration, Education.
UNDERGRADUATE MAJORS: 50. See this chapter: Undergraduate Degree Majors, page 10--68.
CALENDAR: Quarter system. Summer session.
ENROLLMENT: ***Total*** - 5,276. ***Graduate*** - 1,295. ***Undergraduate*** - 3,981: Men - 40%, women - 60%. ***Ethnic distribution of undergraduates:*** Hispanic - 21.9%, Black - 5.8%, Asian/Pacific Islander - 10.3%, Native American/Alaskan - 2.1%, White - 52.4%, Unknown - 7.5%.
LOCATION: Located on a 375-acre site on the western edge of Bakersfield in the southern San Joaquin Valley. One-hundred ten miles north of Los Angeles and three-hundred miles south of San Francisco. One of the fastest-growing areas in California in the heart of the state's oil and agriculture region.
CAMPUS LIFE: ***Clubs and organizations*** - 50. Fraternities and Sororities - yes. ***Athletics:*** Intercollegiate - NCAA, Division II. Intramural sports - yes.
OTHER INFORMATION: ***Founded*** - 1965.
WASC Accredited - yes.

CALIFORNIA MARITIME ACADEMY

P.O. Box 1392
Vallejo, California 94560
Admissions: (707) 648-4222
Financial Aid: (707) 648-4227
Fax: (707) 649-4773
Toll Free: nd

A Specialized California State University That Prepares Students for Careers in Marine-Oriented Industries and Businesses

DISTINGUISHING FEATURES: The California Maritime Academy will become part of the CSU system effective July 1, 1995. It is a state-supported college having the goal of educating men and women for careers in supervisory positions on commercial ships, in the maritime industry ashore, and other businesses and industries. Students earn a Bachelor's degree, a merchant marine officer's license, and if desired, a commission as an ensign in the United States Navy Reserve. Three areas of emphasis at the Academy are the academic program, practical hands-on training, and leadership development. During class time, students wear the traditional uniforms of officers in the merchant marine. Students complement their classroom study with considerable time spent in laboratories and simulators on campus and on board the Academy training ship, the Golden Bear. Each year freshmen, sophomores, and juniors travel aboard the Academy training ship for about eight weeks applying what they have learned in the classroom.
DEGREES OFFERED: Bachelor's.
SPECIAL PROGRAMS: Eight weeks on the Academy training ship applying classroom learning. Minority Engineering Program. ***Education abroad*** - travel on the Golden Bear to places in the Pacific basin such as Alaska, Fiji, Hawaii, Hong Kong, Japan, Mexico, Panama, Peru, Russia, Singapore. Average of two nights in each port. ***Honors programs*** - no.
COLLEGES: na.
UNDERGRADUATE MAJORS: 4 majors. Business Administration (includes deck license), Marine Transportation (includes deck license), Mechanical Engineering (includes engineering license), Marine Engineering Technology (includes engineering license). Preprofessional programs: nd.
CALENDAR: Semester system. No summer school.
FACULTY: Full-time - 28, part-time - 12. Undergraduate classes taught by faculty, not graduate assistants - all. Faculty with Ph.D.'s - 24%. Student/faculty ratio - 15/1. Average class size - 24.
ENROLLMENT: ***Total*** - 500. ***Graduate*** - 0. ***Undergraduate*** - 500: California residents - 82%, out-of-state - 14%, other countries - 4%. Men - 85%, women - 15%. ***Ethnic distribution of undergraduate students:*** Hispanic - 7.0%, Black - 4.0%, Asian/Pacific Islander - 13.0%, Native American/Alaskan - 2.0%, White - 72.0%, International - 3.0%. ***Freshmen graduating within 5 years:*** 70%.
LOCATION: 67 wooded acres in the city of Vallejo, adjacent to the Carquinez Strait at the northeastern extreme of San Francisco Bay. Thirty miles northeast of San Francisco.
CAMPUS LIFE: All first year students must live on campus. ***On-campus housing:*** Spaces - 458, residential students - 85%. ***Clubs and organizations*** - yes. Fraternities and sororities - no. ***Athletics:*** Intercollegiate - yes. Intramural sports - yes. ***Counseling and guidance:*** Academic, personal, career planning, job placement. Faculty advisors - yes. Tutoring - yes. ***Special services/academic programs for:*** Educationally disadvantaged - no, physically disabled - no, learning disabled - no.
FRESHMAN ADMISSION STANDARDS: High school graduation or equivalent. High school units: Total required - nd. English - 4, social science - 0, foreign language - 0, laboratory science - 1, mathematics - 3 (algebra, geometry, and intermediate algebra, Mechanical Engineering majors must have an additional year of algebra and advanced mathematics or science). Candidates for becoming licensed officers in the United States Merchant Marines must meet certain physical requirements.

CALIFORNIA STATE UNIVERSITY

na = not applicable nd = no data available

1993-94 FRESHMAN ADMISSION DATA: ***Applications:*** Received - 375, accepted - 199, enrolled - 130. ***SAT Scores:*** Average verbal/mathematics scores - nd/nd, median verbal/mathematics scores - nd/nd. Verbal/mathematics scores of enrolled freshmen: 1%/2% scored 700-800, 3%/16% scored 600-699, 26%/44% scored 500-599, 36%/265% scored 400-499, 32%/10% scored 300-399. ***ACT composite score:*** Average - nd, median - nd. ***High school GPA:*** Average GPA - nd. ***Class rank:*** nd. ***International students:*** Minimum TOEFL score required - 500.
TRANSFER ADMISSION STANDARDS: ***Transfer units required:*** Minimum - 30, maximum - nd. ***Minimum college GPA*** - 2.0. ***Grades accepted*** - C or better.
1993-94 TRANSFER ADMISSION DATA: ***Applications:*** Received - nd, accepted - nd, enrolled - nd. CCC transfer students enrolled - nd.
ADMISSION PROCEDURES: ***Entrance tests:*** SAT I: Reasoning Test or ACT required. Test deadline for fall admission - January. ***Application process:*** Students should apply in November using the CSU Undergraduate Admission Application. Students admitted for fall semester. Deadlines: Freshmen - 3/1 preferred. Transfers - 3/1 preferred. Application fee - $55. Fee waiver - nd. ***Recommendations:*** 1 - counselor, principal, or employer. ***Interview*** - no. ***Admission notification*** - rolling. Commitment deposit - $nd. ***Advanced placement offered*** - nd. ***Advanced credit given*** - nd. ***Early decision procedure:*** Application deadline - nd, notification - nd.
1994-95 COSTS: ***Total costs*** (approximate, for California residents) - $9,000. Tuition - $0, fees - $2,548, room and board - $4,770, total books, supplies, incidentals (approximate) - $1,200. Nonresidents of California must pay tuition of $6,090 in addition to fees and other expenses.
UNDERGRADUATE FINANCIAL AID: Students receiving financial aid - 55%. Submit financial aid applications by 3/2. Application deadline for institutional scholarships and grants - 3/2. Average financial aid package - $4,750.
OTHER INFORMATION: ***Founded*** - 1929. ***Nonprofit*** - yes. ***WASC Accredited*** - yes.

CHICO

California State University, Chico
1st and Normal Streets
Chico, CA 95929
(916) 898-6886
Admissions: (916) 898-6321
Financial Aid: (916) 898-6451
Housing: (916) 898-6325

DISTINGUISHING FEATURES: California State University, Chico offers a dynamic intellectual and social environment. One of only a few schools nationwide to offer courses via satellite transmission, it is renowned for its Computer Science and Engineering programs. It is a residential campus with eighty percent of the students coming from home towns more than one-hundred miles from Chico. The campus blends a strong liberal arts tradition with innovative programs in computer science, engineering, and communication as well as solid preparation for the professions. Over five-hundred cultural festivals and exhibits, concerts, and other public events occur on campus each year.
DEGREES OFFERED: Bachelor's, Master's.
COLLEGES: Agriculture and Home Economics; Behavioral and Social Sciences; Business; Communications; Education and Physical Education; Engineering, Computer Science, and Technology; Humanities and Fine Arts; Natural Sciences. Institute for Liberal and Interdisciplinary Studies.
UNDERGRADUATE MAJORS: 60. See this chapter: Undergraduate Degree Majors, page 10--68.
CALENDAR: Semester system. Summer sessions.
ENROLLMENT: ***Total*** - 14,706. ***Graduate*** - 1,541. ***Undergraduate*** - 13,165: Men - 50%, women - 50%. ***Ethnic distribution of undergraduates:*** Hispanic - 7.6%, Black - 2.5%, Asian/Pacific Islander - 3.9%, Native American/Alaskan - 1.7%, White - 76.1%, Unknown - 9.2%.
LOCATION: 240-acre campus nestled in the heart of the Sacramento Valley ninety miles north of Sacramento, one-hundred seventy-four miles northeast of San Francisco. The campus is surrounded by a countryside of farms and ranches and is near the 2,400-acre Bidwell Park in the Chico community.
CAMPUS LIFE: ***Clubs and Organizations*** - 180. Fraternities and Sororities - yes. ***Athletics:*** Intercollegiate - NCAA, Division II. Intramural sports- yes.
OTHER INFORMATION: ***Founded*** - 1887.
WASC Accredited - yes.

DOMINGUEZ HILLS

California State University, Dominguez Hills
Carson, CA 90747
(310) 516-3300
Admissions: (310) 516-3600
Financial Aid: (310) 516-3647
Housing: (310) 516-4228

DISTINGUISHING FEATURES: California State University, Dominguez Hills provides a friendly atmosphere with generally small classes and individual attention from faculty. Students are encouraged to meet with academic advisors. There is an emphasis on teaching as well as research. Most classes are offered in the evening; the majority of students are adults working full- or part-time. Dominguez Hills is particularly well known for its health and clinical sciences programs and offers a strong teacher education program. It is the home of CSU's Statewide Nursing Program, which offers to registered nurses courses available throughout the state that lead to Bachelor of Science and Master of Science degrees in nursing. Dominguez Hills pledges that its students will graduate in four years based on a full-time academic program and that it will give priority registration for classes for all terms.
DEGREES OFFERED: Bachelor's, Master's.
COLLEGES: Schools of Education; Health; Humanities and Fine Arts; Management; Science, Mathematics, and Technology; Social and Behavioral Sciences.
UNDERGRADUATE MAJORS: 37. See this chapter: Undergraduate Degree Majors, page 10--68.
CALENDAR: Semester system. Summer sessions.
ENROLLMENT: ***Total*** - 9,671. ***Graduate*** - 2,743. ***Undergraduate*** - 6,928: Men - 38%, women - 62%. ***Ethnic distribution of undergraduates:*** Hispanic - 21.0%, Black - 27.7%, Asian/Pacific Islander - 11.4%, Native American/Alaskan - 1.0%, White - 27.6%, Unknown - 11.3%.
LOCATION: On 346, park-like acres located south of Los Angeles in the heart of a major technological, industrial, and transportation complex. Near major freeways, airports, Los Angeles cultural centers and Southern California resort areas.
CAMPUS LIFE: ***Clubs and Organizations*** - 86. Fraternities and sororities - yes. ***Athletics:*** Intercollegiate - NCAA, Division II. Intramural sports - yes.

OTHER INFORMATION: ***Founded*** - 1960.
WASC Accredited - yes.

FRESNO

California State University, Fresno
Shaw and Cedar Avenues
Fresno, CA 93740
(209) 278-4240
Admissions: (209) 278-2261
Financial Aid: (209) 278-2182
Housing: (209) 278-2345

DISTINGUISHING FEATURES: Cal State Fresno is the major public university in the San Joaquin Valley, the agribusiness center of the state. The campus offers a broad curriculum including the arts, sciences, humanities, agriculture, business, education, engineering, and professional areas such as nursing, industrial technology, social work, and urban planning. An array of multicultural activities that aptly portray a rich, diverse student population are available. The faculty emphasize teaching, individual attention to students, and the practical application of classroom learning.
DEGREES: Bachelor's, Master's, Doctoral.
COLLEGES: Schools of Agricultural Sciences and Technology, Arts and Humanities, Business and Administrative Sciences, Education and Human Development, Engineering, Health and Social Work, Natural Sciences, Social Sciences.
UNDERGRADUATE MAJORS: 63. See this chapter: Undergraduate Degree Majors, page 10--68.
CALENDAR: Semester system. Summer sessions.
ENROLLMENT: ***Total*** - 17,956. ***Graduate - 3,264. Undergraduate*** - 14,692: Men - 44%, women - 56%. ***Ethnic distribution of undergraduates:*** Hispanic - 21.9%, Black - 4.7%, Asian/Pacific Islander - 9.3%, Native American/Alaskan - 1.1%, White - 49.2%, Unknown - 13.8%.
LOCATION: 1,410-acre, park-like campus, including a 327-acre, main campus, in the heart of the San Joaquin Valley. Located about equal distances from San Francisco and Los Angeles, each three to four hours away by car or forty minutes by plane. Within easy driving distance of three national parks: Yosemite, Sequoia, and Kings Canyon.
CAMPUS LIFE: ***Clubs and organizations*** - 200. Fraternities and sororities - yes. ***Athletics:*** Intercollegiate - NCAA, Division I-A. Intramural sports - yes.
OTHER INFORMATION: ***Founded*** - 1911.
WASC Accredited - yes.

FULLERTON

California State University, Fullerton
Fullerton, CA 92634
(714) 773-2011
Admissions: (714) 773-2300
Financial Aid: (714) 773-3125
Housing: (714) 773-2168

DISTINGUISHING FEATURES: CSU Fullerton offers a broad curriculum and is primarily a commuter school. The average class size is twenty-nine. Fullerton emphasizes career internships and cooperative education. Currently, thirty-nine programs offer internships/co-op in fields from the arts to the sciences. The University has an off-campus center at Saddleback Community College in Mission Viejo, which is serving upper-division and graduate students in southern Orange County.
DEGREES OFFERED: Bachelor's, Master's.
COLLEGES: Schools of The Arts, Business Administration and Economics, Communications, Engineering and Computer Science, Human Development and Community Service, Humanities and Social Sciences, Natural Science and Mathematics.
UNDERGRADUATE MAJORS: 46. See this chapter: Undergraduate Degree Majors, page 10--68.
CALENDAR: Semester system. Summer session.
ENROLLMENT: ***Total***-22,565. ***Graduate***-3,737. ***Undergraduate***- 18,828: Men - 43.9%, women - 56.1%. ***Ethnic distribution of undergraduates:*** Hispanic - 16.1%, Black - 2.8%, Asian/Pacific Islander - 20.5%, Native American /Alaskan - 0.7%, White - 47.8% Unknown - 12.4%. ***Freshmen graduating within 5 years*** - nd.
LOCATION: On 225 acres in the city of Fullerton, in northern Orange County about thirty miles southeast of central Los Angeles. Near forty-two miles of beaches, Disneyland, Knotts Berry Farm.
CAMPUS LIFE: ***Clubs and organizations*** - 175. Fraternities and sororities - no. ***Athletics:*** Intercollegiate - NCAA, Division I-AAA. Intramural sports - yes.
OTHER INFORMATION: ***Founded*** - 1957.
WASC Accredited - yes.

HAYWARD

California State University, Hayward
Hayward, CA 94542
(510) 881-3000
Admissions: (510) 727-2624
Financial Aid: (510) 881-3616
Housing: (510) 881-3601

DISTINGUISHING FEATURES: Cal State Hayward has a strong liberal arts and science curricular emphasis. Applied programs are offered in business administration, computer science, counseling, education, health sciences, mass communication, nursing, public administration, and speech pathology and audiology. Hayward prides itself on the quality of the interaction between students and faculty; most classes have fewer than thirty students.
DEGREES OFFERED: Bachelor's, Master's.
COLLEGES: Schools of Arts, Letters, and Social Sciences; Business and Economics; Education; and Science.
UNDERGRADUATE MAJORS: 37. See this chapter: Undergraduate Degree Majors, page 10--68.
CALENDAR: Quarter system. Summer session.
ENROLLMENT: ***Total***-12,583. ***Graduate***-2,834. Undergraduate - 9,749: Men - 38%, women - 62%. ***Ethnic distribution of undergraduates:*** Hispanic - 9.8%, Black - 12.3%, Asian/Pacific Islander - 22.3%, Native American/Alaskan - 0.9%, White - 41.3%, Unknown - 13.4%. ***Freshmen graduating within 5 years*** - nd.
LOCATION: On 400 acres on a hillside overlooking San Francisco Bay. The Pacific Ocean is an hour to the west, San Francisco is about forty minutes away. Close to many Bay Area cities with a multitude of cultural activities.
CAMPUS LIFE: ***Clubs and organizations***-80. Fraternities and Sororities - no. ***Athletics:*** Intercollegiate - NCAA, Division II.

Intramural sports - yes.
OTHER INFORMATION: ***Founded*** - 1957.
WASC Accredited - yes.

HUMBOLDT

Humboldt State University
Arcata, CA 95521
(707) 826-3011
Admissions: (707) 826-4402
Financial Aid: (707) 826-4321
Housing: (707) 826-3451

DISTINGUISHING FEATURES: Humboldt State is best known for its programs in the natural resources in such areas as marine studies, natural resources management, and fisheries. It also offers a broad and balanced curriculum, which is strong in the fine arts, humanities, environmental engineering, computer information systems, and the sciences. The average class size of twenty-five to thirty-five students fosters friendliness and close faculty-student relationships. Most students come from outside the area, traveling at least three-hundred miles to attend, and are likely to be independent and adventuresome. The CSU Summer Arts Program, the largest multidisciplinary arts education program offered on the west coast, takes place on the Humboldt campus.
DEGREES OFFERED: Bachelor's, Master's.
COLLEGES: Arts and Humanities, Behavioral and Social Sciences, Natural Resources and Sciences, Professional Studies.
UNDERGRADUATE MAJORS: 44. See this chapter: Undergraduate Degree Majors, page 10--68.
CALENDAR: Semester system. Summer session.
ENROLLMENT: ***Total*** - 7,854. ***Graduate*** - 980. ***Undergraduate*** - 6,874: Men - 51%, women - 48%. ***Ethnic distribution of undergraduates:*** Hispanic - 6.8%, Black - 1.8%, Asian/Pacific Islander - 3.0%, Native American/Alaskan - 2.5%, White - 73.3%, Unknown - 12.69%. ***Freshmen graduating within 5 years*** - nd.
LOCATION: On 145 acres, two-hundred seventy-five miles north of San Francisco and ninety-five miles south of the Oregon border. Nestled in a spectacular setting of lush redwood forests, rushing rivers, solitary ocean beaches and mountain ranges near the small city of Arcata.
CAMPUS LIFE: ***Clubs and organizations*** - 130. Fraternities and sororities - yes. ***Athletics:*** Intercollegiate - NCAA, Division II. Intramural sports - yes.
OTHER INFORMATION: ***Founded*** - 1913.
WASC Accredited - yes.

LONG BEACH

California State University, Long Beach
1250 Bellflower Boulevard
Long Beach, CA 90840
(310) 985-4111
Admissions: (310) 985-5505
Financial Aid: (310) 985-5581
Housing: (310) 985-4187

DISTINGUISHING FEATURES: CSU Long Beach combines the advantages of a large university with personal attention offered by relatively small classes. It offers a broad range of academic programs and a fast-paced urban atmosphere. The College of Engineering is the largest engineering school in the west, both in terms of total enrollment and in terms of the number of baccalaureate degrees awarded. The campus is eighth in the nation and first in California in the number of engineering degrees awarded to underrepresented minorities. It is known for its dance, graphic design, and public policy and administration programs. Long Beach is the home of the largest fine arts school in California. Long Beach has established a strong research base and a goal of academic excellence. An extensive program of career internships and cooperative education is available. Average class size is thirty-five in lower-division courses; twenty-seven in upper-division.
DEGREES OFFERED: Bachelor's, Master's.
COLLEGES: Arts; Engineering; Health and Human Services; Humanities, Social and Behavioral Sciences; Natural Sciences. School of Business. Graduate School of Education.
UNDERGRADUATE MAJORS: 67. See this chapter: Undergraduate Degree Majors, page 10--68.
CALENDAR: Semester System. Summer session.
ENROLLMENT: ***Total*** - 27,073. ***Graduate*** - 5,647. ***Undergraduate*** - 21,426: Men - 47%, women - 53%. ***Ethnic distribution of undergraduates:*** Hispanic - 15.6%, Black - 7.3%, Asian/Pacific Islander - 22.6%, Native American/Alaskan - 0.9, White - 43.4%, Unknown - 10.2%.
LOCATION: 322-acre urban campus near the major international business center of the Pacific Rim and in the heart of Southern California beaches. Four miles from the Pacific Ocean and forty minutes from downtown Los Angeles.
CAMPUS LIFE: ***Clubs and organizations*** - 300. Fraternities and Sororities - yes. ***Athletics:*** Intercollegiate - NCAA, Division I-AAA. Intramural sports- yes.
OTHER INFORMATION: ***Founded*** - 1949.
WASC Accredited - yes.

LOS ANGELES

California State University, Los Angeles
5151 State University Drive
Los Angeles, CA 90032
(213) 343-3000
Admissions: (213) 343-3901
Financial Aid: (213) 343-3240
Housing: (213) 343-4800

DISTINGUISHING FEATURES: Cal State Los Angeles is a dynamic urban institution offering a diverse, flexible, and practical curriculum. Programs in business, communication studies, international affairs, education, and engineering and computer science lead to a variety of career opportunities. All faculty members serve as academic advisers. Average class size is twenty-three. Many faculty are involved with innovative and exciting programs, allowing students to gain research experience or firsthand experience with the community. Internships and cooperative education programs provide practical experience. Los Angeles is one of the leading CSU campuses in advanced information systems and in providing training in leading-edge computer technology. The university is the largest teacher training institution in the state and offers many unique specializations. The college is a focal point for the arts; the Joffrey Ballet is in residence on the campus.
DEGREES OFFERED: Bachelor's, Master's, Doctoral.
COLLEGES: Schools of Arts and Letters, Business and Eco-

na = not applicable   nd = no data available

nomics, Education, Engineering and Technology, Health and Human Services, Natural and Social Sciences.
UNDERGRADUATE MAJORS: 52. See this chapter: Undergraduate Degree Majors, page 10--68.
CALENDAR: Quarter system. Summer session.
ENROLLMENT: ***Total*** - 17,788. ***Graduate*** - 4,279. ***Undergraduate*** - 13,509: Men - 43%, women - 57%. ***Ethnic distribution of undergraduates:*** Hispanic - 38.2%, Black - 8.4%, Asian/Pacific Islander - 27.0%, Native American /Alaskan - 0.3%, White - 13.6%, Unknown - 12.5%.
LOCATION: 175-acre, hilltop campus, overlooking the city of Los Angeles and the San Gabriel Valley. Just minutes from the Los Angeles downtown financial center, industrial and technological resources, Hollywood studios, museums, and Southern California beaches.
CAMPUS LIFE: ***Clubs and Organizations*** - 100. Fraternities and sororities - yes. ***Athletics:*** Intercollegiate - NCAA, Division II. Intramural sports - yes.
OTHER INFORMATION: ***Founded*** - 1947.
WASC Accredited - yes.

MONTEREY BAY

California State University, Monterey Bay
Del Monte Blvd., CA State Highway 1
Seaside, CA, 93955

CSU Monterey Bay is scheduled to open for freshmen in fall 1995 on 1,300 acres of the former Fort Ord Army Base north of Monterey. The campus will provide innovative, primarily multidisciplinary programs in four academic cluster areas: Visual and Performing Arts and Related Humanities; Marine, Atmospheric and Environmental Sciences; Languages, Cultures, and International Studies; Professional Studies (business and education). The nearby Monterey Bay Aquarium, the Defense Language Institute, and a new University of California research center may provide additional locations for studies.

Plans call for the new university to have state-of-the art telecommunications and multimedia technologies to enhance instruction. The campus also will be largely residential, including condo-style units for students with families and for employees.

NORTHRIDGE

California State University, Northridge
18111 Nordhoff Street
Northridge, CA 91330
(818) 885-1200
Admissions: (818) 885-3700
Financial Aid: (818) 885-2374
Housing: (818) 885-2160

DISTINGUISHING FEATURES: CSU Northridge reflects the friendliness and openness of Southern California. Most students come from Los Angeles and surrounding counties. The campus is known for outstanding programs for educationally disadvantaged students — low-income and minority students. The music department is ranked among the top twenty in the nation and the journalism department is among the top professional programs in the country. The campus is the home of the National Center on Deafness and is very strong in programs for the disabled. Northridge operates an off-campus center to serve upper-division and graduate students in Ventura County.
DEGREES OFFERED: Bachelor's, Master's.
COLLEGES: Schools of the Arts, Business Administration and Economics, Communication, Education, Engineering and Computer Science, Health and Human Services, Humanities, Science and Mathematics, Social and Behavioral Sciences.
UNDERGRADUATE MAJORS: 47. See this chapter: Undergraduate Degree Majors, page 10--68.
CALENDAR: Semester system. Summer session.
ENROLLMENT: ***Total*** - 27,282. ***Graduate*** - 5,603. ***Undergraduate*** - 21,679: Men - 45%, women - 55%. ***Ethnic distribution of undergraduates:*** Hispanic - 17.9%, Black - 7.7%, Asian/Pacific Islander - 16.1%, Native American/Alaskan - 0.7%, White - 45.1%, Unknown - 12.51%.
LOCATION: 350-acre campus in the northwestern part of the San Fernando Valley, a suburban area of Los Angeles. Just twenty-five minutes from downtown Los Angeles.
CAMPUS LIFE: ***Clubs and Organizations*** - 200. Fraternities and sororities - yes. ***Athletics:*** Intercollegiate - NCAA, Division I-AA. Intramural sports - yes.
OTHER INFORMATION: ***Founded*** - 1958.
WASC Accredited - yes.

POMONA

California State Polytechnic University, Pomona
3801 West Temple Avenue
Pomona, CA 91768
(909) 869-4219
Admissions: (909) 869-2000
Financial Aid: (909) 869-3700
Housing: (909) 869-3307

DISTINGUISHING FEATURES: Cal Poly Pomona emphasizes a practical, hands-on system of education that assures students excellent career skills and opportunities. Students apply classroom and laboratory education through service as interns and consultants in industry and government. Nearly one-half of the students are enrolled in one of the majors in the College of Business Administration or Engineering. Most of the students commute from nearby communities. Cal Poly has entered a float in the New Year's Rose Parade for over forty years.
DEGREES OFFERED: Bachelor's, Master's.
COLLEGES: Agriculture, Arts, Business Administration, Engineering, Environmental Design, Science. School of Hotel and Restaurant Management.
UNDERGRADUATE MAJORS: 54. See this chapter: Undergraduate Degree Majors, page 10--68.
CALENDAR: Quarter system. Summer session.
ENROLLMENT: ***Total***-17,050. ***Graduate***-1,846. ***Undergraduate***-15,204: Men - 60%, women - 40%. ***Ethnic distribution of undergraduates:*** Hispanic - 18.5%, Black - 3.4%, Asian/Pacific Islander - 33.4%, Native American/Alaskan - 0.5%, White - 33.8%, Unknown - 10.4%.
LOCATION: 1,300-acre campus set among rolling hills has a rural atmosphere. In the city of Pomona which is forty minutes east of Los Angeles by freeway. Horse shows held monthly on the Kellogg Arabian Horse Center located on campus.
CAMPUS LIFE: ***Clubs and Organizations*** - 100. Fraternities and Sororities - no. ***Athletics:*** Intercollegiate - NCAA, Division II. Intramural sports - yes.
OTHER INFORMATION: ***Founded*** - 1938.
WASC Accredited - yes.

CALIFORNIA STATE UNIVERSITY

na = not applicable nd = no data available

SACRAMENTO

California State University, Sacramento
6000 J Street
Sacramento, CA 95819
(916) 278-6011
Admissions: (916) 278-3901
Financial Aid: (916) 278-6554
Housing: (916) 278-6655

DISTINGUISHING FEATURES: At CSU Sacramento the teaching of undergraduates is the top instructional priority; the faculty are recognized for their research and public service as well. Full professors teach at all class levels. The campus is large enough to offer rich diversity, but not so large that students feel like they are lost in a vast educational machine. The proximity of many state agency headquarters as well as federal offices provides first hand opportunities for research, field work, internships, and part-time jobs in governmental offices. Fewer than four percent of the classes enroll more than fifty students; almost eighty percent enroll thirty or less. The university offers a wide range of academic degrees in the liberal arts, sciences, and professional disciplines such as engineering, computer science, business, and education. The Business Administration program is the largest academic program on campus and one of the largest business administration programs in California. Sacramento offers the only joint Government-Journalism Bachelor's degree in California. Project Success is a partnership between industry and CSU Sacramento's Minority Engineering Program. It provides full-time, paid internships during summers and school breaks for underrepresented students in the engineering and computer sciences fields.
DEGREES OFFERED: Bachelor's, Master's.
COLLEGES: Schools of Arts and Sciences, Business and Public Administration, Education, Engineering and Computer Science, Health and Human Services.
UNDERGRADUATE DEGREE MAJORS: 41. See this chapter: Undergraduate Degree Majors, page 10--68.
CALENDAR: Semester system. Summer session.
ENROLLMENT: ***Total*** - 23,316. ***Graduate*** - 4,558. ***Undergraduate*** - 18,738: Men - 47%, women - 53%. ***Ethnic distribution of undergraduates:*** Hispanic - 10.9%, Black - 5.8%, Asian/Pacific Islander - 13.4%, Native American/Alaskan - 1.5%, White - 56.6%, unknown - 11.4%.
LOCATION: 290-acre, tree-lined campus on the American River in the city of Sacramento just five miles from the State Capitol. The San Francisco Bay area and the Lake Tahoe/Sierra slopes regions are less than two hours away.
CAMPUS LIFE: ***Clubs and organizations*** - 250. Fraternities and sororities - yes. ***Athletics:*** Intercollegiate - NCAA, Division I-AA. Intramural sports - yes.
OTHER INFORMATION: ***Founded*** - 1897.
WASC Accredited - yes.

SAN BERNARDINO

California State University, San Bernardino
5500 University Parkway
San Bernardino, CA 92407
(909) 880-5000
Admissions: (909) 880-5200
Financial Aid: (909) 880-5220
Housing: (909) 880-5246

DISTINGUISHING FEATURES: CSU San Bernardino students enjoy the personal attention possible on a small campus. Small class size fosters close student-faculty contact: More than seventy percent of classes have fewer than twenty-two students. Students have the opportunity for self-paced and independent study. Academic programs emphasize the small lecture/discussion/seminar format. The focus is on hands-on experience through computer applications, special study projects, and internships. Many majors are offered in the late day and evening hours so that working individuals may complete their college degree while maintaining a job. The Coachella Valley Center, serving upper-division and graduate students, is located in Palm Desert on the campus of College of the Desert Community College.
DEGREES OFFERED: Bachelor's, Master's.
COLLEGES: Schools of Business and Public Administration, Humanities, Education, Social and Behavioral Sciences, Natural Sciences.
UNDERGRADUATE MAJORS: 42. See this chapter: Undergraduate Degree Majors, page 10--68.
CALENDAR: Quarter system. Summer session.
ENROLLMENT: ***Total*** - 12,121. ***Graduate*** - 2,931. ***Undergraduate*** - 9,190: Men - 41%, women - 59%. ***Ethnic distribution of undergraduates:*** Hispanic - 19.4%, Black -8.4%, Asian/Pacific Islander - 8.1%, Native American/Alaskan - 1.0%, White - 50.5%, Unknown - 12.6%.
LOCATION: 430-acre, park-like setting in the foothills of the San Bernardino Mountains in Southern California's Inland Empire. Six miles north of San Bernardino and sixty miles east of Los Angeles.
CAMPUS LIFE: ***Clubs and organizations*** - 60. Fraternities and sororities - yes. ***Athletics:*** Intercollegiate - NCAA, Division II. Intramural sports - yes.
OTHER INFORMATION: ***Founded*** - 1960.
WASC Accredited - yes.

SAN DIEGO

San Diego State University
5300 Campanile Drive
San Diego, CA 92182
(619) 594-5000
Admissions: (619) 594-6871
Financial Aid: (619) 594-6323
Housing: (619) 594-6181

DISTINGUISHING FEATURES: San Diego State is a large, diverse institution with an average class size of thirty-five. More students attend San Diego State than any other university in California. The campus holds a special registration program in the Bay Area for northern California students, usually the first Saturday in June. Majors within the CSU system that are unique to San Diego State are Astronomy, Chemical Physics, and European Studies. The largest major is Psychology and the largest college is Business Administration. Several interdisciplinary majors are offered including International Business, one of the largest in the nation. Senior professors instruct lower-division classes as well as upper-division courses.
DEGREES OFFERED: Bachelor's, Master's.
COLLEGES: Arts and Letters, Business Administration, Education, Engineering, Health and Human Services, Professional Studies and Fine Arts, Sciences.
UNDERGRADUATE MAJORS: 77. See this chapter: Undergraduate Degree Majors, page 10--68.
CALENDAR: Semester system. Summer session.

na = not applicable nd = no data available

ENROLLMENT: ***Total*** - 28,131. ***Graduate*** - 5,832. ***Undergraduate*** - 22,299: Men - 48%, women - 52%. ***Ethnic distribution of undergraduates:*** Hispanic - 13.8%, Black - 5.7%, Asian/Pacific Islander - 13.8%, Native American/Alaskan - 0.9%, White - 54.1%, Unknown - 9.5%.
LOCATION: 300-acre campus on a hilltop known as Montezuma Mesa in the eastern part of the city of San Diego. Two hours from Los Angeles. Fifteen miles from the Mexican border and twelve miles from the Pacific Ocean.
CAMPUS LIFE: ***Clubs and organizations*** - 300. Fraternities and sororities - yes. ***Athletics:*** Intercollegiate - NCAA, Division I-A. Intramural sports - yes.
OTHER INFORMATION: ***Founded*** - 1897.
WASC Accredited - yes.

SAN FRANCISCO

San Francisco State University
1600 Holloway Avenue
San Francisco, CA 94132
(415) 338-1111
Admissions: (415) 338-2037
Financial Aid: (415) 338-1851
Housing: (415) 338-1067

DISTINGUISHING FEATURES: San Francisco State provides a diversity of programs in an urban setting. The campus attracts students from a wide variety of cultural backgrounds and socioeconomic levels. Seventy-five percent come from the Bay Area. Most students live in the city and commute. Seminars can be as small as ten students or held in lecture halls for more than two-hundred. The campus is known for its School of Business, the Poetry Center, the Special Education Department, and the School of Creative Arts. On the campus is the largest radio and television facility in Northern California. The Design and Industry Department has helped would-be inventors, designers and entrepreneurs transform their ideas into working prototypes. There are many opportunities to become involved in the Bay Area community through fieldwork, internships, and participation in community-related faculty research projects. SFS has joint doctoral degree programs in Special Education with UC Berkeley. The faculty is involved in research and public service throughout San Francisco. Evening and weekend courses meet the needs of part-time students.
DEGREES OFFERED: Bachelor's, Master's, Doctoral.
COLLEGES: Schools of Behavioral and Social Sciences; Business; Creative Arts; Education; Ethnic Studies; Health, Physical Education, Recreation and Leisure Studies; Humanities; Science, Extended Studies.
UNDERGRADUATE MAJORS: 89. See this chapter: Undergraduate Degree Majors, page 10--68.
CALENDAR: Semester system. Summer session.
ENROLLMENT: ***Total*** - 25,713. ***Graduate*** - 6,612. ***Undergraduate*** - 19,101: Men - 43%. women - 57%. ***Ethnic distribution of undergraduates:*** Hispanic - 10.3%, Black - 7.1%, Asian/Pacific Islander - 32.2%, Native American/Alaskan - 0.7%, White - 34.0%, Unknown - 15.6%.
LOCATION: 95-acre campus in the southwestern corner of the city of San Francisco. One mile from the Pacific Ocean and twenty minutes by freeway or public transportation from downtown.
CAMPUS LIFE: ***Clubs and organizations*** - 200. Fraternities and sororities - yes. ***Athletics:*** Intercollegiate - NCAA, Division II. Intramural sports - yes.
OTHER INFORMATION: ***Founded*** - 1899.
WASC Accredited - yes.

SAN JOSE

San Jose State University
One Washington Square
San Jose, CA 95192
(408) 924-1000
Admissions: (408) 924-2000
Financial Aid: (408) 924-6100
Housing: (408) 924-6160

DISTINGUISHING FEATURES: San Jose State blends classroom learning with practical hands-on experience through its close proximity and interaction with the world center of high technology, Silicon Valley. Nearly seventy-five percent of the total student body comes from the greater San Francisco Bay Area. The campus is especially known for its Schools of Engineering and Business. Unique facilities include the western world's only undergraduate nuclear science laboratory, an aeronautics department at San Jose International Airport, an art foundry/ metal sculpture facility, a deep-sea research ship, state-of-the-art computer-aided design engineering and manufacturing laboratories, and an electro-acoustical recording studio. Many faculty are engaged in applied research that involves students.
DEGREES OFFERED: Bachelor's, Master's.
COLLEGES: Applied Arts and Sciences, Business, Education, Engineering, Humanities and the Arts, Science, Social Sciences, Social Work.
UNDERGRADUATE MAJORS: 87. See this chapter: Undergraduate Degree Majors, page 10--68.
CALENDAR: Semester system. Summer session.
ENROLLMENT: ***Total*** - 27,057. ***Graduate*** - 5,803. ***Undergraduate*** - 21,254: Men - 50%, women - 50%. ***Ethnic distribution of undergraduates:*** Hispanic - 11.9%, Black - 4.7%, Asian/Pacific Islander - 29.3%, Native American/Alaskan - 0.7%, White - 40.9%, Unknown - 12.5%.
LOCATION: In downtown San Jose on nineteen square blocks in the central core of the city. In the heart of Silicon Valley, the world center of high technology research and development. One hour from San Francisco, forty minutes from the mountains and beaches of Santa Cruz.
CAMPUS LIFE: ***Clubs and organizations*** - 220. Fraternities and sororities - yes. ***Athletics:*** Intercollegiate - NCAA, Division I-A. Intramural sports - yes.
OTHER INFORMATION: ***Founded*** - 1857.
WASC Accredited - yes.

SAN LUIS OBISPO

California Polytechnic State University, San Luis Obispo
San Luis Obispo, CA 93407
(805) 756-1111
Admissions: (805) 756-2311
Financial Aid: (805) 756-2927
Housing: (805) 756-1225

DISTINGUISHING FEATURES: Cal Poly San Luis Obispo specializes in preparing students in applied technical and professional fields. Every applicant must declare a major. The institution emphasizes a practical, learning-by-doing, career-oriented approach and provides extensive opportunities for career internships, cooperative education, and field work. Students begin work in their major field of study during the freshman year in a variety of laboratory situations — indoors, outdoors, and on the job. The campus is known nationally for its professional programs in agriculture, architecture, business, computer science, engineering, home economics, science and mathematics. Additionally it offers excellent programs in teacher education, communicative arts, humanities, and social sciences. Small classes allow individual student attention.
DEGREES OFFERED: Bachelor's, Master's.
COLLEGES: Agriculture, Architecture and Environmental Design, Business, Engineering, Liberal Arts, Science and Mathematics, University Center for Teacher Education.
UNDERGRADUATE MAJORS: 55. See this chapter: Undergraduate Degree Majors, page 10--68.
CALENDAR: Quarter system. Summer sessions.
ENROLLMENT: ***Total*** - 15,449. ***Graduate*** - 1,134. ***Undergraduate*** - 14,315: Men - 59%, women - 41%. ***Ethnic distribution of undergraduates:*** Hispanic - 14.5%, Black - 2.0%, Asian/Pacific Islander - 12.6%, American Indian/Alaskan - 1.3%, White - 59.9%, Unknown - 9.7%.
LOCATION: A 374-acre, central campus plus an additional 4,795 acres of rolling campus devoted to student farming, experimental architecture and other outdoor laboratory study. In San Luis Obispo on California's Central Coast, midway between San Francisco and Los Angeles. Friendly, small-campus, small-town feeling.
CAMPUS LIFE: ***Clubs and organizations*** - 350. Fraternities and sororities - yes. ***Athletics:*** Intercollegiate - NCAA, Division I-AA. Intramural sports - yes.
OTHER INFORMATION: ***Founded*** - 1901.
WASC Accredited - yes.

SAN MARCOS

California State University, San Marcos
820 West Vallecitos Boulevard
San Marcos, CA 92096-0001
(619) 752-4000
Admissions: (619) 752-4800
Financial Aid: (619) 752-4850
Housing: (619) 752-4952

DISTINGUISHING FEATURES: San Marcos opened its doors in September 1990 to four-hundred eighty upper-division undergraduate students (juniors and seniors) and graduate students. By fall 1995, the San Marcos campus will be a full-service, comprehensive California State University with a projected enrollment of 2,750. It replaces the North County Center administered by San Diego State University. The campus offers small class size, close interaction with peers and faculty members, and innovative programs. Because of the newness of the institution, students have the unique opportunity to impact the creation of academic programs and services, student governance systems, activities, and athletic programs.
DEGREES OFFERED: Bachelor's.
COLLEGES: Arts and Sciences, Business Administration, Education.
UNDERGRADUATE MAJORS: 15. See this chapter: Undergraduate Degree Majors, page 10--68.
CALENDAR: Semester system. Summer session.
ENROLLMENT: ***Total*** - 2,372. ***Graduate*** - 322. ***Undergraduate*** - 2,050: Men - 33%, women - 67%. ***Ethnic distribution of undergraduates:*** Hispanic - 12.8%, Black - 2.8%, Asian/Pacific Islander - 4.8%, American Indian/Alaskan - 1.2%, White - 67.1%, Unknown - 11.3%.
LOCATION: 304-acre hillside in the southeastern section of the city of San Marcos, twelve miles inland from the northern part of the city of San Diego.
CAMPUS LIFE: ***Clubs and organizations*** - 30. Fraternities and sororities - no. ***Athletics:*** Intercollegiate - no. Intramural sports - no.
OTHER INFORMATION: ***Founded*** - 1990.
WASC Accredited - nd.

SONOMA

Sonoma State University
1801 East Cotati Avenue
Rohnert Park, CA 94928
(707) 664-2880
Admissions: (707) 664-2778
Financial Aid: (707) 664-2389
Housing: (707) 664-2541

DISTINGUISHING FEATURES: Sonoma State offers a distinctive program in the liberal arts and sciences, including traditional majors in the arts and humanities, natural sciences, and social sciences, as well as business, economics, computer science and other professional programs. The campus has grown by one-third in the last five years. Emphasis is on the open exchange of ideas and close human and intellectual relationships among its students and faculty. Average class size is fifteen with less than two percent of classes larger than fifty students. Field experience is available through voluntary community involvement and career internships. The Hutchins School of Liberal Studies offers a different approach to studies, stressing the interrelatedness of knowledge and focusing on major questions of human existence. In Hutchins, general education is provided in interdisciplinary "core" seminars of twelve units each, one each semester for four semesters. Each seminar consists of ten to fifteen students and a single instructor. Students receive Credit/No Credit and a written evaluation of their work at the end of each semester during the first two years; students can get a letter grade as well.
DEGREES OFFERED: Bachelor's, Master's.
COLLEGES: Schools of Arts and Humanities, Business and Economics, Education, Natural Sciences, Social Sciences, Hutchins School of Liberal Studies.
UNDERGRADUATE MAJORS: 37 See this chapter: Undergraduate Degree Majors, page 10--68.

na = not applicable nd = no data available

CALIFORNIA STATE UNIVERSITY

CALENDAR: Semester system. Summer session.
ENROLLMENT: ***Total***-6,551. ***Graduate***- 1,053. ***Undergraduate*** - 5,498: Men - 40%, women - 60%. ***Ethnic distribution of undergraduates:*** Hispanic - 8.5%, Black - 3.4%, Asian/Pacific Islander - 4.4%, Native American/Alaskan - 1.3%, White - 69.2%, Unknown - 13.2%.
LOCATION: 220-acre, park-like campus, nestled between rolling hills and farmland and the town of Rohnert Park. A few miles south of Santa Rosa. Less than an hour's drive north of San Francisco. Near the Napa and Sonoma vineyards and wineries.
CAMPUS LIFE: ***Club and organizations*** - 50. Fraternities and sororities - no. ***Athletics:*** Intercollegiate - NCAA, Division II. Intramural sports - yes.
OTHER INFORMATION: ***Founded*** - 1960.
WASC Accredited - yes.

STANISLAUS

California State University, Stanislaus
801 West Monte Vista Avenue
Turlock, California 95380
(209) 667-3122
Admissions: (209) 667-3152
Financial Aid: (209) 667-3336
Housing: (209) 667-3676

DISTINGUISHING FEATURES: Cal State Stanislaus is a small university with a low student/faculty ratio and limited class size. Staff is available for individualized instruction and interaction. The campus offers a unique 4-1-4 academic calendar consisting of two thirteen-week semesters and a month-long Winter Term in January. The Winter Term provides the opportunity for the uninterrupted, concentrated pursuit of a single area of study. Students may choose from general education courses or courses emphasizing off-campus field work, foreign study, travel, research, and individual study projects designed to immerse them in an environment of interest and supplement regular coursework. The institution offers programs in business, arts, letters, sciences, and education. Psychology is the most popular major. Music, computer science, and biology are also popular. A Cooperative Education program is available to assist students to gain career experience. Classes and degree programs are offered at off-campus sites throughout the six-county area served by Cal State Stanislaus.
DEGREES OFFERED: Bachelor's, Master's.
COLLEGES: Colleges of Arts, Letters, and Sciences. Schools of Business Administration, Education.
UNDERGRADUATE MAJORS: 70. See this chapter: Undergraduate Degree Majors, page 10--68.
CALENDAR: Semester system with a month-long Winter Term in January, 4-1-4 academic calendar; Summer session.
ENROLLMENT: ***Total***-5,857. ***Graduate***- 1,284. ***Undergraduate*** - 4,573: Men - 40%, women - 60%. ***Ethnic distribution of undergraduates:*** Hispanic - 16.2%, Black - 3.6%, Asian/Pacific Islander - 8.2%, Native American/Alaskan - 1.6%, White - 57.3%, Unknown - 13.3%.
LOCATION: 230-acre, park-like campus in the city of Turlock, midway between Sacramento and Fresno. In the heart of Central California between the Sierra Nevada Mountains and Yosemite and the cultural life of the San Francisco Bay Area.
CAMPUS LIFE: ***Clubs and organizations*** - 40. Fraternities and sororities - no. ***Athletics:*** Intercollegiate - NCAA, Division II. Intramural sports - yes.
OTHER INFORMATION: ***Founded*** - 1957.
WASC Accredited - yes.

na = not applicable nd = no data available

CALIFORNIA STATE UNIVERSITY

CALIFORNIA STATE UNIVERSITY

UNDERGRADUATE DEGREE MAJORS

Degree majors are listed alphabetically under descriptive terminologies, which may differ slightly from terminologies in some catalogs. An applicant should select the degree major that best represents the specific academic program sought at the campus to which application is made. The general categories of Agriculture, Business, Education, Engineering, Natural Resources, and Psychology are listed alphabetically, and specific programs within those subject areas appear as subheadings under those general headings. All other programs are listed in alphabetical order. This list does not include all concentrations, and groupings of courses other than degree majors are not shown. Call the campuses or consult campus catalogs for further details. See page 10--74 for additional notes and information on credential programs.

KEY TO SYMBOLS: BA, BS, BFA, etc. = Bachelor of Arts, Bachelor of Science, Bachelor of Fine Arts, etc. b = concentration within another Bachelor's degree major.

Degree Major	Bakersfield	Chico	Dominguez Hills	Fresno	Fullerton	Hayward	Humboldt	Long Beach	Los Angeles	Monterey Bay	Northridge	Pomona	Sacramento	San Bernardino	San Diego	San Francisco	San Jose	San Luis Obispo	San Marcos	Sonoma	Stanislaus
UNDECLARED (1)																					
✓ Freshmen/Sophomores	✓	✓	✓	✓	✓	✓	✓	✓	✓	✓	✓	✓	✓	✓	✓	✓	✓			✓	✓
✓ Juniors/Seniors	✓	✓	✓	✓		✓	✓	✓	✓	✓	✓		✓	✓	✓	✓	✓			✓	✓
Advertising				b	b	b			b								BS				
African-American Studies			BA		b	b		BA	BA		BA		b	b	BA	BA	BA			BA	
AGRICULTURE (Also see Natural Resources)																					
✓ Agricultural Biology	b											BS									
✓ Agricultural Business/Management/Marketing		BS		BS								BS						BS			
✓ Agricultural Economics				b								b									
✓ Agricultural Education & Science				BS								BS						BS			
✓ Agricultural Engineering: See Engineering																					
✓ Agricultural Systems Management		b		b														BS			
✓ Agriculture, Agricultural Science		BS		BS																	
✓ Agronomy, Crop Science		b		b								BS						BS			
✓ Animal Science		b		BS								BS						BS			
✓ Diary Science				b														BS			
✓ Enology				b																	
✓ Equine Industry												b									
✓ Food Science				b								b					b	BS			
✓ Fruit Science & Industry (Horticulture)				b								b						BS			
✓ Ornamental Horticulture				b								b						BS			
✓ Plant Science/Protection				BS														BS			
✓ Poultry Industry																		BS			
✓ Range Management		b		b			BS											BS			
✓ Soil Science				b								BS						BS			
✓ Veterinary, Pre-				b								b									
✓ Viticulture				b																	
American Studies		BA			BA							BA		BA	BA	BA	b				
Anthropology	BA	BA	BA	BA	BA	BA	BA	BA	BA		BA	BS	BA	BA	BA	BA	BA			BA	BA
Applied Studies																					BS
Architecture (Also see City Planning; Engr.; Landscape Arch.)												BArch						BArch			
Art (Also see Graphic Design)	BA	BA	BA	BA	BA	BA	BA	BA	BA	BA	BA	BA	BA	BA	BA	BA	BA			BA	BA
Art (Studio Performance)		BFA			BFA			BFA									BFA			BFA	

KEY TO SYMBOLS: BA, BS, BFA, etc. = Bachelor of Arts, Bachelor of Science, Bachelor of Fine Arts, etc. b = concentration within another Bachelor's degree major.

Degree Major	Bakersfield	Chico	Dominguez Hills	Fresno	Fullerton	Hayward	Humboldt	Long Beach	Los Angeles	Monterey Bay	Northridge	Pomona	Sacramento	San Bernardino	San Diego	San Francisco	San Jose	San Luis Obispo	San Marcos	Sonoma	Stanislaus
Art History	b	b	b		b	b	b	b	b		b			b	b		b			b	b
Asian-American Studies: See Ethnic Studies																					
Asian Studies								BA					BA		BA						
Astronomy															BA,BS	b					
Aviation									b								BS				
Behavioral Sciences			BA							BA		BA					BA				
Bilingual/Bicultural Studies (Also see Education)												b	b	b							
Biochemistry	b	b	b		BS	b	b	BS	BS		BS		b	b	b	BS	b	BS	b		
Biology, Biological Sciences (Also see Botany, Microbiology, etc.)	BS	BS	BS	BS	BA	BA,BS	BS	BA,BS	BS		BA,BS	BS	BA,BS	BA,BS	BA,BS	BA,BS	BA,BS	BS	BS	BA,BS	BA,BS
Biotechnology												BS									
Botany					b		BS					BS				b	b			b	b
BUSINESS ADMINISTRATION																					
✓ Accountancy	b	b	b	b	b	b	b	b	b		b	b	b	b	b	b	b	b	b	b	b
✓ Agri-Business: See Agriculture																					
✓ Banking																b					
✓ Business Administration	BS	BS	BS	BS	BA²	BS	BS	BS²	BS	BS	BS	BS	BS	BA,BS	BS²	BS²	BS²	BS	BS	BS	BS
✓ Business Computer Telecommunications						b															
✓ Business Economics					b	b			b					b						b	
✓ Business Education							b		BS		BS										
✓ Business, Special Interest									b												
✓ Business Statistics									b												
✓ Finance	b	b	b	b	b	b	b	b	b		b	b	b	b	b	b	b	b		b	b
✓ Financial Services				b											b						
✓ High Technology Management																			b		
✓ Hotel & Restaurant/Hospitality Management										b		BS				BS	BS				
✓ Industrial Relations									b							b		b			
✓ Information Systems	b	BS	b	b	b	b	BS	b	BS		b	b	b	b	b	b	b	b			BS
✓ Insurance				b									b								
✓ Internal Auditing																b					
✓ International (World) Business			b	b	BA			b	b	b	b	b	b	b	BA	b	b	b		b	
✓ Management (Business)	b	b	b	b	b	b	b	b	b		b	b	b	b	b	b	b	b			b
✓ Management Science (Operations Research/Management Systems) Also see Quantitative Methods		b			b						b			b						b	b
✓ Marketing (Management)	b	b	b	b	b	b	b	b	b		b	b	b	b	b	b	b	b		b	b
✓ Office Administration/Administrative Services				b					b		b	b				b					
✓ Personnel/Human Resources Management		b	b	b		b		b	b		b	b	b			b	b	b		b	b
✓ Production Operations Management		b	b			b		b	b		b	b	b	b	b		b	b			b
✓ Public Management: See Public Administration																					
✓ Public Relations (Listed alphabetically under P)																					
✓ Quantitative Methods (Also see Management Science)				b				b								b					
✓ Real Estate				b		b			b		b	b	b		b	b					
✓ Retailing									b												
✓ Service Sector Management																			b		
✓ Small Business			b			b			b	b				b		b					
✓ Transportation Management				b					b							b					

CALIFORNIA STATE UNIVERSITY

KEY TO SYMBOLS: BA, BS, BFA, etc. = Bachelor of Arts, Bachelor of Science, Bachelor of Fine Arts, etc. b = concentration within another Bachelor' s degree major.

Degree Major	Bakersfield	Chico	Dominguez Hills	Fresno	Fullerton	Hayward	Humboldt	Long Beach	Los Angeles	Monterey Bay	Northridge	Pomona	Sacramento	San Bernardino	San Diego	San Francisco	San Jose	San Luis Obispo	San Marcos	Sonoma	Stanislaus
Cell Biology					b		b				b					b			b	b	
Chemical Physics															BS						
Chemistry	BS	BS	BA,BS	BA,BS	BA,BS	BA,BS	BA,BS	BA,BS	BA,BS		BA,BS	BS	BA,BS	BA,BS	BA,BS	BA,BS	BA,BS	BS	BS	BA,BS	BA,BS
Child Development	BA	BA		BS	BS	b	b		BA	b	BA		BA	b	BS		BA	b			BA
Chinese																BA	BA				
Cinema (Also See Film)		b														BA					
City/Regional/Urban Planning												BS						BS		b	
Classics															BA	BA					
Clinical Science: See Medical Technology																					
Cognitive Studies																					BA
Communications (Includes Mass Communication. Also see Speech & Radio - Television)	BA	BA	BA	BA	BA	BA				BA		BS	BA	BA						BA	BA
Communicative Disorders: See Speech Pathology																					
Comparative Literature					BA			BA							BA	BA					
Computer Information Systems: See Infor. Systems under Business																					
Computer Science	BS	BS	BS	BS	BS	BS	b	BS	BS		BS	BS	BS	BS	BS	BS	BS	BS	b	BS	BS
Construction		BS		BS				b				b	b					BS			
Corrections: See Criminal Justice or Social Work																					
Creative Writing						b		b			b			b		b					
Criminalistics (Forensic Science)													BS								
Criminal Justice /Criminal Justice Administration	BA	b	b	b	BA	BS		BS	BS				BS	BA	BS	b	BS	b		BA	BA
Criminal Justice - Corrections				b		b		b					b								b
Criminal Justice - Security								b													
Criminology				BS								b									
Cultural Resources Management			b																		
Cytotechnology			b																		
Dance				b	BA	b		BA	b				b		BA	BA	BA			b	
Dance (Performance)								BFA													
Deaf Studies											BA										
Dietetics & Food Administration (Includes Nutritional Science)		BS		BS				BS	BS		b	BS		BS	BS	BS	BS	BS			
Drama: See Theatre Arts																					
Earth Sciences (Also see Geology & Geography)		b	b					BS	BA		BA	BA								b	b
Ecology/Environmental Biology (Also see Environmental Studies)				b	b	b	b			b	b				b	b	b	BS	b	b	
Economics	BA	BA	BA	BA	BA	BA	BA	BA	BA		BA	BS	BA	BA	BA	BA	BA,BS	BS	BA	BA	BA
EDUCATION (Also see Credentials)																					
✓ Bilingual-Crosscultural (Also see alphabetical listing under B)																					b
✓ Child Development	BA	BA		BS	BS	b	b		BA	b	BA		BA	b	BS		BA	b			BA
✓ Communication Handicapped				b																	
✓ Early Childhood Education																		b			
✓ Health & Safety (See Health)																					
✓ Instructional Media/Technology (Audio-Visual)		BS																			
✓ School Psychology: See Psychology																					
ENGINEERING																					
✓ Aeronautical/Aerospace												BS			BS		BS	BS			
✓ Agricultural												BS						BS			

KEY TO SYMBOLS: BA, BS, BFA, etc. = Bachelor of Arts, Bachelor of Science, Bachelor of Fine Arts, etc. b = concentration within another Bachelor's degree major.

Degree Major	Bakersfield	Chico	Dominguez Hills	Fresno	Fullerton	Hayward	Humboldt	Long Beach	Los Angeles	Monterey Bay	Northridge	Pomona	Sacramento	San Bernardino	San Diego	San Francisco	San Jose	San Luis Obispo	San Marcos	Sonoma	Stanislaus
✓ Architectural																		BS			
✓ Biomedical								b													
✓ Chemical								BS				BS					BS				
✓ Civil		BS		BS	BS			BS,CE	b		b	BS	BS		BS	BS	BS	BS			
✓ Computer		BS		BS				b				b	BS				BS	BS			
✓ Electrical				BS				BS	b		b	BS			BS	BS	BS	BS			
✓ Electrical/Electronic		BS			BS								BS								
✓ Electronic												b									
✓ Engineering					BS[2]			BS[2]	BS		BS						BS				
✓ Engineering Materials								b									BS				
✓ Engineering Science					b													BS			
✓ Environmental Engineering												b						BS			
✓ Environmental Resources Engineering							BS														
✓ Industrial & Systems																	BS				
✓ Industrial Engineering				BS							b	BS						BS			
✓ Industrial Management								b													
✓ Manufacturing												BS						BS			
✓ Materials																		BS			
✓ Mechanical		BS		BS	BS			BS	b	BS	b	BS	BS		BS	BS	BS	BS			
✓ Ocean								b													
✓ Petroleum												b									
✓ Structural					b																
✓ Surveying				BS								b									
✓ Water Pollution: See Environmental																					
ENGINEERING TECHNOLOGY (Also See Construction)																					
✓ Electronic Technology								b				b						BS			
✓ Engineering Technology								BS				BS	BS					BS			
✓ Manufacturing Technology								b													
✓ Mechanical Technology													b					b			
English	BA	BA	BA	BA	BA	BA	BA	BA	BA		BA	BA	BA	BA	BA	BA	BA	BA	BA	BA	BA
Entomology																	b				b
Environmental Studies	b	b				BA	BA			b			BA	BA			BA,BS	b		BA	
Ethnic Studies (Includes Asian & Native American. (Also see Afro-American & Mexican American)		BA			BA[2]	BA					b		BA								
European Studies															BA		b				
Exercise Physiology		b																			
Film (Also See Cinema)											b						b				
Film & Creative Arts (Also see Art, Music, & Theatre Arts)										BA						BA	BA		BA		
Fire Protection Administration									BS												
Foods & Nutrition: See Dietetics																					
French		BA		BA	BA	BA	BA	BA	BA		BA		BA	BA	BA	BA	BA			BA	BA
Genetics																					b
Geography		BA	BA	BA	BA	BA,BS	BA	BA	BA		BA	BS	BA	BA	BA	BA	BA			BA	BA
Geology/Geosciences (Also see Earth Science)	BS	BS	BS	BS	BS	BA,BS	BA,BS	BS	BS		BS	BS	BA,BS	BS	BS	BA,BS	BA,BS			BA,BS	BS
German		BA		BA	BA		BA	BA			BA		BA		BA	BA	BA			BA	

CALIFORNIA STATE UNIVERSITY

KEY TO SYMBOLS: BA, BS, BFA, etc. = Bachelor of Arts, Bachelor of Science, Bachelor of Fine Arts, etc. b = concentration within another Bachelor' s degree major.

Degree Major	Bakersfield	Chico	Dominguez Hills	Fresno	Fullerton	Hayward	Humboldt	Long Beach	Los Angeles	Monterey Bay	Northridge	Pomona	Sacramento	San Bernardino	San Diego	San Francisco	San Jose	San Luis Obispo	San Marcos	Sonoma	Stanislaus
Gerontology						b			b				BS		BA						
Government (Also see Political Science)													BA								
Government-Journalism													BA								
Graphic Communications (Printing)		b		b					b									BS			
Graphic Design/Applied Art		b	b	b	b			b	b		b	b		b	b		BS	BS			
Health & Safety Studies													BS								b
Health Care Management/Administration		b	b	b							b		b	b			b				
Health: Community & School		b	b	b				b	b		b		b	b		b	b				
Health: Environmental, Occupational, & Safety				b					b		BS			b	BS		b				
Health Science	BS	BS	BS	BS		BS		BS	BS		BS			BS	BS	BS	BS				
History	BA	BA	BA	BA	BA	BA	BA	BA	BA		BA	BA	BA	BA	BA	BA	BA	BA	BA	BA	BA
Home Economics				BA				BA	BA		BS	BS	BA			BA		BS			
Hotel/Hospitality Management: See Business																					
Human Development						BA		BA						BA				BS			
Humanities		BA									BA	BA	BA	BA	BA	BA	BA				
Human Services			BA		BS									BA							
India Studies																				BA	
Industrial Arts				BA					BA							BA	BA				
Industrial Design								BS									BS				
Industrial Technology		BS		BS			BS		BS							BS	BS	BS			
Information & Communication Studies: See Communications																					
Information Systems (Listed under Business)																					
Interior Design		b		BA				b					BA		b	b	BS	b			
International Relations/Affairs	b	BA									b		b			BA		b			b
International Studies						BA		BA		BA											
Italian																BA					
Japanese					BA			BA	BA							BA	BA				
Journalism (Also see Communications)		BA	b		b	b	BA	BA			BA	b	BA		BA	BA	BS	BS			
Labor Studies			BA													BA					
Land Resourses Management	BS					b															
Landscape Architecture												BS						BLA			
Landscape Irrigation Science												BS									
Language Studies						b				BA											
Latin American Studies		BA			BA	BA			BA						BA						
Liberal Studies	BA	BA	BA	BA	BA	BA	BA	BA	BA	BA	BA	BA	BA	BA	BA	BA	BA	BA	BA	BA 7	BA
Linguistics			b	BA	BA						BA				BA		BA				
Literature (Also see English)	b		b								b					b					
Marine Biology					b		b	BS			b				b	b	b	b		b	
Mass Communication: See Communications																					
Mathematics	BS	BS	BA	BA	BA	BS	BA	BS	BA,BS		BA,BS	BS	BA	BA,BS	BA,BS	BA	BA	BS	BS	BA,BS	BA,BS
Mathematics, Applied		b			b	b	b	b	b		b	b	b			BS	BS			b	
Medical Laboratory Technology (Clinical Science)	b	b	BS			b	b	b	BS		b	b	b		b	BS	b	b		b	
Meteorology																b	BS				
Mexican-American/La Raza Studies	b		BA	BA	b	b		BA	BA		BA		b	b	BA	BA				BA	
Microbiology		BS	b		b		b	BS			b	BS	b		BA,BS	b	b	BS		b	b

KEY TO SYMBOLS: BA, BS, BFA, etc. = Bachelor of Arts, Bachelor of Science, Bachelor of Fine Arts, etc. b = concentration within another Bachelor's degree major.

Degree Major	Bakersfield	Chico	Dominguez Hills	Fresno	Fullerton	Hayward	Humboldt	Long Beach	Los Angeles	Monterey Bay	Northridge	Pomona	Sacramento	San Bernardino	San Diego	San Francisco	San Jose	San Luis Obispo	San Marcos	Sonoma	Stanislaus
Molecular Biology													b		b		b		b		
Museum Studies														b							
Music Education		b	b	b	b		b	b						b	BA					b	
Music	BA	BA	BA	BA	BA	BA	BA	BA	BA		BA	BA	BA	BA		BA	BA	BA		BA	BA
Music (Performing)		b		b	BM			BM	BM		BM		BM		BM	BM	BM			b	
NATURAL RESOURCES																					
✓ Fisheries							BS														
✓ Forestry							BS											BS			
✓ Natural Resources Planning & Interpretation							BS														
✓ Range Land Resource Science		b		b			BS														
✓ Wildlife Management							BS											b			
Natural Science																	BA				
Nuclear Medicine Technology			b																		
Nursing (Also see Health Sciences)	BS	BS	BS[4,5]	BS	BS[4]	BS	BS	BS	BS		BS[4]		BS	BS	BS	BS	BS			BS	BS[4]
Nutrition: See Dietetics																					
Occupational Therapy																	BS				
Oceanography							BS			BS							b				
Park Administration		b											b					b			
Philosophy	BA	BA	BA	BA	BA	BA	BA	BA	BA		BA	BA	BA	BA	BA	BA	BA	BA		BA	BA
Philosophy & Religion																BA					
Physical Education	BS	BA	BA	BS	BS	BS	BA	BA	BS		BA	BS	BS	BS	BS	BS	BS	BS		BS	BA
Physical Science				BA		BS	BS		BS				BA		BS	b	BA	BS			BA
Physical Therapy				BS				BS			b		B,S								
Physics	BS	BS	BS	BA,BS	BS	BS	BA,BS	BA,BS	BA,BS		BS	BS	BA,BS	BA,BS	BA,BS	BA,BS	BA,BS	BS		BA,BS	BA,BS
Physiology				b				b								b	b				
Political Science (Also see Government)	BA	BA	BA	BA	BA	BA	BA	BA	BA		BA	BA		BA	BA	BA	BA	BA	BA	BA	BA
PSYCHOLOGY																					
Psychology (Also see Behavioral Sciences, Education)	BA	BA	BA	BA	BA	BA,BS	BA	BA	BA		BA	BA	BA	BA	BA	BA	BA	BS	BA	BA	BA
✓ Developmental																					b
✓ Educational: See Education																					
✓ Industrial						b											b				
Public Administration	BA	BA	BS	BA	b	b		b	b		b	b		b	BA		b	b			b
Public Relations		b	b	b	b	b	b	b	b								BS				
Quality Assurance								b													
Radiological & Health Physics								b			b										
Radio-Television (Telecommunications & Broadcast Communications)		b	b		b	b		BA	BA		BA	b			BA,BS	BA	BA				
Recreation Administration		BS	BA	BS		BS		BA			BS		BS		BS	BA	BS	BS			
Rehabilitation Counseling									BS												
Religious Studies	BA	BA		b	BA	b	BA	BA			BA		b		BA		BA				
Russian				BA											BA	BA					
Russian Area Studies					BA										BA						
Science																BA					
Social Sciences (Also see Anthropology, Sociology, etc.)		BA		BA			BA		BA	BA		BS	BA	BA	BA	BA	BA	BS	BA		BA
Social Work		BA		BA		b	BA	BA	BA		b	b	BA	b	BA	BA	BA				
Sociology	BA	BA	BA	BA	BA	BA	BA	BA	BA		BA	BA	BA	BA	BA	BA	BA		BA	BA	BA

CALIFORNIA STATE UNIVERSITY

KEY TO SYMBOLS: BA, BS, BFA, etc. = Bachelor of Arts, Bachelor of Science, Bachelor of Fine Arts, etc.   b = concentration within another Bachelor' s degree major.

Degree Major	Bakersfield	Chico	Dominguez Hills	Fresno	Fullerton	Hayward	Humboldt	Long Beach	Los Angeles	Monterey Bay	Northridge	Pomona	Sacramento	San Bernardino	San Diego	San Francisco	San Jose	San Luis Obispo	San Marcos	Sonoma	Stanislaus
Spanish	BA	BA	BA	BA	BA	BA	BA	BA	BA		BA		BA	BA	BA	BA	BA		BA	BA	BA
Special Major/Interdisciplinary Studies	BA	BA,BS	BA,BS	BA	BA	BA,BS	BA,BS	BA	BA,BS	BA	BA	BA	BA,BS	BA		BA	BA,BS		BA	BA,BS	BA,BS
Speech (Communication)	b	b		BA	BA	BA	BA	BA	BA		BA	b			BA	BA	BA	BA			
Speech Pathology and Audiology/Communicative Disorders		BA		BA	BA	BS		BA	BA		BA		BS		BA	BA	BA				
Statistics		b			b	BS		b			b	b			b	BS	b	BS		b	b
Teaching English to Speakers of Other Languages																					b
Technical & Professional Writing																BA					
Theatre Arts/Drama	BA	BA	BA	BA	BA	BA	BA	BA	BA	b	BA	BA	BA	BA	BA	BA	BA			BA	BA
Therapeutic Recreation		b		b		b					b		b				b				
Urban Planning: See City Planning																					
Urban Studies											BA				BA	BA		b			b
Vocational Education		BVEd						BVEd,BS	BVEd					BVEd,BS	BVEd	BVEd		BVEd			BVEd
Women' s Studies															BA	BA			BA		
Zoology					b		BS					BS			b	b	b			b	b
SPECIAL PROGRAMS																					
✓ Hutchins School																				BA[7]	
✓ Interdisciplinary Studies			BA																		

NOTES:
1. Students undecided as to major may be admitted at class levels indicated by ✓.
2. While this is the terminology of the degree awarded, applicants listing this campus as first choice are requested not to use this degree major but one of the concentrations in this subject.
3. Offered in the School of Education.
4. Program available only to upper-division students possessing the R.N. All other programs admit both lower- and upper-division students.
5. Statewide Nursing Program.
6. Pre-Medical, Pre-Dental, Pre-Law, Pre-Engineering, etc.: Preprofessional programs are available on most campuses. Consult the campus catalog or contact the campus for recommended degree majors.
7. Hutchins School Multiple Subjects Waiver Program.

CREDENTIAL PROGRAMS

ALL CREDENTIAL APPLICANTS: The ✓ marks indicate programs approved by the campus and the Commission on Teacher Credentialing. The ✱ marks indicate those programs that will be submitted to the Commission in anticipation of approval. Applicants to programs that are not yet approved should contact the school or department of education on the campus at which they wish to apply. The Commission on Teacher Credentialing has authorized various areas of emphasis, such as bilingual-cross-cultural instruction and adapted physical education, for which individuals holding or pursuing teaching credentials may be certified. Information may be obtained from each campus.

Degree Major	Bakersfield	Chico	Dominguez Hills	Fresno	Fullerton	Hayward	Humboldt	Long Beach	Los Angeles	Monterey Bay	Northridge	Pomona	Sacramento	San Bernardino	San Diego	San Francisco	San Jose	San Luis Obispo	San Marcos	Sonoma	Stanislaus
TEACHING CREDENTIAL																					
Single Subject Instruction	✓	✓	✓	✓	✓	✓	✓	✓	✓	✱	✓	✓	✓	✓	✓	✓	✓	✓		✓	✓
Multiple Subject Instruction	✓	✓	✓	✓	✓	✓	✓	✓	✓	✱	✓	✓	✓	✓	✓	✓	✓	✓	✓	✓	✓
Designated Subjects (Adult, Driver, and Vocational Education)		✱	✓	✱				✓	✓			✓		✓		✓					
Adapted Physical Education Emphasis	✓	✓		✓		✓	✓	✓	✓		✓	✓	✓	✓	✓		✓	✓		✓	
SPECIALIST INSTRUCTION, including:																					
Agriculture Specialist		✓		✓								✓						✓			
Bilingual/Cross Cultural Specialist	✓	✓	✓			✓			✓	✱			✓	✓	✓	✓			✓		
Early Childhood Development				✓				✓												✓	
Language Development Specialist	✓	✓		✱					✓	✱			✓		✓	✓	✓		✓		✓
Mathematics Specialist				✱						✱							✓				
Reading/Language Arts Specialist	✓	✓		✓	✓	✓			✓		✓	✓	✓	✓	✓	✓	✓	✓		✓	✓
Special Education, Including:																					
Communication Handicapped				✓				✓			✓				✓	✓	✓				
Physically Handicapped									✓						✓	✓					
Learning Handicapped	✓	✓	✓	✓	✓	✓	✓	✓	✓		✓	✓	✓	✓	✓	✓	✓	✓	✓	✓	✓
Severely Handicapped	✓	✓	✓	✓	✓	✓		✓	✓		✓	✓	✓	✓	✓	✓	✓	✓	✓		✓
Gifted											✓				✓						
Visually Handicapped									✓							✓					
Special Education Resource Specialist	✓	✓	✓			✓		✓	✓		✓	✓	✓	✓	✓	✓	✓			✓	
SERVICE CREDENTIALS																					
Preliminary Administrative Services	✓	✓	✓	✓	✓	✓	✓	✓	✓		✓		✓	✓	✓	✓	✓	✓		✓	✓
Professional Administrative Services	✓	✓	✓	✓	✓	✓			✓		✓		✓	✓	✓	✓	✓	✓		✓	✓
Health (including School Nursing)				✓				✓	✓		✓		✓	✓	✓		✓				
Librarianship/Media		✓		✱				✓	✓								✓				
Pupil Personnel Services	✓	✓	✓	✓	✓	✓	✓	✓	✓		✓		✓	✓	✓	✓	✓	✓		✓	✓
Clinical Rehabilitative		✓		✓	✓	✓	✓	✓	✓		✓		✓		✓	✓	✓				
School Psychologist		✓	✓	✓		✓	✓	✓	✓		✓		✓		✓	✓	✓				

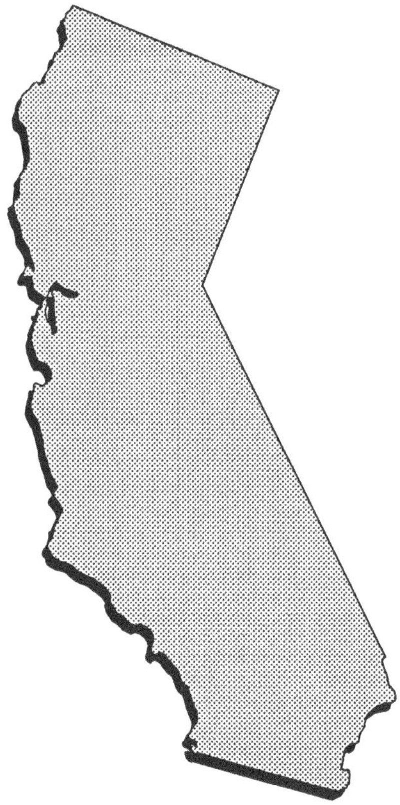

CALIFORNIA STATE UNIVERSITY

Chapter 11

UNIVERSITY OF CALIFORNIA

UNIVERSITY OF CALIFORNIA

The University of California is a state-funded institution, which opened in 1868. With nine campuses throughout California, UC is one of the largest and most renowned centers of higher education in the world. It is California's primary state-supported agency for research. All campuses follow the same admission guidelines and high academic standards, yet each has its own distinct character, atmosphere, and programs.

THE UNIVERSITY OF CALIFORNIA

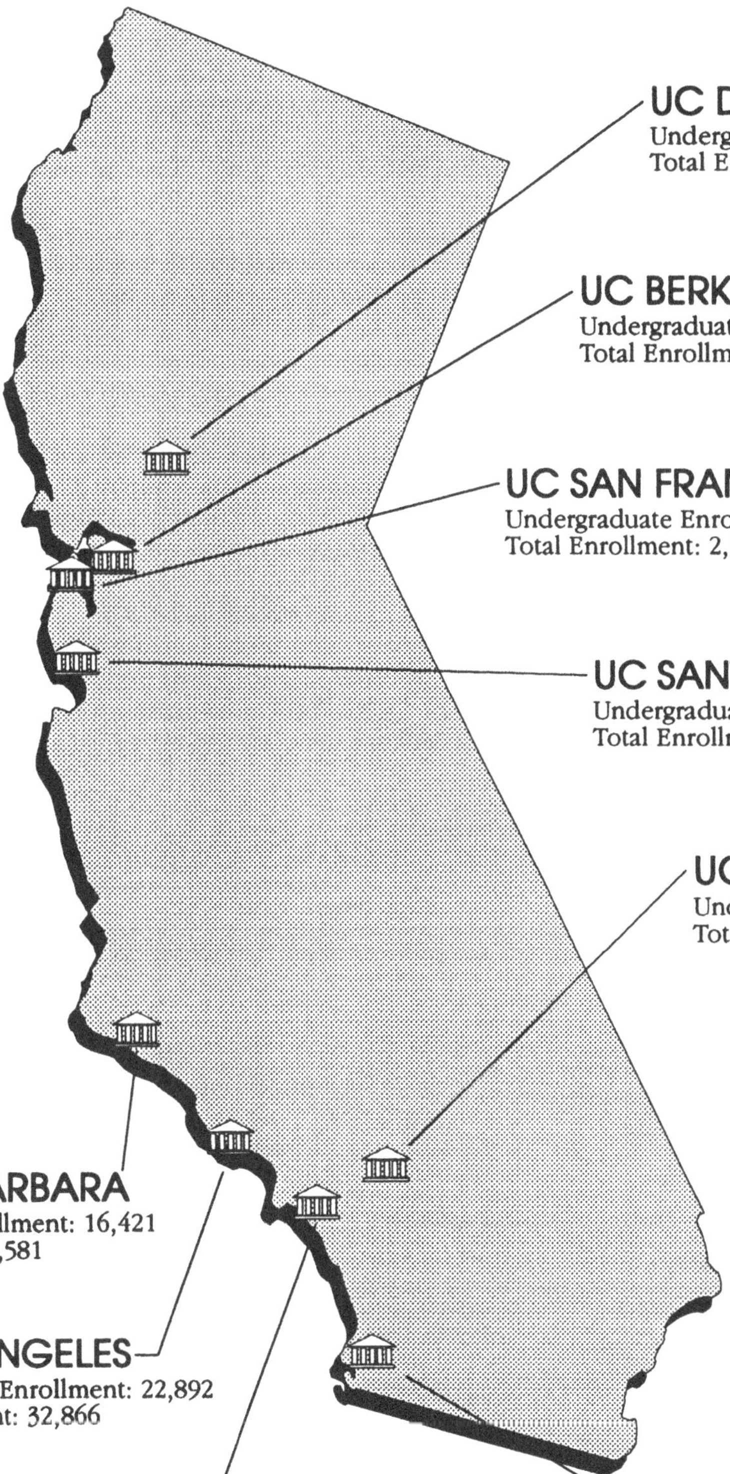

UNIVERSITY OF CALIFORNIA

OVERVIEW

A University of California education is in great demand!

With over 159,000 students, including undergraduate and graduate students, the University of California has nine campuses offering instruction in a wide range of fields. Approximately eighty-four percent of UC students are California residents. About one-fifth study at the graduate level. Among the campuses are five medical schools, three law schools, and a school of veterinary medicine, as well as many professional schools including business administration, education, engineering, and oceanography.

Admission data show that a University of California education is in great demand! 47,063 students applied for freshman admission for fall 1994 to at least one UC campus. This represents an increase of 3.8 percent compared to fall 1993. 88.1% were California residents, an increase of 4.7 percent over 1993. The eight undergraduate campuses that accept freshmen — the San Francisco campus does not — reviewed over 131,000 freshman applications; students applied to an average of 2.8 campuses.

There were 18,486 transfer applicants for fall 1994 admission to at least one UC campus. Nearly 73.3% of transfer applicants were from California Community Colleges, an increase of 1.9% over 1993. Each applicant applied to an average of 2.1 campuses bringing the total number of applications reviewed to almost 39,000.

The eight undergraduate campuses that accept freshmen reviewed over 131,000 freshman applications and almost 39,000 transfer applications.

The following table shows freshman statistics by campus for regularly admitted California residents and transfer statistics by campus for California Community College transfers for fall 1994. 5,409 non-residents applied for freshman admission; 3,012 were admitted, an admit rate of 55.7%. 4,467 students from four-year colleges and other colleges applied for transfer admission; 1,922 were admitted, an admit rate of 43.0%.

FALL 1994 ADMISSION REPORT

Campus	Freshman Level			Transfer Level		
	Applicants	Admits	Admit Rate	Applicants	Admits	Admit Rate
Berkeley	17,968	7,320	40.7%	5,165	1,811	35.1%
Davis	16,018	10,869	67.9%	4,305	2,856	66.3%
Irvine	15,222	10,650	70.0%	3,737	2,185	58.5%
Los Angeles	21,415	10,866	50.7%	6,359	3,388	53.3%
Riverside	9,378	6,516	69.5%	2,152	1,394	64.8%
San Diego	18,778	12,115	64.5%	3,449	2,451	71.1%
Santa Barbara	15,990	12,815	80.1%	4,326	2,604	60.2%
Santa Cruz	9,933	8,023	80.8%	2,962	2,178	73.5%
Total Applications Total Individuals	130,385 43,348	34,770	80.2%	39,148 15,172	11,009	72.6%

MINIMUM ADMISSION REQUIREMENTS

Admission to the University of California is quite competitive. The University selects freshman applicants from the top one-eighth of California's high school graduates. Approximately eight percent of California high school graduates continue their education at a UC campus.

All campuses in the UC system follow the same minimum admission requirements for freshmen. You are a freshman applicant if you have graduated from high school and have not enrolled in a regular session between September and June at any college or university. If you attend a college summer session immediately after graduating from high school, the University considers you to be a freshman applicant.

All campuses in the UC system follow the same minimum admission requirements for freshmen.

To be eligible for admission to UC as a freshman, you must meet the "a-f Subject Requirement," the "Examination Requirement," and the "Scholarship Requirement." Meeting the minimum requirements *does not necessarily guarantee* you a place at a campus or in the major of your choice. Because there are more applicants to the University than there are spaces, admission is very selective. The campuses further screen applicants and generally admit students with higher qualifications than the minimums required. See this chapter: Freshmen Selection Criteria,_page 11--23. However, you must have an understanding of these minimum requirements as a basis for designing your high school program and for setting your goals.

"a-f" SUBJECT REQUIREMENT

To satisfy the "a-f" Subject Requirement for admission, you must successfully complete the specific sequence of college-preparatory high school courses listed on the next two pages. You must achieve at least a C grade each semester for each listed course. Courses in which you receive a D, F, or Incomplete are considered subject omissions and must be made up. See this chapter: Commonly Asked Questions About Admissions, pages 11--13 to 11--15.

The "a-f" Subject Requirement is the sequence of college-preparatory courses that you must complete with a grade of C or higher.

UNIVERSITY OF CALIFORNIA

Each year your California high school submits a list of courses that it certifies as meeting the "a-f" Subject Requirement criteria established by the University of California. This list is the "Official University of California Certified Course List." To be accepted by the University, the courses you take to satisfy the "a-f" Subject Requirement must appear on this list of the high school you attended for the year you took the course. The course titles must appear on your academic record exactly as they appear on this list. Ask your high school for copies of this list for each school year you attend the high school to make sure you are enrolling in the appropriate certified courses.

Courses in mathematics and languages other than English *completed* in the seventh and eighth grades with at least a C grade may be counted toward the "a-f" Subject Requirement. However, your high school principal must certify that these courses are comparable to similar courses offered at your high school. Your high school transcript shows this certification.

"a - f" SUBJECT REQUIREMENT

University of California Freshman Applicants

(Grades of C or better are required)	REQUIREMENT
a. **United States History/ Social Science:** 2 Years Required	Two years of history/social science to include (a) one year of United States history, or one-half year of United States history and one-half year of civics or American government; and (b) one year of world history, cultures, and geography.
b. **English:** 4 Years Required	Four years of college-preparatory English which includes (a) frequent and regular writing and (b) reading of classic and modern literature, poetry, and drama. Not more than two semesters of ninth grade English is accepted for this requirement.
c. **Mathematics:** 3 Years Required, 4 Years Recommended	Three years, including elementary algebra, geometry, and second-year (advanced) algebra.
d. **Laboratory Science:** 2 Years Required, 3 Years Recommended	Two years of laboratory science providing fundamental knowledge in at least two of these three areas: Biology, chemistry, and physics. Laboratory courses in earth/space sciences are acceptable if they have as prerequisites - or provide basic knowledge in - biology, chemistry, or physics. Not more than one year of ninth grade laboratory science can be used to meet this requirement.
e. **Languages Other Than English:** 2 Years Required, 3 Years Recommended	Two years of a language other than English. Courses should emphasize speaking and understanding, and include instruction in grammer, vocabulary, reading, and composition. Alternative methods of certifying competence in a language other than English are described later in this chapter: Commonly Asked Questions About Admissions, page 11--16.
f. **College Preparatory Elective Courses:** 2 Years Required	Two years (four semesters), in addition to those required in "a-e" above, chosen from the following areas: Visual and performing arts, history, social science, English, advanced mathematics, laboratory science, and language other than English (a third year in the language used for the "e" requirement or two years of another language). A ninth grade introductory lab science course is not an acceptable elective.

This sequence of classes adds up to the minimum fifteen units required for admission. You will present a stronger record for admission and be more prepared for the University if you successfully complete work beyond this minimum.

The University uses only those semester grades earned in the "a-f" Subject Requirement courses taken in grades ten, eleven, and twelve to calculate a GPA for admission.

WORKSHEET

Use the worksheet, MY COURSE PLAN, below to monitor your progress toward meeting UC admission requirements.

Summer school: Enter courses completed in the summer following the ninth grade in the tenth grade column; enter courses completed following the tenth and eleventh grades in the eleventh grade column.

MY COURSE PLAN: "a-f" SUBJECT REQUIREMENT

University of California Freshman Applicants

ACADEMIC SUBJECTS	GRADES 7 OR 8	9TH GRADE			USE ONLY GRADES YOU EARNED IN THE 10TH, 11TH, AND 12TH GRADES TO CALCULATE YOUR GPA. 10TH GRADE			11TH GRADE			12TH GRADE		
(Grades of C or better are required)	Course Title	Course Title	Fall Grade	Spring Grade	Course Title	Fall Grade	Spring Grade	Course Title	Fall Grade	Spring Grade	Course Title	Fall Grade	Spring Grade
a. U.S. History/ Social Science: 2 Years Required													
b. English: 4 Years Required													
c. Mathematics: 3 Years Required, 4 Years Recommended													
d. Laboratory Science: 2 Years Required, 3 Years Recommended													
e. Language Other Than English: 2 Years Required, 3 Years Recommended													
f. College Preparatory Elective Courses: 2 Years Required													

You must take a minimum of fifteen units of the high school courses appearing on the Official University of California Certified Course List to fulfill the "a-f" Subject Requirement. At least seven of the fifteen units must be taken in the last two years of high school. (A unit equals an academic year— two semesters of high school study.)

EXAMINATION REQUIREMENT

You must take: (a) the SAT I: Reasoning Test or the ACT and (b) three SAT II: Subject Tests to meet the Examination Requirement.

In addition to successfully completing the appropriate "a-f" Subject Requirement courses, the University of California requires you to take college admissions tests. Your scores on these examinations are important admission criteria.

SAT I: REASONING TEST OR ACT, AND THREE SAT II: SUBJECT TESTS

You must submit the following test scores:

1. Either (a) *or* (b)

   a. Scholastic Assessment Test, SAT I: Reasoning Test. The verbal and mathematics scores on this test must be from the same testing session.
   b. American College Testing, ACT: The ACT composite score must be submitted.

And,

2. Scholastic Assessment Tests: SAT II: Subject Tests that must include *all* of the following:

   a. Writing Test.
   b. Mathematics Level I or Level IIC.
   c. One test in one of the following areas: English literature, foreign languages, sciences, or social studies. The test in English Literature may not be substituted for the Writing Test. You cannot use a second mathematics SAT II: Subject Test for the third Subject Test.

UNIVERSITY OF CALIFORNIA

If you are applying for fall admission, complete all testing no later than December, preferably November, of your senior year.

If you are applying for fall admission, complete all testing no later than December, preferably November, of your senior year to ensure that your scores receive full consideration. The UC campuses require that they receive all test results by January 2nd. UC recommends that for Subject Tests taken in the fall of your senior year, you do not use the Score Choice option of reviewing your SAT II: Subject Test scores before releasing them. You may neglect to release your scores in a timely manner and the processing of your application could be delayed and possibly prevented. See chapter 6: College Entrance Tests, SAT II: Subject Tests, page 6--30.

It is advisable to take all of your admissions tests at least once by the end of the last semester of your junior year. This assures you of having a complete set of test scores on file and alleviates some of the pressure of having to be certain to test in the fall of your senior year. You probably want to retest in the fall, anyway, to try to improve your scores.

TOEFL

If you live in the United States and your first or native language is not English, to be considered for admission to UC, the University may require you to take the Test of English as a Foreign Language (TOEFL) in addition to the SAT I: Reasoning Test or ACT and SAT II: Subject Tests. Individual campuses establish TOEFL requirements and score expectations based upon campus-specific factors. If you are an international student from a country where English is not the primary language, the University *requires* you to take the TOEFL. If you must take the TOEFL, plan to test by January of your senior year. See chapter 6: COLLEGE ENTRANCE TESTS, TOEFL, page 6--43.

If you are an international student from a country where English is not the primary language, UC requires you to take the TOEFL.

This table shows, by campus, when UC requires the TOEFL and the minimum score you must achieve to be admitted.

TOEFL REQUIREMENTS AT UNIVERSITY OF CALIFORNIA CAMPUSES

UC Campus	Minimum TOEFL Score	When is TOEFL Required?
Berkeley	550	Less than one year in a United States high school.
Davis	500	Less than two years in a United States high school.
Irvine	550	All nonimmigrant VISA students and permanent residents with less than two years in a United States high school.
Los Angeles	TOEFL score not used	Campus examination given. TOEFL advised but not required.
Riverside	550	All nonimmigrant VISA students regardless of the number of years in the United States.
San Diego	550	SAT I verbal score below 400 and less than two years in a United States high school.
Santa Barbara	500	Less than two years in a United States high school.
Santa Cruz	550	Less than four years in a United States high school.

Scholarship Requirement

Eligibility for admission as a California resident is based upon a combination of your "a-f" Subject Requirement GPA, and your SAT I or ACT college admissions test scores.

COMPUTING YOUR "A-F" SUBJECT REQUIREMENT GRADE POINT AVERAGE

Because you apply in November of your senior year, UC uses the "a-f" Subject Requirement GPA you report for your sophomore and junior years as your preliminary GPA for admission.

- The University of California uses those semester grades earned in the "a-f" Subject Requirement courses on your high school's Official University of California Certified Course List for grades ten, eleven, and twelve to calculate your grade point average. However, you must submit your GPA when you apply for admission in November of your senior year, well before your senior grades are available. *Therefore, in reality, UC uses only your sophomore and junior year grades to calculate your preliminary GPA for admission.*

- To open admission opportunities for students who distinguish themselves in the supplemental criteria, the admissions evaluators may use senior-year grades to compute the "a-f" Subject Requirement GPA. However, the admissions evaluators use this option infrequently.

Physical education grades are not counted in calculating your GPA, nor are electives that are not on the Official University of California Certified Course List.

- Physical education grades are not counted in calculating your GPA, nor are electives that are not on the Official University of California Certified Course List.

- Grades earned in courses taken in the ninth grade or earlier are not used to calculate your "a-f" Subject Requirement GPA. However, these courses may be used to meet the "a-f" Subject Requirement if they are completed with at least a C grade. For example, courses in foreign language and mathematics completed in grades seven and eight with grades of C or higher may be counted toward meeting the "a-f" Subject Requirement, but their grades are not calculated into your GPA. As another example, an English class completed in grade nine counts toward meeting the "a-f" Subject Requirement of four years of English, but the grade earned is not included in your "a-f" Subject Requirement GPA.

- Honors-level courses taken in your *sophomore, junior, and senior years* in which you earn a C or better are each given one extra point when calculating your GPA. Honors-level courses include (a) those designated as honors courses by your high school, (b) Advanced Placement courses, (c) Higher Level International Baccalaureate courses, and (d) transferable college courses in "a-f" subjects. A more detailed definition of honors-level courses can be found later in this chapter: Commonly Asked Questions About Admissions, page 11--12. Up to eight semester courses (four one-year courses) can be accepted. A maximum of two of these four courses may be taken in grade ten. Extra points are awarded to you as a tenth grader only if you take honors-level courses normally taken by students in the eleventh and twelfth grades.

Grades earned in courses taken in grade nine or earlier are not used to calculate your GPA. However, they may be used to meet your "a-f" Subject Requirement.

- For repeat courses, use both the original grade and the repeat grade. UC instructs you to use on your application *all* grades you receive in "a-f" Subject Requirement courses to calculate a preliminary GPA used to screen you for admission. As explained later in this chapter: Commonly Asked Questions About Admissions, page 11--12, the UC campus admissions evaluator — the admissions officer who reviews your academic record and UC application — has the option of recalculating your GPA using only the higher grade.

- Courses taken in high school summer sessions after the ninth, tenth, and eleventh grades may be used in your GPA calculation if your principal certifies that they are equivalent to regular courses in the "a-f" Subject Requirement. You may clear up "a-f" Subject Requirement deficiencies due to D or F grades by enrolling in appropriate high school or college courses in summer school immediately after graduation. These grades may be used in calculating your high school GPA. However, UC limits you to clearing a total of two semesters (one unit) of "a-f" Subject Requirement courses in which you received a D or F.

Use this worksheet, MY GPA COMPUTATION, and follow these seven steps to calculate your "a-f" Subject Requirement grade point average:

Step 1. Count the number of one-semester "a-f" Subject Requirement courses you have taken in grades ten, eleven, and twelve for which you received a grade of A. Enter this number on line (1) in column (a).

Step 2. Repeat Step (1) for each grade received of B, C, D, and F and enter the corresponding counts on lines (2), (3), (4), and (5) in column (a).

Step 3. For each grade on lines (1) through (5), multiply the number of courses you entered in column (a) by the grade points per grade shown in column (b). Enter the result on the corresponding line in column (c).

Step 4. Total column (a) and enter the result on line (7) and at the bottom of the chart in the boxes marked TOTAL1.

Step 5. Count the number of one-semester honors-level courses you have taken in grades ten, eleven, and twelve. Enter this number to a maximum of eight semester courses on line (8) in column (c).

Step 6. Total column (c) and enter the result on line (9) and at the bottom of the chart in the boxes marked TOTAL2.

Step 7. At the bottom of the worksheet, divide TOTAL2 by TOTAL1 and enter the result to two decimal places in the box marked GPA. This number is MY PRELIMINARY "a-f" SUBJECT REQUIREMENT GPA.

Use only grades earned in the "a-f" Subject Requirement courses taken in the tenth, eleventh, and twelfth grades to calculate your GPA for admission.

MY GPA COMPUTATION

"a-f" Subject Requirement Grade Point Average

		column (a)	column (b)	column (c)
	Letter Grade	Number of Semester Courses	Grade Points per Grade	Total Grade Points Earned column (a) x column (b)
line (1)	A		x 4	
line (2)	B		x 3	
line (3)	C		x 2	
line (4)	D		x 1	
line (5)	F		x 0	
line (7)	TOTAL1			
line (8)	No. of Semester Honors Courses			
line (9)			TOTAL2	

MY PRELIMINARY "a-f" SUBJECT REQUIREMENT GPA

TOTAL2 [ ] ÷ TOTAL1 [ ] = [.]

COLLEGE IN CALIFORNIA: *The Inside Track*

ELIGIBILITY INDEX

ELIGIBILITY INDEX

"a-f" GPA	ACT Composite (1)	SAT I Total (2)	"a-f" GPA	ACT Composite (1)	SAT I Total (2)	"a-f" GPA	ACT Composite (1)	SAT I Total (2)
2.82	36	1590	2.98	29	1220	3.14	20	840
2.83	36	1570	2.99	28	1190	3.15	20	820
2.84	35	1540	3.00	28	1170	3.16	19	800
2.85	35	1520	3.01	27	1150	3.17	19	770
2.86	35	1500	3.02	27	1120	3.18	18	750
2.87	34	1470	3.03	26	1100	3.19	18	730
2.88	34	1450	3.04	26	1080	3.20	17	700
2.89	33	1430	3.05	25	1050	3.21	17	680
2.90	33	1400	3.06	25	1030	3.22	16	660
2.91	33	1380	3.07	24	1010	3.23	16	630
2.92	32	1360	3.08	23	980	3.24	15	610
2.93	31	1330	3.09	23	960	3.25	15	590
2.94	31	1310	3.10	22	940	3.26	14	560
2.95	31	1290	3.11	22	910	3.27	14	540
2.96	30	1260	3.12	21	890	3.28	13	520
2.97	30	1240	3.13	21	870	3.29	12	490

Note 1. ACT composite is scored in intervals of 1 point, from a minimum of 1 to a maximum of 36.

Note 2. SAT I total is scored in intervals of 10 points, from a minimum of 400 to a maximum of 1600.

Equivalence Tables for comparing "before" recentering SAT I total scores with "after recentering" total scores will be available in spring 1995. See Chapter 6: College Entrance Tests, page 6--21 for information on recentering.

California residents must place on this Eligibility Index to meet minimum admission requirements for UC. The Eligibility Index is a combination of your "a-f" Subject Requirement GPA and either your SAT I total or ACT composite college admissions test score. If your "a-f" Subject Requirement GPA is 3.30 or higher, you have met the minimum requirement for admission to the University. If it is below 2.82, you do not qualify for admission. If it is below 3.30 but above 2.81, you have met the minimum requirement if you achieve the necessary college admissions test score.

The Eligibility Index shown here indicates the required SAT I total, *before recentering,* or ACT composite test score for each "a-f" Subject Requirement GPA between 2.82 and 3.29. Students who plan to graduate in June 1996 or later will need to use recentered scores to determine their eligibility. With an "a-f" Subject Requirement GPA of 2.98, you must have a minimum SAT I total score (verbal plus math) of 1220 or a minimum ACT composite score of 29 to meet minimum admission requirements. For the minimum GPA of 2.82, you must achieve the top score of 1590 on the SAT I: Reasoning Test or 36 on the ACT.

If you take the SAT I: Reasoning Test or ACT admissions tests several times, UC uses the highest scores from a single testing session. If you take both the SAT I: Reasoning Test and the ACT, the University uses whichever scores are higher from a single test date.

UNIVERSITY OF CALIFORNIA

The University of California does not use the Eligibility Index as an admission criterion for students who are not California residents for admission purposes. See appendix A: CALIFORNIA RESIDENCY REQUIREMENTS, and in this chapter: Commonly Asked Questions About Admissions, page 11--21.

The University of California does not use the Eligibility Index as an admission criterion for students who are not California residents for admission purposes.

COMMONLY ASKED QUESTIONS ABOUT ADMISSIONS

WHAT ARE HONORS-LEVEL COURSES?

UC considers the following courses as honors-level courses:

- Advanced Placement courses in the "a-f" Subject Requirement that are designed to prepare you for an Advanced Placement Examination of the College Entrance Examination Board. See chapter 6: COLLEGE ENTRANCE TESTS, The AP Program and Examinations, page 6--57.

- College courses in the "a-f" Subject Requirement that are transferable to the University of California; e.g., community college and four-year college courses that you take while still in high school.

- Higher-level courses offered through the International Baccalaureate (IB) Program described later in this chapter: International Baccalaureate, page 11--60.

- High school courses in history, English, advanced mathematics, laboratory science, and languages other than English that are not Advanced Placement courses or Higher Level International Baccalaureate courses, but your high school offers at the honors level. Acceptable honors level courses are specialized, advanced, collegiate-level courses normally offered at the eleventh and twelfth grade levels.

Honors-level courses in which you earn at least a C grade receive an extra point when calculating your GPA.

Honors-level courses can be taken in your sophomore, junior, and senior years. Your high school certifies which courses in its curriculum meet UC's criteria to be considered honors courses. Your high school lists these on its Official University of California Certified Course List described earlier in this chapter. Up to four units (four one-year courses) can be taken as honors-level courses with a limit of two in your tenth grade.

Honors-level courses taken in the eleventh and/or twelfth grades for which you earn at least a C grade receive an extra point when calculating your GPA. Intensive or accelerated courses are not honors-level courses and receive no extra points.

To receive an extra point for an honors-level course taken in the tenth grade, it must be an honors-level course normally taken by eleventh or twelfth grade students. This policy allows the advanced tenth grader, who takes an honors course, to receive the same extra points in his or her GPA calculation as the eleventh or twelfth grader in the class. If the honors course is only for tenth graders and does not appear on the Official University of California Certified Course List, you may not add an extra point in calculating your GPA.

WHAT ARE THE ADVANTAGES OF TAKING TENTH GRADE HONORS COURSES FOR WHICH YOU DO NOT EARN EXTRA GRADE POINTS IN CALCULATING YOUR GPA?

A challenging high school program including Advanced Placement and other honors-level courses is one academic criterion used by the UC campuses to admit freshman applicants.

One primary benefit of taking honors-level courses in the tenth grade is the preparation you receive for more advanced high school classes and for university work. In addition, the admissions evaluator considers the quality of your high school program when reviewing your record for admission. A challenging high school program including Advanced Placement and other honors-level courses is one academic criterion used by the UC campuses to admit freshman applicants.

WHAT ARE THE RULES REGARDING REPEATING COURSES?

If you receive a D or F grade in a course needed to satisfy the "a-f" Subject Requirement, you must repeat the course and earn a grade of C or higher. In some cases — explained in the answer to the next question — the D or F may be cleared by means other than repeating the course. Grades earned in both the original course and the repeated course are used in calculating your preliminary "a-f" Subject Requirement GPA on your admission application. The UC campus admissions evaluator has the option of recalculating your GPA using only the higher grades. *Each course in which you receive a grade of D or F may be repeated only once.*

If you repeat a course used to satisfy the "a-f" Subject Requirement in which you originally earned a grade of C or higher, the repeated grade is not used in calculating your "a-f" Subject Requirement GPA.

HOW DOES THE UNIVERSITY DEAL WITH D'S, F'S, PASSES, CREDITS, AND INCOMPLETES IN "a-f" SUBJECT REQUIREMENT COURSES?

"a-f" Subject Requirement courses in which you earn a D, F or Incomplete are treated as subject omissions and must be repeated.

In calculating your "a-f" Subject Requirement GPA, the University follows the rules listed here regarding the use of D, F, Pass, Credit, and Incomplete grades. The answer to the next question describes special rules regarding D and F grades in chemistry, languages other than English, and mathematics.

1. Courses used to satisfy the "a-f" Subject Requirement taken in the ninth grade or earlier in which you earn D or F grades are treated as subject omissions. As with all ninth grade or earlier courses, their grades are not included in calculating your "a-f" Subject Requirement GPA.

2. Courses used to satisfy the "a-f" Subject Requirement, taken for the first time in the tenth, eleventh, or twelfth grades, in which you earn D or F grades are treated as "a-f" Subject Requirement omissions and scholarship deficiencies. If the courses are not repeated, the D or F grades are used in calculating your "a-f" Subject Requirement GPA. If you repeat a course, the repeated course grade is used for your GPA calculation.

3. D or F grades earned in courses more advanced than those used to satisfy the "a-f" Subject Requirement are not used in calculating your "a-f" Subject Requirement GPA. For example, a D or F grade received in a fourth year of mathematics is disregarded in calculating your GPA, because only three years of mathematics are required for admission under the "c" requirement of the "a-f" Subject Requirement.

4. Courses used to satisfy the "a-f" Subject Requirement may not be taken for Pass/Fail or Credit/No Credit.

5. An Incomplete earned in a course needed to satisfy the "a-f" Subject Requirement is treated as a subject omission.

Courses used to satisfy the "a-f" Subject Requirement may not be taken for Pass/Fail or Credit/No Credit.

For items (2) and (3) above, all "a-f" Subject Requirement courses and grades must be included in your calculation of your preliminary "a-f" Subject Requirement GPA on your admission application. The UC campus admissions evaluator has the option of recalculating your GPA using these rules.

A subject omission is a required course considered missing from your academic record, either because you never took it or received a D, F, or Incomplete grade in it.

WHAT ARE THE SPECIAL RULES REGARDING D'S AND F'S IN CHEMISTRY, LANGUAGES OTHER THAN ENGLISH, AND MATHEMATICS?

Chemistry, languages other than English, and mathematics courses are considered sequential. An advanced semester or year course successfully completed with a grade of C or better clears the previous course omission in the same subject. This means that the course in which you earned the D or F is no longer considered a subject omission. By successfully completing the more advanced course in the subject, you have demonstrated your knowledge of the subject matter. The original D or F grade is averaged with the subsequent C, B, or A in computing your "a-f" Subject Requirement GPA.

CHEMISTRY: If chemistry is used to satisfy the "d" Subject Requirement — one year of laboratory science — a D or F received in the first-semester course is treated as a subject omission and a scholarship deficiency. You may clear the first-semester subject omission by earning a grade of C or better in the second semester of the course. Both semester grades are used in calculating your "a-f" Subject Requirement GPA.

LANGUAGES OTHER THAN ENGLISH: A D or F grade earned in a language other than English is treated as a subject omission and scholarship deficiency in the "e" Subject Requirement — two years of a language other than English. You may clear this subject omission and scholarship deficiency by earning a grade of C or better in a more advanced course in the same language. Both grades are used in calculating your "a-f" Subject Requirement GPA.

MATHEMATICS: A D or F grade earned in algebra or geometry is treated as a subject omission and scholarship deficiency in the "c" Subject Requirement — three years of mathematics. You may clear this subject omission and scholarship deficiency by earning a grade of C or higher in an appropriate, more advanced course in college-preparatory mathematics. Both grades are used in calculating your "a-f" Subject Requirement GPA.

For example, a D or F grade earned in elementary algebra is cleared by earning a grade of C or higher in advanced algebra. A D or F grade earned in geometry is cleared by earning a grade of C or higher in trigonometry. Both grades are used in calculating your "a-f" Subject Requirement GPA.

Chemistry, languages other than English, and mathematics courses are considered sequential. An advanced semester or year course successfully completed with a grade of C or better clears the previous course omission in the same subject.

CAN I TAKE "a-f" SUBJECT REQUIREMENT COURSES IN SUMMER SCHOOL?

Yes, you can, but make sure your high school lists the summer school courses on its Official University of California Certified Course List.

CAN I CLEAR UP DEFICIENCIES DUE TO D AND F GRADES BY ATTENDING SUMMER SCHOOL AFTER GRADUATION?

Yes, you may clear up "a-f" Subject Requirement deficiencies due to D or F grades by enrolling in appropriate high school or college courses in summer school immediately after high school graduation. Grades received in summer school courses may be used in calculating your high school GPA. However, the University limits you to clearing a total of two semesters (one unit) in "a-f" Subject Requirement courses in this manner.

This policy applies only to students planning to enroll at the University in the fall term immediately following high school graduation. Not all UC campuses accept this method of clearing up D and F grade deficiencies. Call the campus admissions office of the UC campus you are planning to attend to learn about their specific policy.

I DID NOT COMPLETE THE FOURTH YEAR OF HIGH SCHOOL ENGLISH. HOW CAN I STILL SATISFY THE "B" SUBJECT REQUIREMENT OF FOUR YEARS OF HIGH SCHOOL ENGLISH?

There are three alternatives to satisfy the fourth year of English requirement.

There are three alternatives to satisfy this requirement:

1. Achieve a score of at least 600 on the College Entrance Examination Board SAT II: Writing Test.

2. Achieve a score of at least 3 on the Advanced Placement Examination in English Language and Composition or on the Advanced Placement Examination in English Composition and Literature. See chapter 6: COLLEGE ENTRANCE TESTS, The AP Program And Examinations, page 6--57.

3. Pass with a grade of C or better an appropriate college course in English composition and literature.

DO COURSES IN SPEECH, DRAMA, DEBATE, OR JOURNALISM MEET THE ENGLISH REQUIREMENT — THE "B" SUBJECT REQUIREMENT?

No, they normally do not. However, they *may* be used to meet the "f" Subject Requirement — the college-preparatory elective requirement — if your high school lists the specific courses in these subjects on its Official University of California Certified Course List.

I AM A BILINGUAL STUDENT WITH COMPETENCE IN A LANGUAGE OTHER THAN ENGLISH. CAN I SATISFY THE "E" SUBJECT REQUIREMENT — THE LANGUAGE-OTHER-THAN-ENGLISH REQUIREMENT — WITHOUT TAKING A LANGUAGE IN HIGH SCHOOL?

Bilingual students may meet the language-other-than-English requirement without taking a language course in high school.

Yes, you can. The University wants to ensure that freshmen have a minimum level of competence in a language other than English. This level corresponds to what UC normally expects of a student who has completed two years of high school study with course grades of C or better. Bilingual students are considered to have met this requirement. You may use any of the following methods as alternatives to coursework to certify satisfaction of the "e" Subject Requirement.

1. Earn a satisfactory score on (a) a recognized test such as an SAT II: Subject Test or Advanced Placement Examination, (b) the Higher Level International Baccalaureate Examination, or (c) a proficiency test administered by a UC campus or another university. See chapter 6: COLLEGE ENTRANCE TESTS, SAT II: Subject Tests, page 6--30 and The AP Program And Examinations, page 6--57. Also see this chapter: International Baccalaureate, page 11--60.

2. Provide proof that you have had two years of formal schooling at the sixth grade or higher in an institution where the language of instruction was not English. A transcript of work completed in your country of origin is acceptable proof.

3. If neither option (1) nor option (2) is available to you, your high school principal can certify on your transcript that you are proficient in a language other than English based upon the judgement of language teachers or other appropriate sources of expertise.

Using one of these options can be very beneficial. It enables you to take electives, or, if you have limited English, courses in English as a second language instead of enrolling in yet another language while you are in high school.

An advanced ESL course may be used to meet the "f" Subject Requirement.

DOES AMERICAN SIGN LANGUAGE (AMESLAN) SATISFY THE LANGUAGE-OTHER-THAN-ENGLISH REQUIREMENT — THE "E" SUBJECT REQUIREMENT?

UC will accept American Sign Language (Ameslan) courses on the Official University of California Certified Course List as meeting the "e" Subject Requirement.

HOW DO ESL — ENGLISH AS A SECOND LANGUAGE — COURSES COUNT TOWARD MEETING THE ENGLISH REQUIREMENT FOR ADMISSION?

If you are a student new to the United States and English is not your native language, typically, your high school schedules you into ESL classes to develop your English skills. A maximum of one unit (one year) of ESL courses may be accepted toward meeting the "b" Subject Requirement — the four-year English requirement. The courses must be (a) advanced ESL courses with strong emphasis upon reading and writing, (b) taken prior to regular college-preparatory English, and (c) listed on your high school's Official University of California Certified Course List.

DO ADVANCED ESL COURSES MEET THE ELECTIVE REQUIREMENT — THE "F" SUBJECT REQUIREMENT?

An advanced ESL course may be used to meet the "f" Subject Requirement — the college-preparatory elective requirement — if your high school lists the course on its Official University of California Certified Course List.

Each UC campus employs a foreign admissions specialist to interpret foreign transcripts.

I HAD COURSES IN BOTH MY NATIVE LANGUAGE AND ENGLISH (OR ANOTHER LANGUAGE) IN HIGH SCHOOL IN MY NATIVE COUNTRY. HOW DOES THE UNIVERSITY EVALUATE THESE COURSES TOWARD MEETING ADMISSION REQUIREMENTS?

If you have a mixed record; i.e., you have had some of your high school education in your native country and some in the United States, the interpretation of your transcript is a complex process. Each UC campus decides the policies it wishes to follow in interpreting your qualifications for admission and employs a foreign admissions specialist to interpret foreign transcripts.

Some campuses may accept your high school courses in your native language of instruction as counting toward meeting the "b" Subject Requirement — the English requirement of four years of college-preparatory English. English or another language taken in your native country may count toward the "e" Subject Requirement — the language-other-than-English requirement. For example, if Chinese is the language of your native country, and you took two years of Chinese in your country's high school, it may count toward meeting the "b" Subject Requirement. If you also took English or another language in your native country, it may count as meeting the "e" Subject Requirement. Other campuses may be unwilling to consider your native country courses in this manner.

The University strongly recommends that you take four years of mathematics in high school, including pre-calculus, during your senior year.

You may wish to contact the foreign admissions specialist at the UC campuses of interest to you to discuss your particular situation and their policies.

THE UNIVERSITY REQUIRES A MINIMUM OF THREE YEARS OF MATHEMATICS TO MEET THE "C" SUBJECT REQUIREMENT FOR ADMISSION. SHOULD I TAKE MORE?

You must take a minimum of three years of high school mathematics to be eligible for admission to the University, but for many fields you need additional training. If you are in an engineering, mathematics, or science program or plan to attend medical, dental, optometry, or veterinary school, you must take calculus in college. Majors in business, agriculture, and many social science fields require statistics and/or calculus.

Most students take calculus or statistics, if required, during their freshman year. The University strongly recommends that you take four years of mathematics in high school, including precalculus, during your senior year. If you are not prepared to take calculus or statistics during your freshman year, you will need to take one or more University preparatory mathematics classes. This could affect your success in other courses and delay your entire undergraduate program.

WHAT MATHEMATICS COURSES ARE ACCEPTABLE TO MEET THE ELECTIVE REQUIREMENT, THE "F" SUBJECT REQUIREMENT?

Acceptable electives are courses in mathematics with second year algebra as a prerequisite — courses such as trigonometry, linear algebra, precalculus (analytical geometry and mathematical analysis), calculus) combinatorics, probability and statistics.

A computer science course is an acceptable mathematics elective if it is a course which enables you to express algorithms in a standard computer language such as PASCAL, BASIC, FORTRAN, OR COBOL. It should be listed on your high school Official University of California Certified Course List.

Many majors require additional science courses for admission.

THE UNIVERSITY REQUIRES A MINIMUM OF TWO YEARS OF LABORATORY SCIENCE TO MEET THE "D" SUBJECT REQUIREMENT FOR ADMISSION. SHOULD I TAKE MORE?

You must take a minimum of two years of laboratory science in high school for admission but many majors require additional science courses. Programs in the biological sciences and some natural resource fields require high school biology, chemistry, and physics. Programs in the physical sciences, mathematics, engineering, agriculture, and the health sciences require chemistry and physics, and recommend biology.

IF I COMPLETE TWO YEARS OF A LANGUAGE OTHER THAN ENGLISH IN HIGH SCHOOL, DO I NEED TO TAKE FOREIGN LANGUAGE IN COLLEGE?

Although two years of a language other than English meets the "e" Subject Requirement — two years of a language other than English — additional language study may be necessary to receive your University degree from a particular college or school at a University campus, or in a particular major. Therefore, UC encourages you to complete the third year of a language other than English in high school. In most cases, doing so eliminates the requirement for further language study at UC. Check the college catalogue of the UC campuses and majors that interest you to learn their language-other-than-English requirement for degree completion.

UC encourages you to complete the third year of a language other than English in high school.

CAN I SATISFY AN "a-f" SUBJECT REQUIREMENT BY EXAMINATION?

Yes, you may satisfy an "a-f" Subject Requirement by earning a score of at least 500 on the appropriate SAT II: Subject Tests as shown in the following table. You also may satisfy an "a-f" Subject Requirement by earning a score of at least 3 on the appropriate Advanced Placement Examination or a minimum score of 5 on Higher Level International Baccalaureate Examinations. See chapter 6: COLLEGE ENTRANCE TESTS, The AP Program And Examinations, page 6--57 and this chapter: International Baccalaureate, page 11--60.

SATISFACTION OF THE "a-f" SUBJECT REQUIREMENT BY EXAMINATION

Subject Requirement	SAT II: SUBJECT TEST	Required Score
a.	American History (satisfies one year)	500
	European History (satisfies one year)	500
b.	Writing or Literature (satisfies first three years)	500
	Writing (satisfies entire requirement)	600
c.	Mathematics Level I (satisfies entire requirement)	550
	Mathematics Level IIC (satisfies entire requirement)	500
d.	Science (each test satisfies one year)	500
e.	Language Other Than English (satisfies entire requirement)	500
f.	Mathematics Level IIC	550
	Writing or Literature	500
	American History	500
	European History	500
	Science (other than that taken to satisfy the "d" requirement above)	500
	Language Other Than English, third year	550
	Language Other Than English (other than that taken to satisfy the "e" requirement above)	500

You may satisfy an "a-f" Subject Requirement by achieving at least 500 on the appropriate SAT II: Subject Tests.

CAN I RECEIVE CREDIT FOR COURSES NOT TAKEN BY TAKING AN ADVANCED COURSE?

Yes, you can. You may receive credit in an introductory course in a language other than English, mathematics, or chemistry, if you earn a grade of C or better in a corresponding advanced course. The advanced course also may be used to meet the "f" Subject Requirement — the college-preparatory elective courses requirement. You need not have taken the introductory course to obtain this credit. For example, if you have not taken French 1 and French 2, you can receive three years of language-other-than-English credit toward your "a-f" Subject Requirement if you earn a grade of C or better in French 3.

You may receive credit in an introductory course in a language other than English, mathematics, or chemistry, if you earn a grade of C or better in a corresponding advanced course.

CAN I MEET THE "a-f" SUBJECT REQUIREMENT BY TAKING COLLEGE COURSES?

Yes, the "a-f" Subject Requirement may be met by taking appropriate college courses.

I HAVE TAKEN PART OF MY HIGH SCHOOL WORK IN ANOTHER COUNTRY. CAN I USE MY FOREIGN SCHOOL RECORD TOWARD ADMISSION?

Yes, you can. You must submit transcripts from both your foreign and American high schools. Each University campus has a foreign admissions specialist in the admissions office to answer specific questions and to evaluate your academic records. If possible, contact this specialist before you go to school abroad to receive guidance in choosing your overseas classes. You also may need assistance in deciding classes to be completed in the United States before you leave. For example, appropriate classes in English, United States history, and American government might not be available in a foreign high school. It might be advantageous to finish these requirements while in an American high school.

CAN I BE ADMITTED BY EXAMINATION ALONE IF I DO NOT MEET THE SUBJECT AND SCHOLARSHIP REQUIREMENTS?

You may be able to qualify for admission to some campuses by examination alone.

Yes, you may be able to qualify for admission to some campuses by examination alone. To do so, you must achieve

a) a total score of at least 1300 on the SAT I: Reasoning Test or a composite score of at least 31 on the ACT, *and*

b) a total score on your three SAT II: Subject Tests of 1650 or higher, with a minimum score of 500 on each test.

If you have completed twelve or more units of transferable college work, you cannot qualify for admission by examination alone. Also, you cannot qualify if you have taken a transferable college course in one or more of the academic subjects covered by the College Entrance Examination Board SAT II: Subject Tests.

If you are currently attending high school, you may qualify for admission to some campuses by examination alone without completing your high school program.

DO I NEED A HIGH SCHOOL DIPLOMA TO BE ADMITTED TO THE UNIVERSITY?

No, you do not. If you are currently attending high school, you may be admitted without completing your high school program if you can qualify by examination alone as described in response to the answer to the previous question.

I DO NOT QUALIFY FOR THE UNIVERSITY BY EXAMINATION ALONE AND DO NOT HAVE MY HIGH SCHOOL DIPLOMA. WHAT CAN I DO?

The University accepts the Certificate of Proficiency awarded by the State Board of Education upon successful completion of the California High School Proficiency Examination. The University also accepts proficiency examinations from other states and the General Education Development Certificate (GED). *However, you must still meet the Subject, Examination, and Scholarship Requirements for admission.*

I LIVE OUT OF STATE, BUT I AM A DEPENDENT OF A GRADUATE OF THE UNIVERSITY OF CALIFORNIA. AM I CONSIDERED A CALIFORNIA RESIDENT FOR ADMISSION PURPOSES?

Yes, UC considers you a California resident for admission purposes, and therefore you are subject to the same admission requirements as California residents. However, the manner in which UC defines legal residence for tuition purposes is different. See appendix A: CALIFORNIA RESIDENCY REQUIREMENTS.

I LIVE OUT OF STATE BUT I AM A DEPENDENT OF A UNIVERSITY OF CALIFORNIA EMPLOYEE. AM I CONSIDERED A CALIFORNIA RESIDENT FOR ADMISSION PURPOSES?

Yes, you are considered a California resident for admission purposes. However, the manner in which legal residence is defined for tuition purposes is different. See appendix A: CALIFORNIA RESIDENCY REQUIREMENTS.

I DO NOT QUALIFY AS A CALIFORNIA RESIDENT FOR ADMISSION PURPOSES. WHAT ARE THE MINIMUM FRESHMAN ADMISSION REQUIREMENTS FOR ME?

The minimum admission requirements are the same as for California residents except for the following:

SCHOLARSHIP REQUIREMENT: Your "a-f" Subject Requirement GPA must be 3.40 or higher, whatever your college admissions test scores. UC uses the Eligibility Index only for California residents.

ADMISSION BY EXAMINATION ALONE: You must score at least 1300 on the SAT I: Reasoning Test, or achieve a composite score of at least 31 on the ACT. Your total score on your th ree SAT II: Subject Tests must be at least 1730 with a minimum score of 500 on any single test.

If you are not a California resident, your "a-f" Subject Requirement GPA must be 3.40 or higher regardless of your admission test scores.

UNIVERSITY OF CALIFORNIA

ADMISSION BY EXCEPTION

Not all students have had the same opportunities to prepare for higher education. The University give special consideration to a limited number of applicants who show potential to succeed at the University, although they do not meet the minimum admission requirements.

A small percentage — up to six percent of newly enrolled freshmen and up to six percent of newly enrolled transfer students — can be admitted in exception to University minimum admission requirements. The University may admit students by exception within the following categories:

A small percentage of students — up to six percent — can be admitted in exception to University minimum admission requirements.

1. Disadvantaged (Those from minority and/or low-income or educationally disadvantaged backgrounds — SAA/EOP/AAP). See this chapter, SAA And EOP, page 11--44.

2. Athletes.

3. Special talent.

4. Other (Those who demonstrate exceptional ability in certain areas or have shown marked improvement in academic performance).

For fall 1993, 4.8% of California entering freshmen and 5.0% of California transfers were admitted by exception.

Each campus has specific requirements for admission by exception. Contact the campus admissions office for information about campus criteria.

Your essay is especially important in applying for admission by exception. It is your opportunity to make a strong case for why you can succeed at the University, although you are deficient in some admission requirements. See chapter 7: STEPS IN THE APPLICATION PROCESS, Writing Your Essay, Page 7--9.

FRESHMEN SELECTION CRITERIA

The University of California has a historic commitment to enroll all eligible applicants who are California residents. Furthermore, UC's goal is to achieve on each campus, a student body that both meets the University's high academic standards, and reflects the cultural, racial, geographic, economic, and social diversity of California itself. However, demand for admission to the UC campuses is very strong.

Because most UC campuses and many of their majors are receiving more eligible applicants than there are spaces available, each campus has developed additional guidelines to further screen applicants. These standards are more demanding than the minimum admission requirements. Reviewing them can help you better understand the actual selection process. The criteria differ from campus to campus and from major to major. They may differ for subsequent terms and years and may become more or less competitive.

There are two categories of criteria for admission: (a) Academic and (b) Supplemental.

Each campus admits at least forty percent and not more than sixty percent of freshmen on the basis of the academic criteria alone. The campuses select the remaining freshmen, other than those admitted through admission by exception — described on page 11--22 — using some or all of the academic criteria *and* supplemental criteria.

ACADEMIC CRITERIA

The academic criteria consist of the following four components:

1. Grade point average, GPA, calculated for all academic courses completed in the "a-f" Subject Requirement specified by the University's minimum admission requirements. Honors-level courses are given extra points. However, the maximum value allowed for your GPA is 4.00, even if extra points for your honors-level courses raise your GPA above 4.00.

2. Test scores on the admissions tests required for admission: (a) SAT I: Reasoning Test or ACT, and (b) SAT II: Subject Tests.

3. The number and content of courses completed in academic subjects beyond the minimum fifteen units of the "a-f" Subject Requirement.

4. The number of University-approved accelerated, Advanced Placement, and honors-level courses completed or in progress.

FALL 1993 ENROLLED FRESHMEN for the University of California System

Average GPA 3.77
GPA of 4.00
or above .... 29% of applicants
36% of admitted students
35% of enrolling students

Average SAT Scores
verbal 496
mathematics 590

SAT Range	% Of Freshmen verbal	math
700 to 800	2.3%	18.1%
600 to 699	16.2%	32.1%
500 to 599	32.7%	31.9%
400 to 499	32.0%	13.9%
Below 400	16.8%	4.0%

SUPPLEMENTAL CRITERIA

The supplemental criteria consist of the following three components:

1. Special talents, interests, or experiences beyond those indicated by the academic criteria that demonstrate unusual promise of leadership, achievement, and service in a particular field such as civic life or the arts.

2. Special circumstances that have adversely affected your life experiences. These circumstances may include, for example, disabilities, personal difficulties, low family income, refugee status, or veteran status.

3. Ethnic identity, gender, and location of residence. These factors are considered to provide cultural, racial, geographic, and socioeconomic diversity in the student population.

FALL 1995 GUIDELINES BY CAMPUS

Fall 1995 freshman admission guidelines are described for each campus on the following pages. These guidelines form the basic framework for making admission decisions. The University has developed them to identify those students who demonstrate the capacity for high academic achievement and have other qualities that can contribute to the strength and diversity of the UC campus. As you review these guidelines note the following:

- The campuses use similar indicators of academic and personal qualifications to evaluate applicants.

- The specific evaluation process and weight of factors, academic and supplemental, differ from campus to campus depending upon enrollment targets — the number of students a campus expects to enroll — and the number and qualifications of applicants.

- *The selection criteria described are for applicants for the fall 1995 term only.* The criteria may differ for the winter and spring terms because enrollment targets and applicant qualifications change. If you apply for the winter or spring terms, contact the appropriate campus admissions offices for more information.

- The number and academic challenge of courses beyond the minimum "a-f" Subject Requirement becomes important. For example, a total of two years of laboratory science taken in grades ten, eleven, and twelve meets the minimum requirement for admission. However, successful completion of three years of laboratory science places you in a more competitive position for admission. Four or five years of mathematics and a language other than English are further examples of courses exceeding the minimum requirement.

- The campuses consider the difficulty level of your courses. How many Advanced Placement and other honors-level courses have you successfully completed?

- Your essay, in which you describe yourself in a way that shows how you stand out from others and what makes you unique — your accomplishments and qualities such as superior motivation, diligence, and creativity — can really make a difference. See chapter 7: STEPS IN THE APPLICATION PROCESS, Writing Your Essay, page 7--9.

- The campuses consider extracurricular activities and personal achievements described in your application.

- The campuses consider special circumstances that may have adversely affected your life and your academic potential. Describe them fully in your essay.

- Your ethnic background can be an important supplemental criterion. UC gives extra consideration to students from groups historically underrepresented at the University.

- Majors differ in student demand and preparation requirements. The relative importance given to academic criteria versus supplemental criteria varies from major to major. Academic criteria may be given greater weight for some majors than others. Note that the criteria for admission to engineering are particularly selective at many campuses because of the high number of well-qualified applicants.

- Your senior year in high school is important. The colleges want to see that you have continued to challenge yourself in your senior year. They examine your record to determine if you have carried through a rigorous academic program including Advanced Placement and other honors-level courses, if possible, and you have maintained a high GPA. A strong senior year will strengthen your chances for admission to the campus and program of your choice.

- *Introducing The University*, a booklet published by the University of California in the spring, provides updated information about admission and selection policies for use by juniors who will apply for fall 1996 admission. Your high school career center or guidance office has copies available for students.

BERKELEY

ALL COLLEGES

ACADEMIC CRITERIA

Academic criteria are used to select approximately fifty percent of admits to the College of Letters and Science, College of Natural Resources, College of Environmental Design, and College of Engineering; and sixty percent of admits to the College of Chemistry.

Academic Index

Berkeley ranks all freshman applicants by college using the following academic index:

+ 1,000 x GPA	(maximum GPA considered is 4.00)
+ SAT I total score	(or ACT composite score)
+ 3 SAT II scores	
= ACADEMIC INDEX	(8,000 is the maximum score)

Additional academic criteria that may be used include college-preparatory courses completed beyond the minimum required and honors or advanced placement courses completed.

COLLEGE OF LETTERS AND SCIENCE: Except for applicants to the Department of Ethnic Studies, which selects applicants by major, all other applicants, including Undeclared majors, are reviewed in a single pool regardless of major.

COLLEGE OF NATURAL RESOURCES: All applicants, including Undeclared majors, are reviewed in a single pool regardless of major.

COLLEGE OF ENVIRONMENTAL DESIGN: Applicants are selected by major.

COLLEGE OF ENGINEERING: Applicants are selected by major. This college is the most competitive for freshman admission.

COLLEGE OF CHEMISTRY: Applicants are selected by major.

Because the Colleges of Environmental Design, Engineering and Chemistry, and the Department of Ethnic Studies in the College of Letters and Science select students by major, your choice of anticipated major can affect you chances of admission.

SUPPLEMENTAL CRITERIA

Supplemental criteria — described on page 11–23 are used to select approximately fifty percent of admits to the College of Letters and Science, College of Natural Resources, College of Environmental Design, and College of Engineering; and forty percent of admits to the College of Chemistry.

Additional consideration is given to these supplemental factors to fill the remaining forty percent to fifty percent of spaces: Personal academic accomplishments and qualities as reflected in your essay, California residency, special hardship circumstances that may have affected your life, and socioeconomic and educational background of your parents. Berkeley reviewed 5,000 applicant files in detail using these supplemental criteria for fall semester 1993.

FALL 1993 ENROLLED FRESHMEN

All colleges at Berkeley are competitive. For fall 1993, 8,345 applicants had GPA's of 4.00 or better; sixty-six percent of *admitted* students had GPA's of 4.00 or better. Eighty-seven percent of admitted students had GPA's of 3.50 or above. For *enrolled* freshmen the median GPA was 4.00; the average GPA was 3.83; the average SAT verbal score was 564; the average mathematics score was 654. Overall, Berkeley admitted forty-two percent of its freshmen applicants.

UC BERKELEY FALL 1993 ENROLLED FRESHMAN CLASS PROFILE						
	Total	Letters & Science	Engineering	Natural Resources	Chemistry	Environmental Design
VERBAL SCORES						
Average	564	565	588	536	543	524
700-800	7.9%	8.3%	10.7%	1.6%	4.8%	1.3%
600-699	35.6%	36.7%	41.2%	24.1%	24.0%	21.1%
500-599	32.2%	30.0%	32.6%	43.5%	44.8%	46.1%
400-499	18.1%	18.6%	11.6%	27.2%	18.4%	23.7%
Below 400	6.9%	6.0%	3.9%	3.7%	8.0%	7.9%
MATH SCORES						
Average	654	640	723	630	694	675
700-800	42.6%	38.1%	72.2%	22.0%	57.6%	40.8%
600-699	31.9%	31.5%	25.0%	46.1%	32.8%	47.4%
500-599	17.2%	20.0%	2.3%	25.7%	8.0%	10.5%
400-499	6.7%	8.3%	0.4%	6.3%	1.6%	1.3%
Below 400	1.5%	2.1%	0.0%	0.0%	0.0%	0.0%
NUMBER OF STUDENTS	3,173	2,337	439	191	125	76

UCB FALL 1993 ENROLLED FRESHMEN

Average GPA 3.83

GPA Range	% Of Freshmen
4.00	59.1%
3.50-3.99	27.7%
3.49 and below	13.2%

FALL 1994 ADMITTED FRESHMEN

The College of Letters and Science granted fall 1994 admission to approximately forty percent of its applicants. The College of Engineering admitted thirty-seven percent; the College of Environmental Design admitted forty-two percent; the College of Chemistry admitted sixty-four percent and the College of Natural Resources admitted fifty percent. Overall, Berkeley admitted forty percent of its freshmen applicants.

DAVIS

ALL COLLEGES

ACADEMIC CRITERIA

Academic criteria are used to select sixty percent of admits. Davis selects freshman applicants who have made the greatest effort to fully prepare academically as measured by the following criteria:

1. Calculated GPA on all academic courses completed in the "a-f" Subject Requirement areas, with additional points given for honors courses (maximum value is 4.00).

2. College entrance test scores: SAT I: Reasoning Test or ACT, and three required SAT II: Subject Tests.

3. The number and content of college-preparatory courses completed in academic subjects beyond UC minimums.

4. The number of University-approved honors or advanced placement courses completed or in progress.

UCD FALL 1993 ENROLLED FRESHMEN

Average GPA 3.73

GPA Range	% Of Freshmen
4.00 and above	28.0%
3.70 to 3.99	27.0%
3.30 to 3.69	33.0%
3.00 to 3.29	11.0%
Below 3.00	1.0%

Average SAT Scores

verbal 485

mathematics 585

SAT Range	% Of Freshmen verbal	math
700 to 800	1.0%	12.6%
600 to 699	12.5%	36.5%
500 to 599	35.7%	34.1%
400 to 499	30.9%	13.5%
Below 400	19.7%	3.3%

SUPPLEMENTAL CRITERIA

Supplemental criteria — described on page 11--23 are used to select the remaining forty percent of admits. Applicants are evaluated using the academic criteria described above in conjunction with supplemental criteria.

IRVINE

ALL SCHOOLS

All freshman applicants are ranked using a selection index based upon GPA in all high school academic courses, SAT I verbal and mathematics scores or ACT equivalent, and scores on three required SAT II: Subject Tests. Additional emphasis is placed on the strength of the your high school curriculum, including the program proposed for the remainder of your senior year. In your senior year, you are expected to improve or maintain the level of performance reported on your application through grade eleven.

ACADEMIC CRITERIA

Academic criteria are used to select sixty percent of admits. Applicants selected are those who rank the highest using the selection index described in the previous paragraph.

UCI FALL 1993 ENROLLED FRESHMEN

Average GPA 3.70

Average SAT Scores

verbal 455

mathematics 573

SAT Range	% Of Freshmen verbal	math
700 to 800	0.6%	11.0%
600 to 699	8.1%	31.4%
500 to 599	23.3%	37.5%
400 to 499	41.9%	16.3%
Below 400	26.0%	3.9%

Additional Screening

BIOLOGICAL SCIENCES AND ECONOMICS: Freshman applicants to Biological Sciences and Economics are subject to additional screening because only a limited number of freshman applicants are admitted directly to these majors. Those admitted usually are selected on the basis of academic criteria alone. Students not selected for the major as freshmen may enroll in lower-division prerequisite courses and petition for the major as juniors based upon performance in the prerequisites.

SCHOOL OF ENGINEERING: Selected applicants rank highest using UCI's academic criteria (described on this page for all schools) with emphasis on mathematics and science preparation. Other students are selected based upon (a) exceptional promise indicated by test scores, (b) relevant academic or extracurricular achievements, (c) unusually rigorous academic preparation, and (d) advanced mathematics and science coursework. Selectivity varies among the engineering majors.

SUPPLEMENTAL CRITERIA

Supplemental criteria are used to select forty percent of the admits. Applicants selected are those whose academic performance is augmented by evidence of academic qualifications and personal circumstances not reflected by the selection index.

LOS ANGELES

COLLEGE OF LETTERS AND SCIENCE

SCHOOL OF ENGINEERING AND APPLIED SCIENCE

ACADEMIC CRITERIA

Academic criteria are used to select approximately fifty to fifty-five percent of admits. UCLA selects students who have taken full advantage of the curriculum available to them and who demonstrate the strongest comprehensive academic preparation. Also considered is how well the student performed in the high school environment and in comparison to peers from that same school. All students applying from the same high school are reviewed together. Selection is based upon performance as indicated by the criteria listed here:

1. GPA calculated for all academic coursework as reported by the student on the undergraduate application.

2. College entrance test scores: SAT I : Reasoning Test or ACT, and three required SAT II: Subject Tests.

3. Quality, content, and level of coursework comprising the entire high school program, including the senior year.

4. Number of college-preparatory courses completed beyond the minimum "a-f" Subject Requirement.

5. Number of Advanced Placement and other honors-level courses completed, particularly in the junior and senior years.

6. For applicants to the School of Engineering and Applied Science, additional emphasis is placed on preparation and performance in mathematics and science. Students who are ready for calculus and have had both chemistry and physics present a stronger record.

UCLA FALL 1993 ENROLLED FRESHMEN

Average GPA 3.90

GPA Range	% Of Freshmen
4.00 & Above	47.8%
3.90 to 3.99	8.6%
3.80 to 3.89	8.3%
3.70 to 3.79	8.1%
3.60 to 3.69	5.9%
3.50 to 3.59	5.0%
3.00 to 3.49	13.6%
2.99 & Below	2.7%

Average SAT Scores
- verbal 518
- mathematics 621

SAT Range	% Of Freshmen verbal	math
700 to 800	1.9%	25.3%
600 to 699	20.4%	37.9%
500 to 599	39.1%	24.5%
400 to 499	28.4%	10.3%
Below 400	10.1%	2.0%

SUPPLEMENTAL CRITERIA

Supplemental criteria — described on page 11--23 are used to select the remaining forty-five to fifty percent of admits. Academic criteria (1) through (6) on this page are used as the basis for selection with consideration given to supplemental factors.

SCHOOL OF THE ARTS, SCHOOL OF THEATER, FILM AND TELEVISION

ACADEMIC AND SUPPLEMENTAL CRITERIA

Both academic and supplemental criteria — described on page 11--23 are used to select one-hundred percent of admits. Students selected (a) are UC-eligible and (b) demonstrate special talent and ability in the specific major chosen. This ability is indicated by audition, portfolio, and/or supplemental information as required by the department.

RIVERSIDE

For the past several years, Riverside has guaranteed admission to the campus for all applicants who met minimum UC-eligibility requirements with further screening used only for admission to the College of Engineering and to the Biomedical Sciences major. For fall 1995, Riverside expects to continue this pattern of admission opportunities.

The academic and supplemental criteria described here are used in the event further screening is necessary.

ALL COLLEGES

ACADEMIC CRITERIA

Applicants accepted for admission are those who demonstrate the strongest comprehensive academic preparation as measured by the following criteria:

1. Academic GPA calculated for all academic courses completed in the "a-f" Subject Requirement, including additional points for completing honors-level courses. The maximum allowable GPA value is 4.00.

2. College entrance test scores: SAT I: Reasoning Test or ACT, and three required SAT II: Subject Tests.

3. The number and content of courses completed in academic subjects beyond the University's minimum eligibility requirements.

4. The number of University-approved accelerated, Advanced Placement, and honors-level courses completed or in progress.

UCR FALL 1993 ENROLLED FRESHMEN

Average GPA 3.58

GPA Range	% Of Freshmen
3.60 to 4.00	45.0%
3.20 to 3.59	31.0%
2.80 to 3.19	19.0%
Below 2.80	5.0%

Average SAT Scores
verbal 431
mathematics 525

SAT Range	% Of Freshmen verbal	math
700 to 800	1.0%	7.2%
600 to 699	5.4%	19.5%
500 to 599	20.1%	34.3%
400 to 499	36.1%	26.3%
Below 400	37.5%	12.7%

Additional Screening

ENGINEERING: Applicants who excel in the academic criteria with additional emphasis upon mathematics and science preparation, and who qualify for first-quarter calculus are selected.

BIOMEDICAL SCIENCES: Applicants who excel in the academic criteria are considered. The following preparation is strongly recommended: (1) At least three high school laboratory courses, (2) mathematics competency sufficient to qualify for college-level calculus, and (3) English composition proficiency sufficient to qualify for placement either in English 1A or Basic Writing 1 at the time of enrollment.

SUPPLEMENTAL CRITERIA

Supplemental criteria — described on page 11--23 are used to select the remaining admits. Applicants are evaluated using the academic criteria previously described in conjunction with supplemental criteria.

SAN DIEGO

ALL COLLEGES

College choice and major do not affect admission.

ACADEMIC CRITERIA

Academic criteria are used to select sixty percent of admits. Applicants are selected upon the basis of their academic index score.

Academic Index

All freshman applicants are ranked using an academic index based upon (a) high school GPA computed for the "a-f" Subject Requirement courses and capped at 4.00, (b) scores on required admissions tests — SAT I: Reasoning Test or ACT, and the SAT II: Subject Tests in Writing and Mathematics, (c) the number of University-approved accelerated, Advanced Placement, and honors-level courses completed or in progress, and (d) the number and content of courses successfully completed in academic subjects beyond the minimum "a-f" Subject Requirement. Intended major is not a factor in the selection process. An academic index selection score is calculated based upon the following formula:

The sum of

a. 1,000 × high school GPA computed for the "a-f" Subject Requirement courses and capped at 4.00;

b. SAT I verbal score;

c. SAT I mathematics score;

d. SAT II: Writing Test score;

e. SAT II: Mathematics score;

f. 25 points for each accelerated, Advanced Placement, or honors-level course completed or in progress, up to a maximum of 200 points; plus

g. 25 points for each academic course successfully completed beyond the minimum "a-f" Subject Requirement, up to a maximum of 600 points.

= ACADEMIC INDEX SELECTION SCORE

By this formula, freshman applicants are assigned an academic index selection score that is used to select approximately sixty percent of the admits.

The maximum ACADEMIC INDEX SELECTION SCORE is 8,000 computed as shown here:	a.	+	1,000 × 4.00
	b.	+	800
	c.	+	800
	d.	+	800
	e.	+	800
	f.	+	200
	g.	+	600
		=	8,000

SUPPLEMENTAL CRITERIA

Supplemental criteria — described on page 11--23 are used to select the remaining forty percent of admits. The files of those not admitted in the top sixty percent (based upon their academic indexes) are further reviewed. Based upon consideration of supplemental criteria, bonus points up to a maximum of two-thousand are added to the academic index selection score, and applicants are then reranked. Those with the highest total scores are admitted.

UNIVERSITY OF CALIFORNIA

UCSD FALL 1993 ENROLLED FRESHMEN

Average GPA 3.83

GPA Range	% Of Freshmen
3.90 to 4.00	46.8%
3.60 to 3.89	31.3%
3.30 to 3.59	15.2%
3.00 to 3.29	5.4%
Below 3.00	1.2%

Average SAT Scores
verbal 515
mathematics 616

SAT Range	% Of Freshmen verbal	math
700 to 800	1.6%	20.3%
600 to 699	17.5%	41.4%
500 to 599	40.7%	30.4%
400 to 499	31.3%	6.9%
Below 400	9.0%	1.1%

SUPPLEMENTAL CRITERIA

Supplemental criteria — described on page 11--23 are used to select the remaining forty percent of admits. The files of those not admitted in the top sixty percent (based upon their academic indexes) are further reviewed. Based upon consideration of supplemental criteria, bonus points up to a maximum of two-thousand are added to the academic index selection score, and applicants are then reranked. Those with the highest total scores are admitted.

SANTA BARBARA

COLLEGE OF LETTERS AND SCIENCE

ACADEMIC CRITERIA

Academic criteria are used to select sixty percent of admits. All UC-eligible applicants are reviewed based upon (a) grades, (b) performance on SAT I: Reasoning Test or ACT and SAT II: Subject Tests, (c) completion of coursework beyond the University's "a-f" Subject Requirement, and (d) completion of Advanced Placement and honors-level courses in grades ten, eleven, and twelve.

Applicants with the strongest qualifications are admitted regardless of major. Forty percent are admitted Undeclared. The level of performance needed to gain admission varies from year to year depending upon the size and academic quality of the applicant pool and the number of enrollment spaces.

SUPPLEMENTAL CRITERIA

Supplemental criteria — described on page 11--23 are used in conjunction with academic criteria to select the remaining forty percent of admits.

COLLEGE OF ENGINEERING

ACADEMIC CRITERIA

Academic criteria are used to select approximately sixty percent of admits. All UC-eligible applicants are reviewed using an academic index based upon (a) grades, (b) performance on SAT I: Reasoning Test or ACT and SAT II: Subject Tests, (c) completion of coursework beyond the University's "a-f" Subject Requirement, and (d) completion of Advanced Placement and honors-level courses in grades ten, eleven, and twelve. Special emphasis is given to preparation and test results in science and mathematics. Applicants must declare a major, and those with the strongest qualifications are admitted. The level of performance needed to gain admission varies from year to year and by major depending upon the size and academic quality of the applicant pool and the number of enrollment spaces.

SUPPLEMENTAL CRITERIA

Supplemental criteria — described on page 11--23 are used in conjunction with academic criteria to select approximately forty percent of admits.

COLLEGE OF CREATIVE STUDIES

ACADEMIC CRITERIA

Academic criteria are used in conjunction with supplemental criteria to select one-hundred percent of admits. All UC-eligible applicants are reviewed based upon (a) grades, (b) performance on SAT I: Reasoning Test or ACT and SAT II: Subject Tests, (c) completion of course-work beyond the University's "a-f" Subject Requirement, and (d) completion of Advanced Placement and honors-level courses in grades ten, eleven, and twelve.

SUPPLEMENTAL CRITERIA

Supplemental criteria — described on page 11--23 are used in conjunction with academic criteria to select one-hundred percent of admits. All applicants must submit for faculty review work in evidence of talent. The faculty recommends for admission those applicants with special talent, outstanding achievement, and capacity for excellence in one of the seven academic areas within the college: Art, biology, chemistry, literature, mathematics, music composition, and physics.

UCSB FALL 1993 ENROLLED FRESHMEN

Average GPA 3.46

GPA Range	% Of Freshmen
3.70 to 4.00	25.0%
3.30 to 3.69	41.0%
3.00 to 3.29	28.0%
Below 3.00	6.0%

Average SAT Scores
- verbal 458
- mathematics 547

SAT Range	% Of Freshmen verbal	% Of Freshmen math
700 to 800	0.4%	5.4%
600 to 699	5.7%	24.6%
500 to 599	28.6%	44.0%
400 to 499	43.1%	20.1%
Below 400	22.3%	6.0%

UCSB FALL 1994 ENTERING FRESHMEN

Average GPA 3.45

GPA Range	% Of Freshmen
3.70 to 4.00	25.0%
3.30 to 3.69	40.0%
3.00 to 3.29	30.0%
Below 3.00	6.0%

Average SAT Scores
- verbal 454
- mathematics 544

UC SANTA BARBARA FALL 1993 ENROLLED FRESHMAN

	College of Letters and Science	College of Engineering	College of Creative Studies
New Freshmen	2995	214	21
Average GPA	3.45	3.53	3.95
Average Test Scores			
SAT Verbal	459	459	543
SAT Math	541	623	665

SANTA CRUZ

ALL COLLEGES

ACADEMIC CRITERIA

Academic criteria are used to select sixty percent of admits. Applicants accepted for admission are those who demonstrate the strongest comprehensive academic preparation measured by the following criteria:

1. GPA for all academic courses completed in the "a-f" Subject Requirement with additional points given for honors-level courses. The maximum calculated GPA cannot exceed 4.00.

2. Test scores on the SAT I: Reasoning Test or ACT, and the three required SAT II: Subject Tests.

3. The number and content of courses taken in academic subjects beyond the minimum required for admission to the University.

4. The number of University-approved honors-level, accelerated, or Advanced Placement courses completed or in progress.

UCSC FALL 1993 ENROLLED FRESHMEN

Average GPA 3.61

GPA Range	% Of Freshmen
3.60 to 4.00	46.1%
3.20 to 3.59	36.7%
2.80 to 3.19	14.0%
2.40 to 2.79	2.2%

Average SAT Scores
- verbal 504
- mathematics 553

SAT Range	% Of Freshmen verbal	math
700 to 800	2.6%	7.7%
600 to 699	16.4%	27.0%
500 to 599	36.6%	39.8%
400 to 499	30.3%	19.1%
Below 400	14.2%	6.4%

SUPPLEMENTAL CRITERIA

Supplemental criteria — described on page 11--23 are used to select the remaining forty percent of admits. Applicants are evaluated using the academic criteria described above in conjunction with supplemental criteria.

UNIVERSITY OF CALIFORNIA

FRESHMAN PROFILE — FALL 1993

The Freshman Profile summarizes by campus the qualifications of applicants and admitted freshmen for fall 1993. The Profile is most useful as a guide to the selection process, rather than to predict your chances for admission. Separate figures are included for non-engineering and engineering programs.

Grade point average, GPA, intervals are listed vertically and SAT composite score (mathematics plus verbal) intervals are listed horizontally. Each block in the chart represents a pool of applicants with GPA and SAT scores within the specific intervals indicated. In each block, the first figure on the first line is the total number of applicants. The second figure on the first line is the number of applicants regularly admitted. The figure in bold type on the second line is the percentage of students who were regularly admitted.

GPA is defined as a student's GPA in the "a-f" Subject Requirement as calculated by a UC admissions evaluator or, if the evaluated GPA was not available, the student's self-reported GPA. Campus overall totals include freshmen whose GPA and/or SAT composite score were out of range or not available. Data is as of October 1993.

LEGEND: applicants/regular admits
% regularly admitted

ALL PROGRAMS EXCEPT ENGINEERING

BERKELEY

GPA ▼ / SAT COMPOSITE	490-790	800-990	1000-1190	1200-1390	1400-1600	OVERALL
2.82-2.99			115/7 **6%**	43/4 **9%**	5/2 **40%**	163/13 **8%**
3.00-3.29	205/14 **7%**	511/90 **18%**	672/105 **16%**	273/43 **16%**	19/7 **37%**	1680/259 **15%**
3.30-3.59	172/36 **21%**	661/175 **27%**	1071/220 **21%**	575/125 **22%**	54/30 **56%**	2533/586 **23%**
3.60-3.89	115/33 **29%**	661/208 **32%**	1472/348 **24%**	1092/420 **39%**	133/109 **82%**	3473/1118 **32%**
3.90-3.99	21/9 **43%**	119/37 **31%**	320/97 **30%**	323/201 **62%**	48/47 **98%**	831/391 **47%**
4.00	41/9 **22%**	399/128 **32%**	1840/679 **37%**	3150/2509 **80%**	1068/1044 **98%**	6498/4369 **67%**
OVERALL	554/101 **18%**	2351/638 **27%**	5490/1456 **27%**	5456/3302 **61%**	1327/1239 **93%**	16926/7062 **42%**

DAVIS

GPA ▼ / SAT COMPOSITE	490-790	800-990	1000-1190	1200-1390	1400-1600	OVERALL
2.82-2.99			183/21 **12%**	44/13 **30%**	4/4 **100%**	231/38 **17%**
3.00-3.29	260/75 **29%**	804/206 **26%**	830/196 **24%**	258/239 **93%**	7/6 **86%**	2159/722 **33%**
3.30-3.59	236/135 **57%**	885/320 **36%**	1247/776 **62%**	419/411 **98%**	20/20 **100%**	2807/1662 **59%**
3.60-3.89	149/93 **62%**	795/489 **62%**	1490/1343 **90%**	656/645 **98%**	49/48 **98%**	3139/2618 **83%**
3.90-3.99	15/12 **80%**	125/100 **80%**	299/284 **95%**	165/161 **98%**	16/16 **100%**	620/573 **92%**
4.00	58/37 **64%**	431/372 **86%**	1440/1404 **98%**	1471/1461 **99%**	261/256 **98%**	3661/3530 **96%**
OVERALL	718/352 **49%**	3040/1487 **49%**	5489/4024 **73%**	3013/2930 **97%**	357/350 **98%**	14206/9413 **66%**

ENGINEERING PROGRAMS

BERKELEY

GPA ▼ / SAT COMPOSITE	490-790	800-990	1000-1190	1200-1390	1400-1600	OVERALL
2.82-2.99			15/1 **7%**	4/0 **0%**	0/0 **0%**	19/1 **5%**
3.00-3.29	16/0 **0%**	49/2 **4%**	72/1 **1%**	43/3 **7%**	5/2 **40%**	185/8 **4%**
3.30-3.59	26/0 **0%**	84/0 **0%**	155/9 **6%**	88/13 **15%**	15/7 **47%**	368/29 **8%**
3.60-3.89	17/0 **0%**	99/1 **1%**	231/23 **10%**	206/72 **35%**	41/32 **78%**	594/128 **22%**
3.90-3.99	3/0 **0%**	14/1 **7%**	67/15 **22%**	72/39 **54%**	14/13 **93%**	170/68 **40%**
4.00	9/0 **0%**	81/6 **7%**	350/102 **29%**	814/530 **65%**	319/305 **96%**	1573/943 **60%**
OVERALL	71/0 **0%**	327/10 **3%**	890/151 **17%**	1227/657 **54%**	394/359 **91%**	3191/1206 **38%**

DAVIS

GPA ▼ / SAT COMPOSITE	490-790	800-990	1000-1190	1200-1390	1400-1600	OVERALL
2.82-2.99			14/2 **14%**	7/1 **14%**	1/1 **100%**	22/4 **18%**
3.00-3.29	15/0 **0%**	58/6 **10%**	103/40 **39%**	43/39 **91%**	5/5 **100%**	224/90 **40%**
3.30-3.59	14/0 **0%**	76/19 **25%**	172/98 **57%**	85/81 **95%**	7/7 **100%**	354/205 **58%**
3.60-3.89	12/0 **0%**	84/43 **51%**	195/177 **91%**	149/147 **99%**	15/15 **100%**	455/382 **84%**
3.90-3.99	0/0 **0%**	11/5 **46%**	36/34 **94%**	44/43 **98%**	4/4 **100%**	95/86 **91%**
4.00	3/0 **0%**	49/43 **88%**	260/254 **98%**	393/392 **99%**	96/95 **99%**	801/784 **98%**
OVERALL	44/0 **0%**	278/116 **42%**	780/605 **78%**	721/703 **98%**	128/127 **99%**	2143/1598 **75%**

LEGEND: applicants/regular admits
% regularly admitted

ALL PROGRAMS EXCEPT ENGINEERING

IRVINE

GPA	SAT 490-790	SAT 800-990	SAT 1000-1190	SAT 1200-1390	SAT 1400-1600	OVERALL
2.82-2.99			157/15 10%	53/11 21%	4/3 75%	214/29 14%
3.00-3.29	362/41 11%	914/228 25%	915/402 44%	239/166 70%	7/71 100%	2437/844 35%
3.30-3.59	315/109 48%	1063/627 59%	1198/955 80%	335/309 92%	17/15 88%	2928/2015 69%
3.60-3.89	249/119 48%	897/639 71%	1326/1214 92%	497/471 95%	30/28 93%	2999/2471 82%
3.90-3.99	19/7 37%	162/128 79%	269/252 94%	110/109 99%	5/4 80%	565/500 89%
4.00	81/45 56%	560/482 86%	1309/1263 97%	1178/1156 98%	211/205 97%	3339/3151 94%
OVERALL	1026/321 31%	3596/2104 59%	5174/4101 79%	2412/2222 92%	274/262 96%	14197/9187 65%

LOS ANGELES

GPA	SAT 490-790	SAT 800-990	SAT 1000-1190	SAT 1200-1390	SAT 1400-1600	OVERALL
2.82-2.99			155/27 17%	56/4 7%	4/1 25%	215/32 15%
3.00-3.29	367/19 5%	867/187 22%	902/175 19%	277/30 11%	15/3 20%	2428/414 17%
3.30-3.59	304/38 13%	1029/311 30%	1466/330 23%	504/116 23%	42/18 43%	3345/813 24%
3.60-3.89	247/32 13%	1068/361 34%	1883/627 33%	1001/689 69%	92/83 90%	4291/1792 42%
3.90-3.99	26/7 27%	183/71 39%	406/188 46%	261/235 90%	26/26 100%	904/527 58%
4.00	67/12 18%	633/245 39%	2171/1279 59%	2771/2638 95%	724/707 98%	6366/4881 77%
OVERALL	1011/108 11%	3780/1175 31%	6985/2626 38%	4870/3712 76%	903/838 93%	19579/8695 44%

RIVERSIDE

GPA	SAT 490-790	SAT 800-990	SAT 1000-1190	SAT 1200-1390	SAT 1400-1600	OVERALL
2.82-2.99			158/52 33%	48/17 35%	2/1 50%	208/70 34%
3.00-3.29	318/78 25%	765/340 44%	637/363 57%	152/94 62%	4/3 75%	1876/878 47%
3.30-3.59	271/166 61%	711/486 68%	730/515 71%	181/118 65%	12/10 83%	1905/1295 68%
3.60-3.89	160/106 66%	597/420 70%	748/545 73%	221/170 77%	19/15 79%	1745/1256 72%
3.90-3.99	10/7 70%	98/65 66%	133/91 68%	49/34 69%	3/3 100%	293/200 68%
4.00	50/36 72%	289/217 75%	629/483 77%	483/382 79%	99/84 85%	1550/1202 78%
OVERALL	809/393 49%	2460/1528 62%	3035/2049 68%	1134/815 72%	139/116 84%	8936/5005 56%

ENGINEERING PROGRAMS

IRVINE

GPA	SAT 490-790	SAT 800-990	SAT 1000-1190	SAT 1200-1390	SAT 1400-1600	OVERALL
2.82-2.99			10/0 0%	8/1 13%	0/0 0%	18/1 6%
3.00-3.29	7/0 0%	47/5 11%	87/45 52%	31/20 65%	2/2 100%	174/72 41%
3.30-3.59	10/0 0%	56/18 32%	141/114 81%	70/63 90%	4/4 100%	281/199 71%
3.60-3.89	5/0 0%	60/23 38%	188/154 82%	109/101 93%	11/11 100%	373/289 78%
3.90-3.99	0/0 0%	7/3 43%	38/32 84%	31/31 100%	1/1 100%	77/67 87%
4.00	4/0 0%	49/36 74%	187/179 96%	215/214 99%	36/35 97%	491/464 95%
OVERALL	26/0 0%	219/85 39%	651/524 81%	464/430 93%	54/53 98%	1505/1113 74%

LOS ANGELES

GPA	SAT 490-790	SAT 800-990	SAT 1000-1190	SAT 1200-1390	SAT 1400-1600	OVERALL
2.82-2.99			12/0 0%	3/0 0%	0/0 0%	15/0 0%
3.00-3.29	28/0 0%	71/0 0%	78/3 4%	43/9 21%	4/2 50%	224/14 6%
3.30-3.59	26/0 0%	82/0 0%	158/20 13%	95/67 71%	8/7 88%	369/94 26%
3.60-3.89	19/0 0%	86/2 2%	213/61 29%	164/131 80%	25/23 92%	507/217 43%
3.90-3.99	2/0 0%	17/0 0%	48/22 46%	56/49 88%	9/9 100%	132/80 61%
4.00	6/0 0%	69/5 7%	267/148 55%	515/496 96%	194/190 98%	1051/839 80%
OVERALL	81/0 0%	325/7 2%	776/254 33%	876/752 86%	240/231 96%	2587/1255 49%

RIVERSIDE

GPA	SAT 490-790	SAT 800-990	SAT 1000-1190	SAT 1200-1390	SAT 1400-1600	OVERALL
2.82-2.99			4/1 25%	5/1 20%	0/0 0%	9/2 22%
3.00-3.29	18/3 17%	62/16 26%	66/41 62%	11/6 55%	0/0 0%	157/66 42%
3.30-3.59	21/12 57%	70/41 59%	77/46 60%	30/17 57%	1/0 0%	199/116 58%
3.60-3.89	14/8 57%	51/31 61%	87/54 62%	36/26 72%	2/1 50%	190/120 63%
3.90-3.99	3/1 33%	8/4 50%	10/7 70%	8/2 25%	0/0 0%	29/14 48%
4.00	6/3 50%	22/15 68%	68/46 68%	49/37 76%	6/4 67%	151/105 70%
OVERALL	62/27 44%	213/107 50%	312/195 63%	139/89 64%	9/5 56%	843/427 51%

UNIVERSITY OF CALIFORNIA

LEGEND: applicants/regular admits
% regularly admitted

ALL PROGRAMS EXCEPT ENGINEERING

GPA / SAT COMPOSITE	490-790	800-990	1000-1190	1200-1390	1400-1600	OVERALL
SAN DIEGO						
2.82-2.99			145/0 0%	55/3 6%	3/1 33%	203/4 2%
3.00-3.29	264/11 4%	742/70 9%	932/76 8%	322/80 25%	11/9 82%	2271/246 11%
3.30-3.59	200/20 10%	866/171 20%	1424/426 30%	565/380 67%	33/33 100%	3088/1030 33%
3.60-3.89	133/28 21%	793/279 35%	1722/1137 66%	913/835 92%	79/76 96%	3640/2355 65%
3.90-399	12/3 25%	140/86 61%	330/279 85%	222/207 93%	29/28 97%	733/603 82%
4.00	41/18 44%	413/307 74%	1731/1602 93%	2228/2161 97%	580/566 98%	4993/4654 93%
OVERALL	650/80 12%	2954/913 31%	6284/3520 56%	4305/3666 85%	735/713 97%	16558/9108 55%
SANTA BARBARA						
2.82-2.99			208/29 14%	56/31 55%	3/3 100%	267/63 24%
3.00-3.29	319/91 29%	1056/661 63%	1202/969 81%	302/276 91%	10/10 100%	2889/2007 70%
3.30-3.59	254/221 87%	1088/1021 94%	1600/1557 97%	438/428 98%	18/18 100%	3398/3245 96%
3.60-3.89	150/140 93%	833/809 97%	1613/1599 99%	585/580 99%	23/23 100%	3204/3151 98%
3.90-3.99	15/14 93%	111/110 99%	294/290 99%	126/126 100%	4/4 100%	550/544 99%
4.00	45/42 93%	359/354 99%	1250/1238 99%	903/898 99%	91/88 97%	2648/2620 99%
OVERALL	783/508 65%	3447/2955 86%	6167/5682 92%	2410/2339 97%	149/146 98%	15452/12832 80%
SANTA CRUZ						
2.82-2.99			162/39 24%	59/36 61%	6/6 100%	227/81 36%
3.00-3.29	241/100 42%	694/388 56%	906/658 73%	321/267 83%	11/10 91%	2173/1423 66%
3.30-3.59	171/128 75%	673/584 87%	1127/1039 92%	410/388 95%	30/30 100%	2411/2169 90%
3.60-3.89	89/75 84%	471/430 91%	1041/1007 97%	496/489 99%	51/50 98%	2148/2051 96%
3.90-3.99	9/6 67%	60/58 97%	182/173 95%	106/104 98%	13/13 100%	370/354 96%
4.00	21/19 91%	153/147 96%	631/624 99%	646/643 99%	104/104 100%	1555/1537 99%
OVERALL	531/328 62%	2051/1607 78%	4049/3540 87%	2038/1927 95%	215/213 99%	10466/7933 76%

ENGINEERING PROGRAMS

GPA / SAT COMPOSITE	490-790	800-990	1000-1190	1200-1390	1400-1600	OVERALL
SAN DIEGO						
2.82- 2.99			12/0 0%	3/1 33%	1/0 0%	16/1 6%
3.00-3.29	23/0 0%	57/15 26%	97/18 19%	41/14 34%	3/3 100%	221/50 23%
3.30-3.59	26/2 8%	93/26 28%	184/66 36%	105/76 72%	12/12 100%	420/182 43%
3.60-3.89	16/2 13%	118/58 49%	285/198 70%	194/179 92%	30/29 97%	643/466 73%
3.90-3.99	4/2 50%	13/10 77%	72/65 90%	59/59 100%	6/6 100%	154/142 92%
4.00	17/7 41%	77/60 78%	337/317 94%	623/605 97%	194/192 99%	1248/1181 95%
OVERALL	86/13 15%	358/169 47%	987/664 67%	1025/934 91%	246/242 98%	2875/2060 72%
SANTA BARBARA						
2.82-2.99			9/2 22%	6/2 33%	1/1 100%	16/5 31%
3.00-3.29	7/0 0%	37/23 62%	74/61 82%	31/29 94%	2/2 100%	151/115 76%
3.30-3.59	6/1 17%	59/52 88%	132/128 97%	68/67 99%	2/2 100%	267/250 94%
3.60-3.89	4/2 50%	39/37 95%	145/144 99%	82/81 99%	8/8 100%	278/272 98%
3.90-3.99	0/0 0%	7/7 100%	27/27 100%	23/23 100%	2/2 100%	59/59 100%
4.00	3/2 67%	28/27 96%	121/121 100%	139/138 99%	17/17 100%	308/305 99%
OVERALL	20/5 25%	170/146 86%	508/483 95%	349/340 97%	32/32 100%	1210/1050 88%
SANTA CRUZ						
2.82-2.99			3/1 33%	1/0 0%	0/0 0%	4/1 25%
3.00-3.29	5/2 40%	15/8 53%	14/10 71%	10/10 100%	1/1 100%	45/31 69%
3.30-3.59	8/4 50%	24/23 96%	23/23 100%	8/7 88%	1/1 100%	64/58 91%
3.60-3.89	6/4 67%	14/13 93%	20/20 100%	13/13 100%	2/2 100%	55/52 95%
3.90-3.99	1/1 100%	1/1 100%	4/4 100%	4/4 100%	2/2 100%	12/12 100%
4.00	1/1 100%	13/11 85%	14/14 100%	17/17 100%	5/5 100%	50/48 96%
OVERALL	21/12 57%	67/56 84%	78/72 92%	53/51 96%	11/11 100%	264/208 79%

MAJORS — APPLICATION AND SCREENING

Some colleges and schools at the University of California campuses have special application requirements and screening procedures for students applying to certain majors and programs of study. For example, if you are applying as a Fine Arts major, you may be required to audition or submit a portfolio as part of the application process. Another program may require you to complete a special application form. Other special application and screening procedures pertain to prerequisite coursework, test scores, grade point average, and entering class level. Several majors accept you for the fall term only.

While some majors do accept incoming freshmen, many accept students only as pre-majors. You must complete substantial pre-major coursework at the college freshman and/or sophomore levels before you are subsequently admitted to your major. Additionally, the campuses expect you to achieve a minimum GPA in these courses, or a minimum overall University GPA, to demonstrate readiness for your major.

State your intended major on your admission application, even if you will not enter it until your sophomore or junior year. Doing this places you in the appropriate program to prepare you for that major.

You may want to consider an alternate major at those campuses to which you apply. Some campuses will not consider you for admission to an alternate major, while others will require or recommend making an alternate choice. Policies regarding consideration of alternate majors are described for each campus. Caution: Review of your application for an alternate choice major does not mean the campus will accept you to this major.

The following are application and screening procedures for freshman applicants to some of the colleges, schools, and majors at specific University campuses. If you do not find your major noted, it is because there are no special application or screening procedures at this time. If you have questions or concerns about majors not noted, call or write to the college or school at the University campus that offers your major.

In all cases, apply during the initial one-month filing period — November for fall admission. Additional information regarding application procedures can be found later in this chapter: Applying To The University Of California, page 11–47.

BERKELEY

In general, Berkeley does not consider applicants for admission to alternate majors.

WALTER A. HAAS SCHOOL OF BUSINESS ADMINISTRATION

Apply for freshman admission to the College of Letters and Sciences as Undeclared. When you become a sophomore at the College, apply for admission to the School of Business Administration for your junior year. Continuing Berkeley students and transfer applicants from other UC campuses and the community colleges compete for a limited number of spaces. Each year the School of Business Administration admits approximately seventy students in the fall semester and forty in the spring semester. The average college GPA for students accepted into the School of Business Administration in their junior year is 3.70 to 3.80. The most important prerequisites are the mathematics and English sequences. You may not earn more than one grade of C in either sequence. Consult the School for lower-division prerequisites and other requirements.

COLLEGE OF CHEMISTRY

Freshmen are accepted for the fall semester only. You must declare a major in either Chemical Engineering or Chemistry at the time of application.

COLLEGE OF ENGINEERING

You must declare a specific engineering major on your undergraduate application to be considered for engineering at Berkeley. Investigate the competition for each engineering major and consider your qualifications before making your decision. Freshmen may apply for admission to engineering for the fall semester only.

Do not enroll in the College of Letters and Science with the intention of transferring to the College of Engineering later. The College of Engineering will not readily admit you. If engineering interests you, apply to other UC campus engineering programs as a backup to Berkeley.

You may major in Computer Science in the College of Letters and Science as well as in the College of Engineering. Chemical Engineering is offered in the College of Chemistry.

COLLEGE OF LETTERS AND SCIENCE

None of the majors in the College of Letters and Science admit freshmen. You may indicate a premajor or apply Undeclared with no specific major on your admissions application. After you complete prerequisite courses and other requirements as specified by the department, you formally apply for admission to your major.

COMPUTER SCIENCE: Computer Science at Berkeley is oversubscribed. You must first complete the majority of lower-division requirements for the major. A GPA of at least 3.50 in the lower division technical requirements is necessary, but GPA's of most students accepted into the major are higher.

MUSIC: Prospective majors must take a placement examination within the department.

ECONOMICS: Although many factors are considered in determining admission to the major, a primary criterion is academic performance measured by GPA in prerequisite courses.

POLITICAL SCIENCE: The most academically qualified and prepared applicants are accepted into this major.

DAVIS

Davis assigns you a faculty advisor based upon the undergraduate major or program of study you indicate on your admission application. All applicants are encouraged to select an alternate major.

If you are undecided, there are two programs available that allow you to explore areas of study before formally declaring a major.

ACADEMIC OPTIONS PROGRAM: This program in the College of Letters and Science offers you the opportunity to apply Undeclared — no specific major — within five broad areas: Fine Arts, Humanities, Life Sciences, Physical Sciences, and Social Sciences. You receive academic advising as you explore your interests.

EXPLORATORY PROGRAM: The College of Agricultural and Environmental Sciences offers this program and provides academic advising. You may ultimately transfer to majors in the three undergraduate colleges.

COLLEGE OF AGRICULTURAL AND ENVIRONMENTAL SCIENCES

If you wish to major in Landscape Architecture or pursue an Individual Major, the College automatically places you in the Exploratory program until you complete the appropriate requirements. The Individual Major program allows you to design your own major and curriculum if existing majors in the College do not satisfy your academic interests and your educational objectives are compatible with those of the College.

COLLEGE OF ENGINEERING

You must indicate a specific major. The College admits freshmen for the fall quarter only.

IRVINE

Applicants to the School of Biological Science and the School of Engineering are advised to select an alternate major (economics or engineering).

SCHOOL OF ENGINEERING

Freshmen are generally accepted in the fall quarter. You must select an engineering discipline on your application: Civil, Electrical, or Mechanical. You are advised to consider second-choice majors such as Applied Physics, Mathematics, or Physics.

Freshman applicants are subject to additional screening beyond minimum UC eligibility requirements. You should have completed four years of college-preparatory mathematics and one year each of college-preparatory chemistry and physics. Special consideration is given to students who have taken honors-level and Advanced Placement courses.

DEPARTMENT OF INFORMATION AND COMPUTER SCIENCE

COMPUTER SCIENCE: If you are interested in a Computer Science major oriented toward theory and application — software — specify Information and Computer Science on your application. If you are interested in a major oriented toward design of computer equipment — hardware — specify Electrical and Computer Engineering.

SCHOOL OF FINE ARTS

DANCE MAJORS AND MUSIC MAJORS: An audition is required.

SCHOOL OF SOCIAL SCIENCES

ECONOMICS AND PSYCHOLOGY: Only a limited number of freshman applicants are admitted directly to these majors. Those admitted are usually selected on the basis of academic criteria alone. If you are not selected for the major as a freshman, you may enroll in lower-division prerequisite courses and petition for the major as a junior based upon performance in the prerequisites.

UNDECLARED MAJORS

Undeclared majors are open to freshman- and sophomore-level applicants only. You can apply under one of these options:

1. If you are uncertain about choosing a major or do not feel ready to declare a major until you have been on campus awhile, you can apply as an Undecided/Undeclared major. You will be advised by the General Studies Advising program.
2. If you are interested in a particular school but have not decided upon a specific major, you can apply as an Undeclared major within that school; e.g., Fine Arts/Undeclared. You will be advised by the School's academic counselor. On your application you may state Undecided/Undeclared, Fine Arts/Undeclared, Humanities/Undeclared, Physical Sciences/Undeclared, or Social Sciences/Undeclared.

LOS ANGELES

You may indicate an alternate major. However, in general, applicants to schools/colleges other than the School of Engineering and Applied Science are not considered for admission to alternate majors.

COLLEGE OF LETTERS AND SCIENCE

You may apply as Undeclared or to an Undeclared major within a general field: Humanities, Life Sciences, Physical Sciences, or Social Sciences.

SCHOOL OF THE ARTS SCHOOL OF THEATER, FILM, AND TELEVISION

The School of the Arts includes the majors of Art, Dance, Design, Ethnomusicology, Music, and World Arts and Cultures. The School of Theater, Film, and Television includes two majors: Theater and Motion Picture/Television.

A limited number of new students are accepted into each major each year. Students are admitted at the freshman, sophomore, and junior levels to all majors except Motion Picture/Television. Motion Picture/Television admits juniors only. The schools admit students in the fall quarter. You may apply for just one major in the Schools; list it as your first choice on your application.

Upon their receipt of your admission application, the School sends you a special questionnaire relating to your previous training and experience in the arts, and your goals and interests. Applicants in all majors must demonstrate artistic ability and potential through submission of a portfolio, auditions, interviews, and/or questionnaires.

Applicants are selected by faculty committees in each major. The committees seek applicants with strong academic backgrounds, good communication skills, demonstrated artistic ability, and potential for success at UCLA. If you are not accepted into a fine arts major, UCLA does *not guarantee admission* to the campus in another area of study.

ART: Applicants must submit a portfolio of five slides of art work in any media.

DANCE: An audition is required.

DESIGN: Design is closed to new applicants until further notice.

MOTION PICTURE/TELEVISION: Only juniors who have satisfied all University and college General Education/Breadth Requirements with a GPA of at least a 3.00 are admitted to the major. A written portfolio is required.

MUSIC: An audition is required.

SCHOOL OF ENGINEERING AND APPLIED SCIENCE

Admission is very competitive. You must select a specific major within the school when applying. The School recommends that you also select a second-choice engineering major. You are considered for your second choice if your record is competitive.

SCHOOL OF NURSING

Fifty students are accepted each year in the fall quarter only. You must be at least at the junior level with a minimum GPA of 2.80.

RIVERSIDE

Applicants to the College of Engineering, Biomedical Sciences, and Business Administration must indicate an alternate major.

COLLEGE OF HUMANITIES AND SOCIAL SCIENCES

BUSINESS: Freshmen interested in the Business Administration major should indicate the pre-Business major on their application.

COLLEGE OF NATURAL AND AGRICULTURAL SCIENCES

BIOMEDICAL SCIENCES: The Biomedical Sciences major, offered in cooperation with the School of Medicine at UCLA, makes it possible for students to earn the M.D. degree in seven years instead of eight. Students complete their undergraduate training in Biomedical Sciences in three years at the Riverside campus. They then formally apply for admission to the medical school phase of the program.

Students complete the first year of medical school at the Riverside campus, the second year at the Harbor/UCLA Medical Center in Torrance, CA under the auspices of UCR, and the final two years at UCLA under the auspices of the UCLA School of Medicine.

This program is open only to new, first-time freshmen who enter UCR in the fall quarter. High school courses in physics, chemistry, biology, and mathematics — at least through trigonometry — are strongly recommended. Applicants who excel in the academic criteria are considered. The following preparation is strongly recommended: At least three high school laboratory courses; mathematics competency to qualify for college-level calculus; and English composition proficiency to qualify for placement in either English 1A or Basic Writing 1 at the time of enrollment.

If you do not qualify for the major, but do meet campus selection criteria, Riverside offers you your alternate major.

This is a rigorous academic program. At the end of each year of the first three years, you are evaluated to determine if you are qualified to continue in the program. Although Biomedical Sciences admits about three-hundred students to the program as freshmen, about thirty remain in it by the end of the third year.

It is the experience of the faculty of the Division of Biomedical Sciences that successful applicants to the medical school phase — the fourth year — are usually from the upper thirtieth to thirty-fifth percentile of high school graduates taking the SAT I. If you meet only the minimum standards for admission to the University, apply for the standard premedical program.

COLLEGE OF ENGINEERING

The College of Engineering accepts applications for the fall quarter only. Freshman applicants who excel in the academic criteria, with additional emphasis upon mathematics and science preparation, and who qualify for first-quarter calculus are selected. If you do not qualify for the major, but meet campus selection criteria, you are offered your alternate major.

SAN DIEGO

In addition to selecting a major, you also must select a college within UCSD as your first choice on your admission application, and rank all others in order of preference. Each of the five colleges — Revelle, John Muir, Marshall, Earl Warren, and Fifth — offers all the undergraduate majors available at the campus. Your major does not determine the College in which you enroll. However, because each college has somewhat different General Education/Breadth Requirements, it benefits you to select the College that best matches your educational goals. You may be reassigned to another college if space is not available in your first choice. If you do not indicate a college preference you are assigned to one. The colleges are fully described later in this chapter: Campus Profiles, pages 11--79 to 11--83.

You do not need to select an alternate major.

DIVISION OF ENGINEERING

If you have previously demonstrated excellent academic performance, you are admitted directly into the engineering major of your choice. If you are not admitted directly into an engineering major, you are initially considered to have pre-Engineering major status. As a pre-Engineering college freshman student, plan to complete the specified prerequisite courses and apply for admission to an engineering major during the spring quarter of your freshman year. Your academic performance in the prerequisite courses is the admission criterion for the engineering major. Because enrollment is limited, you may apply to more than one engineering program. A special application is required.

MATHEMATICS/ COMPUTER SCIENCE

If you apply to this major, you are initially considered to have Pre-Mathematics/Computer Science status. You must successfully complete a prescribed set of courses at UCSD for later admission to the major.

SAN FRANCISCO

UCSF is devoted solely to the study of the health sciences and accepts no freshmen. *You must have completed college study in preprofessional courses before you qualify to apply for admission.* A solid scientific background is indispensable to preparation for education in the health sciences. Good grades and test scores are necessary for admission; however, your academic and career potential, and willingness to work hard are also important considerations.

You are admitted to all programs in the fall quarter. Application filing dates and financial aid procedures differ from those at other UC campuses. Contact the admissions office at the appropriate UCSF school at least eighteen months before you plan to enroll to obtain all the necessary information.

The Schools of Dentistry, Medicine, and Pharmacy admit qualified undergraduates who have completed required college coursework; however, the majority of medical and dental students who enroll have graduated from college. The School of Nursing is open only to college graduates. The program in Dental Hygiene is open to qualified undergraduates with at least two years of preparatory college work.

Shown on the next page is the minimum amount of college study required to be eligible for admission to the various programs.

Program	Undergraduate Preparation	Openings Each Year
Dental Hygiene	2 Years	18
Dentistry	3 to 4 Years, Bachelor's degree recommended	84
Medicine	3 to 4 Years, Bachelor's degree recommended	141
Nursing	Bachelor's degree and R.N. license	297
Pharmacy	2 Years	117
Physical Therapy	Bachelor's degree	32

SANTA BARBARA

COLLEGE OF CREATIVE STUDIES

The College of Creative Studies, CCS, offers a stimulating academic environment to talented, independently productive undergraduates. Each of the approximately two hundred students enjoys close individual advising and academic attention from among the 35-40 faculty members. Each course provides, not an exposure to a predetermined quantity of fixed subject matter, but an occasion for rigorously exploring and modifying a field of knowledge. Through intense creative work and research projects, students acquire a thorough comprehension of their discipline and are encouraged to begin making original contributions to the field.

The grading system is focused upon accomplishment and is a combination of Pass/No Record and variable-unit credit. A Pass in a course is given only for work completed at an above average level — 3.00 or higher. For each course, the student may receive any number of units from 0 to 6; the instructor determines the value of the work completed. If a 0 is received, the course is not recorded on the student's transcript.

Students are selected upon the basis of interests and qualifications in one or more of the following subjects: Art (painting, sculpture, or book arts), biology, chemistry, literature, mathematics, music composition, and physics. If you are not admitted to the College of Creative Studies, you are considered automatically for admission to the College of Letters and Science.

You normally spend at least six quarters in CCS, regardless of previous college credit, to earn a CCS degree.

You must apply to the College of Creative Studies on your admission application. CCS sends you a brochure within six weeks of receipt of filing your UC admission application. It describes CCS application procedures and requests that you provide the following:

1. A completed data form included in the brochure on which you must specify one of the seven CCS disciplines. You cannot be admitted Undeclared.

2. A personal letter of intent in which you state your academic interests, reasons for wanting to study in CCS, and qualifications.

3. High school and any college transcripts. These are in addition to any transcripts requested by UCSB's admissions office.

4. Work in evidence of talent for faculty review. Send slides of art work, samples of fiction and/or verse, original music compositions and audio tape recordings, scientific reports or evidence of completed projects to demonstrate talent.

5. Letters of recommendation from persons well acquainted with your academic background — at least two for Biology, Chemistry, Physics, Mathematics, and Music majors. Letters are helpful, but not essential, for Art and Literature majors.

If you do not receive this brochure by early January, call or write to the College of Creative Studies on the UCSB campus. Their telephone number is (805) 893-2364.

COLLEGE OF ENGINEERING

The College of Engineering admits students in the fall quarter only. You must declare a specific major offered within the College on your application. If you are unsure of which major to select, list both a primary and alternate choice.

Although the Computer Science major is offered by both the College of Engineering and the College of Letters and Science at Santa Barbara, the admission pools for both majors are integrated, and the same screening criteria are used. Select Computer Science in the College of Letters and Science to study the theory and application of computer programming systems — software — or Electrical Engineering in the College of Engineering to study the design of computers and associated equipment — hardware.

Different screening criteria may be used for different majors in the College of Engineering. If you fail to meet the criteria for your primary major and you selected an alternate major requiring different criteria, you are considered for admission to your alternate major in the College. If you are not admitted to the College of Engineering, you are automatically considered for admission to open majors in the College of Letters and Science.

In the majors of Electrical Engineering and Computer Science, you are admitted to pre-major status and must satisfy prerequisites at a certain level before acceptance to the full major.

Once enrolled at UCSB, the opportunity to change to an engineering major is limited to once a year. If you wish to petition for a change of major, you must have achieved an outstanding academic record at UCSB and must have completed a specified sequence of preparatory courses at the University.

The College of Engineering cautions you against applying to an unrelated major to avoid their screening process. Your University record is carefully evaluated before you are allowed to transfer to an Engineering or Computer Science major.

COLLEGE OF LETTERS AND SCIENCE

The following are majors that accept students only as pre-majors: Business Economics/Economics, Communication, Computer Science, Economics/Mathematics, Mathematics, Mathematical Sciences, Political Science, Psychology and Sociology. Subsequent admission to full-major status is contingent upon completion of pre-major courses and achieving a specific minimum GPA. Admission to pre-major status does not guarantee subsequent admission to full-major status.

Dance and Music majors require auditions. Dance auditions take place in February and May of the year preceding intended enrollment. They are also offered during registration week of the fall quarter to applicants unable to attend the winter or spring audition. UCSB advises you to attend one of the earlier auditions to reserve space in the program. Music applicants must take a placement examination prior to enrolling in the first course in music theory and must audition before enrolling in the first performance class. Auditions are held each January.

SANTA CRUZ

You need not declare an alternative major. If you are uncertain about a major or plan to develop an Individual major, apply Undeclared; this does not reduce your chances for acceptance. If you apply for an Individual major, list the specific study area that interests you. The following Individual majors are developed in coordination with faculty sponsors: Ethnic Studies, Medieval Studies, Religious Studies, Russian Studies, South and Southeast Asian Studies, Western Civilization.

The major you select on your application does not determine the residential college within UCSC to which you are assigned. All of UCSC's academic programs and resources are open to students of all the Colleges. The eight residential colleges are fully described later in this chapter in Campus Profiles, page 11--83.

COMPUTER AND INFORMATION SCIENCE: You should have completed four years of mathematics through advanced algebra and trigonometry and three years of science in high school. You are encouraged to take one or both Advanced Placement Examinations in Computer Science — A and/or AB. See chapter 6: COLLEGE ENTRANCE TESTS, AP Program And Examinations, page 6--57.

COMPUTER ENGINEERING: You should have completed four years of mathematics through algebra and trigonometry, one year of chemistry, and one year of physics in high school. You are encouraged to take one or both Advanced Placement Examinations in Computer Science — A and/or AB.

3/2 DUAL DEGREE ENGINEERING PROGRAM: This highly selective, five-year program, in conjunction with Berkeley, is open to freshman applicants in the fall quarter only. You spend three years in this program at Santa Cruz, completing most of the requirements for a Bachelor's degree in one of the fields in the social sciences or humanities. For the fourth and fifth years of the program, you transfer to Berkeley where you complete the requirements for a degree in a chosen engineering specialty. You also complete any remaining courses in your Santa Cruz major. Upon completion of the program, you receive two Bachelor's degrees: a B.A. in a social science or humanities field from Santa Cruz, and a B.S. in engineering from Berkeley. Each student applicant is carefully reviewed on an individual basis.

SAA AND EOP

STUDENT AFFIRMATIVE ACTION
EDUCATIONAL OPPORTUNITY PROGRAM

The University recognizes and values the intellectual and cultural contributions of a student population that reflects the rich diversity of the people of California. To promote this diversity, the University has two special programs to (a) help students interested in attending UC, and (b) provide support services once enrolled: The Student Affirmative Action program, SAA, and the Educational Opportunity Program, EOP.

SAA and EOP are programs to encourage students from diverse ethnic and socioeconomic backgrounds to attend the University.

SAA — STUDENT AFFIRMATIVE ACTION

SAA is a special program of support services for students from groups historically underrepresented at the University, who are academically eligible for regular admission, but who want assistance. Underrepresented groups are those ethnic groups that do not have the same percentage of representation on campus as they do in the general population.

EOP — EDUCATIONAL OPPORTUNITY PROGRAM

EOP — named AAP, Academic Advancement Program, at UCLA — is a special program of support to students meeting the criteria of educationally-disadvantaged and low income. Both criteria must be satisfied to qualify for EOP/AAP. The key qualification component is to demonstrate a history of disadvantage based upon family educational and financial background. Educationally-disadvantaged students are those who have come from homes where family members have traditionally not attended college. Ethnic background is not a factor. Each campus defines its own criteria for admission to the program. Qualifying for EOP at one campus does not ensure that you qualify at another campus.

The program is open to students who meet regular admission requirements. In addition, EOP also provides special assistance to applicants who do not meet regular admission requirements, but can demonstrate the ability and potential to succeed at the University.

EOP applicants must be residents of California. EOP waives this requirement for American Indians. EOP/AAP applicants also must be United States citizens.

ASSISTANCE PROGRAMS

SAA and EOP/AAP representatives may provide services to students in your high school. If so, seek them out.

EARLY ACADEMIC OUTREACH

Early Academic Outreach is a SAA program that provides educational services to motivate students in grades seven through twelve, to help them select appropriate "a-f" Subject Requirement courses in high school, and to strengthen their academic skills. This program (a) assists students to develop their abilities to satisfy more than the minimum course and grade requirements for admission to UC, and (b) prepares them to excel as University students.

IMMEDIATE OUTREACH

Immediate Outreach is the recruitment component of both SAA and EOP/AAP. Its purpose is to (a) identify eligible, underrepresented minority candidates and/or low-income and educationally-disadvantaged candidates, and (b) increase the number of SAA and EOP/AAP students who actually enroll at the University. This program serves twelfth grade and community college students. Students who meet regular admission requirements and the criteria for SAA and EOP/AAP receive extra consideration for admission under the supplemental criteria. See this chapter: Freshmen Selection Criteria, page 11--23.

SAA and EOP/AAP representatives may provide services to students in your high school. If so, seek them out. These contacts can help you in your process of preparing for and getting admitted to the University.

SUPPORT SERVICES

When the University accepts you under SAA and/or EOP/AAP, personal and educational support services become available to you. These services vary from campus to campus. They aid you in adjusting to the University, setting educational goals, and succeeding in classes. Listed here are examples of the programs provided. They are available and optional. Take advantage of them; they can help you to succeed at the University.

Support services aid you in adjusting to the University, setting educational goals, and succeeding in classes.

ORIENTATION TO COLLEGE
TUTORING
ACADEMIC SKILL DEVELOPMENT
PEER COUNSELING: Counseling provided by upper-class SAA or EOP students
FINANCIAL AID ADVISING
GENERAL ACADEMIC ADVISING
HOUSING ASSISTANCE
PERSONAL COUNSELING
CAREER PLANNING
SOCIALS

All campuses offer summer academic readiness programs during the summer following high school graduation.

SUMMER BRIDGE PROGRAM: All campuses offer summer academic readiness programs during the summer following high school graduation. These programs help you prepare for University academic and campus life. Each usually includes academic coursework, learning and study-skills enhancement, and advising. According to students who have participated in these programs, they help smooth the transition between high school and college and are a head start in becoming familiar with the University environment and college study. The programs are mostly optional, although participation may be required on your campus.

- Berkeley: Summer Bridge .... an eight week residential program
- Davis: STEP — Special Transitional Enrichment Program .... a four-week residential program
- Irvine: Student Academic Advancement Services .... a four-and-one-half week residential program
- Los Angeles: Freshmen/Transfer Summer Program .... a six-week residential program
- Riverside: Project Transition .... a five-week residential program
- San Diego: Summer Bridge .... a four-week residential program
  Academic Enrichment Program in Mathematics, Science, and Writing .... an eight-week residential program
- Santa Barbara: Minority Engineering Program .... a three-week residential program
  Summer Transitional Enrichment Program .... a two-week residential program
- Santa Cruz: Summer Bridge .... a five-week residential program

UNIVERSITY OF CALIFORNIA

Your answers to key questions on your UC admission application identify you as an SAA and/or EOP/AAP candidate.

APPLYING TO SAA/EOP

If you wish to apply to SAA/EOP (AAP at UCLA), file your University of California admission application during the regular initial one-month period specified for the term you wish to enter UC — November for fall semester or quarter, July for spring semester or winter quarter, October for spring quarter. Further information regarding filing periods can be found later on the next page.

In the section of the application requesting ethnic identity, check off the ethnic group that best reflects your background to help identify you as eligible for SAA. Also, if you believe you qualify, check off that you wish to apply for EOP/AAP consideration. Questions regarding student and family income, parental education and occupation levels, and participation in pre-University service programs such as Early Academic Outreach, Upward Bound, or MESA are also important in establishing your eligibility for EOP/AAP.

Use your personal essay that you send with your admission application to discuss your interests in EOP and the reasons you are applying to the program. Elaborate on factors that demonstrate a low-income and/or disadvantaged background. Include experiences and circumstances that may have adversely affected your ability to achieve full potential. See Chapter 7: STEPS IN THE APPLICATION PROCESS: Writing Your Essay, page 7–9.

Use your personal essay that you send with your admission application to discuss your interests in EOP and the reasons you are applying to the program.

The financial aid and scholarship application process for SAA/EOP students is the same as that for all UC applicants. The financial aid offices of the UC campuses manage the process. See chapter 4: PAYING FOR COLLEGE.

If you miss the regular deadline for applying for admission, call the SAA/EOP office of the campus that interests you. They may be willing to accept a late application if the number of spaces allotted for admission of SAA/EOP students are not filled.

APPLYING TO THE UNIVERSITY OF CALIFORNIA

The following guidelines are important to remember as you proceed through the process of applying to the University of California system. Because admission to the UC campuses is so competitive, every detail of the admission process is very critical. Besides reviewing these guidelines, read the directions in the admission application booklet and follow the specifics of every step.

When To Apply

Majors and campuses are open to new students in the fall term; closures are common for the winter and spring terms. For this reason, it is advisable — and sometimes only possible — to apply for fall admission.

November is the important month to file for the following fall. Your application must be postmarked between November 1st and November 30th.

November is the important month to file for the following fall. Your application must be postmarked between November 1st and November 30th. If it is postmarked before November 1st, the University will return it to you. If it is postmarked after November 30th, you will lose your priority for admission and reduce your chances for admission to just about zero.

If you are a student who might qualify for admission by exception (see this chapter, page 11--22) or for regular admission through SAA or EOP (see this chapter, page 11--44) it may be possible for you to file a later application. If you miss the November deadline, contact the admission office, the UC campus Educational Opportunity Program office, or the Student Affirmative Action office to determine if your application can still be considered.

How To Apply

YOUR APPLICATION

File just one set of application materials, whether you are applying to one or several campuses.

At the end of September or in early October obtain a copy of the booklet, *Application for Undergraduate Admission and Scholarships 1995-96,* from your high school counselor, guidance administrator, or career center. This booklet contains a review of important dates and deadlines, an information section with detailed directions for completing the application, information about scholarships and majors, and the admission application itself.

Make a copy of the application to use as your worksheet. After you are satisfied that you have completed the worksheet accurately, copy the information onto your application. You may type or print in black ink.

FILING YOUR APPLICATION

Application materials you submit consist of the admission application form, application fees, and your essay.

- ❐ File just one set of application materials, whether you are applying to one campus or several campuses. Indicate on your application those campuses, majors, and alternate majors to which you are applying.
- ❐ Before mailing your application make and keep a copy for future reference and as a backup should the original become lost.
- ❐ Mail your application materials to:

University of California
Undergraduate Application Processing Service
P.O. Box 23460
Oakland, CA, 94623-0460

Get a Certificate of Mailing from the post office. It is your proof of having sent your application during the critical November filing period.

UNIVERSITY OF CALIFORNIA

- ❐ Use the addressed envelope that comes with your application booklet. The processing service makes copies of your application materials and mails them to the campuses to which you apply. Every campus that you indicated on your application receives a copy of your application form and your essay.
- ❐ *Do not send* letters of recommendation, transcripts of your academic record, test score reports, or other supporting documents to the processing service; they will not be forwarded to the campuses, returned to you, or retained — *they will be thrown away.*
- ❐ Get a Certificate of Mailing from the post office. It is your proof of having sent your application during the critical November filing period. If the system loses your application and you have your proof of mailing, the University will accept a duplicate application. UC cautions that *you should not send it* by registered mail or certified mail or by an express mail service, which would require their signature.

APPLICATION FEES

For the 1995-96 school year, the application fee is $40.00 for each campus. For example: The fee for one campus is $40.00; two campuses, $80.00; three campuses, $120.00 .... Send the total fee with your application materials, or your application will not be processed. The fee is nonrefundable.

Be sure to include your total fee with your application materials. If you do not, your admission application will not be processed.

APPLICATION FEE WAIVER PROGRAM

A fee waiver is available. If you previously qualified for a fee waiver for admissions testing (SAT I: Reasoning Test and/or SAT II: Subject Tests), you also may be eligible for an admission application fee waiver. The fee waiver program is for United States residents only. Ask your counselor or high school administrator for a fee waiver application, or request it from the University's admissions, relations with schools, or EOP/Outreach Services office. Mail the fee waiver application with your admission application instead of submitting your fee. If you cannot get a fee waiver application, send a letter requesting one with your admission application. Describe your family income, number of dependents, and the hardship that makes payment of the application fee difficult.

The fee waiver allows you to apply to as many as three campuses without charge. If you qualify for a fee waiver and select more than three campuses, you must pay $40.00 for each additional choice. The University reviews the information about your family income that you provide on the form. If the University decides that you are not qualified for the waiver, it will inform you to submit your fee to have your application processed.

Number Of Dependents	Family Income
1	$20,210
2	$23,730
3	$26,770
4	$29,190
5	$30,830

Family income levels are based upon the Bureau of Labor Statistics low budget standard adjusted for inflation through December 1993.

Students eligible for a fee waiver for the 1995-96 UC admission application meet the income guidelines shown here.

The fee waiver allows you to apply to as many as three campuses without charge.

CHANGE OF CAMPUS CHOICE

If you decide to apply to additional campuses after you have sent in your application, submit a request in writing to the University of California Undergraduate Application Processing Service. Do not submit an additional application form. Include your application ID number that appears on the acknowledgment form sent by the processing service about three weeks after you mail your application. Also, include your social security number, major, new campus choice(s), and $40.00 for each added campus. The campuses consider these requests only if they still have space available — not likely after November 30th.

ADMISSIONS TESTS

When you apply for your admissions testing, you have the opportunity to specify where you want your test scores sent. At that time list the specific UC campuses to which you are applying. The testing company mails your SAT I, ACT, and SAT II scores to those campuses.

If you are applying for the fall term, your official SAT I and/or ACT test scores and your SAT II results must reach the University by early January. Therefore, all testing must be completed by no later than the December testing period. See chapter 6: COLLEGE ENTRANCE TESTS, Admissions Tests, page 6--3.

TRANSCRIPTS

Do not send a transcript of your sixth or seventh semester academic record unless asked for it.

Do not send a transcript of your sixth or seventh semester academic record unless asked for it, and then send it directly to that campus. The campuses do not generally request this transcript, although Santa Cruz has said that this year they are requesting more seventh-semester transcripts than in the past. If you are admitted, you are required to submit an official, final high school transcript showing your date of graduation. This final transcript must arrive by July 15th at the campus at which you will enroll.

It is your responsibility to request your high school office to send an official copy of your record. Usually the high school prefers a written request from you and may ask you to pay a small fee for this service. Order it before you graduate, so that your UC campus receives it by July 15th deadline.

RECOMMENDATIONS

The campuses do not require recommendations as a part of the application process. However, each has their own policy on handling recommendations you may send to them. Those campuses that do review your recommendations generally do so if their admission decision about you is uncertain, and they need more information.

The campuses do not require recommendations as a part of the application process.

Berkeley	places recommendations in your application file but *does not* review them.
Davis	places recommendations in your application file but reviews them *only* if you appeal their admission decision.
Irvine	places recommendations in your application file and *reads* them as part of the admission review process.
Los Angeles	places recommendations in your application file and *reads* them as part of the admission review process.
Riverside	places recommendations in a general file and does *not* review them.
San Diego	places recommendations in your file but reviews them *only* if you appeal their admission decision.
Santa Barbara	places recommendations in your file but reviews them *only* if you appeal their admission decision.
Santa Cruz	places recommendations in your file and *generally does not* review them as part of their admission decision.

Send your recommendations from your teachers, counselor, or administrator directly to those campuses that are willing to consider them in their admission process.

COMPLETING YOUR UC APPLICATION

Read the application booklet carefully and follow the directions exactly. Be honest. If you falsify critical information and are found out, you may be banned for life from attending the University.

UC CAMPUS AND MAJOR CHOICES

Each campus is separate in its admission decisions; admission or rejection to one does not affect admission to another.

Admission to the UC campuses and majors is competitive. You may wish to apply to more than one campus and more than one major. Each campus is separate in its admission decisions. Admission or rejection to one does not affect admission to another.

You have the opportunity on your admission application to state a first choice major and an alternate major for each campus to which you apply. Your selections may differ from campus to campus. There is no guarantee that a campus will accept you in your alternate if it cannot accept you in your first choice major. Policies regarding acceptance to alternate majors vary from campus to campus and from major to major. You may choose Undeclared as an alternate major, if this option appeals to you. These policies are described earlier in this chapter: Majors — Application and Screening, page 11--37 and are important factors to consider in deciding upon campuses and majors to which to apply.

Review your qualifications for admission, your commitment to your major, and your strength of preference of one campus over another. Rank the UC campuses according to (a) desirability, using factors outlined in chapter 2: CHOOSING YOUR COLLEGE; (b) your major, using factors outlined in chapter 3: CHOOSING YOUR MAJOR; and (c) your chances of being accepted. Your admission strategy might be to apply to a campus and a major to which you feel certain of admission, and apply to other campuses and/or majors to which you are less likely to be accepted yet strongly interest you. In this way you can somewhat assure yourself of admission to the University of California while having a chance of admission to your most preferred campus and/or major. The admission application does not ask you to rank these campus choices.

By applying to more than one campus you may increase your chances of being admitted.

If you have a strong preference for a particular campus, you might want to try for admission to a less impacted major at that campus. But, if you are set on a certain major that is difficult to get into at all campuses; e.g., engineering, apply for consideration on several campuses. As a safeguard, state alternate majors that are of some interest to you.

By applying to more than one campus you may increase your chances of being admitted. University research indicates that your chances for admission increase with the number of campuses to which you apply. The admission rate for students applying for freshman admission to three campuses for the fall 1993 term was 86.3%, significantly higher than the overall admission rate of 79.8% percent. 91.3% of freshmen applying to five or more campuses were admitted. The admission rate drops steadily as the number of campuses selected decreases; only 60.6% of freshmen applying to one campus were admitted.

The chances of being admitted to an impacted major later, after you have been attending the University, vary from campus to campus and major to major. The campuses generally advise that you should not count on being able to do this.

Riverside has been accepting all UC-eligible students and expects to continue this pattern for fall 1995. If you are UC-eligible and believe you may not have a sufficiently strong record to compete for admission to other UC campuses, UC Riverside is a fine choice, and it can be your backup. See this chapter: Freshmen Selection Criteria, page 11--23.

The chances of your being admitted to an impacted major later, after you have been attending the University, vary somewhat from campus to campus and major to major. The campuses generally advise that you should not count on being able to do this. Impacted majors usually remain impacted. The campuses often reserve for community college transfers any spaces that open for sophomores or juniors.

For example, Berkeley makes it quite clear that it is unlikely you would be admitted into Electrical Engineering as a sophomore or junior from another major at Berkeley. Students are screened for this program so carefully that there is little dropout — new spaces are few. Whatever spaces are available are most likely given to community college transfer students. The chances of changing your major may differ on other campuses and for other majors.

All undergraduate majors are listed by campus at the back of the application booklet, and each has a code number. Make sure you accurately fill in the code number of your major and alternate major for each campus. A complete listing of all UC majors and the campuses at which they are offered is also at the end of this chapter: Undergraduate Degree Majors, page 11--84.

Each campus has special requirements for applying to some of its majors. A review of this information and special screening requirements for each campus appear earlier in this chapter: Majors — Application and Screening, page 11--37. Also see the section: Freshmen Selection Criteria, page 11--23 earlier in this chapter for its review of freshman admission guidelines by campus.

THE FRESHMAN SELF-REPORTED ACADEMIC RECORD

The Freshman Self-Reported Academic Record is used to make a preliminary review of your academic performance in high school and is an important basis for offering provisional admission.

The application requires you to complete the Freshman Self-Reported Academic Record. This record is a very important section of your application and should be completed with great care and accuracy. It is used to make a preliminary review of your academic performance in high school and is an important basis for offering provisional admission. Full instructions for completing it are given in your application materials.

The Freshman Self-Reported Academic Record requests the following information:

- ❒ Academic courses taken in grades nine, ten, eleven, and twelve, and mathematics and language-other-than-English courses completed in grades seven and eight, if appropriate. *You must list all your "a-f" Subject Requirement courses, even those you repeated.* Use your high school transcript and the Official University of California Certified Course List of your high school. Enter course titles exactly as they appear on your transcript.

- ❒ Summer session courses. If you have completed summer courses in the summer following ninth grade, record their course names and grades earned in the grade ten section. If you have completed courses in the summer following the tenth or eleventh grade, record their course names and grades earned in the section for eleventh grade.

FRESHMAN SELF-REPORTED ACADEMIC RECORD (sample)

NAME — LAST Your Name FIRST

NAME — LAST Your Name FIRST

***VIII. FRESHMAN SELF-REPORTED ACADEMIC RECORD — FRESHMAN APPLICANTS ONLY**

BEFORE YOU COMPLETE THIS SECTION: Read the instructions on pages 13–14 of the application booklet, refer to the completed sample Freshman Self-Reported Academic Record on page 15, and complete the worksheet on pages 16–17. Refer to your high school transcript to complete this section. If you are not sure which courses the University considers academic subject courses and UC approved honors/AP/IB Higher Level courses, check the UC approved certified course list for your school (California high schools only). The information you provide is used to make a preliminary evaluation of your application for admission and will be verified when your final, official high school transcript is received. If your academic record changes after you submit your application, you must notify the Admissions Office at each campus where you have applied *in writing*. DO NOT ATTACH YOUR TRANSCRIPT.

ACADEMIC SUBJECTS	GRADES 7 & 8 (Enter course title for each semester. Note only "D" or "F" grades in parentheses. DO NOT include grades 7 and 8 total in the GPA computation (Item 74 below).) COURSE TITLE	9TH GRADE (Enter course title for each semester. Note only "D" or "F" grades in parentheses. DO NOT include grade 9 total in the GPA computation (Item 74 below).) COURSE TITLE	10TH GRADE (Enter course titles and fall and spring semester grades. Note (H) after any UC approved honors/AP/IB Higher Level courses. Note (C) in parentheses after any college course and list the name of the college.) COURSE TITLE	FALL SEMESTER GRADE	SPRING SEMESTER GRADE	11TH GRADE (Enter course titles and fall and spring semester grades. Note (H) after any UC approved honors/AP/IB higher level courses. Note (C) in parentheses after any college course and list the name of the college.) COURSE TITLE	FALL SEMESTER GRADE	SPRING SEMESTER GRADE	12TH GRADE (Enter titles of courses you are now taking and that you plan to take in the spring. Note (H) after any UC approved honors/AP/IB higher level courses. Note (C) in parentheses after any college course and list the name of the college.) COURSES IN PROGRESS FALL SEMESTER	COURSES PLANNED SPRING SEMESTER	NUMBER OF SEMESTER COURSES (Enter the total number of semester courses.)
*61 HISTORY/SOCIAL SCIENCE — U.S. History; Civics; American Government; World History, Cultures, and Geography.	Do Not Write In This Space	Cultural World History 1,2				AP U.S. History (H)	A	A	U.S. Government		*61 GRADES 9-12 ONLY: 05
*62 ENGLISH — Composition, Literature (American, English, World, etc.).	Do Not Write In This Space	Cultural World Literature 1,2	English 2	A	A	Advanced Composition and Literature (H)	A	A	AP English (H)	AP English (H)	*62 GRADES 9-12 ONLY: 08
*63 MATHEMATICS — Elementary Algebra, Geometry, Advanced Algebra, Trigonometry, Pre-Calculus. (Do not include arithmetic and pre-algebra.)	Algebra 1,2	Geometry 1, 2(D)	Algebra 3,4	A	B	Trigonometry/Math Analysis	B	C	Pre-Calculus	Pre-Calculus	*63A GRADES 7-8 ONLY: 02
			Geometry 2 (repeat)	B							*63B GRADES 9-12 ONLY: 09
*64 LABORATORY SCIENCE — Biology, Chemistry, Physics.	Do Not Write In This Space		Biology (H)	B	B	Chemistry	B	C	Physics 1A (C) (at Rio Community College)	Physics 1B (C) (at Rio Community College)	*64 GRADES 9-12 ONLY: 06
*65 LANGUAGE OTHER THAN ENGLISH — French, German, Spanish, Latin, Mandarin Chinese, Japanese, etc.	Spanish 1,2	Spanish 3,4	Spanish 5,6	C	D	Spanish 6 (repeat)		C			*65A GRADES 7-8 ONLY: 02
											*65B GRADES 9-12 ONLY: 05
*66 COLLEGE PREPARATORY ELECTIVES—UC Approved Only (Do not list courses that are not UC approved college preparatory electives such as PE, typing, drivers education, health, and pep squad.)	Do Not Write In This Space										*66 GRADES 9-12 ONLY: 06
Visual/Performing Arts			Concert Band II	A					Advanced Drama	Advanced Drama	
Social Science (Anthropology, Economics, Psychology, Sociology, etc.)										Economics	*67 TOTAL 61-66 (This total should be the same as the total of Items 68–73.)
Computer Science											
9th Grade Intro Lab Science		Physical Science 1,2									
TOTAL NUMBER OF SEMESTER COURSES	*68 TOTAL 7TH & 8TH GRADE SEMESTER COURSES LISTED ABOVE: 04	*69 TOTAL 9TH GRADE SEMESTER COURSES LISTED ABOVE: 10	*70 TOTAL NUMBER OF 10TH GRADE SEMESTER COURSES: 10			*71 TOTAL NUMBER OF 11TH GRADE SEMESTER COURSES: 09			*72 TOTAL NUMBER OF FALL SEMESTER COURSES IN PROGRESS: 05	*73 TOTAL NUMBER OF SPRING SEMESTER COURSES PLANNED: 05	43

PRELIMINARY ACADEMIC GRADE-POINT AVERAGE

*74 NUMBER OF ACADEMIC SEMESTER COURSES — GRADES 10 & 11

GRADE			GRADE POINTS EARNED
A	08	x4=	32
B	06	x3=	18
C	04	x2=	08
D	01	x1=	01
F	00	x0=	00
ADD: TOTAL	74: 19	ADD: TOTAL	75: 059

NUMBER OF GRADE 10 & 11 UC APPROVED HONORS/AP/IB HIGHER LEVEL SEMESTER COURSES AND TRANSFERABLE COLLEGE COURSES

TOTAL *76: 06

BRING DOWN AND ADD:

TOTAL 75: 059

TOTAL 76: 06

TOTAL *77: 065

DIVIDE AND CARRY TO TWO (2) DECIMAL PLACES:

TOTAL 77: 065 ÷ TOTAL 74: 19

= YOUR PRELIMINARY ACADEMIC GPA *78: 3.42

*79 NUMBER OF GRADE 12 UC APPROVED HONORS/AP/IB HIGHER LEVEL SEMESTER COURSES AND TRANSFERABLE COLLEGE COURSES (in progress or planned): 04

*80 ☐ CHECK THIS BOX IF YOUR HIGH SCHOOL USES A TERM SYSTEM OTHER THAN THE SEMESTER SYSTEM, SUCH AS THE TRIMESTER OR QUARTER SYSTEM.

TEST SCORES AND DATES — Required Of All Freshman Applicants.

Enter your test scores and/or dates you will take the tests in the appropriate spaces below. If you have taken an examination more than once, record your highest score. For the SAT I or SAT record the best total score; verbal and mathematics scores must be from the same sitting.

SAT I: REASONING TEST (or SAT)

- *81 TEST DATE: MO 06 YR 94
- *82 VERBAL SCORE: 560
- *83 MATHEMATICS SCORE: 540
- *84 TOTAL SCORE: 1100

AMERICAN COLLEGE TEST (ACT)

- *85 TEST DATE: MO ___ YR ___
- *86 COMPOSITE SCORE: ___

SAT II: SUBJECT TESTS (and Achievement Tests)

	SCORE	TEST DATE
*87 WRITING (or English Composition)	580	*88 MO 05 YR 94
*89 MATHEMATICS — LEVEL 1	0	*90 MO ___ YR ___
*91 MATHEMATICS — LEVEL 2 OR 2C	550	*92 MO 05 YR 94
*93 THIRD TEST (Refer to the instructions on page 14 and enter in Item 95 the code that corresponds to the third SAT II or Achievement Test you took or plan to take.)	0	*94 MO 1? YR 94
*95 CODE: KH		

*Additional instructions provided in booklet. Please read before completing items marked with this symbol.

*Additional instructions provided in booklet. Please read before completing items marked with this symbol.

- ❐ Senior courses in progress and planned for spring semester. If you make any changes in these courses during your senior year, you must notify the campuses to which you have applied. They can then consider this information as they evaluate you for admission.

- ❐ All honors-level courses taken and planned for grade 12. Be sure to include *all* honors, Advanced Placement, IB, and transferable college-level courses. Write an (H) next to the course name. Write a (C) next to the transferable college-level courses and the name of the college(s).

Complete the Freshman Self-Reported Academic Record with great care and accuracy.

- ❐ Your academic record from a school outside the United States. List these courses as best you can. If they appear on your American high school transcript, list them as stated there. The University recognizes that grade levels and/or methods for reporting coursework may differ in other countries.

- ❐ Semester grades that you achieved in grades ten and eleven only.

- ❐ D or F grades in courses you list for seventh, eighth, or ninth grade. Put the grade in parenthesis next to its course title. Do not include these grades in your calculation.

- ❐ A calculation of your preliminary academic grade point average based upon your semester grades in grades ten and eleven. All grades on your Freshman Self-Reported Academic Record for grades ten and eleven must be used in your calculation, even those of courses you repeated. In computing your preliminary academic GPA, give honors-level courses from grades ten and eleven extra points.

- ❐ A record of your highest test scores from the SAT I: Reasoning Test and/or the ACT test and the SAT II: Subject Tests. The SAT I verbal and mathematics scores must be from the same test sitting. Do not use English Literature scores for the SAT II: Writing Test. A second mathematics score on the SAT II: Subject Tests can be listed, but do not put it in the space for the third SAT II: Subject Tests. If you are going to take the tests again, write the word "retake" in the margin next to your scores with the date on which you intend to retake them. Doing so alerts the campuses to watch for additional scores.

If you are going to take the tests again, write the word "retake" in the margin next to your scores with the date on which you intend to retake them.

University of California admissions personnel are called "admissions evaluators." The admissions evaluators at the individual campuses to which you apply use the Freshman Self-Reported Academic Record to review (a) your academic courses — "a-f" Subject Requirement courses, number of UC-qualifying courses beyond the minimum fifteen required, number of honors-level courses, and senior year courses; (b) the quality of your record — your grades and GPA; and (c) your test scores.

Semester grades in your sophomore and junior years are the most critical in calculating your preliminary GPA for admission. Your application is filed in November before your senior year grades are available. Remember, seventh, eighth, and ninth course grades are not used to calculate your "a-f" Subject Requirement GPA.

The admissions evaluators review your senior year courses in progress and planned for second semester as stated on your Freshman Self-Reported Academic Record. They are looking for a rigorous, challenging list of courses.

If your academic record changes after you submit your application, you must notify *in writing* the Admissions Office at each campus where you have applied.

Your UC application includes a worksheet of the Freshman Self-Reported Academic Record. Complete this worksheet first, then copy the information on to the application. The sample copy of the Freshman Self-Reported Academic Record on page 11--53 is from the 1995-96 UC application. This form changes very little from year to year.

The campus you decide to attend makes a final evaluation of your eligibility for UC admission after you graduate from high school and submit your final high school transcript.

PROVISIONAL OFFERS OF ADMISSION

Important criteria for making provisional offers of admission are

a. your Freshman Self-Reported Academic Record, including your preliminary academic GPA that you calculate — the "a-f" Subject Requirement GPA for grades ten and eleven only;

b. your admissions test scores received by January; and

c. supplemental criteria for at least forty percent of applicants as described earlier in this chapter: Freshmen Selection Criteria, page 11--23.

The campus you decide to attend makes a final evaluation of your eligibility for UC admission after you graduate from high school and after you submit your final official high school transcript. The information on your Freshman Self-Reported Academic Record is verified by this final, official transcript. A provisional offer of admission can be rescinded if you (a) do not meet the admission requirements, (b) have seriously erred on your Freshman Self-Reported Academic Record, or (c) have not followed-through satisfactorily on the senior year program to which you committed on your Freshman Self-Reported Academic Record.

There are several policies regarding the use of D's and F's in calculating your "a-f" Subject Requirement GPA. See this chapter: Commonly Asked Questions About Admissions, page 11--13 to 11--15. However, your preliminary academic GPA on your Freshman Self-Reported Academic Record must include all grades that you received in your sophomore and junior years, even those you repeated for a better grade. This GPA is a factor in determining your provisional admission. Very few GPA's are recalculated by an admissions evaluator using only the repeated grade, which could improve your GPA. This is especially true of impacted campuses and/or majors. However, if your application suggests that you have certain qualifications that might satisfy the supplemental criteria and your academic background deserves further consideration, the admissions evaluator may elect to recalculate your GPA.

Your preliminary academic GPA on your Freshman Self-Reported Academic Record must include all grades that you received in your sophomore and junior years, even those you repeated for a better grade.

YOUR ESSAY

Limit your essay to one side each of two sheets of $8^{1}/_{2}$" x 11" white paper; only two essay pages are copied and sent to the campuses by the University of California Undergraduate Application Processing Service. The campuses are placing more emphasis upon reading the essays; they are a very important part of your application and should be carefully written. Even if you are a top student who expects to be admitted on the basis of your academic index, write your essay carefully. It may be read by the financial aid office as well as the admissions office. See chapter 7: STEPS IN THE APPLICATION PROCESS, Writing Your Essay, page 7--9.

YOUR ACTIVITIES, HONORS, AWARDS, AND EMPLOYMENT

In one section of your application, you are asked to list and describe your extracurricular activities, honors and awards, and jobs. Limited space is supplied for your listing and description; use additional 8 1/2" x 11" pages if you need more space. See chapter 7: STEPS IN THE APPLICATION PROCESS, Activities, page 7--9.

Forty percent to sixty percent of applicants to the University are admitted based upon academic *and* supplemental criteria described earlier in this chapter: Freshman Selection Criteria, page 11--23. Your essay and your description of your activities, honors and awards, and jobs provide important information to the admissions evaluator reviewing your supplemental qualifications for admission. Take time to present yourself clearly and positively.

Answer "yes" on your admission application to the question asking if you wish to apply for scholarships, even if you feel you do not qualify based upon financial need. There are many non–need-based awards for which you may qualify.

SCHOLARSHIPS

Answer "yes" on your admission application to the question asking if you wish to apply for scholarships, even if you feel you do not qualify based upon financial need. There are many non–need-based awards for which you may qualify. A listing and information about merit campus-based scholarships is included in your admission application. See this chapter: Financial Aid, page 11–62. This information includes required qualification criteria, supporting documentation (additional application materials, recommendations, transcripts, test scores), interview requirements, and notification dates. All supporting documentation for these scholarships is due by January 11th of each year.

Also on the application is a list of restricted scholarships limited to students with particular majors or specialties, future career plans, or specific parentage, students from a particular high school or geographical area, students of a special ethnicity, and students meeting other miscellaneous criteria. These restricted scholarships are listed with a code number in your application materials. See this chapter: Financial Aid, page 11--62. If you believe you qualify for any of them, list their code numbers on your application in the appropriate section. Additional restricted scholarships, offered by specific campuses, are awarded based upon information in your application. Not all these scholarships are available at all campuses. Need may or may not be a criterion.

UC ADMISSION PROCEDURES

APPLICATION ACKNOWLEDGMENT

About three weeks after you mail your fall application and not later than December 31st, you should receive an acknowledgment that your application was received. If you do not, call one of the following numbers immediately:

California Residents .... (800) 523-2048

Out-of-state Residents .... (510) 653-0314 or (510) 596-5500
(Ask for UC admissions processing.)

Hearing Impaired Callers .... TDD: (510) 420-1737

When you call, have your social security number handy. Note the name of the person to whom you are speaking, so you can talk with him or her again if any further questions about receipt of your application arise.

About three weeks after you mail your fall application and not later than December 31st, you should receive an acknowledgment that your application was received.

If you need to reapply, be sure to enclose a copy of your Certificate of Mailing from your original application.

NOTIFICATION OF ADMISSION

If you filed your application for fall freshman admission during the priority filing period of November 1st through November 30th, each campus will notify you beginning on March 1st and no later than March 15th if you have been provisionally admitted. The campuses notify transfer students anytime between March 1st and May 1st.

PROVISIONAL ADMISSION

If you are admitted as a freshman, you receive a letter of provisional admission that states certain conditions to be met for your admission to become final. Each University campus sends its own letter, but the points covered generally include the following conditions:

- You must successfully complete the full "a-f" Subject Requirement course pattern before high school graduation.
- You must complete with a C or better all senior year courses indicated as planned or in progress on your Freshman Self-Reported Academic Record.
- You must maintain a senior year grade point average equal to or better than your tenth and eleventh grade preliminary academic GPA reported on your Freshman Self-Reported Academic Record.
- You must tell the UC admissions office if you change your courses during your senior year from those stated on your UC application.

Your letter of provisional admission states certain conditions that must be met for your admission to become final.

The UC campus reviews your final transcript to verify the information you provided on your application about grades earned and courses completed. Your transcript is also checked to determine if you met the conditions of provisional admission. Did you state your record accurately? Did you follow-through and successfully complete the senior year courses you said you would complete?

The admissions office of your chosen campus may reconsider and possibly cancel your offer of admission if your transcript shows that you (a) provided inaccurate information on your Freshman Self-Reported Academic Record, (b) dropped required classes during your senior year, or (c) failed to maintain a high level of scholarship during your senior year. Remember, you have only been provisionally admitted, and your admission can be rescinded. In recent years, individual campuses have canceled from fifteen to thirty admissions a year.

Advise the UC campuses as soon as possible of any difficulties you may have in meeting their conditions for final admission.

If you have any problem meeting the conditions of provisional admission, contact the UC campuses and confer with them regarding your options. If you have dropped a course, if a grade in one of your courses falls below a C, or your senior year GPA has seriously deteriorated, call and openly discuss the matter with an admissions evaluator. All campuses say that the key to maintaining your admission eligibility is to advise them as soon as possible of any difficulties, so they can evaluate the situation and advise you. Options might include retaking courses at a community college or in summer school. Waiting until your final transcript arrives at the UC campus in June or July could jeopardize your admission status. By then it may be too late to remedy a problem.

ACCEPTANCE OF ADMISSION

Each campus that provisionally accepts you sends you a Statement Of Intent To Register form (SIR). Return this form with a nonrefundable deposit of $100 by May 1st to the campus you wish to attend to reserve your space for fall 1995.

You can accept admission to only one campus. Wait until you have heard from each campus to which you have applied, especially your most preferred campuses. You may not transfer your acceptance from one campus to another once you have declared your intent to register and submitted your nonrefundable deposit.

If you decide to apply for admission to another semester, you must file another application during the appropriate filing period.

If you have special circumstances or questions about a unique situation, call the University campus directly to discuss your situation and learn about your options. They may reconsider their policies if you have a compelling reason.

You can accept admission to only one campus; wait until you have heard from each campus to which you have applied.

APPEALS

All campuses are willing to reconsider their decisions if you can provide them with new and convincing information. The campuses do consider a change in circumstances, the possibility of errors, and/or the clarification and amplification of critical criteria. A letter from your counselor clarifying a situation can be effective. However, few appeals are successful. For example, for fall 1993 admission Berkeley received four-hundred appeals and accepted only twenty-five; Los Angeles received six-hundred appeals and accepted about seventy; San Diego received four-hundred appeals and admitted twenty-five.

ALTERNATIVE ADMISSION OPTIONS

UC offers alternative admission options to some students who cannot be accommodated at their first-choice campus and/or major. These options may include

a) fall admission to the campus of choice in an alternate major,

b) deferred admission to the campus of choice for the winter or spring term,

c) fall, winter, or spring admission to another campus,

d) fall enrollment in University extension courses — courses for which admission to UC is not required — with subsequent enrollment in the campus of choice, or

e) enrollment at your campus of choice at a later date following completion of specified coursework at a community college.

UC offers alternative admission options to some students who cannot be accommodated at their first-choice campus and/or major.

PLACEMENT TESTS

THE UNIVERSITYWIDE SUBJECT A EXAMINATION

If the University of California accepts you as an undergraduate, you must demonstrate proficiency in writing. All California students who enter UC for the fall of 1995 must take the Universitywide Subject A Examination to meet this requirement, unless you have satisfied this requirement by April 1, 1995 in any of the following ways:

1. Score a 3 or higher on the College Board Advanced Placement Examination in English. See chapter 6: COLLEGE ENTRANCE TESTS, The AP Program and Examinations, page 6--57.

2. Score 5 or higher on the International Baccalaureate Higher Level Examination (English A only).

3. Score 600 or higher on the College Board SAT II: Writing. See chapter 6: COLLEGE ENTRANCE TESTS, The SAT II: Subject Tests, page 6--30.

4. Complete, with a grade of C or better, an acceptable college course in English Composition.

5. Complete an appropriate English course at the University of California.

If you are accepted as a UC undergraduate, you must demonstrate proficiency in writing.

If you do not demonstrate writing proficiency by any of these means, or by passing the Subject A Examination, you must take the Subject A course, preparatory writing, at the campus you attend, and earn a C or better in it.

Depending on the campus, you receive either no credit, full credit, or reduced credit toward your Bachelor's degree for courses taken to satisfy the Subject A requirement. On a campus where you receive reduced credit, you might, for example, take a four-unit course that counts as four units toward the total number of units in which you are enrolled for the term. However, the course may earn only two units toward your Bachelor's degree.

The campuses require you to complete the course that satisfies your Subject A requirement by a certain deadline, usually by the end of your freshman year. However, it is to your advantage to complete the Subject A requirement before you enter the University. One way is to take an English composition course at a community college, either during your senior year of high school or during the summer before you enter the University.

If you are a California high school student and have not satisfied the Subject A requirement through test scores or college courses, you receive a letter with an application in early April advising you to take the Subject A Examination in May. If you are not a California high school student, you may take the Subject A Examination in the fall after you enter the University. Test results of the Subject A Examination do not affect your admission to UC. The campuses use the scores for course placement purposes only.

If you are a California high school student and have not satisfied the Subject A requirement through test scores or college courses, you receive a letter with an application in early April.

Of 16,164 UC-admitted students taking the May 1994 examination, 47.4 percent passed. The number of UC-enrolled students satisfying the Subject A requirement by all methods remains fairly stable from year to year — between fifty-nine percent and sixty-two percent. See chapter 6: COLLEGE ENTRANCE TESTS, Universitywide Subject A Examination, page 6–49.

ADVANCED PLACEMENT EXAMINATIONS

The University of California gives credit for all College Entrance Examination Board Advanced Placement Examinations in which you receive a score of 3 or higher. See chapter 6: COLLEGE ENTRANCE TESTS, AP Program And Examinations, page 6--57. The credit may count as subject credit, graduation credit, or credit toward the General Education/Breadth Requirement. The admissions evaluators of the individual campuses decide how to award credit. If you are fluent in a language other than English, you may wish to take this opportunity to gain Advanced Placement credit.

The College Entrance Examination Board reports all Advanced Placement Examination results to the University. You may not choose which test scores you wish reported. AP Examination scores do not affect your chances for admission.

The admissions evaluators of the individual campuses determine how credit is awarded for scores of 3 or higher on Advanced Placement Examinations.

If before or after enrolling at the University, you take college courses that duplicate the content of Advanced Placement Examinations, the University may not award credit for both the courses and the examinations.

INTERNATIONAL BACCALAUREATE

The International Baccalaureate, IB, is an internationally recognized two-year curriculum and examination for students sixteen to nineteen years old. Four-hundred schools in fifty-five countries throughout the world, including about 160 high schools in the United States and Canada, have adopted the program. UC grants 8 quarter units ($5\frac{1}{2}$ semester units) of credit for each IB Higher Level Examination for which you score 5 or higher. IB Higher Level Examinations are honors-level courses, which receive an extra point when calculating your "a-f" Subject Requirement GPA; some may be considered equivalent to freshman-level courses in the subject.

1994-95 COSTS

Because the state funds the University of California from state tax revenues, California residents pay no tuition, although they must pay educational fees to attend. These fees are substantially less than tuition costs at private colleges and fees charged to out-of-state students attending the University. University of California's educational fees are the same at all UC campuses. The fees for 1994-95 increased $345 from the prior year; annual educational fees for California residents for 1994-95 are $3,799.

In the following table, figures represent systemwide weighted average expenses for the 1994-95 school year.

No tuition is charged to state residents, although they must pay educational fees to attend UC.

1994-95 ESTIMATED OVERALL COSTS FOR CALIFORNIA RESIDENTS			
Expense Item	For A Single Undergraduate Student		
	Living On-Campus	Living Off Campus	Commuting and Living at Home
Educational Fees	$3,799	$3,799	$3,799
Campus Fees	$95 to $547	$95 to $547	$95 to $547
Books and Supplies	$630 to $882	$630 to $882	$630 to $882
Room and Board	$5,285 to $6,607	$4,811 to $6,350	$1,500 to $2,124
Personal/ Transportation	$1,255 to $2,374	$1,665 to $2,760	$1,191 to $4,275
TOTAL EXPENSES	$11,578 to $13,300	$11,879 to $13,853	$7,333 to $10,299
AVERAGE EXPENSES	$12,603	$12,919	$9,193

Note: Figures as of 8/4/94. All fees are subject to change.

The amounts presented in this table for campus fees, books and supplies, living, personal/transportation, and total expenses are ranges representing averages at all UC campuses.

UNIVERSITY OF CALIFORNIA

Personal/transportation expenses include recreation, clothes, personal items, laundry, local transportation .... Personal expenses may vary depending upon your tastes and life style. Other fees and room and board expenses also may vary from campus to campus. To find out about the specific fees and expenses at the campuses that interest you, read the general catalogue for that campus. You also may contact the financial aid, admissions, and housing offices of the campuses for further information.

Nonresident tuition is $7,699.

NONRESIDENT COSTS

Nonresident tuition, assessed of all nonresident students — out-of-state and foreign students — is $7,699. This amount is in addition to the expenses shown in the above table. See appendix A: CALIFORNIA RESIDENCY REQUIREMENTS.

UNDOCUMENTED ALIEN STUDENTS

Because of a recent court decision, the University now collects nonresident tuition from undocumented alien students, students without legal immigration status. See appendix A: CALIFORNIA RESIDENCY REQUIREMENTS.

FINANCIAL AID

UC offers honorary scholarships, restricted scholarships, unrestricted scholarships, and need-based financial aid.

The University of California has a strong financial aid program offering many types of financial assistance to qualified undergraduates. This financial support program serves a dual role: (1) It recognizes, through scholarships, students' outstanding academic achievement, community involvement, and potential for future achievement. (2) It assists those who demonstrate financial need. In January 1995, all students who applied for undergraduate admission for fall 1995 will receive a copy of the Free Application for Federal Student Aid (FAFSA) and the GPA Verification Form for the Cal Grant Program (See chapter 4: PAYING FOR COLLEGE). The mailing also includes the publications *Student and Parent Guide to Applying for Financial Aid at the University of California* and *Financing Your College Education.* These brochures provide information on financial aid programs and application policies and procedures.

The University offers merit-based scholarships for students with outstanding academic achievement and potential; restricted scholarships for students with specific backgrounds, academic interests, or career objectives; unrestricted scholarships open to all students; and financial aid based upon financial need. By responding "yes" to the statement: "I want to apply for scholarships." in the scholarships section on your UC admission application, you apply for all scholarships the University offers. You are eligible to receive more than one type of award.

MERIT-BASED SCHOLARSHIPS

All documents supporting your application for merit-based scholarships must be postmarked not later than January 11th.

The UC campuses award merit-based scholarships to outstanding students in recognition of academic achievement and potential. Merit-based scholarships range from three-hundred dollars to several thousand dollars. Each campus determines its own criteria. The selection of students for merit-based awards is generally made without regard for their financial need. Once a student is selected for a merit-based award, however, the amount of the award is usually determined on the basis of need. Students who do not demonstrate financial need are typically awarded small honorary scholarships, while those who do have need may receive larger award, which are used to enrich the financial aid package by replacing loan or work-study awards. These scholarships are described for each campus in your admission application in the chart: *Requirements for Campus Scholarships.* Details about eligibility and supporting documentation are included.

UC gives its most prestigious scholarship awards, the Regents Scholarships, to students with the most outstanding academic records. Students who have demonstrated leadership, academic achievement and participation in extracurricular activities receive Alumni Scholarships. You do not need to be a relative of an alumnus to qualify. In addition there are merit-based Chancellor's Scholarships.

To apply for these awards for the fall term, complete the appropriate section on your admission application and submit it by November 30th. Supporting documents, outlined in the same chart, may be required. These documents may consist of letters of recommendation, transcripts, or an essay (in addition to the one required on the admission application form). Send them in one envelope to the appropriate campus office postmarked not later than January 11th. Do not send them with your UC admission application.

The University offers a wide range of scholarships endowed by private individuals

RESTRICTED SCHOLARSHIPS

The University offers a wide range of scholarships endowed by private individuals. These scholarships are limited to students having certain characteristics such as graduation from a particular high school, residence in a specific geographic area, ethnicity, or academic major. You provide much of this information on your admission application. In addition, there is a listing in your admission application booklet of other characteristics that may be used to identify restricted scholarship eligibility. Not all of these scholarships are available at all campuses. Need may or may not be a criterion. Some campuses may require documentation to establish eligibility.

To apply, review the list in your admission application, and specify in the scholarship section of your application any for which you believe you qualify.

UNRESTRICTED SCHOLARSHIPS

By responding "yes" in the scholarship section as previously described, you automatically apply for unrestricted scholarships. Unrestricted scholarships may be awarded by the campuses at their discretion.

NEED-BASED FINANCIAL AID

Forty-nine percent of undergraduates received financial support in 1992-93, the most recent year for which information is available. UC awards most financial aid on the basis of financial need to students who would otherwise be unable to attend the University. Forty-one percent of undergraduates received financial aid that included a need-based award. Financial aid packages contained scholarships, grants, loans, and work-study. Aid packages contained a higher percentage of loans than in past years. Sixty-one percent of financial support for undergraduates was awarded as scholarships and grants. Another thirty-five percent was awarded as loans. The remaining four percent was awarded as work-study earnings.

Each UC campus offers University of California Grants to financially-needy undergraduate students.

Each UC campus offers University of California Fee Grants to financially-needy undergraduate students. In 1992-93, the Fee Grant Program provided awards to all needy students. Ninety-eight percent of financial aid recipients from families with incomes of less than $30,000 received a grant; seventy-nine percent of recipients from families with incomes of more than $60,000 also received one. The size of the Fee Grant was tied to income.

1992-93 FEE GRANT AWARDS
UNIVERSITY OF CALIFORNIA

Parent Income	Fee Grant
Less than $30,000	$1,200(1)
$30,000 to $45,000	$950
$45,000 to $60,000	$750
Above $60,000	$550

(1)The entire amount of the UC fee increase since 1990-91)

UNIVERSITY OF CALIFORNIA

To apply for financial aid based upon financial need, submit a FAFSA. If you are a California resident, apply for need-based financial aid by submitting your application by the March 2nd deadline to the Need Analysis Processor. Each campus continues to accept applications for financial aid after March 2nd and makes awards to late applicants if funds are available. See chapter 4: PAYING FOR COLLEGE, Applying For Financial Aid, page 4--9.

The University requires copies of federal income tax returns to verify information on your FAFSA.

You will receive information from the campuses about additional procedures, including descriptions of any supporting documents required, and a schedule of campus deadlines. The campuses usually require financially independent students and parents of financially dependent students to submit copies of their federal income tax returns, which are used to verify information on your financial aid applications. Applying for financial aid is fully described in chapter 4: PAYING FOR COLLEGE.

The University compares your expected family contribution to your total college expenses for one academic year. If you have financial need, the University offers you a financial aid package consisting of grants, scholarships, loans, and work-study awards to assist you in meeting your need.

The following data about need-based financial aid awarded by UC for the 1992-93 academic year may help you in estimating your financial aid qualifications. This is the latest academic year for which information is available.

UNIVERSITY OF CALIFORNIA
Financial Aid Facts — 1992-93 Academic Year

Undergraduate Financial Aid Recipients

Number of Recipients	60,382
Percent of Students	49%
Average Award	$5,935

Need-based Dependent Undergraduate Financial Aid Recipients

Parent Income	% Receiving Aid
Less than $30,000	54.9%
$30,000 to $44,999	21.5%
$45,000 to $59,999	11.9%
$60,000 or more	7.9%

UNIVERSITY OF CALIFORNIA

The UC campus' financial aid offices generally begin sending notifications of financial aid awards in April.

DEFERRED PAYMENT PLANS

Deferred payment plans make fee and tuition costs more manageable by spreading payment over a period of months rather than requiring the entire amount at the beginning of each term. All campuses except Los Angeles and San Francisco offer deferred payment plans for fees and tuition. The programs require a simple application and nominal participation fee each term. No interest is charged. Los Angeles offers a prepayment plan, which allows you to pay fees and tuition installments prior to the beginning of the term. Many campuses also offer deferred payment plans for housing.

The UC campus' financial aid offices generally begin sending notifications of financial aid awards in April.

UNDOCUMENTED ALIEN STUDENTS

Undocumented alien students receive the same amounts and general types of financial aid as documented nonresident students (for example, those from other states), although the sources of funds differ. Because undocumented alien students are not eligible for state and federal grants and loans, the campuses use University-based grants and loans to meet their financial needs. However, University grants are not normally available to cover nonresident tuition. Therefore, needy undocumented students may have to borrow between $4,000 and $11,000 a year, depending upon campus policies and individual circumstances.

GRADUATING IN FOUR YEARS

Depending upon your academic major, the University of California requires you to complete a minimum of 180 to 200 quarter units to earn your Bachelor's degree. This means you must successfully earn an average of 15 quarter units during each of twelve academic terms to graduate in four years. The typical UC student requires 4.33 academic years — thirteen quarters — to earn an undergraduate degree. Seven out of ten students who enter the University as freshmen earn a degree within six years.

Even with recent budget cuts, the University of California has made these changes to increase student access to faculty and to help students graduate in a timely manner.

- The faculty has agreed to significantly increase the number of courses they teach for undergraduates over the next three years.
- More small, seminar courses for freshmen and sophomores have been added to the curriculum.
- The campuses have expanded opportunities for undergraduates to work with faculty on research projects.
- The University has increased classes and course sections (the number of times the same course is given each term) for undergraduates.
- Teaching effectiveness is assigned more weight in the review of faculty performance.
- Automated registration systems are helping to ensure that more students get the classes they request each term. Several campuses have computerized, interactive telephone registration systems so that students have more success getting the classes they want, and the campuses can track and respond to demand for classes more easily.

The typical UC student requires just over four academic years — thirteen quarters — to earn an undergraduate degree.

It is possible to get the classes you need. You must be flexible.

If your first choice course is not available, you may have to take a second choice course to meet specific General Education, major, or graduation requirements.

You may have to take a class from a less preferred instructor.

You need to be willing to take classes at any time during the day or evening.

Most UC students attend on a full-time basis. Only six to seven percent attend part-time. According to a UC survey of student employment in 1992-93, fifty-eight percent of students worked, averaging 17.6 hours a week.

If you are determined to graduate in four years, make college your first priority and remain strongly focused.

Recent studies by the University indicate that more UC students are now completing their degrees in four years compared to ten years ago. However, many students take more time because of personal decisions to slow their progress. They take time off to work or travel, they take fewer classes one or two terms to participate more fully in an extracurricular activity or to independently pursue an academic interest, they change their major several times or at a relatively late time in their undergraduate years, or they decline to take required classes offered at times they consider inconvenient.

If you are determined to graduate in four years, make college your first priority and remain strongly focused. Decide on your major early in your undergraduate career. Develop an educational plan that includes courses to meet the General Education/ Breadth Requirement as well as classes to complete your major. Select your courses with the assistance of academic advisors. Plan to earn fifteen to eighteen units of academic credit each quarter. Consider taking classes in summer school. Expect to adjust your course selections, choice of instructors, and time schedule to take required classes. Limit your work hours so that you have ample time to carry a full load, and take courses you need when class space is available. Think carefully before you plan to take time off for exchange programs, internships, or travel.

HOUSING

Call or write to the housing offices to receive housing information and application materials. File your housing application well in advance of deadlines.

A variety of undergraduate housing is available: Apartments shared by several students, residence halls with suites, and double and single rooms. Some facilities are two- and three-story low-rises, while others are more like high-rise apartment buildings. Most student housing is coeducational with men and women living in the same building, sometimes on the same floor. At some campuses there are residence halls for students with special interests, such as art, social science, or a foreign language. Apartment-style residences have kitchens. Students in residence halls without kitchens are usually required to purchase a meal plan. Students living off-campus may purchase meal plans at some campuses.

Check the appropriate box on your admission application to receive brochures describing housing options, selection policies, and application information. Also, call or write directly to the housing office of those campuses that interest you to receive supplemental housing information and application materials. Send in your housing applications by the deadlines noted on the following pages for each campus to assure yourself of your best chance to obtain on-campus housing.

CAMPUS HOUSING POLICIES NEW STUDENTS FOR FALL 1994				
Campus	Guarantee Offered To		Application Process	
	Freshmen	Transfers	Deadline	Comments
Berkeley	Yes: 1 year	No	March 31, 1994	Admitted students who submitted housing application and SIR by deadlines were sent housing contract.
Davis	Yes: 1 year	Yes: 1 year	(Note 1.)	Admitted students who submitted SIR by July 1, 1994 were sent housing contracts.
Irvine	Yes: 2 years	Yes: 2 years	May 1, 1994	Admitted students receive housing information and application in March.
Los Angeles	Yes: 2 years	Yes: 2 years	March 31, 1994	Admitted students receive a housing brochure and application with their notification of admission.
Riverside	Yes: All years	Yes: All years	(Note 2.)	Admitted students receive housing information with their notification of admission.
San Diego	Yes: 2 years	Yes: 1 year	May 6, 1994	Students should receive a housing brochure by mid-February.
Santa Barbara	Yes: 1 year	No	April 1, 1994	Applicants receive housing information and application in early February.
Santa Cruz	Yes: 2 years	Yes: 1 year	(Note 3.)	Admitted students request their housing applications when they submit SIR.

Notes: 1. Davis has no separate housing application.
2. For priority placement, Riverside students with special requests are encouraged to submit applications and contracts by June 1st.
3. Deadline depends upon when housing application is obtained and subsequently submitted.
4. "SIR" = "Statement of Intent to Register".

For fall 1994, all campuses guaranteed on-campus housing to all freshmen.

Undergraduate housing availability has improved significantly in recent years with the opening of several large housing projects. For fall 1994, all campuses guarantee on-campus housing to new freshmen who comply with relevant deadlines and procedures. All campuses, with the exception of Berkeley and Santa Barbara, also guarantee housing to new transfers. It is very important to file an application or submit a housing contract by the stated deadlines. At some campuses — Berkeley, Los Angeles, and Santa Barbara — transfer students must apply for housing before they are officially admitted. Admission to the University does not guarantee on-campus housing.

All campuses, with the exception of Berkeley and Santa Barbara, guarantee housing to new transfers.

Some campuses use a random drawing, or lottery, to assign specific accommodations; others do it on a first-come, first-served basis as housing applications are received.

If you are not assigned on-campus housing, or if you do not choose to live on-campus, the off-campus office or the community housing office — campus offices to assist students to find off-campus accommodations — can help you find a suitable place to live. Many students choose to move off-campus after their freshman or sophomore year. Alternative housing may consist of fraternities and sororities, international houses, student cooperatives, apartment rentals, or house rentals in the community. Lists of students seeking roommates are available. For those campuses that have tight housing markets, start looking early in the summer if you wish to live off-campus.

You are encouraged to file your housing application well before the deadline indicated on your housing application.

The following pages present a breakdown by campus of on-campus housing availability for new students for the 1994-95 academic year. The procedures and deadlines noted are for students who entered in fall 1994 and are subject to change. These policies apply only to new students who entered in fall 1994 and complied with all relevant campus housing procedures and deadlines. Contact the appropriate campus housing office for more information. You are encouraged to file your housing application well before the deadline indicated on your housing application.

BERKELEY

Fall 1994: Residence hall housing was guaranteed to all new freshmen who submitted a housing application by March 31st and a Statement of Intent to Register by May 1st. New transfer students needed to submit a housing application by the end of May and an SIR by June 1st. Transfer students were assigned housing by lottery.

Total Spaces: Berkeley has 5,000 on-campus residence hall spaces. Specific hall and room-size assignments are determined by lottery. Berkeley also houses 600 students — primarily at the graduate level — in its International House, a coeducational facility for students from the United States and abroad.

DAVIS

Fall 1994: Between March and April, students admitted for fall 1994 received materials describing residence halls and housing options. No separate housing application was required. All new students who returned the Statement of Intent to Register by July 1st received housing contract offers. Students admitted late were offered housing if space was available.

Total Spaces: Davis has five residence halls housing 3,500 undergraduate students and 178 graduate students. The residence life program supports 12 specialty programs, or theme floors. Ninety percent of new freshmen and twenty-five percent of new transfers are housed on-campus in residence halls.

IRVINE

Fall 1994: UCI guaranteed housing for two years to all new freshmen and transfers entering in the fall of 1994. Housing application materials were sent in March to all fall 1994 applicants who requested housing information on their admission applications. Housing was guaranteed to all new freshman and transfer students under age 25 who submitted their housing application by May 1st and their Statement of Intent to Register on time.

Total Spaces: Irvine has 3,930 on-campus residence hall and apartment spaces. Group housing provides theme housing for 800 undergraduates in the fine arts, engineering, and campuswide honors program as well as group housing for sororities and fraternities. UCI also has a park with limited space for students with their own RV's and trailers.

LOS ANGELES

Fall 1994: Housing is guaranteed for two years to new freshmen and transfer students who apply on time. Newly admitted students received a housing brochure and application with the letter of admission. New fall 1994 undergraduates were required to submit their housing application by March 31st and their SIR by May 1st for freshmen, and June 1st for transfers.

Total Spaces: Los Angeles has 5,630 undergraduate spaces in a variety of on-campus housing facilities. Eighty-five percent of new freshmen chose to live on campus. New transfer students occupied ten percent of the on-campus spaces.

RIVERSIDE

Fall 1994: All new and returning students were guaranteed on-campus housing, unconditionally, for the duration of their undergraduate years. For priority placement, students with special requests were encouraged to submit applications and contracts by June 1st. Admitted students received housing information with their notifications of admission.

Total Spaces: Riverside has 1,800 spaces in two residence halls and 700 spaces in apartment complexes adjacent to the campus. Students may apply for housing in one of the following nine special interest areas: Academic-Science, Academic-Business, Multicultural, Fine Arts, Health and Fitness, Honors, Pan-African, and Outdoors.

SAN DIEGO

Fall 1994: On-campus housing was guaranteed to all new freshmen for two consecutive years and to all transfers for one year. The campus was able to provide on-campus housing for all eligible new students who requested it and was able to honor most requests from continuing students, as well.

Each of UCSD's five colleges has its own housing facilities.

UCSD guaranteed on-campus housing to new students who filed a housing application by May 6th. If you request housing information on your admission application form and do not receive the housing brochure by early March, contact the housing office at UCSD for a copy. You are encouraged to file your housing application well before the deadline.

Total Spaces: San Diego has nearly 5,200 on-campus spaces. Each of UCSD's five colleges has its own housing facilities. Students generally prefer to live with students attending the same college, but this is not always possible because of housing limitations.

SANTA BARBARA

Fall 1994: UCSB met all housing requests from new students for fall 1994. All students who applied for fall admission received information about housing and a housing application in early February. April 1st was the deadline for submitting the housing application for residence halls. University and private residence halls guaranteed housing to new freshmen who observed housing application deadlines. University residence hall space is awarded through a random drawing. Transfer students received priority for two of the three University apartment complexes. Students are assigned apartment space on a first-come, first-served basis.

Total Spaces: Santa Barbara has 3,572 on-campus spaces in six residence halls. Seventy percent of these spaces are reserved for freshmen. In addition, there are three apartment complexes and two family student-housing complexes with 592 units. Additional housing for 2,000 students is available in three privately owned residence halls adjacent to the campus.

Santa Cruz undergraduates belong to one of eight residential colleges, each with its own housing.

SANTA CRUZ

Fall 1994: Santa Cruz guaranteed on-campus housing to new freshmen for two years, new transfer students for one year. About half of UCSC students live on campus. Students who wished to live on campus after the guarantee period participated in a lottery. Admitted students request a housing application when they submit their Statement of Intent to Register.

Total Spaces: Santa Cruz undergraduates belong to one of eight residential colleges, each with its own housing. Cowell, Porter, and Stevenson Colleges have residence halls with dining halls for meals. Kresge houses students in apartments. College Eight, Crown, Merrill, and Oakes offer both residence halls and apartments. UCSC has a park with limited space for students with their own RV's and trailers.

STUDENT SERVICES

STUDENT SUPPORT

Orientation helps you to become familiar with the campus, obtain assistance with course planning and scheduling, and meet other new students.

The University of California campuses offer many student services to assist you with adjustment to college, course and program selection, major and career choice, successful completion of courses, and job placement. Although the campuses may differ in their implementation of these services, the following support services are available throughout the UC system.

- Orientation to college programs are available for new students to obtain an understanding of campus programs and curriculum requirements. Each campus offers orientation programs during the summer or at the beginning of the fall term for newly admitted freshman and transfer students. Orientation helps you to become familiar with the campus, obtain assistance with course planning and scheduling, and meet other new students. Attend this orientation if possible.

  Programs vary in length from one to several days. During two- or three-day programs, you may stay overnight in campus residence halls. Often, parents also are invited to attend. Campuses mail you information about their orientation programs. If you do not receive this information by mid-June, contact the campus.

- Academic advising is provided to help with selecting a major, program planning, academic difficulties, degree requirements, and advanced study and career options. Faculty advisors in each college and department and professional advisors provide this service. Peer advisors — trained upper-division and graduate students — are also available on some campuses.

- Counseling services are provided to assist you with personal adjustment problems.
- Learning or tutorial centers are designed to assist you with developing your academic skills and improving your specific course understanding. All campuses offer tutoring by trained upper-division and graduate students.
- Career-planning programs are provided to assist you to make career decisions. A variety of work-learn programs are offered to help you gain on-the-job experience. These programs include internships, field study, cooperative education, experimental learning, and community service opportunities.
- Job placement services are available to assist you in developing strategies for obtaining a job; e.g., resume writing, interview techniques, and to help you with job placement.
- Information about graduate education is available.
- International student advising services are provided to assist students with questions about immigration, employment, government regulations, financial aid, cultural adjustment, and personal matters.
- Reentry services are designed to assist students who are returning to school after several years of life and work experience.
- Child care is provided for infants, toddlers, and preschool children of students.
- Health, financial aid, and housing services are some other programs provided.

All campuses offer tutoring by trained upper-division and graduate students.

DISABLED STUDENTS

The University provides special assistance and services to help students with disabilities participate fully in campus programs and activities. If you are physically disabled or have a learning disability, contact the disabled student services office at each campus to which you apply to discuss your disability and your special needs. The campuses can then make plans to accommodate you before you enroll. Currently, more than 3,300 undergraduates with learning disabilities attend the University.

Disabled students should contact the disabled student services offices of the campuses to which they apply to initiate services.

A question on the UC admission application asks you to identify your disabilities, but answering it does not necessarily initiate services. It is your responsibility to contact the campuses to begin the process. You will be asked to document your disability as a requirement for eligibility for special assistance. The disabled student services office at each campus will advise you about the types of documentation that are acceptable.

The campus tailors its services and programs, depending upon the nature of your disability, to meet your particular needs. The types of services generally available include assistance with registration and enrollment, accessibility tours and maps, counseling, tutoring, readers, interpreters, notetakers, special test-taking arrangements, adaptive equipment, on-campus van transportation, and equipment loans. For further information about disabled student opportunities, see chapter 8: EDUCATIONAL OPPORTUNITIES, Students With Learning Disabilities, page 8--4.

EDUCATION ABROAD PROGRAM

The University of California, through its Education Abroad Program (EAP), offers UC students the opportunity to study abroad while earning UC credit. In 1995-96, more than fifteen-hundred students are expected to study in over one-hundred host institutions in thirty-two countries worldwide. Most programs run for the full academic year, although there are some short-term programs of one semester/quarter or summer term.

In 1994-95, more than fourteen-hundred students are expected to study in over one-hundred host institutions in thirty-one countries worldwide.

A UC faculty member in residence administers most study centers in these countries. The directors and staff of the study centers advise students about academic matters, assist with housing and specific problems, plan field trips, and provide information about cultural opportunities.

All credit earned abroad applies toward a UC degree, and with careful planning, the courses can count toward your major. While in the EAP, most students make normal progress toward UC graduation. Acceptance of credits earned in the EAP toward your major or graduation requirements depends upon UC departmental or campus criteria. To maximize your educational experience, you must research and plan carefully before you go abroad.

The EAP places you at the finest host universities abroad where you take courses side by side with local students. In some cases, you pursue language study and enroll in special courses designed for the program. You can pursue specialized studies in your major, take courses to add breadth to your general education, concentrate on language or area studies, and conduct research.

The EAP provides on-site orientation to help you adjust to the new culture, environment, and university. In addition, academic-year programs in non-English speaking countries include an intensive language program of four to ten weeks, which takes place before the start of the academic year.

SELECTION CRITERIA

All credit earned for courses taken abroad applies toward a UC degree, and with careful planning, the courses can count toward your major.

Selection of UC undergraduate students is subject to the following minimum qualifications:

- Maturity, flexibility, seriousness of academic purpose, and willingness to work within the program's design as demonstrated by your statement of purpose, previous accomplishments, and personal interview.
- 3.00 cumulative college GPA, or the equivalent at the time of application, and maintained through departure.
- Junior standing — 56 to 60 semester units or 84 to 90 quarter units, varies by campus — by your departure date, except for specific short-term programs abroad of one semester/quarter or summer term.
- Endorsement of your Campus EAP Selection Committee and completion of all campus-specific requirements.

- Completion of language courses and other courses are required with a GPA of 3.00, or the equivalent, at the time of application and maintained until departure. Many programs require two years of college-level training in the language of the host country.

If you are a community college transfer student, you may participate in the EAP as a junior if you transfer to UC Irvine or UC Santa Barbara. At all other campuses, you may participate after fulfilling an initial residency requirement.

Costs are usually comparable to the cost of studying on a UC campus.

COSTS

Costs are usually comparable to the cost of studying on a UC campus, although costs vary from country to country. No overseas tuition is charged. As on a UC campus, you are responsible for UC registration and educational fees; campus fees; and room, board, books, and personal travel and living expenses. The only additional costs directly related to the program are for round-trip transportation and on-site orientation and intensive language program expenses, where applicable.

FINANCIAL ASSISTANCE

While on EAP, you are eligible for many types of financial assistance. Contact your campus EAP office to determine if you qualify.

UC FINANCIAL AID: Students already receiving UC financial aid continue to receive their grants, loans, and scholarships while abroad. Aid is based on the cost of studying at each EAP location. UC students not currently receiving UC financial support may qualify for aid while on EAP.

EAP ALUMNI SCHOLARSHIPS: EAP provides scholarships to financial aid and non-financial aid students who do not have adequate resources to participate in EAP.

EAP OPPORTUNITY GRANT: In order to assist minority and low-income students, EAP provides grants through campus financial aid offices. Grants range from $400 to $1,100.

You are eligible for many types of financial assistance.

PACIFIC REGION SCHOLARSHIPS: First-time EAP participants going to most Pacific Region countries receive scholarships, which range from $200 to $4,000.

OTHER SCHOLARSHIPS AND FELLOWSHIPS: Special campus and Universitywide scholarships and fellowships are available based on country, academic merit, or academic field of study.

COUNTRIES

Most study centers are administered by a UC faculty member in residence.

Countries on the following page have UC study centers:

Most study centers are administered by a UC faculty member in residence.

Australia	Ghana	Netherlands
Austria	Hong Kong	New Zealand
Brazil	Hungary	Russia
Canada	India	Singapore
Chile	Indonesia	Spain
China	Israel	Sweden
Costa Rica	Italy	Taiwan
Denmark	Japan	Thailand
Egypt	Korea	United Kingdom
France	Mexico	& Ireland
Germany		

For information contact the Education Abroad Program at any of the campuses, or write to:

EAP Systemwide Office
Hollister Research Office
University of California
Santa Barbara, CA 93106-1140

SUMMER SESSIONS

Each University of California campus offers a wide range of courses during the summer:

- Programs designed for students to (a) enroll in regular UC summer classes, (b) get an advanced look at college-level academics and campus life, and (c) earn college credit.
- Programs affiliated with SAA/EOP to help students prepare for academics and campus life. See this chapter: SAA and EOP, page 11--44.
- Programs for recent high school graduates to get a head start on their college education.
- Special academic programs for junior high and high school students to develop and explore their academic talents.

Admission to UC summer session does not constitute admission to the University.

Except for SAA/EOP summer programs, it is not necessary for you to be admitted to the University to attend summer session. Conversely, admission to summer session does not constitute admission to the University.

Programs range from one to eight weeks. Costs vary depending upon the campus, the courses, and the program. There are registration and unit fees as well as extra fees for room and board, laboratory, and studio. Some programs are free; several offer financial aid. Most programs give high school or college credit. This information is noted below and on the following pages for each campus. Check with your career center or guidance office in March or April for the latest listing of these programs. Contact the summer session office of the campus for registration, housing, and fee information.

In summer 1994 the following summer programs were available.

BERKELEY

REGULAR SUMMER SESSION: Regular summer session is open to students entering grade twelve with a letter of recommendation from their high school principal. College credit may be earned. Call (510) 642-5641 for additional information.

Special Program: Ten-week intensive language workshops. College credit may be earned.

ACADEMIC TALENT DEVELOPMENT PROGRAMS: Two programs are offered for academic advancement and enrichment:

1. Elementary Division for students who have completed kindergarten through grade six: Students attend a school site near the campus for a three-week experience exploring new academic areas. Application deadline for new applicants: March 31st. Financial aid is available.

2. Secondary Division for students who have completed grades seven through eleven: Students take one or two courses for six weeks on the Berkeley campus. Application deadline for new applicants: February 15th. High school credit may be earned. Financial aid is available.

The duration of summer school programs varies from one to eight weeks.

Students for these two programs are screened on the basis of test scores, course grades, teacher recommendations, and a sample of an intellectual or creative product or an essay on an assigned topic. Call (510) 642-8308 for additional information.

WILDLIFE RESEARCH CAMP: Wildlife Research Camp offers two one-week sessions of scientific research for students between the ages of fourteen and eighteen. The program takes place at UC field stations in the Sierra Nevada mountains. Application deadline: When program is filled, usually in May. Limited financial aid is available. Call (510) 642-4087 for additional information.

PRE-COLLEGE ACADEMY: This six-week, summer enrichment program offers an intensive academic program for 175 underrepresented minority students from Bay Area high schools. Participants take courses in English, mathematics, and science. Application deadline: No information. Call (510) 642-1744 for additional information.

DAVIS

REGULAR SUMMER SESSION: Regular summer session is open to students entering grade twelve with a letter of recommendation from their high school principal. College credit may be earned. Call (916) 752-1641 for additional information.

SUMMER HUMANITIES INSTITUTE: UC Davis offers a six-week residential honors program to high school students who have completed their junior year. Eligible students must have a GPA of 3.25 or higher, or a PSAT verbal score of at least 53. Students take regular summer-session classes. Application deadline: May 6th or when program is filled. College credit may be earned. Financial aid is available. Call (916) 752-7649 for additional information.

UPWARD BOUND SUMMER PROGRAM: This six-week summer residential program is designed to assist first-generation, college-bound students from low-income families. Students may earn up to ten high school credits in mathematics, science, and English plus two electives. The program includes advising, cultural and social activities, and travel to the Oregon Shakespeare Festival and Sequoia Lake at Kings Canyon. There is no cost for eligible students. Application deadline: No information. High school credit. Call (916) 757-3100 for additional information.

ENGINEERING SUMMER PROGRAM FOR HIGH SCHOOL STUDENTS: The College of Engineering is sponsoring a one-week residency program for selected minority and disadvantaged high school students. The program is designed to give students the opportunity to explore the field of engineering. Application deadline: No information: Call (916) 752-3316 for additional information.

You may earn college credit in several of the summer school programs.

IRVINE

REGULAR SUMMER SESSION: Regular summer session is open to students entering grade twelve with a GPA of at least 3.00 in academic subjects. College credit may be earned. Call (714) 856-5493 for additional information.

NATIVE AMERICAN INTERTRIBAL UNIVERSITY PREPARATORY SUMMER PROGRAM: This four-week residential program is available to 120 American Indian high school students entering grades eight and nine from throughout the country. The program includes study in a variety of courses and presentations by American Indian artists and tribal leaders. It is designed to encourage and motivate American Indian students to pursue higher education. Application deadline: When program is filled. Call (714) 856-6281 for additional information.

LOS ANGELES

REGULAR SUMMER SESSION: Regular summer session is open to students entering grades ten through twelve through the Expanding Horizons Program. Call (310) 825-8333 for additional information.

EXPANDING HORIZONS PROGRAM: This program is available to gifted and high-achieving students entering grades ten through twelve. Selection is based upon high school grades, SAT I scores, and counselor/teacher recommendations. Students may take any lower-division college course offered through the regular summer session. Expanding Horizons is offered in cooperation with Bruin Kids/Explore, a cultural and recreational enrichment summer program for teens. There are three six-week sessions. Application deadline: Mid-June. College credit may be earned. Call (310) 825-4191 for additional information.

PREPARING FOR COLLEGE: This four-week session offers motivated students entering grades nine through twelve the opportunity to take courses for high school credit in a variety of subjects. Preparing for College is offered in cooperation with Bruin Kids/Explore, a cultural and recreational enrichment summer program for teens. Application deadline: The first day of class if space is available. Financial aid is available. Call (310) 825-4191 for additional information.

BRUIN KIDS EXPLORE: This program offers students thirteen through seventeen of age activities on the UCLA campus, including classes in sports and the arts, and outdoor adventure trips. Programs vary in length depending upon the activity. Application deadline: When program is filled. High school credit may be earned for some courses. Call (310) 206-5574 for additional information.

RIVERSIDE

REGULAR SUMMER SESSION: Regular session is open to students entering grade twelve with a GPA of at least 3.00. College credit may be earned. Call (714) 787-3044 for additional information.

EXPANDING HORIZONS: This is a two-week nonresidential enrichment program for talented and high-achieving, Riverside area students entering grades eight through twelve. The program includes lectures, demonstrations, and workshops on a variety of academic and enrichment subjects. Students are selected on a first-come, first-served basis. Application deadline: No information. Enrollment packets available after May 1st. Call (909) 787-4361, extension 1655 for additional information.

Several campuses offer summer school programs for high-achieving high school students.

SAN DIEGO

REGULAR SUMMER SESSION: Lower-division courses without prerequisites are open to students entering grade twelve. College credit may be earned. Call (619) 534-4365 for additional information.

SUMMER SCHOLARS PROGRAM: This five-week residential program offers high school juniors the opportunity to sample college life and enroll in a special course in either marine biology or political science. Application deadline: May 6th. College credit may be earned. Call (619) 534-7074 for additional information.

SCIENCE ENRICHMENT PROGRAM: The Howard Hughes Program is an eight-week intensive science research program for San Diego area African American, Hispanic, and Native American students in grades ten through twelve. To be eligible for the program, students must have a GPA of at least 3.00 and experience in completing a science fair project. Students receive a stipend for participating. Application deadline: April 15th. Call (619) 534-7761 for additional information.

SCHOOL OF MEDICINE MINORITY HIGH SCHOOL STUDENT SUMMER RESEARCH APPRENTICE PROGRAM: The UCSD School of Medicine offers an eight-week research apprentice program for San Diego area high school students. Priority is given to students who are African American, Mexican American, Native American, and mainland Puerto Rican. Students are hired as a research apprentices and work thirty-five hours a week under the auspices of a faculty mentor on a self-directed biomedical or scientific research project. The program is limited to twenty-five students. Application deadline: May 30th. Call (619) 534-4170 for additional information.

SANTA BARBARA

REGULAR SUMMER SESSION: Regular session is open to students eighteen and older. College credit may be earned. Call (805) 893-2047 for additional information.

HIGH SCHOOL JUNIORS PROGRAM: This six-week residential program offers high-achieving students, who have completed their junior year, an opportunity to take regular summer-session courses. To be eligible, students must have completed at least twelve academic semester courses with a GPA of 3.30 or better. Application deadline: May 13th. Scholarship application deadline: March 25th. Scholarships are available to students with a GPA of at least 3.50 in twelve semesters of UC "a-f" Subject Requirement courses. College credit may be earned. Call (805) 893-2047 for additional information.

YOUNG SCHOLARS PROGRAM: This six-week residential program offers gifted and talented high school students in grades nine through twelve the opportunity to complete accelerated courses in art, biology, literature, mathematics, and physics. The courses are offered by the College of Creative Studies. Application deadline: May 14th. Scholarship application deadline: March 26th. Limited merit and need-based scholarships are available for California residents. College credit may be earned. Call (805) 893-3872 for additional information.

YOUNG ARTISTS VOCAL INSTITUTE: The Institute is an intensive six-week college-preparatory program for talented young vocalists in grades ten through twelve. Students receive private voice lessons and take classes in vocalization, music theory and history, piano, and body movement. Applicants must submit a high school transcript; letters of recommendation from their high school principal or counselor, and voice teacher or choral director; a brief personal essay; a list of songs performed; and an audition tape including two classical and one musical theatre songs. Application deadline: May 13th. College credit may be earned. Financial aid is available. Call (805) 893-2377 for additional information.

APPRENTICE RESEARCHERS AT QUEST: This six-week nonresidential summer program offers a limited number of Santa Barbara area high school juniors the opportunity to participate in university-level research in microelectronics and related areas. Students are selected on the basis of teacher recommendations, personal interviews, and review of applications by the program coordinator and faculty in the College of Engineering. The program is funded by the National Science Foundation, and students receive a stipend for their participation. Application deadline: April 8th. Call (805) 893-8527 for additional information.

UPWARD BOUND SUMMER PROGRAM: This six-week summer residential program is designed to assist first-generation, college-bound students from low-income families. Students may earn up to ten high school credits in English, mathematics, and science. The program includes college visits and a variety of recreational and cultural activities. There is no cost for eligible students. Application deadline: No information. High school credit. Call (805) 893-3515 for additional information.

SUMMER ACADEMIC INSTITUTE: The two-week residential program is designed to help underrepresented ninth and tenth grade students strengthen academic skills and become eligible for admission to the University. Classes focus on preparing for the SAT I: Reasoning Test and developing writing, computing, and critical thinking skills. Application deadline: No information. Call (805) 893-2400 for additional information.

SANTA CRUZ

REGULAR SESSION: Regular session is open to students entering grade twelve with a letter of recommendation from a counselor. College credit may be earned. Call (408) 459-3544 for additional information.

CAMPUS PROFILES

Profiles of the nine campuses of the University of California present data for the 1993-94 academic year.

BERKELEY

University of California, Berkeley
Berkeley, CA 94720
(510) 642-6000
Admissions: (510) 642-3175
Financial Aid: (510) 642-6442
Housing: (510) 642-3642

DISTINGUISHING FEATURES: UC Berkeley is one of the world's leading intellectual centers, renowned for the size and quality of its libraries and laboratories and the scope of its research and publications. More graduates go on to earn Ph.D. degrees than graduates of any other university in the country. Professors include some of the most distinguished novelists, poets, thinkers, and researchers in the world. The campus has a highly prestigious reputation. A number of special programs for freshmen and sophomores feature small classes and seminars, although lectures may have several hundred students. You can design your own major. It is one of two UC campuses that offers an undergraduate degree in Business Administration. Berkeley is the most ethnically diverse of the campuses.
DEGREES OFFERED: Bachelor's, Master's, Doctoral.
COLLEGES: Chemistry, Engineering, Environmental Design, Letters and Science, Natural Resources.
SCHOOLS: Business Administration, Education, Journalism, Law, Library and Information Studies, Optometry, Public Health, Public Policy, Social Welfare.
UNDERGRADUATE MAJORS: 100. See this chapter: Undergraduate Degree Majors, page 11--84.
CALENDAR: Semester system. Summer sessions.
FACULTY: 2,600 full- and part-time. Undergraduate classes taught by faculty, not graduate students - most. Faculty with Ph.D.'s - 100%. Student/faculty ratio - 12/1.
ENROLLMENT: ***Total*** - 30,337. ***Graduate*** - 8,608. ***Undergraduate*** - 21,729: California residents - 88.0%, out-of-state - 8.0%, other countries - 4.0%. Men - 53.0%, women - 47.0%. ***Ethnic distribution of undergraduates:*** Hispanic - 13.8%, Black - 5.5%, Asian/Pacific Islander - 35.1%, Native American /Alaskan - 1.1%, White - 33.7%, Other/not stated - 10.8%. ***Freshmen graduating within 5 years*** - 73.0%.
LOCATION: On 1,232 acres in an urban setting. Surrounded by wooded hills and the city of Berkeley, known for its cultural diversity, political activity, and dynamic environment. Easily accessible to San Francisco and the Bay Area.
CAMPUS LIFE: ***Undergraduates living on campus*** - 25.0%. ***Clubs and organizations*** - 500. Fraternities and sororities - yes. ***Athletics:*** Intercollegiate - NCAA, Division I-A. Intramural sports - yes.
OTHER INFORMATION: ***Founded*** - 1868.
WASC Accredited - yes.

DAVIS

University of California, Davis
Davis, CA 95616
(916) 752-1011
Admissions: (916) 752-2971
Financial Aid: (916) 752-2390
Housing: (916) 752-2033

DISTINGUISHING FEATURES: UC Davis combines a rich academic environment with the friendly atmosphere of a college town. About two-thirds of UC Davis undergraduates continue their studies at the graduate or professional level. The campus assigns all freshmen an advisor when they enter. Freshman seminars give first-year students the opportunity to interact with faculty in small, informal groups of not more than fifteen students. The Residential Freshman Honors Program offers select students the opportunity to take a specially designed set of honors courses which stimulate thinking across disciplines. Many cultural activities occur on campus — concerts, lectures, etc. Work-Learn Program provides several thousand internships each year. Over sixty percent of all undergraduates take advantage of these part- and full-time internships. The campus is internationally known for its programs in agricultural, environmental, and biological sciences. Programs in the humanities, arts, and social sciences have earned a national reputation. Davis has moved into the ranks of the top twenty general research universities in the United States.
DEGREES OFFERED: Bachelor's, Master's, Doctoral.
COLLEGES: Agricultural and Environmental Sciences, Engineering, Letters and Science.
SCHOOLS: Law, Management, Medicine, Veterinary Medicine.
UNDERGRADUATE MAJORS: 100. See this chapter: Undergraduate Degree Majors, page 11--84.
CALENDAR: Quarter system. Summer sessions.
FACULTY: 1,500 full- and part-time. Undergraduate classes taught by faculty, not graduate students - most. Faculty with Ph.D.'s - 100%. Student/faculty ratio - nd.
ENROLLMENT: ***Total*** - 21,823. ***Graduate*** - 4,506. ***Undergraduate*** - 17,317: California residents - 96.0%, out-of-state - 3.0%, other countries - 1.0%. Men - 48.9%, women - 51.1%. ***Ethnic distribution of undergraduates:*** Hispanic - 10.5%, Black - 4.0%, Asian/Pacific Islander - 25.5%, Native American/Alaskan - 1.2%, White - 51.2%, Other/not stated - 7.7%. ***Freshmen graduating within 5 years*** - 77%.
LOCATION: On 3,600 acres adjacent to the city of Davis, a friendly college town. Seventy miles from San Francisco, fifteen miles from Sacramento. Borders farmlands and orchards. Forty miles of bike paths extend from the central campus through the city of Davis and into the countryside.
CAMPUS LIFE: ***Undergraduates living on campus*** - 21.5%. ***Clubs and organizations*** - 300. Fraternities and sororities - yes. ***Athletics:*** Intercollegiate - NCAA, Division II. Intramural sports - yes.
OTHER INFORMATION: ***Founded*** - 1961.
WASC Accredited - yes.

nd = no data available

IRVINE

University of California, Irvine
Irvine, CA 92717
(714) 856-5011
Admissions: (714) 856-6703
Financial Aid: (714) 856-6261
Housing: (714) 856-6811

DISTINGUISHING FEATURES: UC Irvine is a leading research center with a basic commitment to undergraduate education. It features an interdisciplinary approach, which allows students to focus on a subject from a combination of perspectives. All students must take one course in multicultural studies plus another that focuses on international relations and global issues. Irvine offers a minor in management, so you may complete the major of your choice and learn the basics of managerial processes, finance, accounting and marketing. The campus encourages students to undertake independent study and research projects to complement classroom work and to develop creative talents. The unique 3-2 Program (three years in your undergraduate program and two years in the graduate program) offers a B.A. or B.S. in any major (except Engineering) and a M.B.A. from the Graduate School of Management. The School of Humanities offers a Humanities Core Course for freshmen, which is taught by a team of professors of literature, philosophy, and history. There is a campuswide honors program for students in all majors; in addition, several majors offer upper-division honors courses.
DEGREES OFFERED: Bachelor's, Master's, Doctoral.
COLLEGES: Medicine.
SCHOOLS: Biological Sciences, Engineering, Fine Arts, Humanities, Physical Sciences, Social Ecology, Social Sciences, Management (Graduate only).
ACADEMIC UNITS: Departments of Information and Computer Science, Education, Athletics and Physical Education.
UNDERGRADUATE MAJORS: 47. See this chapter: Undergraduate Degree Majors, page 11--84.
CALENDAR: Quarter system. Summer sessions.
FACULTY: 811 full- and part-time. Undergraduate classes taught by faculty, not graduate students - majority. Faculty with Ph.D.'s - 96%. Student/faculty ratio - 18/1.
ENROLLMENT: ***Total*** - 16,166. ***Graduate*** - 2,625. ***Undergraduate*** - 13,541: California residents - 97.0%, out-of-state - 3.0%, other countries - 0.0%. Men - 47.2%, women - 52.8%. ***Ethnic distribution of undergraduates:*** Hispanic - 11.9%. Black - 2.7%, Asian/Pacific Islander - 44.0%, Native American/ Alaskan - 0.5%, White - 32.3%, Other/not stated - 8.5%. ***Freshmen graduating within 5 years*** - 59.4%.
LOCATION: On 1,489 acres in Orange County in the city of Irvine located in the coastal foothills near Newport Beach. One to two hour drive to Los Angeles, San Diego, and Mexico.
CAMPUS LIFE: ***Undergraduates living on campus*** - 31.0%. ***Clubs and organizations*** - 275, fraternities and sororities - yes. ***Athletics:*** Intercollegiate - NCAA, Division I-AAA. Intramural sports - yes.
OTHER INFORMATION: ***Founded*** - 1965.
WASC Accredited - yes.

LOS ANGELES

University of California, Los Angeles
Los Angeles, CA. 90024
(310) 825-4321
Admissions: (310) 825-3101
Financial Aid: (310) 206-0400
Housing: (310) 825-4271

DISTINGUISHING FEATURES: UCLA has the largest student population among the University of California campuses and is one of the world's most ethnically and culturally diverse university communities. It ranks among the top research universities in the nation and is internationally recognized for its curriculum and faculty. It offers opportunities for research projects and internships. Through the Program in Business and Administration, you may combine a basic business education with any major in the College of Letters and Science. Freshmen and sophomores participate in small seminars and discussion-oriented classes. Through the Honors Collegium in the College of Letters and Science, you may enroll in small, interdisciplinary seminars during your first two years. Students have the opportunity to design their own majors. The campus is an exciting place offering an extensive variety and volume of events.
DEGREES OFFERED: Bachelor's, Master's, Doctoral.
COLLEGES: Letters and Science.
SCHOOLS: Architecture and Urban Planning; Arts; Dentistry; Education; Engineering and Applied Science; Law; Library and Information Sciences; Management; Medicine; Nursing; Public Health; Social Welfare; Theater, Film and Television.
UNDERGRADUATE MAJORS: 109. See this chapter: Undergraduate Degree Majors, page 11--84.
CALENDAR: Quarter system. Summer sessions.
FACULTY: 3,100 full- and part-time. Undergraduate classes taught by faculty, not graduate students - all. Faculty with Ph.D.'s - 100%. Student/faculty ratio - nd.
ENROLLMENT: ***Total*** - 32,866. ***Graduate*** - 9,974. ***Undergraduate*** - 22.892: California residents - 94.3%, out-of-state - 3.6%, other countries - 2.1%. Men - 50.3%, women - 49.7%. ***Ethnic distribution of undergraduates:*** Hispanic - 16.2%, Black - 6.01%, Asian/Pacific Islander - 34.9%, Native American /Alaskan - 1.1%, White - 37.1%, Other/not stated - 4.7%. ***Freshmen Graduating Within 5 Years*** - 66.0%.
LOCATION: On 411 acres in West Los Angeles. Just five miles from the ocean at the foot of the Santa Monica mountains. Downtown LA a few miles to the east.
CAMPUS LIFE: ***Undergraduates living on campus*** - 24.5%. ***Clubs and organizations*** -500, fraternities and sororities - yes, more than 6,000 members. ***Athletics:*** Intercollegiate - NCAA, Division I-A. Intramural sports - yes.
OTHER INFORMATION: ***Founded*** - 1919.
WASC Accredited - yes.

RIVERSIDE

University of California, Riverside
Riverside, CA 92521
(909) 787-1012
Admissions: (909) 787-3411
Financial Aid: (909) 787-3878
Housing: (909) 787-5460

DISTINGUISHING FEATURES: UC Riverside couples the benefits of a large, diverse research university with the personal

nd = no data available

UNIVERSITY OF CALIFORNIA

attention and sense of community usually found only in small liberal arts colleges. The student population is small and the student/faculty ratio is low. The University Honors Program is a four year program providing students with special seminars, projects and classes. Three out of four students go on to graduate or professional school. It is one of the two University campuses that has an undergraduate degree program in Business Administration. It offers the only undergraduate degree in creative writing in the UC system. Through the Biomedical Sciences Program you can earn both a B.S. and M.D. degree in coordination with UCLA Medical School in seven years instead of the usual eight. See this chapter: Majors — Application and Screening, page 11–38.

DEGREES OFFERED: Bachelor's, Master's, Doctoral.

COLLEGES: Engineering, Humanities and Social Sciences, Natural and Agricultural Sciences.

SCHOOLS: Education, Management.

UNDERGRADUATE MAJORS: 54. See this chapter: Undergraduate Degree Majors, page 11--84.

CALENDAR: Quarter System. Summer session.

FACULTY: 500 full- and part-time. Undergraduate classes taught by faculty, not graduate students - most. Faculty with Ph.D.'s - 99%. Student/faculty ratio - 14/1.

ENROLLMENT: ***Total*** - 8,677. ***Graduate*** - 1,336. ***Undergraduate*** - 7,341: California residents - 97.0%, out-of-state - 2.5%, other countries - 0.5%. Men - 47.3%, women - 52.7%. ***Ethnic distribution of undergraduates:*** Hispanic - 13.6%, Black - 4.0%, Asian/Pacific Islander - 32.0%, Native American/Alaskan - 0.6%, White - 40.7%, Other/not stated - 9.0%. ***Freshmen graduating within 5 years*** - 58.0%.

LOCATION: 1,200 acre park-like campus in the rapidly growing valley community of Riverside. Located 50 miles east of Los Angeles.

CAMPUS LIFE: ***Undergraduates living on campus*** - 24.0%. ***Clubs and organizations*** - 170, fraternities and sororities - yes. ***Athletics:*** Intercollegiate - NCAA, Division II. Intramural sports - yes.

OTHER INFORMATION: ***Founded*** - 1954.

WASC Accredited - yes.

SAN DIEGO

University of California, San Diego
9500 Gilman Drive
La Jolla, CA. 92093
(619) 534-2230
Admissions: (619) 534-3160
Financial Aid: (619) 534-4480
Housing: (619) 534-4010

DISTINGUISHING FEATURES: UC San Diego ranks fifth nationally in federal funding for research and development and has an impressive variety of faculty projects, putting the campus on the cutting edge of creativity and discovery in science, technology, the arts, and humanities. The percentage of graduates who go on to earn Ph.D. and M.D. degrees is among the highest of United States public universities and colleges.

DEGREES OFFERED: Bachelor's, Master's, Doctoral.

RESIDENTIAL COLLEGES: There are five undergraduate colleges, each with its own faculty, educational philosophy, general education requirements, traditions, advisors, and housing and dining facilities. The purpose for setting up UC San Diego this way was to give students all the benefits of a great university without the disadvantages of "bigness." There are about 3,000 students in each College, except Eleanor Roosevelt, which is smaller because it first opened to freshmen in 1988. All undergraduate majors and all courses are open to you, regardless of the college you select, so the choice of a college should not depend upon the subjects you wish to study. The decision should be based upon the nature of the environment in which you wish to study these subjects — the setting in which you will do your best work.

The colleges differ in their requirements for general education. In addition to the advanced courses for your major, you must complete the general education requirements assigned by your college. These courses can range from a structured liberal arts program to a program with a broad range of electives. The colleges are listed here in the order of their founding.

Revelle College is the oldest and most traditional. Its structured approach to a liberal arts education prepares its graduates to compete in a complex world. During the first two years a typical class schedule would include

- roughly two-thirds of work in social sciences, humanities, a foreign language, and the fine arts; and,
- one-third of work in calculus and natural science.

In the final years, students concentrate on developing professional competence in a major and a basic understanding of another, unrelated field. This Renaissance curriculum develops three main skills: learning how to use the language of science and scholarship, learning how to think and write creatively, and learning how to learn.

John Muir College features an informal and friendly atmosphere and gives you a great deal of flexibility in planning your program. With an advisor, you design your own course schedule according to the following guidelines:

- one year-long sequence from the social sciences
- one year-long sequence from either mathematics or natural sciences
- two year-long sequences from the humanities, fine arts, or foreign languages
- two expository writing courses.

The flexibility and breadth of options is very appealing to students. Muir is the largest of the colleges.

Thurgood Marshall College emphasizes social awareness and cultural diversity. The educational philosophy is guided by the belief that regardless of a student's major, a liberal arts education must include an awareness and understanding of one's role in society. Therefore, scholarship and social responsibility are mutually compatible. Two programs promote this philosophical thrust: The "Dimensions of Culture" Program is a three-course interdisciplinary sequence. The "Partners at Learning" program gives course credit for tutoring and mentoring at local elementary schools.

Earl Warren College features programs that allow you to make a close connection between your undergraduate education and career goals. You are encouraged to participate in academic internships and field studies in order to gain experiences in the workplace and to test your career choices before graduation. The general education requirements consist of:

- two courses in writing;
- two courses in formal skills (calculus, symbolic logic, computer programming, or statistics); and
- a course called "Ethics and Society."

Besides a major, all students, except engineering majors, are required to complete two, six-course sequences outside their main area of study. Engineering students are required to take a three-course sequence in the humanities and arts and a three-course sequence in the social sciences.

Eleanor Roosevelt College (formerly Fifth College) is UCSD's "international college". The general education curriculum is founded on the tradition of a broad liberal arts program, and shares Eleanor Roosevelt's commitment to an international

nd = no data available

education. To prepare students to be capable world citizens, the curriculum expands writing, analytic, quantitative, and critical thinking skills. These intellectual skills, coupled with the college's international perspective, provide a sound foundation for all majors, including those in physical and applied. sciences. The core course, "The Making off the Modern World," guides students on a global intellectual odyssey, weaving together knowledge about world religions, great empires, and cultural contact. Students may enrich their education by studying or interning abroad.

ACADEMIC UNITS: School of Engineering, School, School of Medicine, Scripps Institution of Oceanography, Graduate School of International Relations and Pacific Studies.

UNDERGRADUATE MAJORS: 75. See this chapter: Undergraduate Degree Majors, page 11--84.

CALENDAR: Quarter system. Summer sessions.

FACULTY: 1,225 full- and part-time. Undergraduate classes taught by faculty, not graduate students - most. Faculty with Ph.D.'s - 99%. Student/faculty ratio - 18/1.

ENROLLMENT: ***Total*** - 17,369. ***Graduate*** - 2,920. ***Undergraduate*** - 14,449: California residents - 94.6%, out-of-state - 4.3%, other countries - 1.1%. Men - 51.1%, women - 48.1%. ***Ethnic distribution of undergraduates:*** Hispanic - 10.9%, Black - 2.5%, Asian/Pacific Islander - 25.4%, Native American/Alaskan - 2.5%, White - 51.2%, Other/not stated - 9.1%. ***Freshmen graduating within 5 years*** - 68% within 6 years.

LOCATION: On a 1,200 acre park-like site high on the bluffs overlooking the Pacific Ocean in the beautiful seaside town of La Jolla. Approximately thirty minutes from San Diego, two hours from Los Angeles and one hour from Mexico.

CAMPUS LIFE: ***Undergraduates living on campus*** - 34.0%. ***Clubs and organizations*** - 250, fraternities and sororities - yes. ***Athletics:*** Intercollegiate - NCAA, Division III. Intramural sports - yes.

OTHER INFORMATION: ***Founded*** - 1961. ***WASC Accredited*** - yes.

SAN FRANCISCO

University of California, San Francisco
San Francisco, California 94143
(415) 476-9000

DISTINGUISHING FEATURES: The UC San Francisco campus concentrates solely on study and research in the health and biomedical sciences, primarily at the graduate level. Its Schools of Medicine, Dentistry, Nursing, and Pharmacy are among the top-ranked professional programs in the country. UCSF offers professional study in medicine, dentistry, nursing, pharmacy, physical therapy, and dental hygiene. The Schools of Dentistry, Medicine, and Pharmacy admit qualified undergraduates who have completed required college coursework. However, most medical and dental students who enroll have graduated from college. The School of Nursing is open only to college graduates. The program in dental hygiene is open to qualified undergraduates with at least two years of preparatory college work. Enrollment consists of 42 undergraduate students and 2,516 graduate students. 37.9% are minority students. See this chapter: Majors — Application and Screening, page 11--38 for further information about programs. UC San Francisco also offers Master's and Doctoral degree programs in the basic health sciences and related social and behavioral sciences.

SANTA BARBARA

University of California, Santa Barbara
Santa Barbara, CA 93106
(805) 893-2327
Admissions: (805) 893-2881
Financial Aid: (805) 893-2432
Housing: (805) 893-2760

DISTINGUISHING FEATURES: UC Santa Barbara is both a friendly and close-knit undergraduate community and an international research center, which attracts outstanding scholars. Senior faculty members regularly teach freshman and sophomore classes. Professors make a special effort to involve students in their research and creative work, and there are many opportunities to work one-on-one with them. During a recent five-year period, seventy-two percent of those who applied to medical school were accepted, sixty-five percent who applied to law school were accepted. UCSB has top-ranked programs in engineering and the sciences, as well as outstanding programs in the humanities, arts, and social sciences. The College of Letters and Science, offering seventy majors, is the largest of UCSB's colleges and has a variety of unique, interdisciplinary programs which reflect the faculty collegiality for which the campus is known. The College encourages students to explore for several quarters before declaring a major. The College Honors Program provides superior students special scholarship and research opportunities. The College of Creative Studies features individualized instruction, small group seminars, tutorials, and requires demonstrated talent in the arts or sciences to be admitted. See this chapter: Majors — Application and Screening, page 11–42 for additional information. The highly competitive College of Engineering offers degree programs in chemical, electrical, and mechanical engineering, and computer science.

DEGREES OFFERED: Bachelor's, Master's, Doctoral.

COLLEGES: Creative Studies, Engineering, Letters and Sciences.

SCHOOLS: Education, Environmental Science and Management.

UNDERGRADUATE MAJORS: 80. See this chapter: Undergraduate Degree Majors,

CALENDAR: Quarter system. Summer sessions.

FACULTY: 700 full- and part-time. Undergraduate classes taught by faculty, not graduate students - most. Faculty with Ph.D.'s - 99%. Student/faculty ratio - nd.

ENROLLMENT: ***Total*** - 18,581. ***Graduate*** - 2,160. ***Undergraduate*** - 16,421: California residents - 94.1%, out-of-state - 4.6%, other countries - 1.2%. Men - 48.4%, women - 51.6%. ***Ethnic distribution of undergraduates:*** Hispanic - 10.7%, Black - 2.6%, Asian/Pacific Islander - 14.7%, Native American/Alaskan - 0.9%, White - 64.0%, Other/not stated - 7.1%. ***Freshmen graduating within 5 years*** - 64.0%.

LOCATION: On an 815 acre promontory bordered on three sides by the Pacific Ocean, and facing the Goleta Valley and the Santa Ynez Mountains to the east. Extensive network of bike paths. Adjacent to the community of Isla Vista. Ten miles north of the city of Santa Barbara and one hundred miles north of Los Angeles.

CAMPUS LIFE: ***Undergraduates living on campus*** - 24.9%. ***Clubs and organizations*** - 300, fraternities and sororities - yes. ***Athletics:*** Intercollegiate - NCAA, Division I-AAA. Intramural sports - yes.

OTHER INFORMATION: ***Founded*** - 1944. ***WASC Accredited*** - yes.

nd = no data available

SANTA CRUZ

University of California, Santa Cruz
Santa Cruz, CA 95064
(408) 459-0111
Admissions: (408) 459-4008
Financial Aid: (408) 459-2963
Housing: (408) 459-2394

DISTINGUISHING FEATURES: UC Santa Cruz provides the intimacy of a small college setting and the resources of a major public university. The Narrative Evaluation System (NES) is a personalized grading system providing a written assessment of your classroom performance from each instructor — your strengths, talents, and areas in need of attention. Letter grades are an option in addition to the narrative in all upper-division courses, and in several lower-division courses as well. Ninety percent of the student body is undergraduate, providing opportunities to collaborate on faculty research, to pursue your own projects, and to have papers published in academic journals. The Dual Degree Program (3/2) with the College of Engineering at UC Berkeley is available. See this chapter: Majors — Application and Screening, page 11--44 for additional information. More than ninety percent of seniors are accepted into one or more of their graduate school choices.
DEGREES OFFERED: Bachelor's, Master's, Doctoral.
RESIDENTIAL COLLEGES: Santa Cruz has a small, private college atmosphere because the campus is divided into eight colleges. Each is a unique social and intellectual community of 900 to 1,300 students with its own affiliated faculty, housing, and recreational facilities. You live, socialize, and study with other students in your college. However, there is ample opportunity to meet students from the other colleges — in your classes and at various college and campus activities. The colleges have faculty and students from all disciplines. You may select any major regardless of your college affiliation because the entire campus curriculum and all academic resources are open to students of all colleges. If after affiliating with one college you decide your interests are better suited to another, you may apply for a transfer. The colleges are primarily residential and social centers, although each has its own academic traditions and a distinctive core course in which all incoming freshmen must enroll. You may choose the college in which you wish to live. The colleges are listed in order of their founding.
Cowell College encourages the study of the traditions of Western civilization and the impact of those traditions on American society, with an emphasis on the humanities. The theme of multiculturalism has emerged as a central concern of the college. The core course, "Idea and Imagination in the Western Cultural Contexts," introduces all freshmen to major classical works. The emphasis is on cross-cultural perspectives, human values, critical thinking, and expository writing.
Stevenson College emphasizes the social sciences concentrating on public service, social responsibility, and international relations. The core course, "Self and Society," introduces students to the world's cultural and social heritage, principally by the study of great books from Western and non-Western traditions.
Crown College emphasizes issues pertaining to the role of science and technology in society. It attracts many natural sciences majors, as well as social science, arts, and humanities students (almost forty percent of the students in Crown). The core course, "World Culture," examines the world's cultures as represented in contemporary California. The goal is to develop a greater sense of how each of us in California is part of a rich and diverse mosaic of peoples, historical backgrounds, points of view, and future ambitions.
Merrill College encourages the enrollment of students from different cultural backgrounds and attracts many foreign students. The core course, "Social Change in the Third World," introduces all first-year students to the social systems and cultures of the Third World, as well as to urgent contemporary questions involving cross-cultural relations.
Porter College encourages students to apply the creative process to all fields of study from composing to computer programming. The faculty includes most of the campus's practicing artists and art scholars, although more than a quarter of the college's faculty (and approximately half its students) specializes in the natural and social sciences. The core course, "Heritage of Arts in a Multicultural Society," concentrates on how artistic heritage impacts upon individual creativity in the multicultural society of California and the Pacific Rim region.
Kresge College emphasizes the humanities and social sciences. The core course, "Cultural Intersections," focuses on American culture: How our belief systems are socially conditioned and how the interaction of race, gender, class, and sexuality defines social practices and representational systems. Kresge draws a growing population of reentry students — those twenty-five years or over who are returning to school — and also serves as a center of graduate student life, thereby mixing typical college age students with older students.
Oakes College emphasizes a broad liberal arts education and a multicultural-community environment. It places special effort on enabling students from groups, including women, who have been historically underrepresented in the natural sciences, to major in those fields. The core course, "Values and Change in a Diverse Society," examines the historical and contemporary aspects of multiculturalism in the United States. Students explore how social inequality based on race, class, and gender occurs among all levels of society.
College Eight focuses on the theme of Environment and Society. The emphasis is on concern for the social, political, scientific, and ethical issues within an environmental context, recognizing the basic interconnections among humans and between humans and other forms of life. The core course, "Global Transformations, Environment, and Community," examines education, identity, nature, community, livelihood, and livability at the local and national level as contemporary global transformations affect them.
UNDERGRADUATE MAJORS: 32. See this chapter: Undergraduate Degree Majors, page 11--84.
CALENDAR: Quarter system. Summer sessions.
FACULTY: 500 full- and part-time. Undergraduate classes taught by faculty, not graduate students - most. Faculty with Ph.D.'s - 96%. Student/faculty ratio - 19/1.
ENROLLMENT: ***Total*** - 10,173. ***Graduate*** - 853. ***Undergraduate*** - 9,320: California residents - 95.0%, out-of-state - 5.0%, other countries - less than 1.0%. Men - 42.3%, women - 57.7%. ***Ethnic distribution of undergraduates:*** Hispanic - 12.6%, Black - 2.6%, Asian/Pacific Islander - 11.7%, Native American/Alaskan - 1.1%, White - 61.6%, Other/not stated - 12.6%. ***Freshmen graduating within 5 years*** - 64.0%.
LOCATION: Nestled in 2,000 acres of beautiful redwood forest and open meadow high above Monterey Bay and the ocean-side city of Santa Cruz. Seventy-five miles south of San Francisco. Thirty-five miles southwest of San Jose.
CAMPUS LIFE: ***Undergraduates living on campus*** - 45.0%. ***Clubs and organizations*** - 100, fraternities and sororities - no. ***Athletics:*** Intercollegiate - NCAA, Division III. Intramural sports - yes.
OTHER INFORMATION: ***Founded*** - 1965.
WASC Accredited - yes.

nd = no data available

UNIVERSITY OF CALIFORNIA

UNDERGRADUATE DEGREE MAJORS

The undergraduate degree programs the University offers are listed by discipline and by campus on the following pages. The indented listings are areas of specialization within the major. For complete information about academic programs, refer to the campus general catalogues.

The majors are listed under the discipline they are most often associated with.

AGRICULTURE, NATURAL RESOURCES, AND ENVIRONMENTAL STUDIES

Berkeley

College of Natural Resources

Bioresource Sciences, B.S.
Conservation and Resource Studies, B.S.
Entomology, B.S.
Forestry, B.S.
Plant Biology, B.S.
Political Economy of Natural Resources, B.S.
Resource Management, B.S.
Soil Environment, B.S.

College of Letters and Science

Environmental Sciences, A.B.
- Biological Sciences
- Physical Sciences
- Social Sciences

Davis

College of Agricultural and Environmental Sciences

Agricultural and Managerial Economics, B.S.
- Consumer Economics

Agricultural Science and Management, B.S.
- Animal Science
- Food Science
- Plant Science
- Range Science

Animal Science, B.S.
- Aquaculture

Avian Sciences, B.S.
Entomology, B.S.
Environmental Biology Management, B.S.
- Environmental Biology
- Environmental Management

Environmental Policy Analysis and Planning, B.S.
- Advanced Policy Analysis
- City and Regional Planning
- Energy Policy
- Environmental Science
- Recreation Policy
- Transportation Planning
- Water Quality

Environmental Resource Sciences, B.S.
Environmental Toxicology, B.S.
Fermentation Science, B.S.
Hydrologic Science, B.S.
International Agricultural Development, B.S.
Plant Biology (Botany), B.S.
- Agronomy
- Floriculture/Nursery Management
- Landscape Horticulture
- Plant Pathology
- Plant Science
- Pomology
- Vegetable Crops
- Viticulture

Range and Wildlands Science, B.S.
Soil and Water Science, B.S.
Wildlife and Fisheries Biology, B.S.

College of Engineering

Biological Systems Engineering, B.S.

Irvine

School of Social Ecology

Applied Ecology, B.S.
Environmental Analysis and Design, B.A.
Social Ecology, B.A.

Los Angeles

College of Letters and Science

Geography/Environmental Studies, B.A.

Riverside

College of Natural and Agricultural Sciences

Botany and Plant Science, B.A., B.S.
- Botany
- Plant Genetics
- Plant Physiology
- Plant Sciences
- Plant Pathology/Nematology

Entomology, B.A., B.S.
Environmental Sciences, B.A., B.S
- Environmental Toxicology
- Natural Science
- Social Science
- Soil Science

Geography, B.A., B.S.
- Biogeography
- Geomorphology
- Locational and Urban/Political Analysis

Santa Barbara

College of Letters and Science

Environmental Studies, B.A.
- Natural Sciences
- Social Science-Humanities

Hydrologic Sciences, B.S.

Santa Cruz

Environmental Studies, B.A.
- Natural History and Wildland Conservation
- Policy, Planning, and Public Values
- Sustainable Agriculture and Agroecology

Environmental Studies/Biology, B.A.
Environmental Studies/Economics, B.A.
Latin American Studies/Environmental Studies, B.A.

ARCHITECTURAL AND ENVIRONMENTAL DESIGN AND PLANNING

Berkeley

College of Environmental Design

Architecture, A.B.
Landscape Architecture, A.B.

Davis

College of Agricultural and Environmental Sciences

Design, B.S.
Environmental Policy Analysis and Planning, B.S.
- Advanced Policy Analysis
- City and Regional Planning
- Energy Policy
- Environmental Science
- Recreation Policy
- Transportation Planning
- Water Quality

Landscape Architecture, B.S.

Irvine

School of Social Ecology

Environmental Analysis and Design, B.A.

San Diego

Urban Studies and Planning, B.A.

UNIVERSITY OF CALIFORNIA

ARTS—APPLIED, FINE, PERFORMING, AND ART HISTORY

Berkeley

College of Letters and Science

Art, History of, A.B.
Art, Practice of, A.B.
Dramatic Art, A.B.
Dramatic Art - Dance, A.B.
Film, A.B.
Music, A.B.

Davis

College of Agricultural and Environmental Sciences

Design, B.S.

College of Letters and Science

Art History, A.B.
Art Studio, A.B.
Dramatic Art, A.B.
Music, A.B.

Irvine

School of Fine Arts

Art History, B.A.
Dance, B.A.
Drama, B.A.
Fine Arts, B.A.
Music, B.A.
Music, B.Mus.
- Bassoon
- Clarinet
- Contrabass
- Flute
- French Horn
- Harp
- Lute and Guitar
- Oboe
- Percussion
- Piano
- Saxophone
- Special String Performance
- Trombone
- Trumpet
- Tuba
- Viola
- Violin
- Violoncello
- Voice

Studio Art, B.A.

School of Humanities

Film Studies, B.A.

Los Angeles

School of the Arts

Art, B.A.
Dance, B.A.
Ethnomusicology, B.A.
Music, B.A.
World Arts and Cultures, B.A.

School of Theater, Film and Television

Motion Picture/Television, B.A.
Theater, B.A.

College of Letters and Science

Art History, B.A.
History/Art History, B.A.
Musicology, B.A.
World Arts and Cultures, B.A.

Riverside

College of Humanities and Social Sciences

Art History, B.A.
Art Studio, B.A.
Dance, B.A.
Music, B.A.
Theatre, B.A.

San Diego

Music, B.A.
Music/Humanities, B.A.
Theatre, B.A.
Visual Arts (Art History/Criticism), B.A.
Visual Arts (Media), B.A.
Visual Arts (Studio), B.A.

Santa Barbara

College of Creative Studies

Creative Studies: Art Emphasis, B.A.
- Book Arts
- Painting
- Sculpture

Creative Studies: Music Composition Emphasis, B.A.

College of Letters and Science

Art History, B.A.
Art, B.A.
Dance, B.A., B.F.A.
Dramatic Art, B.A.
- Directing
- Dramatic Literature, Theory, and Theatre History
- Playwriting
- Theatre Design and Technology

Film Studies, B.A.
Music, B.A.
Music, B.Mus.
- Composition
- Guitar
- Orchestral Instruments
- Piano Performance/Piano Accompanying
- Voice

Theatre, B.F.A.
- Acting

Santa Cruz

Art, B.A.
- Drawing
- Mixed Media
- Painting
- Photography
- Printmaking
- Sculpture

Art History, B.A.
Music, B.A.
Theater Arts, B.A.
- Dance
- Design and Technology
- Drama
- Film/Video

BIOLOGICAL AND LIFE SCIENCES

Berkeley

College of Letters and Science

Human Biodynamics, A.B.
Integrative Biology, A.B.
- General Integrative Biology
- Integrative Human Biology

Molecular and Cell Biology, A.B.
- Biochemistry and Molecular Biology
- Cell and Developmental Biology
- Genetics
- Immunology
- Neurobiology

College of Natural Resources

Bioresource Science, B.S.
Entomology, B.S.
Plant Biology, B.S.

Davis

College of Agricultural and Environmental Sciences

Biochemistry, B.S.
Biological Sciences, B.S.
Entomology, B.S.
Genetics, B.S.
Microbiology, B.S.
Plant Biology (Botany), B.S.
- Agronomy
- Floriculture/Nursery Management
- Landscape Horticulture
- Plant Pathology
- Plant Science
- Pomology
- Vegetable Crops
- Viticulture

Physiology, B.S.
Zoology, B.S.

College of Letters and Science

Biochemistry, B.S.
Biological Sciences, A.B., B.S.
Genetics, B.S.
Microbiology, A.B., B.S.
Physical Education, A.B., B.S.
- Biological
- Biomechanics
- Exercise Physiology
- Psychological

Physiology, B.S.
Plant Biology (Botany), A.B., B.S.
Zoology, A.B., B.S.

Irvine

School of Biological Sciences

Applied Ecology, B.S.
Biological Sciences, B.S.
- Cell Biology
- Developmental Biology
- Ecology
- Evolution
- Genetics
- Microbiology
- Molecular Biology and Biochemistry
- Neurosciences
- Physiology
- Plant Sciences

School of Social Ecology

Applied Ecology, B.S.

Los Angeles

College of Letters and Science

Biochemistry, B.S.
Biology, B.S.
- Ecology, Behavior, and Evolution
- General Biology
- Marine Biology
- Molecular, Cellular, and Developmental Biology
- Plant Biology

Microbiology and Molecular Genetics, B.S.
Physiological Science, B.S.
Psychobiology, B.S.

Riverside

College of Humanities and Social Sciences

Psychobiology, B.A., B.S.

College of Natural and Agricultural Sciences

Biochemistry, B.A., B.S.
- Biology
- Chemistry

Biology, B.A., B.S.
- Cell and Molecular Biology
- Ecology and Evolutionary Biology
- Molecular Genetics
- Organismal Genetics
- Physiology
- Population Biology
- Zoology

Biomedical Sciences, B.S.
Botany and Plant Science, B.A., B.S.
- Botany
- Plant Genetics
- Plant Physiology
- Plant Sciences
- Plant Pathology/Nematology

Entomology, B.A., B.S.
Psychobiology, B.A., B.S.

San Diego

Animal Physiology and Neuroscience, B.S.
Biochemistry and Cell Biology, B.S.
Biology, General, B.S.
Ecology, Behavior, and Evolution, B.S.
Microbiology, B.S.
Molecular Biology, B.S.

Santa Barbara

College of Creative Studies

Creative Studies: Biology Emphasis, B.A.

College of Letters and Science

Aquatic Biology, B.S.
Biochemistry—Molecular Biology, B.S.
Biological Sciences, B.S.
Biopsychology, B.S.
Cell and Developmental Biology, B.S.
Ecology and Evolution, B.S.
Microbiology, B.S.
- Biomedical Sciences
- General Microbiology
- Genetic Engineering

Pharmacology, B.S.
Physiology, B.S.
Zoology, B.S.

Santa Cruz

Biochemistry and Molecular Biology, B.A.
Biology, B.A.
- Ecology, Evolution and Behavior
- Marine Biology
- Molecular, Cellular, and Developmental Biology
- Neurobiology and Behavior
- Plant Sciences

Environmental Studies/Biology, B.A.
Marine Biology, B.A.
Psychobiology, B.A.

BUSINESS AND MANAGEMENT

Berkeley

Walter A. Haas School of Business

Business Administration, B.S.

Irvine

3-2 Program

B.A. or B.S. in any major (except those offered by the School of Engineering) and M.B.A. from Graduate School of Management

Los Angeles

College of Letters and Science

Economics/Business, B.A.

Riverside

College of Humanities and Social Sciences

Business Administration, B.S.
Business Economics, B.A.

San Diego

Management Science, B.S.

Santa Barbara

College of Letters and Science

Business Economics, B.A.
- Accounting

COMMUNICATION

Berkeley
College of Letters and Science
Mass Communications, A.B.

Davis
College of Letters and Science
Rhetoric and Communications, A.B.

Los Angeles
College of Letters and Science
Communication Studies, B.A.
- Interpersonal Communication
- Mass Communication

San Diego
Communication, B.A.

Santa Barbara
College of Letters and Science
Communication, B.A.

ENGINEERING AND COMPUTER SCIENCE

Berkeley
College of Chemistry
Chemical Engineering, B.S.
Chemical Engineering/Materials Science and Engineering, B.S.
Chemical Engineering/Nuclear Engineering, B.S.
Chemical Engineering/Petroleum Engineering, B.S.

College of Engineering
Bioengineering, B.S.
Civil Engineering, B.S.
Earth Resources Engineering, B.S.
Electrical Engineering and Computer Science, B.S.
Engineering Mathematics and Statistics, B.S.
Engineering Physics, B.S.
Environmental Engineering Science, B.S.
Industrial Engineering and Operations Research, B.S.
Manufacturing Engineering, B.S.
Materials Science and Engineering, B.S.
Materials Science and Engineering/Electrical Engineering and Computer Science, B.S.
Materials Science and Engineering/Mechanical Engineering, B.S.
Materials Science and Engineering/Nuclear Engineering, B.S.
Mechanical Engineering, B.S.
Mechanical Engineering/Petroleum Engineering, B.S.
Naval Architecture, B.S.
Nuclear Engineering, B.S.
Nuclear Engineering/Electrical Engineering and Computer Science, B.S.
Nuclear Engineering/Mechanical Engineering, B.S.

College of Letters and Science
Computer Science, A.B.

Davis
College of Engineering
Aeronautical Science and Engineering, B.S.
Biological Systems Engineering, B.S.
Chemical/Biochemical Engineering, B.S.
Chemical Engineering, B.S.
Chemical Engineering/Materials Science and Engineering, B.S.
Civil Engineering, B.S.
Civil Engineering/Materials Science and Engineering, B.S.
Computer Engineering, B.S.
Computer Science and Engineering, B.S.
Electrical Engineering, B.S.
Electrical Engineering/Materials Science and Engineering, B.S.
Food Engineering, B.S.
Materials Science and Engineering, B.S.
Mechanical Engineering, B.S.
Mechanical Engineering/Materials Science and Engineering, B.S.

College of Letters and Science
Computer Science, B.S.

Irvine
School of Engineering
Aerospace Engineering, B.S.
Chemical Engineering, B.S.
Civil Engineering, B.S.
- Environmental Engineering
- Structural Engineering
- Transportation Engineering
- Water Resources Engineering

Computer Engineering, B.S.
Electrical Engineering, B.S.
- Electro-optics and Solid-state Devices
- Power Systems
- Systems and Signal Processing

Engineering, B.S.
- Computer Graphics

Environmental Engineering, B.S.
Mechanical Engineering, B.S.
- Aerospace Engineering
- Combustion/Propulsion
- Heat Transfer/Fluid Mechanics
- Materials Science and Engineering
- Mechanical Systems

Department of Information and Computer Science
Information and Computer Science, B.S.

Los Angeles
School of Engineering and Applied Science
Aerospace Engineering, B.S.
Chemical Engineering, B.S.
- Bioengineering

Civil Engineering, B.S.
Computer Science, B.S.
Computer Science and Engineering, B.S.
Electrical Engineering, B.S.
Materials Engineering, B.S.
Mechanical Engineering, B.S.

College of Letters and Science
Geology - Engineering Geology, B.S.
Linguistics and Computer Science, B.A.

Riverside
College of Engineering
Chemical Engineering, B.S.
Computer Science, B.S.
Electrical Engineering, B.S.
Environmental Engineering, B.S.

San Diego
Applied Mechanics and Engineering Sciences
Aerospace Engineering, B.S.
Applied Science (Bioengineering: Premed), B.A., B.S.
Bioengineering, B.S.
Chemical Engineering, B.S.
Engineering Science, B.S.
Mechanical Engineering, B.S.
Structural Engineering, B.S.

Computer Science and Engineering
Computer Engineering, B.S.
Computer Science, B.A., B.S.

Electrical and Computer Engineering
Applied Physics, B.A.
Computer Engineering, B.S.
Electrical Engineering (Communication Systems), B.S.
Electrical Engineering (Electronic Circuits and Devices), B.S.
Electrical Engineering (Electronic Circuits and Systems), B.S.
Electrical Engineering (Electronic Devices and Materials), B.S.
Electrical Engineering (Photonics), B.S.
Electrical Engineering (Robotics and Control), B.S.
Electrical Engineering (Systems and Control), B.S.
Engineering Physics, B.S.
Information Science, B.A.

ENGINEERING AND COMPUTER SCIENCE *(continued ...)*

Santa Barbara
College of Engineering
Chemical Engineering, B.S.
Computer Science, B.S.
Electrical Engineering, B.S.
Mechanical Engineering, B.S.
College of Letters and Science
Computer Science, B.A.

Santa Cruz
Computer and Information Sciences, B.A.
Computer Engineering, B.S.
Engineering - 3/2 Dual Degree Program (five-year program, available only to freshmen, leading to a B.A. degree in a social science, humanities, or art field from Santa Cruz and a B.S. degree in Engineering from Berkeley)

ETHNIC AND AREA STUDIES

Berkeley
College of Letters and Science
African American Studies, A.B.
American Studies, A.B.
Ancient Near Eastern Archaeology and Art History, A.B.
Asian-American Studies, A.B.
Asian Studies, A.B.
- China
- Japan
- Southeast Asia

Celtic Studies, A.B.
Chicano Studies, A.B.
Dutch Studies, A.B.
Ethnic Studies, A.B.
Latin American Studies, A.B.
Middle Eastern Studies, A.B.
Native American Studies, A.B.
Near Eastern Studies, A.B.
South and Southeast Asian Studies, A.B.
- South Asian Archaeology
- South Asian Civilization
- South Asian Language
- Southeast Asian Language

Women's Studies, A.B.
Special Studies - Unaffiliated
Asian-American Studies, A.B.
Chicano Studies, A.B.
Ethnic Studies, A.B.
Native American Studies, A.B.

Davis
College of Letters and Science
African-American and African Studies (Afro-American) Studies, A.B.
American Studies, A.B.
Chicana/Chicano (Mexican-American) Studies, A.B.
- Humanities
- Sociology

East Asian Studies, A.B.
Native American Studies, A.B.
- North American
- Mexico-Central America
- South America

Women's Studies, A.B.

Irvine
Interdisciplinary Studies
Women's Studies, B.A.
School of Social Sciences
Comparative Culture, B.A.

Los Angeles
College of Letters and Science
Afro-American Studies, B.A.
Ancient Near Eastern Civilizations, B.A.
Chicana and Chicano Studies, B.A.
East Asian Studies, B.A.
Iranian Studies, B.A.
Jewish Studies, B.A.
Latin American Studies, B.A.
- Arts and Humanities
- Ecology and Environment
- Social Sciences

Near Eastern Studies, B.A.
Russian Studies, B.A.
Women's Studies, B.A.
World Arts and Cultures, B.A.

Riverside
College of Humanities and Social Sciences
Asian Studies, B.A.
Ethnic Studies, B.A.
- African American
- Chicano
- Ethnic Studies

Latin American Studies, B.A.
Russian Studies, B.A.
- Civilization
- Language and Literature
- Soviet Area Studies

Womens Studies, B.A.

San Diego
Chinese Studies, B.A.
Ethnic Studies, B.A.
Italian Studies, B.A.
Judaic Studies, B.A.
Russian and Soviet Studies, B.A.
Third Work Studies, B.A.
Women's Studies, B.A.

Santa Barbara
College of Letters and Science
Asian American Studies, B.A.
Asian Studies, B.A.
Black Studies, B.A.
Chicano Studies, B.A.
Latin American and Iberian Studies, B.A.
Women's Studies, B.A.

Santa Cruz
American Studies, B.A.
East Asian Studies, B.A.
Latin American Studies, B.A.
Latin American Studies/Anthropology, B.A.
Latin American Studies/Community Studies, B.A.
Latin American Studies/Economics, B.A.
Latin American Studies/Environmental Studies, B.A.
Latin American Studies/Literature, B.A.
Latin American Studies/Politics, B.A.
Latin American Studies/Sociology, B.A.
Russian Studies, B.A.
South and Southeast Asian Studies, B.A.
Women's Studies, B.A.

FOOD, NUTRITION, AND CONSUMER SCIENCES

Berkeley
College of Natural Resources
Nutrition and Clinical Dietetics, B.S.
Nutrition and Food Science, B.S.

Davis
College of Agricultural and Environmental Sciences
Agricultural and Managerial Economics, B.S.
- Consumer Economics

Community Nutrition, B.S.
- Behavioral-psychological
- Economic and International Development
- Sociocultural

Dietetics, B.S.
Fermentation Science, B.S.
Fiber and Polymer Science, B.S.
- Multidisciplinary
- Marketing/Management

Food Biochemistry, B.S.
Food Science, B.S.
Nutrition Science, B.S.
Textiles and Clothing, B.S.

FOREIGN LANGUAGE AND LITERATURE

Berkeley
College of Letters and Science
Altaic Languages, A.B.
Chinese, A.B.
Classical Languages, A.B.
Comparative Literature, A.B.
Dutch Studies, A.B.
French, A.B.
- Literature
- Civilization

German, A.B.
Greek, A.B.
Italian, A.B.
Japanese, A.B.
Latin, A.B.
Scandinavian, A.B.
- Danish
- Norwegian
- Swedish

Slavic Languages and Literatures, A.B.
- Czech
- Polish
- Russian
- Serbo-Croatian

South and Southeast Asian Studies, A.B.
- South Asian Archaeology
- South Asian Civilization
- South Asian Language
- Southeast Asian Language

Spanish, A.B.
- Hispanic Languages and Bilingual Issues
- Iberian Languages and Literatures
- Latin American Languages and Literatures
- Luzo Brazilian Language and Literature
- Spanish Language and Literature

Davis
College of Letters and Science
Chinese, A.B.
Comparative Literature, A.B.
French, A.B.
German, A.B.
- Area Studies
- General

Greek, A.B.
Italian, A.B.
Japanese, A.B.
Latin, A.B.
Russian, A.B.
- Literature
- Language
- Area Studies

Spanish, A.B.

Irvine
School of Humanities
Chinese Language and Literature, B.A.
Classics, B.A.
- Greek
- Latin
- Linguistics

Comparative Literature, B.A.
French, B.A.
German, B.A.
- Literature
- Linguistics

Japanese Language and Literature, B.A.
Russian, B.A.
Spanish, B.A.
- Bilingualism and English as a Second Language
- Linguistics
- Literature and Culture

Los Angeles
College of Letters and Science
African Languages, B.A.
Arabic, B.A.
Chinese, B.A.
English/Greek, B.A.
English/Latin, B.A.
French, B.A.
- French Studies
- General
- Literature

French and Linguistics, B.A.
German, B.A.
Greek, B.A.
Greek and Latin, B.A.
Hebrew, B.A.
Italian, B.A.
Italian and Special Fields, B.A.
Japanese, B.A.
Latin, B.A.
Linguistics and East Asian Languages and Cultures, B.A.
Linguistics and French, B.A.
Linguistics and Italian, B.A.
Linguistics and Scandinavian Languages, B.A.
Linguistics and Spanish, B.A.
Portuguese, B.A.
Russian Language and Literature, B.A.
Russian Studies, B.A.
Scandinavian Languages, B.A.
Slavic Languages and Literatures, B.A.
Spanish, B.A.
Spanish and Linguistics, B.A.
Spanish and Portuguese, B.A.

Riverside
College of Humanities and Social Sciences
Comparative Literature, B.A.
French, B.A.
- Civilization
- Literature

German, B.A.
- Civilization
- Language
- Literature

Language, B.A.
- Study of two or three of the following languages: Chinese, French, German, Greek, Italian, Japanese, Latin, Portuguese, Russian, and Spanish

Russian Studies, B.A.
- Civilization
- Language and Literature
- Soviet Area Studies

Spanish, B.A.
- Language
- Literature

San Diego
Italian Studies, B.A.
Linguistics (Concentration in "Particular Language"), B.A.
Literature, French, B.A.
Literature, German, B.A.
Literature, Italian, B.A.
Literature, Russian, B.A.
Literature, Spanish, B.A.

Santa Barbara
College of Letters and Science
Chinese, B.A.
- Classical Chinese
- Mandarin Chinese

Classics, B.A.
Comparative Literature, B.A.
French, B.A.
- Cultural Studies
- Linguistics
- Literature

Germanic Languages and Literatures, B.A.
- German Studies
- Literature

Italian Cultural Studies, B.A.
Japanese, B.A.
Portuguese, B.A.
Slavic Languages and Literatures, B.A.
Spanish, B.A.

Santa Cruz
Language Studies, B.A.
- French
- German
- Italian
- Japanese
- Russian
- Spanish
- Spanish for Spanish Speakers

Latin American Studies/Literature, B.A.
Literature, B.A.
- Creative Writing
- French
- General
- German
- Greek
- Italian
- Latin
- Spanish

HEALTH PROFESSIONS

Berkeley
School of Optometry
Optometry, O.D.

Los Angeles
School of Nursing
Nursing, B.S.

San Francisco
School of Dentistry
Dental Hygiene, B.S.
School of Nursing
Nursing, B.S. (open to R.N.s only; taught at UC Davis Medical Center in Sacramento)

HUMANITIES

Berkeley
College of Letters and Science
Ancient Near Eastern Archaeology and Art History, A.B.
Art, History of, A.B.
Classical Civilization, A.B.
Comparative Literature, A.B.
English, A.B.
Linguistics, A.B.
Philosophy, A.B.
Religious Studies, A.B.
Rhetoric, A.B.
Women's Studies, A.B.

Davis
College of Letters and Science
Art History, A.B.
Classical Civilization, A.B.
Comparative Literature, A.B.
English, A.B.
- General
- Teaching
- Writing

Linguistics, A.B.
Medieval Studies, A.B.
Philosophy, A.B.
Religious Studies, A.B.
Rhetoric and Communications, A.B.
Women's Studies, A.B.

Irvine
School of Fine Arts
Art History, B.A.
School of Humanities
Classical Civilization, B.A.
Comparative Literature, B.A.
English, B.A.
- Literary Criticism
- Writing

Humanities, B.A.
- Individualized Program

Philosophy, B.A.
School of Social Sciences
Comparative Culture, B.A.
Linguistics, B.A.
Interdisciplinary Studies
Women's Studies, B.A.

Los Angeles
College of Letters and Sciences
Art History, B.A.
Classical Civilization, B.A.
English, B.A.
- American Studies
- Creative Writing
- General Literature

English/Greek, B.A.
English/Latin, B.A.
French and Linguistics, B.A.
Linguistics, B.A.
Linguistics and Anthropology, B.A.
Linguistics and Computer Science, B.A.
Linguistics and East Asian Languages and Cultures, B.A.
Linguistics and English, B.A.
Linguistics and French, B.A.
Linguistics and Italian, B.A.
Linguistics and Philosophy, B.A.
Linguistics and Psychology, B.A.
Linguistics and Scandinavian Languages, B.A.
Linguistics and Spanish, B.A.
Musicology, B.A.
Philosophy, B.A.
Religion, Study of, B.A.
Spanish and Linguistics, B.A.
Women's Studies, B.A.
World Arts and Cultures, B.A.

Riverside
College of Humanities and Social Sciences
Art History, B.A.
Classical Studies, B.A.
Comparative Literature, B.A.
Creative Writing, B.A.
English, B.A.
Liberal Studies, B.A.
Linguistics, B.A.
Philosophy, B.A.
Religious Studies, B.A.
Women's Studies, B.A.

San Diego
Classical Studies, B.A.
Linguistics, B.A.
Linguistics (Specialization in English as a Foreign Language), B.A.
Linguistics (Specialization in Language & Computers), B.A.
Linguistics (Specialization in Language & Mind), B.A.
Linguistics (Specialization in Language & Society), B.A.
Linguistics (Specialization in Theoretical Linguistics), B.A.
Linguistics (Concentration in "Particular Language"), B.A.
Literature/Composite Major, B.A.
Literature, General, B.A.
Literature/Writing, B.A.
Literatures in English, B.A.
Music/Humanities, B.A.
Philosophy, B.A.
Religious Studies, B.A.
Visual Arts (Art History/Criticism), B.A.
Women's Studies, B.A.

Santa Barbara
College of Creative Studies
Creative Studies: Literature Emphasis, B.A.
College of Letters and Science
Art history, B.A.
Classics, B.A.
- Archaeology
- Civilization
- Language and Culture

Comparative Literature, B.A.
English, B.A.
- Creative Writing

Linguistics, B.A.
Medieval Studies, B.A.
Philosophy, B.A.
- Analytical Reasoning
- Core Philosophy
- Ethics and Public Policy

Religious Studies, B.A.
Renaissance Studies, B.A.
Women's Studies, B.A.

Santa Cruz
Art History, B.A.
Legal Studies/Philosophy, B.A.
Linguistics, B.A.
- Applied
- Computational
- Psycholinguistics
- Theoretical

Literature, B.A.
- Creative Writing
- French
- General
- German
- Greek
- Italian
- Latin
- Spanish

Medieval Studies, B.A.
Philosophy, B.A.
- Religious Thought

Religious Studies, B.A.
Western Civilization, B.A.
Women's Studies, B.A.

INDIVIDUAL MAJORS

Individual majors are available upon petition after enrollment at all campuses as follows:

Berkeley
College of Letters and Science

Davis
College of Agricultural and Environmental Sciences
College of Engineering
College of Letters and Science

Irvine
School of Humanities

Los Angeles
College of Letters and Science

Riverside
College of Humanities and Social Sciences
College of Natural and Agricultural Sciences

San Diego
Thurgood Marshall College Individual Studies Major
John Muir College Special Project Major
Revelle College Individual Major
Eleanor Roosevelt College Individual Major
Earl Warren College Individual Studies Major

Santa Barbara
College of Letters and Science

Santa Cruz
All Colleges

MATHEMATICS

Berkeley
College of Letters and Science
Mathematics, A.B.
Mathematics, Applied, A.B.
Statistics, A.B.

Davis
College of Letters and Science
Mathematics, A.B., B.S.
- Applied
- General
- Graduate Study Preparation
- Teaching

Statistics, A.B., B.S.
- Computer Science
- General

Irvine
School of Physical Sciences
Mathematics, B.S.
- Mathematical Statistics

Los Angeles
College of Letters and Science
Mathematics, B.S.
Mathematics, Applied, B.S.
Mathematics/Applied Science, B.S.
- Actuarial
- Mathematics/Economics
- Operations Research

Mathematics of Computation, B.S.
Mathematics, General, B.S.

Riverside
College of Natural and Agricultural Sciences
Mathematics, B.A., B.S.
- Applied
- Computational
- Physics
- Pure

Statistics, B.A., B.S.

San Diego
Mathematics, B.A.
Mathematics, Applied, B.A.
Mathematics, Applied (Scientific Programming), B.A.
Mathematics - Computer Science, B.A.

Santa Barbara
College of Creative Studies
Creative Studies: Mathematics Emphasis, B.A., B.S.
College of Letters and Science
Economics/Mathematics, B.A.
Mathematical Sciences, B.A.
Mathematical Sciences, B.S.
- Operations Research
- Physical Sciences

Mathematics, B.A.
- High School Teaching
- Liberal Arts

Mathematics, B.S.
Statistical Science, B.A.
Statistical Science, B.S.
- Actuarial Statistics
- Applied Statistics
- Probability and Statistics

Santa Cruz
Mathematics, B.A.
- Computational
- Math Education
- Pure

PHYSICAL SCIENCES

Berkeley
College of Chemistry
Chemistry, B.S.
College of Letters and Science
Astrophysics, A.B.
Chemistry, A.B.
Earth Science, A.B.
Geology, A.B.
Geophysics, A.B.
Physical Sciences, A.B.
Physics, A.B.

Davis
College of Letters and Science
Chemistry, A.B., B.S.
Geology, A.B., B.S.
Physics, A.B., B.S.
Physics, Applied, B.S.
College of Agricultural and Environmental Sciences
Atmospheric Science, B.S.
Hydrologic Science, B.S.
Soil and Water Science, B.S.

Irvine
School of Physical Sciences
Chemistry, B.S.
Physics, B.S.
  Applied
  Astrophysics
  Biomedical

Los Angeles
College of Letters and Science
Astrophysics, B.S.
Atmospheric Sciences, B.S.
Chemistry, B.S.
Chemistry, General, B.S.
Chemistry/Materials Science, B.S.
Cybernetics, B.S.
Earth Sciences, B.A.
Geology, B.S.
Geology - Engineering Geology, B.S.
Geology - Paleobiology, B.S.
Geophysics - Applied Geophysics, B.S.
Geophysics and Space Physics, B.S.
Physics, B.S.
Physics, General, B.A.

Riverside
College of Natural and Agricultural Sciences
Chemistry, B.A., B.S.
  Chemical Physics
  General Chemistry
  Preprofessional Chemistry
Geology, B.A., B.S.
  General Geology
  Paleontology
Geophysics, B.S.
Physical Sciences, B.A.
Physics, B.A., B.S.
  Engineering Physics
  General Physics

San Diego
Biochemistry/Chemistry, B.S.
Chemical Education, B.S.
Chemical Physics, B.S.
Chemistry, B.S.
Chemistry with specialization in Earth Science, B.S.
Earth Sciences, B.A., B.S.
Environmental Chemistry, B.A.
Hydrologic Sciences, B.S.
Physics, B.S.
Physics - Biophysics, B.S.
Physics - Biophysics-Premedical, B.S.
Physics with specialization in Earth Sciences, B.S.
Physics, General, B.A.
Physics, General/Secondary Education, B.A.

Santa Barbara
College of Creative Studies
Creative Studies: Chemistry Emphasis, B.A., B.S.
Creative Studies: Physics Emphasis, B.A., B.S.
College of Letters and Science
Chemistry, B.A., B.S.
Geological Sciences, B.A.
Geological Sciences, B.S.
  Earth Systems Science
  Engineering Geology and Hydrology
  Geochemistry
  Marine Geology
  Paleobiology
Geophysics, B.S.
Physical Geography, B.S.
Physics, B.A., B.S.

Santa Cruz
Chemistry and Biochemistry, B.A., B.S.
Earth Sciences, B.A., B.S.
  Earth History and Global Change
  Solid Earth
  Surface Processes and Environmental Geology
Physics, B.A.
  Applied
  Astrophysics
  Geophysics

SOCIAL SCIENCES

Berkeley
College of Letters and Science
Anthropology, A.B.
Cognitive Science, A.B.
Development Studies, A.B.
Economics, A.B.
Geography, A.B.
History, A.B.
Legal Studies, A.B.
Linguistics, A.B.
Peace and Conflict Studies, A.B.
Political Economy of Industrial Societies, A.B.
Political Science, A.B.
Psychology, A.B.
Social Welfare, A.B.
Sociology, A.B.
Women's Studies, A.B.

Davis
College of Agricultural and Environmental Sciences
Applied Behavioral Sciences, B.S.
  Community Health
  Counseling and Social Work
  Business and Organizational Development
  Education
  Ethnicity
  Urban and Rural Planning
  Recreation
Human Development, B.S.
College of Letters and Science
Anthropology, A.B., B.S.
Economics, A.B.
Geography, A.B., B.S.
  General
  Cultural/Historical
  Economic/Urban, Physical, Regional Planning Analysis
History, A.B.
International Relations, A.B.
  International Relations of the Third World
  Global Resources and Environment
  World Politics
  World Trade and Development
Linguistics, A.B.
Political Science, A.B.
Political Science - Public Service, A.B.
Psychology, A.B.
Psychology, B.S.
  Biology
  Mathematics
Sociology, A.B.
  Comparative Studies and World Development
  General
  Law and Society
  Social Services
Sociology - Organizational Studies, A.B.
Women's Studies, A.B.

UNIVERSITY OF CALIFORNIA

SOCIAL SCIENCES (continued ...)

Irvine
School of Humanities
History, B.A.
School of Social Sciences
Anthropology, B.A.
Comparative Culture, B.A.
Economics, B.A.
Linguistics, B.A.
Political Science, B.A.
Psychology, B.A.
Social Science, B.A.
Sociology, B.A.
School of Social Ecology
Criminology, Law and Society, B.A.
Environmental Analysis and Design, B.A.
Psychology and Social Behavior, B.A.
Social Ecology, B.A.
Interdisciplinary Studies
Women's Studies, B.A.

Los Angeles
College of Letters and Science
Anthropology, B.A., B.S.
Cognitive Science, B.S.
  Quantitative Methods
Development Studies, B.A.
Economics, B.A.
Economics/Business, B.A.
Economics/International Area Studies, B.A.
Geography, B.A.
Geography/Environmental Studies, B.A.
History, B.A.
History/Art History, B.A.
Linguistics, B.A.
Linguistics and Anthropology, B.A.
Linguistics and Psychology, B.A.
Political Science, B.A.
Psychology, B.A.
Sociology, B.A.
Women's Studies, B.A.

Riverside
College of Humanities and Social Sciences
Anthropology, B.A., B.S.
Business Economics, B.A.
Economics, B.A.
History, B.A.
Human Development, B.A.
Liberal Studies, B.A.
Linguistics, B.A.
Political Science, B.A.
Psychobiology, B.A., B.S.
Psychology, B.A.
Public Service - Political Science, B.A.
Social Relations, B.A., B.S.
Sociology, B.A., B.S.
Women's Studies, B.A.
College of Natural and Agricultural Sciences
Geography, B.A., B.S.
  Biogeography
  Geomorphology
  Locational and Urban/Political Analysis
Psychobiology, B.A., B.S.

San Diego
Anthropology, B.A.
Anthropology with Concentration in Archaeology, B.A.
Anthropology with Concentration in Biological Anthropology, B.A.
Cognitive Science, B.A., B.S.
Economics, B.A.
History, B.A.
  Africa
  East Asia
  Europe
  History of Science
  Latin America
  Near East
  U.S. History
Linguistics, B.A.
Linguistics (Specialization in Language & Computers), B.A.
Linguistics (Specialization in Language & Mind), B.A.
Linguistics (Specialization in Language & Society), B.A.
Linguistics (Specialization in Theoretical Linguistics), B.A.
Management Science, B.S.
Political Science, B.A.
Psychology, B.A.
Sociology, B.A.
Sociology with specialization in Regional Studies, B.A.
Third World Studies, B.A.
Urban Studies and Planning, B.A.
Women's Studies, B.A.

Santa Barbara
College of Letters and Science
Anthropology, B.A.
  Cultural Anthropology
  Physical Anthropology
Biopsychology, B.S.
Business Economics, B.A.
  Accounting
Economics, B.A.
Economics/Mathematics, B.A.
Geography, B.A.
History, B.A.
History of Public Policy, B.A.
Linguistics, B.A.
Physical Geography, B.S.
Political Science, B.A.
  International Relations
  Public Service
Psychology, B.A.
Sociology, B.A.
Women's Studies, B.A.

Santa Cruz
Anthropology, B.A.
Community Studies, B.A.
Economics, B.A.
  Business
  Global
History, B.A.
  American
  Asian/African/Latin American
  European
  Mexican/Chicano
  Social and Cultural
Latin American Studies/Anthropology, B.A.
Latin American Studies/Community Studies, B.A.
Latin American Studies/Economics, B.A.
Latin American Studies/Politics, B.A.
Latin American Studies/Sociology, B.A.
Legal Studies, B.A. (part of a double or combined major)
Legal Studies/Economics, B.A.
Legal Studies/Philosophy, B.A.
Legal Studies/Politics, B.A.
Linguistics, B.A.
  Applied
  Computational
  Psycholinguistics
  Theoretical
Politics, B.A.
  Peace and Strategic Studies
Psychobiology, B.A.
Psychology, B.A.
  Developmental
  Experimental
  Personality, Clinical, and Abnormal
  Social
Sociology, B.A.
Western Civilization, B.A.
Women's Studies, B.A.
proposal required)

SPECIAL PROGRAMS

Berkeley
College of Letters and Sciences
Interdisciplinary Studies, B.A.

Riverside
College of Humanities and Social Sciences
Liberal Studies, B.A.
Humanities and Social Sciences Interdisciplinary, B.A.

Santa Barbara
College of Letters and Science
Interdisciplinary Studies, B.A. (proposal required)

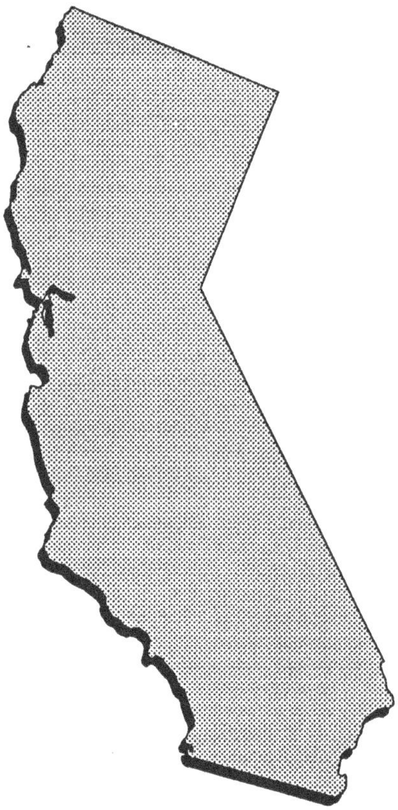

Chapter 12

CALIFORNIA INDEPENDENT COLLEGES

There are more than one-hundred thirty fully-accredited independent (private) colleges in California. They are diverse in size and focus. Each offers a unique educational opportunity.

OVERVIEW

The independent colleges in California, also called the private colleges, enroll 100,000 undergraduate students and 80,000 graduate students. These colleges do not have direct financial support from and control by the state of California. This independence means that they have greater freedom in designing programs, defining admission criteria and procedures, and determining the focus and culture of the school. Because of this self-direction, you will find great diversity among the independents. They are large, medium, and mostly small; nonsectarian and religious; greatly selective to very modestly selective; traditional and innovative; specialized and liberal arts. Some are for women or men only. Some are nonprofit; some are for-profit businesses. Campuses vary widely in location, environment, goals, admission requirements, and programs and degrees offered.

The independent college does not have direct financial support from or control by the state of California.

There are four types of independent, four-year colleges in California:

- Research institutions such as the University of Southern California and Stanford University.
- Small, comprehensive universities such as the University of the Pacific and Santa Clara University.
- Small, specialized schools such as Harvey Mudd College and California Institute of the Arts.
- Small liberal arts colleges such as University of Redlands and Occidental College.

In addition to four-year institutions, which grant the Bachelor's degree, there are two-year colleges, which grant the Associates degree. Some two-year colleges offer liberal arts majors. Others are career colleges that specifically focus on career training. The two-year colleges offer Certificates of Completion or Proficiency and the Associates degree.

CHARACTERISTICS OF THE INDEPENDENT COLLEGES

Student/faculty ratios and average class sizes are often smaller than those of public institutions.

- The independent colleges tend to be small. The majority have enrollments of less than twenty-five hundred students.
- Student/faculty ratios and average class sizes are often smaller than those of public institutions. There is a great deal of opportunity to interact with instructors. Learning is more personal; you receive more individualized attention. You may meet with your professors on an informal basis and even go to their homes. This interaction results in a welcoming, intellectually stimulating environment.
- At most independent colleges, teaching is the primary focus and research is secondary. You will find faculties committed to teaching and accessible to meet your educational needs.

You have an excellent chance of getting into the classes you want and need.

- You have an excellent chance of getting into the classes you want and need. In fact, some independent colleges guarantee that if you satisfactorily complete classes and do not take any terms off, you will graduate and receive a Bachelor's degree in four years. If you do not, you receive the fifth year tuition-free for the classes you still need. The University of the Pacific was the first college to offer this commitment with the following program. Their guarantee states that if you

  a. select a major by the beginning of your sophomore year,
  b. consult with your faculty advisor regularly,
  c. pass courses required for your major (grades of C or better),
  d. and for General Education,
     i. satisfactorily complete 32 semester units a year, and
     ii. maintain a C average or above,

  you will

  a. get the classes needed to graduate,
  b. be charged only for four years' tuition for four-year programs, five years' tuition for five-year programs (Engineering and Pharmacy), and
  c. be ready to graduate on time.

  Of course, the earlier you complete your education, the sooner you can get a job in your profession and earn an income, or continue your education in graduate school.

  Some colleges offer a program which guarantees a Bachelor's degree in four years. This information is noted under the heading Special Programs in the College Profiles beginning on page 12--12.

- You can get involved in student government, athletics, and clubs. The small community atmosphere encourages participation. Also, because there are usually fewer students, there is less competition for positions of leadership.

At most four-year independent colleges, a larger proportion of students live on campus, creating a more intimate sense of community.

- At most four-year independent colleges, a large proportion of students live on campus, creating a more intimate sense of community. Campus life becomes important to students. Housing facilities are designed as an integral part of the campus and are generally available for all students who wish to live in them.

- Private colleges can create and implement new programs, curriculum changes, degree requirements, new majors, and school calendars quickly to meet student needs. This promotes innovation and timeliness, and adds to the dynamic climate of the college.

- The admission committees look beyond the numbers (GPA and test scores), and put more emphasis upon selecting students according to other criteria such as essay, activities, talents — what students offer in diversity, interests, and background. In contrast, the four-year public universities place greater emphasis on the Eligibility Index (GPA and test scores) to determine admission.

- The independent institution may give you personalized and extensive advising because of its strong commitment to students. Many schools allow you to design your own major with the assistance of your advisor.

ADMISSION REQUIREMENTS

Each independent college and university has developed its own admission requirements and standards, and these vary greatly from college to college. Although some colleges accept almost all students who apply, most select students according to a set of criteria based upon the characteristics and needs of their school.

Each independent college and university develops its own admission requirements and standards. These may vary greatly from college to college.

The College Profiles beginning on page 12--12 of this chapter indicate the admission requirements for each institution and present specific information about GPA and test scores for entering students.

The admission committees use some or all of the following factors in making admission decisions. Which of these a college uses and the priority it gives to each depends upon the qualifications it is looking for. The factors are explained more fully in chapter 7: Steps in the Application Process. Whatever a college may require as part of its application process is critical and is reviewed to make final admission decisions. Give the application process your careful attention.

These are factors the colleges may consider:

- Your high school record. Most institutions consider your high school record as the most important factor for determining admission. Many studies have shown that this record of your academic background is the single best predictor of success in college. Your high school record has two parts to it.

  1. Your course pattern. What courses did you take in high school? Did you take a college-preparatory curriculum? What was the level of difficulty of your classes? Did you challenge yourself by enrolling in the most rigorous program your high school had to offer? Did you take more than the minimum number of college-preparatory courses? Were you enrolled in honors and/or Advanced Placement classes? Did you enroll in the more advanced classes even though doing so was a risk to your GPA? Did you continue to take rigorous courses in your senior year?

     If you are planning to be a science or engineering major, did you take more than the minimum number of science and mathematics courses? If you are planning to be a liberal arts major, did you take more than the minimum number or English, history, social science, and/or foreign language classes?

  2. Your grades and class rank. What grades did you achieve in your course work? What are your strengths and weaknesses? How does your grade point average compare with those of your classmates as indicated by your class rank? Did you take more advanced honors and/or Advanced Placement classes and earn lower grades, or did you maintain very high grades in these classes?

Many studies have shown that your high school record is the single best indicator of success in college.

- Your high school. Your high school encloses a profile of itself with transcripts it mails to the colleges. The profile may include a description of the type of community in which it is located (rural, inner-city, affluent, etc.), the percentage of its seniors that go on to four-year colleges, the grading system, the class-ranking system, honors classes, average SAT I: Reasoning Test and ACT scores .... This profile helps the college calibrate the competitiveness of your high school. The college also may rank your high school by how well previous graduates have succeeded at the college.

Ask to see a copy of your high school's profile sheet. It can give you a sense of how your school will look to the colleges to which you are applying.

- College admissions tests. Many of the independent colleges require scores from either the SAT I: Reasoning Test or the ACT. The most competitive schools also may require or recommend scores from the SAT II: Subject Tests. These test scores show how you compare nationally and in California with other candidates. Your test scores alone do not determine academic qualifications for admission. The admissions officers review them in conjunction with your grades and course pattern.

The highly competitive colleges look at activities as one way to differentiate highly-qualified applicants.

- Extracurricular activities. Extracurricular activities both at and outside of high school are important. The colleges are not looking for a long list of activities in which you have been a casual participant. They are interested in the depth of your involvement — the quality of your participation. Have you held leadership positions in some activities? Have you been involved in an activity in which you made a significant contribution? Have you held a job that has given you special responsibilities? The highly competitive colleges look at activities as one way to differentiate between academically highly-qualified applicants.

- Your essays or personal statements. The admissions officer reads your essays or personal statements to evaluate what you choose to say, how well you formulate your thoughts, and the quality of your writing style. Your essay can distinguish you from other qualified candidates.

- Recommendations. Most independent colleges require recommendations from teachers, counselors, administrators, and/or employers. The colleges are interested in information regarding your chances for success at their school. Can the teacher describe incidents or give examples to verify your qualifications? What does the writer say about your personality, talents, work habits, enthusiasm, ambition? How do they rank you in comparison to other students they know or have known?

- Your interview. Most independent colleges require or recommend an interview. The interviewer attempts to get a sense of your personality, your interests, your personal assessment of your academic record, and your level of enthusiasm for their college. Does your interview verify the information about you that is presented on your application materials?

Many independent colleges make an effort to recruit and admit qualified students who are from underrepresented minorities and/or educationally-disadvantaged groups.

- Your special talents and achievements. Are you an outstanding athlete? Musician? Debater? Artist? Have you won an essay contest? Have you been recognized for helping others?

- Your background. Will your background add diversity to the school population? Are you from an underrepresented minority group that the college is encouraging to attend their institution? Are you from an economically or educationally-disadvantaged family background? Many independent colleges make an effort to recruit and admit qualified students who are from underrepresented minorities and/or educationally-disadvantaged groups. Are you disabled? Are you an international student? See chapter 8: Educational Opportunities for a description of the opportunities available to international, disabled, and underrepresented minority and educationally-disadvantaged students.

Are you from a geographical area different from that of the majority of students at the college? Are you a member of a church group affiliated with the college?

COMMONLY ASKED QUESTIONS ABOUT ADMISSIONS

The colleges are impressed by evidence of ambition, intellectual curiosity, and risk-taking.

IS IT BETTER TO TAKE AN HONORS OR ADVANCED PLACEMENT COURSE AND GET A B, OR TO GET AN A IN A REGULAR SECTION OF THE COURSE?

The colleges prefer that you take the more difficult, challenging course and receive the lower grade, than obtain a higher grade in the easier class. They are interested in students who push themselves, who stretch to take the more advanced courses even though these classes are difficult for them. Colleges are impressed by evidence of ambition, intellectual curiosity, and risk-taking.

I RECEIVED C GRADES IN MY FRESHMAN AND SOPHOMORE YEARS BUT HAVE GREATLY IMPROVED MY RECORD DURING MY JUNIOR AND SENIOR YEARS. DO THE INDEPENDENT COLLEGES CONSIDER THIS UPWARD TREND IN MY ACADEMIC RECORD WHEN REVIEWING MY FILE FOR ADMISSION?

The independent colleges are very interested in your academic growth and potential. They analyze your total record and do not look just at your GPA. They seriously consider evidence of academic improvement when making admission decisions. Schools also review your senior course selections to make sure you are not slacking off.

WHEN DO I SEND MY TRANSCRIPT TO THE INDEPENDENT COLLEGES?

The deadline for sending your transcript varies among the independent colleges. Read your application packets carefully for the deadlines of the various schools. Many require your record through your junior year in high school on a form, the Secondary School Report, which also requests a recommendation from your counselor or an administrator. Most colleges require another transcript after the first semester of your senior year on a form known as the 7th Semester Report. This report asks for your grades for first semester and an update from your counselor or administrator of any changes that have occurred since your initial recommendation was written. All schools require a final high school transcript after you have graduated.

Colleges require you to complete with a C or better courses needed to meet college admission requirements.

WHAT IF I RECEIVE A D OR F IN A COURSE REQUIRED FOR ADMISSION?

The colleges generally agree in their evaluation of grades. They require you to complete with a C or better courses needed to meet college freshman admission requirements. Plan to repeat any required courses in which you earned a D or lower.

WHAT HAPPENS IF I REPEAT A COURSE?

The colleges have individual policies for evaluating repeated courses. All grades earned must stay on your high school record — the original grade and the repeated course grade. The colleges decide how to treat your grades when calculating your GPA and evaluating your high school record. Whether a school averages the old and new grade, disregards the lower grade, or disregards your GPA and focuses on your course pattern and improvement varies from college to college.

DO I NEED A HIGH SCHOOL DIPLOMA TO BE ADMITTED?

CAN I BE ADMITTED BY EXAMINATION ALONE IF I DO NOT MEET THE COLLEGE-PREPARATORY AND GPA REQUIREMENTS?

HOW ARE ESL COURSES EVALUATED ON MY TRANSCRIPT?

IF I AM MISSING COLLEGE-PREPARATORY REQUIREMENTS FOR ADMISSION, AM I STILL ADMISSIBLE?

I HAVE TAKEN PART OF MY HIGH SCHOOL WORK IN A FOREIGN COUNTRY. CAN I USE MY FOREIGN SCHOOL RECORD TOWARD ADMISSION?

The independent colleges make a strong commitment to provide financial aid to students who qualify for admission to their institutions.

Each of the independent colleges and universities has its own policies to answer these questions and many others you may think of. Call the admissions office of the college for specific answers.

1994-95 COSTS

The independent colleges do not receive any money for their support from the state of California. They are self-supporting from private funding and tuition payments by students. Generally, it costs much more per year to attend an independent institution than it would a California State University, University of California, or California Community College campus. Public institutions subsidize most of the cost of your education with moneys raised from taxes, but tuition payments are an important source of revenue for the independent colleges. Independent college tuition costs range from $4,620 (Patten College) to $18,669 (Stanford University) for an academic year. To this amount you must add the costs of miscellaneous fees, housing, books, supplies, transportation, recreation, and personal and incidental expenses. Estimated total costs range from $10,000 to $26,475 for the 1994-95 academic year.

FINANCIAL AID

Financial assistance is not limited to students from low-income families.

The independent colleges make a strong commitment to provide financial aid to students who qualify for admission to their institutions. They award both merit-based and need-based scholarships and grants. According to the Association of Independent California Colleges and Universities (AICCU) almost two-thirds of the full-time students enrolled at California independent colleges and universities receive some type of financial assistance (a grant, loan, and/or campus job).

For undergraduate students who obtain financial aid at an independent college or university, the average financial aid package is about $10,000 per student with some students receiving as much as $22,500.

It could cost you less to attend an independent college than a CSU or UC campus.

In addition to financial aid provided directly to students by the colleges, the Cal Grant program, sponsored by the state of California, awards Cal Grant A funds of up to $5,250 a year to cover independent college tuition. The amount of a Cal Grant A award is considerably less for students to attend a CSU or UC campus, because it covers the cost of fees only.

It could cost you less to attend an independent college than a CSU or UC campus. The independent colleges typically are able to offer more generous financial aid packages than the public institutions. They raise large amounts of money through contributions from corporations, foundations, and donations from alumni to use for scholarships and grants. Furthermore, the independent colleges have the resources to provide the classes you need to complete your Associates degree in two years or your Bachelor's degree in four years. You are not as likely to have to attend and pay for additional college years to finish your education.

See chapter 4: PAYING FOR COLLEGE for a full explanation of financial aid.

INDEPENDENTS AT A GLANCE

On the next two pages is a summary of key college profile information, which you can use to compare independent colleges.

For a more detailed review of a particular institution, read its profile in this chapter.

You can safely assume that most applicants to a particular college meet that college's minimum academic requirements, and therefore, the percentage of applicants accepted is a good indicator of the competition to gain admission to the school.

When comparing schools, have your own PSAT and/or SAT/SAT I: Reasoning Test scores available to compare them with those of admitted freshmen. Are your scores competitive? Do you need to raise them?

If personal attention from and interaction with the faculty are important factors to you, give greater consideration to schools with low student/faculty ratios.

Percent of freshmen graduating within five years can indicate how successful the college is in keeping and graduating its students.

Percent of students receiving financial aid is affected by (a) the availability of financial aid moneys, and (b) the overall financial need of students attending the school.

For a more detailed review of a particular institution, read its profile in this chapter, review its own publications, and if the school is one of your high-priority choices, call its admissions office and visit the campus for answers to your remaining questions.

INDEPENDENTS AT A GLANCE
1993-94

School	# of Under-graduates	Freshman Class: % Of Applicant Accepted	Freshman Class: SAT Score Range Of Middle 50%		Freshman Class: Average GPA	Student/ Faculty Ratio	% Of Freshmen Graduating Within Five Years	% Of Students Receiving Financial Aid
			Verbal	Math				
American Academy of Dramatic Arts West	249	nd	nd	nd	2.00	16/1	nd	65%
Art Center College of Design	1,183	nd	nd	nd	2.50	9/1	nd	73%
Azusa Pacific University	2,154	88%	299-699	299-800	3.20	18/1	nd	80%
Biola University	2,058	40%	Average 440	Average 500	3.20	17/1	78%	75%
California Baptist College	870	94%	420-500	480-540	3.00	12/1	nd	79%
California College of Arts & Crafts	1,099	60%	nd	nd	2.80	12/1	30%	55%
California Institute of the Arts	675	nd	nd	nd	nd	7/1	nd	70%
California Institute of Technology	900	27%	600-710	720-780	nd	3/1	80%	65%
California Lutheran University	1,480	nd	300-800	300-800	3.37	15/1	nd	80%
Chapman University	1,871	80%	400-500	430-560	3.05	12/1	45%	65%
Claremont McKenna College	888	41%	560-650	620-710	3.81	9/1	84%	74%
Cogswell Polytechnical College	368	90%	400-650	475-700	3.20	9/1	85%	35%
College of Notre Dame	831	71%	380-470	390-510	3.20	10/1	48%	67%
Concordia University	774	72%	360-480	400-570	3.28	18/1	54%	75%
Dominican College of San Rafael	798	81%	380-470	390-520	3.00	13.5/1	42%	76%
Fresno Pacific College	772	79%	410-530	470-590	3.67	15/1	nd	95%
Golden Gate University	2,066	65%	nd	nd	3.20	16/1	60%	21%
Harvey Mudd College	654	42%	580-690	710-770	nd	8/1	78%	71%
Holy Names College	590	61%	400-470	390-500	2.95	11/1	40%	75%
Humphreys College	761	100%	nd	nd	nd	11/1	50%	81%
La Sierra University	1,318	84%	Average 420	Average 468	3.20	13/1	nd	75%
Loyola Marymount University	3,824	nd	420-530	480-600	3.20	15/1	nd	59%
Marymount College	1,087	nd	340-440	320-480	2.50	16/1	70%	45%
The Master' s College	773	nd	nd	nd	3.27	17/1	nd	88%
Menlo College	560	87%	nd	nd	2.70	15/1	70%	50%
Mills College	824	nd	470-610	480-600	3.40	11/1	69%	71%
Mount Saint Mary' s College	1,241	82%	400-510	430-550	3.49	13/1	68%	80%
Occidental College	1,620	54%	440-560	500-640	nd	11/1	78%	72%
Otis College of Design	655	38%	nd	nd	nd	14/1	78%	80%

COLLEGE IN CALIFORNIA: *The Inside Track*

nd = no data available   na = not applicable

CALIFORNIA INDEPENDENT COLLEGES

INDEPENDENTS AT A GLANCE 1993-94

School	# of Under-graduates	Freshman Class: % Of Applicant Accepted	Freshman Class: SAT Score Range Of Middle 50%: Verbal	Freshman Class: SAT Score Range Of Middle 50%: Math	Freshman Class: Average GPA	Student/ Faculty Ratio	% Of Freshmen Graduating Within Five Years	% Of Students Receiving Financial Aid
Pacific Christian College	736	nd	nd	nd	3.30	19/1	nd	82%
Pacific Union College	1,445	71%	nd	nd	3.26	12/1	53%	87%
Patten College	724	89%	nd	nd	2.90	16/1	70%	85%
Pepperdine University	2,741	65%	440-540	500-620	3.40	13/1	70%	65%
Pitzer College	750	52%	510-630	500-610	3.30	10/1	75%	45%
Point Loma Nazarene College	2,106	85%	360-490	390-540	3.23	15/1	nd	75%
Pomona College	1,382	38%	600-680	650-730	nd	9/1	90%	55%
Saint Mary' s College of California	2,399	73%	460-590	510-600	3.34	16/1	nd	54%
Samuel Merritt College	301	nd	nd	nd	2.99	9/1	nd	90%
San Francisco Art Institute	499	nd	nd	nd	nd	9/1	nd	67%
San Francisco Conservatory of Music	156	55%	440-610	480-650	nd	6/1	48%	64%
Santa Clara University	4,019	69%	440-540	520-630	3.43	13/1	80%	58%
Scripps College	612	74%	540-640	500-610	3.50	9/1	77%	50%
Simpson College	518	nd	nd	nd	nd	14/1	nd	75%
Southern California College	900	88%	Average 443	Average 466	3.20	16/1	34%	80%
Stanford University	6,573	22%	590-690	660-760	nd	10/1	92%	67%
Thomas Aquinas College	208	70%	510-660	550-650	3.41	10/1	67%	84%
United States International University	304	52%	350-490	380-570	2.75	17/1	nd	75%
University of Judaism	100	nd	520-600	510-600	3.38	6/1	nd	70%
University of La Verne	1,110	nd	400-450	440-500	3.15	19/1	nd	75%
University of Redlands	1,500	81%	450-540	470-610	3.45	13/1	60%	75%
University of San Diego	3,914	71%	450-550	500-600	3.45	18/1	65%	55%
University of SanFrancisco	4,291	nd	400-550	450-560	3.40	17/1	nd	65%
University of Southern California	14,676	69%	430-570	520-660	3.52	14/1	63%	60%
University of the Pacific	3,558	81%	400-540	460-620	3.30	15/1	61%	65%
Westmont College	1,285	75%	450-550	480-620	3.52	15/1	nd	80%
Whittier College	1,261	64%	390-510	430-580	3.06	13/1	54%	78%
Woodbury University	956	78%	320-430	380-500	3.05	15/1	nd	60%

COLLEGE IN CALIFORNIA: *The Inside Track*

nd = no data available na = not applicable

INDEPENDENT COLLEGE PROFILES

Over one-hundred and twenty independent California colleges and universities are profiled in this section.

The profiles in this section present data for the 1993-94 and 1994-95 academic years. Over one-hundred and twenty independent California colleges and universities are profiled in two groups. The first group alphabetically lists institutions that grant two-year Associates degrees and/or four-year Bachelor's degrees. A second group lists California career colleges that focus on training for specific careers and offer the Associates degree.

All colleges listed are either accredited or candidates for accreditation. Accreditation certifies that the college meets standards of educational quality established by the agency that accredits them. Under state law, an accredited California institution is allowed to award certificates and degrees without review by the State Superintendent of Public Instruction.

The Western Association of Schools and Colleges (WASC) is one of six regional accrediting associations in the United States. It evaluates and accredits schools in the state of California. WASC accredited schools must meet certain standards of quality. All campuses of the California Community Colleges, California State University, and the University of California are WASC accredited. Many of the independent colleges and universities also are accredited by WASC.

READING THE PROFILES

All figures are approximate and subject to change by the institution.

DISTINGUISHING FEATURES: Describes the institution, its main focus and character. Colleges are nonsectarian and coeducational unless otherwise noted.

DEGREES OFFERED: Lists the degrees granted by the institution. See chapter 3: CHOOSING YOUR MAJOR, page 3--3 for a full description of each of these degrees.

SPECIAL PROGRAMS: Describes special programs offered by the institution including education abroad opportunities. Also noted are whether the school offers honors programs and a program guaranteeing a Bachelor's degree in four years.

COLLEGES: Lists the colleges, schools, or divisions of emphasis in which the institution is organized. Some schools are not organized this way.

UNDERGRADUATE MAJORS: Notes the number of majors offered by the institution. For schools with a limited list of majors and a focused program, the majors offered are named. For other institutions, which offer a broad range of majors, see the chart, UNDERGRADUATE DEGREE MAJORS, beginning on page 12--76. Preprofessional programs offer courses required for later admission into specialized programs or graduate schools in the major.

CALENDAR: Describes the academic calendar.

FACULTY: Presents the number of faculty, whether classes are taught by faculty or graduate assistants, percent of faculty with Ph.D.'s, student/faculty ratio, and average class size information.

ENROLLMENT: Presents size of the student body, where students are from, the percent of males and females, and the ethnic distribution of undergraduate students. Data is based on fall 1993 enrollment. Percent of freshmen who graduate in five years gives a sense of the success rate of the school in keeping and graduating their students.

LOCATION: Describes where in the state the college is located and the size and character of the campus.

CAMPUS LIFE: Presents the number of on-campus housing facilities and percent of total student body who live on campus. Information on clubs, athletic association membership, and counseling and guidance services is provided. Whether the institution provides special services/academic programs for the educationally-disadvantaged, physically-disabled, and learning-disabled students is noted. Chapter 8: EDUCATIONAL OPPORTUNITIES, contains further information for minority, educationally-disadvantaged, and disabled students.

Before you begin your transfer program, contact the college to which you plan to transfer. Determine (a) if the college accepts courses and credits from the college at which they were taken and earned, and (b) the specific courses you must complete to qualify to transfer.

ADMISSION STANDARDS: Describes the specific freshman and transfer admission requirements of the institutions. High school diploma or equivalent as a requirement indicates that the college is willing to accept passing the GED or the California High School Proficiency Test in place of a high school diploma. Unit requirements for transfer students are *semester* units unless otherwise stated.

TRANSFERRING: The institution to which you apply for transfer determines whether the college credits you have already earned are transferable to their institution. *College accreditation does not guarantee that your credits are transferable.* The receiving institution reviews the nature, content, and level of course credit you wish to transfer and whether it is appropriate to the program you will enter. Before you begin your transfer program, contact the college to which you plan to transfer. Determine (a) if the college accepts courses and units from the college at which you completed the courses, and (b) the specific courses and number of units you must complete to qualify to transfer. See chapter 9: CALIFORNIA COMMUNITY COLLEGES, Transfer Programs, page 9--9 for information regarding transfer from a community college.

1993-94 ADMISSION DATA: Indicates how many freshman and transfer applications the school received for the 1993-94 school year, how many applicants were admitted, and how many chose to enroll. 1993-94 freshman SAT and ACT test score results, high school GPA, and high school class rank information present an academic profile of the freshmen admitted. These statistics vary considerably from school to school. Some institutions admit almost all students who apply, others are highly selective and accept only the most qualified according to a set of criteria established by the school. The notation "CCC" in 1993-94 TRANSFER ADMISSION DATA refers to California Community College.

ADMISSION PROCEDURES: Reviews the admission application process including application deadlines and fees; entrance test, recommendation, and interview requirements; admission notification dates and commitment deposit requirements. The term "Rolling" after admission application deadline or admission notification means there is no fixed deadline. The institution processes applications as they receive them, and soon afterward notifies applicants if they are admitted.

- **Fee waiver:** Indicates if the college is willing to waive application fees. Most independent colleges charge an admission application fee varying from $20.00 to $60.00. Many of these schools have agreed to consider waiving admission application fees for those students who cannot afford them.

  Some colleges accept a fee waiver form, the "College Board Request for Waiver of College Application Fee Form", from applicants who qualified for and received a fee waiver for the SAT I: Reasoning Test and/or SAT II: Subject Tests. Ask your counselor for this form and submit it with your admission application. You may receive a total of four forms. Some institutions may require additional information before considering or granting an application fee waiver, and they will mail you supplementary forms to complete. Other colleges may require a letter from your counselor or administrator rather than the College Board form. This letter should accompany your application and verify your inability to afford the application fee.

Some colleges accept a fee waiver form, the College Board Fee Waiver, for applicants who qualified for and received a fee waiver for the SAT I: Reasoning Test and/or SAT II: Subject Tests. Others require a letter verifying your financial need.

- **Advanced placement offered:** Indicates if the college will consider you for placement in an advanced class in the subject or advanced placement as a sophomore if you pass several Advanced Placement Examinations, or you have advanced credit from other sources (college courses, International Baccalaureate). See Chapter 6: COLLEGE ENTRANCE TESTS: The AP Program And Examinations, page 6--57 for further information.

- **Advanced Credit Given:** Indicates if the college gives credit for passing Advanced Placement Examinations.

- **Early decision procedure:** Indicates if this procedure is available, and if so, deadlines for application and testing.

1994-95 COSTS: States the costs to attend the institution for the 1994-95 academic year. These figures are estimates and may change. Contact the colleges or read their catalogues for the latest information.

FINANCIAL AID: Indicates the percentage of undergraduate students who received financial aid and the amount of the average financial aid package offered for 1994-95. Also listed are specific applications required (FAFSA, FAF, institutional) and important deadlines for financial aid applications.

OTHER INFORMATION: Indicates the date the institution was founded, whether the school is nonprofit or operates as a profit-making business, whether it is accredited by WASC or another agency, and whether it is a member of the Association of Independent California Colleges and Universities (AICCU).

Information on the charts Undergraduate Degree Majors was provided by AICCU.

ACADEMY OF ART COLLEGE

79 New Montgomery Street
San Francisco, California 94105
(415) 274-2200
Fax: (415) 546-9737
Toll Free: nd

Art Academy Specializing in the Training of Artists, Designers, and Photographers

DISTINGUISHING FEATURES: Long committed to artistic and educational excellence, the Academy of Art College offers students a broad selection of programs in the arts, design, and photography. Award-winning professionals and instructors with extensive academic experience teach the programs. Co-op program offered with University of San Francisco leading to the BSA degree. Majors are offered in Advertising, Graphic Design, Illustration, Fine Arts, Interior Design, Fashion Illustration, Photography, and Motion Pictures.
DEGREES OFFERED: Certificate, Bachelor's, Master's.
CALENDAR: Semester system.
ENROLLMENT: ***Total*** - 3000.
LOCATION: 5 campuses In the heart of San Francisco.
CAMPUS LIFE: ***On-campus housing:*** Spaces - dormitories available at USF campus.
OTHER INFORMATION: ***Founded*** - 1929. ***Nonprofit*** - no. ***WASC Accredited*** - no. Accredited by the National Association of Schools and Colleges (Senior College).

THE ADVERTISING ARTS COLLEGE

10025 Mesa Rim Road
San Diego, CA 92121
(619) 546-0602
Fax: nd
Toll Free: nd

Professional College with One- to Three-Year Programs

DISTINGUISHING FEATURES: The Advertising Arts College is a professional college serving students seeking specialized education in the advertising field. The emphasis is on hands-on training by professionals who work in the field in which they teach. Majors are offered in Advertising, Graphic Design, Computer Graphics, Fashion Merchandising, Fine Arts, Marketing, and Public Relations. The college offers a comprehensive desktop publishing program with computer laboratory.
DEGREES OFFERED: Certificate, Associate, Bachelor's.
CALENDAR: Quarter system.
ENROLLMENT: ***Total*** - 350.
LOCATION: Just east of the picturesque town of La Jolla and its beaches.
CAMPUS LIFE: ***On-campus housing:*** Spaces - 0.
OTHER INFORMATION: ***Founded*** - 1981. ***Nonprofit*** - no. ***WASC Accredited*** - no. Accredited by the Career College Association.

AMERICAN ACADEMY OF DRAMATIC ARTS WEST

2550 Paloma Street
Pasadena, California 91107
Admissions: (818) 798-0777
Financial Aid: (818) 798-0777
Fax: (818) 798-5047
Toll Free: nd

Professional Conservatory for Actors

DISTINGUISHING FEATURES: The American Academy of Dramatic Arts, West is the California campus of the American Academy of Dramatic Arts, which was founded in New York. America's first conservatory for actors, the Academy is dedicated to a single purpose: to provide a broad and practical education to talented, well-motivated students who desire to make acting their profession. It offers a two-year professional program leading to an Associates degree in Acting.
DEGREES OFFERED: Associates.
SPECIAL PROGRAMS: Offers selected graduates of the two-year professional program an opportunity to be members of the Academy Company for one year. Emphasis of the repertory company is on the continued practical development of the actor through study, rehearsal, and performance of plays and projects in Academy Theatres. Company members receive a Certificate of Advanced Studies in Actor Training. ***Education abroad*** - no. ***Honors programs*** - no.
COLLEGES: na.
UNDERGRADUATE MAJORS: 1 major. Theatre. Preprofessional programs: na.
CALENDAR: Semester system. Summer session.
FACULTY: Faculty closely involved with theater, film, and television. Full-time - nd, part-time - nd. Undergraduate classes taught by faculty, not graduate assistants - all. Faculty with Ph.D.'s - 25%. Student/faculty ratio - 16/1. Average class size - nd.
ENROLLMENT: ***Total*** - 249. ***Graduate*** - 0. ***Undergraduate*** - 249: California residents - 25%, out-of-state and other countries - 75%. Men - 40%, women - 60%. ***Ethnic distribution of undergraduate students:*** Minority - 14%. Hispanic - nd%, Black - nd%, Asian/Pacific Islander - nd%, Native American/Alaskan - nd%, White - nd%. ***Freshmen graduating within 5 years*** - na.
LOCATION: Near Los Angeles and the movie industry.
CAMPUS LIFE: ***On-campus housing:*** Spaces - 0, undergraduate residential students - 0%. ***Clubs and organizations*** - 1, extensive involvement in the arts. Fraternities and sororities - 0. ***Athletics:*** Intercollegiate - no. Intramural sports - no. ***Counseling and guidance:*** Yes. Faculty advisors - nd. Tutoring - nd. ***Special services/academic programs for:*** Educationally disadvantaged - nd, physically disabled - nd, learning disabled - nd.
FRESHMAN ADMISSION STANDARDS: Graduation from high school or equivalent. High school units: nd.
1993-94 FRESHMAN ADMISSION DATA: ***Applications:*** Received - nd, accepted - nd, enrolled - 174. ***SAT Scores:*** nd. ***ACT composite score:*** nd. ***High school GPA:*** Average GPA - 2.00. ***Class rank:*** nd. ***International students:*** Minimum TOEFL score required - nd.
TRANSFER ADMISSION STANDARDS: ***Transfer units required:*** Minimum - 0, maximum - 0. ***Minimum college GPA*** - 2.00. ***Grades accepted*** - nd.

nd = no data available na = not applicable

CALIFORNIA INDEPENDENT COLLEGES

1993-94 TRANSFER ADMISSION DATA: ***Applications:*** Received - nd, accepted - nd, enrolled - 71. CCC transfer students enrolled - nd.
ADMISSION PROCEDURES: ***Entrance tests:*** SAT I: Reasoning Test or ACT required if recent high school graduate. Test deadline for fall admission - nd. ***Application process:*** Students admitted fall and spring. Deadlines: Freshmen and transfers - rolling. Application fee - $35. Fee waiver - no. ***Recommendations*** - 2. ***Interview*** - audition/interview required prior to acceptance. ***Admission notification*** - rolling. Commitment deposit - $nd. ***Advanced placement offered*** - no. ***Advanced credit given*** - no. ***Early decision procedure*** - upon request.
1994-95 COSTS: ***Total costs*** (approximate) - $13,905. Tuition - $8,300, other significant fees - $175, room and board - $4,880, total books, supplies, incidentals (approximate) - $550.
UNDERGRADUATE FINANCIAL AID: Students receiving financial aid - 65%. Submit FAFSA by 3/2. Application deadline for institutional scholarships and grants - none. Average financial aid package - $6,000.
OTHER INFORMATION: ***Founded*** - in New York 1884, in Pasadena 1974. ***Nonprofit*** - yes. ***WASC Accredited*** - yes. ***Member of AICCU*** - yes.

AMERICAN COLLEGE FOR THE APPLIED ARTS LOS ANGELES

1651 Westwood Boulevard
Los Angeles, California 90024
(310) 470-2000
Fax: (310) 477-8640
Toll Free: (800) 333-2652

Small College of Business, Art, and Design

DISTINGUISHING FEATURES: American College for the Applied Arts has campuses in Atlanta, Georgia and London, England. The Los Angeles campus offers small classes coupled with a faculty who are working professionals in various fields of business and design. This provides students with a well-rounded education in their major. Majors are offered in Business Administration (marketing and hotel management concentrations), Commercial Art, Fashion Design, Fashion Merchandising, and Interior Design.
DEGREES OFFERED: Associate, Bachelor's.
CALENDAR: Quarter system; Summer sessions.
ENROLLMENT: ***Total*** - 600.
LOCATION: Westwood area of Los Angeles.
CAMPUS LIFE: ***On-campus housing:*** Spaces - 0.
OTHER INFORMATION: ***Founded*** - 1984. ***Nonprofit***- no. ***WASC Accredited*** - no. Accredited by the Southern Association of Colleges and Schools.

ANTIOCH UNIVERSITY

Two campuses in Southern California:

Marina Del Rey
13274 Fiji Way
Marina Del Ray, California 90292
(310) 578-1090
Fax: (310) 822-4824
Toll Free: (800) 7 ANTIOCH

Santa Barbara
801 Garden Street, Suite 101
Santa Barbara, California 93101
(805) 962-8179
Fax: (805) 962-4786
Toll Free: nd

Small University Offering the Equivalent of the Final Two or Three Years of College for Working Adults

DISTINGUISHING FEATURES: The main campus of Antioch University is in Yellowspring, Ohio. The University degree in Liberal Studies is an alternative to a conventional four-year degree. The program is designed for adults who have already completed 30 to 50 or more quarter units of college work elsewhere and offers the equivalent of the final two or three years of college. The degree program in Liberal Studies provides the student with a broader understanding of the world and contemporary issues as well as a deeper understanding of his/her major field and its fundamental principles and theories. Ethics and values are always emphasized. The college offers a combined Bachelor's/Master's program in Organizational Management in which a Master's degree can be earned in four quarters after the completion of the Bachelor's degree in Business. Majors are offered in Business, Psychology, Gerontology, Gerontology/Psychology, and Human Development.
DEGREES OFFERED: Bachelor's, Master's.
CALENDAR: Quarter system. Summer session.
ENROLLMENT: ***Total*** - Marina Del Rey - 720, Santa Barbara - 260.
LOCATION: Southern California.
CAMPUS LIFE: ***On-campus housing:*** Spaces - 0.
OTHER INFORMATION: ***Founded*** - 1972. ***Nonprofit*** - yes. ***WASC Accredited*** - no. Accredited by the North Central Association of Colleges and Schools (Senior College).

ARMSTRONG UNIVERSITY

2222 Harold Way
Berkeley, California 94704
(510) 848-2500
Fax: (510) 848-9438
Toll Free: nd

Small Business College Catering to International students

DISTINGUISHING FEATURES: Armstrong University is a very small business college, which emphasizes enrolling students from throughout the world. Its curriculum is enhanced by a

nd = no data available na = not applicable

student body from over forty countries and provides an international perspective that is vital in today's multinational world of business. The school's Center for Language and Intercultural Communication (CLIC) offers an intensive English language program for international students. An entering student may enroll in CLIC's "Gateway Program" to receive English language training, study-skill preparation, and an introduction to American business. Upon completion, students may enroll in one of Armstrong's degree programs or transfer to another college or university. Majors are offered in Business Administration with concentrations in Accounting, Finance, International Business, Management, and Marketing.
DEGREES OFFERED: Certificate, Associates, Bachelor's, Master's.
CALENDAR: Quarter system. Summer session.
ENROLLMENT: ***Total*** - 100.
LOCATION: Three-level, Spanish-style building in the heart of Berkeley, near San Francisco.
CAMPUS LIFE: ***On-campus housing:*** Spaces - 0.
OTHER INFORMATION: ***Founded*** - 1918. ***Nonprofit*** - no. ***WASC Accredited*** - no. Accredited by the Association of Independent Schools and Colleges.

ART CENTER COLLEGE OF DESIGN

1700 Lida Street
Pasadena, California 91103
Admissions: (818) 396-2373
Financial Aid: (818) 396-2215
Fax: (818) 405-9104
Toll Free: nd

Specializes in the Training of Artists and Designers

DISTINGUISHING FEATURES: Art Center College of Design focuses on preparing students for the professional world in one of nine specializations within the arts and design. Applicants apply directly to one major. The majority (95%) have attended another college prior to enrolling.
DEGREES OFFERED: Bachelor's, Master's.
SPECIAL PROGRAMS: Exchange programs with Occidental College and California Institute of Technology. ***Education abroad*** - Art Center College of Design, La Tour-de-Peilz, Switzerland. ***Honors programs*** - no.
COLLEGES: na.
UNDERGRADUATE MAJORS: Advertising, Illustration, Fine Arts, Graphic and Packaging Design, Environmental Design, Photography, Film, Product and Transportation Design. Preprofessional programs: na.
CALENDAR: 3 full semesters, fourteen weeks each.
FACULTY: Successful practicing artists and designers. Full-time - nd, part-time - nd. Undergraduate classes taught by faculty, not graduate assistants - all. Faculty with Ph.D.'s - nd%. Student/faculty ratio - 9/1. Average class size - nd.
ENROLLMENT: ***Total*** - 1,244. ***Graduate*** - 61. ***Undergraduate*** - 1,183: California residents - 50%, out-of-state and other countries - 50%. Men - 60%, women - 40%. ***Ethnic distribution of undergraduate students:*** Hispanic - 15%, Black - 2%, Asian/Pacific Islander - 21%, Native American/Alaskan - nd%, White - 62%. ***Freshmen graduating within 5 years*** - nd%.
LOCATION: In the hills above Pasadena's Rose Bowl. Suburban location with easy access to Los Angeles.
CAMPUS LIFE: ***On-campus housing:*** Spaces - 0, undergraduate residential students - 0%. ***Clubs and organizations*** - 5-10. Fraternities and sororities - 0. ***Athletics:*** Intercollegiate - no. Intramural sports - no. ***Counseling and guidance:*** Academic, personal. Faculty advisors - nd. Tutoring - nd. ***Special services/academic programs for:*** Educationally disadvantaged - nd, physically disabled - nd, learning disabled - nd.
FRESHMAN ADMISSION STANDARDS: High school graduation. High school units: Total required - no specific units required. Portfolio required.
1993-94 FRESHMAN ADMISSION DATA: ***Applications:*** Received - nd, accepted - nd, enrolled - 490. ***SAT scores*** - nd. ***ACT composite score:*** nd. ***High school GPA:*** Average GPA - above 2.50. ***Class rank:*** nd. ***International students:*** Minimum TOEFL score required - nd.
TRANSFER ADMISSION STANDARDS: Portfolio oriented toward one major. ***Transfer units required:*** Minimum - variable, maximum - variable. ***Minimum college GPA*** - 2.50. ***Grades accepted*** - nd.
1993-94 TRANSFER ADMISSION DATA: ***Applications:*** Received - 1800, accepted - 660, enrolled - 495. CCC transfer students enrolled - nd.
ADMISSION PROCEDURES: ***Entrance tests:*** SAT I: Reasoning Test or ACT required if in high school. Test deadline for fall admission - nd. ***Application process:*** Students admitted each term. Deadlines: Freshmen and transfers - rolling. Application fee - $45. Fee waiver - yes. ***Recommendations*** - optional. ***Interview*** - optional. ***Admission notification*** - rolling. Commitment deposit - $nd. ***Advanced placement offered*** - yes. ***Advanced credit given*** - yes. ***Early decision procedure*** - no.
1994-95 COSTS: ***Total costs*** (approximate) - $nd. Tuition - $14,225, other significant fees - $nd, room and board - $na, total books, supplies, incidentals (approximate) - $2,400.
UNDERGRADUATE FINANCIAL AID: Students receiving financial aid - 73%. Submit FAFSA and institutional application by 3/2. Application deadline for institutional scholarships and grants - fall 3/1, spring 9/15, summer 2/1. Average financial aid package - $nd.
OTHER INFORMATION: ***Founded*** - 1930. ***Nonprofit*** - yes. ***WASC accredited*** - yes. ***Member of AICCU*** - yes.

ART INSTITUTE OF SOUTHERN CALIFORNIA

2222 Laguna Canyon Road
Laguna Beach, California 92651
(714) 497-3309
Fax: (714) 497-4399
Toll Free: (800) 367-9349 in California,
(800) 255-0762 in other states.

Small College of Fine Arts and Design

DISTINGUISHING FEATURES: Art Institute of Southern California offers fine arts degree programs that are comprehensive, rigorous, and structured. The curriculum is rooted in contemporary aesthetics, and the primary teaching mode is the critique. Bachelor's degree programs are offered in Fine Arts with concentrations in drawing and painting, and Visual Com-

munications with concentrations in illustration, and graphic design and computer. Degree programs include coursework in studio art, art history, social sciences, humanities, and natural sciences.
DEGREES OFFERED: Certificate, Bachelor's.
CALENDAR: 4-1-4 system; Fall semester, Intersession, spring semester.
ENROLLMENT: ***Total*** - 140.
LOCATION: In the beach town of Laguna Beach south of Los Angeles.
CAMPUS LIFE: ***On-campus housing:*** Spaces - 0.
OTHER INFORMATION: ***Founded*** - 1962. ***Nonprofit*** - yes. ***WASC Accredited*** - Candidate. Accredited by the National Association of Schools of Art and Design. Candidate for WASC accreditation.

AZUSA PACIFIC UNIVERSITY

901 E. Alosta Avenue
P.O. Box 7000
Azusa, California 91702
Admissions: (818) 812-3016
Financial Aid: (818) 812-3009
Fax: (818) 969-7180
Toll Free: (800) TALK-APU

Inter-Denominational Christian University of the Liberal Arts

DISTINGUISHING FEATURES: Azusa Pacific is an interdenominational Christian liberal arts university. There are numerous Christian service opportunities, both on and off campus. The residences are divided into seven communities, which provide living-learning experiences based on the assessed needs of the residents.
DEGREES OFFERED: Bachelor's, Master's, Credential.
SPECIAL PROGRAMS: Freshman writing seminar to strengthen writing skills within chosen areas of interest. Career internships and cooperative education. American studies program in Washington, D.C. ***Education abroad*** - programs in Europe, the Far East, Latin America. ***Honors programs*** - yes.
COLLEGES: College of Liberal Arts and Sciences. Schools of Business and Management, Education and Behavioral Studies, Music, Nursing, Theology.
UNDERGRADUATE MAJORS: 32 majors. See this chapter: Undergraduate Degree Majors, page 12--76. Special academic programs: Global Studies, Applied Health, Management Information Systems, Social Work. Preprofessional programs: Dentistry, Engineering, Law, Medicine, Ministry, Social Work.
CALENDAR: Semester system. Summer sessions.
FACULTY: Full-time - 156, part-time - 181. Undergraduate classes taught by faculty, not graduate assistants - all. Faculty with Ph.D.'s - 48%. Student/faculty ratio - 18/1. Average class size - nd.
ENROLLMENT: ***Total*** - 3,923. ***Graduate*** - 1,769. ***Undergraduate*** - 2,154: California residents - 79%, out-of-state - 20%, other countries - 9%. Men - 42%, women - 58%. ***Ethnic distribution of undergraduate students:*** Hispanic - 10%, Black - 4%, Asian/Pacific Islander - 5%, Native American/Alaskan - 2%, White - 79%. ***Freshmen graduating within 5 years*** - nd%.
LOCATION: 71-acre, newly renovated and landscaped residential campus in the foothills of the San Gabriel Valley, twenty-six miles northeast of Los Angeles. An hour from beaches, ski resorts, and desert.
CAMPUS LIFE: ***On-campus housing:*** Spaces - 1,000, undergraduate residential students - 62%. ***Clubs and organizations*** - 14. Fraternities and sororities - 0. ***Athletics:*** Intercollegiate - NAIA. Intramural sports - yes. ***Counseling and guidance:*** Academic, personal, career planning, job placement. Faculty advisors - yes. Tutoring - yes. ***Special services/academic programs for:*** Educationally disadvantaged - limited, physically disabled - limited, learning disabled - limited.
FRESHMAN ADMISSION STANDARDS: High school units: Total required - nd. Recommended: English - 3, social science/history - 2, foreign language - 2, laboratory science - 1 (chemistry or physics), mathematics - 2 (algebra and geometry).
1993-94 FRESHMAN ADMISSION DATA: ***Applications:*** Received - 1080, accepted - 948, enrolled - 599. ***SAT scores:*** Average verbal/mathematics scores - nd/nd, median verbal/mathematics scores - nd/nd. Verbal/mathematics scores of enrolled freshmen: Middle 50% scored 299-699 verbal, 299-800 mathematics, 600-1499 combined verbal and mathematics. 0%/3% scored 700-800, 4%/11% scored 600-699, 18%/28% scored 500-599, 42%/34% scored 400-499, 28%/20% scored 300-399. ***ACT composite score:*** Average - nd, median - nd. ***High school GPA:*** Average GPA - 3.20. Minimum 2.50 required for admission. ***Class rank:*** nd. ***International students:*** Minimum TOEFL score required - 500.
TRANSFER ADMISSION STANDARDS: ***Transfer units required:*** Minimum - none, maximum - 64. ***Minimum college GPA*** - 2.00. ***Grades accepted*** - C or better.
1993-94 TRANSFER ADMISSION DATA: ***Applications:*** Received - 648, accepted - 554, enrolled - 353. CCC transfer students enrolled - nd.
ADMISSION PROCEDURES: ***Entrance tests:*** SAT I: Reasoning Test or ACT required. SAT II: Subject Test in Writing recommended. Test deadline for fall admission - recommended by January. ***Application process:*** Students admitted each term. Deadlines: Freshmen and transfers - 8/15 firm. Application fee - $45. Fee waiver - yes. ***Recommendations:*** 2 - academic from teacher; personal from Pastor, youth director, counselor, or close personal friend. ***Interview*** - contingent upon application materials. ***Admission notification*** - rolling, within two weeks of receipt of application. Commitment deposit - $40. ***Advanced placement offered*** - yes. ***Advanced credit given*** - yes. ***Early decision procedure*** - yes, 3.50 GPA minimum.
1994-95 COSTS: ***Total costs*** (approximate) - $16,574. Tuition - $11,636, other significant fees - $306, room and board - $4,020, total books, supplies, incidentals (approximate) - $612.
UNDERGRADUATE FINANCIAL AID: Students receiving financial aid - 80%. Submit FAFSA (CSS version preferred) by 3/2. Application deadline for institutional scholarships and grants - 5/13, priority deadline - 3/1. Average financial aid package - $3,000.
OTHER INFORMATION: ***Founded*** - 1899. ***Nonprofit*** - yes. ***WASC Accredited*** - yes. ***Member of AICCU*** - yes.

BETHANY COLLEGE

800 Bethany Drive
Santa Cruz, California 95066
(408) 438-3800
Fax: nd
Toll Free: (800) 843-9410

Small Bible College Affiliated with Assemblies of God

DISTINGUISHING FEATURES: Bethany College offers academic majors and ministerial training for students anticipating church related professions, as well as teaching, counseling, social services, and general business. Bethany is denominationally affiliated and residential.
DEGREES OFFERED: Certificate, Associate, Bachelor's, Credential.
CALENDAR: 4-4-1. Two semesters and May term. Summer sessions.
ENROLLMENT: ***Total*** - 450.
LOCATION: Wooded setting in the Santa Cruz mountains, twenty-five miles from San Jose.
CAMPUS LIFE: Students under 21 , unmarried, and not living with parents are required to live on campus. ***On-campus housing:*** Spaces - dormitories and houses available.
OTHER INFORMATION: ***Founded*** - 1919. ***Nonprofit*** - yes. ***WASC Accredited*** - yes.

BIOLA UNIVERSITY

13800 Biola Avenue
La Mirada, California 90639
Admissions: (310) 903-4752
Financial Aid: (310) 903-4742
Fax: (310) 903-4709
Toll Free: (800) 652-4652

The University Combines a Sound Liberal Arts and Christian Program

DISTINGUISHING FEATURES: Biola University has a strong evangelical Christian commitment, which permeates all phases of the university program. The curriculum combines academic excellence with spiritual values. Thirty hours of biblical studies, chapel three times a week, and weekly student ministry are required of all students.
DEGREES OFFERED: Bachelor's, Master's, Credential, First Professional, Doctoral.
SPECIAL PROGRAMS: Double majors possible. Interdisciplinary majors. Career internships. Seniors may take graduate courses with permission. 3/2 program in Engineering with University of Southern California. Work-study program in Washington, D.C. Cooperative program between Biola's music department and the Grove School of Music. ***Education abroad*** - summer program, fall semester in Germany, Biola-Israel program, Latin American Studies Program. ***Honors programs*** - no.
COLLEGES: School of Arts and Sciences, Talbot School of Theology, Rosemead School of Psychology, School of Intercultural Studies, School of Continuing Studies.
UNDERGRADUATE MAJORS: 59 majors. See this chapter: Undergraduate Degree Majors, page 12--76. Preprofessional programs: Law, Medicine.
CALENDAR: 4-1-4 system, January three-week interterm. Summer sessions.
FACULTY: Full-time - 132, part-time - 84. Undergraduate classes taught by faculty, not graduate assistants - all. Faculty with Ph.D.'s - 60%. Student/faculty ratio - 17/1. Average class size - 30.
ENROLLMENT: ***Total*** - 2,883. ***Graduate*** - 825. ***Undergraduate*** - 2,058: California residents - 70%, out-of-state - 22%, other countries - 8%. Men - 40%, women - 60%. ***Ethnic distribution of undergraduate students:*** Hispanic - 9%, Black - 4%, Asian/Pacific Islander - 17%, Native American/Alaskan - 1%, White - 69%. ***Freshmen graduating within 5 years*** - 78%.
LOCATION: 95-acre campus, twenty miles southeast of downtown Los Angeles in the conservative residential community of La Mirada. Quiet suburban setting, but easy access to the cultural life of Los Angeles.
CAMPUS LIFE: Must carry at least 10 units of credit to live on campus. Must be over twenty-one to live off campus. ***On-campus housing:*** Spaces - 1,393, undergraduate residential students - 60%. ***Clubs and organizations*** - numerous. Fraternities and sororities - 0. ***Athletics:*** Intercollegiate - NAIA. Intramural sports - yes. ***Counseling and guidance:*** Academic, personal, career planning, job placement. Faculty advisors - yes. Tutoring - yes. ***Special services/academic programs for:*** Educationally disadvantaged - yes, physically disabled - no, learning disabled - yes.
FRESHMAN ADMISSION STANDARDS: High school units: Total required - 16 including English - 3, social science/history - 2, foreign language - 2 (4 recommended), laboratory science - 1, mathematics - 2 (algebra and geometry), electives - 4. Nursing candidates: Chemistry - 1, algebra - 1. Biology majors: Chemistry - 1, physics - 1, mathematics - 4.
1993-94 FRESHMAN ADMISSION DATA: ***Applications:*** Received - 1,743, accepted - 697, enrolled - 356. ***SAT scores:*** Average verbal/mathematics scores - 440/500, median verbal/mathematics scores - nd/nd. Verbal/mathematics scores of enrolled freshmen: 0%/3% scored 700-800, 6%/16% scored 600-699, 23%/37% scored 500-599, 42%/27% scored 400-499, 22%/15% scored 300-399, 8%/2% scored 200-299. ***ACT composite score:*** Average - 22, median - nd. ***High school GPA:*** Average GPA - 3.20. ***Class rank:*** nd. ***International students:*** Minimum TOEFL score required - 500.
TRANSFER ADMISSION STANDARDS: ***Transfer units required:*** Minimum - none when qualified on basis of high school record, otherwise 12 units. Maximum - 70. ***Minimum college GPA*** - 2.25. ***Grades accepted*** - nd.
1993-94 TRANSFER ADMISSION DATA: ***Applications:*** Received - 359, accepted - 274, enrolled - 192. CCC transfer students enrolled - 55.
ADMISSION PROCEDURES: ***Entrance tests:*** SAT I: Reasoning Test or ACT required (SAT I preferred). Test deadline for fall admission - January preferred. ***Application process:*** Students admitted each term. Must be an evangelical believer in the Christian faith. Deadlines: Freshmen and transfers - 8/1. Application fee - $35. Fee waiver - yes. ***Recommendations:*** 2 - Pastor, and school counselor or employer. ***Interview*** - no. ***Admission notification*** - rolling. Commitment deposit - $100 due 5/1. ***Advanced placement offered*** - yes. ***Advanced credit given*** - yes. ***Early decision procedure*** - no.
1994-95 COSTS: ***Total costs*** (approximate) - $17,886. Tuition - $11,954, other significant fees - $nd, room and board - $4,932, total books, supplies, incidentals (approximate) - $1,000.

UNDERGRADUATE FINANCIAL AID: Students receiving financial aid - 75%. Submit FAFSA and FAF applications by 3/2. Application deadline for institutional scholarships and grants - 5/1, priority deadline - 3/2. Average financial aid package - $7,627.
OTHER INFORMATION: ***Founded*** - 1908. ***Nonprofit*** - yes. ***WASC Accredited*** - yes. ***Member of AICCU*** - yes.

BROOKS INSTITUTE OF PHOTOGRAPHY

801 Alston Road
Santa Barbara, California 93108
(805) 966-3888
Fax: (805) 565-1386
Toll Free: nd

Small, Specialized School of Photography and Filmmaking

DISTINGUISHING FEATURES: Brooks Institute of Photography is a professional school totally dedicated to preparing students for careers in photography and filmmaking. Initially, the emphasis is on technique, followed by applying technical skill to different kinds of photography depending on career goals. General education and business courses complete the career preparation. Students attend year-round and graduate in three years with a Bachelor's degree. A Master's degree takes an additional year. In addition, Brooks offers a three-year Diploma Program to students with a prior Bachelor's degree. Regarded as a world leader in its field, Brooks provides an ideal environment for an education in photography. Still Photography Majors in Color Technology, Commercial, Illustration/Advertising, Industrial/Scientific, Media, and Portraiture are offered as well as a major in Motion Picture/Video.
DEGREES OFFERED: Bachelor's, Master's.
CALENDAR: Trimester system. Each trimester divided into two seven-week sessions. One-week break between sessions, with the exception of a three- or four-week break in midsummer and a two- or three-week break in the winter. Students may enter the program at the beginning of any seven-week session.
ENROLLMENT: ***Total*** - 600.
LOCATION: Three campuses in Santa Barbara; two located in the foothills overlooking the city; the third and newest, housing the Motion Picture/Video Media Center, located downtown.
CAMPUS LIFE: ***On-campus housing:*** Spaces - 0.
OTHER INFORMATION: ***Founded*** - 1945. ***Nonprofit*** - no. ***WASC Accredited*** - no. Accredited by the Association of Independent Colleges and Schools.

CALIFORNIA BAPTIST COLLEGE

8432 Magnolia Avenue
Riverside, California 92504
Admissions: (800) 782-3382
Financial Aid: (714) 689-5771, Ext. 236
Fax: (714) 351-1808
Toll Free: (800) 782-3382

Liberal Arts Christian College Affiliated with the Southern Baptist Convention of California

DISTINGUISHING FEATURES: California Baptist College is the only Southern Baptist college on the West Coast. It offers a quality education in a setting of Christian ideals and values. The college combines a diverse liberal arts curriculum with a value-centered Christian perspective. Each student is encouraged to develop individual potential at his or her own pace and interest against a backdrop of an interested faculty. The accepting, caring atmosphere focuses on individual growth and personal development. The college is service-oriented and students become leaders both on campus and in the community.
DEGREES OFFERED: Bachelor's, Master's, Credential.
SPECIAL PROGRAMS: Career internships in Teacher Education, Behavioral Science, Public Administration, Business Administration, and Religion. ***Education abroad*** - no. ***Honors programs*** - yes.
COLLEGES: Divisions of Business Administration, Fine Arts, Humanities, Natural Science, Professional Services, Religion, social science.
UNDERGRADUATE MAJORS: Known for Education, Behavioral Science, Music, Business Administration and Religion programs. See this chapter: Undergraduate Degree Majors, page 12--76. Special academic programs: Social Work, evening degree in Business Administration and Political Science, Marine Biology. Preprofessional programs: Law, Medicine.
CALENDAR: Early semester with four-and-one-half-week January interterm. Summer session.
FACULTY: Full-time - nd, part-time - nd. Undergraduate classes taught by faculty, not graduate assistants - all. Faculty with Ph.D.'s - 68%. Student/faculty ratio - 12/1. Average class size - nd.
ENROLLMENT: ***Total*** - 921. ***Graduate*** - 51. ***Undergraduate*** - 870: California residents - 68%, out-of-state and other countries - 32%. Men - 49%, women - 51%. ***Ethnic distribution of undergraduate students:*** Minority - 27%. Hispanic - nd%, Black - nd%, Asian/Pacific Islander - nd%, Native American/Alaskan - nd%, White - 73%. ***Freshmen graduating within 5 years*** - nd%.
LOCATION: 75-acre campus of Spanish-style buildings in Riverside, one hour east of Los Angeles.
CAMPUS LIFE: Single and under twenty-one, or those receiving institutional aid are required to live in residence hall or with parents. ***On-campus housing:*** Spaces - 416 plus 96 apartments for married students, undergraduate residential students - 66%. ***Clubs and organizations*** - 20. Fraternities and sororities - 0. ***Athletics:*** Intercollegiate - NAIA. Intramural sports - yes. ***Counseling and guidance:*** Academic, personal, career planning, job placement. Faculty advisors - yes, also peer advisors. Tutoring - nd. ***Special services/academic programs***

for: Educationally disadvantaged - yes, physically disabled - nd, learning disabled - nd.

FRESHMAN ADMISSION STANDARDS: High school units: Total required - nd. Recommended: English - 3, social science/history - 3, foreign language - 2, laboratory science - 2, mathematics - 2, computer - 1.

1993-94 FRESHMAN ADMISSION DATA: ***Applications:*** Received - 343, accepted - 321, enrolled - 289. ***SAT Scores:*** Average verbal/mathematics scores - nd/nd, median verbal/mathematics scores - nd/nd. Verbal/mathematics scores of enrolled freshmen: Middle 50% scored 420-500 verbal, 480-540 mathematics, 840-1010 combined verbal and mathematics. ***ACT composite score:*** Average - nd, median - nd. ***High school GPA:*** Average GPA - 3.00. ***Class rank:*** nd. ***International students:*** Minimum TOEFL score required - 520.

TRANSFER ADMISSION STANDARDS: ***Transfer units required:*** Minimum - 1 semester, maximum - 70 from CCC, 100 from four-year college. ***Minimum college GPA*** - 2.00. ***Grades accepted*** - not more than 6 units total of D, Credit, Pass.

1993-94 TRANSFER ADMISSION DATA: ***Applications:*** Received - 188, accepted - 159, enrolled - 86. CCC transfer students enrolled - nd.

ADMISSION PROCEDURES: ***Entrance tests:*** SAT I: Reasoning Test or ACT required. Test deadline for fall admission - January preferred. ***Application process:*** Students admitted each term. Deadlines: Freshmen and transfers - rolling. Application fee - $30. Fee waiver - yes. ***Recommendations:*** 2 - 1 counselor or principal, 1 Pastor. ***Interview*** - recommended, not required. ***Admission notification*** - rolling. Commitment deposit - $0. ***Advanced placement offered*** - yes. ***Advanced credit given*** - yes. ***Early decision procedure:*** Application deadline - rolling, notification - rolling.

1993-94 COSTS: ***Total costs*** (approximate) - $14,394. Tuition - $7,800, other significant fees - $1,100, room and board - $4,494, total books, supplies, incidentals (approximate) - $1,000.

UNDERGRADUATE FINANCIAL AID: Students receiving financial aid - 79%. Submit FAFSA (CSS version preferred) by 3/2. Application deadline for institutional scholarships and grants - 4/1, priority deadline - 4/1. Average financial aid package - $3,100.

OTHER INFORMATION: ***Founded*** - 1950. ***Nonprofit*** - yes. ***WASC Accredited*** - yes. ***Member of AICCU*** - yes.

CALIFORNIA COLLEGE OF ARTS AND CRAFTS

5212 Broadway at College Avenue
Oakland, California 94618
Admissions: (510) 653-6522
Financial Aid: (510) 653-6522
Fax: (510) 547-5379
Toll Free: (800) 447-1278

College of Fine Arts, Design, and Architecture

DISTINGUISHING FEATURES: CCAC offers a wide range of education in fine arts, design, and architecture. Instruction in design and architectural studies takes place at the San Francisco campus. Courses in fine arts and crafts are taught on the Oakland campus. The college emphasizes a strong foundation studio program and a rigorous humanities and science program. Lectures and seminars are given regularly by visiting artists, scholars, and critics.

DEGREES OFFERED: Bachelor's, Master's.

SPECIAL PROGRAMS: Student exchange program with Mills College, Holy Names College. Career internships required in Graphic Design and Architecture. ***Education abroad*** - no. ***Honors programs*** - no.

COLLEGES: Schools of Art, Architecture, Design.

UNDERGRADUATE MAJORS: 16 majors. Fine Arts: Drawing, Painting, Printmaking, Sculpture, Film/Video/Performance, Photography, Wood/Furniture, Ceramics, Glass, Jewelry/Metal Arts, Textiles. Design: Industrial Design, Graphic Design, Illustration. Architectural Studies: Architecture, Interior Architecture. Preprofessional programs: na.

CALENDAR: Semester system. Summer session.

FACULTY: Practicing artists, designers, craftspeople, and scholars. Full-time - 35, part-time - 168. Undergraduate classes taught by faculty, not graduate assistants - all. Faculty with Ph.D.'s - 92% are working professionals. Student/faculty ratio - 12/1. Average class size - 18.

ENROLLMENT: ***Total*** - 1,178. ***Graduate*** - 79. ***Undergraduate*** - 1,099: California residents - 73%, out-of-state - 16%, other countries - 11%. Men - 43%, women - 57%. ***Ethnic distribution of undergraduate students:*** Hispanic - 6%, Black - 4%, Asian/Pacific Islander - 11%, Native American/Alaskan - 1%, White - 61%. ***Freshmen graduating within 5 years*** - 30%.

LOCATION: Oakland campus - in a residential area of the city, three miles south of the University of California, Berkeley. San Francisco campus - in the heart of San Francisco's design center.

CAMPUS LIFE: ***On-campus housing:*** Spaces - 60, undergraduate residential students - 5%. ***Clubs and organizations*** - 11. Fraternities and sororities - 0. ***Athletics:*** Intercollegiate - no. Intramural sports - no. ***Counseling and guidance:*** Academic, personal, career planning, job placement. Faculty advisors - yes. Tutoring - yes. ***Special services/academic programs for:*** Educationally disadvantaged - no, physically disabled - no, learning disabled - yes.

FRESHMAN ADMISSION STANDARDS: High school diploma or equivalent. High school units: Total required - nd, English - nd, social science/history - nd, foreign language - nd, laboratory science - nd, mathematics - nd.

1993-94 FRESHMAN ADMISSION DATA: ***Applications:*** Received - 247, accepted - 148, enrolled - 59. ***SAT scores:*** Average verbal/mathematics scores - nd/nd, median verbal/mathematics scores - nd/nd. Verbal/mathematics scores of enrolled freshmen: 7%/22% scored over 600, 22%/33% scored 500-599, 48%/11% scored 400-499, 19%/30% scored 300-399, 4%/4% scored below 300. ***ACT composite score:*** Average - nd, median - nd. ***High school GPA:*** Average GPA - 2.80. 12% with 3.50-4.00, 34% with 3.00-3.49, 40% with 2.50-2.99, 14% with 2.49 and below. Overall GPA of 2.00 required. ***Class rank:*** nd. ***International students:*** Minimum TOEFL score required - 500.

TRANSFER ADMISSION STANDARDS: ***Transfer units required:*** Minimum - none, maximum - 72 Bachelor's Degree in Fine Arts, 87 Bachelor's Degree in Architecture. ***Minimum college GPA*** - 2.00. ***Grades accepted*** - C or better.

1993-94 TRANSFER ADMISSION DATA: ***Applications:*** Received - 448, accepted - 212 enrolled - 208. CCC transfer students enrolled - nd.

nd = no data available na = not applicable

ADMISSION PROCEDURES: ***Entrance tests:*** SAT I: Reasoning Test or ACT requested, not required. Test deadline for fall admission - na. Portfolio of art work required. ***Application process:*** Students admitted each term. Deadlines: Freshmen and transfers - rolling, priority date 3/1. Application fee - $30, international students - $45. Fee waiver - yes. ***Recommendations:*** 2 - 1 counselor or principal, 1 art teacher. ***Interview*** - required. ***Admission notification*** - rolling. Commitment deposit - $150. ***Advanced placement offered*** - yes. ***Advanced credit given*** - yes. ***Early decision procedure*** - no.
1994-95 COSTS: ***Total costs*** (approximate) - $20,732. Tuition - $13,760, other significant fees - $100, room and board - $4,425, total books, supplies, incidentals (approximate) - $2,448.
UNDERGRADUATE FINANCIAL AID: Students receiving financial aid - 55%. Submit FAFSA by 3/2. Application deadline for institutional scholarships and grants - 3/2, priority deadline - 3/1. Average financial aid package - $8,000.
OTHER INFORMATION: ***Founded*** - 1907. ***Nonprofit*** - yes. ***WASC Accredited*** - yes. ***Member of AICCU*** - yes.

CALIFORNIA COLLEGE FOR HEALTH SCIENCES

222 West Twenty-Fourth Street
National City, California 91950
(619) 477-4800
Fax: (619) 477-4360
Toll Free: (800) 221 7374

College for the Study of Respiratory Therapy

DISTINGUISHING FEATURES: California College for Health Sciences specializes in the training of respiratory therapists in its campus-based program. Students benefit from small classes and rotate through local San Diego hospitals for their clinical experience. Home study courses offer an Associate degree in Respiratory Therapy, Allied Health, Medical Transcription, and Child Care Studies; a Bachelor's degree in Health Services Management; and a Master's degree program in Wellness Promotion.
DEGREES OFFERED: Associates, Bachelor's, Master's.
CALENDAR: Year-round system.
ENROLLMENT: ***Total*** - 50 in campus-based program.
LOCATION: Near the city of San Diego.
CAMPUS LIFE: ***On-campus housing:*** Spaces - 0.
OTHER INFORMATION: ***Founded*** - 1979. ***Nonprofit*** - no. ***WASC Accredited*** - no. Accredited by the American Medical Association (Respiratory Therapy Technician) and the Career College Association.

CALIFORNIA INSTITUTE OF TECHNOLOGY

1201 East California Boulevard
Pasadena, California 91125
Admissions: (818) 395-6341
Financial Aid: (818) 395-6280
Fax: (818) 564-8136
Toll Free: (800) 568-8324

Theoretically Oriented Institution of Research and Teaching in Science and Engineering

DISTINGUISHING FEATURES: Caltech is one of the world's major research and educational centers. It is dedicated to exceptional instruction and research in engineering and science. Students maintain a high standard of scholarship and intellectual achievement. The Jet Propulsion Lab and the Palomar Observatory are off-campus facilities. The Institute emphasizes the training of creative engineers and scientists. Students become involved in research projects with faculty as early as the freshman year on campus or at nearby Jet Propulsion Laboratory. Humanities are required in the curriculum and some Humanities majors are offered. The school has an unusually small student/faculty ratio and students develop a strong sense of community and close relations with the faculty. Students participate on nearly all Caltech committees, including the admissions committee.
DEGREES OFFERED: Bachelor's, Master's, Doctoral.
SPECIAL PROGRAMS: Summer undergraduate research fellowships for independent research. Student exchange programs with Occidental College, Scripps College, and Art Center College of Design for as little as one course or as much as one full year. Cooperative educational program: 3/2 plan with nine liberal arts colleges. During the freshman year, all grades are Pass/Fail. Students may design their own majors. An honor system governs all scholastic and many extracurricular activities. ***Education abroad*** - no. ***Honors programs*** - no.
COLLEGES: Divisions: Biology; Chemistry and Chemical Engineering; Engineering and Applied Science; Geological and Planetary Sciences; The Humanities and Social Sciences; Physics, Mathematics and Astronomy.
UNDERGRADUATE MAJORS: 19 majors. See this chapter: Undergraduate Degree Majors, page 12--76.
CALENDAR: One twelve-week term, two eleven-week terms. No Summer session.
FACULTY: Full-time - 271, part-time - 0. Undergraduate classes taught by faculty, not graduate assistants - all. Faculty with Ph.D.'s - 100%. Student/faculty ratio - 3/1. Average class size - 15.
ENROLLMENT: ***Total*** - 1,977. ***Graduate*** - 1,077. ***Undergraduate*** - 900: California residents - 34%, out-of-state - 66%, other countries - 6%. Men - 74%, women - 26%. ***Ethnic distribution of undergraduate students:*** Hispanic - 6%, Black - 2%, Asian/Pacific Islander - 25%, Native American/Alaskan - 1%, White - 56%. ***Freshmen graduating within 5 years*** - 80%.
LOCATION: 124-acre campus in a residential area of the city of Pasadena, ten miles northeast of Los Angeles. At the foot of the San Gabriel Mountains, some twenty-five miles inland from the Pacific Ocean.
CAMPUS LIFE: Freshmen must live on campus. ***On-campus housing:*** Spaces - 7 undergraduate, 4 graduate houses, undergraduate residential students - 90%. ***Clubs and***

nd = no data available   na = not applicable

organizations - 100. Fraternities and sororities - 0. ***Athletics:*** Intercollegiate - NCAA Division III. Intramural sports - yes. ***Counseling and guidance:*** Academic, personal, career planning. Faculty advisors - yes. Tutoring - yes. ***Special services/ academic programs for:*** Educationally disadvantaged - no, physically disabled - no, learning disabled - no. Services provided as needed.
FRESHMAN ADMISSION STANDARDS: High school units: Total required - 15. English - 3, social science/history - 1 (U.S. history or Government), foreign language - 0, laboratory science - 2 (physics and chemistry), mathematics - 4. Additional academic units: English, history, foreign language, and/or science - 5.
1993-94 FRESHMAN ADMISSION DATA: ***Applications:*** Received - 1,916, accepted - 510, enrolled - 211. ***SAT Scores:*** Average verbal/mathematics scores - 660/753, median verbal/ mathematics scores - nd/nd. Verbal/mathematics scores of enrolled freshmen: Middle 50% scored 600-710 verbal, 720-780 mathematics, 1320-1490 combined verbal and mathematics. nd%/nd% scored 700-800, nd%/nd% scored 600-699, nd%/ nd% scored 500-599. ***ACT composite score:*** Average - nd, median - nd. ***High school GPA:*** Average GPA - nd. ***Class rank:*** 85% of freshmen in top 10% of class, 14% in top 20%. Approximately 75% have never received lower than A in mathematics and science classes. ***International students:*** Minimum TOEFL score required - nd.
TRANSFER ADMISSION STANDARDS: ***Transfer units required:*** Minimum - 30, 1 or 2 years of college including calculus and physics, maximum - 60, 2 full years of college including calculus and physics. ***Minimum college GPA*** - 3.00. ***Grades accepted*** - D not accepted. Pass grades accepted for credit but not counted in GPA. Other requirements: Transfer examinations in mathematics and physics (and chemistry, if chemistry or Chemical Engineering major.)
1993-94 TRANSFER ADMISSION DATA: ***Applications:*** Received - 175, accepted - 12, enrolled - 12. CCC transfer students enrolled - nd.
ADMISSION PROCEDURES: ***Entrance tests:*** SAT I: Reasoning Test and SAT II: Subject Tests in Writing, Mathematics IIC, and any one of physics, chemistry or biology. Test deadline for fall admission - December. ***Application process:*** Students admitted for fall only. Freshmen deadline - 1/1 firm. Transfer deadlines - United States 3/1, international 3/15. Application fee - $40. Fee waiver - yes. ***Recommendations:*** 3 - 2 teachers, 1 counselor. ***Interview*** - no. ***Admission notification*** - approximately 4/1. Commitment deposit - $100 due by candidate reply date. ***Advanced placement offered*** - through Institute's own placement examinations. ***Advanced credit given*** - through Institute's own placement examinations. ***Early decision procedure:*** Application deadline - 10/15, notification - by 12/10.
1994-95 COSTS: ***Total costs*** (approximate) - $25,457. Tuition - $16,695, other significant fees - $210, room and board - $6,422, total books, supplies, incidentals (approximate) - $2,130.
UNDERGRADUATE FINANCIAL AID: Students receiving financial aid - 65%. Submit FAFSA and FAF by 3/2. Application deadline for institutional scholarships and grants - 2/1. Average financial aid package - $15,000.
OTHER INFORMATION: ***Founded*** - 1891. ***Nonprofit*** - yes. ***WASC Accredited*** - yes. ***Member of AICCU*** - yes.

CALIFORNIA INSTITUTE OF THE ARTS

24700 McBean Parkway
Valencia, California 91355
Admissions: (805) 253-7865
Financial Aid: (800) 443-0480
Fax: nd
Toll Free: (800) 292-ARTS in California,
(800) 545-ARTS in other states.

Professional Institution of the Visual and Performing Arts

DISTINGUISHING FEATURES: Cal Arts was established through the generosity and vision of Walt Disney. The school trains talented and motivated students for professional careers in the visual and performing arts - art, graphic design, photography, film, video, dance, animation, theater, and music. Students are accepted upon evidence of talent and purpose. All students are enrolled in a specific school and progress according to their own needs, preparation, and abilities.
DEGREES OFFERED: Certificate, Bachelor's, Master's.
SPECIAL PROGRAMS: Double majors possible. ***Education abroad:*** Exchange programs with Hochschule der Kunste, Berlin; the Centre International de Recherche Musicale, Nice; and London Contemporary Dance School. ***Honors programs*** - no.
COLLEGES: Professional Schools of Art, Dance, Film/Video, Music, Theatre.
UNDERGRADUATE MAJORS: 5 majors. Art: Art, Graphic Design, Photography. Film/Video: Character Animation, Experimental Animation, Live Action Film and Video. Music: Composition, Performance. Theater: Acting, Performing Arts Design and Technology, Stage and Production Management. Dance. Special academic programs: Animation, Sound Design, Music Technology/New Media, Service Program in Humanities. Preprofessional programs: na.
CALENDAR: Semester system. No summer session.
FACULTY: Composed of professional artists. Full-time - nd, part-time - nd. Undergraduate classes taught by faculty, not graduate assistants - most. Faculty with Ph.D.'s - nd%. Student/faculty ratio - 7/1. Average class size - nd.
ENROLLMENT: ***Total*** - 1,046. ***Graduate*** - 371. ***Undergraduate*** - 675: California residents - 26%, out-of-state and other countries - 68%. Men - 59%, women - 41%. ***Ethnic distribution of all students:*** Minority - 23%. Hispanic - nd%, Black - nd%, Asian/Pacific Islander - nd%, Native American/Alaskan - nd%, White - 77%. ***Freshmen graduating within 5 years*** - nd%.
LOCATION: 60-acre campus in Valencia, a northern suburb of Los Angeles, twenty-seven miles north of Hollywood.
CAMPUS LIFE: ***On-campus housing:*** Spaces - 450, undergraduate residential students - 59%. ***Clubs and organizations*** - 7. Fraternities and sororities - 0. ***Athletics:*** Intercollegiate - no. Intramural sports - no. ***Counseling and guidance:*** Academic, personal, job placement. Faculty advisors - yes. Tutoring - no. ***Special services/academic programs for:*** Educationally disadvantaged - yes, physically disabled - yes, learning disabled - yes.

CALIFORNIA INDEPENDENT COLLEGES

nd = no data available na = not applicable

FRESHMAN ADMISSION STANDARDS: High school diploma or equivalent required. Admission procedures focus on applicant talent and potential as demonstrated by audition, portfolio review and other evidence of achievement and creative potential. Previous academic work, grades, or test scores are not considered. High school units: Total required - nd.
1993-94 FRESHMAN ADMISSION DATA: ***Applications:*** Received - nd, accepted - nd, enrolled - 84. ***SAT Scores:*** na. ***ACT composite score:*** na. ***High school GPA:*** Average GPA - nd. ***Class rank:*** nd. ***International students:*** Minimum TOEFL score required - 550.
TRANSFER ADMISSION STANDARDS: ***Transfer units required:*** Minimum - none, maximum - none. Request requirements for individual professional schools. ***Minimum college GPA*** - none. ***Grades accepted*** - C or better.
1993-94 TRANSFER ADMISSION DATA: ***Applications:*** Received - nd, accepted - nd, enrolled - 201. CCC transfer students enrolled - nd.
ADMISSION PROCEDURES: ***Entrance tests:*** SAT I: Reasoning Test or ACT not required. Portfolio or audition required. Test deadline for fall admission - rolling. ***Application process:*** Students admitted each term. Some programs do not allow spring admission. Deadlines: Freshmen and transfers - rolling, priority dates - 2/1 for fall, 11/15 for spring. Application fee - $50. Fee waiver - yes. ***Recommendations*** - no. ***Interview*** - recommended. ***Admission notification*** - rolling. Commitment deposit - $300. ***Advanced placement offered*** - yes. ***Advanced credit given*** - yes. ***Early decision procedure*** - dependent upon date of portfolio or audition review.
1994-95 COSTS: ***Total costs*** (approximate) - $15,610-$19,210 (varies by major). Tuition - $14,600, other significant fees - $60, room and board - $5,500, total books, supplies, incidentals (approximate) - $400-4,000 (varies by major).
UNDERGRADUATE FINANCIAL AID: Students receiving financial aid - 70%. Submit FAFSA by 3/2. Application deadline for institutional scholarships and grants - 3/2. Average financial aid package - $12,725.
OTHER INFORMATION: ***Founded*** - 1961. ***Nonprofit*** - yes. ***WASC Accredited*** - yes. ***Member of AICCU*** - yes.

CALIFORNIA LUTHERAN UNIVERSITY

60 West Olsen Road
Thousand Oaks, California 91360
Admissions: (805) 493-3135
Financial Aid: (805) 493-3115
Fax: (805) 493-3114
Toll Free: (800) 252-5884

Liberal Arts and Sciences College Owned by the Evangelical Lutheran Church in America

DISTINGUISHING FEATURES: CLU is a small, comprehensive university dedicated to a liberal arts education. Students are challenged in an academic and social environment that allows them to grow as individuals and gain a greater understanding of the world around them. The institution is known for its accessible faculty, friendly atmosphere, and academic excellence.
DEGREES OFFERED: Bachelor's, Master's, Credential.
SPECIAL PROGRAMS: Core cluster of courses for all freshmen. 3/2 cooperative degree program in Engineering with Washington University, St. Louis, Missouri. ***Education abroad:*** Junior year or semester abroad in countries such as Austria, China, England, France, Japan, Mexico, Netherlands, Scandinavia, and Spain. Special postgraduate year in the Netherlands for art students specializing in ceramics. Additional foreign study arrangements made by individual departments. ***Honors programs*** - yes.
COLLEGES: Schools of Arts and Sciences, Business, Education.
UNDERGRADUATE MAJORS: See this chapter: Undergraduate Degree Majors, page 12--76. Special academic programs: Business, Environmental Studies, Premedical. Preprofessional programs: Dentistry, Law, Medicine, Theology, Veterinary Medicine.
CALENDAR: Semester system. Summer sessions.
FACULTY: Full-time - nd, part-time - nd. Undergraduate classes taught by faculty, not graduate assistants - all. Faculty with Ph.D.'s - 84%. Student/faculty ratio - 15/1. Average class size - nd.
ENROLLMENT: ***Total*** - 2,930. ***Graduate*** - 1,450. ***Undergraduate*** - 1,480: California residents - 80%, out-of-state and other countries - 20%. Men - 47%, women - 53%. ***Ethnic distribution of undergraduate students:*** Minority - 19%. Hispanic - nd%, Black - nd%, Asian/Pacific Islander - nd%, Native American/Alaskan - nd%, White - 81%. ***Freshmen graduating within 5 years*** - nd%.
LOCATION: 285-acre campus in the rolling hills that surround the city of Thousand Oaks. One hour north of Los Angeles and one hour south of Santa Barbara. Twelve miles inland from the Pacific Ocean.
CAMPUS LIFE: Freshmen, sophomores, and juniors required to live on campus unless living with relatives. ***On-campus housing:*** Spaces - 968, undergraduate residential students - 48%. ***Clubs and organizations*** - 26. Fraternities and sororities - 0. ***Athletics:*** Intercollegiate - NCAA Division III. Intramural sports - yes. ***Counseling and guidance:*** Academic, personal, career planning, job placement. Faculty advisors - yes. Tutoring - yes. Writing center. ***Special services/academic programs for:*** Educationally disadvantaged - yes, physically disabled - no, learning disabled - no.
FRESHMAN ADMISSION STANDARDS: High school units: Total required - nd. English - 4, social science/history - 2, foreign language - 2, laboratory science - 2, mathematics - 2.
1993-94 FRESHMAN ADMISSION DATA: ***Applications:*** Received - nd, accepted - nd, enrolled - 250. ***SAT Scores:*** Average verbal/mathematics scores - nd/nd, median verbal/mathematics scores - nd/nd. Verbal/mathematics scores of enrolled freshmen: Middle 50% scored 300-800 verbal, 300-800 mathematics, 300-800 combined on verbal and mathematics. ***ACT composite score:*** Average - nd, median - nd. ***High school GPA:*** Average GPA - 3.37. ***Class rank:*** nd. ***International students:*** Minimum TOEFL score required - 530.
TRANSFER ADMISSION STANDARDS: ***Transfer units required:*** Minimum - 24, maximum - 70. ***Minimum college GPA*** - 2.50. ***Grades accepted*** - nd.
1993-94 TRANSFER ADMISSION DATA: ***Applications:*** Received - nd, accepted - nd, enrolled - 190. CCC transfer students enrolled - 153.
ADMISSION PROCEDURES: ***Entrance tests:*** SAT I: Reasoning Test or ACT required. Test deadline for fall admission - December. ***Application process:*** Students admitted each term. Deadlines: Freshmen and transfers - rolling. Application fee - $35. Fee waiver - yes. ***Recommendations:*** 1 - teacher. ***Interview*** - recommended. ***Admission notification*** - rolling. Commitment deposit - $200 due 5/1. ***Advanced placement offered*** - yes. ***Advanced credit given*** - yes. ***Early decision procedure:*** no.

nd = no data available na = not applicable

1994-95 COSTS: ***Total costs*** (approximate) - $18,880. Tuition - $12,950, other significant fees - $180, room and board - $5,300, total books, supplies, incidentals (approximate) - $450.
UNDERGRADUATE FINANCIAL AID: Students receiving financial aid - 80%. Submit FAFSA by 3/2. Application deadline for institutional scholarships and grants - 3/1. Average financial aid package - $9,800.
OTHER INFORMATION: ***Founded*** - 1959. ***Nonprofit*** - yes. ***WASC Accredited*** - yes. ***Member of AICCU*** - yes.

CHAPMAN UNIVERSITY

333 North Glassell Street
Orange, California 92666
Admissions: (714) 997-6711
Financial Aid: (714) 997-6741
Fax: (714) 997-6713
Toll Free: nd

Church-Related (Disciples of Christ)
Liberal Arts and Sciences University

DISTINGUISHING FEATURES: Chapman University offers a comprehensive selection of majors and preprofessional programs. A residential college, the school stresses personal attention and individual development with courses taught in small groups. Average class size is twenty. The interrelationship of learning and work is stressed by encouraging students to participate in work-study programs.
DEGREES OFFERED: Bachelor's, Master's, Credential.
SPECIAL PROGRAMS: Opportunities for undergraduate research. Career internships and field work. Cooperative Education program. Freshman seminar. ***Education abroad:*** Department of English offers a one-semester overseas program with King Alfred's College in Winchester, England suited to majors in Communications, Education, English, or History. ***Honors programs*** - yes.
COLLEGES: Schools of Business and Economics, Communication Arts, Education, Music. Wilkinson College of Letters and Science.
UNDERGRADUATE MAJORS: 92 majors. See this chapter: Undergraduate Degree Majors, page 12--76. Special academic programs: Film and TV Production, Peace Studies, Food Science and Nutrition. Preprofessional programs: Dentistry, Law, Medicine, Psychology, Social Service, Theology, Veterinary Medicine.
CALENDAR: 4-1-4 system, January interterm session. Summer sessions.
FACULTY: Full-time - 115, part-time - 50. Undergraduate classes taught by faculty, not graduate assistants - all. Faculty with Ph.D.'s - 87%. Student/faculty ratio - 12/1. Average class size - 20.
ENROLLMENT: ***Total*** - 2,930. ***Graduate*** - 1,059. ***Undergraduate*** -1,871: California residents - 63%, out-of-state - 25%, other countries - 12%. Men - 39%, women - 61%. ***Ethnic distribution of undergraduate students:*** Hispanic - 9.9%, Black - 4.6%, Asian/Pacific Islander - 9.3%, Native American/Alaskan - 0.6%, White - 71.6%. ***Freshmen graduating within 5 years*** - 45%.
LOCATION: 42-acre, tree-lined campus, thirty miles southeast of Los Angeles. San Diego and Mexico ninety miles south. Ten miles from beach, one-hour from mountains and deserts.
CAMPUS LIFE: Full-time undergraduates under twenty-one must live on campus unless living with parents or otherwise excused. ***On-campus housing:*** Spaces - 909 plus 163 apartments, undergraduate residential students - 65%. ***Clubs and organizations*** - 53. Fraternities and sororities - 9. ***Athletics:*** Intercollegiate - NCAA Division III. Intramural sports - yes. ***Counseling and guidance:*** Academic, personal, career planning, job placement. Faculty advisors - yes. Tutoring - yes. ***Special services/academic programs for:*** Educationally disadvantaged - no, physically disabled - yes, learning disabled - no.
FRESHMAN ADMISSION STANDARDS: B-minus and satisfactory test scores. High school units: Total required - na. Recommended: English - 4, social science/history - 3 (United States history and government), foreign language - 2, laboratory science - 2, mathematics - 3, arts or other elective - 1.
1993-94 FRESHMAN ADMISSION DATA: ***Applications:*** Received - 959, accepted - 771, enrolled - 351. ***SAT scores:*** Average verbal/mathematics scores of enrolled freshmen- 456/501, median verbal/mathematics scores - nd/nd. Verbal/mathematics scores of enrolled freshmen: Middle 50% scored 400-500 verbal, 430-560 mathematics, 830-1050 combined verbal and mathematics. 0.3%/3.1% scored 700-800, 4.9%/10.8% scored 600-699, 21.7%/32.9% scored 500-599, 48.6%-40.9% scored 400-499, 22.7%/11.5% scored 300-399, 1.7%/0.7% scored 200-299. ***ACT composite score:*** Average - 23, median - 23. ***High school GPA:*** Average GPA - 3.05. 28.2% with 3.50-4.00, 25.4% with 3.00-3.49, 25.6% with 2.50-2.99, 20.4% below 2.50. ***Class rank:*** 23% in top 10%, 47.6% in top 25%, 73.3% in top 50%. ***International students:*** Minimum TOEFL score required - 500.
TRANSFER ADMISSION STANDARDS: ***Transfer units required:*** Minimum - 12 completed at time of application. Those with less than 12 are considered freshmen. Maximum - 70. ***Minimum college GPA*** - 2.25 with some exceptions. ***Grades accepted*** - D not accepted if GPA below 2.00. Pass and Credit accepted.
1993-94 TRANSFER ADMISSION DATA: ***Applications:*** Received - 654, accepted - 559, enrolled - 346. CCC transfer students enrolled - 305.
ADMISSION PROCEDURES: ***Entrance tests:*** SAT I: Reasoning Test or ACT required. Test deadline for fall admission - February, before registration preferred. ***Application process:*** Students admitted fall and spring only. Deadlines: Freshmen and transfers: Fall 3/1 priority date, spring 1/15. Application fee - $30. Fee waiver - yes. ***Recommendations:*** 1 - teacher. ***Interview*** - recommended. ***Admission notification*** - rolling. Commitment deposit - $100. ***Advanced placement offered*** - yes. ***Advanced credit given*** - yes, maximum 32 units. ***Early decision procedure:*** Application deadline - 11/1, notification - nd, test deadline - June for fall term, November for spring term.
1994-95 COSTS: ***Total costs*** (approximate) - $23,749. Tuition - $16,624, other significant fees - $529, room and board - $5,896, total books, supplies, incidentals (approximate) - $700.
UNDERGRADUATE FINANCIAL AID: Students receiving financial aid - 65%. Submit FAFSA and FAF applications by 3/2. Application deadline for institutional scholarships and grants - 3/1, priority deadline - 3/1. Average financial aid package - $14,000. Talent scholarships in music, dance, theatre, art, and writing.
OTHER INFORMATION: ***Founded*** - 1861. ***Nonprofit*** - yes. ***WASC Accredited*** - yes. ***Member of AICCU*** - yes.

CHARLES R. DREW UNIVERSITY OF MEDICINE AND SCIENCE

1621 East 120th Street
Los Angeles, California 90059
(213) 563-4800
Fax: (213) 563-4814
Toll Free: (800) 367-3739

Small College of Allied Health Careers

DISTINGUISHING FEATURES: The Drew/UCLA Medical Education Program is especially designed to attract those students who have an interest in addressing the concerns of underserved populations. Undergraduate allied health career students benefit from a combined curriculum at both Drew and UCLA. Among the programs offered are Community Nutrition and Physician Assistant. The school has developed its curriculum to primarily emphasize preventive medicine and health promotion.
DEGREES OFFERED: Associate, Bachelor's, First Professional.
CALENDAR: Semester system.
ENROLLMENT: ***Total*** - 350.
LOCATION: Urban campus in Los Angeles.
CAMPUS LIFE: ***On-campus housing:*** Spaces - 0.
OTHER INFORMATION: ***Founded*** - 1966. ***Nonprofit*** - yes. ***WASC Accredited*** - Candidate. Individual programs are appropriately accredited by agencies specific to their discipline.

CHRISTIAN HERITAGE COLLEGE

2100 Greenfield Drive
El Cajon, California 92019
Admissions: (619) 441-2200
Financial Aid: (619) 441-2200
Fax: (619) 440-0209
Toll Free: (800) 676-2242

Small Liberal Arts Christian College Affiliated with the Baptist Church

DISTINGUISHING FEATURES: Christian Heritage College is a liberal arts college committed to academic excellence and the integration of Biblical values into all areas of life and learning. Majors are offered in Bible, Business, Counseling/Psychology, Education, English, History, Home Economics, International Business, Ministries, Music, Pastoral Studies, Physical Education, and Women and Family Studies.
DEGREES OFFERED: Bachelor's, Credential.
CALENDAR: Semester system.
ENROLLMENT: ***Total*** - 315.
LOCATION: 33-acre campus in a semi-rural area in the small city of El Cajon, twenty miles east of downtown San Diego.
CAMPUS LIFE: Students under twenty-one and not local residents must live on campus. ***On-campus housing:*** Spaces - 230, residential students - 56%.
OTHER INFORMATION: ***Founded*** - 1970. ***Nonprofit*** - yes. ***WASC Accredited*** - yes.

CITY UNIVERSITY

3333 Bowers Avenue, Suite 275
Santa Clara, California 95054
(408) 970-9966
Fax: (408) 970-9969
Toll Free: (408) 648-2489

University Emphasizing Education for Older, Adult Students

DISTINGUISHING FEATURES: City University has as its primary purpose the goal of providing the opportunity for an education to segments of the population not being reached by traditional means. The programs are focused around the three values of accessibility, affordability, and usefulness. Most students have had prior college and are employed professionals. With it open-door policy, City University allows any student who is at least 18 years of age to enroll. Geared to the working adult, it gives academic credit for life experience. The college offers day and evening classes, weekend and "fast track" five-week courses, and Distance Learning independent study classes. Founded in Seattle, City University has sites in Oregon, British Columbia, Germany, Switzerland, and Japan as well as California. The major campus is located in Bellevue, Washington. Undergraduate degrees are offered in Accounting, Aviation Management, Business Administration, Computer Information Systems, Fire Command Administration, Health Care Administration, Hearing Health Care, Law Enforcement Administration, Legal Administration, Liberal Studies, Management, Marketing, Medical Laboratory Technology Nursing, Telecommunications Management, and General Studies.
DEGREES OFFERED: Certificate, Associates, Bachelor's, Master's.
CALENDAR: Quarter system. Summer session.
ENROLLMENT: ***Total*** - 450.
LOCATION: In the heart of Silicon Valley with its numerous high technology companies. Near the city of San Jose and one hour south of San Francisco.
CAMPUS LIFE: ***On-campus housing:*** Spaces - 0.
OTHER INFORMATION: ***Founded*** - 1973 in Washington, 1984 in California. ***Nonprofit*** - yes. ***WASC Accredited*** - no. Accredited by Northwest Association of Schools and Colleges.

CLAREMONT COLLEGES

Claremont, California 91711
Admissions: (909) 621-8000
Financial Aid: (909) 621-8000
Fax: nd
Toll Free: nd

A Cluster of Six Small Colleges, Which Cooperate to Provide Access to Common Services and Facilities

DISTINGUISHING FEATURES: The six Claremont Colleges are:
- Claremont McKenna College: Undergraduate liberal arts college with an emphasis on public affairs (economics, government, and international relations).
- Harvey Mudd College: Undergraduate college with an emphasis on physical sciences and engineering.

nd = no data available   na = not applicable

- Pitzer College: Undergraduate college with an emphasis on behavioral and social sciences.
- Pomona College: Undergraduate college with an emphasis on a traditional, comprehensive liberal arts and sciences curriculum.
- Scripps College (for women): Undergraduate college with an emphasis on humanities and fine arts.
- The Claremont Graduate School: Graduate school, which offers degrees in many academic areas at the master's and doctoral levels.

Each of the undergraduate colleges is described separately in this *GUIDE*. The six colleges have their own faculty, curricular emphasis, distinctive style, and mission. The campuses are adjacent to each other. Students at one campus may take classes and participate in activities at the other campuses. This cooperative arrangement combines the benefits of attending a small college with the advantages of choice of courses, variety of extracurricular activities, and use of the extensive services and facilities of a five-thousand student university. Twenty-five hundred courses are open for cross-enrollment. The Claremont Colleges cooperate to offer programs in which the colleges work together to present a curriculum. These are programs in American Studies, Asian Studies, Black Studies, Chicano Studies, Classics, European Civilization, Film Studies, Fine Arts, Latin American Studies, Music, Speech, Theatre, and Women's Studies.

DEGREES OFFERED: Bachelor's, Master's, Doctoral.

LOCATION: The Claremont Colleges share 500 acres in the residential suburban community of Claremont about forty-five minutes east of downtown Los Angeles. Set at the base of the San Gabriel foothills. Skiing and hiking are nearby, beaches and the desert an hour away.

CLAREMONT MCKENNA COLLEGE

890 Columbia Avenue
Claremont, California 91711
Admissions: (909) 621-8088
Financial Aid: (909) 621-8356
Fax: nd
Toll Free: nd

Small, Highly-Selective, Residential Liberal Arts College with Curricular Emphasis on Economics, Government, and International Relations. A Member of the Claremont Colleges

DISTINGUISHING FEATURES: Claremont McKenna College is one of the Claremont Colleges cluster. (See Claremont Colleges profile on the preceding page.) Students may take courses and participate in activities at the other Claremont Colleges. It is a small college, yet it offers students full access to the resources typical of a comprehensive university through its alliance in the cluster. The focus of this highly-selective school is on economics, government, and international relations. Its goal is to train students for leadership in business, government, the professions, and public affairs. Half the students major in Government or Economics or include one of these two major disciplines as part of a dual or double major. Unusually large numbers of students prefer careers in business, government, politics, and law.

DEGREES OFFERED: Bachelor's.

SPECIAL PROGRAMS: Dual majors. Opportunities to earn both Bachelor's and Master's degrees with coursework at Claremont Graduate School. 3/3 Law degree program with Columbia University School of Law. 3/2 Management Engineering programs with Columbia University, Washington University in St. Louis, Rensselaer Polytechnic Institute, Harvey Mudd, Cal Tech, Stanford, or another engineering institution. Student exchange programs with Colby College in Maine, Haverford College in Pennsylvania, Spelman College in Georgia. Study semester in Washington, D.C. Career internships. ***Education abroad:*** 50% of students study abroad during their CMC studies. Study abroad programs with other Claremont Colleges. ***Honors programs*** - yes.

COLLEGES: na.

UNDERGRADUATE MAJORS: 37 majors. In Social Sciences, Humanities, Sciences, Mathematics, Management/Engineering. See this chapter: Undergraduate Degree Majors, page 12--76. Preprofessional programs: All programs may lead ultimately to professional degrees. 15-20% of graduates go to law schools, 15-20% to schools of business, 20-30% to other graduate programs, 5-8% are premedical and pre-dental students.

CALENDAR: Semester system. No summer session.

FACULTY: Full-time - 96, part-time - 21. Undergraduate classes taught by faculty, not graduate assistants - all. Faculty with Ph.D.'s - 99%. Student/faculty ratio - 9/1. Average class size - 19.

ENROLLMENT: ***Total*** - 888. ***Graduate*** - 0. ***Undergraduate*** - 888: California residents - 63%, out-of-state - 37%, other countries - 4%. Men - 59%, women - 41%. ***Ethnic distribution of undergraduate students:*** Hispanic - 11%, Black - 6%, Asian/Pacific Islander - 19%, Native American/Alaskan - 1%, White - 63%. ***Freshmen graduating within 5 years*** - 84%.

LOCATION: Shares 500 acres with the other Claremont Colleges in the residential suburban community of Claremont about forty-five minutes east of downtown Los Angeles. Set at the base of the San Gabriel foothills. Skiing and hiking are nearby, beaches and the desert an hour away.

CAMPUS LIFE: All students may live on campus. ***On-campus housing:*** Spaces - 840, undergraduate residential students - 97%. ***Clubs and organizations*** - 280. Fraternities and sororities - 0. ***Athletics:*** Intercollegiate - in cooperation with Harvey Mudd and Scripps Colleges, NCAA Division III. Intramural sports - yes. ***Counseling and guidance:*** Academic, personal, career planning, job placement. Faculty advisors - yes. Tutoring - yes. Resident assistants, student sponsors. ***Special services/academic programs for:*** Educationally disadvantaged - no, physically disabled services- yes, learning disabled - no.

FRESHMAN ADMISSION STANDARDS: High school units: Total required - nd. English - 4, social science/history - 1, foreign language - 2, laboratory science - 2, mathematics - 3. Recommended that other courses be chosen from the five college-preparatory fields.

1993-94 FRESHMAN ADMISSION DATA: ***Applications:*** Received - 1,860, accepted - 767, enrolled - 227. ***SAT scores:*** Average verbal/mathematics scores - 601/663, median verbal/mathematics scores - 610/670. Verbal/mathematics scores of enrolled freshmen: Middle 50% scored 560-650 verbal, 620-710 mathematics. 4%/37% scored 700-800, 52%/45% scored 600-699, 38%/17% scored 500-599, 6%/1% scored 400-499, 0%/0% scored 300-399. ***ACT composite score:*** Average - 27.6, median - 28. ***High school GPA:*** Average GPA - 3.81. 78% with 3.50-4.00, 20% with 3.00-3.49, 2% with 2.50-2.99. ***Class rank:***

CALIFORNIA INDEPENDENT COLLEGES

nd = no data available na = not applicable

71% in top 10%, 93% in top 25%. ***International students:*** Minimum TOEFL score required - 600.

TRANSFER ADMISSION STANDARDS: ***Transfer units required:*** Minimum - 1 semester, maximum - 2 years. ***Minimum college GPA*** - usually 3.00 or better. ***Grades accepted*** - C or better.

1993-94 TRANSFER ADMISSION DATA: ***Applications:*** Received - 168, accepted - 64, enrolled - 44. CCC transfer students enrolled - 20.

ADMISSION PROCEDURES: ***Entrance tests:*** SAT I: Reasoning Test or ACT required, SAT I: Reasoning Test preferred. Test deadline for fall admission - January or earlier. ***Application process:*** Students admitted for fall and spring. Deadlines: Freshmen - 1/15 firm, transfers - 4/15 firm. Application fee - $40. Fee waiver - yes. ***Recommendations:*** 2 - counselor and 1 teacher. ***Interview*** - recommended. ***Admission notification*** - 4/1. Commitment deposit - $200 due 5/1. ***Advanced placement offered*** - yes. ***Advanced credit given*** - yes. ***Early decision procedure:*** Application deadline - all credentials by 11/15, notification - 1/10.

1994-95 COSTS: ***Total costs*** (approximate) - $24,500. Tuition - $17,000, other significant fees - $140, room and board - $6,010, total books, supplies, incidentals (approximate) - $1,350.

UNDERGRADUATE FINANCIAL AID: Students receiving financial aid - 74%. Submit FAFSA (CSS version preferred) and FAF applications by 2/1. Application deadline for institutional scholarships and grants - 2/1, priority deadline - 2/1. Average financial aid package - $16,740.

OTHER INFORMATION: ***Founded*** - 1946. ***Nonprofit*** - yes. ***WASC Accredited*** - yes. ***Member of AICCU*** - yes.

COGSWELL POLYTECHNICAL COLLEGE

1175 Bordeaux Drive
Sunnyvale, California 95089
Admissions: (408) 541-0100
Financial Aid: (408) 541-0100
Fax: (408) 747-0764
Toll Free: (800) 264-7955

Non-Residential, Future-Oriented College of Engineering and Engineering Technology

DISTINGUISHING FEATURES: Cogswell Polytechnical College offers both Associate and Bachelor's degree programs in Engineering Technology. Programs may be completed through day and evening classes. Emphasis is on both hands-on and theory. New, modern facilities and laboratories provide access six days a week to state-of-the-art technology. Many students are employed adults studying part-time. College expenses are often paid by employers.

DEGREES OFFERED: Associates, Bachelor's.

SPECIAL PROGRAMS: Trimester calendar allows for completion of degree in three years. Senior project required. ***Education abroad*** - no. ***Honors programs*** - no.

COLLEGES: na.

UNDERGRADUATE MAJORS: Fire Prevention/Technology, Mechanical Engineering Technology, Electrical Engineering (upper division only), Electronics Engineering Technology, Computer Engineering Technology, Fire Administration, Music Engineering Technology, Software Engineering, Computer and Video Imaging. Offers the only B.S. in Music Engineering Technology and B.A. in Computer and Video Imaging in the country. Preprofessional programs: nd.

CALENDAR: Trimester system - fall, spring, summer.

FACULTY: Full-time - 11, part-time - 36. Undergraduate classes taught by faculty, not graduate assistants - all. Faculty with Ph.D.'s - 40%. Student/faculty ratio - 9/1. Average class size - 9.

ENROLLMENT: ***Total*** - 368. ***Graduate*** - 0. ***Undergraduate*** - 368: California residents - 65%, out-of-state - 27%, other countries - 8%. Men - 88%, women - 12%. ***Ethnic distribution of undergraduate students:*** Minority - 36%. Hispanic - nd%, Black - nd%, Asian/Pacific Islander - nd%, Native American/Alaskan - nd%, White - 64%. ***Freshmen graduating within 5 years*** - 85%.

LOCATION: In northern California in the heart of Silicon Valley with its numerous high technology companies. Near the city of San Jose and one hour south of San Francisco.

CAMPUS LIFE: Arranges for housing in private residences in community. ***On-campus housing:*** Spaces - 0, undergraduate residential students - 0%. ***Clubs and organizations*** - 5 professionally oriented. Fraternities and sororities - 0. ***Athletics:*** Intercollegiate - no. Intramural sports - no. ***Counseling and guidance:*** Academic, personal, career planning, job placement. Faculty advisors - yes. Tutoring - yes. ***Special services/academic programs for:*** Educationally disadvantaged - no, physically disabled - no, learning disabled - no.

FRESHMAN ADMISSION STANDARDS: High school units: Total required - college preparatory pattern recommended with emphasis on science and mathematics through trigonometry. English - 4, social science/history - 0, foreign language - 0, laboratory science - 2, mathematics - 4.

1993-94 FRESHMAN ADMISSION DATA: ***Applications:*** Received - 70, accepted - 63, enrolled - 35. ***SAT Scores:*** Test scores not given a great deal of weight in admissions decisions. Deal personally with each student. Average verbal/mathematics scores - nd/nd, median verbal/mathematics scores - nd/nd. Verbal/mathematics scores of enrolled freshmen: Middle 50% scored 400-650 verbal, 475-700 mathematics. 10%/5% scored 700-800, 10%/60% scored 600-699, 40%/35% scored 500-599, 40%/0% scored 400-499, 0%/0% scored 300-399. ***High school GPA:*** Average GPA - 3.20. High school graduation is required with a 2.50 GPA in solid subjects. ***Class rank:*** 5% in top 10%, 40% in top 25%. ***International students:*** Minimum TOEFL score required - 550.

TRANSFER ADMISSION STANDARDS: ***Transfer units required:*** Minimum - 12, maximum - 70. ***Minimum college GPA*** - 2.30. ***Grades accepted*** - C or above.

1993-94 TRANSFER ADMISSION DATA: ***Applications:*** Received - nd,, accepted - nd, enrolled - nd. CCC transfer students enrolled - nd.

ADMISSION PROCEDURES: ***Entrance tests:*** SAT I: Reasoning Test or ACT recommended, not required. Mathematics placement examination required for all accepted students. Test deadline for fall admission - nd. ***Application process:*** Students admitted each term. Deadlines: Freshmen and transfers - rolling for United States citizens, ten weeks before opening of term for international students. Application fee - $30. Fee waiver - no. ***Recommendations:*** Helpful, not required - principal, counselor, teachers, employers. ***Interview*** - recommended, not required. ***Admission notification*** - rolling. Commitment deposit - $0 due na. ***Advanced placement offered*** - yes. ***Advanced credit given*** - yes. ***Early decision procedure*** - no.

1993-94 COSTS: ***Total costs*** (approximate) - $7,560 for 2 trimesters. Tuition - $3,480 per trimester, other significant fees -

nd = no data available   na = not applicable

$nd, room and board - $na, total books, supplies, incidentals (approximate) - $600.
UNDERGRADUATE FINANCIAL AID: Students receiving financial aid - 35%. Submit FAFSA and FAF by 3/2. Application deadline for institutional scholarships and grants - priority 4/15. Average financial aid package - $6,925.
OTHER INFORMATION: ***Founded*** - 1887. ***Nonprofit*** - yes. ***WASC Accredited*** - yes. ***Member of AICCU*** - yes.

COLEMAN COLLEGE

7380 Parkway Drive
La Mesa, California 92042
(619) 465-3990
Fax: nd
Toll Free: nd

Small College Specializing in Computer Training

DISTINGUISHING FEATURES: Coleman College specializes in computer training and education with the latest in computer equipment. The computer laboratories, together with up-to-date curriculum and a well-trained faculty, prepare students for careers in the computer field. Majors offered are Computer Information, Computer Technology, and Office Automation.
DEGREES OFFERED: Certificate, Associates, Bachelor's, Master's.
CALENDAR: Quarter system.
ENROLLMENT: ***Total*** - 1,000.
LOCATION: Urban setting in the city of La Mesa, a suburb of San Diego.
CAMPUS LIFE: ***On-campus housing:*** Spaces - 0.
OTHER INFORMATION: ***Founded*** - 1963. ***Nonprofit*** - yes. ***WASC Accredited*** - no. Accredited by the Association of Independent Colleges and Schools (Senior College of Business).

COLLEGE OF NOTRE DAME

1500 Ralston Avenue
Belmont, California 94002
Admissions: (415) 508-3607
Financial Aid: (415) 508-3509
Fax: (415) 637-0493
Toll Free: nd

Liberal Arts, Catholic Institution

DISTINGUISHING FEATURES: CND was founded by the Sisters of Notre Dame de Namur. The college has a diverse student body and offers a highly personalized education. It serves students of all ethnic, religious, and socioeconomic backgrounds. The liberal arts curriculum requires that all students study both western and nonwestern culture and thought. Career preparation is an integral part of the curriculum and students have ample opportunity for internships.
DEGREES OFFERED: Bachelor's, Master's, Credential.
SPECIAL PROGRAMS: Exchange study programs with Trinity College, Washington, D.C., Emanuel College, Boston, MA. 3/2 Engineering Program with Boston University. Three-unit career development course requirement allowing choice of career planning course or Cooperative Education Internship Program. Campus Ministry program. ***Education abroad*** - junior year in countries such as England, France, Greece, Japan, Kenya, Spain, Switzerland. ***Honors programs*** - no.
COLLEGES: Divisions of Humanities, Natural Sciences and Mathematics, Social and Behavioral Sciences, Visual and Performing Arts, Business Administration.
UNDERGRADUATE MAJORS: 21 majors. In the Humanities, Natural Sciences/Mathematics, Visual/Performing Arts, Social Sciences, and Business Administration. See this chapter: Undergraduate Degree Majors, page 12--76. Special academic programs: Environmental Studies, Interior Design, and Latin American Studies. Preprofessional programs: Dentistry, Elementary Education, Law, Medicine, Physical Therapy, Secondary Education, Veterinary Medicine.
CALENDAR: Semester system. Summer sessions.
FACULTY: Full-time - 61, part-time - 106. Undergraduate classes taught by faculty, not graduate assistants - all. Faculty with Ph.D.'s - 78%. Student/faculty ratio - 10/1. Average class size - 12.
ENROLLMENT: ***Total*** - 1,647. ***Graduate*** -816. ***Undergraduate*** - 831: California residents - 80%, out-of-state - 10%, other countries - 10%. Men - 38%, women - 62%. ***Ethnic distribution of undergraduate students:*** Hispanic - 15%, Black - 7%, Asian/Pacific Islander - 15%, Native American/Alaskan - 1%, White - 48%. ***Freshmen graduating within 5 years*** - 48%.
LOCATION: 80 acres on a wooded hillside on the San Francisco Peninsula, twenty-five miles south of San Francisco.
CAMPUS LIFE: Housing guaranteed to all new students. ***On-campus housing:*** Spaces - 300, undergraduate residential students - 38%. ***Clubs and organizations*** - 22. Fraternities and sororities - 0. ***Athletics:*** Intercollegiate - NCAA Division II. Intramural sports - yes. ***Counseling and guidance:*** Academic, personal, career planning, job placement. Faculty advisors - yes. Tutoring - yes. ***Special services/academic programs for:*** Educationally disadvantaged - no, physically disabled - yes, learning disabled - yes.
FRESHMAN ADMISSION STANDARDS: High school units: Total required - 13, English - 4, social science/history - 2, foreign language - 2, laboratory science - 1, mathematics - 2. Also, one full-year course in two of the following areas: Advanced mathematics, advanced laboratory science, computer science, fine arts, or advanced foreign language.
1993-94 FRESHMAN ADMISSION DATA: ***Applications:*** Received - 372, accepted - 264, enrolled - 97. ***SAT scores:*** Average verbal/mathematics scores - nd/nd, median verbal/mathematics scores - nd/nd. Verbal/mathematics scores of enrolled freshmen: Middle 50% scored 380-470 verbal, 390-510 mathematics, 770-980 combined verbal and mathematics. ***ACT composite score:*** Average - nd, median - nd. Middle 50% scored 18-23. ***High school GPA:*** Average GPA - 3.20. 27% with 3.50-4.00, 38% with 3.00-3.49, 29% with 2.50-2.99, 6% with 2.00-2.49. ***Class rank:*** 11% in the top 10%, 42% in the top 25%, 81% in the top 50%. ***International students:*** Minimum TOEFL score required - 450.
TRANSFER ADMISSION STANDARDS: ***Transfer units required:*** Minimum - 30, maximum - 78. ***Minimum college GPA*** - 2.00 with 30 units or more. ***Grades accepted*** - C or above.
1993-94 TRANSFER ADMISSION DATA: ***Applications:*** Received - 281, accepted - 237, enrolled - 271 total transfers. CCC transfer students enrolled - 179.

nd = no data available na = not applicable

ADMISSION PROCEDURES: ***Entrance tests:*** SAT I: Reasoning Test or ACT required. SAT I: Reasoning Test preferred, ACT accepted. Test deadline for fall admission - December. ***Application process:*** Students admitted each term. Deadlines: Freshmen - Priority date 3/2, final date 6/1, Spring 12/1. Transfers - Priority date 3/2, final date 8/1, Spring 12/1. Application fee - $35. Fee waiver - yes. ***Recommendations:*** 1 - teacher or counselor. ***Interview*** - recommended for marginal students. ***Admission notification*** - rolling, within three weeks after file is completed. Commitment deposit - $200 due 5/1. ***Advanced placement offered*** - yes. ***Advanced credit given*** - yes. ***Early decision procedure:*** Application deadline - nd, notification - nd.
1994-95 COSTS: ***Total costs*** (approximate) - $21,020. Tuition - $12,600, other significant fees - $nd, room and board - $5,700, total books, supplies, incidentals (approximate) - $2,720.
UNDERGRADUATE FINANCIAL AID: Students receiving financial aid - 67%. Submit FAFSA (CSS version preferred) and FAF applications by 3/2. Application deadline for institutional scholarships and grants - 6/1, priority deadline - 3/2. Average financial aid package - $20,000.
OTHER INFORMATION: ***Founded*** - 1851. ***Nonprofit*** - yes. ***WASC Accredited*** - yes. ***Member of AICCU*** - yes.

COLLEGE OF OCEANEERING

272 South Fries Avenue
Los Angeles Harbor
Wilmington, California 90744-6399
(310) 834-2501
Fax: (310) 834-7132
Toll Free: nd

College for the Training of Entry-Level Diving Personnel

DISTINGUISHING FEATURES: The College of Oceaneering is one of the world's largest and best-known diver training facilities. Educational programs include fundamental training in commercial diving complemented by an advanced specialization. All courses include both theoretical education and hands-on in-water practice. Training is on or near the water. Many graduates enter the inland and offshore oil industry. Specializations in underwater welding and burning, underwater inspection and nondestructive testing, and diver medical technology.
DEGREES OFFERED: Certificate, Associates.
CALENDAR: Year-round system with new programs starting every two weeks.
ENROLLMENT: ***Total*** - 300.
LOCATION: Five-acre campus in Los Angeles harbor near the city of Los Angeles.
CAMPUS LIFE: ***On-campus housing:*** Spaces - 0.
OTHER INFORMATION: ***Founded*** - 1969. ***Nonprofit*** - no. ***WASC Accredited*** - yes.

COLUMBIA COLLEGE — HOLLYWOOD

925 North La Brea Avenue
Hollywood, California 90038
(213) 851-0550
Fax: (213) 851-6401
Toll Free: nd

Small College Offering Comprehensive Programs in Television/Video and Motion Picture Arts

DISTINGUISHING FEATURES: Columbia College — Hollywood specializes in film and television/video production. It provides complete television studio, videotape editing, and film editing facilities. The school emphasizes a practical approach with numerous opportunities for hands-on experience. Majors are offered in Cinema and Television/Video.
DEGREES OFFERED: Associates, Bachelor's.
CALENDAR: Quarter system.
ENROLLMENT: ***Total*** - 200.
LOCATION: Hollywood, the entertainment capital of the world.
CAMPUS LIFE: ***On-campus housing:*** Spaces - 0.
OTHER INFORMATION: ***Founded*** - 1952. ***Nonprofit*** - yes. ***WASC Accredited*** - no. Accredited by the Career College Association.

CONCORDIA UNIVERSITY

1530 Concordia West
Irvine, California 92715
Admissions: (714) 854-8002, Ext. 108
Financial Aid: (714) 854-8002, Ext. 118
Fax: (714) 854-6854
Toll Free: (800) 229-1200

Liberal Arts University Owned by the Lutheran Church-Missouri Synod

DISTINGUISHING FEATURES: Formerly called Christ College Irvine, Concordia University is a member of the ten campus, nationwide Concordia University system operated by the Lutheran Church-Missouri Synod. It offers programs in teacher education, liberal arts, business administration, social work and church careers. The emphasis is on intellectual, professional, and spiritual development. There are opportunities for internships and international research.
DEGREES OFFERED: Bachelor's, Master's, Credential.
SPECIAL PROGRAMS: nd. ***Education abroad*** - no. ***Honors programs*** - no.
COLLEGES: Schools of Education, Arts and Sciences, Graduate Studies. Christ College.
UNDERGRADUATE MAJORS: 14 majors. See this chapter: Undergraduate Degree Majors, page 12--76. Preprofessional programs: Law, Medicine, Seminary.
CALENDAR: Quarter system. Summer sessions.
FACULTY: Full-time - 44, part-time - 40. Undergraduate classes taught by faculty, not graduate assistants - all. Faculty with Ph.D.'s - 65%. Student/faculty ratio - 18/1. Average class size - 22.

nd = no data available na = not applicable

ENROLLMENT: *Total* - 916. *Graduate* - 142. *Undergraduate* - 774: California residents - 78%, out-of-state - 15%, other countries - 7%. Men - 40%, women - 60%. *Ethnic distribution of undergraduate students:* Hispanic - 7%, Black - 3%, Asian/Pacific Islander - 12%, Native American/Alaskan - 0%, White - 76%. *Freshmen graduating within 5 years* - 54%.
LOCATION: 65-acre campus on a hilltop in Orange County fifty miles south of Los Angeles, eighty miles north of San Diego. A short distance from UC Irvine.
CAMPUS LIFE: Single students under twenty-two not living with parents or relatives must live on campus. Unique on-campus apartments — each suite designed for four persons, with two bedrooms, a kitchen, bath, and living room. *On-campus housing:* Spaces - 138 apartments with 552 spaces, undergraduate residential students - 58%. *Clubs and organizations* - 21. Fraternities and sororities - 0. *Athletics:* Intercollegiate - NAIA. Intramural sports - yes. *Counseling and guidance:* Academic, personal, career planning, job placement. Faculty advisors - yes. Tutoring - yes. *Special services/academic programs for:* Educationally disadvantaged - no, physically disabled - no, learning disabled - no.
FRESHMAN ADMISSION STANDARDS: High school units: Total required - nd, English - 4, social science/history - 2, foreign language - 2, laboratory science - 3 (2 laboratory courses), mathematics - 3 (algebra, geometry, one elective.)
1993-94 FRESHMAN ADMISSION DATA: *Applications:* Received - 688, accepted - 497, enrolled - 144. *SAT scores:* Average verbal/mathematics scores - 420/485, median verbal/mathematics scores - nd/nd. Verbal/mathematics scores of enrolled freshmen: Middle 50% scored 360-480 verbal, 400-570 mathematics, 800-1060 combined verbal and mathematics. 0%/2% scored 700-800, 3%/14% scored 600-699, 22%/33% scored 500-599, 37%/33% scored 400-499, 28%/14% scored 300-399, 10%/4% scored 200-299. *ACT composite score:* Average - 22, median - nd. *High school GPA:* Average GPA - 3.28. 37% with 3.50-4.00, 38% with 3.00-3.49, 21% with 2.50-2.99, 4% with below 2.50. *Class rank:* 95% in top 50%. *International students:* Minimum TOEFL score required - 525.
TRANSFER ADMISSION STANDARDS: *Transfer units required:* Minimum - none, maximum - 110 quarter. *Minimum college GPA* - 2.50. *Grades accepted* - C or better.
1993-94 TRANSFER ADMISSION DATA: *Applications:* Received - 242, accepted - 175, enrolled - 103. CCC transfer students enrolled - 75.
ADMISSION PROCEDURES: *Entrance tests:* SAT I: Reasoning Test or ACT required. Test deadline for fall admission - nd. *Application process:* Students admitted each term. Deadlines: Freshmen and transfers - 5/1 priority date. Application fee - $25. Fee waiver - yes. *Recommendations:* 1 - teacher or counselor. *Interview* - recommended. *Admission notification* - rolling. Commitment deposit - $100. *Advanced placement offered* - yes. *Advanced credit given* - yes. *Early decision procedure* - no.
1994-95 COSTS: *Total costs* (approximate) - $18,015. Tuition - $10,800, other significant fees - $690, room and board - $4,440, total books, supplies, incidentals (approximate) - $2,085.
UNDERGRADUATE FINANCIAL AID: Students receiving financial aid - 75%. Submit FAFSA (CSS version preferred) by 3/2. Application deadline for institutional scholarships and grants - 4/15, priority deadline - 3/2. Average financial aid package - $8,500.
OTHER INFORMATION: *Founded* - 1972. *Nonprofit* - yes. *WASC Accredited* - yes. *Member of AICCU* - yes.

DEEP SPRINGS COLLEGE

Deep Springs, California
via: Dyer, Nevada 89010
(619) 872-2000
Fax: nd
Toll Free: nd

Very Small, Highly Selective, All-Scholarship Junior College for Men

DISTINGUISHING FEATURES: Deep Springs College is a very small, intimate, highly-selective, all-scholarship junior college for men only. The school is looking for bright young men who express themselves well both verbally and in writing. All accepted students receive a full tuition plus room and board scholarship. The purpose of the college is to prepare students for leadership and service. Deep Springs has a faculty of five to seven professors and features intense instruction in the liberal arts and sciences. A diversity of small, discussion-based classes allows the student to pursue his own interests in a rigorous environment and to sharpen his powers of inquiry. Students work twenty hours a week and are actively involved in the operation and the administration of the college and the alfalfa ranch. After two to three years students transfer to very selective major universities throughout the country to complete their studies.
DEGREES OFFERED: Associates.
CALENDAR: Semester system.
ENROLLMENT: *Total* - 24-26.
LOCATION: Isolated in a high desert valley, thirty miles from the nearest town. On a cattle ranch in the mountains east of Bishop, near the Nevada border.
CAMPUS LIFE: *On-campus housing:* Spaces - dormitories.
OTHER INFORMATION: *Founded* - 1917. *Nonprofit* - yes. *WASC Accredited* - yes.

DESIGN INSTITUTE OF SAN DIEGO

8555 Commerce Avenue
San Diego, California 92121
(619) 566-1200
Fax: (619) 566-2711
Toll Free: nd

Small Interior Design College

DISTINGUISHING FEATURES: The Design Institute of San Diego is devoted exclusively to professional education in the field of interior design. The Bachelor's degree program satisfies the educational requirement for professional membership in the American Society of Interior Designers and the Institute of Business Designers. Students must satisfy the General Education Requirement for the degree by taking classes at other institutions either before or after they attend the Design Institute.
DEGREES OFFERED: Bachelor's.
CALENDAR: nd.
ENROLLMENT: *Total* - 160.
LOCATION: In the city of San Diego.

nd = no data available   na = not applicable

CAMPUS LIFE: ***On-campus housing:*** Spaces - 0.
OTHER INFORMATION: ***Founded*** - 1977. ***Nonprofit*** - no. ***WASC Accredited*** - no. Accredited by the Foundation for Interior Design Education Research.

DEVRY INSTITUTE OF TECHNOLOGY

901 Corporate Center Drive
Pomona, California 91768
(909) 622-9800
Fax: (909) 623-3338
Toll Free: (800) 243-3660

Part of the DeVry System of Eleven Technical Campuses in the United States and Two in Canada

DISTINGUISHING FEATURES: The DeVry Institute of Technology in Los Angeles is one of eleven technical campuses offering Bachelor's degrees. Many classes are offered in the evening to accommodate working adults. Majors are offered in Electronics Engineering Technology, Computer Information Systems, Tele-Communications Management, Business Operations, Accounting. Associate degree programs — Electronics Technician, Digital Electronic Technician.
DEGREES OFFERED: Associate, Bachelor's.
CALENDAR: Trimester system.
ENROLLMENT: ***Total*** - 2,000.
LOCATION: 11.8 acres in the City of Industry, a thriving commercial complex nineteen miles from downtown Los Angeles.
CAMPUS LIFE: ***On-campus housing:*** Spaces - 0.
OTHER INFORMATION: ***Founded*** - 1983. ***Nonprofit*** - no. ***WASC Accredited*** - no. Accredited by the North Central Association of Colleges and Schools (Senior College) and the Career College Association.

DOMINICAN COLLEGE OF SAN RAFAEL

50 Acacia Avenue
San Rafael, California 94901
Admissions: (415) 485-3204
Financial Aid: (415) 485-3204
Fax: (415) 485-3205
Toll Free: (800) 788-3522

Catholic College of Liberal Arts and Sciences

DISTINGUISHING FEATURES: Dominican College of San Rafael was founded by the Dominican Sisters of San Rafael. It is a small, friendly college with a strong liberal arts tradition. Students enjoy an interactive learning environment, personalized attention, and a highly accessible faculty. Stress is placed on developing communication skills. Dominican guarantees graduation within four years of matriculation for all students who meet the prescribed requirements. There will be no fee for any additional units taken by these students. The curriculum is especially strong in Biology, Business, English/Writing, International Studies, Liberal Studies, and Psychology.
DEGREES OFFERED: Bachelor's, Master's, Credential.
SPECIAL PROGRAMS: Cross-registration with UC Berkeley. Exchange programs with several other Dominican colleges. Fieldwork (internships) in all undergraduate degree programs. Choose from over two-hundred internship possibilities in the San Francisco Bay Area. Humanities colloquium. Community service opportunities. Language Institute for English, L.I.F.E., for international students. Program for guaranteeing a Bachelor's Degree in four years. ***Education abroad:*** Special arrangements to study anywhere in the world. ***Honors programs*** - yes.
COLLEGES: na.
UNDERGRADUATE MAJORS: 16 majors. In the Arts and Sciences. Professional programs in Business and Nursing. Student-designed interdisciplinary majors. See this chapter: Undergraduate Degree Majors, page 12--76. Special academic programs in Biology, English/Writing, International Studies, Liberal Studies, and Psychology. Preprofessional programs: Medicine.
CALENDAR: Semester system. Summer session.
FACULTY: Full-time - 41, part-time - 103. Undergraduate classes taught by faculty, not graduate assistants - all. Faculty with Ph.D.'s - 49% of full-time. Student/faculty ratio - 13.5/1. Average class size - 18.
ENROLLMENT: ***Total*** - 1,098. ***Graduate*** - 300. ***Undergraduate*** - 798: California residents - 94%, out-of-state - 3%, other countries - 3%. Men - 21%, women - 79%. ***Ethnic distribution of undergraduate students:*** Hispanic - 10%, Black - 6%, Asian/Pacific Islander - 10%, Native American/Alaskan - 1%, White - 73%. ***Freshmen graduating within 5 years*** - 42%.
LOCATION: 80-acre, wooded campus in Marin County, seventeen miles north of San Francisco and fifteen minutes from the Golden Gate Bridge.
CAMPUS LIFE: ***On-campus housing:*** Spaces - 3 residence halls, undergraduate residential students - 25%. ***Clubs and organizations*** - 10. Fraternities and sororities - 0. ***Athletics:*** Intercollegiate - NAIA. Intramural sports - no. ***Counseling and guidance:*** Academic, personal, career planning, job placement. Faculty advisors - yes, also student assistants. Tutoring - no. ***Special services/academic programs for:*** Educationally disadvantaged - no, physically disabled - no, learning disabled - no.
FRESHMAN ADMISSION STANDARDS: High school units: Total required - nd. English - 4, social science/history - 1, foreign language - 2, laboratory science - 1, mathematics - 2.
1993-94 FRESHMAN ADMISSION DATA: ***Applications:*** Received - 213, accepted - 173, enrolled - 75. ***SAT scores:*** Average verbal/mathematics scores - 432/452, median verbal/mathematics scores - nd/nd. Verbal/mathematics scores of enrolled freshmen: Middle 50% scored 380-470 verbal, 390-520 mathematics, 770-990 combined verbal and mathematics. 0%/0% scored 700-800, 4.5%/4.5% scored 600-699, 16.7%/27.3% scored 500-599, 50.0%/40.9% scored 400-499, 22.7%/22.7% scored 300-399, 6.1%/4.6% scored below 300. ***ACT composite score:*** Average - nd, median - nd. ***High school GPA:*** Average GPA - 3.00. 25% with 3.50-4.00, 30.1% with 3.00-3.49, 32.4% with 2.50-2.99, 4.4% below 2.50. ***Class rank:*** nd. ***International students:*** Minimum TOEFL score required - 550. Below 550 must attend L.I.F.E. before admission.
TRANSFER ADMISSION STANDARDS: ***Transfer units required:*** Minimum -13, maximum - 70. ***Minimum college GPA*** - 2.00. ***Grades accepted*** - Credit, Pass.

nd = no data available   na = not applicable

CALIFORNIA INDEPENDENT COLLEGES

1993-94 TRANSFER ADMISSION DATA: ***Applications:*** Received - 292, accepted - 249, enrolled - 130. CCC transfer students enrolled - 113.
ADMISSION PROCEDURES: ***Entrance tests:*** SAT I: Reasoning Test or ACT required. Test deadline for fall admission - nd. ***Application process:*** Students admitted each term. Deadlines: Freshmen and transfers - 8/15, 3/2 priority date. Application fee - $35. Fee waiver - yes. ***Recommendations:*** 2 - counselor, teachers. ***Interview*** - strongly recommended. ***Admission notification*** - within two weeks after all credentials have been received. Commitment deposit: $150 for commuting students, $300 for campus residents due 8/1. ***Advanced placement offered*** - yes. ***Advanced credit given*** - yes. ***Early decision procedure*** - no.
1994-95 COSTS: ***Total costs*** (approximate) - $19,788. Tuition - $12,790, other significant fees - $250, room and board - $6,100, total books, supplies, incidentals (approximate) - $648. Nursing majors pay an additional $600 per year.
UNDERGRADUATE FINANCIAL AID: Students receiving financial aid - 76%. Submit FAFSA and institutional application by 3/2. Application deadline for institutional scholarships and grants - 3/2. Average financial aid package - $12,080.
OTHER INFORMATION: ***Founded*** - 1890. ***Nonprofit*** - yes. ***WASC Accredited*** - yes. ***Member of AICCU*** - yes.

DOMINICAN SCHOOL OF PHILOSOPHY AND THEOLOGY

2401 Ridge Road
Berkeley, California 94709
(510) 849-2030
Fax: (510) 849-1372
Toll Free: nd

Small Roman Catholic College

DISTINGUISHING FEATURES: The Dominican School of Philosophy and Theology offers students who have successfully completed two years of college a two-year upper-division undergraduate major in Philosophy. The major concentrates on the thought of Aristotle and St. Thomas Aquinas. As a graduate school of theology, it offers Master's degrees in preparation for the teaching of religion and Catholic ministry.
DEGREES OFFERED: Certificate, Bachelor's, Master's, First Professional.
CALENDAR: Semester system.
ENROLLMENT: ***Total*** - 90.
LOCATION: In the city of Berkeley, close to San Francisco.
CAMPUS LIFE: ***On-campus housing:*** Spaces - 0.
OTHER INFORMATION: ***Founded*** - 1932. ***Nonprofit*** - yes. ***WASC Accredited*** - yes.

D-Q UNIVERSITY

Post Office Box 409
Davis, California 95617-1409
(916) 758-0470
Fax: (916) 758-4891
Toll Free: nd

Small, Native American Institution of Higher Learning

DISTINGUISHING FEATURES: D-Q University is the only accredited, private Native American institution of higher learning in California. The school emphasizes basics such as language and mathematics as well as new technologies. It provides educational program extensions to various California reservations and rancherias.
DEGREES OFFERED: Certificate, Associates.
CALENDAR: Semester system.
ENROLLMENT: ***Total*** - 192.
LOCATION: Rural campus near the city of Davis.
CAMPUS LIFE: ***On-campus housing:*** Spaces - dormitories.
OTHER INFORMATION: ***Founded*** - 1971. ***Nonprofit*** - yes. ***WASC Accredited*** - yes.

FRESNO PACIFIC COLLEGE

1717 South Chestnut Avenue
Fresno, California 93702
Admissions: (209) 453-2039
Financial Aid: (209) 453-2041
Fax: (209) 453-2007
Toll Free: (800) 660-6089

Mennonite, Brethren-Sponsored College of Liberal Arts and Sciences

DISTINGUISHING FEATURES: FPC emphasizes developing the whole person, intellectually, socially, physically, and spiritually. It provides a warm environment, which allows you to explore the world from a Christian perspective. Biblical principals of Christian faith and living are dynamically integrated with career preparation in all areas of the liberal arts and sciences. The college is best known for its teacher education programs, with business and Bible/Christian ministries the next largest.
DEGREES OFFERED: Associates, Bachelor's, Master's, Credential.
SPECIAL PROGRAMS: Concurrent enrollment arrangements with CSU, Fresno; Mennonite Brethren Biblical Seminary; and San Joaquin College of Law. Cooperative education program. Choir tours internationally. ***Education abroad*** - Brethren colleges abroad. ***Honors programs*** - no.
COLLEGES: na.
UNDERGRADUATE MAJORS: Liberal Arts, Biblical Studies, Teacher Education, Business Administration. See this chapter: Undergraduate Degree Majors, page 12--76. Preprofessional programs: Dentistry, Law, Medicine, Pharmacy, Veterinary Medicine.
CALENDAR: Semester system. Summer sessions.

CALIFORNIA INDEPENDENT COLLEGES

nd = no data available na = not applicable

FACULTY: Full-time - 58, part-time - 105. Undergraduate classes taught by faculty, not graduate assistants - all. Faculty with Ph.D.'s - 55%. Student/faculty ratio - 15/1. Average class size - 17.
ENROLLMENT: *Total* - 1,560. *Graduate* - 674. *Undergraduate* - 772: California residents - 90%, out-of-state - 10%, other countries - 3.5%. Men - 40%, women - 60%. *Ethnic distribution of undergraduate students:* Hispanic - 14%, Black - 2%, Asian/Pacific Islander - 4%, Native American/Alaskan - 1%, White - 75%. *Freshmen graduating within 5 years* - nd%.
LOCATION: 42-acre campus in the city of Fresno in central California.
CAMPUS LIFE: Single students under twenty-one must get dean's approval for off-campus living. *On-campus housing:* Spaces - 282, undergraduate residential students - 41%. *Clubs and organizations* - 20. Fraternities and sororities - 0. *Athletics:* Intercollegiate - NAIA. Intramural sports - yes. *Counseling and guidance:* Personal. Faculty advisors - nd. Tutoring - nd. *Special services/academic programs for:* Educationally disadvantaged - nd, physically disabled - nd, learning disabled - nd.
FRESHMAN ADMISSION STANDARDS: High school units: Total required - nd. Recommended: English - 4, social science/history - 2, foreign language - 2, laboratory science - 1, mathematics - 3, visual and performing arts - 1.
1993-94 FRESHMAN ADMISSION DATA: *Applications:* Received - 346, accepted - 274, enrolled - 146. *SAT Scores:* Average verbal/mathematics scores - 476/532, median verbal/mathematics scores - nd/nd. Verbal/mathematics scores of enrolled freshmen: Middle 50% scored 410-530 verbal, 470-590 mathematics, 880-1120 combined verbal and mathematics. 0%/4% scored 700-800, 8%/19% scored 600-699, 32%/42% scored 500-599, 44%/27% scored 400-499, 16%/8% scored 300-399. *ACT composite score:* Average - 22, median - nd. *High school GPA:* Average GPA - 3.67. *Class rank:* 51% in top 10%, 87% in top 25%, 100% in top 50%. *International students:* Minimum TOEFL score required - nd.
TRANSFER ADMISSION STANDARDS: *Transfer units required:* Minimum - none, maximum - 94. *Minimum college GPA* - 2.00. *Grades accepted:* Credit, Pass. D not accepted.
1993-94 TRANSFER ADMISSION DATA: *Applications:* Received - 230, accepted - 182, enrolled - 114. CCC transfer students enrolled - nd.
ADMISSION PROCEDURES: *Entrance tests:* SAT I: Reasoning Test or ACT required. Test deadline for fall admission - June. *Application process:* Students admitted each term. Deadlines: Freshmen and transfers - rolling. Application fee - $30. Fee waiver - yes. *Recommendations:* 1 - Pastor or teacher. *Interview* - at request of admissions committee. *Admission notification* - rolling after 2/15. Commitment deposit - $50 due thirty days after notice of admission. *Advanced placement offered* - yes. *Advanced credit given* - yes. *Early decision procedure:* Application deadline - 1/1, notification - nd.
1994-95 COSTS: *Total costs* (approximate) - $14,374. Tuition -$9,900, other significant fees - $174, room and board - $3,670, total books, supplies, incidentals (approximate) - $630.
UNDERGRADUATE FINANCIAL AID: Students receiving financial aid - 95%. Submit FAFSA by 3/2. Application deadline for institutional scholarships and grants - 3/2. Average financial aid package - $9,112.
OTHER INFORMATION: *Founded* - 1944. *Nonprofit* - yes. *WASC Accredited* - yes. *Member of AICCU* - yes.

GOLDEN GATE UNIVERSITY

536 Mission Street
San Francisco, California 94105
Admissions: (415) 442-7200
Financial Aid: (415) 442-7270
Fax: (415) 495-2671
Toll Free: nd

Non-Residential University Specializing in Business, Public Administration, and Law

DISTINGUISHING FEATURES: Golden Gate University is an institution in the work/study tradition offering day and evening classes. The majority of students study part-time and are working adult transfer students wishing to complete their degrees. Emphasis is on the case-study method of instruction in a curriculum of professional education in business management, public administration, and law.
DEGREES OFFERED: Associates, Bachelor's, Master's, First Professional, Doctoral, Juris Doctor (Law).
SPECIAL PROGRAMS: Optional Cooperative Education program with parallel study and employment terms. English Language Skills Center for immigrants and international students. TOEFL preparation. *Education abroad* - no. *Honors programs* - no.
COLLEGES: Schools of Accounting, Finance, Humanities and Social Sciences, Law, Management, Public Administration, Taxation, Technology Management.
UNDERGRADUATE MAJOR: See this chapter: Undergraduate Degree Majors, page 12--76. Preprofessional programs: Pre-Legal Studies.
CALENDAR: Trimester system - fall, spring, summer. Three fifteen-week terms each year.
FACULTY: Full-time - 60, part-time - 448. Undergraduate classes taught by faculty, not graduate assistants - all. Faculty with Ph.D.'s - 60% of full-time. Student/faculty ratio - 16/1. Average class size - nd.
ENROLLMENT: *Total* - 6,934. *Graduate* - 3,960 *Undergraduate* - 2,066: California residents - 80%, out-of-state - 1%, other countries - 19%. Men - 46%, women - 54%. *Ethnic distribution of undergraduate students:* Hispanic - 7%, Black - 11%, Asian/Pacific Islander - 16%, Native American/Alaskan - 1%, White - 63%. *Freshmen graduating within 5 years* - 60%.
LOCATION: In the San Francisco financial district with branch campuses throughout California.
CAMPUS LIFE: *On-campus housing:* Spaces - 0, undergraduate residential students - 0%. *Clubs and organizations* - 25. Fraternities and sororities - 0. *Athletics:* Intercollegiate - no. Intramural sports - no. *Counseling and guidance:* Academic, personal, career planning, job placement. Faculty advisors - yes. Tutoring - yes. *Special services/academic programs for:* Educationally disadvantaged - yes, physically disabled - yes, learning disabled - no.
FRESHMAN ADMISSION STANDARDS: College-preparatory pattern recommended. High school units: Total required - nd. English - nd, social science/history - nd, foreign language - nd, laboratory science - nd, mathematics - nd. Motivation and ability to benefit from educational programs taken into consideration.
1993-94 FRESHMAN ADMISSION DATA: *Applications:* Received - 83, accepted - 54, enrolled - 24. *SAT scores:* nd. *ACT composite score:* nd. *High school GPA:* Average GPA - 3.20.

nd = no data available   na = not applicable

3.00 minimum required, 3.20 for School of Accounting and the School of Taxation. ***Class rank:*** nd. ***International students:*** Minimum TOEFL score required - 525.
TRANSFER ADMISSION STANDARDS: ***Transfer units required:*** Minimum - none, maximum - 70. ***Minimum college GPA*** - 2.00. ***Grades accepted*** - credit in electives only. D's not accepted.
1993-94 TRANSFER ADMISSION DATA: ***Applications:*** Received - 465, accepted - 427, enrolled - 300. CCC transfer students enrolled - 150.
ADMISSION PROCEDURES: ***Entrance tests:*** SAT I: Reasoning Test or ACT not required. Test deadline for fall admission - na. ***Application process:*** Students admitted each term. Deadlines: Freshmen - rolling, transfers and international - six weeks before opening. Application fee - $40-50. Fee waiver - no. ***Recommendations:*** Helpful, but not required - principal, counselor, teachers, employers. ***Interview*** - recommended when feasible. ***Admission notification*** - rolling. Commitment deposit - $0. ***Advanced placement offered*** - yes. ***Advanced credit given*** - yes. ***Early decision procedure*** - no.
1994-95 COSTS: ***Total costs*** (approximate) - $17,430. Tuition - $7,350 (based on $245 per semester unit/30 units per year), other significant fees - $300, room and board - $9,180 (estimate for single person in San Francisco area), total books, supplies, incidentals (approximate) - $600.
UNDERGRADUATE FINANCIAL AID: Students receiving financial aid - 21%. Submit FAFSA (CSS version preferred), FAF, and institutional applications by 3/2. Application deadline for institutional scholarships and grants - priority deadline - 3/2. Average financial aid package - $4,840.
OTHER INFORMATION: ***Founded*** - 1901. ***Nonprofit*** - yes. ***WASC Accredited*** - yes. ***Member of AICCU*** - yes.

HARVEY MUDD COLLEGE

301 East 12th Street
Claremont, California 91711
Admissions: (9094) 621-8011
Financial Aid: (909) 621-8055
Fax: (909) 621-8360
Toll Free: nd

A Highly Selective, Small Residential College of Engineering, Physical Sciences, and Mathematics. A Member of the Claremont Colleges

DISTINGUISHING FEATURES: As one of the six Claremont Colleges, Harvey Mudd College has course choices, activities, and facilities usually found only in a large university. Although the curriculum is focused on mathematics, science, and engineering, a third of the academic program is in the humanities and social sciences. An honor code sets the tone allowing for take-home examinations and twenty-four hour access to all laboratories and facilities. Freshmen are graded Pass/Fail during their first semester of study. Majors are not chosen until the fourth semester. The school emphasizes hands-on experience and most students carry out research for at least one year.
DEGREES OFFERED: Bachelor's, Master's.
SPECIAL PROGRAMS: Engineering and Mathematics Clinics where small project teams of juniors and seniors solve real, company industrial problems. Broad range of undergraduate research opportunities. Individual program of study available. ***Education abroad*** - may participate in Pomona College Study Abroad program to fourteen different countries. ***Honors programs*** - yes.
COLLEGES: na.
UNDERGRADUATE MAJORS: 6 majors. Biology, Chemistry, Computer Science, Engineering, Mathematics, Physics. Individual program of study. See this chapter: Undergraduate Degree Majors, page 12--76. Preprofessional programs: All programs lead to professional degrees.
CALENDAR: Semester system. Summer sessions.
FACULTY: Full-time - 70, part-time - 31. Undergraduate classes taught by faculty, not graduate assistants - all. Faculty with Ph.D.'s - 100% of full-time. Student/faculty ratio - 8/1. Average class size - 16.
ENROLLMENT: ***Total*** - 666. ***Graduate*** - 12. ***Undergraduate*** - 654: California residents - 49%, out-of-state - 49%, other countries - 2%. Men - 77%, women - 23%. ***Ethnic distribution of undergraduate students:*** Hispanic - 4.0%, Black - 2.0%, Asian/Pacific Islander - 22%, Native American/Alaskan - 1%, White - 72%. ***Freshmen graduating within 5 years*** - 78%.
LOCATION: Shares 500 acres with the other Claremont Colleges in the residential suburban community of Claremont about forty-five minutes east of downtown Los Angeles. Set at the base of the San Gabriel foothills. Skiing and hiking nearby. Beaches and the desert an hour away.
CAMPUS LIFE: Students live off campus only with College's permission. Freshmen required to live on campus. ***On-campus housing:*** Spaces - 550, undergraduate residential students - 97%. ***Clubs and organizations*** - 50. Fraternities and sororities - 0. ***Athletics:*** Intercollegiate - in cooperation with Claremont McKenna and Scripps Colleges, NCAA Division III. Intramural sports - yes. ***Counseling and guidance:*** Academic, personal, career planning, job placement. Faculty advisors - yes. Tutoring - yes. Residence hall proctors. ***Special services/academic programs for:*** Educationally disadvantaged - yes, physically disabled - yes, learning disabled - yes.
FRESHMAN ADMISSION STANDARDS: High school units: Total required - nd. English - 4, social science/history - 1 encouraged, foreign language - 2 encouraged, laboratory science - 2 (chemistry and physics required, 1 biology recommended), mathematics - 4 through calculus. Advanced Placement courses are strongly encouraged.
1993-94 FRESHMAN ADMISSION DATA: ***Applications:*** Received - 1,377, accepted - 572, enrolled - 178. ***SAT Scores:*** Average verbal/mathematics scores - nd/nd, median verbal/mathematics scores - nd/nd. Verbal/mathematics scores of enrolled freshmen: Middle 50% scored 580-690 verbal, 710-770 mathematics. 21%/85% scored 700-800, 53%/15% scored 600-699, 24%/0% scored 500-599, 2%/0% scored 400-499. ***ACT composite score:*** Average - nd, median - nd. ***High school GPA:*** Average GPA - nd. 95% with 3.50-4.00. ***Class rank:*** 90% in top 10%, 100% in top 20%. Students have always earned top grades in mathematics and science and have usually done well in other areas. 33% are National Merit Scholars. ***International students:*** Minimum TOEFL score required - 600.
TRANSFER ADMISSION STANDARDS: ***Transfer units required:*** Minimum - varies, maximum - varies. ***Minimum college GPA*** - 3.50. ***Grades accepted*** - B plus or better.
1993-94 TRANSFER ADMISSION DATA: ***Applications:*** Received - 63, accepted - 13, enrolled - 7. CCC transfer students enrolled - nd

nd = no data available   na = not applicable

ADMISSION PROCEDURES: ***Entrance tests:*** SAT I: Reasoning Test or ACT and three SAT II: Subject Tests - Writing, Mathematics Level IIC, and a third one of applicant's choice required. Test deadline for fall admission - January or earlier. ***Application process:*** Students admitted for fall only. Deadlines: Freshmen and transfers -2/1 firm. Application fee - $40. Fee waiver - yes. ***Recommendations:*** 3 - counselor, and 2 teachers in mathematics or science. ***Interview*** - strongly recommended, not required. ***Admission notification*** - fixed 4/1. Commitment deposit - $100 due 5/1. ***Advanced placement offered*** - yes. ***Advanced credit given*** - yes. ***Early decision procedure:*** Application deadline - all credentials by 12/1, notification - early January.

1994-95 COSTS: ***Total costs*** (approximate) - $25,986. Tuition - $17,230, other significant fees - $466, room and board - $6,690, total books, supplies, incidentals (approximate) - $1,600.

UNDERGRADUATE FINANCIAL AID: Students receiving financial aid - 71%. Submit FAFSA, FAF, and institutional applications by 2/1. Application deadline for institutional scholarships and grants - 2/1. Average financial aid package - $15,604.

OTHER INFORMATION: ***Founded*** - 1955. ***Nonprofit*** - yes. ***WASC Accredited*** - yes. ***Member of AICCU*** - yes.

HOLY NAMES COLLEGE

3500 Mountain Boulevard
Oakland, California 94619
Admissions: (510) 436-1321
Financial Aid: (510) 436-1327
Fax: (510) 436-1199
Toll Free: nd

Liberal Arts, Career-Oriented, Catholic College

DISTINGUISHING FEATURES: HNC is owned and operated by the Sisters of the Holy Names. The school emphasizes an integrated liberal arts foundation and strong majors in the humanities and sciences. Writing skills are developed during all four college years. Personal attention is provided both in and out of the classroom and faculty-student mentor relationships are strong. The value of service to others is stressed. Classes are taught in traditional and weekend schedules. The Weekend College (WECO) offers working adults a Bachelor's or Master's degree with classes on Friday nights and Saturdays.

DEGREES OFFERED: Certificate, Bachelor's, Master's, Credential.

SPECIAL PROGRAMS: Emphasis on writing skills. A demanding Humanistic Studies core program traces human experience across centuries and continents. Dual-degree program: 3-2 in Mathematics/Engineering and Science/Engineering with UC Berkeley. Exchange programs with Anna Maria College, Paxton, MA; Central College, IA. Cross-registration available with UC Berkeley; Mills College; St. Mary's College, Moraga; CSU Hayward; California College of Arts and Crafts; Peralta Community College District. May design own course of study. Career internships. ***Education abroad:*** Exchange program with Kansai University, Osaka, Japan. Junior year abroad or other international study programs available. ***Honors programs*** - yes.

COLLEGES: na

UNDERGRADUATE MAJORS: 21 majors. See this chapter: Undergraduate Degree Majors, page 12--76. Preprofessional programs: Health Sciences, Law, Medical Technology, Medicine.

CALENDAR: Semester system. Trimester system for WECO. Summer session.

FACULTY: Full-time - 44, part-time - 81. Undergraduate classes taught by faculty, not graduate assistants - all. Faculty with Ph.D.'s - 75%. Student/faculty ratio - 11/1. Average class size - nd.

ENROLLMENT: ***Total*** - 964. ***Graduate*** - 374. Undergraduate - 590: California residents - 81%, out-of-state and other countries - 19%. Men - 24%, women - 76%. ***Ethnic distribution of undergraduate students:*** Hispanic - 9%, Black - 25%, Asian/Pacific Islander - 7%, Native American/Alaskan - 1%, White - 35%. ***Freshmen graduating within 5 years*** - 40%.

LOCATION: 60-acre, wooded campus in the Oakland Hills overlooking San Francisco Bay and the city of San Francisco. Easy access to activities within the Bay Area.

CAMPUS LIFE: All freshmen not living with family must live on campus. ***On-campus housing:*** Spaces - 300, undergraduate residential students - 34%. ***Clubs and organizations*** - 15. Fraternities and sororities - 0. ***Athletics:*** Intercollegiate - NAIA. Intramural sports - yes. ***Counseling and guidance:*** Academic, personal, career planning, job placement. Faculty advisors - yes. Tutoring - yes. Team and campus ministry. ***Special services/academic programs for:*** Educationally disadvantaged - no, physically disabled - no, learning disabled - yes.

FRESHMAN ADMISSION STANDARDS: High school units: Total required - 15 including: English - 4, social science/history - 1, foreign language - 2 (preferably 3 in same language), laboratory science - 1, mathematics - 3 (algebra 1 and 2 and geometry), additional academic electives for a total of 15 units.

1993-94 FRESHMAN ADMISSION DATA: ***Applications:*** Received - 258, accepted - 157, enrolled - 43. ***SAT scores:*** Minimum total score requirement of 880. Average verbal/mathematics scores - 448/450, median verbal/mathematics scores - nd/nd. Verbal/mathematics scores of enrolled freshmen: Middle 50% scored 400-470 verbal, 390-500 mathematics, 790-970 combined verbal and mathematics. 0%/0% scored above 600, 8%/33% scored 500-599, 67%/29% scored 400-499, 21%/38% scored 300-399, 4%/0% scored 200-299. ***ACT composite score:*** Average - nd, median - nd. Minimum requirement of 21. ***High school GPA:*** Average GPA - 2.95. Minimum requirement of 2.80. ***Class rank:*** nd. ***International students:*** Minimum TOEFL score required - 500.

TRANSFER ADMISSION STANDARDS: ***Transfer units required:*** Minimum - 12, maximum - 66. ***Minimum college GPA*** - 2.20 with fewer than 30 units, 2.10 with 30 or more units. ***Grades accepted*** - nd.

1993-94 TRANSFER ADMISSION DATA: ***Applications:*** Received - 100, accepted - 70, enrolled - 31. CCC transfer students enrolled - nd.

ADMISSION PROCEDURES: ***Entrance tests:*** SAT I: Reasoning Test or ACT required. Test deadline for fall admission - prior to term of enrollment. ***Application process:*** Students admitted each term. Deadlines: Freshmen and transfers - 8/1 for fall, 1/1 for spring. Application fee - $35. Fee waiver - yes. ***Recommendations:*** 2. ***Interview*** - recommended, not required. ***Admission notification*** - rolling. Commitment deposit - $100. ***Advanced placement offered*** - yes. ***Advanced credit given*** - yes. ***Early decision procedure*** - no.

1994-95 COSTS: ***Total costs*** (approximate) - $17,850. Tuition - $11,480, other significant fees - $460, room and board - $5,280, total books, supplies, incidentals (approximate) - $630.

UNDERGRADUATE FINANCIAL AID: Students receiving fi-

nd = no data available   na = not applicable

nancial aid - 75%, 95% of enrolled freshman who applied for aid received financial aid. Submit FAFSA and institutional applications by 3/2. Application deadline for institutional scholarships and grants - priority deadline - 3/2. Average financial aid package - $9,191.
OTHER INFORMATION: ***Founded*** - 1868. ***Nonprofit*** - yes. ***WASC Accredited*** - yes. ***Member of AICCU*** - yes.

HUMPHREYS COLLEGE

6650 Inglewood Avenue (at Benjamin Holt Drive)
Stockton, California 95207
Admissions: (209) 478-0800
Financial Aid: (209) 478-0800
Fax: (209) 478-8721
Toll Free: nd

Two- and Four-Year College of Business, Law, and Liberal Arts

DISTINGUISHING FEATURES: Humphreys College focuses on preparing students for the legal and business professions as lawyers, paralegals, court reporters, legal and executive administrative assistants, business managers, accountants, and computer programmers. Students learn real world problem solving skills while actively pursuing the opportunities afforded by a quality, career-oriented education. Liberal arts is an important part of every academic program. Satellite campuses are located in Sacramento and Modesto.
DEGREES OFFERED: Certificate, Associates, Bachelor's, Juris Doctor (Law).
SPECIAL PROGRAMS: ***Education abroad*** - no. ***Honors programs*** - no.
COLLEGES: na.
UNDERGRADUATE MAJORS: 7 majors. Accounting, Business Management, Computer Management Information Systems, Court-Reporting, Liberal Arts, Office Administration, Paralegal Studies. See this chapter: Undergraduate Degree Majors, page 12--76. Preprofessional programs: Accounting, Law.
CALENDAR: Quarter system. Summer session.
FACULTY: Full-time - 29, part-time - 39. Undergraduate classes taught by faculty, not graduate assistants - all. Faculty with Ph.D.'s - 38%. Student/faculty ratio - 11/1. Average class size - 17.
ENROLLMENT: ***Total*** - 855. ***Graduate*** - 94. ***Undergraduate*** - 761: California residents - 97%, out-of-state - 3%, other countries - 1%. Men - 18%, women - 82%. ***Ethnic distribution of undergraduate students:*** Hispanic - 16%, Black - 8%, Asian/Pacific Islander - 8%, Native American/Alaskan - 2%, White - 66%. ***Freshmen graduating within 5 years*** - 50%.
LOCATION: 7-acre campus within the suburban area of north Stockton in California's central-valley delta. Forty miles south of Sacramento, one-and-one-half hours east of San Francisco.
CAMPUS LIFE: ***On-campus housing:*** Spaces - 64, undergraduate residential students - 10%. ***Clubs and organizations*** -5. Fraternities and sororities - 0. ***Athletics:*** Intercollegiate - no. Intramural sports - yes. ***Counseling and guidance:*** Academic, career planning, job placement. Faculty advisors - yes. Tutoring - yes. ***Special services/academic programs for:*** Educationally disadvantaged - yes, physically disabled - yes, learning disabled - yes.
FRESHMAN ADMISSION STANDARDS: High school diploma or equivalent required. College preparatory program recommended. Open enrollment. High school units: Total required - nd. English - nd, social science/history - nd, foreign language - nd, laboratory science - nd, mathematics - nd.
1993-94 FRESHMAN ADMISSION DATA: ***Applications:*** Received - 92, accepted - 92, enrolled - 84. ***SAT scores:*** nd. ***ACT composite score:*** nd. ***High school GPA:*** Average GPA - nd. ***Class rank:*** nd. ***International students:*** Minimum TOEFL score required - 450.
TRANSFER ADMISSION STANDARDS: ***Transfer units required:*** Minimum - 0, maximum - 96. ***Minimum college GPA*** - 2.00. ***Grades accepted*** - Credit/No Credit grades in electives only. D's not accepted in required courses or in courses that are prerequisites to other required courses.
1993-94 TRANSFER ADMISSION DATA: ***Applications:*** Received - 110, accepted - 110, enrolled - 102. CCC transfer students enrolled - nd.
ADMISSION PROCEDURES: ***Entrance tests:*** SAT I: Reasoning Test or ACT recommended, not required. Test deadline for fall admission - nd. ***Application process:*** Students admitted each term. Deadlines: Freshmen and transfers - Rolling for United States students, ten weeks before opening of term for international students. Application fee - $20. Fee waiver - yes. ***Recommendations:*** Helpful, not required - principal, counselor, teachers, employers. ***Interview*** - recommended. ***Admission notification*** - rolling. Commitment deposit - $20. International students $200. ***Advanced placement offered*** - yes. ***Advanced credit given*** - yes. ***Early decision procedure*** - no.
1994-95 COSTS: ***Total costs*** (approximate) - $10,904. Tuition - $5,082, other significant fees - $0, room and board - $5,010, total books, supplies, incidentals (approximate) - $812.
UNDERGRADUATE FINANCIAL AID: Students receiving financial aid - 81%. Submit FAFSA by 3/2. Application deadline for institutional scholarships and grants - 3/2, priority deadline - 3/2. Average financial aid package - $6,125.
OTHER INFORMATION: ***Founded*** - 1896. ***Nonprofit*** - yes. ***WASC Accredited*** - yes. ***Member of AICCU*** - yes.

ITT TECHNICAL INSTITUTE

9700 Goethe Road
Sacramento, California 95827
(916) 366-3900
Fax: nd
Toll Free: nd

Coeducational Technical Institute With Ten Campuses in California

DISTINGUISHING FEATURES: ITT Technical Institute operates fifty campuses in the United States, ten of them in California. All California campuses offer Computer-Aided Drafting Technology and Electronics Engineering Technology. In addition, each campus offers its own specialized curriculum in technology fields. Day and evening classes are available. ITT emphasizes classroom theory along with hands-on practice.
DEGREES OFFERED: Associate, Bachelor's, depending on the campus.
CALENDAR: Quarter system.
ENROLLMENT: ***Total*** - Each campus has between 400 and 600 students.
LOCATIONS: Buena Park, Carson, Hayward, Oxnard, Sacramento, San Bernardino, San Diego, Santa Clara, Van Nuys, West Covina.

CAMPUS LIFE: ***On-campus housing:*** Spaces - 0.
OTHER INFORMATION: ***Founded*** - 1954. ***Nonprofit*** - no. ***WASC Accredited*** - no. Accredited by the Association of Independent Colleges and Schools and the Career College Association.

JOHN F. KENNEDY UNIVERSITY

12 Altarinda Road
Orinda, California 94563
(510) 254-0200
Fax: (510) 254-6964
Toll Free: nd

University Offering Late Afternoon, Evening, and Weekend Classes for Adult Students

DISTINGUISHING FEATURES: JFK University was established for adult students and offers undergraduate, graduate, and professional programs with late afternoon, evening, and weekend classes. The University is particularly sensitive to life transitions that motivate further education and has developed flexible programs and an array of student services to support such transitions. Most of the students are mature, self-starting adults who maintain home and/or work responsibilities while going to school. They are studying for career change or advancement, re-entering the job market, or for personal growth. The average age of students is thirty-seven. Undergraduate majors are offered in Business Administration and Liberal Studies.
DEGREES OFFERED: Certificate, Bachelor's, Master's, Credential, First Professional, Juris Doctor (Law).
CALENDAR: Quarter system. Summer sessions.
ENROLLMENT: ***Total*** - 1,800. ***Graduate*** - 1,440. ***Undergraduate*** - 356.
LOCATION: Orinda. Other learning centers located in Campbell, Pleasant Hill, and Walnut Creek.
CAMPUS LIFE: ***On-campus housing:*** Spaces - 0.
OTHER INFORMATION: ***Founded*** - 1964. ***Nonprofit*** - yes. ***WASC Accredited*** - yes.

LA SIERRA UNIVERSITY

4700 Pierce Street
Riverside, California 92515
Admissions: (909) 785-2176
Financial Aid: (909) 785-2175
Fax: (909) 785-2901
Toll Free: (800) 874-5587

Seventh-Day Adventist University of the Liberal Arts and Sciences

DISTINGUISHING FEATURES: La Sierra University, formerly Loma Linda University, La Sierra campus, is committed to Christian ideals and values and a wide range of undergraduate programs. The emphasis is on developing each student's full potential — intellectual, social, spiritual, physical. La Sierra has the virtues of a small college combined with the advantages of a multidisciplinary university.
DEGREES OFFERED: Associates, Bachelor's, Master's, Credential, First Professional, Doctoral.
SPECIAL PROGRAMS: Student Missionary Program. Biology courses at Rosario Beach, Washington. Program for guaranteeing a Bachelor's degree in four years. ***Education abroad:*** Extended campus in Hong Kong in Religion and Ministerial Studies. Study tours in South Africa, South America, Antarctica, Middle East. Archaeological excavation at Caesarea Maritima. Year-abroad programs in Austria, France, Spain. ***Honors programs*** - yes.
COLLEGES: College of Arts and Sciences. Schools of Business and Management, Education, Religion.
UNDERGRADUATE MAJORS: 34 majors. In the areas of Liberal Arts, Religion, Natural Science, Social Sciences, Fine Arts, Business, and Education. See this chapter: Undergraduate Degree Majors, page 12--76. Preprofessional programs: Anesthesia, Cytotechnology, Dentistry, Dental Hygiene, Dietetics, Engineering, Law, Medicine, Medical Record Administration, Medical Technology, Nursing, Occupational Therapy, Optometry, Pharmacy, Physical Therapy, Physician's Assistant, Public Health Science, Radiological Technology, Respiratory Therapy, Veterinary Medicine.
CALENDAR: Quarter system. Summer session.
FACULTY: Full-time - 95, part-time - 10. Undergraduate classes taught by faculty, not graduate assistants - all but some freshman composition. Faculty with Ph.D.'s - 75%. Student/faculty ratio - 13/1. Average class size - 12.6.
ENROLLMENT: ***Total*** - 1,469. ***Graduate*** - 151. ***Undergraduate*** - 1,318: California residents - 75%, out-of-state -9%, other countries - 16%. Men - 47%, women - 53%. ***Ethnic distribution of undergraduate students:*** Hispanic - 18%, Black - 7%, Asian/Pacific Islander - 35%, Native American/Alaskan - 1%, White - 39%. ***Freshmen graduating within 5 years*** - nd%.
LOCATION: 350-acre campus in a semi-rural setting fifty miles east of Los Angeles. In the Inland Empire of Southern California.
CAMPUS LIFE: Separate residence halls for men and women. No alcohol, tobacco, drugs, or hallucinogenic drugs permitted. ***On-campus housing:*** Spaces - nd, undergraduate residential students - 50%. ***Clubs and organizations*** - 22. Fraternities and sororities - 0. ***Athletics:*** Intercollegiate - yes. Intramural sports - yes. ***Counseling and guidance:*** Academic, personal, career planning, job placement. Faculty advisors - yes. Tutoring - yes. ***Special services/academic programs for:*** Educationally disadvantaged - yes, physically disabled - yes, learning disabled - yes.
FRESHMAN ADMISSION STANDARDS: High school graduation required. High school units: Total required - na. Recommended: English - 4, social science - 2 (including American and world history), foreign language - 2, laboratory science - 2 (biology and chemistry or physics), mathematics - 2 (algebra 1 and 2, algebra 3 if interested in careers in mathematics, natural sciences, or health sciences), computer literacy and keyboard skills, religion - 1 course per year at a church-related secondary school.
1993-94 FRESHMAN ADMISSION DATA: ***Applications:*** Received - 684, accepted - 576, enrolled - 325. ***SAT scores:*** Average verbal/mathematics scores - 420/468, median verbal/mathematics scores - 410/470. Verbal/mathematics scores of enrolled freshmen: 1%/2% scored 700-800, 6%/11% scored 600-699, 14%/29% scored 500-599, 36%/31% scored 400-499, 32%/22% scored 300-399, 11%/5% scored 200-299. ***ACT composite score:*** Average - 20, median - 20. ***High school GPA:*** Average GPA - 3.20. 69% with 3.00-4.00, 29% with 2.00-2.99, 2% with 1.00-1.99. ***Class rank:*** nd. ***International students:*** Minimum TOEFL score required - 550.

nd = no data available   na = not applicable

CALIFORNIA INDEPENDENT COLLEGES

TRANSFER ADMISSION STANDARDS: ***Transfer units required:*** Minimum - none, maximum - 105 quarter. ***Minimum college GPA*** - 2.00 for most majors. ***Grades accepted*** - D or better.
1993-94 TRANSFER ADMISSION DATA: ***Applications:*** Received - 437, accepted - 305, enrolled - 273. CCC transfer students enrolled - nd.
ADMISSION PROCEDURES: ***Entrance tests:*** SAT I: Reasoning Test or ACT required. Test deadline for fall admission: If GPA is below 2.50, test scores must be submitted as part of application, otherwise prior to registration. ***Application process:*** Students admitted each term. Deadlines: Freshmen and transfers - rolling, 3/1 if applying for financial aid. Application fee - $30. Fee waiver - no. ***Recommendations:*** 3 - 2 teachers, 1 Pastor. ***Interview*** - preferred and may be required. ***Admission notification*** - upon completion of file. Commitment deposit - $0. ***Advanced placement offered*** - yes. ***Advanced credit given*** - yes. ***Early decision procedure*** - no.
1994-95 COSTS: ***Total costs*** (approximate) - $17,027. Tuition - $12,180, other significant fees - $195, room and board - $3,969 total books, supplies, incidentals (approximate) - $683.
UNDERGRADUATE FINANCIAL AID: Students receiving financial aid - 75%. Submit FAFSA (CSS version preferred) and institutional applications by 3/2. Application deadline for institutional scholarships and grants - 5/1, priority deadline - 5/1. Average financial aid package - $12,180.
OTHER INFORMATION: ***Founded*** - 1939. ***Nonprofit*** - yes. ***WASC Accredited*** - yes. ***Member of AICCU*** - yes.

L.I.F.E. BIBLE COLLEGE

1100 Covina Boulevard
San Dimas, California 91773
(909)599-5433
Fax: (909) 599-6690
Toll Free: (800) 356-0001

Small Christian College of Bible Study

DISTINGUISHING FEATURES: L.I.F.E. Bible College emphasizes the Bible, doctrine, and ministry. Majors are offered in Bible and Theology. Within the majors students can concentrate on pastoral ministry, Biblical languages, cross-cultural ministry, Christian teaching, Christian formation, and youth ministry. Student ministry involvement is an integral part of all programs.
DEGREES OFFERED: Bachelor's.
CALENDAR: Semester system.
ENROLLMENT: ***Total*** - 370.
LOCATION: One hour east of Los Angeles near the Los Angeles National Forest and its recreational facilities.
CAMPUS LIFE: ***On-campus housing:*** Spaces - available.
OTHER INFORMATION: ***Founded*** - 1925. ***Nonprofit*** - yes. ***WASC Accredited*** - no. Accredited by the Accrediting Association of Bible Colleges.

LINCOLN UNIVERSITY

281 Masonic Avenue
San Francisco, California 94118
(415) 221-1212
Fax: (415) 387-9730
Toll Free: nd

Small College of Business Administration with an International and Intercultural Orientation

DISTINGUISHING FEATURES: Lincoln University has from its inception maintained an international and intercultural orientation. Accordingly, the University has sought to provide an international setting for its students. The geographical and historical influence of San Francisco has brought many Asian students to the College. The Lincoln student is encouraged to be intellectually curious in pursuit of knowledge and understanding of cultural differences and similarities, and serious in efforts to find solutions to the problems of the world today. Students from the United States, and many Asian, African, European, and Latin American countries are enrolled in the college. A comprehensive English as a Second Language (ESL) program is provided by the college for international students. Majors are offered in Computer Science and in Business Administration with concentrations in Accounting, Economics, Information Science, International Business, Management.
DEGREES OFFERED: Bachelor's, Master's, First Professional.
CALENDAR: Semester system. Summer session.
ENROLLMENT: ***Total*** - 400.
LOCATION: Near the heart of San Francisco.
CAMPUS LIFE: ***On-campus housing:*** Spaces - 0.
OTHER INFORMATION: ***Founded*** - 1919. ***Nonprofit*** - yes. ***WASC Accredited*** - no. Accredited by the Association of Independent Colleges and Schools.

LOMA LINDA UNIVERSITY

Loma Linda, California 92350
(909) 824-4300
Fax: (909) 824-4577
Toll Free: (800) 422-4558

Seventh-day Adventist University for Upper-Division, Graduate , and First Professional Students

DISTINGUISHING FEATURES: There are no freshmen at Loma Linda University. All undergraduates are transfer and graduate students. The university is organized into six schools, the Schools of Allied Health Professions, Dentistry, Graduate, Medicine, Nursing, and Public Health. The Schools of Allied Health Professions, Dentistry, and Nursing accept undergraduates. Undergraduate majors are Clinical Laboratory Science, Dental Hygiene, Health Information Administration, Nursing, Nutrition and Dietetics, Occupational Therapy, Physical Therapy, Radiation Technology, Respiratory Therapy, and Speech-Language Pathology and Audiology.
DEGREES OFFERED: Bachelor's, Master's, Credential, First Professional, Doctoral.

CALENDAR: Quarter system. Summer sessions.
ENROLLMENT: ***Total*** - 2,914. ***Graduate*** - 1,754. ***Undergraduate*** - 1,160.
LOCATION: Seventy miles east of Los Angeles in the San Bernardino area.
CAMPUS LIFE: ***On-campus housing:*** Spaces - residence halls.
OTHER INFORMATION: ***Founded*** - 1905. ***Nonprofit*** - yes. ***WASC Accredited*** - yes. ***Member of AICCU*** - yes.

LOUISE SALINGER ACADEMY OF FASHION

101 Jessie Street
San Francisco, California 94105
(415) 974-6666
Fax: nd
Toll Free: nd

Small College Preparing Students for Careers as Fashion Designers and Merchandisers

DISTINGUISHING FEATURES: The Louise Salinger Academy of Fashion prepares students for careers in fashion designing and/or merchandising. Majors are offered in Fashion Design, Fashion Merchandising, Millinery, Pattern Drafting, and Theatre Costume Construction.
DEGREES OFFERED: Certificate, Associates, Bachelor's.
CALENDAR: Quarter system.
ENROLLMENT: ***Total*** - Less than 100.
LOCATION: Centrally located in the city of San Francisco.
CAMPUS LIFE: ***On-campus housing:*** Spaces - 0.
OTHER INFORMATION: ***Founded*** - 1939. ***Nonprofit*** - yes. ***WASC Accredited*** - no. Accredited by the Career College Association.

LOYOLA MARYMOUNT UNIVERSITY

Loyola Boulevard at West 80th Street
Los Angeles, California 90045
Admissions: (310) 338-2750
Financial Aid: (310) 338-2753
Fax: (310) 338-2797 Admissions
Fax: (310) 338-2793 Financial Aid
Toll Free: (800) LMU-INFO

Catholic University of Liberal Arts and Sciences

DISTINGUISHING FEATURES: LMU is the eighth largest of the nation's twenty-eight Jesuit colleges and universities and the only one in Southern California. It is committed to academic excellence and education for leadership and service. Loyola Marymount offers intensive study in a major and a distinctive core curriculum in the liberal arts and sciences. Strong programs are provided in Liberal Arts, and preprofessional and professional programs in Business, Engineering, Science, Fine Arts, and Communication Arts in Television and Film. In the last three years, eighty-five percent of LMU Science majors applying to professional health and medical schools have been accepted.
DEGREES OFFERED: Bachelor's, Master's, Credential, First Professional, Juris Doctor (Law).
SPECIAL PROGRAMS: Career internships. Service organizations. Nationally ranked debate team. ***Education abroad:*** Affiliated programs available in over ten countries including Austria, England, France, Germany, Ireland, Japan, Spain, and Venezuela. Junior semester or year abroad. LMU programs in England, Germany, and Mexico. ***Honors programs*** - yes.
COLLEGES: Colleges of Liberal Arts, Science and Engineering, Business Administration, Communication and Fine Arts. Loyola Law School.
UNDERGRADUATE MAJORS: 39 majors. See this chapter: Undergraduate Degree Majors, page 12--76. Preprofessional programs: Business, Engineering, Science, Fine Arts, Communication Arts.
CALENDAR: Semester system. Summer session.
FACULTY: Full-time - nd, part-time - nd. Undergraduate classes taught by faculty, not graduate assistants - all. Faculty with Ph.D.'s - 88%. Student/faculty ratio - 15/1. Average class size - nd.
ENROLLMENT: ***Total*** - 6,251. ***Graduate*** - 2,427. ***Undergraduate*** - 3,824: California residents - 81%, out-of-state and other countries - 19%. Men - 44%, women - 56%. ***Ethnic distribution of undergraduate students:*** Minority - 42%. Hispanic - nd%, Black - nd%, Asian/Pacific Islander - nd%, Native American/Alaskan - nd%, White - 58%. ***Freshmen graduating within 5 years*** - nd%.
LOCATION: 128-acre, hilltop mesa above Marina del Rey in a residential neighborhood close to metropolitan Los Angeles.
CAMPUS LIFE: ***On-campus housing:*** Spaces - 1,264 plus 502 apartments, undergraduate residential students - 48%. ***Clubs and organizations*** - 103. Fraternities and sororities - 10. ***Athletics:*** Intercollegiate - NCAA Division I-AAA. Intramural sports - yes. ***Counseling and guidance:*** Academic, personal, career planning, job placement. Faculty advisors - yes. Tutoring - yes. ***Special services/academic programs for:*** Educationally disadvantaged - no, physically disabled - yes, learning disabled - no.
FRESHMAN ADMISSION STANDARDS: High school units: Total required - 16. English - 4, social science/history - 3, foreign language - 3, laboratory science - 3, mathematics - 3. Additional electives to total 16 units. Engineering, Mathematics, and Science majors require additional mathematics and science.
1993-94 FRESHMAN ADMISSION DATA: ***Applications:*** Received - nd, accepted - nd, enrolled - 753. ***SAT Scores:*** Average verbal/mathematics scores - nd, median verbal/mathematics scores - nd. Verbal/mathematics scores of enrolled freshmen: Middle 50% scored 420-530 verbal, 480-600 mathematics, 900-1130 combined verbal and mathematics. nd% scored 700-800, nd% scored 600-699, nd% scored 500-599, nd% scored 400-499, nd% scored 300-399. ***ACT composite score:*** Average - nd, median - nd. ***High school GPA:*** Average GPA - 3.20. ***Class rank:*** nd. ***International students:*** Minimum TOEFL score required - 550.
TRANSFER ADMISSION STANDARDS: ***Transfer units required:*** Minimum - 30. Maximum - 90. ***Minimum college GPA*** - 2.75 for most majors. ***Grades accepted*** - C or better. Credit, Pass in electives.
1993-94 TRANSFER ADMISSION DATA: ***Applications:*** Received - nd, accepted - nd, enrolled - 402. CCC transfer students enrolled - nd.

nd = no data available   na = not applicable

ADMISSION PROCEDURES: ***Entrance tests:*** SAT I: Reasoning Test or ACT required. Test deadline for fall admission - by January preferred. ***Application process:*** Students admitted each term. Deadlines: Freshmen - rolling, priority date for fall - 2/1, for spring - 12/1, transfers - rolling, priority date for fall - 7/1, for spring - 12/1. Application fee - $35. Fee waiver - yes. ***Recommendations:*** 1 - principal or counselor. ***Interview*** - recommended, not required. ***Admission notification*** - rolling, two to three weeks upon completion of file. Commitment deposit - $200 plus $200 for housing due 5/1. ***Advanced placement offered*** - yes. ***Advanced credit given*** - yes. ***Early decision procedure:*** Application deadline - 12/1, notification - nd.

1994-95 COSTS: ***Total costs*** (approximate) - $20,229. Tuition - $13,592, other significant fees - $176, room and board - $5,916 average, total books, supplies, incidentals (approximate) - $545.

UNDERGRADUATE FINANCIAL AID: Students receiving financial aid - 59%. Submit FAFSA and FAF applications by 2/15 for fall term. Application deadline for institutional scholarships and grants - 2/15 for fall term. Average financial aid package - $14,000. Academic scholarships covering full tuition or half-tuition available for incoming freshmen.

OTHER INFORMATION: ***Founded*** - 1914. ***Nonprofit*** - yes. ***WASC Accredited*** - yes. ***Member of AICCU*** - yes.

MARYMOUNT COLLEGE

30800 Palos Verdes Drive East
Rancho Palos Verdes, California 90275
Admissions: (310) 377-5501, Ext. 208
Financial Aid: (310) 377-5501, Ext. 217
Fax: (310) 377-6223
Toll Free: nd

Two-Year Catholic, Liberal Arts College

DISTINGUISHING FEATURES: Marymount College is a small, residential Catholic College that welcomes students of all faiths. It provides the first two years of college study for students wishing to build their academic skills while completing lower-division requirements in a small campus environment. Ninety-five percent of its graduates go on to finish their last two years at a four-year institution. Marymount offers small classes with eighty-five percent of the classes having fewer than twenty-five students; there is a class limit of thirty-five.

DEGREES OFFERED: Associates.

SPECIAL PROGRAMS: Program for students who have completed two or more years of high school and seek early admission to college. ESL program that does not require TOEFL for admission. ***Education abroad:*** Study/travel courses during the interim session and during the summer. Sophomore semester abroad at Regents College, London. Individual study-abroad opportunities in such countries as England, Hong Kong, Kenya, People's Republic of China, Portugal, Russia, Spain, Taiwan. ***Honors programs*** - yes.

COLLEGES: na.

UNDERGRADUATE MAJORS: 39 majors. See this chapter. Undergraduate Degree Majors, page 12--76. Preprofessional programs: Dentistry, Law, Medicine, Pharmacy, Veterinary Medicine.

CALENDAR: 4-1-4 system, one month interim session in January. Summer sessions.

FACULTY: Full-time - 56, part-time - 27. Undergraduate classes taught by faculty, not graduate assistants - all. Faculty with Ph.D.'s - 30%. Student/faculty ratio - 16/1. Average class size - 17.

ENROLLMENT: ***Total*** - 1,087. ***Graduate*** - 0. ***Undergraduate*** - 1,087: California residents - 64%, out-of-state - 13%, other countries - 23%. Men - 48%, women - 52%. ***Ethnic distribution of undergraduate students:*** Hispanic - 17.5%, Black - 5.2%, Asian/Pacific Islander - 8.4%, Native American/Alaskan - 1.0%, White - 50%. ***Freshmen graduating within 5 years*** - 70%.

LOCATION: 22-acre campus on the bluffs of the Palos Verdes Peninsula overlooking the Pacific Ocean and Catalina Island. Forty minutes from downtown Los Angeles and twenty minutes from Long Beach.

CAMPUS LIFE: ***On-campus housing:*** Spaces - 240, undergraduate residential students - 30%. ***Clubs and organizations*** - 20. Fraternities and sororities - 0. ***Athletics:*** Intercollegiate - yes. Intramural sports - yes. ***Counseling and guidance:*** Academic, personal, career planning, job placement. Faculty advisors - yes, and peer counselors. Tutoring - yes. ***Special services/academic programs for:*** Educationally disadvantaged - yes, physically disabled - no, learning disabled - yes.

FRESHMAN ADMISSION STANDARDS: High school diploma or equivalent required. High school units: Total required - depends on program student wishes to enter - Early College, regular Freshmen, or Transfer. College prep curriculum that emphasizes reading, writing skills, and some math recommended. English - nd, social science/history - nd, foreign language - nd, laboratory science - nd, mathematics - nd.

1993-94 FRESHMAN ADMISSION DATA: ***Applications:*** Received - 871, accepted - 740, enrolled - 388. ***SAT scores:*** Average verbal/mathematics scores - nd/nd, median verbal/mathematics scores - nd/nd. Verbal/mathematics scores of enrolled freshmen: Middle 50% scored 340-440 verbal, 320-480 mathematics. ***ACT composite score:*** nd. ***High school GPA:*** Average GPA - 2.50. 31% with 3.00-4.00, 23% with 2.50-2.99, 46% below 2.50. ***Class rank:*** nd. ***International students:*** Minimum TOEFL score required - none.

TRANSFER ADMISSION STANDARDS: ***Transfer units required:*** Minimum - none, maximum - 36. ***Minimum college GPA*** - 2.00. ***Grades accepted*** - A, B, C, D, Credit, Pass.

1993-94 TRANSFER ADMISSION DATA: ***Applications:*** Received - 100, accepted - 93, enrolled - 83. CCC transfer students enrolled - 60.

ADMISSION PROCEDURES: ***Entrance tests:*** SAT I: Reasoning Test recommended for advising purposes. Test deadline for fall admission - nd. ***Application process:*** Students admitted each term. Deadlines: Freshmen and transfers - 8/15. Application fee - $35. Fee waiver - yes. ***Recommendations*** - 1 - teacher or counselor. ***Interview*** - desirable, not required. ***Admission notification*** - rolling. Commitment deposit - $100. ***Advanced placement offered*** - yes. ***Advanced credit given*** - yes. ***Early decision procedure*** - upon request.

1994-95 COSTS: ***Total costs*** (approximate) - $20,414. Tuition - $12,190, other significant fees - $160, room and board - $6,156, total books, supplies, incidentals (approximate) - $1,908.

UNDERGRADUATE FINANCIAL AID: Students receiving financial aid - 45%. Submit FAFSA and institutional applications by 3/1. Application deadline for institutional scholarships and grants - 3/1, priority deadline - 3/1. Average financial aid package - $14,250.

OTHER INFORMATION: ***Founded*** - 1932. ***Nonprofit*** - yes. ***WASC Accredited*** - yes. ***Member of AICCU*** - yes.

THE MASTER'S COLLEGE

21726 West Placerita Canyon Road
P.O. Box 878
Newhall, California 91322
Admissions: (805) 254-6079
Financial Aid: (805) 254-6079
Fax: (805) 254-1998
Toll Free: (800) 568-6248

Liberal Arts Christian College

DISTINGUISHING FEATURES: The Master's College combines academic emphasis with spiritual commitment. The goal is to teach young people how to serve Christ, and the Bible is the centerpiece of all that is studied. All students are involved in an intensive personal discipleship program. Students graduate with a minor in Bible regardless of major. The college offers close faculty-student relationships.
DEGREES OFFERED: Bachelor's, Credential.
SPECIAL PROGRAMS: One-year Bible diploma program called The Master's Institute. Ministry teams. Summer cross-cultural missions. Program for guaranteeing a Bachelor's Degree in four years. ***Education abroad*** - semester in the Holy Land. ***Honors programs*** - no.
COLLEGES: na.
UNDERGRADUATE MAJORS: 13 majors. See this chapter: Undergraduate Degree Majors, page 12--76. Preprofessional programs: Nursing, Seminary.
CALENDAR: Semester system. No summer session.
FACULTY: Full-time - nd, part-time - nd. Undergraduate classes taught by faculty, not graduate assistants - all. Faculty with Ph.D.'s - 43%. Student/faculty ratio - 17/1. Average class size - nd.
ENROLLMENT: ***Total*** - 933. ***Graduate*** - 160. ***Undergraduate*** - 773: California residents - 76%, out-of-state and other countries - 24%. Men - 47%, women - 53%. ***Ethnic distribution of undergraduate students:*** Minority - 14%. Hispanic - nd%, Black - nd%, Asian/Pacific Islander - nd%, Native American/Alaskan - nd%, White - 86%. ***Freshmen graduating within 5 years*** - nd.
LOCATION: 100-acre, tree-filled campus in semi-rural Santa Clarita Valley forty miles north of downtown Los Angeles.
CAMPUS LIFE: Single students not living with parents required to live on campus. ***On-campus housing:*** Spaces - 593, undergraduate residential students - 63%. ***Clubs and organizations*** - 10. Fraternities and sororities - 0. ***Athletics:*** Intercollegiate - NAIA. Intramural sports - yes. ***Counseling and guidance:*** Personal. Faculty advisors - yes. Tutoring - yes. ***Special services/academic programs for:*** Educationally disadvantaged - yes, physically disabled - no, learning disabled - yes.
FRESHMAN ADMISSION STANDARDS: High school units: Total required - 15 including English - 3, social science/history - 2, foreign language - 2, laboratory science - 2, mathematics - 3, electives - 3.
1993-94 FRESHMAN ADMISSION DATA: ***Applications:*** Received - nd, accepted - nd, enrolled - 160. ***SAT Scores:*** Average verbal/mathematics scores - nd/nd, median verbal/mathematics scores - nd. Verbal/mathematics scores of enrolled freshmen: nd% scored 700-800, nd% scored 600-699, nd% scored 500-599, nd% scored 400-499, nd% scored 300-399, nd% scored 200-299. ***ACT composite score:*** Average - nd, median - nd. ***High school GPA:*** Average GPA - 3.27. ***Class rank:*** nd. ***International students:*** Minimum TOEFL score required - 525.
TRANSFER ADMISSION STANDARDS: ***Transfer units required:*** Minimum - 16, maximum - 70 from CCC, 94 from all other colleges. ***Minimum college GPA*** - 2.00. ***Grades accepted*** - C or better.
1993-94 TRANSFER ADMISSION DATA: ***Applications:*** Received - nd, accepted - nd, enrolled - 75. CCC transfer students enrolled - nd.
ADMISSION PROCEDURES: ***Entrance tests:*** SAT I: Reasoning Test or ACT required. Test deadline for fall admission - June. ***Application process:*** Students admitted each term. Deadlines: Freshmen and transfers - 8/15 firm. Application fee - $25. Fee waiver - yes. ***Recommendations:*** 2 - 1 teacher, employer, and 1 Pastor or Youth Pastor. ***Interview*** - no. ***Admission notification*** - rolling. Commitment deposit - $250 due 6/16. ***Advanced placement offered*** - yes. ***Advanced credit given*** - yes. ***Early decision procedure*** - no.
1994-95 COSTS: ***Total costs*** (approximate) - $14,084. Tuition - $9,084, other significant fees - $0, room and board - $4,200, total books, supplies, incidentals (approximate) - $800.
UNDERGRADUATE FINANCIAL AID: Students receiving financial aid - 88%. Submit FAFSA and institutional applications by 3/2. Application deadline for institutional scholarships and grants - 6/1, priority deadline - 3/31. Average financial aid package - $5,995.
OTHER INFORMATION: ***Founded*** - 1927. ***Nonprofit*** - yes. ***WASC Accredited*** - yes. ***Member of AICCU*** - yes.

MENLO COLLEGE

1000 El Camino Real
Atherton, California 94027
Admissions: (415) 688-3753
Financial Aid: (415) 688-3753
Fax: (415) 324-2347
Toll Free: (800) 556-3656

Residential Liberal Arts College

DISTINGUISHING FEATURES: Menlo College emphasizes preparation for careers and the professions in a liberal arts context. The faculty is selected and rewarded for teaching and advising abilities and is devoted to the education of every undergraduate in classes of fewer than fifteen students. This small school is a close-knit community.
DEGREES OFFERED: Bachelor's.
SPECIAL PROGRAMS: Work Internships program emphasized. All students take Menlo Core, the general education curriculum. Freshman Experience program of lectures and seminars. Double majors. ***Education abroad:*** International work internships available. Study abroad during interim session in January. ***Honors programs*** - no.
COLLEGES: School of Business Administration.
UNDERGRADUATE MAJORS: 19 majors. Each major offers a minor and students can mix and match majors and minors. Seven areas of study — Business Administration, Biological Sciences/Biotechnology Management, Communication, Computer Information Systems, Computer Science, Humanities, Psychology/Human Resource Management. See this chapter: Undergraduate Degree Majors, page 12--76. Preprofessional: Biological Science.
CALENDAR: Semester system, January interim session. Summer session.

nd = no data available   na = not applicable

FACULTY: Full-time - 29, part-time - 21. Undergraduate classes taught by faculty, not graduate assistants - all. Faculty with Ph.D.'s - 30%. Student/faculty ratio - 15/1. Average class size - 18.
ENROLLMENT: ***Total*** - 560. ***Graduate*** - 0. ***Undergraduate*** - 560: California residents - 50%, out-of-state - 35%, other countries - 15%. Men - 65%, women - 35%. ***Ethnic distribution of undergraduate students:*** Hispanic - 1%, Black - 4%, Asian/Pacific Islander - 6%, Native American/Alaskan - 0%, White - 74%. ***Freshmen graduating within 5 years*** - 70%.
LOCATION: 62-acre, oak-studded campus located in the suburban town of Atherton, thirty miles south of San Francisco. Within easy reach of high-tech Silicon Valley.
CAMPUS LIFE: Students must live on campus unless twenty-one, or married, or living at home with parents within commuting distance. ***On-campus housing:*** Spaces - 474, undergraduate residential students - 66%. ***Clubs and organizations*** - 20. Fraternities - 2, sororities - 0. ***Athletics:*** Intercollegiate - NCAA Division III (athletic no-cut policy guarantees a spot on roster if student attends practices). Intramural sports - yes. ***Counseling and guidance:*** Academic, personal, career planning, job placement. Faculty advisors - yes. Tutoring - yes. ***Special services/academic programs for:*** Educationally disadvantaged - yes, physically disabled - no, learning disabled - yes.
FRESHMAN ADMISSION STANDARDS: High school units: Total required - minimum 12 college-preparatory units required with grades of C or better. English - nd, social science/history - nd, foreign language - nd, laboratory science - nd, mathematics - nd.
1993-94 FRESHMAN ADMISSION DATA: ***Applications:*** Received - 315, accepted - 275, enrolled - 115. ***SAT scores:*** Average verbal/mathematics scores nd/nd, median verbal/mathematics scores - nd/nd. Verbal/mathematics scores of enrolled freshmen: 0%/3% scored 700-800, 1%/9% scored 600-699, 10%/15% scored 500-599, 30%/34% scored 400-499, 43%/31% scored 300-399, 16%/8% scored 200-299. ***ACT composite score:*** Average - nd, median - 23. ***High school GPA:*** Average GPA - 2.70. Range - 2.70-3.30. Minimum required - 2.00. ***Class rank:*** nd. ***International students:*** Minimum TOEFL score required - 550.
TRANSFER ADMISSION STANDARDS: ***Transfer units required:*** Minimum - 24, maximum - 94. ***Minimum college GPA*** - 2.00. ***Grades accepted*** - A, B, C, Credit, Pass.
1993-94 TRANSFER ADMISSION DATA: ***Applications:*** Received - 139, accepted - 122, enrolled - 88. CCC transfer students enrolled - 62.
ADMISSION PROCEDURES: ***Entrance tests:*** SAT I: Reasoning Test or ACT required. Test deadline for fall admission - through June. ***Application process:*** Students admitted each term. Deadlines: Freshmen and transfers - rolling. Application fee - $40. Fee waiver - yes. ***Recommendations:*** 1. ***Interview*** - no. ***Admission notification*** - rolling. Commitment deposit - $450. ***Advanced placement offered*** - yes. ***Advanced credit given*** - yes. ***Early decision procedure:*** Application deadline - 12/1, notification - nd.
1994-95 COSTS: ***Total costs*** (approximate) - $21,715. Tuition - $14,815, other significant fees - $200, room and board - $6,200, total books, supplies, incidentals (approximate) - $500.
UNDERGRADUATE FINANCIAL AID: Students receiving financial aid - 50%. Submit FAFSA (CSS version preferred) and FAF applications by 3/2. Application deadline for institutional scholarships and grants - rolling, priority deadline - 5/30. Average financial aid package - $16,000.
OTHER INFORMATION: ***Founded*** - 1927. ***Nonprofit*** - yes. ***WASC Accredited*** - yes. ***Member of AICCU*** - yes.

MILLS COLLEGE

5000 MacArthur Boulevard
Oakland, California 94613
Admissions: (510) 430-2135
Financial Aid: (510) 430-2134
Fax: (510) 430-3314
Toll Free: (800) 87 MILLS

Residential, Liberal Arts College For Women

DISTINGUISHING FEATURES: Mills College is a small undergraduate college for women. The graduate program is made up of twenty-two percent men. The undergraduate program aims to educate the whole woman. Academic, creative, and athletic abilities are cultivated and prized. The instruction encourages independence and initiative by the student. Mills is characterized by strong student-faculty relationships and individualized attention. eighty-five percent of the classes contain twenty or fewer students. A wide variety of professional internships provide students with practical work experience to enhance their liberal arts education.
DEGREES OFFERED: Bachelor's, Master's, Credential.
SPECIAL PROGRAMS: Early admission plan allows students to enter Mills after three years of high school. Center for Contemporary Music, a leading innovator of modern music. Cross-registration available with UC Berkeley, California College of Arts and Crafts, and other neighboring institutions. Semester at Wheaton, Mount Holyoke, Agnes Scott, Spelman or five other colleges in the student exchange program. 3/2 program in Engineering with Washington University in St. Louis. Career internships. Independent study. ***Education abroad:*** Study abroad in Austria, Bali, England, France, Germany, Greece, Ireland, Italy, Kenya, Mexico, Netherlands, Scotland, Spain, Switzerland. Other programs of students choice may be acceptable. ***Honors programs*** - no.
COLLEGES: na.
UNDERGRADUATE MAJORS: 33 majors. Known for Mathematics and Computer Science, the Fine Arts, and Creative Writing programs. Major in Political, Legal, and Economic Analysis. See this chapter: Undergraduate Degree Majors, page 12--76. Preprofessional programs: Engineering, Law, Medicine.
CALENDAR: Semester system. No Summer session.
FACULTY: Evenly divided between men and women. Full-time - 74, part-time - 79. Undergraduate classes taught by faculty, not graduate assistants - all. Faculty with Ph.D.'s - 99% of full-time. Student/faculty ratio - 11/1. Average class size - 14.
ENROLLMENT: ***Total*** - 1,137. ***Graduate*** - 313. ***Undergraduate*** - 824: California residents - 91%, out-of-state - 7%, other countries - 1%. Men - 0%, women - 100%. ***Ethnic distribution of undergraduate students:*** Hispanic - 6.3%, Black - 7.0%, Asian/Pacific Islander - 9.4%, Native American/Alaskan - 0.9%, White - 72.0%. ***Freshmen graduating within 5 years*** - 69%.
LOCATION: 135 acres of parklike greenery less than thirty minutes from Oakland, Berkeley, and San Francisco. The largest women's college campus located in an urban setting in the nation.

nd = no data available   na = not applicable

CAMPUS LIFE: Undergraduates who are unmarried and under twenty-one are expected to live on campus or with their own families. ***On-campus housing:*** Spaces - 752, undergraduate residential students - 59%. ***Clubs and organizations*** - 30. Fraternities and sororities - 0. ***Athletics:*** Intercollegiate - NCAA Division III. Intramural sports - yes. ***Counseling and guidance:*** Academic, personal, career planning, job placement. Faculty advisors - yes. Tutoring - yes. ***Special services/ academic programs for:*** Educationally disadvantaged - yes, physically disabled - yes, learning disabled - yes.
FRESHMAN ADMISSION STANDARDS: High school units: Total required - nd. English - 4, social science/history - 2 to 4, foreign language - 3 to 4, laboratory science - 2 to 4, mathematics - 3 to 4.
1993-94 FRESHMAN ADMISSION DATA: ***Applications:*** Received - 529, accepted - nd, enrolled - 132. ***SAT Scores:*** Average verbal/mathematics scores - 535/536, median verbal/mathematics scores - 540/530. Verbal/mathematics scores of enrolled freshmen: Middle 50% scored 470-610 verbal/480-600 mathematics. 3%/6% scored 700-800, 25%/23% scored 600-699, 38%/40% scored 500-599, 27%/25% scored 400-499, 5%/6% scored 300-399. ***ACT composite score:*** Average - 25, median - nd. ***High school GPA:*** Average GPA - 3.40. 42% with 3.50-4.00, 38% with 3.00-3.49, 19% with 2.99 and below. ***Class rank:*** 22% in top 10%, 52% in top 20%. ***International students:*** Minimum TOEFL score required - 550.
TRANSFER ADMISSION STANDARDS: ***Transfer units required:*** Minimum - none, maximum - 67. ***Minimum college GPA*** - 3.00. Individual circumstances considered. ***Grades accepted*** - A, B, C, D, Credit, Pass.
1993-94 TRANSFER ADMISSION DATA: ***Applications:*** Received - 421, accepted - nd, enrolled - 174. CCC transfer students enrolled - nd.
ADMISSION PROCEDURES: ***Entrance tests:*** SAT I: Reasoning Test or ACT required. SAT II: Subject Tests highly recommended including Writing. Test deadline for fall admission - by February. ***Application process:*** Students admitted each term. Deadlines: Freshmen and transfers rolling, 2/15 priority date. Application fee - $35. Fee waiver - yes. ***Recommendations:*** 3 - 2 teachers, and counselor. ***Interview*** - strongly recommended. ***Admission notification*** - rolling. Commitment deposit - $300 plus $150 for housing. ***Advanced placement offered*** - yes. ***Advanced credit given*** - yes. ***Early decision procedure:*** no.
1994-95 COSTS: ***Total costs*** (approximate) - $22,790. Tuition - $14,100, other significant fees - $772, room and board - $6,000, total books, supplies, incidentals (approximate) - $1,920.
UNDERGRADUATE FINANCIAL AID: Students receiving financial aid - 71%. Submit FAFSA (CSS version preferred) and FAF applications by 2/15 for fall, 11/1 for spring. Application deadline for institutional scholarships and grants - 2/15 for fall, 11/1 for spring. Average financial aid package - $13,728.
OTHER INFORMATION: ***Founded*** - 1852. ***Nonprofit*** - yes. ***WASC Accredited*** - yes. ***Member of AICCU*** - yes.

MONTEREY INSTITUTE OF INTERNATIONAL STUDIES

425 Van Buren Street
Monterey, California 93940
(408) 647-4123
Fax: (408) 647-4199
Toll Free: nd

Upper-Division College and Graduate School for International Studies

DISTINGUISHING FEATURES: The Monterey Institute of International Studies specializes in professional Master's degree programs in International Policy Studies, International Business, International Public Administration, Language Teaching, and in Translation and Interpretation. Strongly interdisciplinary, all programs strive to educate professionals for service in public or private sector careers. Programs stress sensitivity to the challenges involved in working across cultures, and the development of strong second-language skills. No freshmen are admitted. There is a small honors Bachelor's degree program in International Studies designed to prepare upper-division (junior, senior) undergraduates for the Institute's rigorous graduate programs. Entering juniors who wish to continue in the Master's programs in International Policy Studies, International Management, or International Public Administration may begin graduate work in the fall of their senior year and complete both the Bachelor's degree and Master's degree in three years. Sixty semester units of lower-division course work are required for admission as a junior. Advanced languages regularly offered during the academic year are: Chinese, English, French, German, Japanese, Russian, and Spanish. The school offers eight- and nine-week summer sessions for intensive language study. This program is open to mature, highly motivated high school students.
DEGREES OFFERED: Bachelor's, Master's.
CALENDAR: Semester system. Summer session.
ENROLLMENT: ***Total*** - 770. ***Graduate*** - 720. ***Undergraduate*** - 50. Over one-third of students are from over 50 countries.
LOCATION: In the historic city of Monterey in Northern California, 130 miles south of San Francisco.
CAMPUS LIFE: ***On-campus housing:*** Spaces - 0.
OTHER INFORMATION: ***Founded*** - 1955. ***Nonprofit*** - yes. ***WASC Accredited*** - yes. ***Member of AICCU*** - yes.

MOUNT ST. MARY'S COLLEGE

12001 Chalon Road
Los Angeles, California 90049
Admissions: (310) 471-9516
Financial Aid: (310) 471-9505
Fax: (310) 440-3258
Toll Free: (800) 999-9893

Catholic, Liberal Arts College, Primarily for Women

DISTINGUISHING FEATURES: MSMC educates women who want to make a difference in their professions, their communities, and their lives. The emphasis is on developing leadership qualities. The Women's Leadership Program is noted for training women in leadership skills. Eighty percent to eighty-five percent of premedical and one-hundred percent of pre-dental students are admitted to medical school. Men are in the undergraduate music, nursing, and physical therapy assistant programs and in all graduate, extended day, and summer programs.
DEGREES OFFERED: Certificate, Associates, Bachelor's, Master's, Credential.
SPECIAL PROGRAMS: Internships in the business community. Clinical experience in health-related and psychology majors. Undergraduate research opportunities in science. Cross registration with UCLA. May design individual major. ***Education abroad:*** Junior year abroad. Summer and January Foreign Study Programs. ***Honors programs*** - yes.
COLLEGES: na.
UNDERGRADUATE MAJORS: 36. Associates degree programs in Business, Early Childhood Education, Liberal Arts, Nursing, Occupational Therapy Assistant, Physical Therapist Assistant. See this chapter: Undergraduate Degree Majors, page 12--76. Preprofessional programs: Dentistry, Law, Medicine.
CALENDAR: Semester system. Summer session.
FACULTY: Full-time - 66, part-time - 133. Undergraduate classes taught by faculty, not graduate assistants - all. Faculty with Ph.D.'s - 86% excluding health services. Student/faculty ratio - 13/1. Average class size - 16.
ENROLLMENT: ***Total*** - 1,498. ***Graduate*** - 257. ***Undergraduate*** - 1,241: California residents - 88%, out-of-state and other countries - 12%. Men - 1%, women - 99%. ***Ethnic distribution of undergraduate students:*** Hispanic - 34.8%, Black - 9.4%, Asian/Pacific Islander - 16.5%, Native American/Alaskan - 0.7%, White - 29.0%. ***Freshmen graduating within 5 years*** - 68%.
LOCATION: On two different beautiful campuses in Los Angeles. Four-year Bachelor's degrees are offered on its Chalon Campus, located in the foothills of the Santa Monica Mountains, overlooking forty miles of the Pacific shoreline. Two-year Associates degrees and Master's programs are offered on the Doheny Campus, located in central Los Angeles within the confines of the old Doheny Estate.
CAMPUS LIFE: ***On-campus housing:*** Spaces - 520, undergraduate residential students - 50%. ***Clubs and organizations*** - 31. Fraternities - 0, sororities - 1. ***Athletics:*** Intercollegiate - yes. Intramural sports - no. ***Counseling and guidance:*** Academic, personal, career planning, job placement. Faculty advisors - yes, also peer counseling. Tutoring - yes. ***Special services/academic programs for:*** Educationally disadvantaged - yes, physically disabled - no, learning disabled - no.
FRESHMAN ADMISSION STANDARDS: High school units: Total required - nd. Recommended for admission to Bachelor's degree programs, the following with a B average: English - 4, social science/history - 1, foreign language - 2, laboratory science - 1, mathematics - 2. Language, science, or mathematics - 1 advanced year. For admission to the Associates degree programs: Ability to benefit from the program is the fundamental criteria. Individual Associates degree programs may have more specific requirements.
1993-94 FRESHMAN ADMISSION DATA: ***Applications:*** Received - 658, accepted - 537, enrolled - 270. ***SAT Scores:*** Average verbal/mathematics scores - nd/nd, median verbal/mathematics scores - nd/nd. Verbal/mathematics scores of enrolled freshmen: Middle 50% scored 400-510 verbal, 430-550 mathematics, 870-1080 combined verbal and mathematics. nd%/nd% scored 700-800, nd%/nd% scored 600-699, nd%/nd% scored 500-599, nd%/nd% scored 400-499, nd%/nd% scored 300-399. ACT composite score: Average - nd, median - nd. ***High school GPA:*** Average GPA - 3.49. ***Class rank:*** nd. ***International students:*** Minimum TOEFL score required - 500.
TRANSFER ADMISSION STANDARDS: ***Transfer units required:*** Minimum - 24 for Bachelor's degree program, 15 for Associates degree program. Maximum - 66 CCC. ***Minimum college GPA*** - 2.25, individual circumstances considered. ***Grades accepted*** - D or better, Credit, Pass.
1993-94 TRANSFER ADMISSION DATA: ***Applications:*** Received - nd, accepted - nd, enrolled - 146. CCC transfer students enrolled - nd.
ADMISSION PROCEDURES: ***Entrance tests:*** SAT I: Reasoning Test or ACT required. Test deadline for fall admission - concurrent with application. ***Application process:*** Students admitted each term. Deadlines: Freshmen and transfers - rolling. 3/1 priority date. Application fee - $30. Fee waiver - yes. ***Recommendations*** - 1 - counselor. ***Interview*** - recommended. ***Admission notification*** - rolling. Commitment deposit - $100 commuter, $200 campus resident. ***Advanced placement offered*** - yes. ***Advanced credit given*** - yes. ***Early decision procedure*** - no.
1994-95 COSTS: ***Total costs*** (approximate) - $18,774. Tuition - $12,474, other significant fees - $440, room and board - $5,060, total books, supplies, incidentals (approximate) - $800.
UNDERGRADUATE FINANCIAL AID: Students receiving financial aid - 80%. Submit FAFSA (CSS version preferred) and FAF applications by 3/2. Application deadline for institutional scholarships and grants - 2/1. Average financial aid package - $13,800.
OTHER INFORMATION: ***Founded*** - 1925. ***Nonprofit*** - yes. ***WASC Accredited*** - yes. ***Member of AICCU*** - yes.

NATIONAL UNIVERSITY

4141 Camino del Rio South
San Diego, California 92108
619) 563-7100
Fax: (619) 563-7596
Toll Free: nd

Institution with Programs Featuring Month-Long Courses Designed for Career Oriented Adults

DISTINGUISHING FEATURES: NU has programs designed primarily for fully-employed, mature, career-oriented adults. The curriculum is structured in a unique, intensive one-course-per-month format for career-oriented adults. This enables working adults to maintain a high degree of flexibility. Although offering primarily evening classes, some day programs are provided. Undergraduate programs are offered in high growth fields in Arts and Sciences, Business, Technology, Psychology, and Education. Majors are offered in Aviation, Behavioral Science, Business, Computer Science, Counseling, Education, Interdisciplinary Studies, Law, Manufacturing Engineering, and Paralegal Studies.
DEGREES OFFERED: Associates, Bachelor's, Master's, Credential, First Professional, Juris Doctor (Law).
CALENDAR: Month long courses. Summer session.
ENROLLMENT: ***Total*** - 14,250. ***Graduate*** - 9,072. ***Undergraduate*** - 5,178.

nd = no data available   na = not applicable

LOCATION: Central campus located in the Mission Valley area of San Diego. Regional Learning Centers in Sacramento, Los Angeles, and Orange Counties. Additional twenty-three learning centers throughout California.
CAMPUS LIFE: ***On-campus housing:*** Spaces - 0
OTHER INFORMATION: ***Founded*** - 1971. ***Nonprofit*** - yes. ***WASC Accredited*** - yes. ***Member of AICCU*** - yes.

NEW COLLEGE OF CALIFORNIA

50 Fell Street
San Francisco, California 94102
(415) 626-1694
Fax: (415) 626-5541
Toll Free: (800) 335-6262

Small, Liberal Arts College Primarily for Older Students

DISTINGUISHING FEATURES: New College of California offers an alternative approach to the study of the humanities for adult students. The average age of New College students is between 25 and 45. Students who attend have a unique opportunity of earning credit in a variety of ways including coursework, independent study, tutorials, and practicums. A weekend degree completion program in the Humanities allows students to earn a degree by attending classes one or two weekends a month. The Science Certificate Program offers accelerated weekend courses in the basic sciences. This program is designed for students needing science courses to prepare for health science careers. Credit is possible for life experience. Undergraduate degrees are offered in the Humanities.
DEGREES OFFERED: Associate, Bachelor's, Master's, First Professional, Juris Doctor (Law).
CALENDAR: Semester system.
ENROLLMENT: ***Total*** - 600.
LOCATION: In the heart of the Mission District of San Francisco.
CAMPUS LIFE: ***On-campus housing:*** Spaces - 0.
OTHER INFORMATION: ***Founded*** - 1971. ***Nonprofit*** - yes. ***WASC Accredited*** - yes.

NEWSCHOOL OF ART & ARCHITECTURE

1249 "F" Street
San Diego, California 92101
(619) 235-4100
Fax: (619) 235-4651

Small Urban College of Art and Architecture

DISTINGUISHING FEATURES: Newschool of Art & Architecture is an urban college dedicated to providing education in the arts and architecture. Students take evening classes in a downtown location. Newschool subscribes to a hands on approach to learning and encourages all students to begin internships as soon as possible. The Fine Arts program supports the professional architectural program and emphasizes painting, sculpture, and graphics. In the architecture program, five to twenty students meet three times per week in design studios.
DEGREES OFFERED: Associate, Bachelor's, Master's.
CALENDAR: Quarter system.
ENROLLMENT: ***Total*** - 120.
LOCATION: In downtown San Diego, central to urban activity and the arts community.
CAMPUS LIFE: ***On-campus housing:*** Spaces - 0.
OTHER INFORMATION: ***Founded*** - 1980. ***Nonprofit*** - no. ***WASC Accredited*** - no. Accredited by Career Schools and Colleges of Technology.

OCCIDENTAL COLLEGE

1600 Campus Road
Los Angeles, California 90041
Admissions: (213) 259-2700
Financial Aid: (213) 259-2548
Fax: (213) 259-2958
Toll Free: nd

Highly Selective Undergraduate Liberal Arts and Science College

DISTINGUISHING FEATURES: Occidental seeks to provide an education in the best tradition of the liberal arts, with emphasis on developing thinking and communication skills through its interdisciplinary cultural studies program presented in team-taught classes. The cultural studies program includes western and nonwestern history and culture, science, mathematics, the arts, and their interrelationship. Its distinguished faculty, committed to excellence in the classroom, promote a highly academic yet relaxed atmosphere. More than seventy-five percent of the classes have fewer than fifteen students. Seventy-five percent of Occidental graduates continue their studies in professional schools.
DEGREES OFFERED: Bachelor's, Master's, Credential.
SPECIAL PROGRAMS: 3/2 and 4/2 Engineering programs with California Institute of Technology and Columbia University. Cross-registration program with Cal Tech and Art Center College, Occidental in Washington, D.C., Occidental-at-the-United Nations in New York. Research opportunities. Student-designed majors. Career internships. ***Education abroad:*** Full-year programs in China, England, France, Germany, Japan, Russia, Spain. Term abroad in Germany, Mexico, Spain. International independent studies available. ***Honors programs*** - yes.
COLLEGES: na.
UNDERGRADUATE MAJORS: 36 majors. In the Humanities, the Fine Arts, Social Sciences, and Sciences. Can choose an independent pattern of study. See this chapter: Undergraduate Degree Majors, page 12--76. Preprofessional programs: Business, Dentistry, Law, Medicine.
CALENDAR: Semester system.
FACULTY: Full-time - 135, part-time - 49. Undergraduate classes taught by faculty, not graduate assistants - all. Faculty with Ph.D.'s - 96%. Student/faculty ratio - 11/1. Average class size - 15.
ENROLLMENT: ***Total*** - 1,650. ***Graduate*** - 30. ***Undergraduate*** - 1,620. California residents - 55%, out-of-state - 42%, other countries - 3%. Men - 47%, women - 53%. ***Ethnic distribution***

nd = no data available   na = not applicable

CALIFORNIA INDEPENDENT COLLEGES

of undergraduate students: Hispanic - 17%, Black -8%, Asian/ Pacific Islander - 17%, Native American/Alaskan - 1%, White - 55%. ***Freshmen graduating within 5 years*** - 78%.
LOCATION: 120-acre campus of hills and trees in the Eagle Rock section of the city of Los Angeles. Fifteen minutes from the center of the city. Urban location unique among the nation's leading small, highly-selective colleges.
CAMPUS LIFE: All freshmen required to live in residence halls. Multicultural special interest housing available. ***On-campus housing:*** Spaces - 1,250, undergraduate residential students - 80%. ***Clubs and organizations*** - 80. Fraternities and sororities - 7. ***Athletics:*** Intercollegiate - NCAA Division III. Intramural sports - yes. ***Counseling and guidance:*** Academic, personal, career planning, job placement. Faculty advisors - yes. Tutoring - yes. ***Special services/academic programs for:*** Educationally disadvantaged - no, physically disabled - yes, learning disabled - no.
FRESHMAN ADMISSION STANDARDS: High school units: Total required - na. Recommended: English - 4, social science/ history - 2, foreign language - 3 to 4, laboratory science - 2 (1 each biological and physical, both chemistry and physics if interested in Science or Engineering), mathematics - 3 (4 if interested in Science or Engineering). Advanced Placement or Honors courses when available.
1993-94 FRESHMAN ADMISSION DATA: ***Applications:*** Received - 2,426, accepted - 1,310, enrolled - 370. ***SAT Scores:*** Average verbal/mathematics scores - nd/nd, median verbal/ mathematics scores - 520/570. Verbal/mathematics scores of enrolled freshmen: Middle 50% scored 440-560 verbal, 500-640 mathematics, 940-1200 combined verbal and mathematics. nd%/nd% scored 700-800, nd%/nd% scored 600-699, nd%/ nd% scored 500-599, nd%/nd% scored 400-499, nd%/nd% scored 300-399. ***ACT composite score:*** nd. ***High school GPA:*** Average GPA - nd. ***Class rank:*** 50.5% in top 10%, 71.3% in top 20%, 96.7% in top 50%. ***International students:*** Minimum TOEFL score required - 600.
TRANSFER ADMISSION STANDARDS: ***Transfer units required:*** Minimum - 30, maximum - none. ***Minimum college GPA*** - 3.00. ***Grades accepted*** - A, B, C, D. Credit, Pass except courses in major.
1993-94 TRANSFER ADMISSION DATA: ***Applications:*** Received - 209, accepted - 125, enrolled - 71. CCC transfer students enrolled - nd.
ADMISSION PROCEDURES: ***Entrance tests:*** SAT I: Reasoning Test or ACT required, SAT I preferred. SAT II: Subject Tests including Writing, Mathematics, and Foreign Language strongly recommended. Test deadline for fall admission - January. ***Application process:*** Students admitted each fall. Deadlines: Freshmen - 2/1 firm, transfers - 4/15 firm. Application fee - $40. Fee waiver - yes. ***Recommendations:*** Freshmen: 3 - 1 counselor, 2 teachers. Transfers: 3 - 2 professors, 1 administrator. ***Interview*** - recommended. ***Admission notification*** - 4/1. Commitment deposit - $200 due 5/1. ***Advanced placement offered*** - yes. ***Advanced credit given*** - yes. ***Early decision procedure:*** Application deadline - 11/15, notification - early January.
1994-95 COSTS: ***Total costs*** (approximate) - $24,044. Tuition - $16,560, other significant fees - $334, room and board - $5,440, total books, supplies, incidentals (approximate) - $1,710.
UNDERGRADUATE FINANCIAL AID: Students receiving financial aid - 72%. Submit FAFSA and FAF applications by 3/2. Application deadline for institutional scholarships and grants - 2/1, parent and student federal tax returns by 4/20. Average financial aid package - $16,141.
OTHER INFORMATION: ***Founded*** - 1887. ***Nonprofit*** - yes. ***WASC Accredited*** - yes. ***Member of AICCU*** - yes.

OTIS COLLEGE OF ART AND DESIGN

2401 Wilshire Boulevard
Los Angeles, California 90057
Admissions: (213) 251-0505
Financial Aid: (213) 251-0542
Fax: (213) 480-0059
Toll Free: (800) 527-6847

College of Art and Design

DISTINGUISHING FEATURES: Otis College offers a curriculum designed to prepare students for professional careers in the art and design fields. Intensive studio courses form the core of the Otis experience. General education classes in critical writing, psychology, science, and art history and theory are designed specifically for art students to insure a broad-based education. The emphasis is on teaching the skills and giving students the resources to balance unique ideas with the demands of the professional marketplace. Otis has state-of-the-art facilities.
DEGREES OFFERED: Associates, Bachelor's, Master's.
SPECIAL PROGRAMS: ***Education abroad*** - May study at more than fifteen arts campuses throughout the world and at several major art schools on the east coast. ***Honors programs*** - no.
COLLEGES: na.
UNDERGRADUATE MAJORS: 8 majors. Ceramics, Design, Environmental Arts, Fashion Design, Illustration, Photographics, Photography, Surface Design. Preprofessional programs: nd.
CALENDAR: Semester system. Summer session.
FACULTY: Leading professional artists and designers. Full-time - 26, part-time - 220. Undergraduate classes taught by faculty, not graduate assistants - all. Faculty with Ph.D.'s - nd%. Student/faculty ratio - 14/1. Average class size - 15.
ENROLLMENT: ***Total*** - 667. ***Graduate*** - 22. ***Undergraduate*** - 655: California residents - 70%, out-of-state - 10%, other countries - 20%. Men - 44%, women - 56%. ***Ethnic distribution of undergraduate students:*** Domestic students- Hispanic - 11%, Black - 5%, Asian/Pacific Islander - 26%, Native American/ Alaskan - 1%, White - 38%. ***Freshmen graduating within 5 years*** - 78%.
LOCATION: In the heart of Los Angeles. Only independent college of fine arts and design in the city of Los Angeles, one of the world's most creative cities.
CAMPUS LIFE: ***On-campus housing:*** Spaces - 175, room only, no food, large communal kitchen, undergraduate residential students - nd%. ***Clubs and organizations*** - 2. Fraternities and sororities - 0. ***Athletics:*** Intercollegiate -no. Intramural sports - no. ***Counseling and guidance:*** Personal, career planning. Faculty advisors - yes. Tutoring - no. ***Special services/academic programs for:*** Educationally disadvantaged - no, physically disabled - no, learning disabled - no.
FRESHMAN ADMISSION STANDARDS: High school diploma or equivalent. High school units: Total required - na. Recommended: English - 4, social science/history - 3, and as many art courses as possible. Considerable emphasis is placed on abilities in drawing, color, and design.

nd = no data available na = not applicable

1993-94 FRESHMAN ADMISSION DATA: ***Applications:*** Received - 635, accepted - 244, enrolled - 180. ***SAT Scores:*** nd. ***ACT composite score:*** nd. ***High school GPA:*** Average GPA - nd. ***Class rank:*** nd. ***International students:*** Minimum TOEFL score required - 550.
TRANSFER ADMISSION STANDARDS: ***Transfer units required:*** Minimum - nd, maximum - 60. ***Minimum college GPA*** - 2.00. ***Grades accepted*** - C or better.
1993-94 TRANSFER ADMISSION DATA: ***Applications:*** Received - 150, accepted - 98, enrolled - 60. CCC transfer students enrolled - nd.
ADMISSION PROCEDURES: ***Entrance tests:*** SAT I: Reasoning Test or ACT not required. Test deadline for fall admission - nd. Portfolio and Home Examination consisting of specific art projects are required and a major part of admission decision. ***Application process:*** Students admitted each term. Deadlines: Freshmen and transfers - rolling. Application fee - $40. Fee waiver - yes. ***Recommendations*** - from art teachers or counselor not required, but encouraged. ***Interview*** - recommended. ***Admission notification*** - rolling, two weeks after file complete. Commitment deposit - $200 due 5/1 or three weeks after admission complete, whichever is later. ***Advanced placement offered*** - yes. ***Advanced credit given*** - yes, but not in AP Studio Art. ***Early decision procedure*** - no.
1994-95 COSTS: ***Total costs*** (approximate) - $18,240. Tuition - $13,140, other significant fees - $600, room and board - $2,700 room only, total books, supplies, incidentals (approximate) - $1,800.
UNDERGRADUATE FINANCIAL AID: Students receiving financial aid - 80%. Submit FAFSA and institutional applications by 3/2. Application deadline for institutional scholarships and grants - priority date 3/1 for fall, 12/1 for January admission. Average financial aid package - $12,000.
OTHER INFORMATION: ***Founded*** - 1918. ***Nonprofit*** - yes. ***WASC Accredited*** - yes. ***Member of AICCU*** - yes.

PACIFIC CHRISTIAN COLLEGE

2500 East Nutwood Avenue
Fullerton, California 92631
Admissions: (714) 879-3901, Ext. 290
Financial Aid: (714) 879-3901, Ext. 231
Fax: (714) 526-0231
Toll Free: nd

Christian College Emphasizing Christian Ministry and Service

DISTINGUISHING FEATURES: PCC focuses personal attention upon each student as an individual and places Christian values at the heart of the whole educational process. The emphasis is on personal accountability and opportunity for growth through interaction with faculty, administrators, and other students. In addition to the majors offered on campus, selected liberal arts majors are available through a Contract Program with California State University, Fullerton.
DEGREES OFFERED: Associates, Bachelor's, Master's.
SPECIAL PROGRAMS: Leadership core curriculum. Cross-cultural service and ministry programs. ***Education abroad*** - no. ***Honors programs*** - no.
COLLEGES: na.
UNDERGRADUATE MAJORS: Emphasizing Christian ministry and service through majors leading to congregational leadership careers and careers in management, education, and the social science professions. All students pursue two majors: one in Biblical studies and another leading to a career. See this chapter: Undergraduate Degree Majors, page 12--76. Preprofessional programs: none.
CALENDAR: 4-1-4 system. Summer session.
FACULTY: Full-time - nd, part-time - nd. Undergraduate classes taught by faculty, not graduate assistants - most. Faculty with Ph.D.'s - 57%. Student/faculty ratio - 19/1. Average class size - nd.
ENROLLMENT: ***Total*** - 879. ***Graduate*** - 143. ***Undergraduate*** - 736: California residents - 56%, out-of-state and other countries - 44%. Men - 63%, women - 37%. ***Ethnic distribution of undergraduate students:*** Minority - 18%. Hispanic - nd%, Black - nd%, Asian/Pacific Islander - nd%, Native American/Alaskan - nd%, White - 82%. ***Freshmen graduating within 5 years*** - nd%.
LOCATION: 11 acres located in the urban, collegiate environment of Fullerton and the Los Angeles-Orange County area.
CAMPUS LIFE: Single full-time students not living at home required to live on campus. ***On-campus housing:*** Spaces - 500, undergraduate residential students - 70%. ***Clubs and organizations*** - 15. Fraternities and sororities - 0. ***Athletics:*** Intercollegiate - yes. Intramural sports - yes. ***Counseling and guidance:*** Academic, personal, career planning, job placement. Faculty advisors - yes. Tutoring - yes. ***Special services/academic programs for:*** Educationally disadvantaged - nd, physically disabled - nd, learning disabled - nd.
FRESHMAN ADMISSION STANDARDS: High school units: Total required - 15 minimum for admission as a regular student.
1993-94 FRESHMAN ADMISSION DATA: ***Applications:*** Received - nd, accepted - nd, enrolled - 162. ***SAT Scores:*** nd. ***ACT composite score:*** nd. ***High school GPA:*** Average GPA - 3.30. ***Class rank:*** nd. ***International students:*** Minimum TOEFL score required - nd.
TRANSFER ADMISSION STANDARDS: ***Transfer units required:*** Minimum - 30, maximum - 68. ***Minimum college GPA*** - 2.00. ***Grades accepted*** - nd.
1993-94 TRANSFER ADMISSION DATA: ***Applications:*** Received - nd, accepted - nd, enrolled - 68. CCC transfer students enrolled - 23.
ADMISSION PROCEDURES: ***Entrance tests:*** SAT I: Reasoning Test or ACT required. Test deadline for fall admission - June. ***Application process:*** Students admitted each term. Deadlines: Freshmen and transfers - rolling, fall 7/1 priority date, spring 12/1 priority date. Application fee - $30. Fee waiver - no. ***Recommendations:*** 2 - teacher or counselor and church leader. ***Interview*** - no. ***Admission notification*** - rolling. Commitment deposit - $nd. ***Advanced placement offered*** - yes. ***Advanced credit given*** - yes. ***Early decision procedure:*** Application deadline - rolling, notification - rolling.
1994-95 COSTS: ***Total costs*** (approximate) - $11,025. Tuition - $7,100, other significant fees - $210, room and board - $3,115, total books, supplies, incidentals (approximate) - $600.
UNDERGRADUATE FINANCIAL AID: Students receiving financial aid - 82%. Submit FAFSA and institutional applications by 3/2. Application deadline for institutional scholarships and grants - 3/2, priority deadline - 3/2. Average financial aid package - $8,700.
OTHER INFORMATION: ***Founded*** - 1928. ***Nonprofit*** - yes. ***WASC Accredited*** - yes. ***Member of AICCU*** - yes.

PACIFIC OAKS COLLEGE

5 Westmoreland Place
Pasadena, California 91103
(818) 397-1300
Fax: (818) 397-1356
Toll Free: nd

An Upper-Division and Graduate College of Programs in the Human Services

DISTINGUISHING FEATURES: Pacific Oaks College offers a wide variety of programs in the human services with a focus on young children and teaching, counseling, bicultural development and clinical child development. The personalized curriculum and class schedule are organized to serve working professionals and mature students as well as regular full-time students. Credit is given for life and work experience. Experiential learning and anti-bias are the heart of the curriculum. The average class size is seventeen. There are two campuses in Pasadena. Undergraduate majors are offered in Human Development, Early Childhood, Teacher Education, Bicultural Development, and Marriage/Family/Child Counseling.
DEGREES OFFERED: Bachelor's, Master's, Credential.
CALENDAR: Semester system.
ENROLLMENT: ***Total*** - 500. ***Graduate*** - 430. ***Undergraduate*** - 192.
LOCATION: 2-acre campus in the city of Pasadena near Los Angeles.
CAMPUS LIFE: ***On-campus housing:*** Spaces - 0.
OTHER INFORMATION: ***Founded*** - 1948. ***Nonprofit*** - yes. ***WASC Accredited*** - yes. ***Member of AICCU*** - yes.

PACIFIC UNION COLLEGE

Angwin, California 94508
Admissions: (707) 965-6336
Financial Aid: (707) 965-7200
Fax: (707) 965-6390
Toll Free: 862-7080

Liberal Arts College Sponsored by the Seventh-Day Adventist Church

DISTINGUISHING FEATURES: Pacific Union College offers a liberal arts education with a Christian perspective. The school is committed to the full intellectual, social, spiritual, and physical development of each of its students. It is one of twelve colleges and universities operated by the Seventh-day Adventists in North America.
DEGREES OFFERED: Associates, Bachelor's, Master's, Credential.
SPECIAL PROGRAMS: nd. ***Education abroad*** - Adventist Colleges abroad in Austria, France, Spain. ***Honors programs*** - yes.
COLLEGES: na.
UNDERGRADUATE MAJORS: Academic and technical curricula in 61 majors. See this chapter: Undergraduate Degree Majors, page 12--76. Preprofessional programs: Dentistry, Engineering, Law, Medicine, Nursing, Pharmacy, Speech Pathology, Veterinary Medicine.
CALENDAR: Quarter system. Summer session.
FACULTY: Full-time - 105, part-time - 20. Undergraduate classes taught by faculty, not graduate assistants - all. Faculty with Ph.D.'s - 51%. Student/faculty ratio - 12/1. Average class size - 13.
ENROLLMENT: ***Total*** - 1,488. ***Graduate*** - 33. ***Undergraduate*** - 1,455: California residents - 84%, out-of-state - 91%, other countries - 7%. Men - 45%, women - 55%. ***Ethnic distribution of undergraduate students:*** Hispanic - 9%, Black - 3%, Asian/Pacific Islander - 17%, Native American/Alaskan - 1%, White - 60%. ***Freshmen graduating within 5 years*** - 53%.
LOCATION: 200-acre, main campus surrounded by approximately 1800 acres of College-owned agricultural and forested land. Atop Howell Mountain in Napa Valley. San Francisco and Oakland are within a two-hour drive.
CAMPUS LIFE: Students under twenty-three and not living with parents must live in dormitories or approved housing. ***On-campus housing:*** Spaces - 1,300, undergraduate residential students - 69%. ***Clubs and organizations*** - 50. Fraternities and sororities - 0. ***Athletics:*** Intercollegiate - yes. Intramural sports - yes. ***Counseling and guidance:*** Academic, personal, career planning, job placement. Faculty advisors - for freshmen. Tutoring - no. ***Special services/academic programs for:*** Educationally disadvantaged - yes, physically disabled - yes, learning disabled - yes.
FRESHMAN ADMISSION STANDARDS: High school units: Total required - no specific units. Minimum: English - 4, social science/history - 1, foreign language - 0, laboratory science - 1, mathematics - 2. Additional units of mathematics, science, history, foreign language, and computer literacy strongly recommended.
1993-94 FRESHMAN ADMISSION DATA: ***Applications:*** Received - 940, accepted - 668, enrolled - 385. ***SAT Scores:*** nd. ***ACT composite score:*** Average - 22, median - 22. ***High school GPA:*** Average GPA - 3.26. Minimum GPA of 2.30 in solid subjects required. 44% with 3.50-4.00, 33% with 3.00-3.49, 14% with 2.50-2.99, 9% with 2.49 and below. ***Class rank:*** 20% in top 10%, 48% in top 25%, 86% in top 50%. ***International students:*** Minimum TOEFL score required - 500.
TRANSFER ADMISSION STANDARDS: ***Transfer units required:*** Minimum - none, maximum - 108 quarter. ***Minimum college GPA*** - 2.00. Individual circumstances considered. ***Grades accepted*** - D, Credit, Pass except courses in major.
1993-94 TRANSFER ADMISSION DATA: ***Applications:*** Received - 288, accepted - 287, enrolled - 242. CCC transfer students enrolled - nd.
ADMISSION PROCEDURES: ***Entrance tests:*** ACT required. Test deadline for fall admission - may be admitted without test scores, but ACT scores required before registration. ***Application process:*** Students admitted each term. Deadlines: Freshmen and transfers rolling, 4/30 priority date. Application fee - $30. Fee waiver - yes. ***Recommendations:*** 3 - high school personnel, Pastor, employer. ***Interview*** - if admissions committee requests one. ***Admission notification*** - rolling. Commitment deposit - $100 room deposit. ***Advanced placement offered*** - yes. ***Advanced credit given*** - yes. ***Early decision procedure*** - no.
1994-95 COSTS: ***Total costs*** (approximate) - $16,380. Tuition - $11,925, other significant fees - $nd, room and board - $3,825, total books, supplies, incidentals (approximate) - $630.
UNDERGRADUATE FINANCIAL AID: Students receiving financial aid - 87%. Submit FAFSA and FAF applications by 3/2. Application deadline for institutional scholarships and grants - 3/2. Average financial aid package - $7,564.
OTHER INFORMATION: ***Founded*** - 1882. ***Nonprofit*** - yes. ***WASC Accredited*** - yes. ***Member of AICCU*** - yes.

PATTEN COLLEGE

2433 Coolidge Avenue
Oakland, California 94601
Admissions: (510) 533-8306, Ext. 263
Financial Aid: (510) 533-8306, Ext. 247
Fax: (510) 534-8564
Toll Free: nd

Christian College of Biblical and Liberal Studies

DISTINGUISHING FEATURES: Patten is a very small, coeducational, Christian college with a fifty year history of providing individualized education within an interdenominational and ethnically diverse setting. The college is a member of the National Association of Evangelicals. Students feel a strong network of support from faculty, staff, and fellow students in the warm, caring intercultural environment. The opportunities for practical Christian experience and service help to define and develop students' talents and ministries.
DEGREES OFFERED: Associates, Bachelor's, Credential.
SPECIAL PROGRAMS: Day and evening programs. Christian service program into the community. Program for guaranteeing a Bachelor's degree in four years. ***Education abroad*** - no. ***Honors programs*** - no.
COLLEGES: na.
UNDERGRADUATE MAJORS: 7 majors. In the Bachelor's degree program, the Biblical Studies major is balanced by general education and a second major in Christian Education, Pastoral Studies, Sacred Music, or Business Management or by a preprofessional option in Pre-seminary or Liberal Studies. Preprofessional programs: nd.
CALENDAR: Semester system. Summer session.
FACULTY: Full-time - 16, part-time - 12. Undergraduate classes taught by faculty, not graduate assistants - all. Faculty with Ph.D.'s - 65%. Student/faculty ratio - 16/1. Average class size - 25.
ENROLLMENT: ***Total*** - 724. ***Graduate*** - 0. ***Undergraduate*** - 724: California residents - 95%, out-of-state - 2%, other countries - 3%. Men - 55%, women - 45%. ***Ethnic distribution of undergraduate students:*** Hispanic - 8%, Black - 27%, Asian/Pacific Islander - 23%, Native American/Alaskan - 2%, White - 40%. ***Freshmen graduating within 5 years*** - 70%.
LOCATION: 5-acre, park-like campus centrally located in the Oakland's Fruitvale district. San Francisco is twenty minutes away by train or the Bay Bridge.
CAMPUS LIFE: Must be a full-time student to live on campus. ***On-campus housing:*** Spaces - 50, undergraduate residential students - 30%. ***Clubs and organizations*** - 5. Fraternities and sororities - 0. ***Athletics:*** Intercollegiate - yes. Intramural sports - yes. ***Counseling and guidance:*** Academic, career planning. Faculty advisors - yes. Tutoring - yes. ***Special services/academic programs for:*** Educationally disadvantaged - no, physically disabled - no, learning disabled - no.
FRESHMAN ADMISSION STANDARDS: High school units: Total required - 16 recommended minimum including English - 4, social science/history - 4, foreign language - 1, laboratory science - 2, mathematics - 2, fine arts - 1, other courses to complete a high school program - 2.
1993-94 FRESHMAN ADMISSION DATA: ***Applications:*** Received - 180, accepted - 160, enrolled - 140. ***SAT Scores:*** nd. ***ACT composite score:*** nd. ***High school GPA:*** Average GPA - 2.90. ***Class rank:*** nd. ***International students:*** Minimum TOEFL score required - 550.
TRANSFER ADMISSION STANDARDS: ***Transfer units required:*** Minimum - none, maximum - 70. ***Minimum college GPA*** - 2.50. ***Grades accepted*** - C or better.
1993-94 TRANSFER ADMISSION DATA: ***Applications:*** Received - nd, accepted - nd, enrolled - 60. CCC transfer students enrolled - nd.
ADMISSION PROCEDURES: ***Entrance tests:*** SAT I: Reasoning Test or ACT strongly recommended. Test deadline for fall admission - June. ***Application process:*** Students admitted each term. Deadlines: Freshmen and transfers - fall 12/15, spring 7/15. Application fee - $30. Fee waiver - Yes. ***Recommendations:*** 2 - Pastor, teacher, or employer. ***Interview*** - recommended. ***Admission notification*** - rolling. Commitment deposit - $35 housing. ***Advanced placement offered*** - no. ***Advanced credit given*** - no. ***Early decision procedure:*** Application deadline - rolling, notification - rolling.
1994-95 COSTS: ***Total costs*** (approximate) - $10,355. Tuition - $4,620, other significant fees - $160, room and board - $5,075, total books, supplies, incidentals (approximate) - $500.
UNDERGRADUATE FINANCIAL AID: Students receiving financial aid - 85%. Submit FAFSA and FAF applications by 3/2. Application deadline for institutional scholarships and grants - 3/1. Average financial aid package - up to $6,000.
OTHER INFORMATION: ***Founded*** - 1945. ***Nonprofit*** - yes. ***WASC Accredited*** - yes. ***Member of AICCU*** - yes.

PEPPERDINE UNIVERSITY

24255 Pacific Coast Highway
Malibu, California 90263
Admissions: (310) 456-4392
Financial Aid: (310) 456-4301
Fax: (310) 456-4861
Toll Free: nd

Liberal Arts, Christian University Related to the Church of Christ

DISTINGUISHING FEATURES: Seaver College is the undergraduate, residential, value-centered liberal arts college of Pepperdine. It is small and selective with a friendly, supportive environment encouraging interaction and independent growth. The school features a serious commitment to rigorous academics and an emphasis on Judeo-Christian values. Pepperdine is independent of control from any religious body though it is affiliated with the Church of Christ.
DEGREES OFFERED: Bachelor's, Master's, Credential, First Professional, Doctoral, Juris Doctor (Law).
SPECIAL PROGRAMS: Great Books Colloquium in which students engage in close, critical reading of the masterpieces of Western Civilization. Opportunities for research. 3/2 Engineering programs with University of Southern California and Washington University in St. Louis. Career internships. Semester in Washington, D.C. ***Education abroad*** - may spend up to two semesters in Pepperdine facilities in Australia, England, France, Germany, Italy, Japan, Spain ***Honors programs*** - accelerated three years honors program.

COLLEGES: Divisions of Business Administration, Communication, Fine Arts, Humanities, Natural Science, Religion, Social Science and Teacher Education, Interdisciplinary/International Programs. Seaver College, Schools of Law, Business and Management. Graduate School of Education and Psychology.
UNDERGRADUATE MAJORS: 51 majors. See this chapter: Undergraduate Degree Majors, page 12--76. Preprofessional programs: Dentistry, Law, Medicine, Pharmacy, Social Work.
CALENDAR: Semester system. Summer session.
FACULTY: Full-time - 153, part-time - 144. Undergraduate classes taught by faculty, not graduate assistants - most. Faculty with Ph.D.'s - 99%. Student/faculty ratio - 13/1. Average class size - 18.
ENROLLMENT: ***Total*** - 7,023. ***Graduate*** - 4,282. Undergraduate - 2,741: California residents - 61%, out-of-state - 31%, other countries - 8%. Men - 45%, women - 55%. ***Ethnic distribution of undergraduate students:*** Hispanic - 7%, Black - 3%, Asian/Pacific Islander - 6%, Native American/Alaskan - 1%, White - 83%. ***Freshmen graduating within 5 years*** - 70%.
LOCATION: 830-acre campus in the Santa Monica Mountains overlooking the Pacific Ocean in the city of Malibu, less than an hour west of downtown Los Angeles.
CAMPUS LIFE: All freshmen and sophomores under twenty-one and not living with parents must live in on-campus residence homes. Juniors and seniors may reside in University apartments or in off-campus facilities. ***On-campus housing:*** Spaces - 1,608, undergraduate residential students - 70%. ***Clubs and organizations*** - 35. Fraternities and sororities - 13. ***Athletics:*** Intercollegiate - NCAA Division I-AAA. Intramural sports. ***Counseling and guidance:*** Academic, personal, career planning, job placement. Faculty advisors - special for freshmen. Tutoring - yes. ***Special services/academic programs for:*** Educationally disadvantaged - yes, physically disabled - yes, learning disabled - yes.
FRESHMAN ADMISSION STANDARDS: High school units: Total required - nd, a strong college-preparatory program preferred. English - 4, social science/history - nd, foreign language - 2, laboratory science - 3, mathematics - 3, course-work in speech, humanities, and social science.
1993-94 FRESHMAN ADMISSION DATA: ***Applications:*** Received - 3,123, accepted - 2,037, enrolled - 590. ***SAT Scores:*** Average verbal/mathematics scores - 502/569, median verbal/mathematics scores - nd/nd. Verbal/mathematics scores of enrolled freshmen: Middle 50% scored 440-540 verbal, 500-620 mathematics, 940-1160 combined verbal and mathematics. 1%/8% scored 700-800, 10%/29% scored 600-699, 43%/45% scored 500-599, 39%/16% scored 400-499, 7%/2% scored 300-399. ***ACT composite score:*** Average - 24, median - nd. ***High school GPA:*** Average GPA - 3.40. ***Class rank:*** 28% in top 10%, 26% in top 25%, 91% in top 50%. ***International students:*** Minimum TOEFL score required - 550.
TRANSFER ADMISSION STANDARDS: ***Transfer units required:*** Minimum - 30, maximum - 70 from two year college, 100 from four year college. ***Minimum college GPA*** - 30 units, 2.70 GPA. ***Grades accepted*** - C and above.
1993-94 TRANSFER ADMISSION DATA: ***Applications:*** Received - 353, accepted - 200, enrolled - 90. CCC transfer students enrolled - nd.
ADMISSION PROCEDURES: ***Entrance tests:*** SAT I: Reasoning Test or ACT required. Test deadline for fall admission - December. ***Application process:*** Students admitted each term. Deadline: Freshmen and transfers - 2/1 firm. Application fee - $45. Fee waiver - yes. ***Recommendations:*** 2 - teacher and personal reference. ***Interview*** - strongly recommended. ***Admission notification*** - 4/1. Commitment deposit - $400 (includes housing deposit) due 5/1. ***Advanced placement offered*** - yes. ***Advanced credit given*** - yes. ***Early decision procedure:*** Application deadline - 11/15, notification - nd.
1994-95 COSTS: ***Total costs*** (approximate) - $25,860. Tuition - $18,200, other significant fees - $nd, room and board - $6,770, total books, supplies, incidentals (approximate) - $880.
UNDERGRADUATE FINANCIAL AID: Students receiving financial aid - 65%. Submit FAFSA, FAF, and institutional applications by 3/2. Application deadline for institutional scholarships and grants - 2/15, priority deadline - 2/15. Average financial aid package - $18,000.
OTHER INFORMATION: ***Founded*** - 1937. ***Nonprofit*** - yes. ***WASC Accredited*** - yes. ***Member of AICCU*** - yes.

PHILLIPS JUNIOR COLLEGE

Phillips Junior College, Condie Campus
One West Campbell Avenue
Campbell, California 95008
(408) 866-6666
Fax: (408) 866-5542
Toll Free: nd

A Private Junior College Specializing In Career Programs

DISTINGUISHING FEATURES: Phillips Junior College operates forty-seven campuses throughout the United States, including five campuses in California. It offers programs that target specific career goals through relatively small class sizes, hands-on instruction in laboratories, and access to a highly successful job placement program. Programs are offered in Accounting, Business, Computers, Court Reporting, Electronics, Legal Assistant, Medical Assisting, Office Administration, Paralegal, Travel and Hospitality.
DEGREES OFFERED: Diploma, Associates.
CALENDAR: Quarter system.
ENROLLMENT: ***Total*** - Each campus has between 500 and 600 students.
LOCATIONS: Campbell, Carson, Fresno, Northridge, Riverside.
CAMPUS LIFE: ***On-campus housing:*** Spaces - 0.
OTHER INFORMATION: ***Founded*** - 1945. ***Nonprofit*** - no. ***WASC Accredited*** - yes, Condie campus. Accredited by the Career College Association.

PITZER COLLEGE

1050 North Mills Avenue
Claremont, California 91711
Admissions: (909) 621-8129
Financial Aid: (909) 621-8208
Fax: (909) 621-8521
Toll Free: nd

Residential Liberal Arts College. A Member of the Claremont Colleges

DISTINGUISHING FEATURES: Students who are socially and politically aware, mature, responsible, independent and involved are particularly well-suited to Pitzer. The College prizes lively student-faculty interaction and student involvement in all aspects of college governance. Emphasis is on the social sciences. Pitzer's membership in the Claremont Colleges allows students the opportunities of a university while maintaining the individual attention of a small college. Students may take up to one third of their classes at any of the other Claremont Colleges. The college has the course choices, activities, and facilities usually found only in a large university.
DEGREES OFFERED: Bachelor's.
SPECIAL PROGRAMS: Off-campus study programs in the United States. Freshman seminars limited to twelve students in each section. Combined Bachelor's/Master's degree programs with the Claremont Graduate School in Mathematics, Business Administration, Public Policy. Interdisciplinary programs and courses. Career internships. Independent study. Program in American College English for International students (PACE) provides language training for non-native English speakers wishing to prepare for attending college in the United States. New Resources program for older adults. Program for guaranteeing a Bachelor's degree in four years. ***Education abroad*** - programs in Africa, Asia, Australia, Caribbean, Europe, North America. ***Honors programs*** - yes.
COLLEGES: na.
UNDERGRADUATE MAJORS: 32 majors. Emphasizes the Social Sciences. Most popular majors are Psychology, Anthropology, Sociology, English, and Political Science. See this chapter: Undergraduate Degree Majors, page 12--76. Preprofessional programs: nd.
CALENDAR: Semester system. Summer session.
FACULTY: Full-time - 65, part-time - 15. Undergraduate classes taught by faculty, not graduate assistants - all. Faculty with Ph.D.'s - 100%. Student/faculty ratio - 10/1. Average class size - 18.
ENROLLMENT: ***Total*** - 750. ***Graduate*** - 0. ***Undergraduate*** - 750: California residents - 48%, out-of-state - 52%, other countries - 6%. Men - 45%, women - 55%. ***Ethnic distribution of undergraduate students:*** Hispanic - 16%, Black - 6%, Asian/Pacific Islander - 13%, Native American/Alaskan - 1%, White - 64%. ***Freshmen graduating within 5 years*** - 75%.
LOCATION: Shares 500 acres with the other Claremont Colleges in the residential suburban community of Claremont about forty-five minutes east of downtown Los Angeles. Set at the base of the San Gabriel foothills.

CAMPUS LIFE: All freshmen must live on campus, unless married or living with parents within ten miles of Claremont. Some off-campus housing for limited numbers. ***On-campus housing:*** Spaces - 650, undergraduate residential students - 90%. ***Clubs and organizations*** - 100+. Fraternities and sororities - 0. ***Athletics:*** Intercollegiate - joint programs in major sports with Pomona College for both men and women. NCAA, Division III. Intramural sports - yes. ***Counseling and guidance:*** Academic, personal, career planning, job placement. Faculty advisors - yes. Faculty advisor and upper-class mentor for each new student. Tutoring - yes. ***Special services/academic programs for:*** Educationally disadvantaged - no, physically disabled - yes, learning disabled - no.
FRESHMAN ADMISSION STANDARDS: High school units: Total required - na. Recommended: English - 4 including courses that require extensive writing, social science/history - 3 or more, foreign language - 3, laboratory science - 3, mathematics - 3.
1993-94 FRESHMAN ADMISSION DATA: ***Applications:*** Received - 1,135, accepted - 590, enrolled - 220. ***SAT scores:*** Average verbal/mathematics scores - nd, median verbal/mathematics scores - nd. Verbal/mathematics scores of enrolled freshmen: Middle 50% scored 510-630 verbal, 500-610 mathematics, 1050-1200 combined on verbal and mathematics. nd%/nd% scored 700-800, nd%/nd% scored 600-699, nd%/nd% scored 500-599, nd%/nd% scored 400-499, nd%/nd% scored 300-399. Average total score - 1190. ***ACT composite score:*** Average - 27, median - nd. ***High school GPA:*** Average GPA - 3.30. ***Class rank:*** Most students in the top 25% of class. 99% in top 50%. ***International students:*** Minimum TOEFL score required - 550.
TRANSFER ADMISSION STANDARDS: ***Transfer units required:*** Minimum - none, maximum - 60. ***Minimum college GPA*** - none. ***Grades accepted*** - C or better.
1993-94 TRANSFER ADMISSION DATA: ***Applications:*** Received - 136, accepted - 68, enrolled - 30. CCC transfer students enrolled - 12.
ADMISSION PROCEDURES: ***Entrance tests:*** SAT I: Reasoning Test or ACT required. SAT II: Subject Tests recommended - one in Writing and two others of student's choice. Test deadline for fall admission - January. ***Application process:*** Students admitted each term. Deadlines: Freshmen - 2/1 firm, transfers - 4/15 firm. Application fee - $40. Fee waiver - yes. ***Recommendations:*** 2 - school official and teacher. ***Interview*** - strongly recommended, not required. ***Admission notification*** - freshmen 4/1, transfers 5/15. Commitment deposit - $100 plus $200 tuition deposit. ***Advanced placement offered*** - yes. ***Advanced credit given*** - yes. ***Early decision procedure:*** Application deadline - 12/1, notification - 1/1.
1994-95 COSTS: ***Total costs*** (approximate) - $26,500. Tuition - $19,170, other significant fees - $nd, room and board - $5,910, total books, supplies, incidentals (approximate) - $1,600.
UNDERGRADUATE FINANCIAL AID: Students receiving financial aid - 45%. Submit FAFSA (CSS version preferred) and FAF applications by 2/1. Application deadline for institutional scholarships and grants - 2/1, priority deadline - 2/1. Average financial aid package - $18,900.
OTHER INFORMATION: ***Founded*** - 1963. ***Nonprofit*** - yes. ***WASC Accredited*** - yes. ***Member of AICCU*** - yes.

nd = no data available   na = not applicable

POINT LOMA NAZARENE COLLEGE

3900 Lomaland Drive
San Diego, California 92106
Admissions: (619) 221-2273
Financial Aid: (619) 221-2296
Fax: (619) 221-2579
Toll Free: nd

Liberal Arts and Science College Affiliated with the Church of the Nazarene

DISTINGUISHING FEATURES: PLNC is a church-related institution dedicated to providing higher education in the liberal arts and preparation for service and leadership in selected professions. The school seeks to promote a community of students who pursue an understanding of persons and things in the context of the Christian faith.

DEGREES OFFERED: Bachelor's, Master's, Credential.

SPECIAL PROGRAMS: Campus service/ministries into the community and into Mexico. Career internships. Summer Field Biology Institute. Capitol Campus program in Sacramento. Semester in Washington, D.C. ***Education abroad*** - summer ministries program at Institute of Holy Land Studies in Jerusalem. ***Honors programs*** - yes.

COLLEGES: na.

UNDERGRADUATE MAJORS: 50 majors. See this chapter: Undergraduate Degree Majors, page 12--76. Preprofessional programs: Architecture, Dentistry, Engineering, Law, Medicine, Nursing.

CALENDAR: Semester system. Summer session.

FACULTY: Full-time - 116, part-time - 25. Undergraduate classes taught by faculty, not graduate assistants - all. Faculty with Ph.D.'s - 72%. Student/faculty ratio - 15/1. Average class size - 18.

ENROLLMENT: ***Total*** - 2,484. ***Graduate*** - 378. ***Undergraduate*** - 2,106: California residents - 86%, out-of-state - 11%, other countries - 3%. Men - 38%, women - 62%. ***Ethnic distribution of undergraduate students:*** Hispanic - 7%, Black - 3%, Asian/Pacific Islander - 4%, Native American/Alaskan - 1%, White - 85%. ***Freshmen graduating within 5 years*** - nd%.

LOCATION: 90-acre, oceanfront campus five miles from San Diego proper. Branch campus in Pasadena.

CAMPUS LIFE: ***On-campus housing:*** Spaces - 1,330, undergraduate residential students - 59%. ***Clubs and organizations*** - 47. Fraternities and sororities - yes. ***Athletics:*** Intercollegiate - NAIA. Intramural sports - yes. ***Counseling and guidance:*** Academic, personal, career planning, job placement. Faculty advisors - religious counseling. Tutoring - yes. ***Special services/academic programs for:*** Educationally disadvantaged - yes, physically disabled - yes, learning disabled - yes.

FRESHMAN ADMISSION STANDARDS: High school units: Total required - nd. English - 4, social science/history - 1, foreign language - 2, laboratory science - 1, mathematics - 2 (algebra and geometry).

1993-94 FRESHMAN ADMISSION DATA: ***Applications:*** Received - 809, accepted - 687, enrolled - 428. ***SAT Scores:*** Average verbal/mathematics scores - 425/472, median verbal/mathematics scores - nd/nd. Verbal/mathematics scores of enrolled freshmen: Middle 50% scored 360-490 verbal, 390-540 mathematics, 770-1010 combined verbal and mathematics 0.5%/2.0% scored 700-800, 3.5%/11.0% scored 600-699, 19%/28% scored 500-599, 39%/33% scored 400-499, 31%/21% scored 300-399. ***ACT composite score:*** Average - 21, median - nd. ***High school GPA:*** Average GPA - 3.23. 64% have 3.00 or higher. ***Class rank:*** 20% in top 10%, 43% in top 25%, 69% in top 50%. ***International students:*** Minimum TOEFL score required - 550.

TRANSFER ADMISSION STANDARDS: ***Transfer units required:*** Minimum - none, maximum - 70. ***Minimum college GPA*** - 2.00. ***Grades accepted*** - D if higher grades will average 2.00.

1993-94 TRANSFER ADMISSION DATA: ***Applications:*** Received - 614, accepted - 522, enrolled - 282. CCC transfer students enrolled - 203.

ADMISSION PROCEDURES: ***Entrance tests:*** SAT I: Reasoning Test required, ACT accepted. Test deadline for fall admission - as early as possible. ***Application process:*** Students admitted each term. Deadlines: Freshmen and transfers - rolling. Application fee - $20. Fee waiver - yes. ***Recommendations:*** 2 - Minister or youth Pastor and teacher. ***Interview*** - preferred, not required. ***Admission notification*** - rolling. Commitment deposit - $200 room deposit due with housing application. ***Advanced placement offered*** - yes. ***Advanced credit given*** - yes. ***Early decision procedure:*** Application deadline - rolling, notification - rolling.

1994-95 COSTS: ***Total costs*** (approximate) - $17,510. Tuition - $10,176, other significant fees - $144, room and board - $4,190, total books, supplies, incidentals (approximate) - $3,000.

UNDERGRADUATE FINANCIAL AID: Students receiving financial aid - 75%. Submit FAFSA, FAF, and institutional applications by 3/2. Application deadline for institutional scholarships and grants - 4/10, priority deadline - 4/10. Average financial aid package - $6,973.

OTHER INFORMATION: ***Founded*** - 1902. ***Nonprofit*** - yes. ***WASC Accredited*** - yes. ***Member of AICCU*** - yes.

POMONA COLLEGE

Claremont, California 91711
Admissions: (909) 621-8134
Financial Aid: (909) 621-8205
Fax: (909) 621-8952
Toll Free: nd

Highly Selective College of the Liberal Arts and Sciences. Founding Member of the Claremont Colleges

DISTINGUISHING FEATURES: Pomona is a highly selective college offering a traditional, comprehensive liberal arts and sciences curriculum. Cooperation and collaboration among students rather than competition is emphasized. Student and faculty interaction is perhaps the most important element of a Pomona education. As one of the six Claremont Colleges, Pomona has course choices, activities, and facilities usually found only in a large university. Approximately seventy-five percent of its graduates attend graduate school in medicine, law, arts and sciences, or media studies.

DEGREES OFFERED: Bachelor's.

SPECIAL PROGRAMS: Special programs in modern languages, international relations, and public policy analysis. Opportunities to participate in faculty research. Independent study. Individual majors. 3/2 Engineering program with California Institute of Technology and Washington University in St. Louis, MO. Research opportunities. Oldenborg Center dormitory for modern language study in sections devoted to culture and language programs. Noncredit ten-week job internships available in a variety of professional settings. Student exchange programs for a semester or a year with Colby College, Fisk University, Smith College, Swarthmore College, and Spelman College. Washington, D.C. semester at American University. Program for guaranteeing a Bachelor's degree in four years. ***Education abroad:*** Over forty-five percent of students study abroad for a semester or a year. A variety of programs are offered including tutorial programs conducted by both native and Pomona faculty, independent study in fourteen countries, and study at Pomona programs in major foreign cities. ***Honors programs*** - no.
COLLEGES: na.
UNDERGRADUATE MAJORS: 36 majors. See this chapter: Undergraduate Degree Majors, page 12--76. Preprofessional programs: Business, Dentistry, Law, Medicine, Veterinary Medicine.
CALENDAR: Semester system. No summer session.
FACULTY: Full-time - 161, part-time - 30. Undergraduate classes taught by faculty, not graduate assistants - all. Faculty with Ph.D.'s - 100%. Student/faculty ratio - 9/1. Average class size - 14.
ENROLLMENT: ***Total*** - 1,382. ***Graduate*** - 0. ***Undergraduate*** - 1,382: California residents - 42%, out-of-state - 58%, other countries - 3%. Men - 51%, women - 49%. ***Ethnic distribution of undergraduate students:*** Hispanic - 11%, Black - 4.5%, Asian/Pacific Islander - 21%, Native American/Alaskan - 1%, White - 56%. ***Freshmen graduating within 5 years*** - 90%.
LOCATION: Shares 500 acres with the other Claremont Colleges in the residential suburban community of Claremont about forty-five minutes east of downtown Los Angeles. Set at the base of the San Gabriel foothills.
CAMPUS LIFE: Freshmen must live in dormitories. Upperclassmen permitted to live off campus. ***On-campus housing:*** Spaces - 1,300, undergraduate residential students - 95%. ***Clubs and organizations*** - 280. Fraternities and sororities - 7 coed. ***Athletics:*** Intercollegiate - NCAA Division III. Intramural sports - yes. ***Counseling and guidance:*** Academic, personal, career planning, job placement. Faculty advisors - yes. Tutoring - yes. Peer advising. ***Special services/academic programs for:*** Educationally disadvantaged - no, physically disabled - no, learning disabled - no.
FRESHMAN ADMISSION STANDARDS: Recommended high school units: Total required - nd. English - 4, social science/history - 2 to 3, foreign language - 3, laboratory science - 2 to 3, mathematics - 3 (4 for Science or Mathematics majors).
1993-94 FRESHMAN ADMISSION DATA: ***Applications:*** Received - 3,036, accepted - 1,150, enrolled - 390. ***SAT scores:*** Average verbal/mathematics scores - 623/687, median verbal/mathematics scores - 640/700. Verbal/mathematics scores of enrolled freshmen: Middle 50% scored 600-680 verbal, 650-730 mathematics, 1250-1410 combined verbal and mathematics. 13%/51% scored 700-800, 59%/38% scored 600-699, 22%/8% scored 500-599, 6%/3% scored 400-499. ***ACT composite score:*** Average - nd, median - 31. ***High school GPA:*** Average GPA - nd. ***Class rank:*** 79% in top 10%, 96% in top 25%, 100% in top 40%. ***International students:*** Minimum TOEFL score required - 600.
TRANSFER ADMISSION STANDARDS: ***Transfer units required:*** Minimum - 24, maximum - 64. ***Minimum college GPA*** - approximately 3.00. ***Grades accepted*** - C and better in arts and science courses only. Two-year enrollment as full-time Pomona student required for graduation.
1993-94 TRANSFER ADMISSION DATA: ***Applications:*** Received - 236, accepted - 54, enrolled - 22. CCC transfer students enrolled - nd.
ADMISSION PROCEDURES: ***Entrance tests:*** SAT I: Reasoning Test or ACT required. SAT II: Subject Tests recommended. Test deadline for fall admission - December. ***Application process:*** Students admitted for fall term. Deadlines: Freshmen - 1/15 firm, transfers - fall 3/15 firm, spring 11/1 firm. Application fee - $50. Fee waiver - yes. ***Recommendations:*** 3 - counselor, 2 teachers. ***Interview*** - highly recommended. ***Admission notification*** - freshmen 4/10, transfers fall 5/15, spring 12/1. Commitment deposit - $300 due prior to candidate reply date. ***Advanced placement offered*** - yes. ***Advanced credit given*** - yes. ***Early decision procedure:*** Application deadline - 11/15, notification - 12/15.
1994-95 COSTS: ***Total costs*** (approximate) - $26,920. Tuition - $17,720, other significant fees - $180, room and board - $7,220, total books, supplies, incidentals (approximate) - $1,800.
UNDERGRADUATE FINANCIAL AID: Students receiving financial aid - 55%. Submit FAFSA (CSS version preferred) and FAF applications by 3/2. Application deadline for institutional scholarships and grants - 2/1, priority deadline - 2/1. Average financial aid package - $18,300.
OTHER INFORMATION: ***Founded*** - 1887. ***Nonprofit*** - yes. ***WASC Accredited*** - yes. ***Member of AICCU*** - yes.

QUEEN OF THE HOLY ROSARY COLLEGE

43326 Mission Boulevard
Fremont, California 94539
(510) 657-2468
Fax: (510) 657- 1734
Toll Free: nd

Two-Year College to Prepare Dominican Sisters

DISTINGUISHING FEATURES: The two-year program at Queen of the Holy Rosary prepares Dominican Sisters for their life and ministry as Catholic educators. The single major in Religious Studies is complemented with coursework in philosophy, music, and educational principles.
DEGREES OFFERED: Associates.
CALENDAR: Semester system.
ENROLLMENT: ***Total*** - 270.
LOCATION: In the California Mission San Jose area of Fremont in the San Francisco Bay area.
CAMPUS LIFE: ***On-campus housing:*** Spaces - 0.
OTHER INFORMATION: ***Founded*** - 1930. ***Nonprofit*** - yes. ***WASC Accredited*** - yes.

CALIFORNIA INDEPENDENT COLLEGES

nd = no data available   na = not applicable

SAINT JOHN'S SEMINARY COLLEGE

5012 East Seminary Road
Camarillo, California 93012
(805) 482-2755
Fax: nd
Toll Free: nd

College to Prepare Men for the Catholic Priesthood

DISTINGUISHING FEATURES: St. John's is a freestanding Seminary College that emphasizes the liberal arts and has a curriculum that leads to the degree of Bachelor of Arts in Philosophy. Its overall purpose is to prepare men for the Catholic priesthood.
DEGREES OFFERED: Bachelor's.
CALENDAR: Semester system.
ENROLLMENT: ***Total*** - 116 men.
LOCATION: 100-acre campus near Los Angeles.
CAMPUS LIFE: ***On-campus housing:*** Spaces - dormitories.
OTHER INFORMATION: ***Founded*** - 1939. ***Nonprofit*** - yes. ***WASC Accredited*** - yes.

SAINT MARY'S COLLEGE OF CALIFORNIA

Moraga, California 94575
Admissions: (510) 631-4224
Financial Aid: (510) 631-4370
Fax: (510) 376-7193
Toll Free: nd

Roman Catholic College of the Liberal Arts

DISTINGUISHING FEATURES: Saint Mary's College of California is a traditional liberal arts college run by the Christian Brothers. The curriculum is flexible and innovative. The Collegiate Seminar, of not more than twenty students, is required of all students. It is the core of the curriculum. Students take four classes in which they read and discuss the classics of Western Civilization. A community atmosphere is created throughout the campus. Students participate in the College's decision-making process and the student body president is an ex-officio member of the Board of Trustees.
DEGREES OFFERED: Certificate, Associates, Bachelor's, Master's, Credential.
SPECIAL PROGRAMS: Integral Program of Liberal Arts is a unique major that studies the Great Books. Students study all the areas of human learning through reading the authors who founded these disciplines. 3/2 program in Engineering with the University of Southern California and Washington University in St. Louis, MO. Partnership program with Samuel Merritt College offering a four-year curriculum that leads to a Bachelor's Degree in Nursing. Internship programs in cooperation with various community agencies. ***Education abroad*** - junior year and/or January term in Argentina, England, France, Greece, Ireland, Italy, Mexico, and Spain. ***Honors programs*** - yes.
COLLEGES: Schools of Education, Economics and Business Administration, Liberal Arts, Science, plus an Intercollegiate Nursing Program with Samuel Merritt College.
UNDERGRADUATE MAJORS: 29 majors. See this chapter: Undergraduate Degree Majors, page 12--76. Preprofessional programs: Dentistry, Law, Medicine, Pharmacy.
CALENDAR: 4-1-4 system, January interterm. Summer session for graduate students only.
FACULTY: Full-time - 124, part-time - 32. Undergraduate classes taught by faculty, not graduate assistants - all. Faculty with Ph.D.'s - 93%. Student/faculty ratio - 16/1. Average class size - 20.
ENROLLMENT: ***Total*** - 3,217. ***Graduate*** - 818. ***Undergraduate*** - 2,399: California residents - 75%, out-of-state - 22%, other countries - 3%. Men - 47%, women - 53%. ***Ethnic distribution of undergraduate students:*** Hispanic - 12%, Black - 4%, Asian/Pacific Islander - 7%, Native American/Alaskan - 1%, White - 73%. ***Freshmen graduating within 5 years*** - nd%.
LOCATION: 450-acre campus in the rolling hills of Moraga Valley in the San Francisco Bay Area. San Francisco is a half-hour away.
CAMPUS LIFE: ***On-campus housing:*** Spaces - 1,378, undergraduate residential students - 70%. ***Clubs and organizations*** - 45. Fraternities and sororities - 0. ***Athletics:*** Intercollegiate - NCAA Division I-AA. Intramural sports - yes. ***Counseling and guidance:*** Academic, personal, career planning, job placement. Faculty advisors - yes. Tutoring - yes. ***Special services/academic programs for:*** Educationally disadvantaged - yes, physically disabled - yes, learning disabled - no.
FRESHMAN ADMISSION STANDARDS: High school units: Total required - 15 units completed with minimum B average. English - 4, social science/history - 3, foreign language - 3, laboratory science - 2, mathematics - 3.
1993-94 FRESHMAN ADMISSION DATA: ***Applications:*** Received - 2,651, accepted - 1,945, enrolled - 465. ***SAT Scores:*** Average verbal/mathematics scores - nd/nd, median verbal/mathematics scores - nd/nd. Verbal/mathematics scores of enrolled freshmen: Middle 50% scored 460-590 verbal, 510-600 mathematics, 950-1180 combined verbal and mathematics. nd%/nd% scored 700-800, nd%/nd% scored 600-699, nd%/nd% scored 500-599, nd%/nd% scored 400-499, nd%/nd% scored 300-399. ***ACT composite score:*** Average - nd, median - nd. ***High school GPA:*** Average GPA - 3.34. ***Class rank:*** nd. ***International students:*** Minimum TOEFL score required - 525.
TRANSFER ADMISSION STANDARDS: ***Transfer units required:*** Minimum - 23, maximum - 64 from CCC. ***Minimum college GPA*** - 2.30. ***Grades accepted*** - A, B, C, Credit, Pass.
1993-94 TRANSFER ADMISSION DATA: ***Applications:*** Received - 647, accepted - 377, enrolled - 190. CCC transfer students enrolled -136.
ADMISSION PROCEDURES: ***Entrance tests:*** SAT I: Reasoning Test or ACT required. Test deadline for fall admission - January. ***Application process:*** Students admitted each term. Deadline: Freshmen and transfers - 3/1 firm. Application fee - $35. Fee waiver - yes. ***Recommendations:*** 1 - principal, counselor, or teacher. ***Interview*** - optional. ***Admission notification*** - 3/15. Commitment deposit - $250. CA resident, $100 non-CA resident, due 5/15. ***Advanced placement offered*** - yes. ***Advanced credit given*** - yes. ***Early decision procedure:*** Application deadline - 11/15, SAT I: Reasoning Test taken by Nov of senior year, notification - 1/15.
1994-95 COSTS: ***Total costs*** (approximate) - $20,402. Tuition - $13,332, other significant fees - $1160, room and board - $6,354, total books, supplies, incidentals (approximate) - $600.

nd = no data available na = not applicable

UNDERGRADUATE FINANCIAL AID: Students receiving financial aid - 54%. Submit FAFSA and FAF by 3/2. Application deadline for institutional scholarships and grants - 3/1, priority deadline - 3/1. Average financial aid package - $9,942.
OTHER INFORMATION: ***Founded*** - 1863. ***Nonprofit*** - yes. ***WASC Accredited*** - yes. ***Member of AICCU*** - yes.

SAMUEL MERRITT COLLEGE

370 Hawthorne Avenue
Oakland, California 94609
Admissions: (510) 420-6076
Financial Aid: (510) 420-6131
Fax: (510) 420-6025
Toll Free: nd

College of Nursing

DISTINGUISHING FEATURES: Samuel Merritt College and Saint Mary's College in Moraga offer an Intercollegiate Nursing Program and jointly confer a Bachelor of Science degree in Nursing. The four-year curriculum provides students with in-depth nursing experience and well-rounded academic studies in both the sciences and liberal arts. Students take their first nursing course in the freshman year and are offered a variety of clinical experiences in numerous facilities throughout the Bay Area. Multiple entry options are designed to facilitate admission of students to advanced standing. The college Graduate FasTrak, an accelerated nursing enrollment option, allows completion of degree requirements in seventeen months for those students who already have a Bachelor's degree.
DEGREES OFFERED: Bachelor's, Master's.
SPECIAL PROGRAMS: Affiliation with Saint Mary's College for liberal arts education. Features extensive clinical instruction. ***Education abroad*** - no. ***Honors programs*** - no.
COLLEGES: na.
UNDERGRADUATE MAJORS: 1 major. Nursing. Preprofessional programs: none.
CALENDAR: 4-1-4 system, January interterm. Summer session.
FACULTY: Full-time - nd, part-time - nd. Undergraduate classes taught by faculty, not graduate assistants - all. Faculty with Ph.D.'s - 20%. Student/faculty ratio - 9/1. Average class size - nd.
ENROLLMENT: ***Total*** - 445. ***Graduate*** - 144. ***Undergraduate*** - 301: California residents - 95%, out-of-state and other countries - 5%. Men - 11%, women - 89%. ***Ethnic distribution of undergraduate students:*** Minority - 24%. Hispanic - nd%, Black - nd%, Asian/Pacific Islander - nd%, Native American/Alaskan - nd%, White - 76%. ***Freshmen graduating within 5 years*** - nd%.
LOCATION: In the Merritt Peralta Medical Center complex in downtown Oakland. San Francisco is a half-hour away.
CAMPUS LIFE: ***On-campus housing:*** Spaces - 93, undergraduate residential students - 10%. ***Clubs and organizations*** - 7. Fraternities and sororities - 0. ***Athletics:*** Intercollegiate - available through Saint Mary's College. Intramural sports - available through Saint Mary's College. ***Counseling and guidance:*** Academic, personal, career planning, job placement. Academic advisement and counseling available through Saint Mary's College. Faculty advisors - yes. Tutoring - nd. ***Special services/academic programs for:*** Educationally disadvantaged - nd, physically disabled - nd, learning disabled - nd.
FRESHMAN ADMISSION STANDARDS: High school units: Total required - nd. English - 3, social science/history - 2, foreign language - 0, laboratory science - 2 (including one year of chemistry and 1 year Biology), mathematics - 2 (algebra and geometry).
1993-94 FRESHMAN ADMISSION DATA: ***Applications:*** Received - nd, accepted - nd, enrolled - 14. ***SAT Scores:*** nd. ***ACT composite score:*** Average - nd, median - nd. ***High school GPA:*** Average GPA - 2.99. Minimum - 2.50. ***Class rank:*** nd. ***International students:*** Minimum TOEFL score required - 550.
TRANSFER ADMISSION STANDARDS: ***Transfer units required:*** Minimum - 30, maximum - nd. ***Minimum college GPA*** - 2.50. ***Grades accepted*** - C or better, Credit, Pass.
1993-94 TRANSFER ADMISSION DATA: ***Applications:*** Received - nd, accepted - nd, enrolled - 24. CCC transfer students enrolled - nd.
ADMISSION PROCEDURES: ***Entrance tests:*** SAT I: Reasoning Test or ACT required. Test deadline for fall admission - March. ***Application process:*** Students admitted each term - fall, spring, summer. May submit application for joint admission to Samuel Merritt and St. Mary's College. Deadlines: Freshmen and transfers - rolling. Application fee - $35. Fee waiver - no. ***Recommendations:*** 1 - teacher or counselor. ***Interview*** - yes. ***Admission notification*** - rolling, within eight to ten weeks after completed application received. Commitment deposit - $200 tuition plus $100 housing. ***Advanced placement offered*** - yes. ***Advanced credit given*** - yes. ***Early decision procedure:*** no.
1994-95 COSTS: ***Total costs*** (approximate) - $20,450. Tuition - $12,460, other significant fees - $65, room and board - $3,150 (room only), total books, supplies, incidentals (approximate) - $4,775.
UNDERGRADUATE FINANCIAL AID: Students receiving financial aid - 90%. Submit FAFSA by 3/2. Application deadline for institutional scholarships and grants - 3/2. Average financial aid package - $13,000.
OTHER INFORMATION: ***Founded*** - 1909. ***Nonprofit*** - yes. ***WASC Accredited*** - yes. ***Member of AICCU*** - yes.

SAN FRANCISCO ART INSTITUTE

800 Chestnut Street
San Francisco, California 94133
Admissions: (415) 749-4580
Financial Aid: (415) 749-4520
Fax: (415) 749-4590
Toll Free: nd

Institute of the Visual Arts

DISTINGUISHING FEATURES: The San Francisco Art Institute stands for creative freedom. It is one of the only exclusively fine arts colleges in the United States. Many of the nation's most accomplished artists have been either its students or teachers. Outstanding students have the opportunity in their junior year to compete for private studio space for their senior year. Eighty percent of the students are over the age of twenty-five. The majority of students transfer from other schools, mainly from California Community Colleges.
DEGREES OFFERED: Bachelor's, Master's.
SPECIAL PROGRAMS: Independent study. Career internships. ***Education abroad*** - no. ***Honors programs*** - no.

nd = no data available na = not applicable

COLLEGES: na.
UNDERGRADUATE MAJORS: 6 majors. Painting, Printmaking, Photography, Filmmaking, Sculpture/Ceramic Sculpture, Performance/Video: New Genres. Preprofessional programs: nd.
CALENDAR: Semester system. Summer session.
FACULTY: Full-time - nd, part-time - nd. Undergraduate classes taught by faculty, not graduate assistants - all. Faculty with Ph.D.'s - nd%, 100% have highest degree in their field. Student/faculty ratio - 9/1. Average class size - nd.
ENROLLMENT: ***Total*** - 626. ***Graduate*** - 127. ***Undergraduate*** - 499: California residents - 50%, out-of-state and other countries - 50%. Men - 43%, women - 57%. ***Ethnic distribution of undergraduate students:*** Minority - 11%. Hispanic - nd%, Black - nd%, Asian/Pacific Islander - nd%, Native American/Alaskan - nd%, White - 89%. ***Freshmen graduating within 5 years*** - nd%.
LOCATION: In the heart of San Francisco on Russian Hill in a Mediterranean-styled building overlooking Fisherman's Wharf.
CAMPUS LIFE: ***On-campus housing:*** Spaces - 0, undergraduate residential students - 0%. ***Clubs and organizations*** - 5. Fraternities and sororities - 0. ***Athletics:*** Intercollegiate - no. Intramural sports - no. ***Counseling and guidance:*** Academic, personal, job placement. Faculty advisors - yes. Tutoring - yes. ***Special services/academic programs for:*** Educationally disadvantaged - no, physically disabled - no, learning disabled - yes.
FRESHMAN ADMISSION STANDARDS: Graduation from high school or equivalent. High school units: Total required - nd. English - nd, social science/history - nd, foreign language - nd, laboratory science -nd, mathematics - nd.
1993-94 FRESHMAN ADMISSION DATA: ***Applications:*** Received - nd, accepted - nd, enrolled - 41. ***SAT Scores:*** nd. ACT composite score: nd. ***High school GPA:*** Average GPA - minimum C+ or better. ***Class rank:*** nd. ***International students:*** Minimum TOEFL score required - 500.
TRANSFER ADMISSION STANDARDS: ***Transfer units required:*** Minimum - 0, maximum - 90. ***Minimum college GPA*** - none. ***Grades accepted*** - C or better.
1993-94 TRANSFER ADMISSION DATA: ***Applications:*** Received - nd, accepted - nd, enrolled - 164. CCC transfer students enrolled - nd.
ADMISSION PROCEDURES: ***Entrance tests:*** SAT I: Reasoning Test or ACT and portfolio required. Test deadline for fall admission - rolling. ***Application process:*** Students admitted each term. Deadlines: Freshmen and transfers - rolling. Application fee - $50. Fee waiver - yes. ***Recommendations*** - none. ***Interview*** - recommended. ***Admission notification*** - rolling. Commitment deposit - $300. ***Advanced placement offered*** - yes. ***Advanced credit given*** - yes. ***Early decision procedure*** - no.
1994-95 COSTS: ***Total costs*** (approximate) - $22,820. Tuition - $14,500, other significant fees - $nd, room and board - $5,600, total books, supplies, incidentals (approximate) - $2,720.
UNDERGRADUATE FINANCIAL AID: Students receiving financial aid - 67%. Submit FAFSA (CSS version preferred) and FAF by 3/2. Application deadline for institutional scholarships and grants - 9/1, priority deadline - 4/1. Average financial aid package - $11,060.
OTHER INFORMATION: ***Founded*** - 1871. ***Nonprofit*** - yes. ***WASC Accredited*** - yes. ***Member of AICCU*** - yes.

SAN FRANCISCO COLLEGE OF MORTUARY SCIENCE

1598 Delores Street
San Francisco, California 94110
(415) 824-1313
Fax: (415) 824-1390
Toll Free: nd

College Providing Funeral Service Education

DISTINGUISHING FEATURES: The San Francisco College of Mortuary Science provides a program in funeral service education to men and women from throughout the United States and the world. Classroom and practical laboratory training in all phases of funeral service are provided on campus under the direct supervision of licensed funeral directors/embalmers. The college has an on-site mortuary. To receive a degree students must take their general education courses at other institutions.
DEGREES OFFERED: Associates.
CALENDAR: Trimester system.
ENROLLMENT: ***Total*** - 70.
LOCATION: In the city of San Francisco.
CAMPUS LIFE: ***On-campus housing:*** Spaces - 0.
OTHER INFORMATION: ***Founded*** - 1930. ***Nonprofit*** - yes. ***WASC Accredited*** - yes.

SAN FRANCISCO CONSERVATORY OF MUSIC

1201 Ortega Street
San Francisco, California 94122
Admissions: (415) 759-3431
Financial Aid: (415) 759-3422
Fax: (415) 759-3499
Toll Free: nd

Conservatory of Music

DISTINGUISHING FEATURES: The San Francisco Conservatory of Music has attracted gifted students from all over the world and trained them for careers as professional symphony musicians, concert artists, opera singers, composers, conductors, and teachers. The Conservatory is especially noted for its outstanding faculty, low student-teacher ratio, and extensive opportunities for performance. More than two-thirds of the alumni are employed in the music professions.
DEGREES OFFERED: Bachelor's, Master's.
SPECIAL PROGRAMS: Community service program sends students into the community to perform. Music as Reality course on practical aspects of career as musician. Student required to perform before faculty jurors at the end of each academic year. ***Education abroad*** - no. ***Honors programs*** - yes.
COLLEGES: na.
UNDERGRADUATE MAJORS: Applied Music, Music Composition. Areas of Concentration: Keyboard Instruments, Orchestral Instruments, Classical Guitar, Voice, and Composition. Preprofessional programs: none.
CALENDAR: Semester system. Summer session.

FACULTY: Most faculty are professional musicians. Full-time - 23, part-time - 30. Undergraduate classes taught by faculty, not graduate assistants - all. Faculty with Ph.D.'s - 28%. Student/faculty ratio - 6/1. Average class size - 13.
ENROLLMENT: ***Total*** - 274. ***Graduate*** - 108. ***Undergraduate*** - 156: California residents - 55%, out-of-state - 19%, other countries - 26%. Men - 42%, women - 58%. ***Ethnic distribution of undergraduate students:*** Hispanic - 3%, Black - 3%, Asian/Pacific Islander - 22%, Native American/Alaskan - 0%, White - 72%. ***Freshmen graduating within 5 years*** - 48%.
LOCATION: In the heart of San Francisco in a residential neighborhood near Golden Gate Park three miles from the University of San Francisco.
CAMPUS LIFE: Off-campus housing available at the University of San Francisco. ***On-campus housing:*** Spaces - 0, undergraduate residential students - 0%. ***Clubs and organizations*** - 3. Fraternities and sororities - 0. ***Athletics:*** Intercollegiate - no. Intramural sports - no. ***Counseling and guidance:*** Academic, career planning, job placement. Faculty advisors - yes. Tutoring - yes. ***Special services/academic programs for:*** Educationally disadvantaged - yes, physically disabled - nd, learning disabled - nd.
FRESHMAN ADMISSION STANDARDS: Graduation from high school. May be waived if music qualifications are extraordinary. High school units: Total required - nd. English - 3, social science/history - 0, foreign language - 3 preferred, laboratory science - 0, mathematics - 0.
1993-94 FRESHMAN ADMISSION DATA: ***Applications:*** Received -69, accepted - 38, enrolled - 24. ***SAT scores:*** Average verbal/mathematics scores - 468/457, median verbal/mathematics scores - nd/nd. Verbal/mathematics scores of enrolled freshmen: Middle 50% scored 400-610 verbal, 480-650 mathematics, 860-1200 combined verbal and mathematics. 6%/6% scored 700-800, 20%/38% scored 600-699, 25%/13% scored 500-599, 19%/31% scored 400-499, 12%/12% scored 300-399, 18%/0% scored 200-299. ***ACT composite score:*** Average - nd, median - nd. ***High school GPA:*** Average GPA - nd. ***Class rank:*** nd. ***International students:*** Minimum TOEFL score required - 500.
TRANSFER ADMISSION STANDARDS: ***Transfer units required:*** Minimum - none, maximum - determined by committee on academic standing. ***Minimum college GPA*** - 2.00. ***Grades accepted*** - C or better.
1993-94 TRANSFER ADMISSION DATA: ***Applications:*** Received - nd, accepted - nd, enrolled - 40. CCC transfer students enrolled - 9.
ADMISSION PROCEDURES: ***Entrance tests:*** SAT I: Reasoning Test or ACT and audition required. Test deadlines for admission: Prefer by 4/30 for fall, 11/15 for spring. ***Application process:*** Students admitted each term. Deadlines: Freshmen and transfers - 3/1 priority date. Application fee - $60. Fee waiver - no. ***Recommendations:*** 2 including one from a musician. ***Interview*** - audition on applicant's major instrument required. Consult Conservatory Catalogue for repertoire. ***Admission notification*** - rolling. Commitment deposit - $200 due 6/1. ***Advanced placement offered*** - yes. ***Advanced credit given*** - yes. ***Early decision procedure*** - no.
1994-95 COSTS: ***Total costs*** (approximate) - $22,020. Tuition - $13,000, other significant fees - $250, room and board - $5,600, total books, supplies, incidentals (approximate) - $3,170.
UNDERGRADUATE FINANCIAL AID: Students receiving financial aid - 64%. Submit FAFSA, FAF, and institutional applications by 3/2. Application deadline for institutional scholarships and grants - 3/15, priority deadline - 3/15. Average financial aid package - $9,637.
OTHER INFORMATION: ***Founded*** - 1917. ***Nonprofit*** - yes. ***WASC Accredited*** - yes. ***Member of AICCU*** - yes.

SAN JOSE CHRISTIAN COLLEGE

790 South 12th Street
San Jose, California 95112
(408) 293-9058
Fax: nd
Toll Free: nd

Evangelical Christian College

DISTINGUISHING FEATURES: San Jose Christian College is a non-denominational evangelical Christian college educating church leaders in Bible, preaching, youth ministry, Christian education, missions, counseling, and music. It emphasizes excellence and integrity in its academic programs and practical internships.
DEGREES OFFERED: Associates, Bachelor's.
CALENDAR: Quarter system.
ENROLLMENT: ***Total*** - 230.
LOCATION: 9-acre campus in the city of San Jose forty-five miles south of San Francisco.
CAMPUS LIFE: ***On-campus housing:*** Spaces - dormitories.
OTHER INFORMATION: ***Founded*** - 1939. ***Nonprofit*** - yes. ***WASC Accredited*** - no. Accredited by the American Association of Bible Colleges.

SANTA CLARA UNIVERSITY

Santa Clara, California 95053
Admissions: (408) 554-4700
Financial Aid: (408) 554-4505
Fax: (408) 554-5255
Toll Free: nd

Undergraduate and Graduate Catholic University of the Arts and Sciences, Business, and Engineering

DISTINGUISHING FEATURES: Governed by a Board of Trustees of laymen and Jesuits, Santa Clara University is selective and comprehensive. The principal objective of the school is to provide superior undergraduate education in the liberal arts and sciences and in the professions of business and engineering to a student body of limited size and high ability. Academic life is characterized by a competitive, hard-working attitude tempered by a spirit of cooperation among students and faculty. Students are attracted by its strong academic reputation, supportive community, and successful athletic programs. Santa Clara is able to blend its traditional, historical, Jesuit origins with a commitment to innovation, multiculturalism, and the nurturing of scholars who will also be leaders. The campus environment encourages reflection and collaborative learning. It is California's oldest institution of higher learning.

DEGREES OFFERED: Certificate, Bachelor's, Master's, Credential, First Professional, Doctoral, Juris Doctor (Law).
SPECIAL PROGRAMS: Core liberal arts curriculum for all undergraduates regardless of major. International Business Studies program supplements academic majors in liberal arts and business. Integration of foreign language proficiency and understanding of foreign culture with education in international business. Retail Studies program open to all majors with overview of careers in retailing. Ethnic Studies Interdisciplinary program. Women's Study program. Da Vinci Interdisciplinary program in Engineering. Combined Sciences program combining study in both the natural and social sciences. Career internships. ***Education abroad*** - junior semester or year abroad in Austria, England, France, Germany, Hong Kong, Indonesia, Italy, Japan, Singapore, Spain, Thailand. ***Honors programs*** - yes.
COLLEGES: College of Arts and Sciences. Leavey School of Business and Administration. Schools of Engineering, Law. Division of Counseling Psychology and Education.
UNDERGRADUATE MAJORS: 31 majors. See this chapter: Undergraduate Degree Majors, page 12--76. Special academic programs: International Studies and Business, Retail Management Institute, Center for Applied Ethics. Preprofessional programs: Dentistry, Education, Law, Medicine.
CALENDAR: Quarter system. Summer session.
FACULTY: Full-time - 296, part-time - 120. Undergraduate classes taught by faculty, not graduate assistants - all. Faculty with Ph.D.'s - 90%. Student/faculty ratio - 13/1. Average class size - 26.
ENROLLMENT: ***Total*** - 7,725. ***Graduate*** - 3,706. ***Undergraduate*** - 4,019: California residents - 66%, out-of-state - 34%, other countries - 3%. Men - 49%, women - 51%. ***Ethnic distribution of undergraduate students:*** Hispanic - 13%, Black - 3%, Asian/Pacific Islander - 19%, Native American/Alaskan - 0.5%, White - 64.5%. ***Freshmen graduating within 5 years*** - 80%.
LOCATION: 103-acre campus in the heart of Silicon Valley, center of high technology. Less than one hour from San Francisco. Spanish-style architecture, picturesque campus.
CAMPUS LIFE: Freshmen not required to live on campus, but ninety-five percent choose to do so. ***On-campus housing:*** Spaces - 1,931, undergraduate residential students - 42%. ***Clubs and organizations*** - 100. Fraternities and sororities - 7. ***Athletics:*** Intercollegiate - NCAA Division I-AAA. Intramural sports - yes. ***Counseling and guidance:*** Academic, personal, career planning, job placement. Faculty advisors - yes. Tutoring - yes. ***Special services/academic programs for:*** Educationally disadvantaged - no, physically disabled - yes, learning disabled - yes.
FRESHMAN ADMISSION STANDARDS: High school units: Total required - 16 including English - 4, social science/history - 2, foreign language - 3, laboratory science - 1 (physics and chemistry recommended for Science and Engineering majors), mathematics - 3 (2 algebra, 1 geometry, trigonometry for Science, Mathematics, Engineering majors). Elective courses in advanced foreign languages, mathematics, laboratory science, or other solid college-preparatory classes - 4.
1993-94 FRESHMAN ADMISSION DATA: ***Applications:*** Received - 4,019, accepted - 2,779, enrolled - 888. ***SAT Scores:*** Average verbal/mathematics scores - nd/nd, median verbal/mathematics scores - nd/nd. Middle 50% scored 440-540 verbal, 520-630 mathematics. Verbal/mathematics scores of enrolled freshmen: 1%/8% scored 700-800, 10%/33% scored 600-699, 36%/43% scored 500-599, 43%/14% scored 400-499, 9%/2% scored 300-399. ***ACT composite score:*** Average - nd, median - nd. ***High school GPA:*** Average GPA - 3.43. 48% with 3.50-4.00, 41% with 3.00-3.50, 11% with 2.50-2.99. ***Class rank:*** 35% in top 10%, 73% in top 25%, 95% in top 50%. ***International students:*** Minimum TOEFL score required - 550.
TRANSFER ADMISSION STANDARDS: ***Transfer units required:*** Minimum - 45 quarter, maximum - determined by committee on academic standing in each school, generally 88 quarter. ***Minimum college GPA:*** For Arts and Sciences and Engineering - 3.00, for Business - 3.40. ***Grades accepted*** - C or better. Other requirements: SAT I required of all transfer students with less than 45 quarter units.
1993-94 TRANSFER ADMISSION DATA: ***Applications:*** Received - 892, accepted - 534, enrolled - 346. CCC transfer students enrolled - 231.
ADMISSION PROCEDURES: ***Entrance tests:*** SAT I: Reasoning Test or ACT required. Test deadline for fall admission - January. ***Application process:*** Deadlines: Freshmen - fall 2/1 firm, transfers - fall 5/15, winter 10/15, spring 12/1 - all firm. Application fee - $40. Fee waiver - yes. ***Recommendations:*** 1 - teacher or counselor. ***Interview*** - not required, but available. ***Admission notification*** - rolling. Commitment deposit - $200 due 5/1. ***Advanced placement offered*** - yes. ***Advanced credit given*** - for score of 4 or 5 on Advanced Placement Tests. ***Early decision procedure*** - no.
1994-95 COSTS: ***Total costs*** (approximate) - $22,300. Tuition - $13,584, other significant fees - $250, room and board - $5,928, total books, supplies, incidentals (approximate) - $2,538.
UNDERGRADUATE FINANCIAL AID: Students receiving financial aid - 58%. Submit FAFSA and FAF applications by 3/2. Application deadline for institutional scholarships and grants - 2/1, priority deadline - 2/1. Average financial aid package - $11,529.
OTHER INFORMATION: ***Founded*** - 1851. ***Nonprofit*** - yes. ***WASC Accredited*** - yes. ***Member of AICCU*** - yes.

SCRIPPS COLLEGE

1030 Columbia Avenue
Claremont, California 91711
Admissions: (909) 621-8149
Financial Aid: (909) 621-8275
Fax: (909) 621-8323
Toll Free: (800) 770-1334

Highly Selective, Liberal Arts College for Women, Emphasizing the Humanities, Fine Arts, Social and Natural Sciences. A Member of the Claremont Colleges

DISTINGUISHING FEATURES: Scripps College is an innovative college for women. Its traditional strengths in the humanities and the fine arts are fully supplemented by a major science program and an broad range of social science options. A member of the Claremont Colleges, Scripps is rare among American women's institutions in that it offers its six hundred students the academic advantages of a women's college as well as the educational and social benefits of a large coeducational institution. Students actively cross-register at the other Claremont Colleges. This highly cooperative college cluster offers approximately 2,500 courses to over 5,000 students. The six Claremont campuses are adjacent to each other, so students can easily walk from campus to campus for classes, meals, lectures, films, and concerts. The college is viewed

nd = no data available na = not applicable

as exceptionally innovative because of its interdisciplinary Humanities Program and commitment to the career development of women. It is characterized by close faculty relationships, small classes, and extensive opportunities to get involved in activities. The core of the curriculum is a sequence of courses in humanities with distinctive offerings in fine arts, social science, languages, literature, and science.

DEGREES OFFERED: Bachelor's.

SPECIAL PROGRAMS: Three-credit Humanities Internship Program for sophomores, juniors, and seniors to relate college to work experience. Combined Bachelor's and Master's degree programs with Claremont Graduate School in Government, International Studies and Public Policy, and Business Administration. Combined Bachelor's degree program in Engineering with Stanford University and other leading institutions. Off-campus semester study available at American University, Washington, D.C.; the United Nations; Colby College, ME; Spelman College, GA; California Institute of Technology. Design own major. ***Education abroad:*** Scripps study-abroad programs in Ecuador, France, Germany, Hungary, Zimbabwe. Thirty additional countries such as Australia, China, Ireland, Japan, Nigeria, Russia and Spain may be arranged through affiliated programs. ***Honors programs*** - yes.

COLLEGES: na.

UNDERGRADUATE MAJORS: 48 majors. See this chapter: Undergraduate Degree Majors, page 12--76. Preprofessional programs: Architecture and Urban Planning, Arts Management, Education, Health, Law, Librarianship, Medicine, Natural History/Environment, Veterinary Medicine.

CALENDAR: Semester system. No summer session.

FACULTY: Full-time - 60, part-time - 26. Undergraduate classes taught by faculty, not graduate assistants - all. Faculty with Ph.D.'s - 95%. Student/faculty ratio - 9/1. Average class size - 14.

ENROLLMENT: ***Total*** - 612. ***Graduate*** - 0. ***Undergraduate*** - 612: California residents - 54%, out-of-state - 42%, other countries - 4%. Men - 0%, women - 100%. ***Ethnic distribution of undergraduate students:*** Hispanic - 8%, Black - 5%, Asian/Pacific Islander - 13%, Native American/Alaskan - 1%, White - 69%. ***Freshmen graduating within 5 years*** - 77%.

LOCATION: Shares 500 acres with the other Claremont Colleges in the residential suburban community of Claremont about forty-five minutes east of downtown Los Angeles. Set at the base of the San Gabriel foothills.

CAMPUS LIFE: Freshmen must live in dormitories or at home; upperclassmen permitted to live off campus. ***On-campus housing:*** Spaces - 550, undergraduate residential students - 96%. ***Clubs and organizations*** - 150. Fraternities and sororities - 0. ***Athletics:*** Intercollegiate - NCAA III. Intramural sports - yes. ***Counseling and guidance:*** Academic, personal, career planning, job placement. Faculty advisors - yes. Tutoring - yes. ***Special services/academic programs for:*** Educationally disadvantaged - no, physically disabled - yes, learning disabled - no.

FRESHMAN ADMISSION STANDARDS: High school units: Total required - na. Recommended: English - 4, social science/history - 3, foreign language - 3 (or 2 years of 2 foreign languages), laboratory science - 3, mathematics - 4. Enrollment in Honors or Advanced Placement courses encouraged.

1993-94 FRESHMAN ADMISSION DATA: ***Applications:*** Received - 855, accepted - 632, enrolled - 139. ***SAT Scores:*** Average verbal/mathematics scores - 560/590, median verbal/mathematics scores - 550/600. Verbal/mathematics scores of enrolled freshmen: Middle 50% scored 540-640 verbal, 500-610 mathematics, 1040-1250 combined verbal and mathematics. 6%/10% scored 700-800 30%/42% scored 600-699, 45%/37% scored 500-599, 19%/.% scored 400-499, 1%/2% scored 300-399. ***ACT composite score:*** Average - 26, median - 26. ***High school GPA:*** Average GPA - 3.50. 56% with 3.50-4.00, 31% with 3.00-3.49, 11% with 2.50-2.99, 2% with 2.49 and below. ***Class rank:*** 60% in top 10%, 82% in top 25%, 97% in top 50%. ***International students:*** Minimum TOEFL score required - 550.

TRANSFER ADMISSION STANDARDS: ***Transfer units required:*** Minimum - open if freshmen or sophomores, maximum - 62. ***Minimum college GPA*** - 3.00. ***Grades accepted*** - C or better.

1993-94 TRANSFER ADMISSION DATA: ***Applications:*** Received - 100, accepted - 49, enrolled - 29. CCC transfer students enrolled - 9.

ADMISSION PROCEDURES: ***Entrance tests:*** SAT I: Reasoning Test or ACT required. SAT II: Subject Tests recommended especially Writing and a foreign language test. Test deadline for fall admission: SAT I: Reasoning Test or ACT no later than December. SAT II: Subject Tests no later than January. ***Application process:*** Students admitted each term. Deadlines: Freshmen - 2/1 firm, transfers - 4/1 firm. Application fee - $40. Fee waiver - yes. ***Recommendations:*** 3 - counselor and 2 teachers. ***Interview*** - strongly recommended. ***Admission notification*** - freshmen 4/1, transfers 5/1. Commitment deposit - $350 due 5/1 for freshmen, 6/1 for transfers. ***Advanced placement offered*** - yes. ***Advanced credit given*** - yes. ***Early decision procedure:*** Application deadline - 11/15, notification - 12/15.

1994-95 COSTS: ***Total costs*** (approximate) - $26,100. Tuition - $17,238, other significant fees - $112, room and board - $7,350, total books, supplies, incidentals (approximate) - $1,400.

UNDERGRADUATE FINANCIAL AID: Students receiving financial aid - 50%. Submit FAFSA (CSS version preferred) and FAF applications by 2/1. Application deadline for institutional scholarships and grants - 2/1. Average financial aid package - $17,664.

OTHER INFORMATION: ***Founded*** - 1926. ***Nonprofit*** - yes. ***WASC Accredited*** - yes. ***Member of AICCU*** - yes.

SIMPSON COLLEGE

2211 College View Drive
Redding, California 96003
Admissions: (916) 224-5606
Financial Aid: (916) 224-5600
Fax: (916) 224-5627
Toll Free: (800) 598-2493

Small Christian College of Liberal Arts and Professional Studies

DISTINGUISHING FEATURES: A member of the Christian College Coalition, Simpson College offers a choice of professional studies leading to the ministry, missions, business education, and other career fields. Liberal arts and biblical studies form the core of each program. The focus is on personal development and educating Christian students for life and service in a global community. Students from many evangelical backgrounds learn both on and off campus. There are plentiful ministry and job opportunities.

DEGREES OFFERED: Certificate, Associates, Bachelor's, Master's, Credential.

SPECIAL PROGRAMS: Student ministries. Independent study. ***Education abroad*** - no. ***Honors programs*** - no.

COLLEGES: na.

nd = no data available   na = not applicable

UNDERGRADUATE MAJORS: 19 majors. See this chapter: Undergraduate Degree Majors, page 12--76. Christian Education and Youth Ministries Concentration. Preprofessional programs: Seminary.
CALENDAR: Semester system. Summer sessions.
FACULTY: Full-time - 27, part-time - 20. Undergraduate classes taught by faculty, not graduate assistants - all. Faculty with Ph.D.'s - 50%. Student/faculty ratio - 14/1. Average class size - nd.
ENROLLMENT: ***Total*** - 652. ***Graduate*** - 374. Undergraduate - 518: California residents - 87%, out-of-state - 12%, other countries - 1%. Men - 42%, women - 58%. ***Ethnic distribution of undergraduate students:*** Hispanic - 2%, Black - 1%, Asian/Pacific Islander - 8%, Native American/Alaskan - 3%, White - 86%. ***Freshmen graduating within 5 years*** - nd%.
LOCATION: 60-acre, northern California campus in Shasta recreation area in small city setting in Shasta County.
CAMPUS LIFE: Single students not living with parents or relatives must live on campus, unless twenty-three or older. ***On-campus housing:*** Spaces - 200, undergraduate residential students - 63%. ***Clubs and organizations*** - 20. Fraternities and sororities - 0. ***Athletics:*** Intercollegiate - yes. Intramural sports - yes. ***Counseling and guidance:*** Academic, personal, career planning, job placement. Faculty advisors - yes, also spiritual life advisor. Tutoring - yes. ***Special services/academic programs for:*** Educationally disadvantaged - no, physically disabled - no, learning disabled - no.
FRESHMAN ADMISSION STANDARDS: High school diploma. High school units: Total required - na. College-preparatory program recommended including English - 4, social science/history - 3, foreign language - 2, laboratory science - 3, mathematics - 3.
1993-94 FRESHMAN ADMISSION DATA: ***Applications:*** Received - nd, accepted - nd, enrolled - nd. ***SAT Scores:*** nd. ***ACT composite score:*** Average - nd, median - nd. ***High school GPA:*** Average GPA - nd, minimum required - 2.00. ***Class rank:*** nd. ***International students:*** Minimum TOEFL score required - 500.
TRANSFER ADMISSION STANDARDS: ***Transfer units required:*** Minimum - 0, maximum - nd. ***Minimum college GPA*** - 2.00. ***Grades accepted*** - C or better.
1993-94 TRANSFER ADMISSION DATA: ***Applications:*** Received - nd, accepted - nd, enrolled - nd. CCC transfer students enrolled - nd.
ADMISSION PROCEDURES: ***Entrance tests:*** SAT I: Reasoning Test or ACT required. Test deadline for fall admission - June. ***Application process:*** Students admitted each term. Deadlines: Freshmen and transfers - rolling. Application fee - $20. Fee waiver - yes. ***Recommendations:*** 2 - academic and spiritual. ***Interview*** - required. ***Admission notification*** - rolling. Commitment deposit - $100 due sixty days after acceptance. ***Advanced placement offered*** - yes. ***Advanced credit given*** - yes. ***Early decision procedure*** - no.
1994-95 COSTS: ***Total costs*** (approximate) - $11,394. Tuition - $6,600, other significant fees - $504, room and board - $3,690, total books, supplies, incidentals (approximate) - $600.
UNDERGRADUATE FINANCIAL AID: Students receiving financial aid - 75%. Submit FAFSA and institutional applications by 3/2. Application deadline for institutional scholarships and grants - rolling, priority deadline - 3/2. Average financial aid package - $7,250.
OTHER INFORMATION: ***Founded*** - 1921. ***Nonprofit*** - yes. ***WASC Accredited*** - yes. ***Member of AICCU*** - yes.

SOUTHERN CALIFORNIA COLLEGE

55 Fair Drive
Costa Mesa, California 92626
Admissions: (714) 556-3610, Ext. 218
Financial Aid: (714) 556-3610, Ext. 355
Fax: (714) 957-9317
Toll Free: (800) 722-6279

Liberal Arts College Affiliated with the Assemblies of God Church

DISTINGUISHING FEATURES: Southern California College is a charismatic Christian College. It is unique in that it is the only liberal arts college in the Pentecostal tradition west of the Rockies. The College is committed to encouraging in its students an appreciation of the finest intellectual and moral values and is dedicated to the integration of faith and learning. SCC is characterized by quality of faculty, small classes, close interpersonal relationships and strong spiritual commitment.
DEGREES OFFERED: Bachelor's, Master's, Credential.
SPECIAL PROGRAMS: Career internships. ***Education abroad*** - yes. ***Honors programs*** - no.
COLLEGES: Divisions of Business, Humanities and Fine Arts, Natural Sciences and Mathematics, Professional Studies, Religion, Social Sciences, Interdisciplinary Studies.
UNDERGRADUATE MAJORS: 29 majors. Church Leadership and Biblical Studies. See this chapter: Undergraduate Degree Majors, page 12--76. Preprofessional programs: Dentistry, Law, Medicine, Veterinary Medicine.
CALENDAR: 4-1-4 system. Summer session.
FACULTY: Full-time - 43, part-time - 7. Undergraduate classes taught by faculty, not graduate assistants - all. Faculty with Ph.D.'s - 58%. Student/faculty ratio - 16/1. Average class size - 16.
ENROLLMENT: ***Total*** - 965. ***Graduate*** - 65. ***Undergraduate*** - 900: California residents - 75%, out-of-state - 23%, other countries - 2%. Men - 45%, women - 55%. ***Ethnic distribution of undergraduate students:*** Hispanic - 12%, Black - 3%, Asian/Pacific Islander -6%, Native American/Alaskan - 1%, White - 74%. ***Freshmen graduating within 5 years*** - 34%.
LOCATION: 40-acre campus in the suburban town of Costa Mesa in Orange County close to Los Angeles.
CAMPUS LIFE: Single students not living with parents or relatives must live on campus unless approved by petition. ***On-campus housing:*** Spaces - 528, undergraduate residential students - 62%. ***Clubs and organizations*** - 17. Fraternities and sororities - 0. ***Athletics:*** Intercollegiate - NAIA. Intramural sports - yes. ***Counseling and guidance:*** Academic, personal. Faculty advisors - yes. Tutoring - yes. ***Special services/academic programs for:*** Educationally disadvantaged - yes, physically disabled - yes, learning disabled - yes.
FRESHMAN ADMISSION STANDARDS: High school units: Total required - na. Recommended: English - 4, social science/history - 3, foreign language - 0, laboratory science - 2, mathematics - 2.
1993-94 FRESHMAN ADMISSION DATA: ***Applications:*** Received - 502, accepted - 444, enrolled - 222. ***SAT scores:*** Average verbal/mathematics scores - 443/466, median verbal/mathematics scores - 410/460. Average total score - 884. Verbal/mathematics scores of enrolled freshmen: 1%/1% scored 700-800, 4%/10% scored 600-699, 15%/23% scored 500-599, 34%/31% scored 400-499, 36%/28% scored 300-399, 10%/7%

nd = no data available   na = not applicable

CALIFORNIA INDEPENDENT COLLEGES

scored 200-299. ***ACT composite score:*** Average - nd, median - 22. ***High school GPA:*** Average GPA - 3.20, minimum required - 2.50. ***Class rank:*** 22% in top 10%, 53% in the top 25%, 78% in top 50%. ***International students:*** Minimum TOEFL score required - 550.
TRANSFER ADMISSION STANDARDS: ***Transfer units required:*** Minimum - none, maximum - 70 from CCC, unlimited from other colleges. ***Minimum college GPA*** - 2.00. ***Grades accepted*** - D not accepted for Bachelor's degree but course will not need to be retaken to meet general education requirements.
1993-94 TRANSFER ADMISSION DATA: ***Applications:*** Received - 221, accepted - 189, enrolled - 121. CCC transfer students enrolled - nd.
ADMISSION PROCEDURES: ***Entrance tests:*** SAT I: Reasoning Test or ACT required. Test deadline for fall admission - nd. ***Application process:*** Students admitted each term. Deadlines: Freshmen and transfers - rolling. Application fee - $30. Fee waiver - no. ***Recommendations:*** 2 - Pastor and teacher or counselor. ***Interview*** - preferred, required only for missing data. ***Admission notification*** - rolling. Commitment deposit - $50 for housing. ***Advanced placement offered*** - yes. ***Advanced credit given*** - yes. ***Early decision procedure*** - no.
1994-95 COSTS: ***Total costs*** (approximate) - $16,092 Tuition - $9,220, other significant fees - $300, room and board - $4,124, total books, supplies, incidentals (approximate) - $2,448.
UNDERGRADUATE FINANCIAL AID: Students receiving financial aid - 80%. Submit FAFSA and institutional applications by 3/2. Application deadline for institutional scholarships and grants - priority deadline 3/2. Average financial aid package - $7,378.
OTHER INFORMATION: ***Founded*** - 1920. ***Nonprofit*** - yes. ***WASC Accredited*** - yes. ***Member of AICCU*** - yes.

SOUTHERN CALIFORNIA INSTITUTE OF ARCHITECTURE

5454 Beethoven Street
Los Angeles, CA 90066
(310) 574-1123
Fax: (310) 574-3801
Toll Free: nd

Professional School of Architectural Design

DISTINGUISHING FEATURES: The Southern California Institute of Architecture is a professional school of architectural design. It is an autonomous, self-governing institution based on the premise that the students and faculty together determine its academic direction. The educational methodology centers around design exploration. Students investigate possibilities of architecture through close contact with award winning current practitioners.
DEGREES OFFERED: Bachelor's, Master's.
CALENDAR: Trimester system.
ENROLLMENT: ***Total*** - 420.
LOCATION: Located in west Los Angeles, a short distance to the ocean and many cultural facilities and events.
CAMPUS LIFE: ***On-campus housing:*** Spaces - 0.
OTHER INFORMATION: ***Founded*** - 1972. ***Nonprofit*** - yes. ***WASC Accredited*** - candidate. Accredited by the National Architectural Accrediting Board, Inc.

STANFORD UNIVERSITY

Stanford, California 94305
Admissions: (415) 723-2091
Financial Aid: (415) 723-3058
Fax: (415) 725-2846
Toll Free: nd

Highly Selective University with Undergraduate and Graduate Programs in the Humanities, Sciences, and Engineering

DISTINGUISHING FEATURES: Stanford University has an outstanding reputation, is a major research university, and is one of the most selective colleges in the country. Approximately twenty-two percent of applicants are admitted. Students who add both excellence and diversity are selected. The University offers a broad, rigorous curriculum in the liberal arts as well as professional training. The challenging academic and extracurricular atmosphere takes place within an informal setting. Undergraduate and graduate programs are offered in the Humanities and Sciences, Earth Sciences, and Engineering. The schools of Business, Education, Law, and Medicine offer only graduate degrees. Some classes in the graduate schools are open to undergraduates.
DEGREES OFFERED: Bachelor's, Master's, Credential, First Professional, Doctoral, Juris Doctor (Law).
SPECIAL PROGRAMS: Honor code underlies academic life. Year-long sequence of three courses in Culture, Ideas, and Values. Freshman English (composition) courses designed for freshmen. May design own major. Independent study options. Student-initiated courses. Over 2,000 students per year participate in public service activities. Undergraduate Research Opportunities Program to encourage individual research. Eighteen different interdisciplinary majors. Stanford-in-Washington, D.C. Stanford-Howard University Exchange Program for one quarter. ***Education abroad:*** About thirty percent of Stanford undergraduates will attend an overseas studies center by the time they earn their degrees. Centers in Chile, England, France, Germany, Italy, Japan, Poland. ***Honors programs*** - yes.
COLLEGES: Schools of Business, Humanities and Sciences, Earth Sciences, Education, Engineering, Law, Medicine.
UNDERGRADUATE MAJORS: 57 majors. See this chapter: Undergraduate Degree Majors, page 12--76. Preprofessional programs: Business, Law, Medicine.
CALENDAR: Quarter system. Summer session.
FACULTY: Full-time - 1,408, part-time - less than 1%. Undergraduate classes taught by faculty, not graduate assistants - all except some freshman sections. Faculty with Ph.D.'s - 99%. Student/faculty ratio - 10/1. Average class size - nd.
ENROLLMENT: ***Total*** - 13,174. ***Graduate*** - 6,601. ***Undergraduate*** - 6,573: California residents - 42%, out-of-state - 55%, other countries - 3%. Men - 53%, women - 47%. ***Ethnic distribution of undergraduate students:*** Hispanic - 11%, Black - 8%, Asian/Pacific Islander - 24%, Native American/Alaskan - 1%, White - 52%. ***Freshmen graduating within 5 years*** - 92%.
LOCATION: 8,800-acre campus adjacent to the town of Palo Alto in the heart of Silicon Valley in northern California. Forty minutes south of San Francisco. Picturesque residential campus.
CAMPUS LIFE: All freshmen must live on campus. Housing guaranteed for four years for all undergraduates. New housing

nd = no data available   na = not applicable

under construction to guarantee housing for all four undergraduate years. ***On-campus housing:*** Spaces - 5,013 plus 251 apartment units, undergraduate residential students - 93%. ***Clubs and organizations*** - 512. Fraternities and sororities - 29. ***Athletics:*** Intercollegiate - NCAA Division I-A. Intramural sports - yes. ***Counseling and guidance:*** Academic, personal, career planning, job placement. Faculty advisors - yes. Resident and upper-class advisors as well. Tutoring - yes. ***Special services/ academic programs for:*** Educationally disadvantaged - yes, physically disabled - yes, learning disabled - yes.
FRESHMAN ADMISSION STANDARDS: Students are evaluated on how well they have used the resources available in their secondary school and in their community. Students should take the most intellectually challenging high school program available in courses that span the humanities, social sciences, mathematics, and sciences as well as course work in the creative and performing arts. High school units: Total required - no required courses for entrance, although the following strong academic program is recommended in grades 10 to 12. English - 3, social science/history - at least 2, foreign language - 3 in one language, laboratory science - 2 or more, mathematics - 3 (algebra; plane, solid, and analytic geometry; trigonometry), creative and performing arts - 1, computer science - some computer literacy.
1993-94 FRESHMAN ADMISSION DATA: ***Applications:*** Received - 13,608, accepted - 2,926, enrolled - 1,616. Admit rate - 22%. ***SAT scores:*** Average verbal/mathematics scores - nd/nd, median verbal/mathematics scores - nd/nd. Verbal/mathematics scores of enrolled freshmen: Middle 50% scored 590-690 verbal, 660-760 mathematics. 22%/59% scored 700-800, 50%/30% scored 600-699, 22%/10% scored 500-599, 6%/1% scored below 500. ***ACT composite score:*** Average - nd, median - nd. ***High school GPA:*** Average GPA - 73% have GPA of 3.80-4.00. ***Class rank:*** 88% in top 10%. ***International students:*** Minimum TOEFL score required - at least 600.
1994-95 FRESHMAN ADMISSION DATA: ***Applications:*** Received - 14,609, accepted - 2,937, enrolled - 1,606. Admit rate - 21%. ***SAT scores:*** Verbal/mathematics scores of admitted freshmen: 27%/61% scored 700-800, 48%/29% scored 600-699, 21%/9% scored 500-599, 4%/1% scored below 500. ***Class rank:*** 91% in top 10%.
TRANSFER ADMISSION STANDARDS: ***Transfer units required:*** Minimum - 39 quarter, maximum - 90 quarter. ***Minimum college GPA*** - 3.20 recommended. ***Grades accepted*** - A, B, C. Other requirements: SAT above 1,100 recommended.
1993-94 TRANSFER ADMISSION DATA: ***Applications:*** Received - 1,341, accepted - 159, enrolled - 120. Admit rate -12%. CCC transfer students enrolled - nd. ***College GPA of Admitted Transfers:*** 82% with 3.50-4.00, 18% below 3.50.
1994-95 TRANSFER ADMISSION DATA: ***Applications:*** Received - 1,418, accepted - 191, enrolled - 146. Admit rate - 13%. CCC transfer students enrolled - nd. ***College GPA of Admitted Transfers:*** 84% with 3.50-4.00, 16% below 3.50.
ADMISSION PROCEDURES: ***Entrance tests:*** SAT I: Reasoning Test or ACT required. At least three SAT II: Subject Tests strongly recommended. Test deadline for fall admission - no later than December. ***Application process:*** Students admitted for fall only. Intended major not taken into account in the admission decision. Freshmen deadline - 12/15 firm, transfers - 3/15 firm. Application fee - $50 domestic, $65 international. Fee waiver - yes. ***Recommendations:*** 3 - 2 teachers (from 11th and 12th grades) and 1 counselor. ***Interview*** - not available. ***Admission notification*** - First week in April. Commitment deposit - $100 due 5/1. ***Advanced placement offered*** - yes. ***Advanced credit given*** - yes. ***Early decision procedure*** - no.
1994-95 COSTS: ***Total costs*** (approximate) - $26,475. Tuition - $18,669, other significant fees - $200, room and board - $6,796, total books, supplies, incidentals (approximate) - $810.
UNDERGRADUATE FINANCIAL AID: Students receiving financial aid - 67%. Submit FAFSA (CSS version preferred), FAF, and institutional applications by 3/2. Application deadline for institutional scholarships and grants - rolling, priority deadline - 2/1. Average financial aid package - $11,463.
OTHER INFORMATION: ***Founded*** - 1885. ***Nonprofit*** - yes. ***WASC Accredited*** - yes. ***Member of AICCU*** - yes.

THOMAS AQUINAS COLLEGE

10,000 North Ojai Road
Santa Paula, California 93060
Admissions: (800) 634-9797
Financial Aid: (805) 525-4417
Fax: (805) 525-0620
Toll Free: (800) 634-9797

Catholic College Wholly Devoted to Liberal Education

DISTINGUISHING FEATURES: TAC is an independent, coeducational Catholic college totally committed to liberal education. Students of exceptional ability and from diverse backgrounds are drawn by a unique Great Books program into a close-knit community of learning. The Great Books program is a prescribed, four-year, interdisciplinary course of studies based on the original works of the best, most influential authors, poets, scientists, mathematicians, philosophers, and theologians of Western civilization. The course is essentially a sustained conversation in tutorials, seminars, and laboratories guided by tutors who assist students in the work of reading, analyzing, and evaluating these great works. Classics from Aristotle to Einstein replace textbooks. There are no majors or minors, no electives, no lectures. All students take the same demanding curriculum. Classes are Socratic in method and do not exceed twenty students. Faculty are dedicated exclusively to teaching and are well-prepared to lead rigorous and lively conversations about classic works in the arts and sciences. Thomas Aquinas College aims at providing its students with a thorough grounding in the arts of thinking, a broad and integrated vision of the whole of life and learning.
DEGREES OFFERED: Bachelor's.
SPECIAL PROGRAMS: ***Education abroad*** - no. ***Honors programs*** - no.
COLLEGES: na.
UNDERGRADUATE MAJORS: 1 major - Liberal Education. Preprofessional programs: none.
CALENDAR: Semester system. No summer session.
FACULTY: Full-time - 19, part-time - 2. Undergraduate classes taught by faculty, not graduate assistants - all. Faculty with Ph.D.'s - 65%. Student/faculty ratio - 10/1. Average class size - 14-18.
ENROLLMENT: ***Total*** - 208. Graduate - 0. ***Undergraduate*** - 208: California residents - 31%, out-of-state - 55%, other countries - 14%. Men - 52%, women - 48%. ***Ethnic distribution of undergraduate students:*** Hispanic - 3%, Black - 1%, Asian/Pacific Islander - 4%, Native American/Alaskan - 0%, White - 92%. ***Freshmen graduating within 5 years*** - 67%.
LOCATION: 159 acres in a small town not far from Los Angeles.

CAMPUS LIFE: Students must live on campus unless living with family. ***On-campus housing:*** Spaces - 224, undergraduate residential students - 99%. ***Clubs and organizations*** - 1. Fraternities and sororities - 0. ***Athletics:*** Intercollegiate - no. Intramural sports - yes. ***Counseling and guidance:*** yes. Faculty advisors - yes. Tutoring - yes. ***Special services/academic programs for:*** Educationally disadvantaged - no, physically disabled - no, learning disabled - no.
FRESHMAN ADMISSION STANDARDS: High school units: Total required - nd. English - 4, social science/history - 4, foreign language - 2, laboratory science - 2, mathematics - 3.
1993-94 FRESHMAN ADMISSION DATA: ***Applications:*** Received - 125, accepted - 87, enrolled - 67. ***SAT scores:*** Average verbal/mathematics scores - 583/590, median verbal/mathematics scores - 571/580. Verbal/mathematics scores of enrolled freshmen: Middle 50% scored 510-660 verbal, 550-650 mathematics, 1060-1310 combined verbal and mathematics. 14%/10% scored 700-800, 30%/36% scored 600-699, 36%/42% scored 500-599, 26%/12% scored 400-499, 0%/0% scored 300-399. ***ACT composite score:*** Average - 26, median - 27. ***High school GPA:*** Average GPA - 3.41. 77% with 3.00-4.00, 21% with 2.00-2.99, 2% with 1.00-1.99,. ***Class rank:*** 22% in top 10%, 58% in top 25%, 88% in top 50%. ***International students:*** Minimum TOEFL score required - nd.
TRANSFER ADMISSION STANDARDS: No transfer students accepted, mandatory four-year program.
1993-94 TRANSFER ADMISSION DATA: No transfer students accepted, mandatory four-year program.
ADMISSION PROCEDURES: ***Entrance tests:*** SAT I: Reasoning Test or ACT required. Test deadline for fall admission - June. ***Application process:*** Students admitted fall term. Deadlines: Freshmen - rolling. Application fee - $0. Fee waiver - na. ***Recommendations:*** 3 - at least 2 from teachers. ***Interview*** - sometimes required. ***Admission notification*** - rolling. Commitment deposit - $100. ***Advanced placement offered*** - no. ***Advanced credit given*** - no. ***Early decision procedure*** - no.
1994-95 COSTS: ***Total costs*** (approximate) - $20,300. Tuition - $13,300, other significant fees - $0, room and board - $5,300, total books, supplies, incidentals (approximate) - $1,700.
UNDERGRADUATE FINANCIAL AID: Students receiving financial aid - 84%. Submit FAFSA, FAF, and institutional applications by 3/2. Application deadline for institutional scholarships and grants - nd. Average financial aid package - $11,500.
OTHER INFORMATION: ***Founded*** - 1968. ***Nonprofit*** - yes. ***WASC Accredited*** - yes. ***Member of AICCU*** - yes.

UNITED STATES INTERNATIONAL UNIVERSITY

10455 Pomerado Road
San Diego, California 92131
Admissions: (619) 693-4772
Financial Aid: (619) 693-4559
Fax: (619) 693-4739
Toll Free: nd

International University with Associated Campuses in Nairobi and Mexico City

DISTINGUISHING FEATURES: An international focus is an integral part of all degree programs at United States International University. Each of its four campuses is an intercultural community offering the chance to learn from an international faculty and to study with fellow students from around the globe. USIU fosters student growth through an interdisciplinary approach to learning. The faculty has a commitment to a multinational, multicultural thread throughout the curriculum. Programs are designed to help students become more complete human beings with potential for providing positive leadership in the world community. Community service and internships provide experiential learning.
DEGREES OFFERED: Certificate, Associates, Bachelor's, Master's, Credential, Doctoral.
SPECIAL PROGRAMS: Can transfer to another USIU campus.
The Freshman Experience is a one year interdisciplinary, international look at the world through natural science, social sciences, and humanities. The Senior Experience is comprised of an interdisciplinary seminar, a senior project or thesis, and an internship. ***Education abroad:*** Programs offered at associated campuses in Kenya, Nairobi, and Mexico City. ***Honors programs*** - no.
COLLEGES: College of Liberal Arts. Schools of Business and Management, Education, Hospitality Management, Human Behavior.
UNDERGRADUATE MAJORS: 13 majors. See this chapter: Undergraduate Degree Majors, page 12--76. Preprofessional programs: Law.
CALENDAR: Quarter system, optional three-week terms between quarters. Summer session.
FACULTY: Full-time - 51, part-time - 61. Undergraduate classes taught by faculty, not graduate assistants - most. Faculty with Ph.D.'s - 93%. Student/faculty ratio - 15-20/1. Average class size - 15-20.
ENROLLMENT: ***Total*** - 1,485. ***Graduate*** - 4,282. ***Undergraduate*** - 304: California residents - 50%, out-of-state - 15%, other countries - 35%. Men - 48%, women - 52%. ***Ethnic distribution of undergraduate students:*** Hispanic - 9.5%, Black - 5.0%, Asian/Pacific Islander - 6.5%, Native American/Alaskan - 1.0%, White - 78.5%. ***Freshmen graduating within 5 years*** - nd%.
LOCATION: 160-acre, wooded campus twenty minutes from downtown San Diego. Los Angeles is two hours north, Mexico an hour south.
CAMPUS LIFE: Freshmen required to live on campus unless twenty-one or older. ***On-campus housing:*** Spaces - 600, undergraduate residential students - 30%. ***Clubs and organizations*** - 20. Fraternities and sororities - 0. ***Athletics:*** Intercollegiate - NAIA. Intramural sports - yes. ***Counseling and guidance:*** Academic, personal, career planning, job placement. Faculty advisors - yes. Tutoring - yes. ***Special services/academic programs for:*** Educationally disadvantaged - no, physically disabled - no, learning disabled - no.
FRESHMAN ADMISSION STANDARDS: High school units: Total required - nd. English - 4, social science/history - 2, foreign language - 2, laboratory science - 2, mathematics - 2, electives - 2.
1993-94 FRESHMAN ADMISSION DATA: ***Applications:*** Received - 322, accepted - 168, enrolled - 51. ***SAT Scores:*** Average verbal/mathematics scores - 440/440, median verbal/mathematics scores - 435/440. Verbal/mathematics scores of enrolled freshmen: Middle 50% scored 350-490 verbal, 380-570 mathematics, 750-1030 combined verbal and mathematics. 0%/7% scored 700-800, 7%/0% scored 600-699, 14%/21% scored 500-599, 36%/43% scored 400-499, 36%/29% scored 300-399, 7%/0% scored 200-299. ***ACT composite score:*** Aver-

age - 18, median 17. ***High school GPA:*** Average GPA - 2.75. Minimum 2.50 required. ***Class rank:*** nd. ***International students:*** Minimum TOEFL score required - 550. Lower score requires English proficiency test upon enrollment for course placement.

TRANSFER ADMISSION STANDARDS: ***Transfer units required:*** Minimum - 16 quarter, maximum - 108 quarter. ***Minimum college GPA*** - 2.50. ***Grades accepted*** - C or better.

1993-94 TRANSFER ADMISSION DATA: ***Applications:*** Received - 78, accepted - 47, enrolled - 17. CCC transfer students enrolled - nd.

ADMISSION PROCEDURES: ***Entrance tests:*** SAT I: Reasoning Test or ACT required. Test deadline for fall admission - nd. ***Application process:*** Students admitted each term. Deadlines: Freshmen and transfers - rolling, no more than thirty days prior to quarter applying for. Application fee - $30. Fee waiver - yes. ***Recommendations:*** 1 - teacher or counselor. ***Interview*** - sometimes required. ***Admission notification*** - rolling, one to three weeks after application received. Commitment deposit - $100 due within four weeks of admission. ***Advanced placement offered*** - yes. ***Advanced credit given*** - yes. ***Early decision procedure*** - no.

1994-95 COSTS: ***Total costs*** (approximate) - $18,873. Tuition - $11,760, other significant fees - $nd, room and board - $5,150, total books, supplies, incidentals (approximate) - $500.

UNDERGRADUATE FINANCIAL AID: Students receiving financial aid - 75%. Submit FAFSA and institutional applications by 3/2. Application deadline for institutional scholarships and grants - 3/2, priority deadline - 4/15. Average financial aid package - $8,000.

OTHER INFORMATION: ***Founded*** - 1952. ***Nonprofit*** - yes. ***WASC Accredited*** - yes. ***Member of AICCU*** - yes.

UNIVERSITY OF JUDAISM — LEE COLLEGE

15600 Mulholland Drive
Los Angeles, California 90077
Admissions: (310) 476-9777, Ext. 261
Financial Aid: (310) 476- 9777, Ext. 252
Fax: (310) 471-1278
Toll Free: nd

Selective, Academic Institution Dedicated to the Study of Higher Jewish and Liberal Education

DISTINGUISHING FEATURES: Lee College at the University of Judaism offers a small-college experience in a large, vibrant city. Its core curriculum, which applies the great traditions of Jewish and Western cultures to classic liberal arts subjects, reflects a unique approach to higher education. Lee's challenging academic environment offers an outstanding six to one student/faculty ratio encouraging close relationships with professors and provides an atmosphere of open inquiry. Individual majors or self-designed interdisciplinary majors are available.

DEGREES OFFERED: Bachelor's, Masters.

SPECIAL PROGRAMS: Freshman year Study-in Israel program. Core curriculum which integrates Jewish and other Western civilization studies. ***Education abroad:*** Programs in Israel. ***Honors programs*** - nd.

COLLEGES: nd.

UNDERGRADUATE MAJORS: 6 majors. Bioethics, Business, Jewish Studies, Literature, Political Science, and Psychology. Preprofessional programs: nd.

CALENDAR: Semester system. Summer sessions - nd.

FACULTY: Full-time - nd, part-time - nd. Undergraduate classes taught by faculty, not graduate assistants - all. Faculty with Ph.D.'s - 56%. Student/faculty ratio - 6/1. Average class size - nd.

ENROLLMENT: ***Total*** - 202. ***Graduate*** - 102. ***Undergraduate*** - 100: California residents - 55%, out-of-state and other countries - 45%. Men - 47%, women - 53%. ***Ethnic distribution of undergraduate students:*** Minority - 3%. Hispanic - nd%, Black - nd%, Asian/Pacific Islander - nd%, Native American/Alaskan - nd%, White - 97%. ***Freshmen graduating within 5 years*** - nd%.

LOCATION: 28-acre campus in the Santa Monica mountains in the residential neighborhood of Bel Air, minutes from the heart of Los Angeles.

CAMPUS LIFE: ***On-campus housing:*** Spaces - nd, undergraduate residential students - 52%. ***Clubs and organizations*** - 20. Fraternities and sororities - 0 ***Athletics:*** Intercollegiate - no. Intramural sports - nd ***Counseling and guidance:*** Academic, personal, career planning, job placement. Faculty advisors - yes. Tutoring - yes. ***Special services/academic programs for:*** Educationally disadvantaged - nd, physically disabled - nd, learning disabled - nd.

FRESHMAN ADMISSION STANDARDS: High school units: Total required - nd. College prep program. English - nd, social science/history - nd, foreign language - nd, laboratory science - nd, mathematics - nd.

1993-94 FRESHMAN ADMISSION DATA: ***Applications:*** Received - nd, accepted - nd, enrolled - 18. ***SAT Scores:*** Average verbal/mathematics scores - nd/nd, median verbal/mathematics scores - nd/nd. Verbal/mathematics scores of enrolled freshmen: Middle 50% scored 520-600 verbal, 510-600 mathematics, 1040-1230 combined verbal and mathematics. nd%/nd% scored 700-800, nd%/nd% scored 600-699, nd%/nd% scored 500-599, nd%/nd% scored 400-499, nd%/nd% scored 300-399, nd%/nd% scored 200-299. ***ACT composite score:*** Average - nd, median - nd. ***High school GPA:*** Average GPA - 3.38. ***Class rank:*** nd. ***International students:*** Minimum TOEFL score required - nd.

TRANSFER ADMISSION STANDARDS: ***Transfer units required:*** Minimum - none, maximum - none. ***Minimum college GPA*** - 3.00. ***Grades accepted*** - nd.

1993-94 TRANSFER ADMISSION DATA: ***Applications:*** Received - nd, accepted - nd, enrolled - 18. CCC transfer students enrolled - nd.

ADMISSION PROCEDURES: ***Entrance tests:*** SAT I: Reasoning Test or ACT required. Test deadline for fall admission - nd. ***Application process:*** Students admitted each term. Deadlines: Freshmen and transfers - 1/31 priority date. Application fee - $25. Fee waiver - yes. ***Recommendations:*** 2. ***Interview*** - no. ***Admission notification*** - rolling. Commitment deposit - $100 due approximately 5/1. ***Advanced placement offered*** - yes. ***Advanced credit given*** - yes. ***Early decision procedure*** - Application deadline - 11/15.

1994-95 COSTS: ***Total costs*** (approximate) - $20,458. Tuition - $10,560, other significant fees - $428, room and board - $6,320, total books, supplies, incidentals (approximate) - $3,150.

UNDERGRADUATE FINANCIAL AID: Students receiving financial aid - 70%. Submit FAFSA, FAF, and institutional applications by 3/2. Application deadline for institutional schol-

CALIFORNIA INDEPENDENT COLLEGES

nd = no data available na = not applicable

arships and grants - 3/2. Average financial aid package - $9,300.
OTHER INFORMATION: ***Founded*** - 1982. ***Nonprofit*** - yes. ***WASC Accredited*** - yes. ***Member of AICCU*** - yes.

UNIVERSITY OF LA VERNE

1950 Third Street
La Verne, California 91750
Admissions: (909 593-3511, Ext. 4026
Financial Aid: (909) 593-3511, Ext. 4135
Fax: (909) 546-1451
Toll Free: (800) 876-4858

Liberal Arts College

DISTINGUISHING FEATURES: ULV has a firm commitment to the individual student and offers undergraduate degrees in widely diverse concentrations in the liberal arts and graduate degrees in education, business, counseling, public administration, and law. There is an emphasis on a wide variety of learning options form traditional approaches to highly innovative nontraditional teaching and learning opportunities. The faculty is organized to work with each student in designing curriculum and programs to encourage student responsibility for learning and self-fulfillment. Graduate students make up half of the student body.
DEGREES OFFERED: Associates, Bachelor's, Master's, Credential, First Professional, Doctoral, Juris Doctor (Law).
SPECIAL PROGRAMS: Emphasis on professional internships in all majors. Child Life Specialist program to prepare Child Development majors to work with children in hospital settings. Six-year Law degree program - three years undergraduate, three years law school. Seven year medical program with College of Osteopathic Medicine - three year undergraduate, four years medical school. ***Education abroad:*** Programs in universities in China, Ecuador, England, France, Germany, Japan, Spain. Semester programs in China, Ecuador, England, Greece, Japan, and Mexico. January interterm foreign study. ***Honors programs*** - yes.
COLLEGES: Colleges of Arts and Sciences, Graduate and Professional Studies, Law.
UNDERGRADUATE MAJORS: 75 majors. Undergraduate concentrations in Business, Education, Communications, the Physical and Social Sciences, Languages, Humanities, International Studies. See this chapter: Undergraduate Degree Majors, page 12--76. Preprofessional programs: Dentistry, Law, Medicine, Theology.
CALENDAR: 4-1-4 system. Summer sessions.
FACULTY: Full-time - nd, part-time - nd. Undergraduate classes taught by faculty, not graduate assistants - all. Faculty with Ph.D.'s - 69%. Student/faculty ratio - 19/1. Average class size - 19.
ENROLLMENT: ***Total*** - 1,110. ***Graduate*** - 0. ***Undergraduate*** - 1,110: California residents - 90%, out-of-state and other countries - 10%. Men - 44%, women - 56%. ***Ethnic distribution of undergraduate students:*** Minority - 40%. Hispanic - nd%, Black - nd%, Asian/Pacific Islander - nd%, Native American/Alaskan - nd%, White - 60%. ***Freshmen graduating within 5 years*** - nd%.
LOCATION: 26-acre campus at the foot of the San Gabriel Mountains in the town of La Verne forty-five minutes east of Los Angeles. Satellite campuses mainly for graduate students in California, Alaska, and Europe.
CAMPUS LIFE: ***On-campus housing:*** Spaces - 426, undergraduate residential students - 48%. ***Clubs and organizations*** - 67. Fraternities and sororities - 6. ***Athletics:*** Intercollegiate - NCAA Division III. Intramural sports - yes. ***Counseling and guidance:*** Academic, personal, career planning, job placement. Faculty advisors - yes. Individual academic program for each student under faculty counselor. Tutoring - yes. ***Special services/academic programs for:*** Educationally disadvantaged - yes, physically disabled - no, learning disabled - yes.
FRESHMAN ADMISSION STANDARDS: High school units: Total required - 15. Recommended, but not required - at least 7 additional units in such academic fields as algebra, geometry, foreign language, science, social science/history. English - nd, social science/history - nd, foreign language - nd, laboratory science - nd, mathematics - nd.
1993-94 FRESHMAN ADMISSION DATA: ***Applications:*** Received - nd, accepted - nd, enrolled - 248. ***SAT Scores:*** Average verbal/mathematics scores - nd/nd, median verbal/mathematics scores - nd/nd. Verbal/mathematics scores of enrolled freshmen: Middle 50% scored 400-450 verbal, 440-500 mathematics, 840-900 combined verbal and mathematics. nd%/nd% scored 700-800, nd%/nd% scored 600-699, nd%/nd% scored 500-599, nd%/nd% scored 400-499, nd%/nd% scored 300-399, nd%/nd% scored 200-299. ***ACT composite score:*** Average - nd, median - nd. ***High school GPA:*** Average GPA - 3.15. ***Class rank:*** nd. ***International students:*** Minimum TOEFL score required - nd.
TRANSFER ADMISSION STANDARDS: ***Transfer units required:*** Minimum - 30, maximum - none. ***Minimum college GPA*** - 2.00. ***Grades accepted*** - A, B, C.
1993-94 TRANSFER ADMISSION DATA: ***Applications:*** Received - nd, accepted - nd, enrolled - 115. CCC transfer students enrolled - nd.
ADMISSION PROCEDURES: ***Entrance tests:*** SAT I: Reasoning Test or ACT required. Test deadline for fall admission - nd. ***Application process:*** Deadline: Freshmen and transfers - 3/1 priority date or until filled. Application fee - $25. Fee waiver - yes. ***Recommendations:*** 1 - teacher, counselor, or principal. ***Interview*** - highly recommended. ***Admission notification*** - rolling. Commitment deposit - $100 due approximately 5/1. ***Advanced placement offered*** - yes. ***Advanced credit given*** - yes. ***Early decision procedure*** - no.
1994-95 COSTS: ***Total costs*** (approximate) - $18,790. Tuition - $13,540, other significant fees - $nd, room and board - $4,550, total books, supplies, incidentals (approximate) - $700.
UNDERGRADUATE FINANCIAL AID: Students receiving financial aid - 75%. Submit FAFSA and institutional applications by 3/2. Application deadline for institutional scholarships and grants - 3/2. Average financial aid package - $12,000.
OTHER INFORMATION: ***Founded*** - 1891. ***Nonprofit*** - yes. ***WASC Accredited*** - yes. ***Member of AICCU*** - yes.

UNIVERSITY OF REDLANDS

1200 Colton Avenue
P.O. Box 3080
Redlands, California 92373-0999
Admissions: (909) 335-4074
Financial Aid: (909) 335-4047
Fax: (909) 335-4089
Toll Free: nd

Liberal Arts University

DISTINGUISHING FEATURES: The University of Redlands of-

nd = no data available   na = not applicable

fers a caring environment, which promotes close interaction between students and faculty and a strong sense of community. Traditional and experimental approaches to liberal arts, preprofessional programs and programs for mature learners are emphasized. Undergraduates have the opportunity to participate in research projects with the faculty. In some cases students may receive performance evaluations instead of grades. Single, month-long classes are offered between conventional semesters permitting in-depth study of various subjects.

DEGREES OFFERED: Bachelor's, Master's, Credential.

SPECIAL PROGRAMS: Johnson Center for Individualized Learning - alternative program in a traditional framework, individualized learning program in which students write contracts with instructors to design their courses and curriculum for graduation and receive detailed narratives instead of grades, good program for exceptionally bright, highly motivated, self-reliant and creative students who do not fit into regular curriculum, enrolls ten percent to fifteen percent of college population. Work internships. Interdisciplinary honors program for qualified students. Freshman seminars with small groups of students. Double-major option. Cooperative education program with Waseda University in Tokyo. Semester seminar at American University in Washington, D.C. ***Education abroad*** - study abroad in more than sixty locations such as Australia, Austria, France, Ecuador, England, Germany, Hong Kong, Ireland, Italy, Kenya, Japan, Mexico, Russia, Scotland, Singapore, Spain, Wales. ***Honors programs*** - yes.

COLLEGES: School of Music. The Johnson Center. College of Arts and Sciences.

UNDERGRADUATE MAJORS: 35 majors. Professional programs in Education, Business, Accounting, Computer Science, and Communicative Disorders. See this chapter: Undergraduate Degree Majors, page 12--76. Preprofessional programs: Law, Medicine, Music.

CALENDAR: 4-1-4 system. January interterm. No summer classes.

FACULTY: Full-time - 135, part-time - nd. Undergraduate classes taught by faculty, not graduate assistants - all. Faculty with Ph.D.'s - 87%. Student/faculty ratio - 13/1. Average class size - 17.

ENROLLMENT: ***Total*** - 1,600. ***Graduate*** - 100. ***Undergraduate*** - 1,500 not including students enrolled at off-campus Whitehead Center: California residents - 70%, out-of-state - 30%, other countries - 5%. Men - 49%, women - 51%. ***Ethnic distribution of undergraduate students:*** Hispanic - 9%, Black - 4%, Asian/Pacific Islander - 9%, Native American/Alaskan - 1%, White - 74%. ***Freshmen graduating within 5 years*** - 60%.

LOCATION: 130-acre campus in a residential neighborhood of the small town of Redlands, sixty-five miles east of Los Angeles and forty miles west of Palm Springs.

CAMPUS LIFE: Freshmen required to live on campus, limited number of upperclassmen may petition to live off campus. ***On-campus housing:*** Spaces - 1,225, undergraduate residential students - 89%. ***Clubs and organizations*** - 60. Fraternities and sororities - 10. ***Athletics:*** Intercollegiate - NCAA Division III. Intramural sports - yes. ***Counseling and guidance:*** Academic, personal, career planning, job placement. Faculty advisors - yes. Tutoring - yes. ***Special services/academic programs for:*** Educationally disadvantaged - yes, physically disabled - no, learning disabled - no.

FRESHMAN ADMISSION STANDARDS: High school units: Total required - at least 16 academic units. Should have completed a minimum of: English - 4, social science/history - 3, foreign language - 2, laboratory science - 3, mathematics - 3.

1993-94 FRESHMAN ADMISSION DATA: ***Applications:*** Received - 1,498, accepted - 1,219, enrolled - 306. ***SAT scores:*** Average verbal/mathematics scores - nd/nd, median verbal/mathematics scores - nd/nd. Verbal/mathematics scores of enrolled freshmen: Middle 50% scored 450-540 verbal, 470-610 mathematics. 3%/5% scored 700-800, 7%/20% scored 600-699, 32%/39% scored 500-599, 45%/29% scored 400-499, 11%/6% scored 300-399. ***ACT composite score:*** Average - nd, median - nd. 26% scored 25-36, 64% scored 19-24, 10% scored 13-18, 0% scored 1-12. ***High school GPA:*** Average GPA - 3.45. ***Class rank:*** 26% in top 10%, 63% in top 25%, 89% in top 50%. ***International students:*** Minimum TOEFL score required - 550.

TRANSFER ADMISSION STANDARDS: ***Transfer units required:*** Minimum - 24, maximum - 66. ***Minimum college GPA*** - 2.50. ***Grades accepted*** - A, B, C.

1993-94 TRANSFER ADMISSION DATA: ***Applications:*** Received - nd, accepted - nd, enrolled - 120. CCC transfer students enrolled - 90.

ADMISSION PROCEDURES: ***Entrance tests:*** SAT I: Reasoning Test or ACT required. Test deadline for fall admission - December. ***Application process:*** Students admitted each term, no later than one month prior to term's start. Deadlines: Freshmen - 2/1 if applying for need-based financial aid, 12/15 if applying for academic or merit scholarships. Transfers - 3/1. Application fee - $40. Fee waiver - yes. ***Recommendations:*** 2 - teacher, and administrator or counselor. ***Interview*** - recommended. ***Admission notification*** - rolling, within four weeks of a completed file and start of phase. Commitment deposit - $200 due 5/1. ***Advanced placement offered*** - at the discretion of the department. ***Advanced credit given*** - for scores of 3, 4, and 5. ***Early decision procedure*** - no.

1994-95 COSTS: ***Total costs*** (approximate) - $23,560. Tuition - $16,530, other significant fees - $225, room and board - $6,205, total books, supplies, incidentals (approximate) - $600.

UNDERGRADUATE FINANCIAL AID: Students receiving financial aid - 75%. Submit FAFSA (CSS version preferred), FAF, and institutional applications by 2/1. Application deadline for institutional scholarships and grants - 12/15, priority deadline - 2/1. Average financial aid package - $nd.

OTHER INFORMATION: ***Founded*** - 1907. ***Nonprofit*** - yes. ***WASC Accredited*** - yes. ***Member of AICCU*** - yes.

UNIVERSITY OF SAN DIEGO

5998 Alcala Park
San Diego, California 92110
Admissions: (619) 260-4506
Financial Aid: (619) 260-4514
Fax: (619) 260-6836
Toll Free: (800) 248-4873

Catholic University of the Liberal Arts

DISTINGUISHING FEATURES: USD offers a value-oriented education with a strong academic emphasis. Critical thinking and attention to values are encouraged. The school has created academic and extracurricular programs oriented to help students grow in personal and professional competence, international sensitivity, responsibility, and voluntary civic action. Small classes promote close student-faculty rapport.

DEGREES OFFERED: Certificate, Bachelor's, Master's, Credential, First Professional, Doctoral.

SPECIAL PROGRAMS: Orientation to academic life through Freshman Preceptorial course, which examines one of the major disciplines in an innovative approach with a small group of not more than twenty students. Team-taught interdisciplinary courses. Independent research project for students of superior ability. Independent study. ***Education abroad:*** Sophomore or junior semester abroad in England, France, Germany, Italy, or Spain. Summer program in Guadalajara, Mexico. ***Honors programs*** - yes.

COLLEGES: College of Arts and Sciences. Schools of Business Administration, Education, Law, Nursing.

UNDERGRADUATE MAJORS: 30 majors. See this chapter: Undergraduate Degree Majors, page 12--76. Special academic programs: Marine Science and Ocean Studies programs affiliated with Hubbs Research/Sea World. Interdisciplinary studies: Diversified Liberal Arts, Hispanic Studies, Humanities, International Relations. Preprofessional programs: Dentistry, Education, Foreign Service, Law, Medicine, Optometry, Pharmacy, Veterinary Medicine.

CALENDAR: 4-1-4 system. Summer sessions.

FACULTY: Full-time - 275, part-time - 206. Undergraduate classes taught by faculty, not graduate assistants - all. Faculty with Ph.D.'s - 97%. Student/faculty ratio - 18/1. Average class size - 15-25.

ENROLLMENT: ***Total*** - 6,083. ***Graduate*** - 2,169. ***Undergraduate*** - 3,914: California residents - 58%, out-of-state - 38%, other countries - 4%. Men - 44%, women - 56%. ***Ethnic distribution of undergraduate students:*** Hispanic - 13%, Black - 4%, Asian/Pacific Islander - 10%, Native American/Alaskan - 1%, White - 68%. ***Freshmen graduating within 5 years*** - 65%.

LOCATION: 180-acre setting in the city of San Diego overlooking the Pacific Ocean and San Diego Bay and harbor. Spanish Renaissance architecture.

CAMPUS LIFE: All freshmen must live on campus if not living with relatives. ***On-campus housing:*** Spaces - 2,550, undergraduate residential students - 55%. ***Clubs and organizations*** - 65. Fraternities and sororities - 8. ***Athletics:*** Intercollegiate - NCAA Division I-AA. Intramural sports - yes. ***Counseling and guidance:*** Academic, personal, career planning, job placement. Faculty advisors - yes. Tutoring - yes. ***Special services/academic programs for:*** Educationally disadvantaged - yes, physically disabled - nd, learning disabled - nd.

FRESHMAN ADMISSION STANDARDS: High school units: Total required - balanced program with a minimum of 16 academic subjects including college-preparatory courses. At least 4 academic subjects required each year. English - 4, social science/history - 3 to 4, foreign language - 3 to 4, laboratory science - 3 to 4, mathematics - 4.

1993-94 FRESHMAN ADMISSION DATA: ***Applications:*** Received - 3,834, accepted - 2,735, enrolled - 886. ***SAT Scores:*** Average verbal/mathematics scores - nd/nd, median verbal/mathematics scores - nd/nd. Verbal/mathematics scores of enrolled freshmen: Middle 50% scored 450-550 verbal, 500-600 mathematics, 950-1150 combined verbal and mathematics. 1%/3% scored 700-800, 7%/23% scored 600-699, 31%/44% scored 500-599, 48%/25% scored 400-499, 13%/5% scored 300-399. ***ACT composite score:*** Average - nd, median - nd. ***High school GPA:*** Average GPA - 3.45. 82.4% with 3.00-4.00, 17.6% with 2.00-2.99. ***Class rank:*** nd. ***International students:*** Minimum TOEFL score required - 550.

TRANSFER ADMISSION STANDARDS: ***Transfer units required:*** Minimum - 24 of acceptable college work if not admissible from high school, maximum - none. ***Minimum college GPA*** - 2.70. ***Grades accepted*** - C, Credit, Pass.

1993-94 TRANSFER ADMISSION DATA: ***Applications:*** Received - 892, accepted - 566, enrolled - 301. CCC transfer students enrolled - nd.

ADMISSION PROCEDURES: ***Entrance tests:*** SAT I: Reasoning Test or ACT required. SAT II: Writing required for English placement. Test deadline for fall admission - December preferred. ***Application process:*** Students admitted each term. Deadlines: Freshmen and transfers - fall 1/15 priority date, spring 11/1 priority date. Application fee - $45. Fee waiver - yes. ***Recommendations:*** 2 - counselor and teacher. ***Interview*** - not required. ***Admission notification*** - 4/15. Commitment deposit - $100 tuition plus $150 housing due 5/1. ***Advanced placement offered*** - yes. ***Advanced credit given*** - yes. ***Early decision procedure:*** Application deadline - 12/1, notification - 1/31.

1994-95 COSTS: ***Total costs*** (approximate) - $20,800. Tuition - $13,600, other significant fees - $100, room and board - $6,600, total books, supplies, incidentals (approximate) - $500.

UNDERGRADUATE FINANCIAL AID: Students receiving financial aid - 55%. Submit FAFSA and institutional applications by 2/20. Application deadline for institutional scholarships and grants - 2/20. Average financial aid package - $12,950.

OTHER INFORMATION: ***Founded*** - 1949. ***Nonprofit*** - yes. ***WASC Accredited*** - yes. ***Member of AICCU*** - yes.

UNIVERSITY OF SAN FRANCISCO

2130 Fulton Street
San Francisco, California 94117
Admissions: (415) 666-6563
Financial Aid: (415) 666-6303
Fax: (415) 666-2217
Toll Free: nd

Jesuit University of the Liberal Arts

DISTINGUISHING FEATURES: The Catholic Jesuit tradition of scholarship and dedication to the humanities is the core of all academic programs at USF. The General Education Curriculum (GEC) is the foundation of the education and is combined with the study of a major discipline. Small classes ensure extensive interaction between students and faculty. Research projects with faculty are available.

DEGREES OFFERED: Bachelor's, Master's, Credential, First Professional, Doctoral, Juris Doctor (Law).

SPECIAL PROGRAMS: Freshmen Seminar program designed to develop critical thinking and analytical skills. Sophomore Erasmus Project, a living and learning experience focused on a topical issue. 3 Plus 3, a combined undergraduate and law degree program allowing completion of both degrees in six years. Ignatius Institute, an in-depth examination of philosophy, theology, and the humanities based on great books of Western civilization with emphasis on great works of Christianity. Semester Jesuit Exchange program with Boston College, Boston or Fordham University, New York City. Cooperative education with Academy of Art College and the Consortium with eight member universities and colleges. ***Education abroad*** - semester abroad in Austria, England, France, Germany, Italy, Japan, Mexico, Singapore, Spain. ***Honors programs*** - yes.

COLLEGES: College of Arts and Sciences, McLaren School of Business. Schools of Nursing, Education, Law. College of Professional Studies for working adults.

UNDERGRADUATE MAJORS: Liberal Arts, Business Administration, Science, Nursing. See this chapter: Undergraduate Degree Majors, page 12--76. Preprofessional programs: Dentistry, Engineering, Medicine, Medical Technician, Pharmacy, Physical Therapy, Veterinary Medicine.

nd = no data available   na = not applicable

CALENDAR: 4-1-4 system. January intersession. Summer sessions.
FACULTY: Full-time - nd, part-time - nd. Undergraduate classes taught by faculty, not graduate assistants - all. Faculty with Ph.D.'s - 88%. Student/faculty ratio - 17/1. Average class size - nd.
ENROLLMENT: ***Total*** - 7,119. ***Graduate*** - 2,828. ***Undergraduate*** - 4,291: California residents - 65%, out-of-state and other countries - 35%. Men - 43%, women - 57%. ***Ethnic distribution of undergraduate students:*** Minority - 37%. Hispanic - nd%, Black - nd%, Asian/Pacific Islander - nd%, Native American/Alaskan - nd%, White - 63%. ***Freshmen graduating within 5 years*** - nd%.
LOCATION: 56-acre, wooded hilltop campus in the heart of San Francisco near Golden Gate Park. Just minutes from downtown and the Pacific Ocean. Advantages of an urban campus while maintaining the serenity of a more suburban, hilltop. College of Professional Studies classes conducted at regional centers in San Francisco, Cupertino, Fresno, Oakland, Orange, Sacramento, San Jose, and San Ramon.
CAMPUS LIFE: All freshmen and sophomores must live on campus if not living at home, unless twenty-one years or older. ***On-campus housing:*** Spaces - 1,334, residential students - 45%. ***Clubs and organizations*** - 50. Fraternities and sororities - 5. ***Athletics:*** Intercollegiate - NCAA Division I-AAA. Intramural sports - yes. ***Counseling and guidance:*** Academic, personal, career planning, job placement. Faculty advisors - yes. Tutoring - nd. ***Special services/academic programs for:*** Educationally disadvantaged - nd, physically disabled - nd, learning disabled - nd.
FRESHMAN ADMISSION STANDARDS: High school units: Total required - nd. English - 4, social science - 3, history - 0, foreign language - 2, laboratory science - 2, mathematics - 3.
1993-94 FRESHMAN ADMISSION DATA: ***Applications:*** Received - nd, accepted - nd, enrolled - 540. ***SAT Scores:*** Average verbal/mathematics scores - nd/nd, median verbal/mathematics scores - nd. Verbal/mathematics scores of enrolled freshmen: Middle 50% scored 400-550 verbal, 450-560 mathematics. ***ACT composite score:*** Average - nd, median - nd. ***High school GPA:*** Average GPA - 3.40. ***Class rank:*** nd. ***International students:*** Minimum TOEFL score required - nd.
TRANSFER ADMISSION STANDARDS: ***Transfer units required:*** Minimum - 24, maximum - 70. ***Minimum college GPA*** - C+ or better if admissible on basis of high school record. ***Grades accepted*** - D acceptable.
1993-94 TRANSFER ADMISSION DATA: ***Applications:*** Received - nd, accepted - nd, enrolled - 550. CCC transfer students enrolled - 250.
ADMISSION PROCEDURES: ***Entrance Tests:*** SAT I: Reasoning Test or ACT required. Test deadline for fall admission - January preferred. ***Application process:*** Students admitted each term. Deadlines: Freshmen and transfers - 2/15 priority date. Application fee - $35. Fee waiver - yes. ***Recommendations:*** 1 - counselor, teacher, or dean. ***Interview*** - recommended, not required. ***Admission notification*** - rolling. Commitment deposit - $100 plus $250 for housing due 5/1 for fall. ***Advanced placement offered*** - yes. ***Advanced credit given*** - yes. ***Early decision procedure*** - no.
1994-95 COSTS: ***Total costs*** (approximate) - $22,178. Tuition - $13,226, other significant fees - $100, room and board - $6,452, total books, supplies, incidentals (approximate) - $2,400.
UNDERGRADUATE FINANCIAL AID: Students receiving financial aid - 65%. Submit FAFSA and FAF applications by 3/2. Application deadline for institutional scholarships and grants - 3/2. Priority deadline - 2/15. Average financial aid package - $8,500.
OTHER INFORMATION: ***Founded*** - 1855. ***Nonprofit*** - yes. ***WASC Accredited*** - yes. ***Member of AICCU*** - yes.

UNIVERSITY OF SOUTHERN CALIFORNIA

University Park
Los Angeles, California 90089
Admissions: (213) 740-1111
Financial Aid: (213) 740-1111
Fax: (213) 740-8826
Toll Free: nd

Large, Urban Research University

DISTINGUISHING FEATURES: USC is one of the largest private colleges in the United States and is the second-largest, private research university in the country. With an average class size of twenty-six, it prides itself on combining the enrichment advantages of a large institution with the opportunity for close student-faculty interaction. A few introductory courses may have as many as two-hundred fifty students; however, these break down into smaller groups of approximately twenty-five students for discussion and/or laboratory. Undergraduates have many opportunities to participate in faculty research. The University's extensive curriculum is centered in the College of Letters, Arts, and Sciences and complemented by specialized education in eighteen professional schools. USC has an extensive network of alumni support to help investigate career interests.
DEGREES OFFERED: Certificate, Bachelor's, Master's, Credential, First Professional, Doctoral, Juris Doctor (Law).
SPECIAL PROGRAMS: Program guaranteeing a Bachelor's degree in four years. Freshmen seminar program of interdisciplinary courses limited to fifteen students. Freshmen-only general education courses. Double majors available. Semester in Washington, D.C. and Los Angeles to work with federal and community agencies. Career internships. Individually tailored, interdisciplinary majors available. Engineering Cooperative program with Industry. Baccalaureate/MD Program: Eight year medical degree program with guaranteed admission to USC School of Medicine for a select number of entering freshmen. For 1994-95 those admitted had an average total SAT of 1400, an average high school GPA of 3.97. Medical school admission guaranteed provided student maintains a minimum 3.20 college GPA overall and in the sciences; receives a minimum score of eight (national average) on the MCAT; and successfully completes the Bachelor's Degree. ***Education abroad:*** Programs of one semester or year offered in countries such as Australia, Austria, China, England, France, Germany, Greece, Israel, Italy, Japan, Kenya, Russia, Spain, and Zimbabwe. ***Honors programs*** - yes. Thematic Option is an alternative way for 150 freshmen to meet their general education requirements. Its curriculum is arranged around four core courses which focus on the history of Western civilization. The program combines interaction with faculty in small classes; intensive writing tutorials; and films, dinners and seminars. Typically, Thematic Option students have a minimum total SAT of 1250 and a minimum GPA of 3.50. Resident Honors program allows exceptional students to begin at USC after the junior year of high school and to complete their high school diploma while enrolled as college freshmen.

nd = no data available na = not applicable

COLLEGES: College of Letters, Arts and Sciences. Schools of Architecture, Business Administration, Accounting, Cinema-Television, Communication, Dentistry, Education, Engineering, Fine Arts, Gerontology, Medicine, Music, Pharmacy, Public Administration, Social Work, Urban and Regional Planning. Division of Drama. Institute of Safety and Systems Management. Independent Health Professions of Nursing, Occupational Therapy, Physical Therapy. Law Center.
UNDERGRADUATE MAJORS: 170 majors. See this chapter: Undergraduate Degree Majors, page 12--76. Preprofessional programs: Dentistry, Law, Medicine, Occupational Therapy, Pharmacy, Physical Therapy, Planning, Secondary Teaching.
CALENDAR: Semester system. Summer sessions.
FACULTY: Full-time - 3,086, part-time - 914. Undergraduate classes taught by faculty, not graduate assistants - most. Faculty with Ph.D.'s - 97%. Student/faculty ratio - 14/1. Average class size - 26.
ENROLLMENT: ***Total*** - 27,734. ***Graduate*** - 13,058. ***Undergraduate*** - 14,676: California residents - 56%, out-of-state - 36% and other countries - 7%. Men - 51%, women - 49%. ***Ethnic distribution of undergraduate students:*** Hispanic - 13%, Black - 6%, Asian/Pacific Islander - 21%, Native American/Alaskan - 1%, White - 53%. ***Freshmen graduating within 5 years*** - 63%.
LOCATION: 150-acre, park-like campus, ten minutes south of downtown Los Angeles offering the advantages of a major metropolitan setting. Health Sciences campus adjacent to the Los Angeles County/USC Medical Center.
CAMPUS LIFE: On-campus living recommended, but not required. ***On-campus housing:*** Spaces - 5,715, undergraduate residential students - 65% including fraternities and sororities. ***Clubs and organizations*** - 450. Fraternities and sororities - 29/19. ***Athletics:*** Intercollegiate - NCAA Division I-A. Intramural sports - yes. ***Counseling and guidance:*** Academic, personal, career planning, job placement. Faculty advisors - yes. Tutoring - yes. ***Special services/academic programs for:*** Educationally disadvantaged - yes, physically disabled - yes, learning disabled - no.
FRESHMAN ADMISSION STANDARDS: High school units: Total required - 16. Recommended pattern of courses: English - 4, social science/history - 2, foreign language - 2, laboratory science - 2 (as many as possible for Business, Engineering, Natural Sciences, and Health professions), mathematics - 3 (4 for Business, Engineering, Natural Sciences, or Health professions), additional courses in computer science, drama, fine arts, journalism, music, speech - 3.
1993-94 FRESHMAN ADMISSION DATA: ***Applications:*** Received - 12,229, accepted - 8,498, enrolled - 2,420. ***SAT Scores:*** Accepts highest individual verbal score and highest individual mathematics score from different sittings. Average verbal/mathematics scores - nd/nd, median verbal/mathematics scores - nd/nd. Verbal/mathematics scores of enrolled freshmen: Middle 50% scored 430-570 verbal, 520-660 mathematics, 950-1230 combined verbal and mathematics. nd%/nd% scored 700-800, nd%/nd% scored 600-699, nd%/nd% scored 500-599, nd%/nd% scored 400-499, nd%/nd% scored 300-399. ***ACT composite score:*** Average - nd, median - nd. ***High school GPA:*** Average GPA - 3.52. 45% with 3.60-4.30, 51% with 2.30-3.59, 4% with 2.40-2.70, nd% with 2.39 and below. ***Class rank:*** 45% in top 10%, 76% in top 25%, 95% in top 50%. ***International students:*** Minimum TOEFL score required - for Journalism or Cinema majors only.
TRANSFER ADMISSION STANDARDS: ***Transfer units required:*** Minimum: 30 for students with insufficient high school records or SAT I scores. Maximum: 80 (no more than 70 from a two-year college). ***Minimum college GPA*** - C+, B recommended. Some schools and departments recommend at least a 3.00. ***Grades accepted*** - nd.
1993-94 TRANSFER ADMISSION DATA: ***Applications:*** Received - 4,291, accepted - 2,663, enrolled - 1,629. CCC transfer students enrolled - nd.
ADMISSION PROCEDURES: ***Entrance tests:*** SAT I: Reasoning Test or ACT required. Urged to take 3 SAT II: Subject Tests, one of which should be Writing. Test deadline for fall admission - no later than November for greatest scholarship consideration. ***Application process:*** Students admitted each term to most majors. Deadlines: Freshmen and transfers - 2/1 firm, 12/15 priority date or until class filled. After these deadlines, applicants considered for programs of choice on a space-available basis only. Apply for admission by 11/1 for early financial aid estimate, by 12/15 for scholarships. Some schools and departments close earlier. Application fee - $50. Fee waiver - yes. ***Recommendations*** - not required by most departments, but strongly recommended. ***Interview*** - not required by most departments, but encouraged. ***Admission notification*** - 4/1. Commitment deposit - $250. ***Advanced placement offered*** - yes. ***Advanced credit given*** - yes. ***Early decision procedure:*** Application deadline - 12/1, notification - 1/15.
1994-95 COSTS: ***Total costs*** (approximate) - $26,900. Tuition - $17,230, other significant fees - $nd, room and board - $6,500, total books, supplies, incidentals (approximate) - $2,800.
UNDERGRADUATE FINANCIAL AID: Students receiving financial aid - 60%. Submit FAFSA, FAF, and institutional applications by 3/2. Application deadline for institutional scholarships and grants - 3/2. Priority deadline - 2/15. Average financial aid package - $17,800.
OTHER INFORMATION: ***Founded*** - 1880. ***Nonprofit*** - yes. ***WASC Accredited*** - yes. ***Member of AICCU*** - yes.

UNIVERSITY OF THE PACIFIC

3601 Pacific Avenue
Stockton, California 95211
Admissions: (209) 946-2211
Financial Aid: (209) 946-2421
Fax: (209) 946-2689
Toll Free: (800) 959-2867

Comprehensive University with Liberal Arts and Professional Programs

DISTINGUISHING FEATURES: UOP is a comprehensive university offering an extensive liberal arts and sciences curriculum as well as professional preparation in several areas. Its student body size offers the opportunity for educational diversity while preserving the values of a smaller and personalized academic environment. The school is noted for its exceptionally strong student residential life program. The Conservatory of Music is the oldest in the Western United States and emphasizes performance. The School of International Studies is the only such university-based undergraduate school of its kind in California. All students in this program spend at least one semester abroad, and overseas internships are available and encouraged.
DEGREES OFFERED: Bachelor's, Master's, Credential, First Professional, Doctoral, Juris Doctor (Law).
SPECIAL PROGRAMS: Interdisciplinary programs. Individualized study and self-designed majors. Independent study. Opportunities for research. Five-year School of Engineering Co-

nd = no data available   na = not applicable

op Work-Study program beginning in the junior year and required of all United States students. Co-op education and/or internship programs are available in virtually all majors. United Nations semester. Washington, D.C. semester. Capitol Campus program in Sacramento. Program guaranteeing a Bachelor's degree in four years. ***Education abroad*** - year or semester program through two-hundred programs in over sixty countries in Europe, Asia, Africa, North and Central America and the Caribbean, Middle East, Oceania, South America. ***Honors programs*** - yes.

COLLEGES: College of the Pacific, Conservatory of Music, Schools of Business and Public Administration, Education, Engineering, International Studies, Pharmacy. University College for adult reentry students. McGeorge School of Law in Sacramento, School of Dentistry in San Francisco.

UNDERGRADUATE MAJORS: 100 majors. See this chapter: Undergraduate Degree Majors, page 12--76. Preprofessional programs: Dentistry, Law, Medicine, Nursing, Optometry, Pharmacy, Physical Therapy, Veterinary Medicine.

CALENDAR: Semester system. Trimester system for Pharmacy. Summer session.

FACULTY: Full-time - 247, part-time - 75. Undergraduate classes taught by faculty, not graduate assistants - all. Faculty with Ph.D.'s - 84%. Student/faculty ratio - 15/1. Average class size - 25.

ENROLLMENT: ***Total*** - 4,140. ***Graduate*** - 582. ***Undergraduate*** - 3,558: California residents - 70%, out-of-state - 24%, other countries - 6%. Men - 45%, women - 55%. ***Ethnic distribution of undergraduate students:*** Hispanic - 9%, Black - 4%, Asian/Pacific Islander - 23%, Native American/Alaskan - 1%, White - 59%. ***Freshmen graduating within 5 years*** - 61%.

LOCATION: 150-acre campus in the residential area of Stockton two hours from San Francisco. Eastern look with red brick and ivy buildings.

CAMPUS LIFE: Freshmen and sophomores required to live on campus unless living with relatives. ***On-campus housing:*** Spaces - 2,450, undergraduate residential students - 50%. ***Clubs and organizations*** - 90. Fraternities and sororities - 9. ***Athletics:*** Intercollegiate - NCAA Division I-A. Intramural sports - yes. ***Counseling and guidance:*** Academic, personal, career planning, job placement. Faculty advisors - yes. Peer advisors assigned to entering freshmen. Tutoring - yes. ***Special services/academic programs for:*** Educationally disadvantaged - yes, physically disabled - yes, learning disabled - yes.

FRESHMAN ADMISSION STANDARDS: High school units: Total required - na. 15 recommended including English - 4, social science/history - 4, foreign language - 2, laboratory science - 2, mathematics - 3 (2 algebra, 1 geometry). Additional academic courses in the previously mentioned areas plus visual and performing arts. Recommend at least 4 academic courses per semester including senior year. Students interested in Economics or Business Administration should take advanced mathematics. Students interested in Mathematics, Science, Engineering, or Pharmacy should take biology, chemistry, physics, and advanced mathematics. Encouraged to take honors and Advanced Placement courses.

1993-94 FRESHMAN ADMISSION DATA: ***Applications:*** Received - 2,459, accepted - 1,997, enrolled - 582. ***SAT Scores:*** Average verbal/mathematics scores - 444/531, median verbal/mathematics scores - nd/nd. Verbal/mathematics scores of enrolled freshmen: Middle 50% scored 400-540 verbal, 460-620 mathematics. nd%/nd% scored 700-800, nd%/nd% scored 600-699, nd%/nd% scored 500-599, nd%/nd% scored 400-499, nd%/nd% scored 300-399, nd%/nd% scored 200-299. ***ACT composite score:*** Average - nd, median - nd. ***High school GPA:*** Average GPA - 3.30. ***Class rank:*** 36% in top 10%, 66% in top 25%, 84% in top 50%. ***International students:*** Minimum TOEFL score required - 475.

TRANSFER ADMISSION STANDARDS: ***Transfer units required:*** Minimum - 15. Maximum - 64 from CCC. ***Minimum college GPA*** - 2.30. ***Grades accepted*** - nd.

1993-94 TRANSFER ADMISSION DATA: ***Applications:*** Received - 1,786, accepted - 793, enrolled - 496. CCC transfer students enrolled - 336.

ADMISSION PROCEDURES: ***Entrance tests:*** SAT I: Reasoning Test or ACT required. Test deadline for fall admission - January. ***Application process:*** Students admitted each term. Deadlines: Freshmen and transfers - fall - 3/1 priority date or until space filled, spring - 12/14 or until space filled. Application fee - $50. Fee waiver - yes. ***Recommendations:*** 1 - teacher or counselor. ***Interview*** - not required, but recommended. ***Admission notification*** - rolling after 2/1. Commitment deposit - $200 due 5/1. ***Advanced placement offered*** - yes. ***Advanced credit given*** - yes. ***Early decision procedure:*** Application deadline - 12/15, notification - nd.

1994-95 COSTS: ***Total costs*** (approximate) - $23,793. Tuition - $16,320, other significant fees - $330, room and board - $5,326, total books, supplies, incidentals (approximate) - $1,817.

UNDERGRADUATE FINANCIAL AID: Students receiving financial aid - 65%. Submit FAFSA by 3/2. Application deadline for institutional scholarships and grants - 3/2. Average financial aid package - $17,000.

OTHER INFORMATION: ***Founded*** - 1851. ***Nonprofit*** - yes. ***WASC Accredited*** - yes. ***Member of AICCU*** - yes.

UNIVERSITY OF WEST LOS ANGELES

1155 West Arbor Vitae
Inglewood, California 90301
(310) 215-3339
Fax: (310) 670-9331
Toll Free: nd

University Offering Programs in Law and Paralegal Studies Serving Primarily Working Adults

DISTINGUISHING FEATURES: One of the University of West Los Angeles' special purposes is to serve working and career-change adults in addition to traditional full-time students. No freshmen are admitted. The faculty is composed primarily of practitioner attorneys. The majority of students are working and many are married with families. In addition to the Bachelor's degree, the school offers a certificate program for college graduates. Because it is small, the school is able to give students personal attention from admission counseling to graduate placement assistance in a friendly, relaxed, and supportive atmosphere. An undergraduate major in Para-Legal Studies is offered.

DEGREES OFFERED: Certificate, Bachelor's, First Professional, Juris Doctor (Law).

CALENDAR: Paralegal - Trimester. Summer session.

ENROLLMENT: ***Total*** - 222. ***Graduate*** - 97. ***Undergraduate*** - 125.

LOCATION: 6-acre campus near Los Angeles International Airport.

CAMPUS LIFE: ***On-campus housing:*** Spaces - 0.

nd = no data available   na = not applicable

CALIFORNIA INDEPENDENT COLLEGES

OTHER INFORMATION: ***Founded*** - 1966. ***Nonprofit*** - yes. ***WASC Accredited*** - yes. ***Member of AICCU*** - yes.

WEST COAST UNIVERSITY

Los Angeles Center and Administrative Offices for all Centers
440 Shatto Place
Los Angeles, California 90020-1765
(213) 427-4400
Fax: (213) 380-4362
Toll Free: (800) 248-4928 in California

Urban, Commuting University Primarily Organized for Mature, Employed Persons Seeking to Continue Their Education Entirely in Evening and Weekend Programs

DISTINGUISHING FEATURES: WCU has been devoted for over forty years to the educational needs of mature men and women for whom it has developed programs in a variety of professional and technical fields. Ranging from accounting to engineering to management information systems, the programs are designed and scheduled so that students can complete requirements for the Bachelor's degree in four-and-one-half years, the Master's degree in Business Administration and in Science in one-and-one-half years. Most students carry 3 to 5 units per eight-week term for a total of 18 to 30 semester units per year in evening and weekend classes. Classes are taught by a core of full-time faculty and a compliment of adjunct practicing professionals. They are offered at learning centers in Los Angeles, Orange, San Diego, Santa Barbara, and Ventura counties. Undergraduate degree majors are offered in Accounting, Acquisition and Contract Management, Business Administration, Business Information Systems, Computer Science, Configuration and Data Management, Engineering, Industrial Technology, and Logistics.
DEGREES OFFERED: Certificate, Associates, Bachelor's, Master's.
CALENDAR: Six eight-week terms, including summer sessions.
ENROLLMENT: ***Total*** - 1,500. ***Graduate*** - 1,000. ***Undergraduate*** - 500.
LOCATION: Learning Centers in Los Angeles, Orange, San Diego, Vandenberg AFB, and Camarillo, California.
CAMPUS LIFE: ***On-campus housing:*** Spaces - 0.
OTHER INFORMATION: ***Founded*** - 1909. ***Nonprofit*** - yes. ***WASC Accredited*** - yes. ***Member of AICCU*** - yes.

WESTMONT COLLEGE

955 La Paz Road
Santa Barbara, California 93108
Admissions: (805) 565-6200
Financial Aid: (805) 565-6063
Fax: (805) 565-6234
Toll Free: (800) 777-9011

Christian, residential Liberal Arts and Sciences College

DISTINGUISHING FEATURES: Westmont's commitment lies in a student's spiritual, academic, and emotional growth. These goals are accomplished by integrating a rigorous liberal arts and science curriculum with an enthusiasm for the historic Christian faith. Opportunities are available for Christian service. There are about thirty different Christian outreach programs for ministering to those in need, both in the community of Santa Barbara and outside of the country. Close interaction between students and faculty is emphasized.
DEGREES OFFERED: Bachelor's, Credential.
SPECIAL PROGRAMS: Leadership Development Program involving academic seminars, leadership projects, peer reflection groups, and a relationship with a mentor. Career internships and practicums. Individually designed majors called Alternative Majors. Part of the thirteen-member Christian College Consortium offering study on other Christian College campuses. Urban semester program in San Francisco. Washington, D.C. semester in government. Film studies program in Los Angeles. Program guaranteeing a Bachelor's degree in four years. ***Education abroad:*** Short-term study excursions abroad during Mayterm Seminars in Europe and the Orient. Summer business institutes in European and Russian business capitols. Term at the Institute of Holy Land Studies in Jerusalem. Europe semester in England, France, Greece, Israel, Italy. Latin American studies in Costa Rica. Southeast Asia program in China, Hong Kong, Japan, Taiwan. African program in Kenya. ***Honors programs*** - yes.
COLLEGES: na.
UNDERGRADUATE MAJORS: 26 majors. See this chapter: Undergraduate Degree Majors, page 12--76. Preprofessional programs: Dentistry, Engineering, Law, Medicine, Ministry, Missions, Pharmacy, Physical Therapy, Veterinary Medicine.
CALENDAR: Semester system, Mayterm. Summer sessions.
FACULTY: Full-time - 79, part-time - 36. Undergraduate classes taught by faculty, not graduate assistants - all. Faculty with Ph.D.'s - 81%. Student/faculty ratio - 15/1. Average class size - 22.
ENROLLMENT: ***Total*** - 1,285. ***Graduate*** - 0. ***Undergraduate*** - 1,285: California residents - 73.3%, out-of-state - 25.4%, other countries - 1.3%. Men - 40%, women - 60%. ***Ethnic distribution of undergraduate students:*** Hispanic - 3.5%, Black - 1.0%, Asian/Pacific Islander - 3.6%, Native American/ Alaskan - 1.2%, White - 88.1%. ***Freshmen graduating within 5 years*** - nd.
LOCATION: 133-acre, tree-filled campus between the Santa Ynez Mountains and the Pacific Ocean in Montecito, a residential suburb of Santa Barbara, ninety miles north of Los Angeles.
CAMPUS LIFE: On-campus living strongly recommended for freshmen. Off-campus housing for upperclassmen and married students. ***On-campus housing:*** Spaces - 1,145, undergraduate residential students - 85%. ***Clubs and organizations*** - 40. Fraternities and sororities - 0. ***Athletics:*** Intercollegiate - NAIA. Intramural sports - yes. ***Counseling and guidance:*** Academic, personal, career planning, job placement. Faculty advisors - yes. Tutoring - yes. ***Special services/academic programs for:*** Educationally disadvantaged - yes, physically disabled - yes, learning disabled - yes.
FRESHMAN ADMISSION STANDARDS: High school units: Total required - na. Minimum of 16 strong academic units recommended including English - 4, social science/history - 4, foreign language - 2, laboratory science - 3 (including 2 physical science, 1 biological science), mathematics - 3 (including 2 algebra, 1 geometry).
1993-94 FRESHMAN ADMISSION DATA: ***Applications:*** Received - 950, accepted - 713, enrolled - 351. ***SAT scores:*** Average verbal/mathematics scores - 501/550, median verbal/ mathematics scores - 500/550. Verbal/mathematics scores of enrolled freshmen: Middle 50% scored 450-550 verbal, 480-

nd = no data available na = not applicable

CALIFORNIA INDEPENDENT COLLEGES

620 mathematics, 930-1170 combined verbal and mathematics. 1.2%/6.6% scored 700-800, 11.7%/24.7% scored 600-699, 42.8%/39.8% scored 500-599, 35.0%/24.4% scored 400-499, 8.7%/4.5% scored 300-399, 0.6%/0% scored 2.00-2.99. ***ACT composite score:*** Average - 24, median - 24. ***High school GPA:*** Average GPA - 3.52. 56% with 3.50-4.00, 33% with 3.00-3.49, 11% with 2.50-2.99. ***Class rank:*** 42% in top 10%, 70% in top 25%, 91% in top 50%. ***International students:*** Minimum TOEFL score required - 560.

TRANSFER ADMISSION STANDARDS: ***Transfer units required:*** Minimum - 24 transferable units to disregard high school record, maximum - 64 from CCC, no maximum from a four-year college. ***Minimum college GPA*** - 2.50. ***Grades accepted*** - C or better, Credit. Pass accepted if accumulated GPA of graded courses meets requirement.

1993-94 TRANSFER ADMISSION DATA: ***Applications:*** Received - 292, accepted - 184, enrolled - 112. CCC transfer students enrolled - 69.

ADMISSION PROCEDURES: ***Entrance tests:*** SAT I: Reasoning Test or ACT required. Test deadline for fall admission - January preferred. ***Application process:*** Students admitted each term, but on a space-available basis in spring. Deadlines: Freshmen - 2/15 priority date, transfers - fall 3/15, spring 11/1. Application fee - $30. Fee waiver - yes. ***Recommendations:*** Encouraged but not usually required. ***Interview*** - strongly recommended. ***Admission notification:*** Freshmen - 3/15, transfers - 4/1. Commitment deposit - $200. ***Advanced placement offered*** - yes. ***Advanced credit given*** - yes. ***Early decision procedure*** - Application deadline - 12/1, notification 1/15.

1994-95 COSTS: ***Total costs*** (approximate) - $22,390. Tuition - $14,320, other significant fees - $866, room and board - $5,304, total books, supplies, incidentals (approximate) - $1,900.

UNDERGRADUATE FINANCIAL AID: Students receiving financial aid - 80%. Submit FAFSA (CSS version preferred) and FAF applications by 3/2. Application deadline for institutional scholarships and grants - 3/1, priority deadline - 3/1. Average financial aid package - $11,750.

OTHER INFORMATION: ***Founded*** - 1940. ***Nonprofit*** - yes. ***WASC Accredited*** - yes. ***Member of AICCU*** - yes.

WHITTIER COLLEGE

13406 E. Philadelphia Street
Whittier, California 90608
Admissions: (310) 907-4238
Financial Aid: (310) 907-4285
Fax: (310) 907-4870
Toll Free: nd

Small Liberal Arts College

DISTINGUISHING FEATURES: Whittier College, founded by the Society of Friends, seeks to provide the student with an approach to learning that will lead to an understanding of man and his environment and a social concern for practical human service. A core curriculum, Whittier's Liberal Education Program, which represents approximately one third of student coursework, is made up of paired courses that explore a common topic. Professors from different academic disciplines connect these courses in team-taught sequences. The school emphasizes individual choice, self-direction, and preprofessional preparation in a liberal arts setting. Whittier offers several research and internship opportunities with senior faculty.

DEGREES OFFERED: Bachelor's, Master's, Credential, First Professional, Juris Doctor (Law).

SPECIAL PROGRAMS: House system in which senior faculty live on campus with their families in housing adjacent to student residence halls, providing social and cultural interaction. Whittier Scholars program allowing students to structure individualized course of study, twenty-five percent of Whittier students in the program. Student-run radio station. 3/2 Engineering program with Dartmouth, Columbia, University of Southern California, Colorado State University, Washington University in St. Louis, University of Minnesota. Career internships available. ***Education abroad:*** Fall semester in Denmark. Study abroad in China, India, Japan, Mexico and over forty additional universities in Europe, Latin America, Australia, and Asia. ***Honors programs*** - no.

COLLEGES: School of Law.

UNDERGRADUATE MAJORS: 35 majors. See this chapter: Undergraduate Degree Majors, page 12--76. Preprofessional programs: Athletic Training, Dentistry, Engineering, Law, Medicine, Nursing, Social Work, Theology, Therapy, Veterinary Medicine, Communicative Disorders.

CALENDAR: 4-1-4 system, January interterm. Summer sessions.

FACULTY: Full-time - 110, part-time - 58. Undergraduate classes taught by faculty, not graduate assistants - all. Faculty with Ph.D.'s - 92%. Student/faculty ratio - 13/1. Average class size - nd.

ENROLLMENT: ***Total*** - 1,922. ***Graduate*** - 661. ***Undergraduate*** - 1,261: California residents - 68%, out-of-state - 29%, other countries - 3%. Men - 46%, women - 54%. ***Ethnic distribution of undergraduate students:*** Hispanic - 23%, Black - 4%, Asian/Pacific Islander - 9%, Native American/Alaskan - 1%, White - 59%. ***Freshmen graduating within 5 years*** - 54%.

LOCATION: 95-acre campus in the foothills of the suburban town of Whittier, eighteen miles east of Los Angeles. School of Law located in Los Angeles.

CAMPUS LIFE: All freshmen and sophomores not living with parents or relatives must live on campus the first three years. ***On-campus housing:*** Spaces - 670, undergraduate residential students - 60%. ***Clubs and organizations*** - 60. Fraternities and sororities - 9. ***Athletics:*** Intercollegiate - NCAA Division III. Intramural sports - yes. ***Counseling and guidance:*** Academic, personal, career planning, job placement. Faculty advisors - yes. Tutoring - yes. ***Special services/academic programs for:*** Educationally disadvantaged - no, physically disabled - no, learning disabled - no.

FRESHMAN ADMISSION STANDARDS: High school units: Total required - nd. Most entering freshmen enter with: English - 4, social science/history - 2 or 3, foreign language - 2 or more, laboratory science - 3, mathematics - 3 or more.

1993-94 FRESHMAN ADMISSION DATA: ***Applications:*** Received - 1,681, accepted - 1.069, enrolled - 345. ***SAT scores:*** Average verbal/mathematics scores - 454/507, median verbal/mathematics scores - nd/nd. Verbal/mathematics scores of enrolled freshmen: Middle 50% scored 390-510 verbal, 430-580 mathematics, 850-1070 combined verbal and mathematics. 2%/3% scored 700-800, 6%/17% scored 600-699, 23%/37% scored 500-599, 44%/31% scored 400-499, 23%/12% scored 300-399. ***ACT composite score:*** Average - nd, median - nd. ***High school GPA:*** Average GPA - 3.06. ***Class rank:*** 35% in top 10%, 63% in top 25%, 85% in top 50%. ***International students:*** Minimum TOEFL score required - 550.

CALIFORNIA INDEPENDENT COLLEGES

nd = no data available na = not applicable

TRANSFER ADMISSION STANDARDS: ***Transfer units required:*** Minimum - 12. Maximum - 90. ***Minimum college GPA*** - 2.50. ***Grades accepted*** - C, Credit, Pass.
1993-94 TRANSFER ADMISSION DATA: ***Applications:*** Received - 319, accepted - 155, enrolled - 99. CCC transfer students enrolled - 45.
ADMISSION PROCEDURES: ***Entrance tests:*** SAT I: Reasoning Test or ACT required. Test deadline for fall admission - January. ***Application process:*** Students admitted each term. Deadlines: Freshmen - 2/15 priority date, open until spaces filled. transfers - 4/15 priority date, open until spaces filled. Application fee - $35. Fee waiver - yes. ***Recommendations:*** 2 - counselor and teacher, principal, or dean. ***Interview*** - recommended not required. ***Admission notification*** - rolling, beginning 3/1. Commitment deposit - $300 tuition plus $100 housing due 5/1. ***Advanced placement offered*** - yes. ***Advanced credit given*** - yes. ***Early decision procedure*** - Application deadline 12/5, notification - nd.
1994-95 COSTS: ***Total costs*** (approximate) - $25,025. Tuition - $16,249, other significant fees - $579, room and board - $5,699, total books, supplies, incidentals (approximate) - $2,498.
UNDERGRADUATE FINANCIAL AID: Students receiving financial aid - 78%. Submit FAFSA (CSS version preferred) and FAF applications by 3/2. Application deadline for institutional scholarships and grants - 2/15, priority deadline - 2/15. Average financial aid package - $17,006.
OTHER INFORMATION: ***Founded*** - 1887. ***Nonprofit*** - yes. ***WASC Accredited*** - yes. ***Member of AICCU*** - yes.

WOODBURY UNIVERSITY

P.O. Box 7846
7500 Glenoaks Boulevard
Burbank, California 91510
Admissions: (818) 767-0888
Financial Aid: (818) 767-0888
Fax: (818) 504-9320
Toll Free: (800) 327-6343

Small University of Business, Architecture, and Design

DISTINGUISHING FEATURES: Woodbury integrates undergraduate career-oriented professional programs with instruction in the liberal arts. It is known for programs in the majors of Business, Architecture, Fashion and Interior Design. Involved faculty, small classes, and personal attention all help students focus their education toward individual goals. The curriculum emphasizes relating theory to practice. Woodbury's proximity to Burbank's media and entertainment district, and the greater Los Angeles community provides ample opportunities for field experience in the business and design industries. The college offers evening and weekend courses for working adults.
DEGREES OFFERED: Bachelor's, Master's.
SPECIAL PROGRAMS: Five-year Bachelor of Architecture program. Emphasis on strong business background, encourages business courses for all students, not just Business majors. Career internships available. ***Education abroad*** - no. ***Honors programs*** - no.
COLLEGES: Architecture and Design, Arts and Sciences, Business and Management.
UNDERGRADUATE MAJORS: 16 majors. See this chapter: Undergraduate Degree Majors, page 12--76. Special academic programs: Fashion Design with a minor in Costuming for motion pictures/television. Preprofessional programs: Architecture, Business.
CALENDAR: Quarter system. Summer sessions.
FACULTY: Drawn from professional educators and practicing professionals in the business and design fields. Full-time - 30, part-time - 100. Undergraduate classes taught by faculty, not graduate assistants - all. Faculty with Ph.D.'s - nd%. Student/faculty ratio - 15/1. Average class size - 18.
ENROLLMENT: ***Total*** - 1,049. ***Graduate*** - 93. ***Undergraduate*** - 956: California residents - 70%, out-of-state - 17%, other countries - 13%. Men - 44%, women - 56%. ***Ethnic distribution of undergraduate students:*** Hispanic - 21%, Black - 7%, Asian/Pacific Islander - 17%, Native American/Alaskan - 1%, White - 41%. ***Freshmen graduating within 5 years*** - nd%.
LOCATION: 22-acre, wooded campus on a hillside in the residential community of Burbank twenty-five minutes north of downtown Los Angeles.
CAMPUS LIFE: ***On-campus housing:*** Spaces - 184, undergraduate residential students - 20%. ***Clubs and organizations*** - 25. Fraternities and sororities - 6. ***Athletics:*** Intercollegiate - no. Intramural sports - yes. ***Counseling and guidance:*** Academic, personal, career planning, job placement. Faculty advisors - yes. Tutoring - yes. ***Special services/academic programs for:*** Educationally disadvantaged - no, physically disabled - no, learning disabled - no.
FRESHMAN ADMISSION STANDARDS: High school units: Total required - 16. College-preparatory program recommended. English - 4, social science/history - 4, foreign language - 3, laboratory science - 2, mathematics - 3.
1993-94 FRESHMAN ADMISSION DATA: ***Applications:*** Received - 400, accepted - 313, enrolled - 111. ***SAT Scores:***. Average verbal/mathematics scores - nd/nd, median verbal/mathematics scores - nd/nd. Verbal/mathematics scores of enrolled freshmen: Middle 50% scored 320-430 verbal, 380-500 mathematics, 710-950 combined verbal and mathematics. nd%/nd% scored 700-800, nd%/nd% scored 600-699, nd%/nd% scored 500-599, nd%/nd% scored 400-499, nd%/nd% scored 300-399, nd%/nd% scored 200-299. ***ACT composite score:*** Average - nd, median - nd. Middle 50% scored 19-22. ***High school GPA:*** Average GPA - 3.05. Middle 50% averaged 2.63- 3.25. ***Class rank:*** nd. ***International students:*** Minimum TOEFL score required - 500.
TRANSFER ADMISSION STANDARDS: ***Transfer units required:*** Minimum - none, maximum - none. ***Minimum college GPA*** - 2.00. ***Grades accepted*** - A, B, C.
1992-93 TRANSFER ADMISSION DATA: ***Applications:*** Received - 257, accepted - 184, enrolled - 95. CCC transfer students enrolled - nd.
ADMISSION PROCEDURES: ***Entrance tests:*** SAT I: Reasoning Test or ACT. Test deadline for fall admission - nd. ***Application process:*** Students admitted each term. Deadlines: Freshmen - rolling, 3/1 priority date, transfers - rolling 4/15 priority date. Winter, spring, summer quarters: one month prior to beginning of quarter. Application fee - $30 domestic, $50 international. Fee waiver - yes. ***Recommendations:*** 2 - people familiar with academic work. Teacher, counselor, principal, employer, church official, coach. ***Interview*** - strongly recommended. ***Admission notification*** - rolling. Commitment deposit - $100. ***Advanced placement offered*** - yes. ***Advanced credit given*** - yes. ***Early decision procedure*** - no.
1994-95 COSTS: ***Total costs*** (approximate) - $19,410, Architecture - $19,890. Tuition - $12,180, Architecture - $12,660, other significant fees - $840, room and board - $5,490, total books, supplies, incidentals (approximate) - $900.

nd = no data available   na = not applicable

CALIFORNIA INDEPENDENT COLLEGES

UNDERGRADUATE FINANCIAL AID: Students receiving financial aid - 60%. Submit FAFSA (CSS version preferred) by 3/1. Application deadline for institutional scholarships and grants - rolling, priority 3/1. Average financial aid package - $11,590.
OTHER INFORMATION: ***Founded*** - 1884. ***Nonprofit*** - yes. ***WASC Accredited*** - yes. ***Member of AICCU*** - yes.

YESHIVA OHR ELCHON ON CHABAD WEST COAST TALMUDICAL SEMINARY

7215 Waring Avenue
Los Angeles, California 90046
(213) 937-3763
Fax: nd
Toll Free: nd

Rabbinical College for Men Only

DISTINGUISHING FEATURES: The Seminary is noted for its academic excellence and highly respected faculty. Students enjoy a relaxed atmosphere that promotes their intellectual growth. They benefit from small classes and personal attention and have the opportunity to participate in community projects. There are two programs for attaining a Bachelor's Degree in Religious Studies — the New Direction Program and the Advanced Talmud option.
DEGREES OFFERED: Bachelor's.
CALENDAR: Semester system.
ENROLLMENT: ***Total*** - 50 men.
LOCATION: 2.1-acre campus in the city of Los Angeles.
CAMPUS LIFE: ***On-campus housing:*** Spaces - yes.
OTHER INFORMATION: ***Founded*** - 1953. ***Nonprofit*** - yes. ***WASC Accredited*** - no. Accredited by the Association of Advanced Rabbinical and Talmudical Schools.

CAREER COLLEGES

The following career colleges are accredited schools and offer the Associates degree. Curriculums focus on career training.

BUSINESS COLLEGES

HEALD COLLEGES
1453 Mission Street, 4th Floor
San Francisco, California 94103
(415) 864-5060
Total Enrollment for all campuses: 4,275
Business College campuses: Concord, Fresno, Hayward, Oakland, Sacramento, Salinas, San Francisco, San Jose, Santa Rosa, Stockton.

MTI COLLEGE
2011 West Chapman Avenue, Suite 100
Orange, California 92668
(714) 385-1132
Total Enrollment: nd

SAN JOAQUIN COLLEGE
8400 West Mineral King Avenue
Visalia, California 93291
(209) 651-2500
Total Enrollment: nd

CULINARY ARTS

CULINARY ARTS ACADEMY
625 Polk Street
San Francisco, California 94102
(415) 771-3536
Total Enrollment: nd

FASHION AND INTERIOR DESIGN

BROOKS COLLEGE
4835 East Pacific Coast Highway
Long Beach, California 90804
(310) 597-6611
Total Enrollment: 583

INTERIOR DESIGNERS INSTITUTE
1061 Camelback Road
Newport Beach, California 92660
(714) 675-4451
Total Enrollment: nd

THE FASHION INSTITUTE OF DESIGN AND MERCHANDISING
919 South Grand Avenue
Los Angeles, California 90015
(213) 624-1200
Total Enrollment for all campuses: 2,484
Branch campuses: Costa Mesa, San Diego, San Francisco.

TECHNICAL COLLEGES

CAREER DEVELOPMENT INSTITUTE
1950 East Seventeenth Street
Santa Ana, California 92701
(714) 648-0214
Total Enrollment: nd

DON BOSCO TECHNICAL INSTITUTE
1151 San Gabriel Boulevard
Rosemead, California 91770
(818) 307-6500
Total Enrollment: 205

HEALD COLLEGES
Institutes of Technology Campuses: Hayward, Martinez, Sacramento, San Francisco.

MTI COLLEGE
2011 West Chapman Avenue, Suite 100
Orange, California 92668
(714) 385-1132

SAN JOAQUIN COLLEGE

nd = no data available na = not applicable

UNDERGRADUATE DEGREE MAJORS

	Azusa Pacific University	Biola University	California Baptist College	California Institute of Technology	California Lutheran University	Chapman University	Claremont McKenna College	College of Notre Dame	Concordia University	Dominican College	Fresno Pacific College	Golden Gate University	Harvey Mudd College	Holy Names College	Humphreys College	John F. Kennedy University	La Sierra University	Loma Linda University	Loyola Marymount University	Marymount College	The Master's College	Menlo College	Mills College	Mount St. Mary's College	National University
ARCHITECTURE/MANUFACTURING																									
Architecture/Manufacturing																									
Industrial Arts/Tech Design																									
Interior Design								B												A					
Quality Assurance																									
AREA STUDIES																									
Area Studies																									
African																									
American							B																B	B	
Asian/Chinese							B																		
European							B												B				B		
Latin American							B	B															B		
Russian/Slavic																									
ART/FINE ARTS/PROFESSIONAL ARTS																									
Art/Fine Arts/Professional Arts		B						B	B	B				B									B	B	
Advertising						B											B					B			
Crafts		B																							
Drawing/Painting	B	B	B		B	B				B							B		B	A				B	
Fashion Design																				A					
Filmmaking		B				B													B	A					
Graphics	B	B			B	B		B									B								
Photography					B												B								
Printmaking		B			B					B													B		
Sculpture		B			B	B																			
BIOLOGICAL SCIENCES																									
Biological Sciences	B	B	B	B	B	B	B	B	B	B	B		B	B			B		B	A	B	B	B	B	
Biochemistry/Biophysics	B	B		B	B		B	B									B		B				B	B	
Marine Studies/Sciences		A																		A					
Psychobiology							B										B								
BUSINESS ADMINISTRATION/MANAGEMENT																									
Business Administration/Management	B	B	B		B	B		B	B	B	B	B		B	A,B	B	B		B	A	B	B	B	B	B
Accounting	B	B			B	B	B	B	B	B	B	B			A,B	B	B		B	A				B	B
Banking						B						B													B
Marketing	B	B			B	B		B		B	B	B					B		B			B		B	B
Hotel Management												B													
Industrial Relations					B																				B
International Business							B	B		B		B							B			B		B	
Sports Management											B														
CHEMISTRY																									
Chemistry	B	B		B	B	B	B				B		B				B		B	A			B	B	
COMMUNICATIONS																									
Communications	B	B				B															B	B			B
Broadcasting		B			B	B																B			
Cinema/TV		B				B													B						
Communication	B	B	B		B	B		B	B		B						B		B	A		B	B		
Court Reporting															A										
Journalism	B	B			B	B											B					B			
Public Relations		B				B																			
Speech	B	B	B		B	B											B		B	A					
COMPUTER/INFORMATION SCIENCE																									
Computer/Information Science	B	B		B	B	B	B	B			B	B	B	B	A,B		B		B	A	B	B	B	A	B
EARTH SCIENCES																									
Earth Sciences																									
Environmental Studies					B	B	B	B			A														
Geology				B	B															A					

KEY TO SYMBOLS: A = Associate's Degree Programs or Transfer Credit
B = Bachelor's Degree Programs

	Occidental College	Pacific Christian College	Pacific Union College	Pepperdine University (Seaver)	Pitzer College	Point Loma Nazarene College	Pomona College	Saint Mary's College	Santa Clara University	Scripps College	Simpson College	Southern California College	Stanford University	United States International University	University of La Verne	University of the Pacific	University of Redlands	University of San Diego	University of San Francisco	University of Southern California	West Coast University	Westmont College	Whittier College	Woodbury University
ARCHITECTURE/MANUFACTURING																								
Architecture/Manufacturing																				B				B
Industrial Arts/Tech Design			B																		A,B			
Interior Design			A,B																					B
Quality Assurance																					B			
AREA STUDIES																								
Area Studies																B		B					B	
African										B			B			B								
American	B			B	B		B			B			B	B	B									
Asian/Chinese	B			B	B		B			B			B			B	B			B				
European				B	B					B						B	B							
Latin American	B				B			B		B			B	B		B	B	B						
Russian/Slavic													B			B				B				
ART/FINE ARTS/PROFESSIONAL ARTS																								
Art/Fine Arts/Professional Arts	B		B	B				B	B	B			B		B	B	B	B	B	B		B	B	B
Advertising				B												B			B					
Crafts																								
Drawing/Painting	B		B	B		B	B			B					B	B	B		B					
Fashion Design			B																					B
Filmmaking	B																			B				
Graphics			A	B		B										B			B					B
Photography			A				B			B					B									
Printmaking																								
Sculpture				B			B										B							
BIOLOGICAL SCIENCES																								
Biological Studies	B	B	B	B	B	B	B	B	B	B		B	B		B	B	B	B	B	B		B	B	
Biochemistry/Biophysics	B		B	B	B	B	B			B			B			B				B			B	
Marine Studies/Sciences	B												B					B		B				
Psychobiology	B				B					B										B				
BUSINESS ADMINISTRATION/MANAGEMENT																								
Business Administration/Management		B	B	B		B		B	B		B	B		B	B	B	B	B	B	B	A,B	B	B	B
Accounting			B	B		B		B	B	B	B	B			B	B	B	B	B	B	A,B			B
Banking									B			B				B								B
Marketing			B						B			B		B	B	B			B		B			B
Hotel Management																			B					
Industrial Relations			B	B		B										B								
International Business			B	B					B	B				B	B	B			B					B
Sports Management			B													B								
CHEMISTRY																								
Chemistry	B		B	B	B	B	B	B	B	B		B	B		B	B	B	B	B	B		B	B	
COMMUNICATIONS																								
Communications				B				B	B	B			B		B	B						B		
Broadcasting				B								B			B	B			B	B				
Cinema/TV					B							B			B					B				
Communication		B	B	B		B		B	B			B			B	B		B	B	B		B		
Court Reporting																								
Journalism			B	B		B						B			B	B			B	B				
Public Relations			B	B												B				B				
Speech				B		B						B			B	B								
COMPUTER/INFORMATION SCIENCE																								
Computer/Information Science	B		B	B		B	B		B	B			B		B	B	B	B	B	B	A,B	B		B
EARTH SCIENCES																								
Earth Sciences																						B	B	
Environmental Studies	B				B		B			B			B	B	B		B		B	B	A,B			
Geology	B						B			B			B			B				B			B	

CALIFORNIA INDEPENDENT COLLEGES

UNDERGRADUATE DEGREE MAJORS (cont ...)

	Azusa Pacific University	Biola University	California Baptist College	California Institute of Technology	California Lutheran University	Chapman University	Claremont McKenna College	College of Notre Dame	Concordia University	Dominican College	Fresno Pacific College	Golden Gate University	Harvey Mudd College	Holy Names College	Humphreys College	John F. Kennedy University	La Sierra University	Loma Linda University	Loyola Marymount University	Marymount College	The Master's College	Menlo College	Mills College	Mount St. Mary's College	National University
ENGINEERING																									
Engineering		A					B										A								
General	B	B		B									B	A											
Aerospace				B																					
Biomedical																									
Chemical				B																					
Civil				B															B						
Computer				B															B						
Electrical				B															B						
Electronics				B																					
Industrial/Management							B																		B
Mechanical				B															B						
Music																									
Petroleum																									
HEALTH SCIENCES																									
Health Sciences						B											B			A				B	
Dental Hygiene																	A	B							
Dietetics																	A	A,B							
Gerontology																								B	
Health Services Management																								B	B
Human Development																	A								
Medical Records Administration																	A	B						A	
Medical Technology																	A	B							
Nursing	B	B								B				B			A	A,B		A				A,B	
Optometry																	A								
Pharmacy																	A								
Physical Therapy	B					B											A	A						A	
Speech Pathology		B															A	B							
Sports Medicine	B																								
HUMANITIES																									
Humanities		B				B		B	B	B												B			
Classics							B												B						
Comparative Literature						B	B													A			B		
English Language & Literature	B	B	B	B	B	B	B	B	B	B	B			B			B		B	A	B		B	B	
Liberal Studies	B		B		B	B		B	B	B	A,B			B	A	B	B		B	A	B		B	B	
Linguistics																									
Philosophy	B	B			B	B	B	B			A			B					B	A		B	B	B	
Religious Education	B	B			B	B			B								B								
Religious Studies/Theology	B	B	B		B	B	B	B	B	B	B			B			B		B	A	B			B	
LANGUAGES																									
Languages																									
Chinese							B																		
French					B	B	B	B									B		B	A			B	B	
German					B		B																B		
Italian							B																		
Japanese							B													A					
Russian							B																		
Spanish		A	B		B	B	B				B			B			B		B	A			B	B	
MATHEMATICS																									
Mathematics	B	B	B	B	B	B	B		B	B	B		B	B			B		B	A	B		B	B	B
PERFORMING ARTS																									
Performing Arts						B			B																
Dance						B													B				B		
Dramatic Arts					B	B	B	B	B		A								B	A			B		
Music	B	B	B		B	B	B	B	B	B	B			B			B		B	A	B		B	B	

KEY TO SYMBOLS: A = Associate's Degree Programs or Transfer Credit
B = Bachelor's Degree Programs

CALIFORNIA INDEPENDENT COLLEGES

	Occidental College	Pacific Christian College	Pacific Union College	Pepperdine University (Seaver)	Pitzer College	Point Loma Nazarene College	Pomona College	Saint Mary's College	Santa Clara University	Scripps College	Simpson College	Southern California College	Stanford University	United States International University	University of La Verne	University of the Pacific	University of Redlands	University of San Diego	University of San Francisco	University of Southern California	West Coast University	Westmont College	Whittier College	Woodbury University
ENGINEERING																								
Engineering				B												B							B	
General			B						B	B						B					A	B		
Aerospace																				B				
Biomedical																				B				
Chemical													B							B				
Civil									B				B			B				B				
Computer													B			B				B				
Electrical									B				B			B		B		B	A,B			
Electronics			B																					
Industrial/Management			B										B			B				B	A,B			
Mechanical									B				B			B				B	A,B			
Music												B	B							B				
Petroleum													B							B				
HEALTH SCIENCES																								
Health Sciences								B							B	B					A			
Dental Hygiene																				B				
Dietetics				B																				
Gerontology																				B				
Health Services Management															B				B	B				
Human Development																								
Medical Records Administration																								
Medical Technology			B																					
Nursing			A,B			B		B										B	B	B				
Optometry																								
Pharmacy																B				B				
Physical Therapy		B																						
Speech Pathology																B	B						B	
Sports Medicine	B	B		B		B						B				B			B					
HUMANITIES																								
Humanities																		B						B
Classics	B			B	B		B	B	B	B			B			B				B				
Comparative Literature	B			B			B						B	B		B	B			B		B		
English Language & Literature	B		B	B	B	B	B	B	B	B	B	B	B		B	B	B	B	B	B		B	B	
Liberal Studies		B	B	B		B		B			B	B		B		B	B					B		
Linguistics	B			B	B		B			B			B			B				B				
Philosophy	B			B	B	B	B	B	B	B			B		B	B	B	B	B	B		B	B	
Religious Education		B	A,B	B		B					B	B							B					
Religious Studies/Theology	B	B	B	B		B	B	B	B	B	B	B	B		B	B	B	B	B	B		B	B	
LANGUAGES																								
Languages										B						B								
Chinese	B						B			B			B							B				
French	B		B	B	B		B	B	B	B			B		B	B	B	B	B	B		B	B	
German	B			B	B		B	A	B	B			B		B	B	B		B	B				
Italian				B				A	B	B			B							B				
Japanese	B			B			B			B			B			B			B	B				
Russian	B			B			B			B			B							B				
Spanish	B		B	B	B	B	B	B	B	B			B		B	B	B	B	B	B		B	B	
MATHEMATICS																								
Mathematics	B		B	B	B	B	B	B	B	B		B	B		B	B	B	B	B	B		B	B	
PERFORMING ARTS																								
Performing Arts								B								B								
Dance							B			B			B											
Dramatic Arts	B	B		B	B	B	B	B	B	B		B	B		B	B				B		B	B	
Music	B	B	B	B	B	B	B	A	B	B	B	B	B		B	B	B	B		B		B	B	

UNDERGRADUATE DEGREE MAJORS (cont ...)

	Azusa Pacific University	Biola University	California Baptist College	California Institute of Technology	California Lutheran University	Chapman University	Claremont McKenna College	College of Notre Dame	Concordia University	Dominican College	Fresno Pacific College	Golden Gate University	Harvey Mudd College	Holy Names College	Humphreys College	John F. Kennedy University	La Sierra University	Loma Linda University	Loyola Marymount University	Marymount College	The Master's College	Menlo College	Mills College	Mount St. Mary's College	National University
PHYSICAL EDUCATION																									
Physical Education	B	B	B		B	B			B		B						B				B				
Recreation	B																								
Sports Management											B														
PHYSICAL SCIENCES																									
Physical Sciences	B	B	B			B			B		A			A						A			B		
Astronomy				B																					
Physics		B		B	B		B						B				B		B	A					
SOCIAL SCIENCES																									
Social Sciences	B	B	B	B	B	B		B	B		B			B	A	B	B			A				B	
Anthropology									B								B			A			B		
Behavioral Science	B	B	B					B	B							B	B			A					B
Child/Human Development		B									B						B			A			B	B	
Economics		B		B	B	B	B					B					B		B	A			B		
Environmental Studies						B	B				A					B							B		
Ethnic Studies						B			B										B				B		
Geography																				A					
History	B	B	B	B	B	B	B	B	B	B	B			B			B		B	A	B	B	B	B	
Home Economics																					B				
International Relations/Studies	B	B			B	B	B			B				B									B		
Paralegal Studies															B										
Political Science/Government	B		B	B	B	B	B	B		B	A	B							B	A	B		B	B	
Psychology	B	B	B		B	B	B	B	B		B	B		B		B	B		B	A		B	B	B	B
Social Welfare/.Service	B	B	B						B		B						B			A					
Sociology	B	B	B		B	B		B	B		B			B			B		B	A			B	B	
Women' s/Gender Studies							B																B		

KEY TO SYMBOLS: A = Associate's Degree Programs or Transfer Credit
B = Bachelor's Degree Programs

COLLEGE IN CALIFORNIA: *The Inside Track*

SOURCE: *1994-95 AICCU Guide for Students, Parents, and Counselors,* 1994, AICCU.

	Occidental College	Pacific Christian College	Pacific Union College	Pepperdine University (Seaver)	Pitzer College	Point Loma Nazarene College	Pomona College	Saint Mary's College	Santa Clara University	Scripps College	Simpson College	Southern California College	Stanford University	United States International University	University of La Verne	University of the Pacific	University of Redlands	University of San Diego	University of San Francisco	University of Southern California	West Coast University	Westmont College	Whittier College	Woodbury University
PHYSICAL EDUCATION																								
Physical Education		B	B	B		B		B				B			B	B			B	B		B	B	
Recreation			B																				B	
Sports Management			B													B			B					
PHYSICAL SCIENCES																								
Physical Sciences	B		B	B			B		B	B					B	B				B		B	B	
Astronomy							B			B			B							B				
Physics	B		B		B	B	B	B	B	B			B		B	B	B	B	B	B		B	B	
SOCIAL SCIENCES																								
Social Sciences	B	B	B	B			B		B	B	B	B			B	B				B		B	B	B
Anthropology	B				B		B	B	B	B		B	B			B	B	B		B		B	B	
Behavioral Science	B		B												B	B						B		
Child/Human Development		B	A,B			B									B	B							B	
Economics	B			B	B	B	B	B	B	B			B		B	B	B	B	B	B		B	B	
Environmental Studies	B				B					B					B		B		B	B			B	
Ethnic Studies					B		B			B				B		B	B			B				
Geography																				B				
History	B	B	B	B	B	B	B	B	B	B	B	B	B		B	B	B	B	B	B		B	B	B
Home Economics			B			B																		
International Relations	B		B	B	B		B			B			B	B	B	B	B	B		B		B	B	
Paralegal Studies															B			B						
Political Science/Government	B	B	B	B	B	B	B	B	B	B		B	B		B	B	B	B	B	B		B	B	B
Psychology	B	B	B	B	B	B	B	B	B	B	B	B	B	B	B	B	B	B	B	B		B	B	B
Social Welfare/.Service		B	B																				B	
Sociology	B	B	B	B	B	B	B	B	B	B		B	B		B	B	B	B	B	B		B	B	
Women' s Gender Studies	B				B		B			B			B				B			B			B	

CALIFORNIA INDEPENDENT COLLEGES

PROGRAMS FOR PROFESSIONAL EDUCATORS

	Azusa Pacific University	Biola University	California Baptist College	California Lutheran University	Chapman University	College of Notre Dame	Concordia University	Dominican College	Fresno Pacific College	Holy Names College	John F. Kennedy University	La Sierra University	Loyola Marymount University	Marymount College	The Master's College	Mills College	Mount St. Mary's College	National University
Adult & Continuing Education		B		C											B			
Art Education	B	B,C	B,C	C	C	C						C	B,C					
Bilingual/Cross Cultural		B							C									C
Business/Commerce/Distrib Education		B,C	B,C	C					C			C						
Career Counselor					C							C	C					
Child Care												B					A	
Child Welfare & Attendance																		
Communication Handicapped					C													
Community College Teaching				C	C													
Early Childhood Education				C	C		B,C							A		B,C	A,C	
Education Administration	C	B,C		C	C	C	C		C			C	C				C	C
Educational Supervision				C	C		C											
Elementary Teaching	C	B,C	B,C	C	B,C	C	B,C	C	C	C	C	B,C	C		B,C	C	B,C	B,C
English as a Second Language	C	B,C										B						
Health Science Education					B							B					B	
Industrial Arts/Technical Education																		
Learning Handicapped				C	C				C	C		C	C					C
Mathematics Education		B,C		C			B,C		C			C	C		B,C		B,C	
Montessori						C												
Music Education	B	B,C		C	C	C	B,C		C			B	B		B,C		B,C	
Physical Education	B	B,C	B,C	B	B,C		B,C		B,C			B,C			B,C			
Physically Handicapped					C													
Pupil Counselor	C			C	C				C			C	C				C	C
Reading Education	C			C	C				C				C					
School Psychologist				C	C							C	C					C
School Social Worker	C				C							B						
Science Education		B,C	B,C	C	C	C	B,C		C			B	C				B,C	
Secondary Teaching	C	B,C	B,C	C	B,C	C	B,C	C	C	C	C	C	C		B,C	C	B,C	B,C
Severely Handicapped									C			C						

KEY TO SYMBOLS:
A = Associate's Degree Programs
B = Bachelor's Degree Programs
C = Teaching Credential Programs

	Occidental College	Pacific Christian College	Pacific Oaks College	Pacific Union College	Patten College	Pepperdine University (Seaver)	Point Loma Nazarene College	Saint Mary's College	Santa Clara University	Simpson College	Southern California College	United States International University	University of La Verne	University of the Pacific	University of Redlands	University of San Diego	University of San Francisco	University of Southern California	Westmont College	Whittier College
Adult & Continuing Education													B				C			
Art Education	B,C		B			C	B	C					B	B,C	B,C	B			B,C	
Bilingual/Cross Cultural							C							C		C	C	C		
Business/Commerce/Distrib Education				B,C	B		B													
Career Counselor														C		C				
Child Care			B										B,C							
Child Welfare & Attendance																C				
Communication Handicapped														B,C	B,C			C		
Community College Teaching								C								C				
Early Childhood Education		A,B	B	A,B			B,C	C					B,C					C		C
Education Administration							C	C		C		C	B,C	C	C	C	C			
Educational Supervision								C						C						
Elementary Teaching	C	B	C	B,C	C	C	C	C	C	B,C	C	B,C	B,C	B,C	B,C	B,C	B,C	B,C	C	C
English as a Second Language				C								C		B,C			C			
Health Science Education								C								B			B,C	
Industrial Arts/Technical Education				B,C																
Learning Handicapped			C				C	C	C		C		C	C				C		
Mathematics Education	B,C			C		C		C			B,C			B,C	B,C	B,C			B,C	
Montessori								C												
Music Education	B,C	B		B,C		C	B,C			B	B,C		B,C	B,C	B,C	B		B,C	B,C	
Physical Education		B		B,C		C	B	B,C			B,C		B,C	B,C			B		B,C	C
Physically Handicapped																C				
Pupil Counselor							C	C						C	C	C	C			
Reading Education							C	C					B,C	C		B,C				C
School Psychologist														C			C			
School Social Worker																				
Science Education	B,C										C		B,C	B,C	B,C				B,C	
Secondary Teaching	C	B		C		C	C	C	C	B,C	C	B,C	B,C	B,C	B,C	B,C	B,C	C	C	C
Severely Handicapped			C											C		C				

COLLEGE IN CALIFORNIA: *The Inside Track*

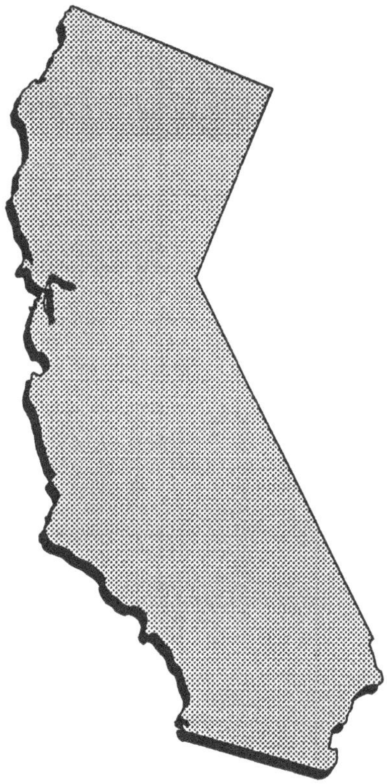

Appendix A

CALIFORNIA RESIDENCY REQUIREMENTS

California Residency Requirements For Tuition Purposes

As a general rule, you must have been a California resident for at least one year immediately preceding the residence determination date.

Your eligibility as a resident of the State of California determines whether you must pay nonresident tuition fees at California public colleges and universities. These tuition fees are in addition to the regular enrollment fees paid by California residents. California residency status also affects your eligibility for financial aid from the state. California law defines state residency qualifications.

RESIDENCE DETERMINATION DATES

As a general rule, you must have been a California resident for at least one year immediately preceding the residence determination date in order to qualify as a "resident student" for (a) tuition purposes or (b) financial aid from the state. If you have not been a resident of California for at least one year prior to this date for the term in which you plan to attend the public college, you must pay nonresident tuition in addition to enrollment fees. The California Student Aid Commission residence determination date establishes your eligibility for student aid from the state.

UNIVERSITY OF CALIFORNIA

University of California residence determination dates vary each year.

A residence determination date is set for each academic term. It is the date from which residence is determined for that term. Residence determination dates vary each year, depending upon the date instruction begins for the quarter or semester.

Quarter-term campuses .... The day instruction begins at the last of the University of California campuses to open for the quarter.

Semester-term campuses .... The day instruction begins for the semester.

CALIFORNIA STATE UNIVERSITY

A residence determination date is set for each academic term. It is the date from which residence is determined for that term. The residence determination dates are the same every year.

Quarter term campuses	Fall:	September 20th
	Winter:	January 5th
	Spring:	April 1st
	Summer:	July 1st
Semester-term campuses	Fall:	September 20th
	Winter:	January 5th — Stanislaus only
	Spring:	January 25th

CALIFORNIA COMMUNITY COLLEGES

Quarter and semester-term campuses	The day before instruction begins. The day is totally dependent upon the date instruction begins at each campus, and therefore varies from campus to campus.

CALIFORNIA STUDENT AID COMMISSION

The residence determination date is September 20th of the first year of the award.

DETERMINATION OF CALIFORNIA RESIDENCY

If you are under the age of eighteen, your residence is considered to be that of your parent, parents, or non-parent adult

If you are a minor, under the age of eighteen, your residence is considered to be that of your parent, parents, or non-parent adult who is responsible for your direct care and control and with whom you last lived. One year of residency in California is required for either your parent or your non-parent adult for you to qualify as a California resident. To qualify as a non-parent, responsible adult, he/she must have had continuous direct care and control of you for two years prior to the residency determination date.

If you are an adult (age eighteen or older) and wish to be classified as a resident for tuition purposes, you must have given up your prior residence and been physically present within the state for more than one year prior to the residence determination date for the term in which you wish to enroll as a resident. You must not only have been physically present within the state for one year, you also must have shown intent to make the state your permanent home. The one-year time period begins when both your presence and intent to stay are demonstrated.

Physical presence in the state for educational purposes alone does not establish California residence.

The steps necessary to show California residency intent vary from case to case. The steps may include, but are not limited to:

a. Registering to vote and voting in California elections.

b. Designating California as your permanent address on all school, employment, and military records.

c. Obtaining a California driver's license or, if a non-driver, a California identification card.

d. Paying California income taxes as a resident, including income taxes on income earned outside California from the date residence is established.

e. Obtaining a California vehicle registration.

f. Establishing a place to live in California where your personal belongings are kept.

g. Residing in California during summers and other academic holidays.

h. Licensing for professional practice in California.

i. Not doing any of the above — (a) through (h) — in other states during any period during which you claim to be a California resident.

Physical presence in the state for educational purposes alone does not establish California residence.

Documentary evidence of the above may be required. All relevant evidence is considered in determining your residency classification.

THE UNIVERSITY OF CALIFORNIA FINANCIAL INDEPENDENCE REQUIREMENT

Effective the fall quarter 1993, students at the University of California whose parents are not residents of California will be required to be financially independent in order to be considered for classification as residents for tuition purpose.

You will be considered financially independent if you meet *any* of the following qualifications:

All relevant evidence is considered in determining your residency classification.

1. You are at least twenty-four years of age by December 31st of the calendar year resident classification is sought.
2. You are a veteran of the United States Armed Forces.
3. You are a ward of the court, or both parents are deceased.
4. You have legal dependents other than a spouse.
5. You are married or in a graduate or professional program, and you were not claimed as an income tax deduction by your parents or any other individual for the tax year immediately preceding the term for which your request for resident classification is made.

6. You are a single undergraduate student, your annual income is at least $4,000, you were not claimed as an income tax deduction by your parents or any other individual for *two tax years* immediately preceding the term for which your request for resident classification is made, and you demonstrate self-sufficiency for those years.

RESIDENCY RULES

The rules regarding California residency for tuition and state financial aid purposes are complex and far more extensive than described here. There are numerous regulations pertinent to many special circumstances, and there are some exemptions from nonresident tuition. Contact the admissions office of the campus in which you are interested and/or the California Student Aid Commission for answers to your specific questions about individual circumstances. The colleges and universities and the California Student Aid Commission may use professional judgement on a case-by-case basis when evaluating individual situations.

The public California colleges and universities and the California Student Aid Commission may use professional judgement on a case-by-case basis when evaluating individual situations.

UNDOCUMENTED ALIEN STUDENTS

If you are in the United States without legal immigration status, you are an undocumented alien student. Recent court rulings have affected your eligibility to qualify (a) as a resident of the state of California for tuition purposes to attend public colleges and universities, and (b) for financial aid from the state and federal governments.

At this time, if you are an undocumented alien student —

a. At California Community Colleges and the University of California, you are considered a nonresident for tuition purposes and must pay, in addition to regular fees, non-resident tuition at California Community Colleges and the University of California.

b. At California State University, you may or may not be considered a nonresident for tuition purposes. (No final determination has been made at this time.)

c. You are not eligible for state and federal grants and loans. Your eligibility for college and private grants, scholarships, and loans is not affected.

Non-resident tuition costs and financial aid opportunities are described in chapter 9, CALIFORNIA COMMUNITY COLLEGES, page 9--8; chapter 10, CALIFORNIA STATE UNIVERSITY, page 10--48; and chapter 11, UNIVERSITY OF CALIFORNIA, page 11--61.

Appendix B

SOURCE MATERIALS

CHAPTER 4: PAYING FOR COLLEGE

The Student Guide, Financial Aid from the U.S. Department of Education 1994-95. Washington, D.C.: United States Department of Education, Government Printing Office, 1994.

New Recipient Cal Grant Reference Manual, 1994-95 Academic Year. Sacramento, CA: California Student Aid Commission, April 1994.

Financial Aid For Students Workbook, 1994-95 School Year. Sacramento, CA: California Student Aid Commission, October 1993.

Financial Aid For Students Counselors Guide, 1994-95 School Year. Sacramento, CA: California Student Aid Commission, October 1993.

"Cal Grant Workshop for Counselors." Sacramento, CA: California Student Aid Commission, November 1993.

Financial Aid Need Estimator. Iowa City, IO: American College Testing Program, 1994.

The Facts About Army ROTC. Elliott City, MD: Department of the Army, College Army ROTC, November 1991.

1995 Navy-Marine Corps ROTC College Scholarship Bulletin. Gaithersburg, MD: Department of the Navy, Navy-Marine Corps ROTC Scholarship Program, 1993.

Air Force ROTC and Your Future. Maxwell AFB, AL: Air Force Reserve Officer Training Corps, 1993.

Title IV Provisions in 1992 HEA Conference Agreement, Higher Education Amendments of 1992, Student Aid Provisions. Washington, D.C.: United States Department of Education, July 1992.

Cooperative Education Undergraduate Program Directory, 5th Edition, 1991-92. Boston, MA: National Commission for Cooperative Education, 1991.

CHAPTER 5: ATHLETICS

A Guide for the College Bound Student. Kansas City, MO: National Association of Intercollegiate Athletics, June, 1994.

1994-95 NCAA Guide for the College-Bound Student-Athlete. Overland Park, KA: National Collegiate Athletic Association, March 1994.

Making Sure You Are Eligible to Participate in College Sports. Iowa City, IA: NCAA Initial-Eligibility Clearinghouse, 1994.

Making Sure Your High School Students Will Be Eligible to Participate in College Sports. Iowa City, IA, NCAA Initial-Eligibility Clearinghouse, 1994.

CHAPTER 6: COLLEGE ENTRANCE TESTS

Working with the New PSAT, Preparation, Administration, Interpretation. Princeton, NJ: The College Entrance Examination Board, 1993.

1994 PSAT/NMSQT Student Bulletin. Princeton, NJ: The College Entrance Examination Board, 1994.

1993 About Your PSAT/NMSQT Scores. Princeton, NJ: The College Entrance Examination Board, 1993.

1993 PSAT/NMSQT Interpretive Manual. Princeton, NJ: The College Board, 1993.

Verbal Practice Questions for the New PSAT/NMSQT and SAT I: Reasoning Test. Princeton, NJ: The College Entrance Examination Board, 1992.

Mathematics Practice Questions for the New PSAT/NMSQT and SAT I: Reasoning Test. Princeton, NJ: The College Entrance Examination Board, 1992.

1994-95 Registration Bulletin for the SAT Program, Western Edition. Princeton, NJ: The College Entrance Examination Board, 1994.

1994-95 Registration Bulletin for the SAT Program, International Edition. Princeton, NJ: The College Board, 1994.

Taking the SAT I : Reasoning Test. The Official Guide to the SAT. Princeton, NJ: The College Entrance Examination Board, June, 1994.

Taking the SAT II: Subject Tests. The Official Guide to the SAT II: Subject Tests. Princeton, NJ: The College Entrance Examination Board, 1994.

Fee Waiver Service, SAT Program, 1994-95. Princeton, NJ: The College Entrance Examination Board, 1994.

May 1994 Advanced Placement Examinations Bulletin for Students. Princeton, New Jersey: The College Entrance Examination Board, 1993.

Some Questions and Answers About the Advanced Placement Program 1993-94. Princeton, NJ: The College Entrance Examination Board, 1993.

AP Yearbook 1993-94. Princeton, NJ: The College Entrance Examination Board, 1993.

ATP Services for Handicapped Students, Admissions Testing Program 1993-94, 1994-95. Princeton, NJ: The College Entrance Examination Board, 1994.

Counselor's Handbook for the New SAT Program, Answers to your Questions about the SAT I: Reasoning Test, SAT II: Subject Tests. Princeton, NJ: The College Entrance Examination Board, 1994.

1994-95 Bulletin of Information for TOEFL/TWE and TSE, United States Edition. Princeton, NJ: Educational Testing Service, 1994.

1994-95 Bulletin of Information for TOEFL/TWE and TSE, Canada, Europe, Overseas, Middle East and North Africa Editions. Princeton, NJ: Educational Testing Service, 1994.

English Placement Test (EPT) and Entry Level Mathematics Test (ELM) Information Bulletin 1994-95. Princeton, NJ: Educational Testing Service, 1994.

University of California: An Information Booklet for the Universitywide Subject A Examination, April 1994 Oakland, CA: Office of the President, University of California, 1994.

Registering for The ACT Assessment 1994-95. Iowa City, IO: American College Testing Program, 1994.

Preparing for the ACT Assessment 1994-95. Iowa City, IO: American College Testing Program, 1994. Iowa City, IO: American College Testing Program, 1994.

User Handbook, ACT Assessment 1994-95. Iowa City, IO: American College Testing Program, 1994.

CHAPTER 9: CALIFORNIA COMMUNITY COLLEGES

California Community Colleges, Since You Asked, Revised January 1994. Sacramento, CA: Office of the President, California Community Colleges, 1994.

Answers for Transfers, University of California 1995-96. Oakland, CA: Office of the President, University of California, June 1994.

CSU What a Difference: A Guide for California Community College Transfers to The California State University. Long Beach, CA: Office of the Chancellor, California State University, June 1991.

CHAPTER 10: CALIFORNIA STATE UNIVERSITY

Admission Handbook, CSU Policies for Determining Undergraduate Admission. Long Beach, CA: Academic Affairs, Educational Support, Office of the Chancellor, California State University, September 1992.

The California State University 1995-96 Undergraduate Admission Application. Long Beach, CA: Academic Affairs, Educational Support, Office of the Chancellor, California State University, August 1994.

Educational Opportunity Program, Information and Supplementary Forms 1995-96. Long Beach, CA: Academic Affairs, Educational Support, Office of the Chancellor, California State University, August 1994.

Campus Highlights for High School and Community College Counselors 1994-95. Long Beach, CA: Academic Affairs, Educational Support, Office of the Chancellor, California State University, Academic Affairs, Educational Support, 1994.

CSU Review. Long Beach, CA: Academic Affairs, Educational Support, Office of the Chancellor, California State University, September 1992 to May 1994.

CSU Origin of Fall Term Enrollment, Fall 1993. Long Beach, CA: Division of Analytical Studies, Office of the Chancellor, California State University, August 1994.

CSU Enrollment by Ethnic Group, Fall 1993. Long Beach, CA: Division of Analytical Studies, Office of the Chancellor, California State University, March 1994.

CHAPTER 11: UNIVERSITY OF CALIFORNIA

Quick Reference for Counselors 1994-95. Oakland, CA: Student Academic Services, Office of the President, University of California, August 1994.

Frequency Distribution of College Entrance Examination Board (CEEB) Test Scores for Entering Freshmen, Fall 1993 Term. Student Academic Services, Office of the President, University of California, January, 1994.

Introducing the University 1995-96. Oakland, CA: Student Academic Services, Office of the President, University of California, March 1994.

Application for Undergraduate Admission and Scholarships 1995-96. Oakland, CA: Student Academic Services, Office of the President, University of California, August 1994.

California Notes, a Newsletter for Schools and Colleges from the University of California. Oakland, CA: Student Academic Services, Office of the President, University of California, September 1992 to May 1994.

CHAPTER 12: CALIFORNIA INDEPENDENT COLLEGES

California Independent Colleges and Universities, the Guide for Students, Parents, and Counselors: 1994-95 Sacramento, CA: Association of Independent California Colleges and Universities (AICCU), August 1994.

California Colleges and Universities 1990. Sacramento, CA: California Postsecondary Education Commission, December 1989.

Western Association of Schools and Colleges (WASC) 1993-94. Aptos, CA: Western Association of Schools and Colleges, Inc., September 1993.

Index

A

INDEX

C

INDEX

D

INDEX

E

F

G

H

I

L

M

N

S

T

U

V

W

YES! I want to order my own copy of

COLLEGE IN CALIFORNIA: *The Inside Track*

O.K. Here' s how . . .

✓ **By telephone:** Grab your VISA or Master Charge bank card and call **(408) 354-7975** to place your order.

✓ **By fax:** Fill out this coupon completely and fax it to **(408) 354-5977** to place your order.

✓ **By mail:** Fill out this coupon completely and mail it with your payment to:

BAYWOOD HOUSE Inc.
P.O. Box 33022
Los Gatos, CA 95031

TO ORDER *your own copy of*

COLLEGE IN CALIFORNIA: *The Inside Track*

Mail or fax this coupon now to → BAYWOOD HOUSE Inc.
P.O. BOX 33022
LOS GATOS, CA 95031

Fax: (408) 354--5977
Tel: (408) 354-7975

You will receive your books within ten days.
Phone orders also accepted.

Your name: ______________________

Title: ______________________

School or Institution: ______________________

Shipping Address: ______________________

City: ____________ State: ___ Zip: ________

Tel #: (_____) -________ - __________

Please send [ ] books @ 21.95 each [ ]

Add 8 1/4 % ($1.81 per book) CA mailing addresses only — sales tax [ ]

U.S.: $3.00 1st book, $2.00 each additional book (*) — shipping & handling [ ]

TOTAL [ ]

How do you wish to pay? ☐ Visa ☐ Mastercard

☐ check or moneyorder enclosed (payable to BAYWOOD HOUSE Inc.)

____-____-____-____ Card #

___/___ expiration date

Print cardholder's name

X ______________ Cardholder's signature

(*) *More shipping information —*

To any location in the U.S. and its territories:
normal delivery (please allow 10 days)
1st book - $3.00... each additional book - $2.00

express delivery (please allow 3 days)
add additional $10.00 each book

To locations outside the U.S. and its territories:
Call for surface/air rates and delivery times.

I found out about

COLLEGE IN CALIFORNIA: *The Inside Track*

from:

- ☐ high school staff
- ☐ friend/colleague
- ☐ consultant/advisor
- ☐ college speaker
- ☐ newspaper article
- ☐ newspaper ad
- ☐ magazine article
- ☐ magazine ad
- ☐ TV talk show
- ☐ radio talk show
- ☐ radio ad
- ☐ library
- ☐ other ______________

☐ I am a student in grade ________

☐ I am a parent with a student in grade ________

☐ I am an educator at ________

my position is ________